Money, Expectations, and Business Cycles

Essays in Macroeconomics

This is a Volume in
ECONOMIC THEORY, ECONOMETRICS, AND MATHEMATICAL
ECONOMICS

A series of Monographs and Textbooks

Consulting Editor: KARL SHELL

A complete list of titles in this series appears at the end of this volume.

Money, Expectations, and Business Cycles

Essays in Macroeconomics

Robert J. Barro

The University of Rochester
Rochester, New York

and

National Bureau of Economic Research
Cambridge, Massachusetts

ACADEMIC PRESS 1981
A Subsidiary of Harcourt Brace Jovanovich, Publishers
New York London Toronto Sydney San Francisco

ACADEMIC PRESS, INC.
111 Fifth Avenue, New York, New York 10003

United Kingdom Edition published by
ACADEMIC PRESS, INC. (LONDON) LTD.
24/28 Oval Road, London NW1 7DX

Library of Congress Cataloging in Publication Data

Barro, Robert J.
  Money, expectations, and business cycles.

  (Economic theory, econometrics, and mathematical
economics series)
  Includes bibliographies and index.
  1. Macroeconomics——Addresses, essays, lectures.
I. Title.
HB172.5.B37   339   80–1770
ISBN 0–12–079550–7

PRINTED IN THE UNITED STATES OF AMERICA

81 82 83 84   9 8 7 6 5 4 3 2 1

To Jennifer, who shows great promise as an economist.

Contents

③ Rational Expectations and the Role of Monetary Policy   **79**

From *Journal of Monetary Economics*, 1976

④ A Capital Market in an Equilibrium Business Cycle Model   **111**

From *Econometrica*, 1980

⑤ Unanticipated Money Growth and Economic Activity in the United States   **137**

ⅠⅠⅠ Alternative Approaches to Macroeconomics

⑥ A General Disequilibrium Model of Income and Employment   **173**

With Herschel I. Grossman
From *American Economic Review*, 1971

Preface

This volume brings together my principal published articles in the money/ macro area with two new essays. The first new paper, "The Equilibrium Approach to Business Cycles," is intended to be a comprehensive survey of theoretical and empirical developments in this major new branch of macroeconomics. The second unpublished paper, "Unanticipated Money Growth and Economic Activity in the United States," sythesizes a number of my empirical papers that attempt to implement and test some aspects of the "new classical macroeconomics."

The book is assembled in five parts, the first of which contains the survey paper on monetary theory that I coauthored with Stan Fischer. The main section of this paper that seems out-of-date is the one entitled "Rational Expectations and the Phillips Curve." The recent surge of research in this area is discussed in my new survey paper.

Part II includes the two new essays plus two theoretical papers on the "equilibrium approach to business cycles." Part III contains papers that deal with the non-market-clearing approach to macroeconomics, sluggish price adjustment, and the macro significance of long-term contracts. Part IV has three papers on public debt. Part V includes two papers that use the inventory approach to money demand and one theoretical paper on the workings of the gold standard.

I have benefited substantially from research support by the National Science Foundation and the National Bureau of Economic Research.

SURVEY OF DEVELOPMENTS IN MONEY AND MACROECONOMICS

1

Recent Developments in Monetary Theory*

WITH STANLEY FISCHER

This paper surveys recent work in monetary theory, with primary emphasis on material that has appeared since the writing of Harry Johnson's 1962 survey. The discussion deals with the following topics: (1) the theory of money demand, with special attention to inventory approaches; (2) money, inflation and growth; (3) the welfare cost of inflation, the optimum quantity of money, and inflationary finance; (4) disequilibrium theory; (5) the general equilibrium approach to monetary theory; (6) the new microfoundations of money; and (7) rational expectations and the Phillips Curve.

1. Introduction

Over the last thirty years there have been substantial changes in the role attached to money as a determinant of the price level and the rate of economic activity. However, these changes reflect more the accumulation of empirical evidence and the corresponding shift in theoretical emphasis, rather than an alteration of basic analytical structure. Comparison of Modigliani's (1944) exposition of the Keynesian system with Friedman's (1970) framework for monetary analysis reveals little change in the basic short-run macroeconomic model. Nonetheless, today's monetary theory and the profession's current view of money are very different from those of thirty years ago. The major changes can be indicated by some concepts that are now commonplace, but were unfamiliar thirty years ago: (1) the distinction between real and nominal rates of interest as implied by nonzero expectations of inflation, (2) the short-run Phillips Curve tradeoff associated with unanticipated movements in money and prices, and (3) the absence of a long-run Phillips Curve, implying a natural rate of unemployment in a situation where price expectations are fulfilled.

Perhaps the most striking contrast between current views of money and those of thirty years ago is the rediscovery of the endogeneity of the price level and inflation and their relation to the behavior of money. This last point can be

*This paper was prepared for the 50th anniversary volume of the Central Bank of Mexico. Portions of the paper are extensions of the material contained in Fischer (1975a).

3

Reprinted from *Journal of Monetary Economics*, 2, April 1976, 133–167, by permission of North-Holland Publishing Company, Amsterdam, and the authors.

highlighted by contrasting Milton Friedman's original version of his paper, 'Discussion of the Inflationary Gap,' in the 1942 *American Economic Review* with the amended version that appears in the 1953 volume, *Essays in Positive Economics*.[1] The original paper discusses inflation without any mention of monetary factors, while the later version adds material on money supply, the demand for money, inflationary expectations, etc. In Friedman's words (1953, p. 253): 'As I trust the new material makes clear, the omission from the [earlier] version of monetary effects is a serious error which is not excused but may perhaps be explained by the prevailing Keynesian temper of the times.' Friedman's own transition to a belief in the potency of money summarizes the direction of change, if not the magnitude of change, in the profession's approach to macroeconomic phenomena.

The present survey of developments in monetary theory should be regarded as complementary with Johnson's (1962) paper, which comprehensively covers earlier material. Our discussion deals with the following topics: (1) the theory of money demand; (2) money, inflation and growth; (3) the welfare cost of inflation, the optimum quantity of money, and inflationary finance; (4) disequilibrium theory; (5) the general equilibrium approach to monetary theory; (6) the new microfoundations of money; and (7) rational expectations and the Phillips Curve.

2. The theory of money demand

2.1. Deterministic inventory models

The seminal papers that use an inventory approach to model the demand for money in a deterministic setting are those of Baumol (1952) and Tobin (1956, 1959). The simplest models assume only two stores of value – money and an interest-bearing alternative asset – and exogenous receipt and expenditure streams. The key elements in the model are a lumpy cost of transacting between the two stores of value, an interest rate differential between the earning asset and money that creates a holding cost for money, and a lack of synchronization between receipts and expenditures. In one form of the model there is a lack of synchronization between lump-sum income receipts (say, wage payments) and a continuous stream of (consumption) expenditures. In another, essentially equivalent, version there is a continuous stream of income receipts and lumpy expenditures. An important aspect of extensions of the Baumol–Tobin models, as discussed below, is that the synchronization between receipts and expenditures becomes, at least partially, endogenous.

Economic units are assumed to act to maximize interest earnings (on the earning asset and also on money if money bears explicit interest) net of trans-

---

[1] Friedman makes very clear the changes that appear in the 1953 version.

action costs; equivalently, they can be viewed as minimizing the costs of managing their money balances, where these costs comprise the interest foregone by holding money and the transaction costs of moving between money and earning assets. More frequent transactions enable the economic unit to reduce interest costs by holding smaller money balances on average, at the expense of higher transaction costs. The optimal transaction frequency obviously involves a balance between the increase in transaction costs and the reduction in interest costs. In the Baumol version, where integer constraints on the number of transactions is ignored, the implied average real balances are determined by the well-known square root formula: the money demand elasticities are $+\frac{1}{2}$ with respect to income (expenditures) and the lumpy cost of transacting, and $-\frac{1}{2}$ with respect to the interest rate differential between the earning asset and money. A notable result is the prediction of economies-of-scale in cash holding. This result reflects the lumpy nature of transaction costs – as income rises the increase in foregone interest costs motivates individuals to transact more frequently between cash and earning assets, so that money holding falls as a ratio to income.

In Tobin's formulation integer constraints on numbers of transactions (over the exogenous interval between income receipts) are explicitly taken into account. Individuals now react in a jumpy fashion to changes in interest rates or in costs of transacting. In the Tobin model it is possible (and perhaps likely, quantitatively) for individuals who receive lumpy payments in the form of money to be at a corner solution where the earning asset is not used at all. Average money holding for these individuals, which equals one-half of each lumpy income receipt, responds with unit elasticity to income and the receipt interval, but is insensitive at the margin to interest rates and the cost of transacting between money and earning assets. These results correspond to those obtained in the simple model constructed by Fisher (1922, p. 84) to illustrate the effect on velocity of a shift in the receipt interval.

An aggregation of the integer-constrained solutions from the Tobin model is presented in Barro (1976), assuming a continuous, gamma-distributed cross-sectional distribution of income. The aggregated behavior displays money-demand elasticities that are averages of the Baumol square-root values and those values associated with the corner solution in which the earning asset is not used at all. Hence, economies-of-scale in cash holding are less pronounced (a conclusion that is reinforced when proportional costs of transfer are also included in the model), the magnitude of the interest-rate and transaction-cost elasticities are nonzero but below one-half, and the elasticity with respect to the (exogenous) interval between income receipts is positive, but less than one. However, these conclusions do not hold for general forms of income distribution, and it is not yet clear what minimal restrictions on the distribution will yield these or similar results.

Karni (1973) has extended the Baumol model by viewing transaction costs as partly a time cost, so that changes in the value of time have an effect on money demand through an effect on the cost of transacting. Since money demand in the Baumol (or Tobin) model is unit elastic in income and transaction costs taken together, economies-of-scale result only when transaction costs rise less than proportionately with income (either cross-sectionally or in aggregate time series, depending on the context). If transaction costs are primarily a time cost and if the value of time moves proportionately with (real, per capita) income, then the predicted economies-of-scale would be small.

Although this extended Baumol–Tobin model seems to provide reasonable predictions for the magnitude of income and interest rate elasticities, the model does not seem to account for the absolute volume of household money holdings. If the average receipt interval is one month, the maximum average holding of money predicted by the Tobin formulation would be two weeks' income. This figure substantially underestimates household money holdings in the United States, which are about $1\frac{1}{2}$ months' income in 1973.[2] However, the extensions of the basic model that are described below may account for some of the remainder of money holding.

The Baumol–Tobin framework has been extended to incorporate additional assets; in particular, Feige and Parkin (1971) and Santomero (1974), following a suggestion by Clower (1970), have added commodity stocks as a store-of-value alternative to money and earning assets. A new lumpy cost of transacting is introduced for purchases of commodities with money, where the frequency of commodity purchases is assumed to be larger than (in fact, an integer multiple of) the frequency of exchanges between money and earning assets. The nominal interest rate on commodity stores (assumed to be less than the interest rate on money, which could be zero) is the expected rate of inflation less the rate of physical depreciation and storage costs. The new implications for money demand derive from the extra margin of substitution between money and commodities. An increase in the expected rate of inflation, which raises the interest rate on commodities, reduces money holding (and raises commodity holding) even if the nominal rate of return on earning assets is held fixed. An increase in the transaction cost for purchasing commodities reduces money holding by inducing less frequent, but larger size, commodity purchases – hence, the positive effect of transaction costs on money holding in the Baumol–Tobin model is special to the particular type of transaction that is included in that model.

A more rigorous treatment of the Feige and Parkin model, with special attention to integer and nonnegativity constraints, has been carried out by P. Miller (1973). Unfortunately, the solutions in his model cannot be written in closed form, and it is correspondingly difficult to evaluate the properties of the

---

[2]Using GNP data and flow-of-funds figures on household money holdings from the *Federal Reserve Bulletin*, October 1974.

asset demand functions. However, his results suggest that at least the detailed conclusions of the Feige and Parkin model stem from their neglect of integer constraints on the number of transactions and nonnegativity constraints on money balances and commodity inventories.

Grossman and Policano (1975) point out that commodity inventories and money are always substitutes in the Feige and Parkin model only because the commodities are purchased more frequently than income is received. If some commodities are purchased less frequently than income receipts, then money and total commodity holdings can end up as complements, with both being substitutes for earning assets. In this situation an increase in the expected inflation rate, with the real rate of return on earning assets held fixed, would lower money holding, as expected, but commodity holdings would also decline. Further, if the nominal rate of return on earning assets is held fixed while the expected rate of inflation rises, commodity holdings would rise, and, surprisingly, money holdings would also increase.

Barro (1970) uses the inventory framework to analyze the determination of the interval between income receipts. In a model where earning assets are excluded, increases in the expected inflation rate and decreases in the lumpy costs of making income payments reduce money holding by raising the frequency of income receipts. In a more general context, variations in the income receipt interval can be viewed as an alternative to earning asset exchanges as a mechanism for economizing on cash balances. Accordingly, households may be at a corner solution where it does not pay to conduct earning asset exchanges between income receipts precisely because the receipt interval has been selected in an optimal manner. Moreover, the endogenous determination of the receipt interval implies a dependence of money holdings on interest rates and transaction costs (for making income payments) even in the 'corner solution' case. The determination of the receipt interval has been discussed in the context of a larger model in Santomero (1974), who includes financial earning assets and commodity inventories, and by Clower and Howitt (1975), who include commodity inventories and focus on issues of integer constraints and 'bunching costs' associated with synchronizing different types of transactions.

2.2. Stochastic models

The inventory approach to money demand is applied in a stochastic context in two articles by Miller and Orr (1966, 1968), with some modifications of these results appearing in Orr (1971, chs. 3–6). The basic difference from the Baumol–Tobin setup appears in the description of receipts and expenditures. In Miller and Orr (1966) an economic unit's (a 'firm's') net cash flow from receipts and expenditures (which are treated as exogenous) is entirely random – specifically, the net flow is generated by a trendless random walk characterized by daily variance, σ^2. The firm designs a cash-management policy to minimize the sum of transaction costs (where each exchange between money and an earning asset costs a lump-sum amount) and foregone interest costs from holding money. The tradeoff between these two cost components is qualitatively similar to that in the Baumol–Tobin model. The firm's behavior can be characterized by an inventory rule of the (S, s) type – namely, if the level of cash produced by the exogenous flows reaches zero or a selected ceiling level, S, then the firm reacts with the appropriate exchange between money and the earning asset to end up with a selected return level of cash, s. With cash flow generated by a random walk it is possible to derive closed-form solutions for optimal values of the ceiling and return point. An important aspect of the implied solution for average cash holdings is that the scale variable (which appears with an elasticity of $\frac{1}{3}$) is now σ^2, the variance of net cash flow. As in the Baumol/Tobin model, the prediction is for economies-of-scale in cash holdings (derived partly from the lumpy transaction cost and partly from the implication that the variance of cash flows would typically not rise as the square of sales or any other measure of gross cash flow). There is also a negative interest rate effect on money holding (elasticity of $-\frac{1}{3}$), and a positive effect (elasticity of $\frac{1}{3}$) of transaction costs associated with money–earning asset exchanges. Thus, the differences between the Miller and Orr elasticities and the Baumol elasticities involve a substitution of $\frac{1}{3}$ for $\frac{1}{2}$. In both models foregone interest costs are proportional to average money holdings. However, in the Baumol model, transaction costs vary with the reciprocal of average cash holding, while in the Miller and Orr model, transaction costs depend on the inverse of the square of average cash holdings. Hence, optimal cash holdings in the Baumol model involve a square-root formula, while those in the Miller and Orr model appear in a cube-root formula.

Attempts to extend the Miller and Orr framework to include elements of cash flow trend along with the random movements (modeled by a random walk with unequal probabilities of increases or decreases in cash) have not yet produced clear results [Orr (1971, pp. 74–80)]. The inclusion of proportional transfer costs [Eppen and Fama (1969) and Orr (1971, p. 104)] reduces the predicted economies-of-scale in cash holdings. Miller and Orr (1968) also introduce a third asset – viewed as a less 'liquid,' but higher interest-bearing, alternative to cash – but the implications on which interest rates and transaction costs are most relevant to money demand have not yet been clearly established. Frost (1970) extends the Miller and Orr framework to include direct, bank-service type returns as a function of cash balance holdings. This view rationalizes a part of firm's demand for money as arising from compensating balance-type considerations. Fischer (1974) presents a stochastic model of a firm's demand for cash in a context where cash shortages can reduce the volume of sales.

A model of precautionary demand for money is presented in Patinkin (1965, section V.2 and appendix V) (the work is in collaboration with A. Dvoretzky). In this setup an economic unit faces a given amount of net expenditures over a discrete interval, but the timing of cash inflows and outflows during the period is uncertain. The unit holds a precautionary cash balance to guard against the possibility of a string of cash outflows that would otherwise exhaust liquid resources during the period. One implication of the model is that an increase in the overall volume of transactions (assumed to occur by an increase in the number of payments rather than by an increase in the size of each payment) would lead to a less than proportional increase in money holding. This prediction of economies-of-scale in cash holdings is similar to the one found in the Miller and Orr model.

Tsiang (1969) directly extends the Baumol–Tobin framework to make the expenditure rate stochastic, while maintaining a deterministic, lumpy (exogenous) receipt pattern. In this setting the exogenous net cash flows that occur between income receipts are always negative, but the rate of flow is uncertain. The model introduces another new element – a delay in the receipt of funds from liquidation of 'short' or 'long' assets, with penalty costs associated with each type of liquidation. The conclusions suggested by Tsiang (1969, pp. 112–17) with respect to income, interest rate and transaction cost effects on money demand do not show important differences from the deterministic case. Unfortunately, the impact of randomness, per se – for example, the impact of a change in the variance of expenditures – was not explored.

2.3. Portfolio approach

In his classic article on the demand for assets, Tobin (1958) presented two ways of obtaining an interest-elastic demand for money. The first was essentially the Keynesian speculative demand in which portfolio-holders hold money in the expectation that interest rates will rise and that they will therefore avoid capital losses on bonds. An assumed diversity of expectations and a relationship between the current bond interest rate and the expected interest rate are used to produce a demand for money function with negative interest rate elasticity. The second approach uses expected utility maximization to develop a demand for assets that depends on the expected return and variance of return of the portfolio.

In 'Liquidity Preference as Behavior Toward Risk,' Tobin identifies the safe asset that has no uncertainty of return as money, and this identification is made also by Arrow (1971). However, money is not a safe asset since it is subject to the risk of price level changes,[3] and risk aversion does not provide a basis for the demand for money, narrowly defined, since there are assets, such as time deposits, that have precisely the same risk characteristics as money and yield higher returns. Accordingly, although the Markowitz (1959)–Tobin portfolio framework has provided the basis for significant advances in the field of finance

---

[3]See Fischer (1975b), in which the safe asset is an indexed bond.

and is the basic analytical tool for studying the demand for risky assets, it does not explain the demand for money.

3. Money, inflation and growth

The major questions discussed in the money and growth literature (which, in fact, has little to do with growth) are the 'superneutrality' of money[4] – in particular, the relationships among the steady-state rate of inflation, the real rate of return and capital intensity – and the stability and more detailed dynamic properties of the processes of inflation and capital accumulation. Since the steady-state results have themselves been a matter of controversy, it is not surprising that there is little agreement on appropriate dynamic analyses.

In the simplest neoclassical monetary growth model, there is only one good and two assets, money and capital. Money is entirely of the outside variety and new issues enter the economy in the form of lump-sum transfers to individuals.[5] The first monetary growth models [Tobin (1965) and Sidrauski (1967b)] assume that savings is a constant proportion of disposable income, which includes transfer payments from the government. In a steady state, in which the actual and expected rates of inflation are equal, the rate of inflation is equal to the growth rate of the nominal money stock minus the growth rate of population – a type of long-run quantity theory. The major result in the Tobin model is that capital intensity increases with the inflation rate, or, equivalently, that the real interest rate falls with the inflation rate.[6] This result depends on both portfolio and savings behavior. Consider an increase in the steady-state inflation rate. For a given capital stock, portfolio behavior implies that real balances will be reduced, which implies that less of disposable income has to be saved to provide newly-born individuals with real balances.[7] Given the assumption of a constant savings rate, a larger fraction of savings takes the form of capital, thus raising capital intensity.

---

[4]Money is superneutral when steady-state real variables are independent of the growth rate of money.

[5]If new money accrued to individuals in proportion to their existing holdings of nominal balances, the process would be equivalent to paying interest on money at a rate equal to the growth rate of money. In this situation money growth is always superneutral.

[6]Mundell (1971) obtains a similar interest rate result in a short-run model with an independent investment function. According to his analysis, an increase in the expected rate of inflation reduces real balances, thereby reducing household wealth and causing a drop in aggregate demand. In order to maintain clearing of the commodity market, the real interest rate must fall, implying an increase in capital accumulation. However, this result does not go through if it is assumed that consumption demand depends on real balances relative to desired real balances. In this situation an increase in the expected inflation rate would lower actual and desired real balances by the same amount, and the commodity market would still clear at the initial real interest rate.

[7]The depreciation on real balances associated with inflation is financed from the transfer payments that correspond to the growth rate of money.

However, in the descriptive (nonoptimizing) framework, the steady-state effect of inflation on capital intensity can go in either direction [see Levhari and Patinkin (1968)]. Dornbusch and Frenkel (1973) point out that the key question is the effect of anticipated inflation on consumption demand – the original Tobin–Sidrauski result can be reversed by assuming a sufficiently strong direct positive effect of anticipated inflation on consumption demand.

The steady-state effects of inflation on the real rate of return and capital intensity have been considerably clarified by the model of Sidrauski (1967a), in which saving behavior is derived from intertemporal maximization of utility. Sidrauski deals with an 'immortal family,' whose membership is growing at rate n, that is concerned with maximizing the 'present value' of its intertemporal stream of utility per head. Utility per head is a positive function of consumption and real balances per head – the latter intended as a proxy for the saving in transaction costs, etc., at higher levels of real cash balances. The discount rate for the present-value calculation is a subjective rate of time preference, δ, which is treated as a constant (independent of wealth, etc.). In the Sidrauski model both the real rate of return and the capital–labor ratio in the steady state are invariant with respect to the inflation rate. The reason for these strong results is that the real rate of interest is determined by the modified golden rule of optimal growth theory, namely that the real interest rate, r, is given by $r = \delta + n$.

An intuitive explanation for this result is as follows. Consider a steady-state situation, so that the immortal family's consumption per head is constant over time. Suppose that the real rate of return in this steady state is r. In order for the situation actually to be a steady state it must be that the present value of the family's utility would diminish by any rearrangement, at the rate of return r, of the consumption stream away from uniform consumption. For example, an increase in current saving would reduce current consumption per head, but could be used to augment consumption per head at a later date. The net effect on the present value of utility involves the rate of return r (which indicates the number of units of future consumption that can be obtained by foregoing a unit of present consumption), the subjective rate of time preference δ (which indicates the terms on which the family would trade today's utility per head for future utility per head), and the population growth rate n (which indicates the number of heads that deflate total future consumption relative to the number for present consumption). In order for the family to be just satisfied with uniform consumption per head, there must be a balance among these three forces – in particular, $r = \delta + n$ must apply in the steady state. Since δ and n are exogenous (by assumption), it is immediate that the steady-state real rate of return – and, hence, the steady-state capital–labor ratio, which is determined by equating the marginal product of capital to r – is invariant with respect to the inflation rate. Hence, the nominal rate of interest increases one-to-one with the inflation rate. The only real steady-state effects of higher inflation are a reduction in per capita real cash balances and a consequent reduction in per head utility.

One question about the Sidrauski conclusions is how much they depend on the context of an immortal family that applies a fixed discount rate to a stream of future utilities per head. In an overlapping-generations model with physical capital [Diamond (1965)], the steady-state real rate of return does not generally coincide with the value, $\delta + n$, that emerges in the (effectively) infinite-life case. However, these results seem to depend on the exclusion of operative inter-generational transfers [Barro (1974)],[8] which can transform finite-lived individuals into immortal families with effectively infinite horizons. In any case the subjective rate of time preference[9] becomes an endogenous consideration in an overlapping-generations model, rather than being pinned down exogenously as in the Sidrauski model. Once the rate of time preference is variable, it is at least conceivable that the steady-state real rate of return can be affected by variables like the rate of inflation. The use of an over-lapping-generations model to study money and growth questions was suggested by Tobin (1968), but, to our knowledge, has not yet been followed up.

The Sidrauski model can be extended to make the labor–leisure choice endogenous. In this situation [Brock (1974)], the steady-state values of the real rate of return and (assuming constant-returns-to-scale) the capital–labor ratio remain invariant to the inflation rate, but the steady-state ratios of labor and capital to population can be affected through induced changes in the labor force participation rate. The model can also be extended to view money explicitly as a productive input (either for firms or households), rather than entering it into the utility function [see Levhari and Patinkin (1968), Dornbusch and Frenkel (1973), and Fischer (1974)]. The steady-state real rate of return is again invariant to inflation, but the capital–labor ratio will change if real balances differentially affect the marginal productivity of capital and labor (that is, if the industry that produces transactions has a technology that differs from that of the industry that produces commodities). In the cases mentioned in this paragraph money is not superneutral.

The dynamics of inflation in monetary growth models depends heavily on the process by which expectations are formed. In particular, Sidrauski (1967b), using adaptive expectations, finds a stability condition similar to Cagan's (1956), requiring a lag in the adjustment of expectations to actual inflation. This lag overcomes the familiar instability problem of monetary models in which the demand for real balances is negatively related to the expected rate of inflation. Stability can alternatively be obtained, as Cagan pointed out, by

[8]Corresponding considerations arise in analyzing the burden of the public debt.
[9]The expression, 'subjective rate of time preference,' refers here to the terms at which households are just willing to exchange current for future consumption. The discount factor on future flows of utility (either during an individual's finite lifetime or during the lifetime of a descendant) could still be constant.

assuming a lag in the adjustment of actual to desired real balances. The response of prices in the Cagan and Sidrauski models to changes in the growth rate of money does not reflect the stylized fact that real balances rise at the beginning of inflationary periods. A reformulation of expectations formation [Frenkel (1975)] or adjustment lags for real balances can produce the desired pattern.

The determination of price dynamics in these models is only implicit. Prices change to maintain portfolio balance – that is, to equate the demand for nominal balances to the supply of nominal balances. Models with explicit price-determination equations, in which prices change because they are expected to and/or because there is an excess supply of real balances, are presented in Hadjimichalakis (1971) and Goldman (1972).

The determinants of investment in the one-sector, full-employment neoclassical model are unclear – output that is not consumed is invested. The two-sector model of Foley and Sidrauski (1970, 1971), in which the relative price of capital can change, presents a more carefully worked out view of investment, close in spirit to Tobin's (1971, ch. 18) approach. In short-run (instantaneous) equilibrium the price level, the interest rate, and the relative price of capital adjust to obtain portfolio (stock) equilibrium and equilibrium in the market for consumption goods (flow equilibrium). The rate of investment is, through the supply decisions of firms, an increasing function of the relative price of capital; firms can also be interpreted as selling equity shares to finance investment. The Foley–Sidrauski model adds a third asset – bonds – to the asset menu so that it becomes possible to study policy other than increases in the growth rate of money.

An alternative approach to the determination of investment is advanced in Keynes–Wicksell models [Rose (1966) and Stein (1971)], in which there is an independent (of savings) demand for investment goods. Such models can be viewed as dynamizing *IS–LM* analysis. Prices are assumed to change in response to excess demand in the goods markets, and asset markets may be out of equilibrium. In conditions of excess demand, it is necessary to specify the allocation of frustrations between consumers and investors. The Keynes–Wicksell approach makes possible a more interesting analysis of short-run dynamics than the neoclassical models [Fischer (1972)]; the approach can also be used to model unemployment in monetary growth models [Nagatani (1969)]. The insights of the general disequilibrium models (section 5, below) could be used in refining the specification of disequilibrium behavior in the Keynes–Wicksell models.

4. The welfare cost of inflation, the optimum quantity of money, and inflationary finance

Since the Sidrauski (1967a) model incorporates real balances into the utility function, it can be used to analyze the welfare cost of steady-state inflation. In particular, the first-order maximization condition associated with the substitution between consumption and money holding implies that marginal reductions in real balances should be multiplied by the nominal interest rate (the opportunity-cost rate of holding money) in order to express the welfare loss in terms of the equivalent loss of consumption. This consumer surplus approach to measuring the welfare cost of inflation, which amounts to calculating the area under the money demand function beyond the prevailing level of real balances, was first employed by Bailey (1956) and has since been used by a number of authors. A reduction in the rate of inflation reduces the nominal interest rate (at least if the real rate is held fixed) and thereby raises real balances and lowers the welfare cost of inflation.

The question posed as the optimum quantity of money is what steady-state rate of inflation maximizes steady-state welfare (minimizes the welfare cost of inflation). The answer, provided explicitly by Friedman (1969) and implicitly by Bailey (1956), is that rate of inflation which makes the nominal interest rate (the private cost of holding money) equal to zero.[10] Since this interest rate equates the private cost of holding money with the social cost of producing it (assumed to be zero), it leads to a social optimum. Gramm (1974) points out that the private economy does not automatically reach this point because real balances are produced by a government monopoly. Since the achievement of a zero nominal interest rate typically requires deflation, it may be necessary to impose lump-sum taxes in order to finance the implied rate of reduction in the money stock.

A frequent objection to the optimum quantity of money conclusion is that the increases in real balances produced by decreases in the inflation rate would displace real capital. This displacement occurs in some of the descriptive money and growth models, as discussed above, but does not occur in the Sidrauski optimizing model. Superficially, the limiting properties of that model as the nominal rate of interest approaches zero are curious – namely, why would the private sector hold any real capital at all when the opportunity cost of holding money is driven all the way down to zero? (In this sense the prescription for the optimum quantity of money may indirectly be a call for the government to hold all of the socially-determined quantity of capital.) It seems that a satisfactory resolution of these issues will require a model with uncertainty that explicitly recognizes the differences in risk characteristics of capital and other stores of value, such as money.

The welfare cost of inflation topic is often discussed in connection with the government revenue from (high-powered) money issue [Keynes (1923, ch. 2)]. In the approach of Cagan (1956), Bailey (1956) and Friedman (1971), the present value of government revenue is based entirely on the future flows of new money. If the rate of monetary expansion, μ, is constant and the resulting

---

[10]See Johnson (1969) and Stein (1970) for further discussion of the optimum quantity of money.

constant rate of price change (assumed to be fully perceived) is denoted by π, then the revenue from note issue depends on $m(\pi+n)$, where m is current real balances (of high-powered money) and n is the real growth rate of the economy.[11] The constant rate of inflation that maximizes this revenue can then be shown to occur at a point where the (absolute) elasticity of money demand with respect to the nominal interest rate, $\pi+r$, is above unity. If the real rate of return is determined in accordance with the modified Golden Rule formula, $r = \delta+n$, it can be shown that the revenue-maximizing value of π declines with the real growth rate, n, but that the revenue-maximizing value of μ is independent of n.

A modification to the standard revenue calculations is presented in Auernheimer (1974). His essential argument is that the above calculations omit consideration of the initial stock sale of cash corresponding to the creation of real balances of amount m (or of the stock sale associated with a change in the real balance level from any intial value, m_1, to any final value, m_2). For example, in a nongrowth context ($n = 0$), the value of a license to print (costlessly producible) money, subject to a constraint of zero inflation, would not have zero value, as indicated by the standard approach, but would rather have a value equal to the real amount of cash issued, in exchange for commodities, at the initial date. If the initial lump-sum amount of cash balances is added to the present value from future note issue, the revenue from printing money turns out to depend on $m(\pi+r)$, rather than $m(\pi+n)$. In this formulation the maximization of government revenue from printing money entails setting the (absolute) elasticity of money demand with respect to $\pi+r$ equal to unity – that is, the usual monopoly formula appears in the Auernheimer formulation. Hence, the departure from unit elasticity in the standard approach is a consequence of omitting the initial stock sale of cash.[12] The Auernheimer setup has the same implications as before for the effects of changes in n on the revenue-maximizing values of π and μ (although there would be differences in the case of changes in the subjective discount rate, δ).

Phelps (1973) has argued that setting $\pi+r = 0$ is not generally optimal in a second-best situation where other sources of government revenue also generate dead-weight burdens. The optimal rate of money issue must be derived within an overall public finance framework. In this context the welfare cost of inflation can be expressed in terms of the relation between amounts of dead-weight loss per amount of revenue collected. Using the Auernheimer formulation for revenue, and basing the welfare cost measure on the area under the money demand curve, it can be shown that the marginal collection cost for inflationary finance (the increment in welfare cost expressed as a ratio to the increment in revenue) is equal to $-\eta/(1+\eta)$, where η is the (negative) elasticity of real

---

[11] This calculation assumes that the demand for real per capita balances is unit elastic in real per capita income.

[12] Swan (1970) points out that erroneous conclusions in parts of the monopoly and durable goods literature result from a similar omission.

balances with respect to the nominal interest rate.[13] For example, for the elasticity of $\eta = -\frac{1}{2}$ from the Baumol-type inventory-demand model, the marginal collection cost is one – that is, each dollar of revenue collected would have an associated dollar of dead-weight burden. Accordingly, while the Phelps' proposition that inflationary finance should be chosen as part of the optimal public finance package is incontestable in principle, it may be that, quantitatively, this argument would not lead to the choice of very much monetary expansion (and would likely lead to a negative rate of inflation).

Auernheimer (1974) has pointed out another difficulty with the determination of revenue-maximizing rates of inflation – namely, the calculations of maximum revenue from note issue assume constant (and fully perceived) values for μ and π. The basic difficulty, which occurs in any situation where a monopolist determines the quantity of durable goods to sell, is that the government has a revenue incentive to induce unanticipated capital losses on money holders once they have built up their cash balances under the assumption that the rate of inflation will be constant. In particular, once the government has engineered its initial stock sale of cash, it could increase the present value of its revenue by accelerating money and prices beyond the rates implied by the setting of the money-demand elasticity at -1. Of course, this proposition assumes that price expectations – and the corresponding initial holdings of real balances – do not take into account the government's subsequent incentive to accelerate money and prices. The case where price expectations are based on the assumption that the government will (dynamically) maximize its revenue, together with a knowledge of how the model works to determine prices (that is, a rational expectations assumption – see section 8, below), has not yet been worked out.

As a concluding note, the major lesson of the welfare cost of inflation literature seems to be that economists have very little basis for discussing desirable rates of anticipated inflation. The costs of anticipated inflation in this literature are only liquidity costs. It is hard to take a strong view on why permanent 10 percent inflation is bad on this basis. An urgent order of business remains clarification of the reason for the public's dislike of inflation: if it is merely unanticipated inflation that is objected to, is the public under some illusion, or are economists under some illusion? A lengthy discussion of the costs of inflation is contained in Phelps (1972).

5. Disequilibrium theory

The interpretation of the Keynesian system as an equilibrium system except in the labor market had become widely entrenched in the textbooks by the 1960s, in the shape of the familiar *IS–LM* apparatus. The apparatus was strongly

---

[13]Note that the marginal collection cost is positive as long as $\eta > -1$. If $\eta < -1$, the revenue-maximizing rate of inflation has been exceeded and further expansions of inflation would raise welfare cost while reducing revenue.

criticized as essentially non-Keynesian by Clower (1965) and Leijonhufvud (1968). We shall avoid the exegetical issue and focus instead on disequilibrium models as frameworks for studying the cyclical behavior of the economy.

The distinction between notional and effective demands is critical in disequilibrium analysis. Notional demands and supplies are calculated by individuals and firms on the assumption that they can buy and sell as much as they want of any good at prevailing prices. This assumption can be true only in equilibrium. In disequilibrium there are constraints on the amounts of some goods an individual can buy or sell. Effective demands are calculated conditional on the quantity constraints, or any other nonprice constraints, the individual perceives. For instance, if there is an excess supply of labor, the effective demand for goods by an individual who cannot sell as much labor as he wants is less than the notional demand for goods at prevailing prices. Further, his demand for goods in that situation will be directly a function of the amount of labor he can sell. This is the essence of Clower's (1965) dual decision hypothesis in which one set of demands is expressed if markets clear and another set if individuals are constrained. Clower applied his analysis to the consumption function, thus justifying the Keynesian consumption function with income rather than the real wage as an argument.

The most useful definition of effective demands is not yet settled. For instance, Grossman (1971) assumes that individuals express demands in each market that are based only on the quantity constraints perceived in other markets. Thus, the effective supply of labor when the individual is constrained only in the labor market is the notional supply. This is a convenient but not compelling hypothesis. It also implies that effective demands do not necessarily obey Walras' Law, although the effective demand for money can be (arbitrarily) defined so that Walras' Law holds in a formal sense. Since Grossman views quantities in a monetary exchange economy as determined by the smaller of the effective supply and demand of each commodity other than money (which does not have a market of its own), this redefinition of effective money demand would have no substantive implications in his model.

An analysis of the behavior of firms in demanding labor when they are unable to sell all the goods they want at the prevailing price level had earlier been provided by Patinkin (1965, ch. 13). In that situation, firms' demand for labor is a function of the level of demand rather than (or, possibly, in addition to) the real wage. The Clower and Patinkin analyses are combined by Barro and Grossman (1976, ch. 2) in a simple model with one perishable consumption good, labor services, and money. In this model households supply labor, purchase goods, and can attempt to save by adding to money balances. Firms hire labor to produce goods and both firms and households take prices as given.

For any specified wage and price levels, except for the general market-clearing values, firms and/or households will be constrained in some markets. In particular, on the assumption that quantities are determined by the minimum of effective supply or demand in the commodity and labor markets, there exist wage and price levels – for example, those that are equiproportionately above the general market-clearing values – at which there are excess effective supplies of both labor and goods.[14] In such situations, the Keynesian cross becomes the model of output determination, and any change in demand (caused, say, by an increase in the nominal money stock) has the full multiplier effect on output – provided the change does not move the system into a different configuration of excess effective demands. Significantly, for this Keynesian case to prevail, the real wage may even be below the general market-clearing level if the absolute price level is sufficiently high to reduce the effective demand for goods below the general market-clearing level, through the real balance effect. This model does not require counter-cyclical variations in the real wage rate in order to generate a direct relation between aggregate demand shifts and movements in output and employment.

If the price and wage levels are equiproportionately below the general market-clearing levels, then general excess demand results. The amount of goods available for households to purchase then has an influence on effective labor supply that is analogous to the impact of employment on effective consumption demand in the familiar excess supply case. There is a (labor) supply multiplier for the general excess demand case that parallels the usual (consumption) demand multiplier.

The introduction of a capital market does not alter the basic disequilibrium story. If the rate of return moves rapidly to equate the (effective) supply and demand for loanable funds, then a situation of simultaneous excess supply in the commodity and labor markets corresponds to the standard less-than-full-employment *IS–LM* analysis.

What does money have to do with all this? Leijonhufvud (1968, p. 90) argues that the fact that the offer to work takes the form of a demand for additions to money balances rather than goods is crucial in generating the disequilibrium states. In a one-factor model in which the only market is one in which labor trades for a single good, it is, of course, possible to have unemployment if the real wage is too high; presumably, Leijonhufvud is arguing that the real wage could not be too high in the simplest nonmonetary model. It is also clear that unemployment can arise at disequilibrium prices – and probably even at a real wage below the general market-clearing level – in models with many goods but no money. Grossman (1974) constructs a model in which money's role as a medium of exchange is important in determining the existence of multipliers, though not essential for the existence of unemployment. The key element of the medium of exchange property in his model is that it determines the pattern of trades, and therefore the actual volume of transactions implied by a short-end

---

[14]The fact that households can plan to save by adding to money balances is important in this regard.

(supply, demand) rule for a given set of (exogenous) prices. The role of money in disequilibrium trading has also been studied by Benassy (1974).[15] In any event, it is clear that the argument that money is crucial in generating disequilibrium cannot be adequately studied in models with exogenous prices.

Expectations are obviously important in disequilibrium analysis. To the extent that current unemployment is regarded as transitory, effective demand will be little reduced by constraints in the labor market, since individuals will draw down assets, if they have them, to maintain consumption. This point is developed in the context of a consumer's life cycle model in Barro and Grossman (1976, ch. 2). The role of capital market imperfections and the distribution of unemployment relative to that of asset-holdings in determining the size of the multiplier are studied by Fleming (1973). Liquidity constraints are also analyzed in the work by Clower (1967) and Arrow and Hahn (1971, ch. 13). Tobin and Dolde (1971) present some theoretical and simulation analyses of liquidity effects on aggregate consumption behavior.

The Walrasian assumption that prices move instantly to clear markets is replaced in disequilibrium analysis by the assumption that quantities can move instantaneously (rapidly) while prices remain fixed (move slowly). Thus, a discrete change in the stock of money or in expectations, say, results in substantial movements in output in these models, while prices are held fixed. The outstanding problem in macroeconomic disequilibrium theory is the working out of joint price and quantity determination.[16] The large information and search-theory literature on price determination will undoubtedly play a role in this synthesis. While disequilibrium analysis has succeeded in presenting models in which many Keynesian notions – notably that of effective demand – are clarified, it remains to be seen whether the same analytical structure will prove useful when applied to situations in which price determination is endogenous.

6. The general equilibrium approach to monetary theory

The general equilibrium approach has been advanced in a number of papers by Tobin (1971, chs. 13, 16–21) (chs. 17 and 21 are jointly with Brainard) and in a paper by Brainard (1964). A key element in the approach is that money is viewed as just one among a spectrum of imperfectly substitutable assets, the demands for some of which can be determined on the risk-aversion basis

---

[15]Benassy also rigorously demonstrates the existence of a quantity equilibrium at a prespecified set of prices under fairly general conditions.

[16]Barro and Grossman (1976, Ch. 2) append the 'law of supply and demand' to a static model to discuss dynamics and stability. Assumptions about the demands expressed in markets which do not clear, as discussed above, are obviously important in this regard. See Iawi (1974) for an analysis of joint price and quantity determination.

of the portfolio approach. The nature of these models is indicated by Tobin (1971, ch. 13, p. 225):

'The structure of rates may be pictured as strung between two poles, anchored at one end by the zero own-rate conventionally borne by currency (and by the central bank discount rate) and at the other end by the marginal productivity of the capital stock. Among assets that are not perfect substitutes, the structure of rates will depend upon relative supplies. In general, an increase in the supply of an asset – e.g., long-term government bonds – will cause its rate to rise relative to other rates, but less in relation to assets for which it is directly or indirectly a close substitute.

In such a synthesis, monetary policy falls in proper perspective. The quantity of money can affect the terms on which the community will hold capital, but it is not the only asset supply that can do so. The net monetary position of the public is important, but so is its composition.'

Tobin has used the approach to analyze whether a decrease in long-term government debt (through increased taxation) is expansionary or contractionary.[17] The basic answer is that the operation will be contractionary (raising the required rate of return on capital) if long-term government debt is a better substitute for money than for capital. One shortcoming with this specific analysis, though not necessarily with the general technique, is that it neglects the future tax liabilities associated with the government debt as an element of household balance sheets. If these tax liabilities were a perfect substitute for the debt itself,[18] then changes in the stock of debt would not exert any pressure at all on the spectrum of interest rates. The conclusion may be different depending on whether the taxes are lump-sum or based on income, on whether there is uncertainty about future income or tax rates, and on the distribution of risk attitudes in the economy. The more general point is that the nature of taxes must be brought into a full analysis of changes in government debt within a framework of asset market equilibrium.

The application of the approach to financial intermediation [Tobin (1971, ch. 17) – a joint paper with Brainard] leads to the conclusion that autonomous growth in an intermediary would be expansionary (lowering the required rate of return on capital). In a discussion of government regulation of interest rates, Tobin (1971, ch. 18) stresses that the fixing of money's (currency's) nominal interest rate at zero is important in macroeconomic analyses. The effect of

---

[17]This discussion [Tobin, (1971, ch. 13, p. 225)] explicitly abstracts from the deflationary short-run multiplier effects of the tax increase (which arise if future tax liabilities associated with government debt are not fully capitalized).

[18]By a perfect substitute we mean here that households are concerned only with the difference between the amount of government bonds and the amount of capitalized tax liabilities in their portfolio. This issue is related to, but not identical with, the question of whether government bonds are net wealth [Barro (1974)].

Regulation Q-type interest rate ceilings on time deposits [Tobin (1971, ch. 19)] turns out to be contractionary if time deposits are a better substitute for money than for capital. However, this analysis may take the legal fixing of interest rates too literally – M. Klein (1971) and B. Klein (1974) have stressed the importance of implicit interest payments that can avoid the legal interest rate prohibitions.

The general equilibrium approach can also be applied to standard monetary policy instruments, such as changes in commercial bank reserve require- ments and shifts in the central bank discount rate, as well as to less conventional questions, such as the impact of paying interest on commercial bank reserves held at the central bank and the effect of prohibition of interest payments on demand deposits (which is likely to be only partially effective). In all of these questions, a crucial issue is the relative substitutabilities among currency, demand deposits, and the variety of earning assets.

Finally, it should be noted that the 'general equilibrium' in the description of most applications of the above approach should be understood as referring to equilibrium in the asset markets alone, conditional on the values of other economic variables, such as the level of output or the price level. These other variables are themselves endogenously determined when the asset markets are combined with the goods and factor markets.

7. The new microfoundations of money

Monetary analysis typically starts from an informal and usually picturesque explanation of the use of money, involving, as in Jevons (1875), the double coincidence of wants and the four functions of money. A demand for money is then postulated and money is treated as one of the assets in a macromodel, distinguished from other assets in one or more ways: since money is the medium of exchange demanded for its command over goods and services, the demand is a demand for real balances; since it is a medium of exchange the real income elasticity of demand is positive; its interest return may be fixed exogenously; its nominal quantity, if it is a fiat money, can be exogenously determined.

The criticism 'that the foundations of monetary theory have not yet been laid'[19] turns primarily on the argument that there is no role for money in macro- models, which are all small Walrasian general equilibrium models. Essentially, it is argued that there is no role for money in intertemporal general equilibrium models since all trades can be arranged in the first period the auctioneer opens the market. Money, serving as a store of value, can be introduced into such an economy in a manner suggested by Arrow (1964), but money is, in Hahn's terminology, 'inessential' in that the equilibrium allocation of goods in the economy with money is precisely the same as the equilibrium without it. Alter- natively, within each trading period, there is no obvious need for a medium of

---

[19]Hahn (1973a, p. 233). This article is a useful survey of one branch of the modern literature.

exchange since all trade takes place with the market at equilibrium prices. Even if it is assumed that trade is between individuals rather than with the market, there appears to be no reason why one good rather than another should be used to balance trade between two individuals whose needs do not doubly coincide – nor is there a good reason why trade should balance between individuals. While these are compelling criticisms of the general equilibrium model as a description of modern economies, their practical import applied to the standard macro-models is less clear, since several features of the demand for money in such models do reflect the medium of exchange function of money.

Recent literature on the foundations of monetary theory has attempted: to make precise the notion of the double coincidence of wants; to present criteria for the selection of the medium or media of exchange (also, under the guise of 'portability,' 'divisibility,' etc., a concern of the early monetary theorists); and, fundamentally, to explain how it is that the use of money enables an economy to attain equilibria that are not possible without money. At the risk – amounting to certainty – of oversimplification, we can distinguish three approaches. The first approach deals with a single period and investigates the possibility and num-ber of exchanges required to attain a competitive equilibrium allocation of goods under various constraints on the exchanges that can be made when all trading is strictly bilateral. The papers by Starr (1972), Ostroy (1973), and Jones (1974) assume that prices are fixed throughout at their competitive equilibrium values, while Feldman (1973) allows each pair of trading partners to negotiate their own exchange rates. The second approach, associated with Foley (1970), Niehans (1969, 1971), and Kurz (1974b), examines single-period exchanges in an economy in which transactions are costly, and determines market equilibrium and the nature of exchanges for that economy. The third approach, used by Hahn (1973b), Kurz (1974a), Starr (1974), Starrett (1973) and Heller (1974), involves a multiperiod general equilibrium framework in which exchange within periods is with the market, but in which money can be useful in making inter-temporal transfers. Transaction costs and/or informational considerations are involved in all the analyses. Many of these models can be viewed as developments of work by Hicks (1967), attempting to relate traditional explanations of the use of money to Keynes' three motives for holding money.

The difficulties of barter and the double coincidence of wants in the context of bilateral trading can be illustrated in a three-person, three-good exchange economy in which individuals have the initial allocations of goods $(1, 0, 0)$, $(0, 1, 0)$, $(0, 0, 1)$, and in which the equilibrium allocation is $(0, 1, 0)$, $(0, 0, 1)$ and $(1, 0, 0)$. The equilibrium price vector can be taken as $(1, 1, 1)$. Impose the double coincidence requirement by forbidding trades in which an individual increases either his (positive) excess demand for or (positive) excess supply of any good. If exchanges take place at equilibrium prices and trade is required to balance in each exchange, there is no set of bilateral trades by which the equili-brium allocation can be reached from the initial allocation. The introduction of an extra commodity, not subject to the double coincidence requirement with each individual ending with as much of that good as he started, or the relaxation of the requirement of budget balance in each transaction, makes the equilibrium allocation attainable. This is the spirit of the more general results proved in Starr (1972).

But why impose budget balance? The reasons are elucidated in Ostroy (1973), who asks what constraints have to be imposed on individuals who have limited information about the excess demand of other traders to ensure that the Walrasian equilibrium is attained. The requirement given trade at equilibrium prices is that budgets balance over the entire sequence of trades. But since individuals cannot monitor the sequences of trades of others, budget balance over the sequence of trades can be ensured only by having balance at each trade. Given the latter constraint, the use of money – or a record keeping system – provides more rapid convergence to equilibrium than is possible without it. Similar results, in which the use of a commodity (rather than a fiat) money permits the attainment of the equilibrium allocation with less information than is required without it, are proved in Ostroy and Starr (1973).

As an example of the second approach, we consider the trading-post model used by Niehans (1971), in which there are potentially $n(n-1)/2$ markets in which each of n goods can be traded for every other good. Thus, trade is with the market rather than explicitly between individuals; one of Niehans' concerns is to obtain restrictions on transactions costs such that one of the goods emerges as money. Some of each good is used up in the process of its being traded for another, with these transaction costs assumed proportional to the amount of the good being given up. An equilibrium for such an economy exists, and in general each of the trading posts may be open. However, if there is one good that has zero transaction costs, in that none of it is used up when it is exchanged for another good, then there will be only $(n-1)$ operative trading posts, with the one good appearing on one side of all transactions. Again, there is a medium of exchange arising in this case because it saves transaction costs.[20] Niehans (1971) also discusses the extension of the model to account for the holding of a fiat money that does not yield direct utility. In this context a multi-period model is needed with some constraint imposed to ensure the holding of money at the end – such a constraint is always required in finite-horizon fiat money models.

The work by Hahn (1973b) emphasizes both transaction costs and the temporal sequence of exchanges.[21] The basic results are once more best understood by means of an example, due to Starrett (1973). Consider a two-person, two-

[20]Karni (1972) points out that no economy is fully monetized and examines the conditions under which exchanges are or are not mediated by money in the context of a model similar to Niehans'.
[21]An influential paper by Radner (1968) also emphasizes the sequential nature of transactions and the importance of the unfolding of new information over time.

period, one-good economy. Endowments of the good are $(0, 1)$ and $(1, 0)$. There are potentially a spot and futures market in period 1 and a spot market in period 2. For simplicity, let each individual have the Leontief utility function $U(C_1, C_2) = \min (C_1, C_2)$. Then, Pareto optimal allocations are $(a, a), (1-a, 1-a)$, $0 \leq a \leq 1$. Assume that use of the forward market is costly but the spot markets are operated costlessly. Then Starrett shows that in competitive equilibria, in which budgets have to balance in each period, the second-period spot market is not used but the forward market is – which is costly. Therefore, the competitive equilibrium is not Pareto optimal.[22] However, if a paper asset is introduced such that budgets do not have to balance over goods transactions within each period, but only over both periods, then the spot markets are used in both periods and efficient equilibrium results. Transactions in the paper asset are taken to be costless. The example appears closely related to the results obtained in the consumption loans model, though inefficiency occurs here in a finite horizon model.

In most of the contributions discussed above, money makes the attainment of equilibria that are unattainable without it possible by permitting the unbalancing of budgets in goods within a period or transaction. The reasons for balance at each transaction have to do with restrictions on the information that an individual is likely to have about other traders' solvency and the saleability of goods taken in exchange. Those models that concentrate on market equilibrium in intertemporal models do so because it is argued that the sequential nature of exchange is important, but then implicitly allow simultaneous trade within a period. Indeed, they provide more reason for the use of bonds than for the use of a medium of exchange.[23]

There are few formal attempts to explain the emergence of money from barter systems; Kurz (1974b) argues that this social choice is fundamentally not analyzable by conventional economists' methods, though analysis of transaction costs, as in Niehans, is likely to at least restrict the choice of media of exchange. The work by Jones (1974) provides an interesting start on the dynamics of the emergence of a medium of exchange. The literature mentioned here has assumed nonincreasing returns to scale in transactions, though there are attempts to study money in nonconvex transactions technologies.[24] The relationship between the existence of organized markets and the use of a medium of exchange is as yet unclear. Further, uncertainty has not been given a prominent role in any of these models, except in Brunner and Meltzer (1971).

This work is obviously both difficult and only at a beginning. It is not clear where, if anywhere, it will lead. It will no doubt provide more convincing and

---

[22]Starrett shows that this result is not dependent on the assumption that only the futures market has costly transactions, or that the utility functions are Leontief.

[23]It may well be, though, that only trivial transaction costs account for the failure of bonds to be used as a medium of exchange. See Heller (1974).

[24]See Niehans (1969), Heller (1974) and Heller and Starr (1973).

carefully worked out explanations for the use of a medium of exchange than we now have, but it is probable that those explanations will not be fundamentally different from the traditional verbal explanations. Furthermore, it is doubtful that this work will have any major consequences for the way in which macro-models are built.

8. Rational expectations and the Phillips Curve

It is, no doubt, peculiar to discuss rational expectations as a branch of mone-tary theory, but recent applications of the notion to monetary theory are im-portant. We shall discuss both the hypothesis and some of its implications. The dependence of the dynamics of the price level on the process of expectations formation is obvious from both the money and growth and the new micro-economic foundations of inflation literature. Although adaptive expectations was widely used, explanations for its use were few: adaptive expectations seemed reasonable and proved useful in explaining data, as in Cagan's (1956) pioneering work on hyperinflation. However, even in Cagan's model, adaptive expectations are systematically wrong in predicting, say, the behavior of the inflation rate in response to a change in the growth rate of money.

In proposing rational expectations, Muth (1961, p. 316) argued 'that expecta-tions, since they are informed predictions of future events, are essentially the same as the predictions of the relevant economic theory.' In deterministic models, rational expectations are equivalent to perfect foresight, so that the expected path of prices in a model is the path that, according to the model, subsequently ensues, given the expectations. Perfect foresight in monetary growth models implies instability of the inflationary process if no jumps in the price level are permitted; alternatively, if jumps in the price level can take place, perfect fore-sight implies there are many possible paths for prices, only one of which is stable [see Black (1974) and Sargent and Wallace (1973)]. This saddle point indeterminacy–instability result is similar to the well-known Hahn paradox of capital theory, and raises the question of whether the unique stable path will be followed in a competitive economy. Brock (1974) presents an optimizing money and growth model in which the economy follows the stable perfect foresight path because it is utility-maximizing.

The types of policy actions that are consistent with the perfect foresight assumption are limited: in perfect foresight models, preannounced changes in the growth rate of money lead to changes in the inflation rate before the change in the money growth rate occurs. Since there are no long-run sources of money illusion in these models, changes in money growth have real effects only through the inflation effect on the demand for real balances. There is no counter-cyclical policy role for money. In a rational expectations framework, and given wage and price flexibility and long-run neutrality of money, a necessary, but not sufficient, condition for money to affect real variables in the 'short run' is uncertainty about both money and the real economy.

In a stochastic model, the rational expectations assumption is that the subjective probability distributions used in decision-making by private agents are the same as the probability distributions for the relevant variables implied by the model. More generally, if individuals do not have all the information used in the model, expectations are rational if they are optimal predictions based on the information available to the individual.

It is important to distinguish the rational expectations hypothesis per se, which says only that individuals make the best use of the information they are assumed to have and is entirely unexceptionable, from the models known as rational expectations models that have usually been constructed so that money is neutral aside from possible expectations phenomena. In the context of existing rational expectations models with uncertainty, three key issues arise with respect to the cyclical role of money. First, does the model generate a short-run Phillips Curve, which in this context can be viewed as an effect of unanticipated movements in money on the levels of output and employment? Second, if the Phillips Curve exists, is it exploitable, so that monetary policy can systematically affect the economy's time path of output and employment? Third, if an active policy role for money is feasible, is it also desirable?

It was already suggested above that uncertainty would be a necessary condition for generating a Phillips Curve in a rational expectations model. The additional ingredient that turns out to be needed is some limitation on current information that allows individuals to become confused between monetary and real shocks. The point can be brought out within a simple uncertainty model that includes only one type of commodity and money (with new money entering as lump-sum transfer payments). We shall sketch such a model here and also briefly indicate the mechanics of calculating 'rational expectations.' The difficulty in these calculations is that expectations, say of the general price level, must be determined simultaneously with the price level itself.

The first version of the model will turn out to allow individuals too much information to generate a Phillips Curve. We shall then discuss informational limitations that do result in a Phillips Curve. The key relation in the model is a positive response of supply (of commodities and/or factor services) to the relative values of actual and anticipated prices. Friedman (1968) rationalizes this effect by arguing that labor suppliers would deflate their nominal wage offers (one of the actual prices in a larger model) by the expected price of a market basket of goods. Hence, when wages increase faster then expected prices during a period of unanticipated inflation, labor supply rises above its normal level. Lucas and Rapping (1969) arrive at a similar conclusion, although by a route that stresses the dependence of labor supply on current nominal wages relative to expected future nominal wages. Similar effects of prices relative to expected prices on factor supplies arise in optimal search models [for example, Alchian

(1970), Mortensen (1970) and McCall (1970)]. In these models a decline in nominal wage offers relative to expected wages (over space) reduces labor supply by increasing the amount of time devoted to job search.

A simple supply function that embodies these ideas would take the form,

$$y_t^s = \alpha[P_t - E_t(P_{t+1})] + u_t^s, \tag{1}$$

where y^s is the supply of commodities and/or factor services (above or below some 'normal' level that we do not deal with explicitly), P is the actual price of commodities, and u^s is a random term that shifts supply through unanticipated changes in productivity, tastes, etc.[25] The time subscript represents the date to which each variable refers. $E_t(P_{t+1})$ denotes the expectation, formed at date t, of the price level that will prevail next period, $t+1$.

The second element of the model is a description of aggregate demand. Money enters the model through its effects on aggregate demand. A simple form is

$$y_t^d = \beta[M_t - E_t(P_{t+1})] + u_t^d, \tag{2}$$

where y^d is aggregate demand, M is the nominal stock of money, and u^d is a random demand shift term. Increases in M_t relative to $E_t(P_{t+1})$ raise demand through a real balance effect.

The price level and output are determined by a market-clearing condition equating aggregate supply and demand. Denoting the random net excess demand shift by $u_t \equiv u_t^d - u_t^s$, the equation of supply and demand from (1) and (2) implies

$$P_t = (1 - \beta/\alpha)E_t(P_{t+1}) + (\beta/\alpha)M_t + (1/\alpha)u_t \tag{3}$$

and

$$y_t = \beta[M_t - E_t(P_{t+1})] + u_t^d. \tag{4}$$

The M_t and u_t terms in (3) illustrate standard 'demand-pull' effects on the price level. The $E_t(P_{t+1})$ term can be viewed as a 'cost-push' effect, where an increase in the expected future price level raises the current price level for given values of the excess demand terms if $\alpha > \beta$ applies (amounting to a dominance of substitution over income effects). Note that, in this case, the partial effect on P_t of an increase in M_t is less than one – that is, with future price expectations held fixed, an increase in money produces a less than proportionate response in prices. It is this less than unitary response that introduces the possibility of short-run effects of money on output. Note, however, that equal increases in M_t and $E_t(P_{t+1})$ will produce an equal increase in P_t – a response that will characterize at least the long-run effect of money when price expectations are

---

[25]The variables y_t, P_t, etc. are actually the logarithms of output, the price level, etc.

endogenous to the model. The important properties of eq. (4) are that increases in M_t, for a given value of $E_t(P_{t+1})$, raise output, but equal movements in M_t and $E_t(P_{t+1})$ do not affect output.

Eq. (4) would produce a Phillips Curve relation if it were assumed that expected prices were fixed [corresponding to the results discussed by Grossman (1973)] or, somewhat less stringently, if expected prices reacted gradually to actual prices according to a fixed rule, such as an adaptive expectations formula. In these situations there would also be an active role for monetary policy – in particular, movements in money that offset the real demand shifts, u_t^d, would work to stabilize output.

The Phillips Curve interpretation of eq. (4) obviously hinges on the way in which price expectations are formed. The idea of the rational expectations approach is to base expectations on the model itself – in particular, expectations of P_{t+1} are based on the knowledge that prices in all periods are determined from market-clearing relations of the form of eq. (3). To use the model to take expectations requires a specification of the stochastic structure of the model: we make the simple assumption that increments to M and u are statistically independent over time with zero mean, so that M and u are generated by trendless random walks.[26] Then, the expectation formed at date t of any future value of M (or u) is simply M_t (or u_t).

Now, observe that M_t and u_t completely determine the current state of the economy, since lagged values do not appear in eqs. (3) and (4) and all expectations must also depend only on M_t and u_t (in the random walk case). Since the model is linear, it is reasonable to postulate that P_t will itself be a (log) linear function of M_t and u_t – that is,

$$P_t = \pi_1 M_t + \pi_2 u_t, \tag{5}$$

where π_1 and π_2 are as yet undetermined coefficients.[27] Using the trial solution (5) and the random walk assumption, we have

$$E_t(P_{t+1}) = \pi_1 M_t + \pi_2 u_t,$$

so that, substituting into eq. (3), the π's are given by

$$\pi_1 = 1, \qquad \pi_2 = 1/\beta.$$

[26]Inclusion of trends would not affect the conclusions.

[27]Use of this solution procedure requires the model to be stable. An alternative procedure, that is equivalent in the stable case, involves repeated substitution into expectations equations obtained by updating eq. (3) and taking expectations. The solution by repeated substitution involves an infinite sum of coefficients in M_t and u_t which converges since $|1 - \beta/\alpha| < 1$, as long as expected future prices can be bounded away from plus or minus infinity. This convergence condition, which is also the stability condition, has been termed the 'absence of speculative bubbles' by Sargent and Wallace (1975). The stability issue has been explored in perfect foresight models by Sargent and Wallace (1973) and Brock (1974), but has not been examined rigorously in the uncertainty context.

Hence, the solution for prices and output is

$$P_t = E_t(P_{t+1}) = M_t + (1/\beta)u_t,$$

$$y_t = u_t^s. \tag{6}$$

A first observation is that money now affects prices equiproportionately. From the perspective of eq. (3), the explanation is that expected future prices – determined now within the model – also move in proportion to money. The implication, consistent with eq. (4), is that movements in money have no output effects. Output is determined in eq. (6) only by real variables ('tastes and technology') and there is no Phillips Curve in the model.*

The reason for the above result is that individuals have too much information – namely, full current information – for movements in money to have real effects. The information structure must be complicated in some way in order to generate a Phillips Curve. One modification that turns out not to be sufficient is to introduce a lag in information transmittal. Current information could be limited to an observation of the price level (of the single type of commodity), while information of more detail – namely, about M and u – is received only with a one-period lag. The essence of individual information problems in the model concerns the forecasting of future prices – that is, the calculation of $E_t(P_{t+1})$. In the present setting, where the underlying determinants of prices – the monetary and real shocks, M and u – are generated by random walks, it also turns out that the price level itself will move as a random walk. The current price level, P_t, is then the best prediction for any future price level. Therefore, when individuals observe P_t, they already possess full current information with respect to predictions of future prices. Removing knowledge of the breakdown of current demand movements into monetary and real components does not present a substantive information problem and, therefore, does not lead to a Phillips Curve.

From this point there are two alternative ways to proceed to set up an extended rational expectations model that does yield a Phillips Curve. First, remaining within the setting of the above model, it can be assumed that monetary and real shocks are generated by stochastic processes with different intertemporal characteristics. For example, money could still be generated by a random walk (so that money growth is serially independent), but the real shock, u, could have a tendency to return to a normal level, so that movements in u are negatively correlated over time. In this situation predictions of future price levels would be sharpened if currently observed (unanticipated) price movements could be dichotomized into underlying monetary and real components. In particular, under the above specification, movements in P associated with movements in

---

* An error has been corrected in the originally published form of equation (6). The absence of U_t^d from the output solution would not obtain if a real balance term had been included in the supply function of equation (1).

M would tend to be 'permanent' – in the sense of determining the most likely point for all future prices – while those associated with u would be at least partially temporary. Note that, in this case, the separation of price movements into permanent versus transitory components amounts to a separation of demand shifts into monetary versus real sources.

Individuals will form $E_t(P_{t+1})$ based on their best guesses of how much the (unanticipated) price movements are attributable to money versus real sources. In effect, the weight attached to the currently observed price, P_t, in forming $E_t(P_{t+1})$ will be higher the larger the fraction of (unanticipated) price movements that, on the average, are associated with money movements. The latter depends on the variance of money relative to the variance of real shocks. In particular, the higher the relative variance of money, the more sensitive will $E_t(P_{t+1})$ be to current price observations, because individuals think that observed price movements are more likely to be caused by money, and are therefore more likely to be 'permanent.'

To see the implications for output, suppose for expository purposes that the real variable, u, does not shift (and has not shifted for some time, so that a zero shift corresponds to ex ante expectations). The price level will then be unexpectedly high or low depending only on whether money is unexpectedly high or low. If money is higher than anticipated, prices will be unexpectedly high, but, in the general case, individuals will not attribute the full amount of the unanticipated price rise to a monetary disturbance. To the extent that individuals incorrectly attribute some part of the price rise to a real (temporary) demand shift, price expectations – and therefore also actual prices [eq. (3)] – will rise less than proportionately with money. It follows that the monetary disturbance will have some positive effect on output [eq. (4)]. Accordingly, there is now a Phillips-type relation between unanticipated money movements and output. However, in the long run (one period of time in the simplest models where full information is obtained with a one-period lag),[28] the monetary disturbance is perceived as entirely monetary, and output effects vanish.

The extent of the output response to a money shock varies inversely with the responsiveness of price expectations to current price observations. Hence, if money is relatively more variable, expectations will be more sensitive and output will be correspondingly less sensitive to a (given size) money shock. In other words the magnitude of the Phillips Curve slope – viewed here as expressing the positive relation between output and unanticipated money shocks – diminishes as the variance of money rises. This proposition was developed by Lucas (1973, p. 330) in a somewhat different context (see below). This example of the dependence of a reduced form coefficient on the underlying stochastic structure has been stressed as a general proposition by Lucas (1972b). Namely, econometric

---

[28]Lucas (1975) has extended the rational expectations framework to allow for a monetary effect on output that lasts longer than one period. His model incorporates gradual information spread and persistence effects associated with the accumulation of physical capital (which lasts more than one period).

models estimated from past data may not be relevant for policy evaluation, since the parameters of such models can be expected to change along with policy.

The second general approach that yields a Phillips Curve is one that was suggested by Phelps (1970) and used in a rational expectations context by Lucas (1972a, 1973) and Barro (1976). Production and exchange are viewed as taking place at physically separated locations, so that a distinction between local and global information can arise. Local markets are now subjected to an additional random disturbance that describes shifts in relative supplies and demands (unanticipated changes in the composition of tastes and technology). Current information of individuals is now limited to the observation of a single local price, and this observation conveys (blurred) information about three underlying shocks: monetary, aggregate real, and relative (real). For convenience, we can return to the initial specification of the aggregate disturbances in which money and the aggregate real shock are generated by random walks, so that all the aggregate shifts are 'permanent.' A simple assumption about the relative shifts is that they are purely transitory – amounting to the assumption that perfect arbitrage of anticipated relative price differentials occurs over one period of time. The problem of separating price movements into permanent versus temporary components in order to predict future prices then amounts to a separation of demand shifts into aggregate versus relative components.[29] In this case monetary disturbances have output effects because they are partly confused with the relative shocks. The magnitude of the output effect now depends on the relative values of the total aggregate demand variance and the relative demand variance. Again, the Phillips Curve slope coefficient declines in magnitude when money becomes more unpredictable.

Implications for monetary policy

Models in which the Phillips Curve is a result only of expectational errors, with expectations formed in a rational manner based on limited information, have radical implications for monetary policy. The effects of money variance, per se, have been considered in Barro (1976). It is demonstrated there that an increase in this variance, holding fixed the variance of real shocks, would increase the variance of output about the level that would have been obtained under conditions of full current information. This result obtains although increased money variance appears, in one respect, to be 'stabilizing.' That is, the inverse effect of money variance on the magnitude of the Phillips Curve slope implies a smaller amount of fooling associated with monetary shocks. However, the increased errors associated with real shocks turn out to more than balance the gains on the monetary side. Essentially, an increased variance of money reduces the information content of observed prices and therefore makes it more difficult

---

[29]In the more general case where aggregate real shocks are partly transitory, the division into permanent versus transitory involves two types of demand divisions: aggregate versus relative and monetary versus real.

for individuals to respond 'appropriately' to changing patterns of relative supplies and demands. On these grounds there is an efficiency argument for making
money as predictable as possible – a conclusion that is obviously reminiscent
of the constant growth rate rule that has been advocated by Simons (1948)
and Friedman (1960).

The usual view of activist monetary policy refers to systematic feedback
from economic variables to money, rather than to money variance, per se.
The implications of systematic money rules in rational expectations models
depend crucially on the relative information positions of the policymaker and
the public. In the situation considered by Sargent and Wallace (1975), the policymaker determines M_t as a function of a set of variables (for example, P_{t-1} and
y_{t-1}) that have already been fully perceived at date t by all individuals. Further,
the form of the feedback rule is, itself, a part of individual information sets.
In this situation – where the policymaker possesses no superior information –
the feedback effects of money are fully taken into account in the formation of
price expectations. Accordingly, the existence of the feedback rule for money has
no effect on (the entire probability distribution of) output. Hence, although a
Phillips Curve exists, it is not exploitable by monetary policy.

In a second situation, the monetary rule is again general knowledge, but the
policymaker has superior information about the economy – for example, he
obtains information more rapidly than the public about aggregate prices and
output. Under these conditions, it is shown in Barro (1976) that countercyclical
monetary policy (that offsets shifts in aggregate real shocks) can work to move
the economy toward the level of output that would be chosen under full current
information. The reason for the potential effectiveness of monetary policy
under these circumstances is that a policy can be designed that induces individuals to act as though they were aware of the extra information that is possessed
by the policymaker. This interpretation suggests the obvious alternative to an
activist monetary policy of providing the extra information directly to the public.
In effect, the case for activist monetary policy in a situation where the authority
has superior economic information reduces to arguments for economies-of-
scale in information gathering and processing.

Finally, there is the situation in which the monetary authority has superior
information about its own actions, though not necessarily about the economy.
In this context Taylor (1975) demonstrates that a deceptive monetary policy
can have systematic output effects during 'transition periods' in which the public
gradually learns the nature of policy. Sargent and Wallace (1976) have raised
some general questions about the feasibility of this sort of deception, even in
the short run. In any event, if the deceptive policy is feasible, there is still a
question about its desirability. At least in the situation where the policymaker
lacks superior information about the economy, it is clear that systematic policy
deception will move output away from its full current information position.
Hence, the normative case for policy deception must rely on arguments for the

nonoptimality of the full current information position. Phelps (1972) and Tobin (1972) have presented heuristic arguments for external effects of the congestion-type, though Prescott's (1975) analysis suggests that the main external effects would arise from income taxation, unemployment compensation and the like, that produce a gap between marginal product and the net real wage rate. Although external effects of this type would argue for economic policies that lower the average rate of unemployment below the natural rate (if such policies were feasible), it is not clear that there are any implications here for the cyclical policy role of money.

Although the rational expectations hypothesis provides a consistent explanation of some cyclical phenomena, it arouses a number of strong reactions. One reaction is that it is absurd to assume individuals can make the necessary calculations since most economists still cannot do so (Fisher, 1972); this is reminiscent of criticisms of microeconomic theory on the grounds that most consumers have never seen a Lagrangean, and it is equally beside the point. Individuals and firms do read newspapers and buy consulting services, and their expectations are influenced by model predictions (although most present models use adaptive expectations). The rational expectations assumption may be excessively strong in that it ignores uncertainty over model selection, but it is a more persuasive starting point than the alternative of using a rule of thumb for expectations formation that is independent of the stochastic properties of the time path of the variable about which expectations are formed. A fundamental difficulty with theories of expectations that are not based on the predictions of the relevant economic model (rational expectations) is that they require a theory of systematic mistakes. Such theories are inherently more difficult to formulate than those based on rational behavior, and it seems to be a reasonable strategy to try to do without them. A second reaction is not so much to rational expectations as a theory of expectations as to expectational Phillips Curves. It is argued that there are real reasons for short-run price or wage inflexibility that produce a short-run Phillips Curve, so that the policy implications of the usual rational expectations models mentioned above are incorrect. Fischer (1975c) has constructed a model in which the existence of long-term labor contracts allows room for stabilizing monetary policy even though expectations are formed rationally.[30] However, the sensitivity of these results to the specified form of contracting remains an issue for future investigations. A third reaction is to the perfect foresight models and the restrictive role for policy in them. While perfect foresight is surely an unattractive assumption, the cure is not necessarily to use nonrational assumptions, but instead to use non-deterministic models.

---

[30]This paper uses some results of the recent literature on price inflexibility associated with long-term nominal contracting. Two references are Baily (1974) and Azariadis (1975).

9. Conclusions

Conclusions on each of the branches of the literature surveyed here and some comments on gaps that need filling are presented in the preceding sections. There are other areas in which theoretical research is required and is taking place: analysis of the effects of indexing on the operation of financial markets and economic stability, incorporation of advances in the theory of finance into macro models, theories of money supply and financial intermediation, incorporation of monetary theory into trade theory. However, it is clear from this paper that many of the major outstanding questions in monetary theory and macroeconomics more generally are related to the Phillips Curve (or the famous missing equation), and concern the short-run dynamics and costs of inflation and unemployment. Considerable progress has been made on these questions recently, but, as we need no reminding, there is room for further progress.

References

Alchian, A., 1970, Information costs, pricing, and resource unemployment, in: E. Phelps, ed., Microeconomic foundations of employment and inflation theory (Norton, New York).

Arrow, K., 1964, The role of securities in the optimal allocation of risk bearing, Rev. Econ. Studies 31, April, 91–96.

Arrow, K., 1971, The theory of risk aversion, in: K. Arrow, Essays in the theory of risk bearing (Markham, Chicago).

Arrow, K. and F. Hahn, 1971, General competitive analysis (Holden-Day, San Francisco).

Auernheimer, L., 1974, The honest government's guide to the revenue from the creation of money, J. Polit. Econ. 82, May/June, 598–606.

Azariadis, C., 1975, Implicit contracts and underemployment equilibria, J. Polit. Econ. 83, Dec., 1183–1202.

Bailey, M., 1956, The welfare cost of inflationary finance, J. Polit. Econ. 64, April, 93–110.

Baily, M.N., 1974, Wages and Employment Under Uncertain Demand, Rev. Econ. Studies 41, Jan., 37–50.

Barro, R., 1970, Inflation, the payments period, and the demand for money, J. Polit. Econ. 78, Nov./Dec., 1228–63.

Barro, R., 1974, Are government bonds net wealth? J. Polit. Econ. 82, Nov./Dec., 1095–1118.

Barro, R., 1976, Integral constraints and aggregation in an inventory model of money demand, J. of Finance, forthcoming.

Barro, R., 1976, Rational expectations and the role of monetary policy, Journal of Monetary Economics 2, Jan., 1–32.

Barro, R. and H. Grossman, 1976, Money, employment, and inflation (Cambridge Univ. Press, Cambridge).

Baumol, W., 1952, The transaction demand for cash: An inventory theoretic approach, Quart. J. Econ. 66, Nov., 545–56.

Benassy, J.P., 1974, NeoKeynesian disequilibrium theory in a monetary economy, unpublished.

Black, F., 1974, Uniqueness of the price level in monetary growth models with rational expectations, J. Econ. Theory 7, Jan., 53–65.

Brainard, W., 1964, Financial intermediaries and a theory of monetary control, Yale Econ. Essays 4, 431–82.

Brock, W., 1974, Money and growth: The case of long-run perfect foresight, Int. Econ. Rev. 15, Oct., 750–77.

Brunner, K. and A. Meltzer, 1971, The uses of money: Money in the theory of an exchange economy, Amer. Econ. Rev. 61, Dec., 784–805.

Cagan, P., 1956, The monetary dynamics of hyperinflation, in: M. Friedman, ed., Studies in the quantity theory of money (Univ. of Chicago Press, Chicago).

Clower, R., 1965, The Keynesian counter-revolution: A theoretical appraisal, in: F. Hahn and F. Brechling, eds., The theory of interest rates (St. Martin's, New York).

Clower, R., 1967, A reconsideration of the microfoundations of monetary theory, Western Econ. J. 6, Dec., 1–8.

Clower, R., 1970, Introduction, in: R. Clower, Monetary theory (Penguin, Baltimore).

Clower, R. and P. Howitt, 1975, The optimal timing of transactions, unpublished.

Diamond, P., 1965, National debt in a neoclassical growth model, Amer. Econ. Rev. 55, Dec., 1126–50.

Dornbusch, R. and J. Frenkel, 1973, Inflation and growth: Alternative approaches, J. Money, Credit, and Banking 5, Feb., 141–56.

Eppen, G. and E. Fama, 1969, Cash balance and simple dynamic portfolio problems with proportional costs, Int. Econ. Rev. 10, June, 119–33.

Feige, E. and M. Parkin, 1971, The optimal quantity of money, bonds, commodity inventories, and capital, Amer. Econ. Rev. 61, June, 335–49.

Feldman, A., 1973, Bilateral trading processes, pairwise optimality, and Pareto optimality, Rev. Econ. Studies 40, Oct., 463–74.

Fischer, S., 1972, Keynes–Wicksell and neoclassical models of money and growth, Amer. Econ. Rev. 62, Dec., 880–90.

Fischer, S., 1974, Money and the production function, Econ. Inquiry 12, Dec., 517–33.

Fischer, S., 1975a, Recent developments in monetary theory, Amer. Econ. Rev. Proceedings 65, May, 157–66.

Fischer, S., 1975b, The demand for index bonds, J. Polit. Econ. 83, June, 509–34.

Fischer, S., 1975c, Long-term contracts, rational expectations and the optimal money supply rule, unpublished.

Fisher, F., 1972, Comment on paper by R. Lucas, in: O. Eckstein, ed., The econometrics of price determination (Washington, DC).

Fisher, I., 1922, The purchasing power of money (Macmillan, New York).

Flemming, J., 1973, The consumption function when capital markets are imperfect: The permanent income hypothesis reconsidered, Oxford Econ. Papers 25, July, 160–72.

Foley, D., 1970, Economic equilibrium with costly marketing, J. Econ. Theory 2, Sept., 276–91.

Foley, D. and M. Sidrauski, 1970, Portfolio choice, investment and growth, Amer. Econ. Rev. 60, March, 44–63.

Foley, D. and M. Sidrauski, 1971, Monetary and fiscal policy in a growing economy (Macmillan, New York).

Frenkel, J., 1975, Inflation and the formation of expectations, Journal of Monetary Economics 1, Oct., 403–21.

Friedman, M., 1953, Discussion of the inflationary gap, in: M. Friedman, Essays in positive economics (Univ. of Chicago Press, Chicago).

Friedman, M., 1960, A program for monetary stability (Fordham U. Press, New York).

Friedman, M., 1968, The role of monetary policy, Amer. Econ. Rev. 58, March, 1–17.

Friedman, M., 1969, The optimum quantity of money (Aldine, Chicago).

Friedman, M., 1970, A theoretical framework for monetary analysis, J. Polit. Econ. 78, March/Apr., 193–238.

Friedman, M., 1971, Government revenue from inflation, J. Polit. Econ. 79, July/Aug., 846–56.

Frost, P., 1970, Banking services, minimum cash balances, and the firm's demand for money, J. of Finance 25, Dec., 1029–40.

Goldman, S., 1972, Hyperinflation and the rate of growth in the money supply, J. Econ. Theory 5, Oct., 250–57.

Gramm, W., 1974, Laissez faire and the optimum quantity of money, Econ. Inquiry 12, March, 125–32.

Grossman, H., 1971, Money, interest, and prices in market disequilibrium, J. Polit. Econ. 79, Sept./Oct., 943–61.

Grossman, H., 1973, Aggregate demand, job search, and employment, J. Polit. Econ. 81, Nov./Dec., 1353–69.

Grossman, H., 1974, Effective demand failures: A comment, Swed. J. Econ. 76, Sept., 358–65.
Grossman, H., and A. Policano, 1975, Money balances, commodity inventories, and infla-
  tionary expectations, J. Polit. Econ. 83, Dec., 1093–1112.
Hadjimichalakis, M., 1971, Money, expectations, and dynamics – An alternative view, Int.
  Econ. Rev. 12, Oct., 381–402.
Hahn, F., 1973a, On the foundations of monetary theory, in: M. Parkin and A.R. Nobay,
  eds., Essays in modern economics (Barnes and Noble, New York).
Hahn, F., 1973b, On transaction costs, inessential sequence economies, and money, Rev.
  Econ. Studies 40, Oct., 449–62.
Heller, W., 1974, The holding of money balances in equilibrium, J. Econ. Theory 7, Jan., 93–108.
Heller, W. and R. Starr, 1973, Equilibrium in a monetary economy with non-convex trans-
  actions costs, unpublished.
Hicks, J., 1967, Critical essays in monetary theory (Oxford Univ. Press, Oxford).
Iwai, K., 1974, The firm in uncertain markets and its price, wage and employment adjustment,
  Rev. Econ. Stud. 41, April, 257–76.
Jevons, W.S., 1875, Money and the mechanism of exchange (D. Appleton, London).
Johnson, H., 1962, Monetary theory and policy, Amer. Econ. Rev. 52, June, 335–84.
Johnson, H., 1969, Money in a neo-classical one-sector growth model, in: H. Johnson, Essays
  in monetary economics, 2nd ed. (Harvard Univ. Press, Cambridge, MA).
Jones, R.A., 1974, The origin and development of media of exchange, unpublished.
Karni, E., 1972, Transactions costs and the demand for media of exchange, Western Econ. J.
  10, Dec., 71–80.
Karni, E., 1973, The transactions demand for cash: incorporation of the value of time into the
  inventory approach, J. Polit. Econ. 81, Sept./Oct., 1216–25.
Keynes, J.M., 1923, A tract on monetary reform (Macmillan, London).
Klein, B., 1974, Competitive interest payments on bank deposits and the long-run demand for
  money, Amer. Econ. Rev. 64, Dec., 931–49.
Klein, M., 1971, A theory of the banking firm, J. Money, Credit and Banking 3, May, 205–18.
Kurz, M., 1974a, Equilibrium in a finite sequence of markets with transaction cost, Econo-
  metrica 42, Jan., 1–20.
Kurz, M., 1974b, Equilibrium with transaction cost and money in a single market exchange
  economy, J. Econ. Theory 7, Apr., 418–52.
Leijonhufvud, A., 1968, On Keynesian economics and the economics of Keynes (Oxford Univ.
  Press, New York).
Levhari, D. and D. Patinkin, 1968, The role of money in a simple growth model, Amer. Econ.
  Rev. 58, Sept., 713–53.
Lucas, R., 1972a, Expectations and the neutrality of money, J. Econ. Theory 4, April, 103–24.
Lucas, R., 1972b, Econometric testing of the natural rate hypothesis, in: O. Eckstein, ed.,
  The econometrics of price determination (Washington, DC).
Lucas, R., 1973, Some international evidence on output–inflation tradeoffs, Amer. Econ. Rev.
  63, June, 326–34.
Lucas, R., 1975, An equilibrium model of the business cycle, J. Polit. Econ. 83, Dec., 1113–44.
Lucas, R. and L. Rapping, 1969, Real wages, employment, and inflation, J. Polit. Econ. 77,
  Sept./Oct., 721–54.
Markowitz, H., 1959, Portfolio selection (Yale Univ. Press, New Haven).
McCall, J., 1970, Economics of information and job search, Quart. J. Econ. 84, Feb., 113–26.
Miller, M. and D. Orr, 1966, A model of the demand for money by firms, Quart. J. Econ. 80,
  Aug., 413–35.
Miller, M. and D. Orr, 1968, The demand for money by firms – Extensions of analytical re-
  sults, J. of Finance 23, Dec., 735–59.
Miller, P., 1973, The transactions demand for money in a three-asset economy, unpublished.
Modigliani, F., 1944, Liquidity preference and the theory of interest and money, Econometrica
  12, Jan., 45–88.
Mortensen, D., 1970, A theory of wage and employment dynamics, in: E. Phelps, ed., Micro-
  economic foundations of employment and inflation theory (Norton, New York).
Mundell, R., 1971, Inflation, saving, and the real rate of interest, in: R. Mundell, Monetary
  theory, (Goodyear, Pacific Palisades).

Muth, J., 1961, Rational expectations and the theory of price movements, Econometrica 29, July, 315–35.

Nagatani, K., 1969, A monetary growth model with variable employment, J. Money, Credit, and Banking 1, May, 188–206.

Niehans, J., 1969, Money in a static theory of optimal payment arrangements, J. Money, Credit, and Banking 1, Nov., 706–26.

Niehans, J., 1971, Money and barter in general equilibrium with transactions costs, Amer. Econ. Rev. 61, Dec., 773–83.

Orr, D., 1971, Cash management and the demand for money (Praeger, New York).

Ostroy, J., 1973, The informational efficiency of monetary exchange, Amer. Econ. Rev. 53, Sept., 597–610.

Ostroy, J. and R. Starr, 1973, Money and the decentralization of exchange, unpublished.

Patinkin, D., 1965, Money, interest and prices, 2nd ed. (Harper and Row, New York).

Phelps, E., 1970, The new microeconomics in employment and inflation theory, in: Microeconomic foundations of employment and inflation theory (Norton, New York).

Phelps, E., 1972, Inflation policy and unemployment theory: The cost–benefit approach to monetary planning (Norton, New York).

Phelps, E., 1973, Inflation in the theory of public finance, Swedish J. of Econ. 75, March, 67–82.

Prescott, E., 1975, Efficiency of the natural rate, J. Polit. Econ. 83, Dec., 1229–36.

Radner, R., 1968, Competitive equilibrium under uncertainty, Econometrica 36, Jan., 31–58.

Rose, H., 1966, Unemployment in a theory of growth, Int. Econ. Rev. 7, Sept., 50–58.

Santomero, A., 1974, A model of the demand for money by households, J. of Finance 29, March, 89–102.

Sargent, T. and N. Wallace, 1973, The stability of models of money and growth with perfect foresight, Econometrica 41, Nov., 1043–48.

Sargent, T. and N. Wallace, 1975, Rational expectations, the optimal monetary instrument, and the optimal money supply rule, J. Polit. Econ. 83, April, 241–54.

Sargent, T. and N. Wallace, 1976, Rational expectations and the theory of economic policy, Journal of Monetary Economics 2, April, 169–183.

Sidrauski, M., 1967a, Rational choice and patterns of growth in a monetary economy, Amer. Econ. Rev. Proceedings 57, May, 534–44.

Sidrauski, M., 1967b, Inflation and economic growth, J. Polit. Econ. 75, Dec., 796–810.

Simons, H., 1948, Economic policy for a free society (Univ. of Chicago Press, Chicago).

Starr, R., 1972, Exchange in barter and monetary economies, Quart. J. Econ. 86, May, 290–302.

Starr, R., 1974, The price of money in a pure exchange monetary economy with taxation, Econometrica 42, Jan., 45–54.

Starrett, D., 1973, Inefficiency and the demand for money in a sequence economy, Rev. Econ. Studies 40, Oct., 437–48.

Stein, J., 1970, Monetary growth theory in perspective, Amer. Econ. Rev. 60, March, 85–106.

Stein, J., 1971, Money and capacity growth (Columbia Univ. Press, New York).

Swan, P., 1970, Durability of consumption goods, Amer. Econ. Rev. 60, Dec., 884–94.

Taylor, J., 1975, Monetary policy during a transition to rational expectations, J. Polit. Econ. 83, Oct., 1009–22.

Tobin, J., 1956, The interest-elasticity of transactions demand for cash, Rev. Econ. and Stat. 38, Aug., 241–47.

Tobin, J., 1958, Liquidity preference as behavior towards risk, Rev. Econ. Studies 25, Feb., 65–86.

Tobin, J., 1959, The demand for money, ch. 4 of unpublished manuscript.

Tobin, J., 1965, Money and economic growth, Econometrica 33, Oct., 671–84.

Tobin, J., 1968, Notes on optimal monetary growth, J. Polit. Econ. 76, July/Aug., 833–59.

Tobin, J., 1971, Essays in economics, volume 1: Macroeconomics (Markham, Chicago).

Tobin, J., 1972, Inflation and unemployment, Amer. Econ. Rev. 62, March, 1–18.

Tobin, J. and W. Dolde, 1971, Wealth, liquidity, and consumption, unpublished.

Tsiang, S.C., 1969, The precautionary demand for money: An inventory theoretical analysis, J. Polit. Econ. 77, Jan./Feb., 99–117.

THE EQUILIBRIUM APPROACH
TO BUSINESS CYCLES

The *new classical macroeconomics* has been a major development of the 1970s. This approach attempts to understand business cycles from an equilibrium perspective in which imperfect information and rational expectations play a major role. The survey paper (no. 2) discusses the principal theoretical arguments and relates these to the conception and execution of empirical tests. There are detailed considerations of policy implications and of the identification problems concerning unobserved expectational variables that arise in testing natural rate hypotheses. The principal empirical findings in the literature are also summarized. The concluding section indicates the areas in which substantial advances have been made, but suggests that a satisfactory understanding of business cycles is not yet at hand.

My two theoretical papers (nos. 3 and 4) develop in greater detail the type of analytical apparatus that is used in the first part of the survey paper. The first (no. 3) uses a "Phelpsian islands" setup to consider the effects of monetary and other disturbances on outputs and prices under circumstances of local commodity market clearing, incomplete current information about some aggregate variables, and rational formation of expectations. The "reduced forms" exhibit the Lucas-type effects of nominal shocks on real variables, which derive from a confusion of general inflation for relative price changes. The framework is used to discuss price dispersion and a variety of topics in monetary policy. The main results reflect the type of systematic policy neutrality that has been highlighted by Sargent and Wallace.

The second theoretical paper (no. 4) adds an economy-wide bond market to the array of localized commodity markets. The contemporaneous observation of a global nominal interest rate alters the informational setup in a major way. However, in many respects the relations between money and output resemble those derived in simpler frameworks. The extended model permits an analysis of monetary and other effects on anticipated and realized real rates of return. In the present setup, systematic monetary changes—whether permanent or temporary—are reflected entirely in the time path of prices; anticipated real rates of return and output are invariant with respect to the perceived portions of monetary changes.

The empirical paper (no. 5) synthesizes results from several published papers of mine. These analyses deal primarily with reduced-form effects of constructed money shocks on the unemployment rate, output (real GNP), and the price level (GNP deflator). Substantial space is devoted to tests of natural rate hypotheses, which imply that some real variables are invariant with respect to anticipated monetary movements. Some related implications are drawn for the effects of anticipated and unanticipated monetary changes on the general price level. This paper and the discussion in the survey article stress the difficulties in successful execution of these types of expectational tests. On the whole, the empirical results for the unemployment rate and output seem reasonable, but those for the price level are in a less satisfactory state.

2

The Equilibrium Approach to Business Cycles*

Important developments have occurred in recent years in modeling business fluctuations as equilibrium phenomena. The new approach is often referred to as rational expectations macroeconomics because this treatment of expectations is a key element of the analysis. More generally, the class of models that will be surveyed exhibit the following major characteristics: (a) continuous market clearing; (b) imperfect information about some current aggregate variables; (c) a variant of the "Lucas supply function," which allows nominal shocks to have temporary effects on real variables; (d) some version of the natural rate hypothesis, which rules out real effects of perceived nominal variables like the money stock; and (e) rational formation of expectations.

This paper first considers the equilibrium approach as a positive theory of business cycles. A specific, simplified framework is used to illustrate propositions that apply generally to this class of models. The discussion then deals with implications for policy. The next sections cover econometric policy evaluation, estimation and hypothesis testing in models that include expectational variables, and some specific empirical findings. The final section contains general reflections on the insights provided by the *new classical macroeconomics*.

Equilibrium Business Cycle Theory

The models considered here account for booms and recessions as equilibrium phenomena; specifically, movements of output and employment are explained as responses to changes in relative price variables. Although some components of GNP

*This research was supported by the National Science Foundation. I have benefited from comments by William Brock, Ray Fair, Herschel Grossman, Bob Hall, Bob King, Bob Lucas, Ben McCallum, Ed Prescott, Bob Shiller, John Taylor, and Larry Weiss.

41

are cyclically more volatile than others, it seems fundamental that the business cycle is an aggregate phenomenon that involves co-movements of numerous variables; for example, of various components of production, employment, and investment. For this reason it seems to be a reasonable modeling strategy to concentrate initially on aggregate concepts of demand and supply, which entails a focus on relative prices that stimulate co-movements in the supply of various types of current goods and services, rather than contemporaneous substitutions among these categories. Therefore, the stress is on intertemporal substitution variables—relative price shifts that induce substitution of current aggregate supplies of goods and services for future supplies—rather than contemporaneous relative price variables, such as the real wage rate. The principal analysis considers these aggregative effects without distinguishing final products from factor inputs, durables from nondurables, and so on.

Setup of the Basic Model

Consider the type of model where goods and services are traded in a large number of localized markets or "islands," indexed by a parameter z. A simple version of the imperfect information story, due to Phelps (1970) and Lucas and Rapping (1969) and related to ideas advanced by M. Friedman (1968), allows individuals to receive current information on local prices $P_t(z)$, but at most lagged information about the economy-wide average price level P or other nominal aggregates like the money stock. The underlying idea is that local prices reflect a mixture of the unperceived nominal aggregates and a variety of local factors that are specific to markets, individuals, occupations, etc. Fluctuations in these local elements; which involve changes in the composition of technology and tastes, reevaluation of individual talents or opportunities, and the like; are viewed as having far more significance than general business conditions for individual fortunes (Lucas, 1977, pp. 19-20). In particular, the exploitation of these local opportunities may require rapid and large responses by individuals; whether in terms of accepting or offering a job, making a sale, undertaking an investment project, and so on. Under imperfect information conditions, individuals attempt to purge the general price component from their observed price signals in order to make the appropriate allocative decisions.

Specifically, suppliers in a local market compare their observed current price or wage opportunities with their expectations of prices or wages at alternative times and places. In a simplified setting where individuals visit only one market each period and where intermarket mobility over time is sufficient to make all markets look equally attractive one period ahead, the margin of substitution will involve a comparison of $P_t(z)$ with $E_z P_{t+1}$, which is the expectation formed today in market z of next period's general price level. In this setting the expected price next period represents the perceived long-run reward for the pertinent type of commodity or labor service. Changes in current actual prices (wages) relative to anticipated future prices (wages) are viewed as inducing substantial intertemporal substitution on the supply side. Some evidence on the importance of this mechanism for labor supply, including results from negative income tax experiments, is discussed in Hall (1979, pp. 17–19). From the standpoint of commodities, the supply response may involve the holding of inventories as well as shifts in the timing of production. Models that involve as a central element a response of supply to this or similar relative price variables include Lucas (1972a, 1973), Sargent (1973), Sargent and Wallace (1975), and Barro (1976a).[1]

A direct comparison of next period's expected nominal price with currently observed prices is appropriate only if stores of value earn a zero nominal rate of return; that is, if paper money is the only available asset. More generally—as noted in Lucas and Rapping (1969), McCallum (1978), Barro (1980), and King (1978)— the anticipated future prices would effectively be discounted by the available nominal interest rate over the applicable horizon. Instead of specifying a supply response to $P_t(z)$ relative to $E_z P_{t+1}$, which is a measure of the anticipated one-period real rate of return on money from the perspective of market z, the pertinent variable would be the expected real rate of return based on the holding of assets that earn a nominal interest rate R_t.

Equilibrium business cycle models typically incorporate a positive speculative response of supply to perceived excesses of observed prices over anticipated (future) normal values; that is, to unusual real rate of return opportunities. An analogous type of speculation implies a negative effect of the same type of relative price variable on the demand side (Barro, 1976a, p. 5; B. Friedman, 1978, p. 76). In a specification that employs an anticipated real rate of return measure as the relative price variable, the aggregate demand equation when considered as an average over the markets would exhibit the conventional negative substitution effect of expected real interest rates on consumption and investment.

The existence of a speculative demand effect suggests as a modeling strategy a symmetric treatment of the aggregate demand and supply functions, which has not been the standard practice in macroeconomics. One argument for an asymmetric treatment of supply and demand in the labor market has been presented by M. Friedman (1968). Labor suppliers are influenced by a variable like $P_t(z) - E_z P_t$ (or $E_z P_{t+1}$)—where $P_t(z)$ now represents an observed wage and P_t is the price of a market basket of goods—while demanders are influenced by a variable like $P_t(z) -$

---

[1]Lucas (1973, p. 327) writes his supply variable in logarithmic terms as $P_t(z) - E_z P_t$; that is, $E_z P_t$ appears without explanation instead of $E_z P_{t+1}$. However, most of the results would be unaffected by this difference in form. Sargent (1973, p. 434) and Sargent and Wallace (1975, p. 242) use the variable $P_t - E_{t-1} P_t$, where $E_{t-1} P_t$ is the average expectation formed last period of this period's price level. A direct comparison of P_t with $E_{t-1} P_t$ is difficult to reconcile with the intertemporal substitution or search stories of labor supply. However, $E_{t-1} P_t$ may be viewed as a proxy for the average over a set of local markets of $E_z P_t$ or possibly $E_z P_{t+1}$ in the context of an incomplete information setup where P_t is not observed contemporaneously. A direct comparison of P_t with a variable like $E_{t-1} P_t$ has been rationalized along long-term nominal contracting grounds by Gray (1976) and Fischer (1977). The argument is that previous expectations of current prices determine some portion of current contractual nominal wages, which would then be compared with current prices to determine the supply of commodities by firms. This interpretation is disputed in Barro (1977b) on the grounds that efficient contracts would not permit quantity variables like employment to be influenced by perceived, purely nominal disturbances.

$P_t(z')$, where $P_t(z')$ is the observed contemporaneous product price for an individual firm. The idea is that firms' concentrated interest in a small number of prices, such as individual commodity prices or the costs of specific factors, implies—without any assumption of superior information capabilities on the part of firms—that labor demand will be less influenced by unanticipated inflation than will workers' labor supply. The shortcoming of Freidman's model is that a comparison of observed wages with an anticipated price of a general market basket of goods does not suggest much positive responsiveness of today's labor supply to the posited relative price variable. The strong point of the intertemporal substitution model is the expectation of a high elasticity of supply in the face of a perceived temporary opportunity for unusual gains, which in this case reflect wages that differ from average expected (discounted) future wages (Lucas, 1977, pp. 16, 17).

Suppose that aggregate supply and demand are influenced by the same relative price variable; for example, by an anticipated real rate of return with comparable information on prices, etc., on both sides of each local market. If the other right-hand side variables for supply and demand are exogenous real variables, then an equilibrium solution would involve a dichotomy between monetary variables and the real sector. The equation of supply to demand would determine output and the anticipated real rate of return in each local market as functions of exogenous real variables. Therefore, in this type of model with a single form of relative price variable, it is essential for obtaining a link between nominal disturbances and real variables that the monetary shocks impact directly on excess commodity demand.[2] One possibility would be a real balance-type effect on commodity and demand supply. In Lucas's (1972a, p. 106) overlapping-generations model in which money is the only store of value, a positive real balance effect on aggregate demand corresponds to the older generation's incentive to spend all of its savings from the previous period.[3] For the context of households that have access to interest-bearing assets and that effectively plan over an infinite horizon (perhaps because they have an operative bequest motive), it is argued in Barro (1980, Part I) that the principal direct monetary effect on excess demand would involve the discrepancy between the money stock and its contemporaneously perceived value. Essentially, this setup ignores the wealth effect corresponding to changes in the excess burden due to inflation. This formulation implies, in particular, that equal increases in total money and in the desired money stock have no direct effect on excess commodity demand. The distinction between this type of specification of the direct monetary effect and the real balance type of specification arises primarily in analyses of anticipated inflation, which involve changes in real balances but no changes in money relative to

[2]In Sargent (1973, p. 434) and Sargent and Wallace (1975, p. 242), supply depends on $P_t - E_{t-1}P_t$, while demand depends on an expected real interest rate. Therefore, a direct monetary effect on excess commodity demand is unnecessary. Similarly, in Lucas (1973, pp. 327–328), nominal income is exogenous and supply depends on $P_t(z) - E_z P_t$.

[3]This model assumes also (Lucas 1972a, p. 105) that new money enters as governmental transfers that are proportional to individual money holdings. The implicit interest rate on holding money in this circumstance leads to neutral effects of changes in the anticipated monetary growth rate.

perceived money. If last period's money stock is viewed as observable, the latter variable becomes the unperceived part of current money growth, denoted by $m_t - E_z m_t$.

A simple log-linear model of local commodity markets that reflects the above discussion is (Barro, 1980, Part I):

$$y_t^s(z) = \alpha_s r_t(z) - \beta_s(m_t - E_z m_t) + \epsilon_t^s(z), \tag{1}$$

$$y_t^d(z) = -\alpha_d r_t(z) + \beta_d(m_t - E_z m_t) + \epsilon_t^d(z), \tag{2}$$

where $y(z)$ is the log of local output, $r_t(z) \equiv P_t(z) - E_z P_{t+1} + R_t$ is the anticipated one-period[4] real rate of return from the perspective of market z (neglecting effects associated with the variance of future prices), $P(z)$ is the log of the local price, P is the log of the average of prices across markets, R is a one-period nominal interest rate on an asset that is traded economy-wide, $(\alpha_s, \alpha_d) > 0$ are relative prices elasticities, $(\beta_s, \beta_d) > 0$ are "wealth" elasticities, and the $\epsilon(z)$'s are local disturbance terms that add to zero in summations across the markets. Constants, economy-wide real shocks, or systematic effects on natural outputs could readily be added to equations (1) and (2).

The assumptions that goods not travel across markets during a period and that local prices are completely flexible generate the equilibrium condition for each commodity market, $y_t^s(z) = y_t^d(z)$. Equations (1) and (2) then imply conditions for local output and expected real rate of return, which can be written as

$$y_t(z) = (1/\alpha)(\alpha_s\beta_d - \alpha_d\beta_s)(m_t - E_z m_t) + (\alpha_s/\alpha)\epsilon_t^d(z) + (\alpha_d/\alpha)\epsilon_t^s(z), \tag{3}$$

$$r_t(z) = (1/\alpha)[\beta(m_t - E_z m_t) + \epsilon_t(z)], \tag{4}$$

where $\alpha \equiv \alpha_s + \alpha_d$, $\beta \equiv \beta_s + \beta_d$, $\epsilon_t(z) \equiv \epsilon_t^d(z) - \epsilon_t^s(z)$.

Some Properties of the Model

Equations (3) and (4) are not final solutions for $y_t(z)$ and $r_t(z)$ because they contain the endogenous expectation $E_z m_t$. Further, the model would have to be closed to determine R_t and the array of $P_t(z)$'s by specifying some sort of portfolio balance condition. However, even before the remainder of the model is specified and the expectational problems are solved, the intermediate equations (3) and (4) reveal several properties that typify a class of equilibrium business cycle models.[5]

---

[4]The neglect of future anticipated real rates of return is satisfactory because these values are constant in the present setup. This type of model stresses departures of currently perceived returns from normal values, rather than changes in the normal rate of return.

[5]The absence of actual or expected price levels from the right side of equations (3) and (4) depends on some features of the specification in equations (1) and (2). For example, this absence would not obtain if commodity supply and demand depended on the level of real cash balances, with either the actual or expected price level used as a deflator for nominal money. These changes would require an analysis of expectational equilibrium and portfolio balance before discussing any solution properties. Ultimately, the substantive differences would involve the real effects of anticipated inflation, as indicated in the text.

Output and the anticipated real rate of return are influenced by monetary factors in equations (3) and (4) only to the extent that money growth is unperceived as such, $m_t \neq E_z m_t$. As stressed by Sargent (1973, pp. 442–444), there is a direct tie between departures of output from its natural value (which is itself treated as constant on average across markets in the present setting) and departures of the anticipated real rate of return from the natural rate. It is clear from equations (1) and (2) that the crucial role of the unperceived part of money growth follows from the specification of the direct excess demand effect of money shocks—that is, from the β_d and β_s terms—and does not depend on the particular definition of $r_t(z)$, as long as the same form of this relative price variable appears in the supply and demand functions, which is not the case in some models mentioned above. However, the substitution of a real balance type variable for the $m_t - E_z m_t$ terms in equations (1) and (2), as in Barro (1976a, pp. 4–5), would preserve most of the results discussed in the following. The principal differences arise for effects of anticipated inflation, which are implicitly being treated here as minor issues from the standpoint of business cycle analysis.

My conjecture—based on suggestions from Bob King—is that the role of direct monetary wealth effects will prove to be less important in models that incorporate more than one type of intertemporal substitution variable. Lucas's model (1975, pp. 1124–1125), which allows investment demand to respond to perceptions of locally persisting unusual price opportunities, is suggestive in this context. However, a fully satisfactory specification of this type has not yet been presented.[6]

The conclusion that unperceived money growth, $m_t - E_z m_t$, is the key monetary influence on real variables emphasizes the role of incomplete information on nominal aggregates. If the quantity of money were observed directly without a significant time lag, or if its value could be inferred quickly from contemporaneous observations on commodity prices or financial returns (see in the following), then the present real effects of money shocks would disappear.[7] Reliance on this sort of information gap is a shortcoming of this type of theory. In particular, if more rapid observation and assimiliation of general price indices or money stock measures would substantially lessen the amplitude of business fluctuations, then it is surprising that this more rapid observation does not take place through a combination of

[6]The transmission mechanism for investment in Lucas's (1975, pp. 1124–1125) model involves the relative price variable, $r_{kt}(z) \equiv E_z P_{t+1}(z) - E_z P_{t-1}$. In this setting local profit opportunities persist long enough so that all markets do not appear identical one period ahead.

[7]Lucas (1977, p. 24) argues that these types of models are compatible with observable money as long as general price movements cannot be inferred accurately from published monetary statistics. However, this line of argument cannot explain the apparently strong output and employment effects of money shocks as measured by published monetary figures (see the empirical section). King (1979a) demonstrates that errors in the measurement or conception of the money stock would also not account for a relation between reported monetary data and real variables. Barro and Hercowitz (1980) distinguish initial reports on money from the revised data, but argue that this distinction has not been important empirically.

individual information-gathering efforts and improved government reporting. A counterargument (Lucas, 1977, p. 21) is that because individual fortunes are more dependent on relative price and income changes than on general business fluctuations, it would not pay for the representative individual to spend a great deal of effort in processing aggregate signals.

BEHAVIOR OF RATES OF RETURN

Since money shocks impact positively on excess commodity demand, the relative price variable $r_t(z)$ moves positively with $m_t - E_z m_t$ in equation (4) in order to maintain clearing of the local commodity market. It should be stressed that the pertinent variable here is the anticipated real rate of return; monetary shocks tend to move the realized real rate of return in a direction opposite to that of the anticipated rate in incomplete information models with an economy-wide nominal interest rate, as discussed in Barro (1980, Part III). Given the specification of the anticipated real rate of return, $r_t(z) \equiv P_t(z) - E_z P_{t+1} + R_t$, there is no immediate implication for the behavior of the nominal interest rate R_t. A typical—though not inevitable—conclusion from the full model solution (discussed next) is that the economy-wide nominal interest rate declines with a money shock through a sort of liquidity effect in which $P_t(z)$ rises by less than M_t; that is, real balances increase in the "short-run." $P_t(z)$ must rise in this case relative to $E_z P_{t+1}$ in order to generate the requisite increase in $r_t(z)$. Positive serial correlation in the money growth process can reverse the predicted negative effect on R_t, essentially by introducing the feature that the perceived parts of current money shocks signal future money creation and inflation, which lead to increases in current nominal interest rates.

ASSOCIATION BETWEEN MONEY SHOCKS AND OUTPUT

The direction of association of output with money shocks in equation (3) depends on the relative magnitudes of some elasticities. The speculative supply coefficient α_s, which is stressed in these types of models, entails a positive relation, but the demand coefficient α_d has an opposite implication. A sufficient condition for obtaining the "normal" net positive relation is that money shocks impact directly mostly on the demand side; that is, β_d is much greater than β_s. The direct monetary effect on supply—which can be viewed as reflecting a wealth effect on the demand for leisure—is, in fact, typically assumed to be negligible in macroanalysis.

PERSISTENCE EFFECTS

The present type of model does not account for effects of money shocks on output that last more than one "period"; that is, the model does not account for persisting effects of shocks. If a period is viewed as an interval of no more than a few months, corresponding to the interval over which significant information on nominal aggregates can plausibly be lacking, then this property conflicts with empirical evidence. That evidence (see Part VII) suggests a continuing effect of money shocks on output and unemployment rates in the United States over a 1–2 year period. Hall (1975, pp. 311–314) has criticized rational expectation macro models on this ground, essentially by noting that first, if full information is received with a one-period lag then shocks to money and prices from period to period would not be serially correlated under rational expectations, and second, unemployment rates are, in fact, strongly serially correlated over corresponding periods; say, from quarter to quarter. Tobin (1977, p. 461) and Modigliani (1977, pp. 5–6) have raised similar objections to rational expectation models.

Lucas and Sargent (1978, p. 65) point out that the above criticisms fail to distinguish between *sources of impulses* and *propagation mechanisms*. There is no inconsistency in serially uncorrelated shocks producing serially correlated movements in a response variable, as was noted in a purely statistical way by Slutzky (1937) and has been illustrated by a number of concrete theoretical models.

Lucas's (1975) model exhibits serially correlated output movements as a consequence of two assumptions: a lag of more than one period in information acquisition, and more importantly, the presence of a stock variable like productive capacity. Suppose that capacity responds positively to a money shock during the period when the shock is not fully understood. As information on nominal aggregates becomes available in future periods, individuals are likely to regret some of their earlier decisions on employment, production, investment, and so on. However, these decisions are bygones that typically alter the initial conditions for future periods by changing the value of productive capacity. Since the existence of this heightened capacity is likely to imply at least a temporary outward shift in labor demand and commodity supply, the monetary shock will tend to have persisting effects on output and employment. (Note that the positive impact effect of monetary shocks on the anticipated real rate of return is likely to be reversed in future periods that are characterized by excess capacity.) Conceivably, productive capacity does not exhibit sufficient cyclical variability to operate as an empirically important channel for persistence. However, Lucas's modeling of capacity can be generalized beyond the explanation of this particular variable. The approach applies to any variable that responds initially to monetary shocks and then has a durable aspect that implies a change in future initial conditions. For example, inventories of goods-in-process show dramatic cyclical fluctuations (Feldstein and Auerbach, 1976, p. 357) and would function theoretically in a manner analogous to Lucas's productive capacity. Similarly, adjustment costs for variations in employment, which were utilized by Sargent (1979a, Chapter 16) to explain persistence, amount to treating labor as a capital-like input. Blinder and Fischer (1978, p. 5) stress the role of finished goods inventories. A monetary shock would induce a rundown of producers' inventories, which would show up in future periods as a short-fall of stocks below normal desired levels. The incentive to rebuild stocks would apply after the nature of the initial monetary shock was understood, which would generate a persistence of output effects.

One empirical difficulty with some adjustment-cost explanations for persistence is the implication that the responses of investment, and so on, would peak contemporaneously with shocks and follow a persisting, but declining, pattern therafter. Empirical evidence (given later) suggests a period of several quarters of rising output (and investment) response to monetary disturbances. It seems that this behavior can be explained by the model of Kydland and Prescott (1980, pp. 175,ff.), in which planning-type costs for capital projects imply a delay in the peak response of investment to shocks.

The arguments for persistence that depend on stock variables like capital goods imply future periods in which excess capacity would deter investment. However, unlike the initial response periods in which rapid reactions to the perception of temporary profit opportunities are warranted, these later periods may involve a relatively small amount of contraction. This possibility may account for the empirical evidence, which does not indicate an important contractionary effect of monetary shocks on the levels of output and employment in the periods following the roughly 2-year interval of net expansionary effect.

Adjustment-cost-type explanations for persisting effects tend also to lessen the impact effects on supply of relative price variables like the anticipated real rate of return. Therefore, the extensions to account for persistence may undermine the quantitative role of the underlying intertemporal substitution mechanism as the basis for fluctuations in output and employment.

Expectational Equilibrium

The above discussion of issues proceeded without a determination of the expectational equilibrium related to the intermediate equations (3) and (4). The relation of unperceived money movements and some other variables to output and employment seems to involve more the modeling of supply and demand functions along natural rate lines than the use of rational expectations as a basis for equilibrium analysis. (See, however, note 5.) On the other hand, an expectational theory is essential for determining which movements in money and other variables would be unperceived. These considerations have major implications for policy and for assessment of econometric results, as discussed later.

The model set out in equations (1)–(4) can be solved by specifying a portfolio balance condition—for example, a standard money demand function that exhibits an inverse effect of R_t, as in Barro (1980, Part I)—and appealing to rational expectations to determine $E_z m_t$, which appears directly in equations (3) and (4), and $E_z P_{t+1}$, which appears in the definition of the expected real rate of return, $r_t(z)$. The solution is sensitive to the specification of individual information sets. If individuals have full current information, so that $E_z m_t = m_t$ applies, equations (3) and (4) imply immediately that output and the anticipated real rate of return are equal to their natural values. In this case all monetary movements are neutral. The model could still be employed to determine the price level and nominal interest rate, but the results would be of no interest from the standpoint of business cycle analysis. The present class of models requires some aspect of incomplete current information about nominal aggregates in order to generate output effects of monetary disturbances.

Incomplete information has been modeled by assuming that individuals observe a subset of current prices, but receive information about the general price level and some other variables only with a lag. Equilibrium models in which quantity variables like sales, inventories, and so on, convey information have not yet been constructed (Lucas, 1977, p. 17). In the models of Lucas (1972a, 1973) and Barro (1976a), individuals have contemporaneous observations on local commodity prices. There are no economy-wide capital markets in these models and $R_t = 0$ can be thought of as applying to equations (1)–(4) above. Individuals face the problem of inferring variables like $E_z m_t$ and $E_z P_{t+1}$, based on current price information and knowledge of lagged variables. The central rational expectations assumption, following Muth (1961), is that individuals effectively use the model's stochastic equilibrium solution to solve this inference problem. More precisely, the solution for current prices and expected values of future prices, and so forth, is a simultaneous process in which first, market-clearing conditions like those specified in equations (3) and (4) are satisfied and second, expectations are consistent with this solution, given the specification of individual information sets. This approach has been criticized, as in Fisher (1972) and Shiller (1978, pp. 33–34), as assuming an unreasonable amount of information about model structure in individual hands, although alternative procedures for isolating systematic effects on expectations seem to be arbitrary. Notably, manageable approaches to the concept of learning about model structure have not yet been advanced. Sargent (1979b, pp. 26–28) argues that technical difficulties in expectational calculations and problems with the specification of prior distributions make it impractical to incorporate Bayesian learning methods into these types of stochastic equilibrium models. Lucas (1977) stresses that the rational expectations approach is likely to be most fruitful in the context of recurring types of stochastic events:

> Insofar as business cycles can be viewed as repeated instances of essentially similar events, it will be reasonable to treat agents as reacting to cyclical changes as "risk," or to assume their expectations are rational, that they have fairly stable arrangements for collecting and processing information, and that they utilize this information in forecasting the future in a stable way, free of systematic and easily correctable biases [p. 15].

The mechanics of solution procedures in models that exploit the rational expectations hypothesis are discussed in the papers cited previously and will not be considered here. I will discuss first the nature of the results in standard cases where prices, and so on, are determined uniquely as stationary functions of the state of the economy, and then mention some puzzling issues about uniqueness that have arisen in the literature.

In the models of Lucas (1972a, 1973) and Barro (1976a), locally observed prices reflect a mixture of aggregate (monetary) noise and local (real) disturbances. Confusions between monetary and real shocks prevent individuals from inferring accurately the aggregate state of the economy, given their incomplete, localized information. In particular, monetary shocks produce movements in actual prices $P_t(z)$ relative to perceived general prices $E_z P_{t+1}$; that is, movements in the anticipated real rate of return variable $r_t(z)$ in equations (1) and (2). The response of output to money shocks depends on the combination of elasticity parameters shown in equation (3) and also on the conditional expectation calculation for $E_z m_t$. As the population variance of money shocks rises relative to that of real shocks, the fraction of price variance due to the monetary source increases. Accordingly, individuals subject to incomplete information will rationally associate a larger fraction of observed price changes with monetary movements and will therefore be less fooled by a given size money shock. As demonstrated by Lucas (1973, p. 328), the slope of the relation between output and money shocks will be flatter the larger the variance of money. This proposition is often stated in terms of a more nearly vertical Phillips curve—in a relation of money-wage change to the unemployment rate—in economies where nominal aggregates are historically less predictable.

An economy-wide capital market plays an informational role in the models because observation of the nominal interest rate conveys current global information to individuals. In some circumstances knowledge of the current nominal rate of return and a single commodity price would amount to full current information; in particular, $E_z m_t = m_t$ would follow in equations (3) and (4). Basically, with individuals possessing one piece of current global information and one item of local information, money shocks will have real effects only if there are more independent sources of noise that one global (monetary) shock and one relative disturbance. In particular, the nominal interest rate is likely to allow identification of the unobserved monetary aggregate[8] unless there are some additional economy-wide disturbances; for example, shocks to aggregate velocity or to aggregate commodity supply. These results indicate the uneasy balance in modeling strategy here between allowing for private incentives to develop markets or other institutions that disseminate information and the necessity for retaining information gaps that allow for business cycle effects of monetary disturbances. A related discussion of the balance between creating markets that convey price signals and the maintenance of private incentives to gather underlying information is contained in S. Grossman (1979, Section 5).

If some additional aggregate disturbances are added to the model with an economy-wide capital market—and additional markets are not introduced—as in Barro (1980) and King (1978), the relation of output to money shocks can resemble that derived in simpler frameworks. One conclusion from these models with endogenous nominal interest rates is that stress on confusions between temporary and permanent monetary shocks has been overdone. The real effects of temporary, but perceived, money shocks would be eliminated by the appropriate adjustment in the nominal rate of return. The models can be used also to examine the effects of autonomous velocity shifts. Although these shifts appear in a parallel fashion to money supply shocks in the portfolio balance condition, the change in velocity does not exert a similar wealth-type effect on excess commodity demand. In one specific setting (Barro, 1980, Part III), velocity disturbances turn out to be important only

---

[8]There are some degenerate cases in which the nominal interest rate, being invariant to money shocks, cannot reveal the value of these shocks; see King (1978, p. 17).

because they influence the relation of perceived money growth $E_z m_t$ to actual growth. In this situation velocity shocks have a positive effect on the price level, but a negative effect on output, which involves an increase in expectations of money and prices. However, it is likely that the output effects of velocity shocks would be reversed in models with more than one type of intertemporal substitution variable where the direct monetary wealth effect is deemphasized.

Some interesting monetary issues that have not yet been examined with this type of model include the impact of open-market operations, as opposed to money-financed transfers or government purchases, and the distinction between inside and outside money. The models have tended also to neglect nonmonetary disturbances associated with changes in government expenditures or public debt. Some preliminary theoretical analyses of these effects appear in McCallum and Whitaker (1979), Hall (1979), and Barro (1979c).

Extensions of the analysis to open economies will not be considered in this paper; however, relevant work includes Mussa (1976, Appendix), Barro (1978a), Stockman (1980), Saidi (1979), and Blejer and Fernandex (1979). In flexible exchange rate models the observable exchange rate can play an information role that parallels that of the nominal interest rate in closed-economy models with a global capital market.

A different modification to the information structure of the models is considered by Cukierman (1979), who allows individuals to obtain price quotes from more than one local commodity market during each period. One conclusion here is that an increased population variance of money raises the number of markets visited each period, which works to reinforce the proposition that a higher money variance reduces the output effect of a given size money shock.

Price Dispersion

The models can be used also to analyze the distribution of prices over time and across markets. Not surprisingly, an increased variance of money or an increased variance of real shocks, which are assumed to be uncorrelated with the monetary disturbances, tend to raise the forecast variance of future prices. More interestingly, as demonstrated in Barro (1976a, pp. 13–14), an increase in money variance raises the dispersion of relative prices and of price expectations across markets. The latter effect is stressed in Cukierman and Wachtel (1979). The basic mechanism for these effects involves the Lucas slope relationship, which implies a reduced sensitivity of excess commodity demand to observed local prices when the variance of money rises. The market-specific disturbances then require a larger movement of local prices in order to satisfy the individual market equilibrium conditions, which implies the increase in price dispersion. The increase in dispersion of expectations arises because each observed price is perceived by local market participants as being more closely associated with the general price level and hence—in the typical case—with expected future prices. Therefore, expected price levels become more sensitive to local shocks, which generates the increased dispersion of price expectations.

II THE EQUILIBRIUM APPROACH TO BUSINESS CYCLES

Hercowitz (1979, Section I) has extended the theory to incorporate heterogeneity of supply elasticities across markets. In this setting the realized value of a money shock affects prices and outputs differentially across markets. Price dispersion is then positively related to the magnitude of realized money shocks, which differs from the effect of the population variance of money that was discussed previously.

Uniqueness of Equilibrium

A number of not well understood (by me) issues have arisen concerning the uniqueness and stability of rational expectations equilibria. One class of problems involves speculative bubble equilibria; essentially situations where, starting from a stationary solution such as an equality between the growth rates of money and prices, an arbitrary change in the current price level is supported by a corresponding perturbation to the entire path of future prices. The situation can be illustrated with the following general form of equation that relates the anticipated future price to the current actual price,

$$EP_{t+1} = \delta_0 + (1 + \delta_1)P_t + u_t, \tag{5}$$

where P_t and EP_{t+1} are in logarithmic terms, the δ's are constants, and u_t is a serially independent error term with zero mean. The variable u_t could involve innovations to the money stock or other stochastic influences. Systematic growth of money or other variables could readily be incorporated. A relation like equation (5) would emerge from a Cagan (1956) type formulation where real money demand varied inversely with the expected inflation rate, as used in Sargent and Wallace (1973a, p. 330; 1973b, p. 1043). Equation (5) would arise also in the model of Barro (1976a, p. 6) or in a variant of Taylor's (1977, p. 1379) model. Typically, since a higher value of P_t means lower current real balances, EP_{t+1} will be associated on a more than one-to-one basis with P_t; that is, $\delta_1 > 0$ will apply. In the Cagan model this assumption follows from an inverse dependence of real money demand on the anticipated inflation rate. In Barro (1976a) an equiproportional move in P_t and $E_t P_{t+1}$ implies a negative real balance effect, which generates excess supply of commodities. Assuming a dominance of substitution over income effects, a further rise in EP_{t+1} would then be required in order to clear the commodity market. In this situation $\delta_1 > 0$ would apply in equation (5). Taylor (1977) considers the possibility $\delta_1 < 0$, as discussed below.

The "natural" solution to equation (5) determines P_t solely as a function of the current state variable u_t; in particular, the result is

$$P_t = \pi_0 + \pi_1 u_t,$$

where $\pi_0 = -\delta_0/\delta_1$, $\pi_1 = -1/(1+\delta_1)$. Consider, however, the addition of the arbitrary quantity X to the *initial* price level P_0. Equation (5) would again be satisfied if EP_1 were raised by the amount $(1+\delta_1)X$, if EP_2 were raised by $(1+\delta_1)^2 X$, and so on. Speculative bubbles appear possible because, when $\delta_1 > 0$, an arbitrary increase in the current price level can be validated by the appropriate acceleration in the mean value of future prices, with the mean of P_t (which is in logarithmic terms) approaching $\pm\infty$ as $t\to\infty$. (For a more general discussion of these paths see Flood and Garber, 1979, pp. 4,5.) Since, with $\delta_1 > 0$, these bubble solutions involve odd types of limiting behavior, such as expected real balances approaching infinity or zero, they can in many cases be shown to be inconsistent with transversality conditions that arise from the maximizing behavior of individual agents in an intertemporal context (Brock, 1975). (Similar considerations involving the "Hahn problem" in models with heterogenous capital goods have been discussed by Shell and Stiglitz [1967].) In one context (Brock, 1980), equilibria in which real balances approach zero asymptotically can be ruled out if money is "essential enough" for the operation of the economy.

Taylor (1977) and Calvo (1978) discuss nonunique solutions that do not involve explosive limiting behavior of prices. These cases fall also within the realm of equation (5), except that the parameter δ_1 is now such that $|1+\delta_1| < 1$ applies.[9] In this situation the addition of the arbitrary quantity X to P_0 still requires the addition of $(1+\delta_1)X$ to EP_1, $(1+\delta_1)^2X$ to EP_2, and so on, but the perturbations to the mean values of future prices are now described by a damped, rather than an explosive, process. Taylor (1977, pp. 1382–1383) points out that price solutions in this situation may involve a reaction to some intrinsically irrelevant variable that everyone decides to employ as a "leading indicator" (see also Shiller, 1978, p. 33). Parameter configurations that yield these types of paradoxical results seem to be unusual: In Taylor's model (1977, p. 1382) a positive supply effect of real money balances must be sufficiently strong to reverse the normal relative slopes of "I/S and L/M curves," and in one of Calvo's models (1978, p. 324) the income effect of interest rates on saving must dominate over the substitution effect. However, the general conditions for ruling out these possibilities are unclear.

A third type of nonuniqueness problem involves incomplete current information as an essential property. A central element in equilibrium business cycle models concerns inferences of contemporaneously unobserved variables from limited current information sets. In effect, conditional expectations are calculated as regressions of unobservable variables on observable economic characteristics. The coefficients in these regressions are determined simultaneously with the equilibrium solution for prices. In some cases described in King (1978, pp. 18–19) and Barro (1980, Appendix), it is possible to find more than one coefficient configuration for these regressions that are, in turn, consistent with an array of coefficients that describe an equilibrium price solution. Plausible parameter restrictions can rule out multiple equilibria, but the generality of the uniqueness result is again at issue.[10]

[9]Black (1974) discusses a related case that involves feedback from the inflation rate to money growth. Nonunique solutions with nonexplosive price behavior emerge if (a) the feedback is positive and greater than one to one; and (b) the magnitude of the inflation rate elasticity of money demand exceeds unity.

[10]It is interesting to note the divergent reactions to these types of uniqueness problems. One set of opinion regards these problems as symptomatic of the inadequacy of equilibrium analysis and even as evidence that private markets require governmental intervention. Another set regards them as empirically irrelevant intellectual curiosities, which will eventually be disposed of by deeper theoretical arguments.

Policy Implications

The Policy-Irrelevance Argument

The major implications for monetary policy derive from the dependence of real variables, such as output and the anticipated real rate of return in equations (3) and (4), only on unperceived parts of a variable like money growth, $m_t - E_z m_t$. Suppose that monetary policy is viewed as the choice among systematic feedback rules from the state of the economy to money growth, $m_t = F(\theta_t)$, where θ_t represents the current state and F is the function to be selected. In this approach policy is viewed not as a one-time choice of money supply or the government deficit, but rather as a regular way of operating in relation to the economy. The vector θ_t could include current and lagged values of output, inflation rate, government spending, and so forth. In the case stressed by Sargent (1973) and Sargent and Wallace (1975, 1976), θ_t includes only observations that are available also to individuals for estimating variables like contemporaneous money growth $E_z m_t$ or future prices $E_z P_{t+1}$.

The simple policy-irrelevance argument, which turns out not to be generally correct, is the following. Given that the policy function F is known and that individuals exploit fully the information contained in the observed variables θ_t, it follows that the systematic policy feedback $F(\theta_t)$ affects m_t and $E_z m_t$ equally. Under rational expectations and an equal information basis for the policymaker and the private sector, systematic policy cannot generate departures of money from its perceived value. If it is only these departures that count for output, as in equation (3), it follows that the entire probability distribution of output is invariant to the selection of the systematic policy response function $F(\theta)$.

Differential Information and Policy Irrelevance

The above policy-irrelevance argument is satisfactory in the context where Sargent and Wallace (1975) derived it, because expectations like $E_z m_t$ are conditioned on full lagged information and zero current information. That is, expectations appear as $E_{t-1} m_t$ or $E_{t-1} P_t$ and are therefore insensitive to current realizations of random variables. When the pertinent expectations are based on partial current information and are therefore sensitive to some current shocks—as, for example, in the models of Lucas (1973, 1975) and Barro (1976a)—it is possible that the choice of systematic feedback function $F(\theta)$ will influence the relation of current disturbances to contemporaneous expectations like $E_z m_t$, essentially by altering the information content of current prices. Theoretical examples of this phenomenon have been reported by King (1978) and Weiss (1979, 1980). King (1979b) demonstrates that a necessary condition for overturning the policy-irrelevance proposition in the present context is differential information across individuals who also have access to a common price. For example, agents in local commodity market z may have individual-specific information about next period's money growth rate or velocity shock. Similarly, participants of an economy-wide capital market may possess a commodity price observation that was obtained from their contemporaneous experience in a local market.

Consider the example discussed by King (1979b, pp. 16–20) for the setup of localized commodity markets, where there is an economy-wide supply disturbance but no capital market. The monetary authority is assumed to react with a lag to an intrinsically irrelevant *target* variable g:

$$m_t = \Psi g_{t-1} + \text{error term,}$$

where Ψ is a known constant and the g_t variable is distributed as white noise. Note that the authority is assumed to observe g_t only at date $t+1$, at which time it will also be common knowledge for individuals. If there were no policy feedback ($\Psi = 0$), or if g_t were observable currently up to a common error term across individuals (which could, as special cases, have either a zero or infinite variance), the policy-irrelevance result would go through. However, suppose that there is individual-specific contemporaneous information about g_t, which can be expressed as the observation by individual i of the noisy signal, $\tilde{g}_t(i) = g_t + \xi_t(i)$, where the individual error $\xi_t(i)$ is distributed like white noise. Possibly, $\tilde{g}_t(i)$ would represent the aggregate information that individuals receive by observing their own current transfer payment or an announcement of a future transfer from the government. Knowledge of g_t would be valuable for individuals as a predictor for m_{t+1} and therefore for P_{t+1}. Individuals will combine their observation of $P_t(z)$ with $\tilde{g}_t(i)$ to form money growth and price expectations, taking account of the interaction between the average opinion (expectation) of future prices and the determination of $P_t(z)$ through market-clearing conditions. The particular realization for g_t will typically matter for output, and so on, because each of the $\tilde{g}_t(i)$ will be affected correspondingly, but partially informed individuals will incorrectly assign some of this effect to the individual-specific noise term $\xi_t(i)$. That is, the typical agent will believe incorrectly that his observation $\tilde{g}_t(i)$ has shifted relative to the average of these observations across individuals; Weiss (1979, Section II) refers to this outcome as an error in average opinion about average opinion. Inferences about other random variables, such as the aggregate supply shock or $\epsilon_t(z)$, will be affected in this situation. The magnitude of policy feedback, as determined by the Ψ parameter, will count because it determines the extent to which errors in average opinion about average opinion of the g variable are transmitted to prices and outputs.

The models that allow for real effects of policy feedback have ambiguous normative implications. King's (1979b, p. 23) discussion of the above example, which concerned feedback from an intrinsically irrelevant target, suggests that optimal monetary policy would amount to elimination of feedback ($\Psi = 0$). However, Weiss's (1979, Section 5) conclusions are different for a case of differential information about shifts in future velocity (which he assumes is intrinsically irrelevant). In this setting, optimality would call for a monetary policy that reacts actively to past velocity changes in order to eliminate the link between prices and current information about future velocity shocks. Positive and normative analyses with these types of models becomes complicated in the more interesting cases where differential information and policy feedback apply not only to intrinsically irrelevant variables, but also to disturbances that appear directly in commodity supply and demand functions.

King (1979b, Section 4) demonstrates the existence of private indexing arrangements that reproduce the outcomes generated by feedback monetary policy. For example, the real effects produced by the reaction of next period's money growth rate to the target variable g_t could be offset completely by a universally applied private indexing scheme of the general form proposed in Barro (1976b), which would relate terms of trade ex post to the realized value of g_t. Similarly, private indexing arrangements would be an alternative to policy activism as a mechanism for insulating the economy from the real effects of Weiss's (1979, Section 5) differential information about future velocity shocks. The parallel between monetary policy and private indexing applies even when feedback is extended from intrinsically irrelevant variables to a vector of disturbances that appear directly in the structural model. However, in an environment with an economy-wide capital market and localized commodity markets, it is necessary that indexing apply to the globally observed price that is set in the capital market.

The analysis in Barro (1976b) indicated that the parameters of an indexation rule were irrelevant for the distribution of output, because these rules had no significance for the information on which ex ante allocative decisions were based. This conclusion turns out to hold only under the conditions where the policy irrelevance result is also valid. Under conditions of differential information, a change in indexing rules can have real effects by altering the information content of prices. Since policy activism and private indexation produce equivalent outcomes under some circumstances, optimal policy choice may involve an assessment of the relative *transaction costs* of operation. A full analysis of alternatives would necessarily include consideration of individual incentives to adopt indexing arrangements.

Other Aspects of the Policy-Irrelevance Argument

STOCHASTIC ELEMENTS OF POLICY

When the original policy-irrelevance argument is valid, it does not imply an independence of real variables from the random parts of policy. As indicated above, pure variance of money has real effects involving a diminished signaling value of observed nominal prices. In this sense the argument for irrelevance of systematic policy can be modified to generate a call for predictable behavior of money, such as a constant growth rate rule (M. Friedman, 1960) or other "stable rules of the game" (Simons, 1948, p. 169). These results conform in spirit to government's fostering the information role of the price system that is stressed by Hayek (1945).

INFORMATIONAL ADVANTAGES OF THE POLICYMAKER

The analysis is consistent with real and possibly desirable effects of policy that reflect an informational advantage of the policymaker (Sargent and Wallace, 1975, p. 251; Barro, 1976a, p. 21). To the extent that the θ_t variables discussed above incorporate information that was not exploited in deriving a conditional expectation like $E_z m_t$, a reaction of m_t to θ_t—that is, the choice of the F function—would have real effects. In a model where other sources of aggregate disturbances are included, such as supply shocks or velocity shifts, it is possible that adjustments of money to the parts of these disturbances that were not universally observed would have beneficial effects. Essentially, it is feasible to construct a form of policy reaction that induces the private sector to act as if it had observed these aggregate disturbances directly. In these cases provision of information by the policymaker is likely to be a substitute for activist monetary policy. The efficacy of policy activism then requires an appeal to an information or computational advantage for the government.

DECEPTIVE POLICY

A different case for policy activism hinges on the government's having superior information about its own behavior $F(\theta)$ (Taylor, 1975; B. Friedman, 1979). The basic argument is that the policymaker can create *innovations* to money and prices—and thereby influence real economic activity—during transition periods where the parameters of policy are known to the monetary authority but not to the public. (The normative basis for this type of policy deception is considered below.) It is doubtful that the government can keep *systematically* ahead of expectations of inflation, money expansion, and so on, especially if the private sector believes that the government is pursuing this type of game. For example, a rule to expand the money supply at a rate 1% faster than expected either at all times or during recessions does not generally describe a feasible mode of behavior. To the extent that policy changes reflect shifting public attitudes rather than policymaker *discretion,* these possibilities will be further limited. For example, there is no reason to believe that average expectations lag behind major shifts in the structure of policy, such as movements off the gold standard or adoption of a ''Full Employment Act'' economic policy.

The desirability of deceptive government policy is, in any case, difficult to defend in a broad perspective that values governmental credibility. The principal arguments that have been offered in favor of deceptive policy, as outlined in Phelps (1972, Chapter 4) and Hall (1976, p. 141), involve the nonoptimality of private market outcomes under full current information conditions. The main *externality* elements that have been pinpointed in this context, as discussed in Prescott (1975, pp. 1230–1234), involve government-engineered distortions like income taxation and unemployment compensation. The disincentive effects of tax and welfare programs are important, but they seem unlikely to serve as a normative basis for a regular program of deceptive countercyclical policy.

RULES VERSUS DISCRETION

The possibility for shifts in the parameters of policy relates to the distinction between rules and discretion, as discussed by Kydland and Prescott (1977). As an example, an optimal rule for patient policy would weigh the costs of monopoly against the beneficial stimuli to new inventions. At any point in time, however,

     II THE EQUILIBRIUM APPROACH TO BUSINESS CYCLES

optimal policy might seem to involve the abolition of all past patents—thereby achieving the benefits of competitive supply with the existing technology—combined with a promise to honor patents on all future inventions. As time evolves, new inventions become old and a similar argument leads again to revocation of patents. In other words the policy that optimizes at all dates subject to the initial conditions applying at those dates is subject to a time-inconsistency property where earlier plans are not followed through. When this policy behavior is anticipated by the private sector, the outcome is likely to be a time-consistent policy with a suboptimal amount of inventions. Analogous propositions can be generated for areas like honoring foreign debt, choosing the rate of monetary growth, regulating profits on new and old energy sources, building dams for flood plains. If one limits attention to situations where the actual policy process is understood by all economic agents, the common future of the examples is that some amount of precommit-ment—that is a rule not subject to change via current discretion—is a necessary ingredient for optimal policy. In the patent case it is necessary for the govern-ment—presumably utilizing a system of laws—to constrain itself against the future confiscation of patent rights, even if that action would in some respects appear desirable when conditioned later on the existing stock of inventions. With respect to constraining the rate of monetary expansion, the problem arises in the con-text of the government's exploiting the inflationary expectations that led indi-viduals to hold a particular amount of fixed nominal claims on the government. In earlier times this discretion was limited by the gold standard and fixed exchange rates, which have now been abandoned. New mechanisms for precommitment on monetary behavior seem presently to be lacking.

AUTOMATIC STABILIZERS

McCallum and Whitaker (1979) argue that automatic stabilizers can have real effects even in circumstances where natural rate characteristics of the economy and the absence of an informational advantage for the government imply that systematic feedback from economic variables to fiscal instruments would be impotent. Under a tax law that relates individual liability to individual income, persons who experience a decline in income—which is assumed to be individually observable with no lag—are immediately aware of a partially compensating reduction in tax obliga-tions. If a contemporaneous general business recession is not perceived, individuals will view this tax cut as a reduction in relative liabilities. Therefore, even in the case where a perceived general tax cut financed by public debt issue would not influence aggregate demand—that is, in the Ricardian equivalence case discussed in Barro (1974) where the anticipated future taxes implied by perceived government deficits are fully capitalized by current taxpayers—the tax cut produced through the automa-tic stabilizer could have a temporary expansionary effect.

ALLOCATIVE POLICIES

The present discussion does not rule out real effects of perceived government policies that have direct effects on relative prices. For example, unemployment insurance and tax laws have real effects even (especially) when they are fully perceived. Shifts between taxes and debt issue can have real effects involving the timing of non-lump-sum taxation (Barro, 1979b; Kydland and Prescott, 1980, pp. 185–186). In certain cases rational expectations alter the effects of policy without implying that such policies are irrelevant. For example, the aggregate demand effects of government purchases would depend on the relation of current spending to anticipated future spending (Hall, 1979, pp. 10–11; Barro, 1979c). An analysis of the investment tax credit program, as discussed in Kydland and Prescott (1977, pp. 482–486), would consider private expectations about the relation of the credit to economic activity. If the credit is varied countercyclically, firms may postpone investment projects at the start of recessions and accelerate spending during booms in order to cash in on the largest possible credit. Hence the full effect of the program may be an increased amplitude of business fluctuations, in contrast to the stated objective of economic stabilization. It is also likely that systematic inflation has real effects—such as the traditional welfare cost of inflation calculation—that were not included in the simple model described by equations (1) and (2).

Market Clearing

Equilibrium business cycle models have often been criticized for their reliance on continuous market clearing; see, for example, Modigliani (1977, p. 6) and some counterarguments in Lucas and Sargent (1978, pp. 64–65) and Barro (1979a, pp. 54–56). The equation of supply to demand implies that market transactions have proceeded to the point where perceived mutually advantageous trades have been exhausted. Imperfect information about exchange opportunities, production conditions, and so forth, or various transactions and mobility costs could be incorporated in these models, but they would appear as explicit influences in the supply and demand functions. The rejection of continuous market clearing as a modeling device requires the substitution of an alternative mechanism. A popular formulation in the disequilibrium literature (e.g., Barro and Grossman, 1976, Chapter 2) postulates arbitrary dynamic processes for price formation and arbitrary rules for determining quantities in non-market-clearing situations. The modeling implies easily correctable ways in which private markets malfunction; not surprisingly, the problems can be overcome by simple forms of activist government policy with respect to money supply or other variables.

McCallum (1979c) has investigated the sensitivity of policy irrelevance conclusions to a type of wage or price stickiness that involves slow adjustment to *excess demand* plus a one-to-one effect of the expected change in the market-clearing price on actual wage–price change. This type of relation is justified in terms of optimal response to wage–price adjustment costs. The policy-irrelevance proposition holds in this model despite the presence of sluggish wage–price adjustment. Essentially, systematic monetary policy influences the expected market-clearing price, which affects actual wages and prices one-to-one, and thereby leaves output unchanged.

The result depends on a correspondence between the policy feedback lag and the lag with which expectations of market-clearing prices are allowed to affect actual wages and prices. In this respect the conclusions parallel results of Fischer (1977, Part II) and Phelps and Taylor (1977, p. 165), where the argument for policy activism requires the period over which nominal wages are precommitted to exceed the time delay for policy feedback. These analyses reflect the general point (Barro, 1979a, p. 55) that the case for policy activism requires some aspect of resource allocation in which the government is superior to the private sector. Costs of changing prices, as discussed by Phelps and Taylor (1977, pp. 165–166) and McCallum (1979c, p. 21), may not be a quantitatively important basis for this argument. It is difficult to see how the private sector's potential for making long-term wage commitments, as stressed by Fischer (1977, pp. 202–204), can support an underlying argument for the superiority of government-influenced allocations; see the subsequent discussion.

The long-term contracting approach to wage–price stickiness was introduced to macroanalysis in papers by Azariadis (1975), Baily (1974), and D. Gordon (1974). Although these models do not explain the pre-setting of wages or prices in nominal terms, they can rationalize some precommitment—and thereby stickiness—with regard to real terms of trade. The argument in Barro (1977b) is that a similar application of efficient contracting analysis to the determination of quantities—which is implicit in the above theories—would rule out effects on output and employment of perceived nominal shocks. Basically, efficient contracts would allow output and employment to be determined as if prices had been flexible. It is therefore not satisfactory to refer to contracting theory as a rationale for wage–price stickiness and to retain features of quantity determination—such as equation of the marginal product of labor to the realized real wage—that would be inconsistent with the contracting model. It is possible that more mileage will come out of analyses that account for limitations on contractual contingencies, enforcement costs, and so on; see, for example, H. Grossman (1978) and Hall and Lillien (1979). At present, contracting analysis seems mostly to suggest that continuous market clearing would be a useful *as if* device for analyzing the determination of output and employment.

Econometric Policy Evaluation

Lucas (1972b, 1976a) has constructed a broad attack on the use of estimated econometric models to simulate the impact of alternative policy rules. His argument is that these estimated models reflect a particular process for expectation formation with respect to prices, money, taxes, and so on, that would shift in major ways along with changes in the structure of policy. For example, suppose that a model was estimated over a sample where the monetary rule was given by

$$m_t = \alpha_0 + \alpha_1 X_t + u_t, \qquad (6)$$

where X_t is a set of current and lagged variables influencing current money growth and u_t is a random term. Suppose further that output is determined by

$$y_t = \beta_0 + \beta_1(m_t - E_t m_t) + \beta_2 X_t + v_t, \tag{7}$$

which is of the form of equation (3), where v_t is another error term. Using equation (6) and rational expectations to calculate $E_t m_t = \alpha_0 + \alpha_1 X_t$ (with X_t treated as fully observable and u_t as entirely unobservable at date t, so that the problem of partial current information does not arise), and substituting into equation (7) yields the reduced form for output,

$$y_t = (\beta_0 - \beta_1\alpha_0) + \beta_1 m_t + (\beta_2 - \beta_1\alpha_1)X_t + v_t$$
$$= \gamma_0 + \gamma_1 m_t + \gamma_2 X_t + v_t. \tag{8}$$

Observable data on (y, m, X) could be used to estimate the γ coefficients on the right side of equation (8). Frequently, the estimated coefficients from a reduced-form equation of this type would be used to design an optimal feedback response of m_t to the variables X_t. For example, the choice of the policy rule $m_t = -(\gamma_2/\gamma_1)X_t$ appears to make output insensitive to variations in X_t in accordance with equation (8). In fact, the adoption of this new policy, which would amount to a shift in the coefficients of equation (6), implies that the estimated reduced form is no longer valid. The coefficient γ_2 in equation (8) shifts along with the change in α_1 in equation (6). In this example it is clear from equation (7) that—since $m_t - E_t m_t$ would just equal the error term u_t in equation (6)—y_t is actually invariant to the choice of the monetary rule coefficients (α_0, α_1). With systematic feedback from X_t to m_t filtered out, the impact of X_t on y_t is fixed by the coefficient β_2 in equation (7).

More generally, the implementation of rational expectations in the context of shifting policy structure does not inevitably lead to policy irrelevance or to the proposition that econometric analysis of policy is impossible (Shiller, 1978, pp. 28,29), but does imply a different evaluation from that derived by direct implementation of an estimated reduced form model. Lucas and Sargent (1978, pp. 56–57) argue further that the coefficient shifts associated with policy changes may account for the continual necessity of updating the forms and coefficients of estimated econometric models. Accordingly, the econometric problems posed by shifting policy structure are likely to be quantitatively important in practice.

Empirical Testing: Observational Equivalence Problems

The preceding theoretical discussion stressed the role of unperceived changes in money or other variables. A major issue, which has substantial implications for policy, concerns the testing of the proposition that only these unperceived components—and not the recognized movements in money—affect real variables like output, employment, and real rates of return. Sargent (1976a, pp. 9–12; 1976b) and Sims (1980, pp. 6–11) have raised some basic questions concerning the possibility of testing this type of theoretical proposition involving unobserved expectational variables.

The Observational Equivalence of Natural and Unnatural Rate Models

Consider the two-equation natural rate model, which is a modification of equations (6) and (7),

$$m_t = a + b_1 m_{t-1} + b_2 m_{t-2} + \cdots + c_0 X_t$$
$$+ c_1 X_{t-1} + \cdots + d_0 Z_t + d_1 Z_{t-1} + \cdots + u_t, \tag{9}$$

$$y_t = e + f_0 (m_t - E_t m_t) + f_1 (m_{t-1} - E_{t-1} m_{t-1}) + \cdots + g_0 X_t$$
$$+ g_1 X_{t-1} + \cdots + h_0 Z_t + h_1 Z_{t-1} + \cdots + v_t. \tag{10}$$

Equation (9) indicates a dependence of money growth on its own history, as represented by the sequence of arbitrary length in the lagged values $m_{t-1}, m_{t-2}, \ldots$, and on two vectors of exogenous variables (X, Z). In equation (10), y_t depends on current and an arbitrary number of lagged monetary shocks, where the lagged effects would reflect the persisting influences discussed in the theoretical section. In each case the lagged value of money growth m_{t-i} is matched with the contemporaneous expectation $E_{t-i} m_{t-i}$. Additional issues, discussed later, arise if the impact of m_{t-i} is relative to expectations formed at earlier dates, $E_{t-i-j} m_{t-i}$. The variables (X, Z)—which might include lagged values of y—appear also in equation (10). The error terms u_t and v_t are assumed to be mutually and serially independent. Equations (9) and (10), together with rational expectations, deliver the strong policy invariance propositions that were discussed previously, at least for cases where partial current information is not introduced into the calculation of expectations. Changes in the coefficients of the policy equation (a, b, c, d) have no implications for the determination of output.

Consider the alternative *unnatural* rate theory,

$$y_t = k + p_0 m_t + p_1 m_{t-1} + \cdots + q_0 X_t$$
$$+ q_1 X_{t-1} + \cdots + r_0 Z_t + r_1 Z_{t-1} + \cdots + \epsilon_t, \tag{11}$$

which might appear as part of a reduced form of an econometric model. If the coefficients (k, p, q, r) could be held fixed while the parameters of the money rule (a, b, c, d) were varied, then the choice of rule would have important implications for the behavior of output. The crucial empirical question is whether equation (10) or (11) (if either) is invariant to the shift of parameters in equation (9).

Suppose that equation (10)—the natural rate theory—is correct and that the expectations $E_{t-i} m_{t-i}$ can be determined by direct substitution from equation (9) with $(X_{t-i}, Z_{t-i}, m_{t-i-1})$ assumed observable at date $t - i$. The expression for output with expectations substituted out involves current and lagged values of the m, X, and Z variables; in particular, the reduced form of the natural rate model coincides in form with equation (11). For example, the coefficients in equation (11), when derived from equations (9) and (10), turn out to be: $p_0 = f_0, p_1 = f_1 - b_1 f_0, \ldots;$ $q_0 = g_0 - c_0 f_0, q_1 = g_1 - c_0 f_1 - c_1 f_0, \ldots$. At least if there were no finite truncation in the number of lag values included in equations (9) and (10), this pattern of coefficients would impose no constraints on the estimated reduced-form coefficients corresponding to equations (9) and (10). The coincidence in reduced forms implies that, with no further restrictions imposed on the model, it is impossible empirically to distinguish the system composed of equations (9) and (10) from that comprising equations (9) and (11). Put another way, the choice between equations (10) and (11) as invariant relationships would determine the effect of policy in the sense of the impact on the determination of output of shifts in the parameters that appear in equation (9). If the data provide no variation in policy, in the sense of shifts in the relevant coefficients, it is not surprising that the data cannot identify these effects.

Methods of Identification

One method for identifying the coefficients in equation (10) is to constrain the system ex ante so that some variables that shift money growth in equation (9) do not directly affect output in equation (10). For example, suppose that the X variables, which appear in equation (9) in accordance with the c coefficients, are absent from equation (10). With $g_i = 0$ imposed, equations (9) and (10) determine a reduced form that can be written as equations (9) and (11) with some testable restrictions imposed across the coefficients of the two equations. Essentially, the X variables are now constrained to influence output in equation (11) only to the extent that these variables serve as conditional estimators for money growth, as dictated from the coefficients in equation (9). These restrictions would not appear if the X variables were allowed also to affect output directly. This exclusion method of testing natural rate–rational expectations hypotheses was carried out in Barro (1977a, pp. 109–111; 1978b, pp. 557–560). In those papers a federal expenditure relative to normal variable and a lagged unemployment rate variable are entered into a money growth equation, but are excluded ex ante from having direct effects in equations for the unemployment rate, output and the price level. Statistical tests that are carried out in this setting amount to joint tests of the natural rate–rational expectations hypotheses and the exclusion restrictions. Similarly, in McCallum (1976), the hypothesis that the expected inflation rate affects the rate of wage change with a unit coefficient is testable because the predictors of inflation are constrained not to enter directly into the wage–change equation.

Another possibility, which amounts to a special case of the above type of exclusion restriction, is to limit ex ante the number of lag values of money growth or other variables that affect output. Suppose that only the contemporaneous money shock were relevant in equation (10)—that is, $f_i = 0$ for $i = 1, 2, \ldots$, were imposed (recall that X or Z might represent a lagged value of y)—but that coefficients $b_1, b_2 \cdots \neq 0$ were permitted in equation (9). In this situation lagged values of m are constrained to affect y in the reduced form only to the extent that they influence the conditional expectation $E_t m_t$, as determined from the coefficients in equation (9). Testable restrictions on coefficients across the equations in the reduced form would be implied, although problems would arise if the error term in equation (10) were serially correlated (McCallum, 1979a, pp. 399–401). Restrictions on numbers of lag values are usually not available ex ante, but McCallum (1979a, pp. 397–399) has defended the applicability of this type of restriction in the present context. He contends that, with initial conditions truly held constant, lagged values of money shocks could not be relevant for current output. Theoretically, initial conditions would include not only last period's values of output and employment, but also the most recent values of capacity, inventories, decisions, and so on. Empirically, it is not clear how to hold constant the relevant initial conditions. Lucas (1973, p. 328) and Sargent (1976c, p. 235) rely on lagged values of dependent variables. However, the results in Barro (1977a, p. 108; 1978b, p. 555) indicate that lagged values of money shocks have important unemployment rate and output effects even when lagged values of the dependent variables are held constant. This finding can be rationalized by a theory that recognizes many channels for persisting output effects—not all of which have been isolated—but the upshot of this discussion is to question the usefulness of this avenue of identification.

A different avenue for identification, mentioned by Shiller (1978, p. 17) and used by Sheffrin (1978, pp. 209–210), involves a priori restrictions on the signs or magnitudes of coefficients in the output equation (10). For example, a restriction that all monetary shocks have expansionary effects, $f_i \geq 0$, can be tested in conjunction with the natural rate–rational expectations hypotheses. (However, this restriction on the f_i coefficients would not apply generally in models that utilize stock adjustment as an explanation for persistence; see the discussion earlier in this chapter.) If a variable such as government spending that appears as one of the X_t variables in the money growth equation (9) were restricted to appear directly in equation (10) with a nonnegative coefficient, then hypotheses could again be tested.

Finally, as stressed by Sargent (1976a, pp. 12–13; 1976b), identification can be achieved if observations are pooled from different monetary regimes—that is, subsamples with different coefficients or error term distributions in equation (9)—if the output equation (10) or other relationships are assumed either to be stable across the regimes or at least to shift in a limited fashion. An example of the latter specification would allow the error variance from equation (9), but not the coefficients, to influence the determination of output. Different policy regimes might correspond to different countries, as in Lucas (1973), in which case the homogeneity of the output equation across countries becomes an issue. There is no difficulty in allowing some country-specific coefficients in equation (10) as long as some parts of the equation are constrained ex ante to coincide across the countries. Alternatively, different policy regimes could be associated with a given country at distinct points in time, as in the comparison of United States experience under the gold standard from 1880 to 1914 with that under the fiat money standard of the post–World War II period that is carried out in a preliminary way in Rush (1978). Similarly, Neftci (1978) isolates a structural break in monetary behavior for the post–World War II period corresponding to pre- and post-1962. In Saidi and Barro (1976), Canadian monetary behavior under a flexible exchange rate regime is distinguished from that under fixed exchange rates. In all of these cases the testing of natural rate hypotheses would require some ex ante restirctions on the stability of the output equation (10) or other relations across the different policy regimes.

Identification through pooling over different policy regimes is actually another special case of the general idea introduced at the start of this section. The general requirement is to specify some variables that shift the policy variable (m_t in equation (9)) without independently affecting output in equation (10) (or an equation for some other variable of interest). A shift in regime that does not correspond to a simultaneous shift in the output equation provides candidates for these sorts of "variables."

Unanticipated versus Unperceived Money Growth

Even more difficult identification problems arise if output or other variables depend on values of money growth m_{t-i} relative to prior expectations $E_{t-i-j} m_{t-i}$. That is, money growth at date $t-i$ that was unanticipated as of some prior date $t-i-j$ appears in addition to the portion of date $t-i$ money growth that was contemporaneously unperceived. Fischer (1977, 1980) has argued for the importance of these types of unanticipated money growth variables on the grounds that some nominal contracts that are in force at date $t-i$ will have been based on prior monetary expectations. Suppose that a string of one-period-ahead prediction errors — $(m_t - E_{t-1} m_t)$, $(m_{t-1} - E_{t-2} m_{t-1})$, ... —were added to the output equation (10). Consider the case where natural and unnatural rate models are distinguished, as discussed previously, by the presence of a single variable X_t that appears in the money growth equation (9) but is excluded from the output equation (10). The distinction between the natural and unnatural rate models corresponds in this case to restrictions on the coefficients of the m and X variables in the reduced-form equation (11), as related to the coefficients in equation (9). However, the introduction of the extra string of unanticipated money growth variables into equation (10) implies a corresponding new string of free coefficients attached to the m and X variables in the reduced form equation (11).[11] In effect, the reduced-form restrictions are eliminated by this change in the model.[12] Therefore, a test for the irrelevance of the string of one-period-ahead unanticipated money growth variables in equation (10) is essentially the same as the test of the natural rate model that was discussed earlier. With a single X_t variable as the basis for identification it is impossible to distinguish (a) rejection of equation (10) on the grounds that a set of one-period-ahead unanticipated money growth variables is also pertinent for output, from (b) rejection because current and lagged values of the X variable appear for any other reason in the "wrong" way in the reduced-form equation (11). Distinction between these possibilities would require exclusion restrictions on at least two independent variables,

---

[11]Prior expectations of the X variable, $E_{t-i-1} X_{t-i}$, come into the analysis. It is being assumed that these priors cannot be based on some new variables that do not appear in the output equation (10).

[12]This statement is inexact because there are some remaining restrictions that relate to the length of the lag b_i (and c_i) in equation (9). (Lags involved with the determination of $E_{t-i-1} X_{t-i}$—see note 11—would also come into play.) As the length of the lag f_i in equation (10) becomes large, these restrictions become weaker, in the sense that the ratio of free coefficients to independent variables in the reduced form approaches one. Because the number of lag terms is arbitrary, I have neglected restrictions that depend on lag lengths.

X_t^1 and X_t^2.[13] Accordingly, a direct distinction between the output effects of unperceived versus unanticipated money growth is likely to be a difficult one to make in practice.

Some Invalid Testing Procedures

A basic element in the preceding discussion is the cross-equation nature of tests involving natural rate–rational expectations hypotheses. A test that only the unperceived part of money influences output involves joint consideration of money and output equations. Lucas (1972b, p. 57) and Sargent (1971; 1976a, pp. 3–6) discuss examples of invalid tests that have ignored the joint nature of expectational hypotheses. As an illustration of the nature of this problem, consider equation (11), which describes output as a function of current and lagged money growth and other variables. An investigator may wish to use this equation to test the hypothesis that the rate of monetary growth does not have a *long-run* effect on output, which is an implication of the natural rate view. Roughly speaking, if the money growth rate rises from an average value of say 1% per year to an average of 5% per year the mean value of output (and its entire distribution) should be unaffected. If equation (11) is viewed as a structural relation with coefficients that are invariant to policy changes, this property can hold only if the sum of the money growth rate coefficients equals zero. The restriction $\Sigma p_i = 0$ in equation (11) is testable, but is generally not an implication of a properly specified natural rate–rational expectations model. From the perspective of equation (9), the posited change in the mean money growth rate amounts to a shift in the constant term by an amount Δa. This shift implies, via substitution for the $E_{t-i} m_{t-i}$ terms in equation (10), a change in the constant term of the reduced form expression for output in equation (11) by the amount $\Delta k = -\Delta a (f_0 + f_1 + \cdots) = -\Delta a \Sigma f_i$. This shift in the constant delivers the long-run invariance of output to the mean rate of monetary expansion, independently of the configuration of the p_i coefficients in equation (11), which do not shift in the present case.

The restriction $\Sigma p_i = 0$ would arise under special forms of the monetary process; notably, if money growth were generated as a form of random walk where $b_1 + b_2 + \cdots = \Sigma b_i = 1$ in equation (9). It can be verified via substitution into equation (10) that the sum of the coefficients in equation (11) is given by $\Sigma p_i = \Sigma f_i (1 - \Sigma b_i)$. Therefore, $\Sigma p_i = 0$ holds in the random walk case where $\Sigma b_i = 1$, independently of the values of the f_i coefficients in equation (10). It should be recalled that the random walk process is nonstationary and therefore implies an ever-

[13]More generally, the number of independent X variables must exceed the number of additional strings of unanticipated money growth variables that are introduced into the output equation. For example, if the two-period-ahead string, $(m_t - E_{t-2} m_t)$, $(m_{t-1} - E_{t-3} m_{t-1})$, . . . , were included also in equation (1), the *structural* coefficients would be underidentified if only one X variable were available. Two X variables would not be sufficient in this case to distinguish the different grounds for rejecting the natural rate model that were discussed above.

increasing variance for the growth rate of money (and prices) as the forecast date is advanced. Empirical estimates for recent U.S. experience are in the stationary range where $0 < \Sigma b_i < 1$; see, for example, Barro (1978b, p. 551). Therefore, if the typical monetary effect on output is expansionary in the sense that $\Sigma f_i > 0$ holds in equation (10), then $\Sigma p_i > 0$, but smaller in magnitude than Σf_i, would be expected from the natural rate view. In fact, the empirical estimates conform with this view (Barro, 1978b, pp. 555–556). The general point is that natural rate hypotheses cannot be applied to a relation of the form of equation (11) without consideration of the form of the policy process, as described by equation (9).

Sargent (1971; 1976a, pp. 3–6) describes problems that are analogous to the above example, although dealing with expectations of price change in the context of an interest rate or Phillips curve equation, rather than with money growth. The type of tests carried out by Solow (1968, pp. 11–17) for a long-run tradeoff between inflation and unemployment are shown by Sargent to hinge on the empirically invalid restriction that the inflation rate evolve as a form of random walk, as in the above example pertaining to money growth. The same criticism invalidates estimates of expectational Phillips curves that have been carried out by R. Gordon (1971, 1972). At the least, modeling of expected inflation in wage-change or other equations must take account of the actual process by which inflation is generated, as exemplified by the later work of McCallum (1976).

Empirical Findings

Lucas's Cross-Country Evidence

Lucas's (1973) empirical investigation is aimed primarily at the slope coefficient in the Phillips curve; in particular, at the proposition that the reaction of output to nominal shocks is positive but declining in size as the variance of nominal shocks rises.[14] The empirical procedure uses an annual time series of data from 1951 to 1967 to estimate a regression of detrended output on the change in nominal income and lagged detrended output for each of the 18 countries in the sample. There is no attempt to distinguish change in nominal income from the unanticipated movement in nominal income, it merely being assumed that change in nominal income has a constant mean over time within each country. The estimated coefficients on the change in nominal income variable are typically positive—averaging .51 over the countries—and most are significantly different from zero. Lucas (1973, p. 332) observes that the estimated coefficients are much smaller (in fact, essentially zero) for the two volatile price countries in the sample (Argentina and Paraguay) than for the remaining relatively low price variance countries. However, there is a negligible correlation between coefficient estimate and price variance among the 16 moderate

[14]Lucas (1976b) has pointed out that his ''cross-equation'' comparisons of output and inflation are not meaningful. Given the value of nominal income, which is assumed exogenous, there is an identity relation between the inflation rate equation and a first-difference form of the output equation.

inflation countries. Basically similar findings are reported by Alberro (1980), who applies Lucas's methodology to 50 countries. The six volatile price countries in Alberro's sample (Argentina, Brazil, Chile, Indonesia, Korea, Uruguay) have low estimated coefficients on the nominal income change variable, but there is again little relation of estimated coefficients to nominal income change variance among the more stable countries (Alberro, 1980, Figure 1).

The low slope coefficients for the volatile price countries accord with the usual view that countries can differ much more in terms of nominal income or price variance than in terms of output variance (Lucas, 1973, Table 1; Alberro, 1980, Table 1). However, there is a serious question whether this finding and the generally positive estimated slope coefficients for the relatively stable countries are closely related to the Phillips curve theories proposed by Lucas and others.

Consider an extreme natural rate model where the log of detrended output y in a country is determined independently of monetary events by an autoregressive process,

$$y_t = \alpha y_{t-1} + u_t,$$

where u is a white-noise error term. Suppose that the log of the detrended price level P for this country is determined by a similar process,

$$P_t = \beta P_{t-1} + v_t,$$

where v is another white-noise error; in particular, v and u are independently distributed. One questionable element in this setup is the independence of price level determination from shifts in real output, which requires some endogeneity of money supply or velocity. This type of model might apply under a fixed exchange rate regime (which characterizes most of the moderate inflation countries for Lucas's and Alberro's samples) or other monetary setup that would to a large extent insulate a country's price level changes from its output fluctuations.

If one runs Lucas's regression,

$$\hat{y}_t = \hat{\pi} \cdot \Delta X_t + \lambda y_{t-1},$$

where $\Delta X_t \equiv y_t - y_{t-1} + P_t - P_{t-1}$ is the change in nominal income, on an infinite sample of data generated from the above model, it can be shown that

$$\hat{\pi} = \kappa(1+\alpha)/[2 - \kappa(1-\alpha)],$$

where κ is the fraction of nominal income change variance due to variance in output: $\kappa \equiv 2(1-\alpha)\sigma_y^2/\sigma_{\Delta X}^2$, σ_y^2 is the variance of y, and $\sigma_{\Delta X}^2$ is the variance of ΔX. In particular, $0 < \hat{\pi} < 1$ applies and $\hat{\pi}$ is increasing in κ, and therefore decreasing in $\sigma_{\Delta X}^2$ for a given value of σ_y^2. (For values of α close to 1, $\hat{\pi} \approx \kappa$ applies.) This model accounts readily for the generally positive empirical estimates $\hat{\pi}$, and for the tendency of $\hat{\pi}$ to approach zero as $\sigma_{\Delta X}^2$ (or σ_p^2) approaches infinity. In this model the coefficient of nominal income change is positive because this variable corresponds to the dependent variable plus independent price change noise (less lagged output, which is held fixed separately). As the noise variance becomes relatively large, the estimated coefficient declines and eventually approaches zero.

These results indicate that the Lucas (1973) and Alberro (1978) cross-country findings are consistent with a mechanical model in which Phillips curve effects are entirely absent. On the other hand, this alternative model is surely consistent with the natural rate view; it seems that the cross-country evidence cannot be reconciled with theories that imply the same stable tradeoff across countries between the rate of inflation and the level of output.

Further information from the cross-country evidence could be obtained by using money or price level shocks, rather than the change in nominal income, as independent variables. However, these alternatives would also have to deal with simultaneity problems, as discussed below. Hypotheses concerning the relation of money or price variance to a Phillips curve coefficient could be tested also on time series data if changes in underlying variances can be isolated. These changes might correspond to discrete breaks in monetary regime, as in Neftci (1978), or to continuous evolution of variances, as treated in a preliminary way in Hercowitz (1979).

Sargent's Classical Macroeconometric Model

Sargent (1976c) uses quarterly, post–World War II, U.S. data to test whether lagged values of several variables including the money stock influence the unemployment rate (and the labor force participation rate and the long-term nominal interest rate) once a number of lags of the dependent variable are held fixed. As Sargent points out (1976c, pp. 221–222), the relation of this test to a natural rate model of the form of equations (9) and (10) above is unclear. Specifically, this type of natural rate model is consistent with unemployment effects of either lagged money shocks or lagged values of other variables, given the past history of the unemployment rate.

An important finding in Sargent's estimated model (1976c, p. 235) is the minor explanatory role in the unemployment rate equation that is played by the price-surprise term, $P_t - E_{t-1}P_t$, which has an estimated coefficient that is negative, but with a t value of only 2.0. When the model is reestimated by Fair (1979, pp. 703–708) with a second-order autoregressive error term and with a constraint that the expectation $E_{t-1}P_t$ be formed in an internally consistent manner, the estimated coefficient becomes insignificant. It seems likely that these estimates are confounded by simultaneity problems; clearly, in an OLS regression the sign of the estimated coefficient on the price-surprise term would depend on whether demand or supply shocks were dominant over the sample. Fair (1979, p. 704) uses only the nominal money stock and population as exogenous variables for carrying out two-stage least squares, deleting Sargent's (1976c, p. 234) government purchases, employment, and surplus variables because they were absent from the structural model. (The treatment of the surplus as exogenous is surprising in any case.) Since the contemporaneous realizations of the two exogenous variables and of the long-term nominal interest rate (which is treated by Fair as predetermined) are the main basis for distinguishing supply effects of the current price level from those of the expected price level, $E_{t-1}P_t$,[15] it is unclear that the estimates can be interpreted as supply parameters. For example, one would question the independence of the interest rate from supply disturbances. These doubts are reinforced by the dramatic reversal in sign for the price-surprise coefficient that arises when Fair (p. 706) adds the years 1974–1977 to the sample. The natural interpretation is that adverse supply shocks were important since 1974, with these shocks producing a positive correlation between the unemployment rate and price movements (and nominal interest rate changes).

If the major purpose in the above type of estimation is to isolate monetary effects on the unemployment rate, prices, and so on, it would be instructive to examine reduced forms in which monetary shocks appear as explanatory variables (see in the following). Dependent variables would be the unemployment rate, output, or the price-surprise variable, although difficult problems arise concerning the information set for determining the expected price level. An additional issue concerns the replacement of the price surprise term used in the Sargent and Fair studies, $P_t - E_{t-1}P_t$, by the anticipated real rate of return variable, $r_t \equiv R_t + P_t - E_t P_{t+1}$, that was discussed earlier in the theoretical sections.

Barro on "Unanticipated Money Growth"

The empirical analyses of annual U.S. data since World War II in Barro (1977a, 1978b) deal primarily with reduced-form effects of money shocks on the unemployment rate, output, and the price level. The analysis is modified and extended to quarterly data in Barro and Rush (1980). Money growth is divided into *anticipated* and *unanticipated* components by identifying the anticipated part with the prediction derivable from a money growth equation that was estimated with a single set of coefficients over samples beginning in 1941. As indicated in the following, the empirical distinction between anticipated and perceived money growth is a slippery one. The monetary equation includes as regressors lagged values of money growth, current real federal spending relative to "normal" (generated as a distributed lag of past values), and lagged unemployment rates. The residuals, labeled as unanticipated money growth, are shown to have significant and quantitatively important expansionary influences.[16] Given the relatively minor role played by price surprises in the results of Sargent (1976c) and Fair (1979) discussed earlier, it appears that monetary influences on output involve channels that have yet to be isolated.

The intertemporal pattern of reduced form monetary effects is most clear in the quarterly results (Barro and Rush, 1980, Table 2.1), where the positive response of

[15]Another distinction arises from the nonlinear restrictions on the reduced form that are imposed in the calculation of $E_{t-1}P_t$.

[16]Analogous results are reported for the United Kingdom in Attfield, Demery, and Duck (1979), for Canada in Wogin (1980), and Saidi and Barro (1976), and for Mexico in Blejer and Fernandez (1979). The last study includes an explicit analysis of an open economy under fixed exchange rates, with stress on the distinction between traded and nontraded goods.

output to a money shock rises to a peak at a 3–4-quarter lag, then gradually diminishes to become insignificant after 7 quarters. The negative response of the unemployment rate is similar, although possibly revealing a slightly longer lag relative to that of output.[17] Quantitatively, a 1-percentage-point money shock is estimated to affect real GNP by somewhat more than 1% during the first year and by a slightly smaller amount in the second year. Correspondingly, the unemployment rate would (starting from a 6% rate) change by about .6 percentage points in each year. The estimated equations for output and the unemployment rate include also a contemporaneous expansionary influence of a *fiscal* variable, which is represented either by a measure of military personnel or by real federal purchases (Barro and Rush, 1980, pp. 30–32 and Table 2.1). Further investigation of the role of these variables, with special attention to the distinction between temporary and permanent government purchases, is contained in Barro (1979c).

Tests are carried out for the hypothesis that money growth at date $t-i$ appears only as a divergence from $E_{t-i}m_{t-i}$ in affecting output and the unemployment rate. As discussed above, cross-equation coefficient restrictions derived from this hypothesis depend on the omission of some money growth predictors—in this case the real federal spending relative to normal and lagged unemployment rate variables—from output and unemployment rate relations of the form of equation (10). In the present context the hypothesis receives overall support (Barro, 1977a, pp. 109–111; 1978b, p. 557).

The robustness of the test results to changes in the specification of the money growth equation and to alterations of the associated exclusion restrictions is a serious issue. (See the discussions in McCallum, 1979b, p. 244; Small, 1979; Barro 1979d; and Germany and Srivastava, 1979.) As examples, a more appropriate measure of normal federal spending could be designed, feedback effects to money from interest rate changes might be important, and shifts in the U.S. money growth structure since 1941 may be isolated. When a large number of candidate variables are considered for the money growth equation, it becomes important (Barro, 1979d, pp. 1005–1006) to use the appropriate statistical procedure, which entails joint estimation of equations for money growth and output and/or the unemployment rate (Leiderman, 1980; Barro and Rush, 1980, pp. 27–30). Estimation and testing by this method appropriately allows the choice of estimated coefficients in the money growth equation to consider the effects—through the calculation of the unantici-pated money growth series—on the fit of the output and/or unemployment rate relations. Earlier procedures, which involved separate estimation of the money growth equation, have less desirable statistical properties; in particular, the intro-

---

[17]These lag patterns apply to equations that use seasonally adjusted data and in which a correction was made for second-order serial correlation of residuals. The role of seasonal factors in the estimation warrants further investigation. The residual serial correlations turns out to be strongly positive from quarter to quarter, but much weaker from year to year. The lagged response pattern of output or the unemployment rate to money shocks appears somewhat longer—out to 8–10 quarters—if the correction for serial correlation of residuals is omitted. Autocorrelation of residuals was not a problem when annual data were used; see for example Barro and Rush (1980, Part I). The lag patterns found in the annual data are consistent with those estimated from the quarterly figures.

duction of irrelevant variables into the money growth equation will produce small-sample bias in the estimation of the output and unemployment rate equations. More general discussions of estimation procedures in the context of the nonlinear, cross-equation coefficient restrictions that arise in this type of analysis are contained in Hansen and Sargent (1979a,b).

An empirical form for a price level equation is derived from combination of a money demand function with an equation that relates output to a distributed lag of monetary shocks (Barro, 1978b, pp. 558–560). This analysis includes the nominal interest rate—a determinant of money demand—as a right-hand side variable, although a full model would relate interest rates to exogenous variables. The form of the price equation implies a one-to-one, contemporaneous effect of money in the sense that, with the array of current and past money shocks and the current nominal interest rate held fixed, the coefficient on the current money stock is unity and those on lagged money stocks are zero. Since a distributed lag of money shocks affects output positively, there would be a corresponding string of negative effects on the price level. Results in Barro (1978b, pp. 560–570) confirm some of these hypotheses, but the pattern of price level response to unanticipated money movements is elongated substantially relative to that of output. Results in Barro and Rush (1980) indicate further difficulties with the price equation, which concern discrepancies from hypothesized cross-equation patterns with the money growth relation and a lack of robustness in results obtained from quarterly data. At this stage the source of these problems has not been isolated.

The present set of empirical results does not distinguish the effects of unperceived money growth, $m_{t-i} - E_{t-i} m_{t-i}$, from those of unanticipated growth, $m_{t-i} - E_{t-i-j} m_{t-i}$. As indicated previously, it is at least difficult to differentiate tests for the separate effect of unanticipated money variables from the tests of cross-equation restrictions that have already been discussed. In particular, this distinction would put even more weight on exclusion restrictions that are already regarded as tenuous. Sheffrin (1978) argues against the unanticipated money form on the grounds that the pattern of estimated coefficients is implausible. An attempt to test directly for effects of unperceived money growth is discussed in Barro and Hercowitz (1980). Money stock revisions, which are interpreted as components of contemporaneously unperceived money, are shown to lack explanatory value for output and the unemployment rate. If the initial reports on the money stock are viewed as observable with a negligible time lag, this finding would support the view that unanticipated, rather than unperceived, money were the important stimulus for output.

Concluding Comments

It seems reasonable to ask where these developments in the new classical macroeconomics leave us in terms of understanding business cycles. On a theoretical level the central arguments rely on an interplay between temporarily unperceived inflation and economic activity; misperceptions of general price level movements for shifts in relative prices are a hallmark of these models. A significant weakness of the approach is the dependence of some major conclusions on incomplete contemporaneous knowledge of monetary aggregates, which would presumably be observed cheaply and rapidly if such information were important. The role of incomplete current information on money in equilibrium business cycle theory parallels the use of adjustment costs to explain sticky wages and prices with an associated inefficient determination of quantities in Keynesian models. The underpinning of the two types of macroeconomic models are both vulnerable on a priori grounds.

The equilibrium approach has revitalized macro policy analysis, especially by shifting consideration from the impact of one-time realizations of variables like the money stock or government spending to a study of different methods for operating policy in relation to the economy. Government *policies* with respect to money, expenditures, and so forth, are parts of the model's structure. The new approach has shown how models that exhibit business cycle characteristics may also be consistent with the irrelevance of systematic policy feedback and with the harmful effects of unpredictable government behavior. More generally, the approach stresses the necessity of identifying calls for macro policy activism with a demonstration that the proposed form of government intervention would improve private sector outcomes in a setting where individual rationality prevails.

On an empirical level there is evidence that money shocks—but not price level surprises—are involved with expansions of economic activity. The results do not isolate effects of contemporaneously unperceived monetary movements from those changes that would merely have been unpredictable at earlier dates. This distinction is important from the standpoint of positive theories of business cycles and also from the viewpoint of policy analysis. Possibly, the most important gap in current theories is an explanation for the real effects of monetary and price changes that are contemporaneously perceived but were unanticipated as of some time in the past. Attempted explanations that have relied on price adjustment costs or long-term contracts seem inadequate.

The new macroeconomic approach has produced econometric insights concerning expectations that will remain even if other aspects of the theory are questioned. These developments involve the appropriate methods for testing natural rate hypotheses and the interplay between expectations and policy shifts.

It is important to appreciate that doubts about the explanatory value for business cycles of currently available equilibrium theories do not constitute support for Keynesian disequilibrium analysis. The disequilibrium theories are essentially incomplete models that raise even larger questions about the consistency of model structure with underlying rational behavior.

It remains a fair observation that existing macroeconomic theories—including new and old approaches—provide only limited knowledge about the nature of business cycles.

References

Alberro, J., "The Lucas Hypothesis on the Phillips Curve: Further International Evidence," *Journal of Monetary Economics*, 6, 1980.

Attfield, C. L. F., D. Demery, and N. W. Duck, "A Quarterly Model of Unanticipated Monetary Growth and Output in the U.K., 1963-1978," unpublished, University of Bristol, September 1979.

Azariadis, C., "Implicit Contracts and Underemployment Equilibria," *Journal of Political Economy*, 83, December 1975, 1183-1202.

Baily, M. N., "Wages and Employment under Uncertain Demand," *Review of Economic Studies*, 41, January 1974, 37-50.

Barro, R. J., "Are Government Bonds Net Wealth?" *Journal of Political Economy*, 82, November-December 1974, 1095-1117.

Barro, R. J., "Rational Expectations and the Role of Monetary Policy," *Journal of Monetary Economics*, 2, January 1976a, 1-32.

Barro, R. J., "Indexation in a Rational Expectations Model," *Journal of Economic Theory*, 13, October 1976b, 229-44.

Barro, R. J., "Unanticipated Money Growth and Unemployment in the United States," *American Economic Review*, 67, March 1977a, 101-115.

Barro, R. J., "Long-Term Contracting, Sticky Prices, and Monetary Policy," *Journal of Monetary Economics*, 3, July 1977b, 305-316.

Barro, R. J., "A Stochastic Equilibrium Model of an Open Economy under Flexible Exchange Rates," *Quarterly Journal of Economics*, 92, February 1978a, 149-164.

Barro, R. J., "Unanticipated Money, Output, and the Price Level in the United States," *Journal of Political Economy*, 86, August 1978b, 549-580.

Barro, R. J., "Second Thoughts on Keynesian Economics," *American Economic Review*, Proceedings, 69, May 1979a, 54-59.

Barro, R. J., "On the Determination of the Public Debt," *Journal of Political Economy*, 87, October 1979b, 940-971.

Barro, R. J., "Output Effects of Government Purchases," unpublished, University of Rochester, December 1979c, forthcoming in *Journal of Political Economy*.

Barro, R. J., "Unanticipated Money Growth and Unemployment in the United States: Reply," *American Economic Review*, 69, December 1979d, 1004-1009.

Barro, R. J., "A Capital Market in an Equilibrium Business Cycle Model," *Econometrica*, 48, September 1980, 1393-1417.

Barro, R. J., and H. I. Grossman, *Money, Employment, and Inflation*, Cambridge, Cambridge University Press, 1976.

Barro, R. J., and Z. Hercowitz, "Money Stock Revisions and Unanticipated Money Growth," *Journal of Monetary Economics*, 6, 1980, 257-267.

Barro, R. J., and M. Rush, "Unanticipated Money and Economic Activity," in S. Fischer, ed., *Rational Expectations and Economic Policy*, Chicago, University of Chicago Press for the National Bureau of Economic Research, 1980.

Black, F., "Uniqueness of the Price Level in Monetary Growth Models with Rational Expectations," *Journal of Economic Theory*, 7, January 1974, 53-65.

Blejer, M. I., and R. B. Fernandez, "The Effects of Unanticipated Money Growth on Prices, Output, and its Composition in a Fixed Exchange-Rate Open Economy," unpublished, Hebrew University of Jerusalem, April 1979.

Blinder, A. A., and S. Fischer, "Inventories, Rational Expectations and the Business Cycle," unpublished, June 1978, forthcoming in *Journal of Monetary Economics*.

Brock, W. A., "A Simple Perfect Foresight Monetary Model," *Journal of Monetary Economics*, 1, April 1975, 133-150.

Brock, W. A., "A Note on Hyper-Inflationary Equilibria in Long Run Perfect Foresight Monetary Models: A Correction," unpublished, University of Chicago, 1980.

Cagan, P., "The Monetary Dynamics of Hyperinflation," in M. Friedman, ed., *Studies in the Quantity Theory of Money*, Chicago, University of Chicago Press, 1956.

Calvo, G. A., "On the Indeterminacy of Interest Rates and Wages with Perfect Foresight," *Journal of Economic Theory*, 19, December 1978, 321-337.

Cukierman, A., "Rational Expectations and the Role of Monetary Policy: A Generalization," *Journal of Monetary Economics*, 5, April 1979, 213-230.

Cukierman, A., and P. Wachtel, "Differential Inflationary Expectations and the Variability of the Rate of Inflation: Theory and Evidence," *American Economic Review*, 69, September 1979, 595-609.

Fair, R. C., "An Analysis of the Accuracy of Four Macroeconometric Models," *Journal of Political Economy*, 87, August 1979, 701-718.

Feldstein, M. S., and A. Auerbach, "Inventory Behavior in Durable Goods Manufacturing: the Target-Adjustment Model," *Brookings Papers on Economic Activity*, 2, 1976, 351-396.

Fischer, S., "Long-Term Contracts, Rational Expectations and the Optimal Money Supply Rule," *Journal of Political Economy*, 85, February 1977, 191-205.

Fischer, S., "On Activist Monetary Policy with Rational Expectations," in S. Fischer, ed., *Rational Expectations and Economic Policy*, Chicago, University of Chicago Press for the National Bureau of Economic Research, 1980.

Fisher, F., Comment on paper by R. Lucas, in O. Eckstein, ed., *The Econometrics of Price Determination*, Washington, D.C., 1972.

Flood, R. P., and P. M. Garber, "Market Fundamentals vs. Price Level Bubbles: the First Test," unpublished, University of Virginia, September 1979, forthcoming in *Journal of Political Economy*.

Friedman, B., Discussion of paper by Lucas and Sargent, in *After the Phillips Curve: Persistence of High Inflation and High Unemployment*, Boston, Federal Reserve Bank of Boston, 1978.

Friedman, B., "Optimal Expectations and the Extreme Information Assumptions of 'Rational Expectations' Macromodels," *Journal of Monetary Economics*, 5, January 1979, 23-42.

Friedman, M., *A Program for Monetary Stability*, New York, Fordham University Press, 1960.

Friedman, M., "The Role of Monetary Policy," *American Economic Review*, 58, March 1968, 1-17.

Germany, J. D., and S. Srivastava, "Empirical Estimates of Unanticipated Policy: Issues in Stability and Identification," unpublished, M.I.T., June 1979.

Gordon, D., "A Neo-Classical Theory of Keynesian Unemployment," *Economic Inquiry*, 12, December 1974, 431-459.

Gordon, R. J., "Inflation in Recession and Recovery," *Brookings Papers on Economic Activity*, 1, 1971, 105-158.

Gordon, R. J., "Wage-Price Controls and the Shifting Phillips Curve," *Brookings Papers on Economic Activity*, 2, 1972, 385-421.

Gray, J. A., "Wage Indexation: A Macroeconomic Approach," *Journal of Monetary Economics*, 2, April 1976, 221-236.

Grossman, H. I., "Risk Shifting, Layoffs and Seniority," *Journal of Monetary Economics*, 4, November 1978, 661-686.

Grossman, S., "Rational Expectations and the Allocation of Resources under Asymmetric Information: A Survey," unpublished, University of Pennsylvania, July 1979.

Hall, R. E., "The Rigidity of Wages and the Persistence of Unemployment," *Brookings Papers on Economic Activity*, 2, 1975, 301-335.

Hall, R. E., "The Phillips Curve and Macroeconomic Policy," *Journal of Monetary Economics*, supplement, 1976, 127-148.

Hall, R. E., "Labor Supply and Aggregate Fluctuations," presented at the Carnegie-Rochester Conference, April 1979, revised September 1979.

Hall, R. E., and D. Lillien, "Efficient Wage Bargains under Uncertain Supply and Demand," *American Economic Review*, 69, December 1979, 868-879.

Hansen, L. P., and T. J. Sargent, "Formulating and Estimating Dynamic Linear Rational Expectations Models," unpublished, Federal Reserve Bank of Minneapolis, March 1979a.

Hansen, L. P., and T. J. Sargent, "Linear Rational Expectations Models for Dynamically Interrelated Variables," unpublished, Federal Reserve Bank of Minneapolis, July 1979b.

Hayek, F. A., "The Use of Knowledge in Society," *American Economic Review*, 35, September 1945, 519-530.

Hercowitz, Z., "Money and the Dispersion of Relative Prices," unpublished, University of Rochester, September 1979, forthcoming in *Journal of Political Economy*.

King, R. G., "Asset Markets and the Neutrality of Money: An Economy-wide Bond Market," unpublished, University of Rochester, October 1978.

King, R. G., "Monetary Information and Monetary Neutrality," unpublished, University of Rochester, 1979a, forthcoming in *Journal of Monetary Economics*.

King, R. G., "Monetary Policy and the Information Content of Prices," unpublished, University of Rochester, October 1979b, forthcoming in *Journal of Political Economy*.

Kydland, F. E., and E. C. Prescott, "Rules Rather than Discretion: The Inconsistency of Optimal Plans," *Journal of Political Economy*, 85, June 1977, 473–491.

Kydland, F. E., and E. C. Prescott, "A Competitive Theory of Fluctuations and the Feasibility and Desirability of Stabilization Policy," in S. Fischer, ed., *Rational Expectations and Economic Policy*, Chicago, University of Chicago Press for the National Bureau of Economic Research, 1980.

Leiderman, L., "Macroeconometric Testing of the Rational Expectations and Structural Neutrality Hypotheses for the United States," *Journal of Monetary Economics*, 6, January 1980, 69–82.

Lucas, R. E., "Expectations and the Neutrality of Money," *Journal of Economic Theory*, 4, April 1972a, 103–124.

Lucas, R. E., "Econometric Testing of the Natural Rate Hypothesis," in O. Eckstein, ed., *The Econometrics of Price Determination*, Washington, D.C., 1972b.

Lucas, R. E., "Some International Evidence on Output-Inflation Tradeoffs," *American Economic Review*, 63, June 1973, 326–334.

Lucas, R. E., "An Equilibrium Model of the Business Cycle," *Journal of Political Economy*, 83, December 1975, 1113–1144.

Lucas, R. E., "Econometric Policy Evaluation: a Critique," *Journal of Monetary Economics*, supplement, 1976a, 19–46.

Lucas, R. E., "Some International Evidence on Output-Inflation Tradeoffs: Errata," *American Economic Review*, 66, December 1976b, 985.

Lucas, R. E., "Understanding Business Cycles," *Journal of Monetary Economics*, supplement, 1977, 7–30.

Lucas, R. E., and L. Rapping, "Real Wages, Employment, and Inflation," *Journal of Political Economy*, 77, September/October 1969, 721–754.

Lucas, R. E., and T. J. Sargent, "After Keynesian Macroeconomics," Federal Reserve Bank of Boston, *After the Phillips Curve: Persistence of High Inflation and High Unemployment*, 1978.

McCallum, B. T., "Rational Expectations and the Natural Rate Hypothesis: Some Consistent Estimates," *Econometrica*, 44, January 1976, 43–52.

McCallum, B. T., "Dating, Discounting, and the Robustness of the Lucas-Sargent Proposition," *Journal of Monetary Economics*, 4, January 1978, 121–130.

McCallum, B. T., "On the Observational Inequivalence of Classical and Keynesian Models," *Journal of Political Economy*, 87, April 1979a, 395–402.

McCallum, B. T., "The Current State of the Policy-Ineffectiveness Debate," *American Economic Review*, proceedings, 69, May 1979b, 240–245.

McCallum, B. T., "A Macroeconomic Model with Predetermined Wages, Markup Pricing, and Classical Properties," unpublished, University of Virginia, September 1979c.

McCallum, B. T., and J. K. Whitaker, "The Effectiveness of Fiscal Feedback Rules and Automatic Stabilizers under Rational Expectations," *Journal of Monetary Economics*, 5, April 1979, 171–186.

Modigliani, F., "The Monetarist Controversy or, Should We Forsake Stabilization Policies," *American Economic Review*, 67, March 1977, 1–19.

Mussa, M., "The Exchange Rate, the Balance of Payments and Monetary and Fiscal Policy under a Regime of Controlled Floating," *Scandinavian Journal of Economics*, 78, No. 2, 1976, 229–248.

Muth, J., "Rational Expectations and the Theory of Price Movements," *Econometrica*, 29, July 1961, 315–335.

Neftci, S. N., "Unanticipated Money Growth and the Stability of Economic Relationships," unpublished, August 1978.

Phelps, E. S., "The New Microeconomics in Employment and Inflation Theory," in E. Phelps, ed., *Microeconomic Foundations of Employment and Inflation Theory*, New York, Norton, 1970.

Phelps, E. S., *Inflation Policy and Unemployment Theory*, New York, Norton, 1972.

Phelps, E. S., and J. B. Taylor, "Stabilizing Powers of Monetary Policy under Rational Expectations," *Journal of Political Economy*, 85, February 1977, 163–190.

Prescott, E. C., "Efficiency of the Natural Rate," *Journal of Political Economy*, 83, December 1975, 1229–1236.

Rush, M., "Money, Output and Inflation in the United States under the Gold Standard," unpublished, University of Rochester, 1978.

Saidi, N. H., "Essays on Rational Expectations and Flexible Exchange Rates," unpublished Ph.D. Dissertation, University of Rochester, 1979.

Saidi, N. H., and R. J. Barro, "Unanticipated Money, Output, and Unemployment in Canada," unpublished, University of Rochester, July 1976.

Sargent, T. J., "A Note on the 'Accelerationist' Controversy," *Journal of Money, Credit, and Banking,* 3, August 1971, 721-725.

Sargent, T. J., "Rational Expectations, the Real Rate of Interest, and the Natural Rate of Unemployment," *Brookings Papers on Economic Activity,* 2, 1973, 429-472.

Sargent, T. J., *Testing for Neutrality and Rationality,* Federal Reserve Bank of Minneapolis, June 1976a.

Sargent, T. J., "The Observational Equivalence of Natural and Unnatural Rate Theories of Macroeconomics," *Journal of Political Economy,* 84, June 1976b, 631-640.

Sargent, T. J., "A Classical Macroeconometric Model for the United States," *Journal of Political Economy,* 84, April 1976c, 207-237.

Sargent, T. J., *Macroeconomic Theory,* New York, Academic Press, 1979a.

Sargent, T. J., "Interpreting Economic Time Series," unpublished, University of Minnesota, November 1979b.

Sargent, T. J., and N. Wallace, "Rational Expectations and the Dynamics of Hyperinflation," *International Economic Review,* 14, June 1973a, 328-350.

Sargent, T. J., and N. Wallace, "The Stability of Models of Money and Growth with Perfect Foresight," *Econometrica,* 41, November 1973b, 1043-1048.

Sargent, T. J., and N. Wallace, "Rational Expectations, the Optimal Monetary Instrument, and the Optimal Money Supply Rule," *Journal of Political Economy,* 83, April 1975, 241-254.

Sargent, T. J., and N. Wallace, "Rational Expectations and the Theory of Economic Policy," *Journal of Monetary Economics,* 2, April 1976, 169-183.

Sheffrin, S. M., "Discriminating between Rational Expectation Models," *Economic Letters,* 1, December 1978, 205-210.

Shell, L., and J. E. Stiglitz, "The Allocation of Investment in a Dynamic Economy," *Quarterly Journal of Economics,* 81, November 1967, 592-609.

Shiller, R. J., "Rational Expectations and the Dynamic Structure of Macroeconomic Models: A Critical Review," *Journal of Monetary Economics,* 4, January 1978, 1-44.

Simons, H. C., "Rules versus Authorities in Monetary Policy," in H. Simons, *Economic Policy for a Free Society,* Chicago, University of Chicago Press, 1948.

Sims, C. A., "Macroeconomics and Reality," *Econometrica,* 48, January 1980. 1-48.

Small, D. H., "Unanticipated Money Growth and Unemployment in the United States: Comment," *American Economic Review,* 69, December 1979, 996-1003.

Slutzky, E., "The Summation of Random Causes as the Source of Cyclic Processes," *Econometrica,* 5, April 1937, 105-146.

Solow, R. M., "Recent Controversy on the Theory of Inflation: An Eclectic View," in *Inflation: its Causes, Consequences and Control,* New York, 1968.

Stockman, A. C., "A Theory of Exchange Rate Determination," *Journal of Political Economy,* 88, August 1980, 673-698.

Taylor, J., "Monetary Policy during a Transition to Rational Expectations," *Journal of Political Economy,* 83, October 1975, 1009-1022.

Taylor, J., "Conditions for Unique Solutions in Stochastic Macroeconomic Models with Rational Expectations," *Econometrica,* 45, September 1977, 1377-1386.

Tobin, J., "How Dead is Keynes?" *Economic Inquiry,* 15, October 1977, 459-468.

Weiss, L., "Information Aggregation and Policy," unpublished, Yale University, July, 1979.

Weiss, L., "The Role for Active Monetary Policy in a Rational Expectations Model," *Journal of Political Economy,* 88, April 1980, 221-233.

Wogin, G., "Unemployment and Monetary Policy under Rational Expectations: Some Canadian Evidence," *Journal of Monetary Economics,* 6, January 1980, 59-68.

Rational Expectations and the Role of Monetary Policy*

1. Introduction

The purpose of this paper is to analyze the role of monetary policy in a model with three major characteristics: (1) prices and quantities are competitively determined by market-clearing relationships – that is, by the solution of a competitive equilibrium system; (2) information is imperfect; and (3) expectations of future variables are formed rationally, in the sense of being optimal predictions based on the available information. The focus of the analysis is on the effects of monetary expansion on prices and outputs.

Part 2 of the paper generates a Phillips-curve-type relation in a framework that builds on the work of Friedman (1968) and Lucas (1973). The source of the Phillips curve is a lack of full current information that prevents individuals from dichotomizing unanticipated price movements into relative and absolute components. Hence, although suppliers and demanders in any market form their expectations about future prices (in other markets) in a rational manner, the implied behavior of output in each market does not separate unanticipated supply and demand shifts into relative and aggregate parts. In this framework changes in money that are not fully perceived as nominal disturbances can lead to movements in output. It also follows here that an increase in the variance of the monetary growth rate (which is one component of the variance of aggregate excess demand) induces individuals to attribute a larger fraction of observed price movements to monetary forces, and thereby leads to a reduced responsiveness of output to a given monetary disturbance. Thus, as in Lucas's model, the magnitude of the Phillips curve slope is inversely related to the variance of the monetary growth rate.

Part 2 of the paper also discusses the determination of the variance of relative

*This research was supported by a grant from the Liberty Fund. I have benefited from discussions of earlier versions of this paper at the Federal Reserve Bank of Minneapolis Seminar on Rational Expectations, and at seminars at Chicago, M.I.T., Rochester, and Pennsylvania. I am particularly grateful to Bob Lucas for a number of important suggestions.

79

Reprinted from *Journal of Monetary Economics*, 2, January 1976, 1–32, by permission of North-Holland Publishing Company, Amsterdam.

prices and the variance of future prices about their currently predictable values. One interesting conclusion is that an increase in the variance of aggregate excess demand would lead to an increase in the variance of relative prices.

The third part of the paper follows Sargent and Wallace (1975) by inquiring into the role of monetary policy in this type of rational expectations model. Pure variance of money leads to an increase in the variance of output about its full current information position and to an increased variance of future prices about their currently predictable values. Essentially, an additional amount of monetary noise makes it more difficult for individuals to isolate real shifts, and therefore tends to move output away from full information output. Accordingly, to the extent that direct costs of controlling money are neglected, a zero variance of money would be optimal.

I then consider the implications of feedback effects from observed economic variables to money. When the monetary authority lacks superior information, it turns out that this sort of feedback is irrelevant to the determination of output. Essentially, when individuals know the form of the feedback rule and also perceive the variables to which money is reacting, this type of monetary behavior would be taken into account in the formation of expectations. When the monetary authority possesses superior information there is the potential for beneficial countercyclical policy. However, the provision of the superior information to the public has identical implications for output if the costs of providing this information are neglected.

Finally, I consider the case where the monetary authority has superior information about its own monetary rule. This situation might permit a form of systematic policy deception in the 'short run', when the public does not appreciate the nature of the deception. However, in my model where the policy criterion concerns the gap between actual and full information output, this type of policy deception is not desirable.

2. A rational expectations model with imperfect information

2.1. Setup of the model

The model is an extension to the one developed by Lucas (1973). There is one type of nondurable commodity, denoted by y, that can be viewed as a personal service. With this view, the supply of the commodity corresponds to the supply of factor services, and the demand for the commodity corresponds to the demand for factor services. The commodity is transacted in various markets, indexed by $z = 1, \ldots, n$, that are at physically separated locations. The variety of locations for a single good is intended to serve as a proxy for markets in a variety of goods, since the multilocation context seems easier to formalize. There is assumed to be an instantaneous flow of information within any market, but a lag in the flow of information across markets. Hence, at a given point in time, there can be a different commodity price across markets, but only a single price within each market.

The model is constructed in a discrete time period framework, where the length of the period signifies the time delay with which information travels across markets. In the present setup market participants possess full information about the relevant economy-wide variables with a one-period lag. During a single period an individual can visit any of the n markets, but it is assumed to be impossible to visit more than one market during a period.[1] Further, it is supposed that there is sufficient information about last period's prices across markets so that current arbitrage insures that all markets offer the same ex ante distribution of price. In this respect the setup resembles the one used by Mortensen (1975).

Aside from lagged knowledge of aggregate variables a participant in market z also possesses current information that is assumed to be limited to an observation of the current price in that market, $P_t(z)$. The crucial idea is that certain types of local information are received more rapidly than some aspects of global information – such as prices in other markets. It is this differential information structure that allows for a confusion between relative and absolute shifts, and thereby allows for temporary real effects of unperceived money movements. Of course, the use of a fixed-length information lag and the distinction of only two types of information, local and global, are abstractions made solely for technical convenience.

Aside from the nondurable commodity, the only other good in the economy is fiat money, M.[2] Money is held by individuals because it is the only available store of value. New money enters the economy as transfer payments from the government. These transfers are received by individuals at the start of each period in an amount that is independent of each individual's money holding during the previous period. It is assumed, for simplicity, that the government does not participate directly in the commodity markets.

In order to keep the model analytically manageable, I have constructed the equations in log-linear form. All of the variables used below in these equations are to be interpreted in logarithmic terms.

The supply of the commodity at date t in market z, denoted by $y_t^s(z)$, is assumed to depend on the following set of variables: (1) A systematic supply term, $k_t^s(z)$, that is intended to capture systematic changes in technology, popu-

---

[1] The present analysis does not deal with optimal search for information across markets. Further, the manner in which aggregate information is transmitted (with a one-period lag) is not explored. Extensions to incorporate optimal search could be very interesting.

[2] Sargent and Wallace (1975) have constructed a model that is similar in some respects, but which also includes a capital market. As Bob Lucas has pointed out to me, the existence of a single, economy-wide capital market implies that the observation of the price (rate of return) on this market conveys important aggregate information. This sort of current aggregate information is very different from the current local information that I assume is available in the present model. I plan to deal at a later time with the different type of information structure that is implied by the existence of an economy-wide capital market.

lation, etc. (2) A term that measures the current price of output in market z, $P_t(z)$, relative to the price that is expected to prevail next period.[3] Because all of next period's markets have the same ex ante distribution of price, it can be assumed that this expectation applies to P_{t+1}, the (geometric, unweighted) average of prices across the markets at date $t+1$. If $I_t(z)$ denotes the information possessed at date t by participants in market z,[4] then $EP_{t+1}|I_t(z)$ is the relevant price expectation. A positive response of supply to the term $P_t(z) - EP_{t+1}|I_t(z)$ can be viewed as an effect of speculation over time associated with the intertemporal substitutability of leisure. This type of effect has been discussed in Lucas and Rapping (1970) and Lucas (1972). (3) A wealth variable, measured as $[M_t + E\Delta M_{t+1}|I_t(z) - EP_{t+1}|I_t(z)]$,[5] that is assumed to have a positive effect on desired leisure, and hence a negative effect on factor supply and a negative effect on $y_t^s(z)$. The inclusion of the (log of the) aggregate money stock, M_t, reflects a simplifying assumption that the total money possessed by participants in market z, $M_t(z)$, is always the same fraction of the aggregate money stock.[6] The term $E\Delta M_{t+1}|I_t(z)$, where $\Delta M_{t+1} \equiv M_{t+1} - M_t$, accounts for the expected governmental transfer at the start of the next period. (4) Random terms u_t^s and $\varepsilon_t^s(z)$, where u_t^s is a shift term on aggregate supply, and $\varepsilon_t^s(z)$ is a shift term on relative supply in market z. The sample mean of $\varepsilon_t^s(z)$ across the markets is zero by definition. Other properties of the distributions of these random variables will be discussed below, after the introduction of the demand side of the model.

The specific form of the supply function (in log-linear terms) is

$$y_t^s(z) = k_t^s(z) + \alpha_s[P_t(z) - EP_{t+1}|I_t(z)]$$
$$- \beta_s[M_t + E\Delta M_{t+1}|I_t(z) - EP_{t+1}|I_t(z)] + u_t^s + \varepsilon_t^s(z), \qquad (1)$$

where α_s and β_s are, respectively, the (absolute values of the) relative price and wealth elasticities of current commodity supply. It should be noted that the wealth term in eq. (1) does not hold constant the appropriate measure of wealth when $P_t(z)$ changes. The price deflator for the wealth term should be a (weighted) price index that includes $P_t(z)$ as well as EP_{t+1}. The full effect of $P_t(z)$ on $y_t^s(z)$ includes a positive substitution effect plus a reinforcing effect that derives from the reduction in appropriately measured wealth. However,

---

[3]The inclusion of expected prices at dates further into the future does not seem to have any important effects in the present model.

[4]The present framework is sufficiently simple so that all participants in a single market at a given point in time have the same information set. In this respect, Lucas (1975) considers a more complicated setup.

[5]It would seem preferable to subtract off the expected desired real money holding at date $t+1$. However, this change would complicate the exposition of the model without affecting the main results. See the discussion at the end of appendix 2.

[6]Lucas (1972) develops a model in which this fraction is a random variable. In my model the random relative disturbance terms, discussed next, serve the same purpose.

II THE EQUILIBRIUM APPROACH TO BUSINESS CYCLES

this wealth effect would be negligible if the weight of the current period, during which $P_t(z)$ applies, is small relative to the weight of the future period(s), during which EP_{t+1} applies. Subsequently, the important issue concerns the net effect of EP_{t+1} on $y_t^s(z)$, which depends from eq. (1) on the sign of $\beta_s - \alpha_s$. If the current period is viewed as short relative to the length of the future, then the substitution effect, as measured by α_s, would tend to dominate over the wealth effect β_s. It is assumed below that the substitution effect is dominant, so that $\alpha_s > \beta_s$ and the net effect of EP_{t+1} on $y_t^s(z)$ is negative.

The specification of the demand side of the model is parallel to that of the supply side,

$$
\begin{aligned}
y_t^d(z) = k_t^d(z) - \alpha_d[P_t(z) - EP_{t+1}|I_t(z)] \\
+ \beta_d[M_t + E\Delta M_{t+1}|I_t(z) - EP_{t+1}|I_t(z)] + u_t^d + \varepsilon_t^d(z).
\end{aligned} \tag{2}
$$

Price speculation by demanders implies a negative effect of $[P_t(z) - EP_{t+1}| I_t(z)]$ on $y_t^d(z)$, as measured by the elasticity $-\alpha_d$. Note that demanders in market z are assumed to possess the same information set, $I_t(z)$, as suppliers to this market.[7] The positive effect of wealth on commodity demand is measured by the elasticity β_d. As discussed in the case of supply, it is assumed that the substitution effect of EP_{t+1} is dominant, so that $\alpha_d > \beta_d$ applies. Finally, u_t^d and $\varepsilon_t^d(z)$ are stochastic shift terms that are analogous to those introduced into the supply function.

2.2. Market-clearing determination of prices and outputs

Before deriving the market-clearing conditions, it is useful to define the excess demand variables,

$$
k_t(z) \equiv k_t^d(z) - k_t^s(z),
$$

$$
u_t \equiv u_t^d - u_t^s,
$$

$$
\varepsilon_t(z) \equiv \varepsilon_t^d(z) - \varepsilon_t^s(z).
$$

The determination of prices depends solely on excess demand measures, but the determination of output (below) requires also the specification of separate supply and demand functions. I assume in the main text that u_t is generated by a random walk process,

$$
u_t = u_{t-1} + v_t,
$$

$$
v_t \sim N(0, \sigma_v^2),
$$

---

[7]In the present setup an individual supplies and demands commodities simultaneously in the same market. It would be possible to allow each individual to visit two markets in each period, one for supply and one for demand, but the resulting complications in information sets are considerable. Separate concepts of supply and demand can be maintained here if one thinks of the commodity that an individual supplies as not being identical to those he demands (for example, back-scratching services?).

where N refers to the normal distribution. The random variable v_t is serially independent and represents the current period's 'innovation' to real aggregate excess demand. Because u_t has a one-to-one effect on u_{t+1}, the v-innovations are 'permanent' in the sense of determining the most likely position of all future values of u. I consider in appendix 1 the implications of substituting a first-order Markov process, $u_t = \lambda u_{t-1} + v_t$, where $0 \leq \lambda \leq 1$. In this formulation, smaller values of λ signify that v_t has more of a transitory and less of a permanent effect on excess demand.

I assume that $\varepsilon_t(z)$ is serially independent and independent of u_t,[8] where

$$\varepsilon_t(z) \sim N(0, \sigma_\varepsilon^2).$$

The ε-shifts are purely transitory, in the sense of lasting only one period. This assumption seems best viewed as reflecting substantial arbitrage possibilities across markets over one period of time, rather than implying that relative shifts in taste, technology, etc., are short-lived.

Finally, it is useful to define the (absolute value of the) price elasticity of excess demand,

$$\alpha \equiv \alpha_s + \alpha_d,$$

and the wealth elasticity,

$$\beta \equiv \beta_s + \beta_d.$$

The earlier assumptions on the dominance of substitution effects imply $\alpha > \beta$.

The price at date t in market z is determined to equate supply and demand in that market.[9] Equating the expressions in eqs. (1) and (2), and using the above definitions, leads to the market-clearing condition for market z,

$$\alpha P_t(z) = (\alpha - \beta)EP_{t+1}|I_t(z) + \beta[M_t + E\Delta M_{t+1}|I_t(z)]$$
$$+ k_t(z) + u_t + \varepsilon_t(z). \tag{3}$$

[8]Since the sample mean of $\varepsilon_t(z)$ is zero by definition, the distribution of $\varepsilon_t(z)$ would actually depend on the number of markets. However, this consideration seems unimportant if the number of markets is large, as I am implicitly assuming. It is also possible that certain markets have positive or negative correlations of their relative excess demand shifts with the aggregate excess demand shifts (u_t or the monetary disturbance that is discussed below). In that case there would be different information about the aggregate picture in different markets. The analysis would then have to consider the implications of this differential information on the choice of which market to enter. I do not deal with these possibilities here.

[9]The model does not include any elements of adjustment costs for price changes that would inhibit price flexibility. In this respect see Barro (1972). In particular, there is no consideration of the role of long-term nominal contracting in the present analysis. The role of price stickiness in Keynesian models is discussed in detail in Barro and Grossman (1975, ch. 2). It would be of interest to incorporate price adjustment costs into a rational-expectations-type model.

It is apparent from the form of eq. (3) and the assumed serial independence of $\varepsilon_t(z)$ that the distribution of $P_t(z)$ can be independent of the market index, z, only if $k_t(z)$ is constant across markets. That is, the arbitrage condition that insures that all markets have the same ex ante distribution of price is that the ratio of systematic demand to supply, $k_t(z) \equiv k_t^d(z) - k_t^s(z)$, be the same for all markets.[10] It is then permissible to drop the z subscript from the $k_t(z)$ term in eq. (3).

Eq. (3) indicates that $P_t(z)$ is determined by a set of 'demand-pull' variables that include the money stock plus expected next period's transfer and the sum of systematic and random excess demand terms, $k_t + u_t + \varepsilon_t(z)$. There is also a 'cost-push' term, $EP_{t+1}|I_t(z)$,[11] that has an effect in the direction of the sign of $\alpha - \beta$. Under the assumption of a dominant substitution effect, the impact of EP_{t+1} on $P_t(z)$ is positive.

The key element of the rational expectations approach is that the EP_{t+1} term in eq. (3) is not determined by an ad hoc expectations mechanism from outside of the model, but is instead based on the knowledge – implied by an assumed knowledge of the model – that prices are determined by market-clearing conditions of the form of eq. (3). Hence, current market-clearing prices and (the set of) expectations about future prices are determined through a simultaneous process. In order to implement this approach, it is necessary to complete the specification of the model by describing the processes that generate M_t and k_t. I assume, provisionally, that changes in money are generated by a constant growth rate, g, plus a random term, denoted by m_t. That is,

$$M_t - M_{t-1} \equiv \Delta M_t = g + m_t,$$
$$m_t \sim N(0, \sigma_m^2), \tag{4}$$

where m_t is assumed to be serially independent, as well as uncorrelated with v_t and the array of $\varepsilon_t(z)$. I examine the implications of more complicated money supply processes in a later part of the paper. In order to focus on the short-run, cyclical effects of money, I also abstract in the main text from long-term monetary growth – that is, $g = 0$ is assumed. This abstraction amounts to neglecting the effects of systematic inflation. Appendix 2 deals with the case where $g \neq 0$. When $g = 0$, eq. (4) implies that $E\Delta M_{t+1}|I_t(z) = 0$.

I assume that the k_t process takes the form,

$$k_t = k_0 - \beta \rho t, \tag{5}$$

where $k_0 = 0$ can be assumed subsequently through an appropriate normalization of output units. It turns out, as shown in Appendix 2, that the form for k_t

---

[10]Alternatively, if some serial dependence in $\varepsilon_t(z)$ had been introduced, then $k_t(z)$ could be such as to just offset the implications of this serial dependence for $P_t(z)$.

[11]The terms on the right side of eq. (3) can be viewed equivalently as negative forces on the current excess demand for money.

in eq. (5) amounts to assuming that the systematic growth rate of output is equal to ρ. Again, it is convenient to abstract in the main text from the effects of long-term growth so that $\rho = 0$ is assumed. Since $k_t = 0$ in this case, the systematic excess demand term no longer appears in the analysis. Appendix 2 deals with the case where $\rho \neq 0$.

The next step is to solve the model in the sense of determining prices and outputs as functions of exogenous variables. The simplest procedure for solving the model involves, first, writing out the (log-linear) form of the solution for $P_t(z)$ in terms of a vector of unknown coefficients on the set of relevant independent variables. Second, the market-clearing condition expressed in eq. (3) is used to determine the values of the unknown coefficients. This solution method has been used before in a parallel context by Lucas (1972, 1973). The procedure is analogous to applying the method of undetermined coefficients to a trial solution in the case of differential or difference equations. In the present situation $P_t(z)$ depends on the following variables (in a log-linear form),[12]

$$P_t(z) = \Pi_1 M_{t-1} + \Pi_2 m_t + \Pi_3 v_t + \Pi_4 \varepsilon_t(z) + \Pi_5 u_{t-1}, \tag{6}$$

where the Π's are the unknown coefficients. Since M_{t-1} is included in current information sets, previous values of M do not appear in the price solution. Since m_t, v_t and $\varepsilon_t(z)$ are serially independent, past values of these variables do not appear.[13] Since, for a given value of v_t, u_t depends only on u_{t-1}, it follows that values of u prior to $t-1$ do not appear.

If individuals know that prices in each period are determined by eq. (6), then the expected price for next period must be

$$\begin{aligned} EP_{t+1}|I_t(z) &= \Pi_1 EM_t|I_t(z) + \Pi_5 Eu_t|I_t(z) \\ &= \Pi_1 E(M_{t-1} + m_t)|I_t(z) + \Pi_5 E(u_{t-1} + v_t)|I_t(z), \end{aligned}$$

since the expected values of m_{t+1}, v_{t+1} and $\varepsilon_{t+1}(z)$, conditioned on $I_t(z)$, are all zero. The information set, $I_t(z)$, is assumed to include observations (or sufficient data to infer the values) of M_{t-1} and u_{t-1}. The additional information contributed by an observation of $P_t(z)$[14] amounts, from eq. (6), to an observation

---

[12]In the case where g and ρ are nonzero, the solution includes the additional terms $\Pi_6 t + \Pi_7$ – that is, a time trend and a constant term. See appendix 2.

[13]If a variable such as v_{t-1} had been entered, it would eventually be determined that its associated Π-coefficient was zero.

[14]I have not included an individual's own value of ΔM_t, which arrives as a government transfer, as an additional element of $I_t(z)$. This exclusion is satisfactory if the relation between individual and aggregate transfers is sufficiently noisy so that the individual transfer provides a negligible increment of information over $P_t(z)$. This assumption need not be inconsistent with my earlier simplifying assumption that $M_t(z)$ was a constant fraction of M_t, since $M_t(z)$ refers to the total money contained in market z. If individual and aggregate M were always proportionately related, then M_t would, itself, become an element of $I_t(z)$, and the principal information gap in the model would disappear.

of the sum $\Pi_2 m_t + \Pi_3 v_t + \Pi_4 \varepsilon_t(z)$. The key to the formation of price expectations is then the calculation of the two expectations, Em_t and Ev_t, conditioned on the observation of $P_t(z)$. In effect, these two conditional expectations are obtained by running regressions of m_t and v_t, respectively, on the observed sum $\Pi_2 m_t + \Pi_3 v_t + \Pi_4 \varepsilon_t(z)$. That is,

$$Em_t | I_t(z) = \frac{\theta_1}{\Pi_2} \left[\Pi_2 m_t + \Pi_3 v_t + \Pi_4 \varepsilon_t(z) \right],$$

where

$$\theta_1 = \frac{(\Pi_2)^2 \sigma_m^2}{(\Pi_2)^2 \sigma_m^2 + (\Pi_3)^2 \sigma_v^2 + (\Pi_4)^2 \sigma_\varepsilon^2},$$

and

$$Ev_t | I_t(z) = \frac{\theta_2}{\Pi_3} \left[\Pi_2 m_t + \Pi_3 v_t + \Pi_4 \varepsilon_t(z) \right], \tag{7}$$

where

$$\theta_2 = \frac{(\Pi_3)^2 \sigma_v^2}{(\Pi_2)^2 \sigma_m^2 + (\Pi_3)^2 \sigma_v^2 + (\Pi_4)^2 \sigma_\varepsilon^2}.$$

The θ_1-coefficient measures the fraction of the total price variance (of $P_t(z)$ about its best estimate given I_{t-1}) that is produced by (aggregate) money variance m, and the θ_2 coefficient measures the fraction produced by aggregate real variance v. The remaining fraction of price variance, $1 - \theta_1 - \theta_2$, is attributable to relative real variance ε. The expected price at $t+1$ can then be written as

$$EP_{t+1} | I_t(z) = \Pi_1 M_{t-1} + \left(\frac{\Pi_1 \theta_1}{\Pi_2} + \frac{\Pi_5 \theta_2}{\Pi_3} \right) \left[\Pi_2 m_t + \Pi_3 v_t + \Pi_4 \varepsilon_t(z) \right]$$

$$+ \Pi_5 u_{t-1}. \tag{8}$$

The Π-coefficients must be such that the market-clearing condition, eq. (3), holds as an identity, given eqs. (6) and (8). This identity relation implies five (independent) conditions corresponding to term-by-term coefficient equalities for the variables that appear in eq. (6). The algebra is straightforward and I will limit the discussion here to a presentation and interpretation of the results. The five Π-coefficients can be determined to be

$$\Pi_1 = 1,$$

$$\Pi_2 = (\theta_1 + \theta_2) + (\beta/\alpha)(1 - \theta_1 - \theta_2),$$

$$\Pi_3 = \Pi_2 / \beta,$$

$$\Pi_4 = \Pi_2 / \beta,$$

$$\Pi_5 = 1/\beta. \tag{9}$$

These coefficients imply the price solution

$$P_t(z) = M_{t-1} + [\theta_1 + \theta_2 + (\beta/\alpha)(1 - \theta_1 - \theta_2)]$$
$$\times [m_t + (1/\beta)(v_t + \varepsilon_t(z))] + (1/\beta)u_{t-1}. \tag{10}$$

Before discussing this result, it is convenient to define the variance of the total aggregate disturbance, $\beta m_t + v_t$, as

$$\sigma_A^2 \equiv \beta^2 \sigma_m^2 + \sigma_v^2.$$

The θ-coefficients in eq. (10) are then determined, using eqs. (7) and (9), as

$$\theta_1 + \theta_2 = \frac{\beta^2 \sigma_m^2 + \sigma_v^2}{\beta^2 \sigma_m^2 + \sigma_v^2 + \sigma_\varepsilon^2} = \frac{\sigma_A^2}{\sigma_A^2 + \sigma_\varepsilon^2}. \tag{11}$$

An aggregate 'price index', P_t, can be calculated for future reference as a (geometric, unweighted) average of the prices determined in eq. (10),

$$P_t = M_{t-1} + [\theta_1 + \theta_2 + (\beta/\alpha)(1 - \theta_1 - \theta_2)][m_t + (1/\beta)v_t] + (1/\beta)u_{t-1}. \tag{12}$$

The relative disturbances, $\varepsilon_t(z)$, are averaged out in determining P_t.

The main results for $P_t(z)$ in eq. (10) can be interpreted as follows. First, M_{t-1}, which is contained in the information set $I_t(z)$, has a proportional effect on $P_t(z)$ ($\Pi_1 = 1$). On the other hand, m_t, the random part of M_t, is not a part of $I_t(z)$. Since market participants do not have separate observations of $P_t(z)$ and the aggregate price index, P_t, they cannot separate the impact of m_t from the impact of the other excess demand shifts, $v_t + \varepsilon_t(z)$. Hence, m_t and $(1/\beta)(v_t + \varepsilon_t(z))$ enter with a common coefficient in eq. (10). This coefficient is less than one as long as the substitution effect of a change in EP_{t+1} outweighs the income effect ($\alpha > \beta$). Because m_t has a coefficient that generally differs from one, it also turns out that this part of money can have a nonzero effect on output.

The expected future price level follows from eqs. (8) and (9) as

$$EP_{t+1} | I_t(z) = M_{t-1} + (\theta_1 + \theta_2)[m_t + (1/\beta)(v_t + \varepsilon_t(z))] + (1/\beta)u_{t-1}. \tag{13}$$

Note that $\theta_1 + \theta_2$ is the fraction of total excess demand variance that is accounted for by aggregate shifts (m and v). Since M and u are generated by random walk processes, it follows that the m_t and v_t shifts persist into the next period and therefore continue to affect P_{t+1}. On the other hand, the $\varepsilon_t(z)$ shift is transitory and does not affect P_{t+1}. Accordingly, the current excess demand shift, $m_t + (1/\beta)(v_t + \varepsilon_t(z))$, is weighted by $\theta_1 + \theta_2$ in forming EP_{t+1}. This weighting would change if the processes that generated M_t, u_t, and $\varepsilon_t(z)$ were altered. Appendix 2 deals with the case where u_t is no longer a random walk.

The difference between current observed price in market z and the expected future price (in any market) is determined from eqs. (10) and (13) as

$$P_t(z) - EP_{t+1}|I_t(z) = (\beta/\alpha)(1 - \theta_1 - \theta_2)[m_t + (1/\beta)(v_t + \varepsilon_t(z))]. \qquad (14)$$

The weighting term on the current demand shift depends on $1 - \theta_1 - \theta_2$, which measures the fraction of total excess demand variance that is attributable to relative (hence, in this model, transitory) shifts.

The price solutions from eqs. (13) and (14) can be substituted into either the supply or demand function for commodities (eqs. (1) or (2)) to obtain an expression for output. It is convenient to define here the parameter

$$H \equiv \alpha_s \beta_d - \alpha_d \beta_s.$$

Then, the result for output is [15]

$$
\begin{aligned}
y_t(z) = {} & (H/\alpha)(1 - \theta_1 - \theta_2)m_t + (1/\alpha)[\alpha_s - (H/\beta)(\theta_1 + \theta_2)][v_t^d + \varepsilon_t^d(z)] \\
& + (1/\alpha)[\alpha_d + (H/\beta)(\theta_1 + \theta_2)][v_t^s + \varepsilon_t^s(z)] + (\beta_s/\beta)u_{t-1}^d \\
& + (\beta_d/\beta)u_{t-1}^s.
\end{aligned}
\qquad (15)
$$

There are a number of interesting aspects of the output expression. First, (only) the unperceived part of the current money stock, m_t, has an impact on output. The sign of the effect depends on the substitution and wealth elasticities of the commodity supply and demand functions, as measured by the combination $H \equiv \alpha_s \beta_d - \alpha_d \beta_s$. In Lucas's (1973) model, the substitution effect on demand, α_d, and the wealth effect on supply, β_s, were both assumed to be zero. In that case unperceived monetary expansion has, unambiguously, a positive effect on output. More generally, this result follows if the substitution effect on supply, α_s, and the wealth effect on demand, β_d, are the dominant influences.[16] I will treat the case where $H > 0$ as the normal one, although there is nothing in my particular model that suggests that this case would typically arise.[17]

Second, the magnitude of the effect of m_t on $y_t(z)$ – which could be called a (reverse) Phillips curve slope – depends, through the $1 - \theta_1 - \theta_2$ term, on the relation between the variances of relative and aggregate disturbances. In particular,

$$1 - \theta_1 - \theta_2 = \frac{\sigma_\varepsilon^2}{\sigma_A^2 + \sigma_\varepsilon^2} = \frac{\sigma_\varepsilon^2}{\beta^2 \sigma_m^2 + \sigma_v^2 + \sigma_\varepsilon^2}$$

is the fraction of total excess demand variance that is attributable to relative disturbances. For given varances of the real disturbances, σ_ε^2 and σ_v^2, the magnitude of the Phillips-type response diminishes with the variance of the monetary

[15]The output expression neglects any differences in the sizes of markets – that is, there are no remaining systematic effects on $y_t(z)$ that are associated with the z-index.
[16]Barro and Grossman (1975, ch. 7) contains a related discussion for a model that has separate labor and commodity markets, but which treats expectations in an ad hoc manner.
[17]In an overlapping-generations model with a retirement period, this case may be typical. In this sort of model working households would have a small fraction of total wealth, so that β_s would be small. Further, the retired households, with a relatively large fraction of total wealth, would have short time horizons, so that β_d would be large.

growth rate, σ_m^2.[18] That is, when the monetary growth rate is less predictable, individuals are more inclined to associate observed price fluctuations in their markets with (aggregate) monetary movements. In that case, the reaction of output to a given monetary disturbance, m_t, would be correspondingly smaller. This type of effect has been discussed previously by Lucas (1973, p. 330), and it can be appropriately called the Lucas-hypothesis on the Phillips curve slope.[19] Given the negative effect of σ_m^2 on the Phillips slope, there is a sense in which more variable monetary growth has a 'stabilizing' effect on output. However, since this process reflects a monetary clouding that lessens the extent to which observed prices are a signal about relative prices, it seems intuitive that this type of stabilization would not be desirable in a full sense. Section 3.1 of this paper confirms that intuition.

Third, this type of model does not yield real effects of monetary disturbances that persist beyond one period – that is, only the current value of m_t enters into eq. (15). Some elements that could result in persistent effects are (1) the recognition that aggregate information is attained only gradually over time, rather than fully with a one-period lag; (2) elements of capital accumulation that would allow current changes in stocks to have a continued effect into subsequent periods; (3) adjustment costs in the supply and demand functions. Lucas's (1975) paper contains aspects of the first two of these elements. However, my analysis in the present paper does not incorporate any of these effects.

Fourth, the manner in which the current real shifts affect output brings out the key aspect of the information structure of the model – namely, each aggregate shift, v_t^d or v_t^s, has the same effect as the corresponding relative shift, $\varepsilon_t^d(z)$ or $\varepsilon_t^s(z)$. This behavior derives from the underlying assumption that participants in market z cannot tell what fraction of the observed movement in $P_t(z)$ reflects a relative price shift rather than an absolute shift. The precise way in which individuals would like to discriminate between these two types of shifts will be brought out below in section 3.1. It can also be noted here that the existence of an effect of unperceived monetary expansion on output, as discussed above, depends entirely on the inability of market participants to distinguish immediately between relative and absolute price shifts.

2.3. Price distributions

Given the price solutions in eqs. (10) and (12), the model determines distributions of prices both across markets and over time. It is convenient to focus

---

[18]If monetary disturbances had differential effects across markets – either systematic or random – one would anticipate a positive association between $\sigma_m{}^2$ and $\sigma_\varepsilon{}^2$. However, if the movement in $\sigma_\varepsilon{}^2$ is much less than one-to-one with $\sigma_m{}^2$, the qualitative conclusion about the Phillips curve slope would remain valid.

[19]I am currently attempting to test this hypothesis for the United States over the period 1890 to 1973. Lucas (1973) has performed some related tests for a cross section of countries during the post-World War II period. Lucas's results support the hypothesis, but his main evidence seems to rest on two outlying Latin American cases.

the discussion of these distributions on the problem of predicting the future price in a (randomly-selected) market z', based on information currently possessed by participants in market z. That is, I focus on the gap between $P_{t+1}(z')$ and $EP_{t+1}|I_t(z)$.[20] This gap can be usefully broken down into three independent components,

$$P_{t+1}(z')-EP_{t+1}|I_t(z) \equiv [P_{t+1}(z')-P_{t+1}]+[P_{t+1}-EP_{t+1}|I_t]$$
$$+[EP_{t+1}|I_t-EP_{t+1}|I_t(z)], \qquad (16)$$

where I_t denotes full current information. The information set I_t includes separate observations of m_t and v_t, whereas $I_t(z)$ includes only the combination of m_t, v_t, and $\varepsilon_t(z)$ that is implicit in an observation of $P_t(z)$. It turns out that the three components in eq. (16) are independently, normally distributed with zero mean, so that the variance of each component fully specifies its distribution. I will refer to these variances as τ_1^2, σ^2, and τ_2^2, respectively, and will use the symbol V to denote the sum of the three variances.

The first component corresponds to the distribution of relative prices at a point in time. Eqs. (10) and (12) (updated by one period) imply

$$P_{t+1}(z')-P_{t+1} = (1/\beta)[\theta_1+\theta_2+(\beta/\alpha)(1-\theta_1-\theta_2)]\varepsilon_{t+1}(z'),$$

which has zero mean (conditioned on $I_t(z)$). Using the expression for $\theta_1+\theta_2$ in eq. (11), the variance of relative prices can then be determined as

$$\tau_1^2 \equiv E[P_{t+1}(z')-P_{t+1}]^2|I_t(z)$$
$$= \frac{\sigma_\varepsilon^2[\sigma_A^2+(\beta/\alpha)\sigma_\varepsilon^2]^2}{\beta^2(\sigma_A^2+\sigma_\varepsilon^2)^2} . \qquad (17)$$

Not surprisingly, a key determinant of the relative price variance is σ_ε^2, the variance of relative excess demand.[21] More interestingly, there is also an effect of σ_A^2. This effect is positive as long as $\alpha > \beta$ holds, as I have been assuming. Therefore, an increase in the variance of aggregate excess demand leads to an increase in the variance of relative prices.[22] The reasoning for this effect is as follows. When σ_A^2 increases, the responsiveness of excess demand to locally

[20]Recall that $EP_{t+1}(z') = EP_{t+1}$ for all z' in this model.
[21]However, the effect is not unambiguously positive. Two sufficient conditions for a positive effect are $\alpha < 3\beta$ or $\sigma_\varepsilon{}^2 < \sigma_A{}^2$.
[22]Vining (1974) has a preliminary, I believe inconclusive, discussion of some post-World War II United States evidence on this issue. Graham (1930, p. 175) discusses some observations from the German hyperinflation that appear to support this hypothesis. Cairnes (1873) discusses the general idea that changes in money (gold) would have short-run effects on the dispersion of relative prices. His emphasis is on the (nonproportional) manner in which new money enters different parts of the economy, and on differences in the responsiveness of supply and demand for various types of commodities. Mills (1927 pp. 252–69) calculates measures of price dispersion for the United States from 1891 to 1926.

observed prices diminishes, because individuals are less inclined to associate price movements with shifts in relative excess demand. Accordingly, a given-size relative disturbance, $\varepsilon_t(z)$, requires a larger price movement in order to achieve clearing of the local market. This accentuated response of $P_t(z)$ to $\varepsilon_t(z)$ implies the increase in relative price variance, τ_1^2.

The second component of eq. (16) is the future price net of the price that is predictable based on full current information, I_t. Eqs. (12) and (13) imply

$$P_{t+1}-EP_{t+1}|I_t = (1/\beta)[\theta_1+\theta_2+(\beta/\alpha)(1-\theta_1-\theta_2)](\beta m_{t+1}+v_{t+1}).$$

Note that this component has zero mean (conditioned on $I_t(z)$) and is independent of the first component. The variance of the future absolute price level can then be calculated as

$$\begin{aligned}
\sigma^2 &\equiv E[P_{t+1}-EP_{t+1}|I_t]^2|I_t(z) \\
&= \frac{\sigma_A^2[\sigma_A^2+(\beta/\alpha)\sigma_\varepsilon^2]^2}{\beta^2(\sigma_A^2+\sigma_\varepsilon^2)^2}.
\end{aligned} \tag{18}$$

The effect of σ_A^2 on σ^2 is unambiguously positive if $\alpha > \beta$. The effect of σ_ε^2 is negative when $\alpha > \beta$ holds.

Finally, the third component in eq. (16) involves the distribution of relative information in terms of its implications for EP_{t+1}. Eqs. (12) and (13) imply

$$EP_{t+1}|I_t-EP_{t+1}|I_t(z) = (1/\beta)[(1-\theta_1-\theta_2)(\beta m_t+v_t)-(\theta_1+\theta_2)\varepsilon_t(z)].$$

It can be verified that this expression has zero mean conditioned on $I_t(z)$. This component is also independent of the first two components. The variance of relative information can then be calculated as

$$\begin{aligned}
\tau_2^2 &= E[EP_{t+1}|I_t-EP_{t+1}|I_t(z)]^2|I_t(z) \\
&= \frac{\sigma_A^2\sigma_\varepsilon^2}{\beta^2(\sigma_A^2+\sigma_\varepsilon^2)}.
\end{aligned} \tag{19}$$

This variance is increasing in both σ_A^2 and σ_ε^2.

The full variance of $P_{t+1}(z')$ about $EP_{t+1}|I_t(z)$ is the sum of the three component variances,

$$\begin{aligned}
V &\equiv E[P_{t+1}(z')-EP_{t+1}|I_t(z)]^2|I_t(z) \\
&= \tau_1^2+\sigma^2+\tau_2^2 \\
&= \frac{1}{\beta^2(\sigma_A^2+\sigma_\varepsilon^2)}\left\{\left[\sigma_A^2+(\beta/\alpha)\sigma_\varepsilon^2\right]^2+\sigma_A^2\sigma_\varepsilon^2\right\}.
\end{aligned} \tag{20}$$

It can be shown by straightforward differentiation that V is unambiguously increasing in σ_ε^2,[23] and is unambiguously increasing in σ_A^2 as long as $\alpha > \beta$.

One aspect of the next part of the paper is an analysis of the impact of monetary policy on the predictability of future prices, as measured inversely by V in eq. (20). That analysis would be more meaningful if price predictability played some direct role in the commodity supply and demand functions – perhaps by affecting the costs of long-term nominal contracting. However, the present treatment does not incorporate this type of effect.

3. Monetary policy

Following Sargent and Wallace (1975), I now consider the role of monetary policy in a rational expectations framework. Monetary policy is identified here with a stochastic control rule for determining the time path of the money stock. My procedure differs from that of Sargent and Wallace in two major respects: first, the criterion for evaluating policy is different; and second, my analysis incorporates the dependence of certain coefficients of the model – in particular, the Phillips curve slope – on the underlying distributions of the excess demand shifts. Sargent and Wallace (1975, p. 5) evaluate policy by using a loss function that gives credit to stabilizing a measure of aggregate output, where this output measure is an aggregate analogue to my eq. (15). Their model corresponds in essential respects to dealing with the (geometric) average of the $y_t(z)$'s across the markets, where this averaging of eq. (15) over the n markets leads to an aggregate output expression in which the relative excess demand shifts, $\varepsilon_t^s(z)$ and $\varepsilon_t^d(z)$, do not appear. Stabilizing this measure of aggregate output would amount to giving no credit to changes in the composition of output that were responses to changes in relative supply and demand – that is, to changes in the composition of tastes, technology, etc. It seems clear that a loss function based on this simple measure of aggregate output would not be appropriate.

My earlier discussion of the output expression in eq. (15) stressed that the key aspect of the partial information structure of the model is the confusion between aggregate and relative shifts. It is possible to determine the output that would arise in each market if all participants were able to discriminate perfectly between these shifts – that is, under full current information where $I_t(z)$ includes observations on P_t and M_t. The output level under full current information (subsequently called full information output) can be compared with the output level determined in eq. (15). My proposed criterion for monetary policy is to minimize the expected squared gap between actual and full information output in each market.[24]

---

[23]That is, the positive effect on τ_2^2 in eq. (19) and the ambiguous (though likely positive) effect on τ_1^2 in eq. (17) dominate over the negative effect on σ^2 in eq. (18).

[24]My basic idea for this measure is that it should serve as an approximation to the expected loss of consumer surplus. Ideally, the criterion would be based directly on the behavior of individual expected utilities. Unfortunately, the present model is not set up to proceed in that fashion.

3.1. Prices and outputs under full current information

This model coincides with the one developed in part 2 except that P_t and M_t (and, hence, m_t, v_t and $\varepsilon_t(z)$) are now included in $I_t(z)$. The analysis proceeds as in section 2.2 until the derivation of $EP_{t+1}|I_t(z)$. Given the new information assumption, eq. (8) is now replaced by the simpler expression,

$$EP_{t+1}|I_t(z) = \Pi_1(M_{t-1}+m_t)+\Pi_5 u_t.$$

The remainder of the analysis follows the form of section 2.2. Using an asterisk to denote the full (current) information situation, the price level in market z turns out to be

$$P_t^*(z) = M_{t-1}+m_t+(1/\beta)(u_{t-1}+v_t)+(1/\alpha)\varepsilon_t(z). \tag{21}$$

It is convenient to rewrite here the price that arises under partial information, from eq. (10),

$$P_t(z) = M_{t-1}+[\theta_1+\theta_2+(\beta/\alpha)(1-\theta_1-\theta_2)][m_t+(1/\beta)(v_t+\varepsilon_t(z))]$$
$$+(1/\beta)u_{t-1}.$$

In contrast with its effect on $P_t(z)$, the unanticipated change in the money stock, m_t, has a one-to-one effect on $P_t^*(z)$. Further, the current real disturbances, v_t and $\varepsilon_t(z)$, have different effects on $P_t^*(z)$. In particular, if $\alpha > \beta$, the response of $P_t^*(z)$ to the aggregate disturbance, v_t, is larger than that to the relative disturbance, $\varepsilon_t(z)$.

The result for full information output is

$$y_t^*(z) = (1/\alpha)(\alpha_s - H/\beta)v_t^d+(1/\alpha)(\alpha_d+H/\beta)v_t^s+(\alpha_s/\alpha)\varepsilon_t^d(z)$$
$$+(\alpha_d/\alpha)\varepsilon_t^s(z)+(\beta_s/\beta)u_{t-1}^d+(\beta_d/\beta)u_{t-1}^s, \tag{22}$$

where $H \equiv \alpha_s\beta_d-\alpha_d\beta_s$. Again, it is convenient to rewrite the partial information result, this time from eq. (15),

$$y_t(z) = (H/\alpha)(1-\theta_1-\theta_2)m_t+(1/\alpha)[\alpha_s-(H/\beta)(\theta_1+\theta_2)]$$
$$\times [v_t^d+\varepsilon_t^d(z)]+(1/\alpha)[\alpha_d+(H/\beta)(\theta_1+\theta_2)][v_t^s+\varepsilon_t^s(z)]$$
$$+(\beta_s/\beta)u_{t-1}^d+(\beta_d/\beta)u_{t-1}^s.$$

There are several interesting contrasts between the results for $y_t(z)$ and those for $y_t^*(z)$. First, m_t has no effect on $y_t^*(z)$, which corresponds to the one-to-one effect of m_t on $P_t^*(z)$. Second, each aggregate shift, v_t^d or v_t^s, has a different effect on $y_t^*(z)$ from the corresponding relative shift, $\varepsilon_t^d(z)$ or $\varepsilon_t^s(z)$. From inspection of the $y_t(z)$ and $y_t^*(z)$ expressions, it is clear that the two responses to the v_t's would coincide if $\theta_1 + \theta_2 = 1$. This result obtains because $\theta_1 + \theta_2 = 1$ signifies $\sigma_\varepsilon^2 = 0$, so that the aggregate – relative confusion cannot arise, and all aggregate shifts induce the appropriate output response. Note that the effect of m_t on $y_t(z)$ is zero in this case. It also follows that the response of $y_t(z)$ and $y_t^*(z)$ to the ε_t's would coincide if $\theta_1 + \theta_2 = 0$, since $\sigma_A^2 = 0$ in that case. When $\theta_1 + \theta_2$ is between zero and one, there will be divergences between the responses of $y_t(z)$ and $y_t^*(z)$ to m_t, v_t and $\varepsilon_t(z)$. This observation can be seen more easily by writing out an expression for the gap between actual and full information output,

$$y_t(z) - y_t^*(z) = (H/\alpha\beta)[(1 - \theta_1 - \theta_2)(\beta m_t + v_t) - (\theta_1 + \theta_2)\varepsilon_t(z)]. \quad (23)$$

If $H > 0$ and $0 < \theta_1 + \theta_2 < 1$, it is clear from eq. (23) that (in relation to the full information situation) $y_t(z)$ reacts too much to the aggregate shifts, m_t and v_t, and not enough to the relative shifts, $\varepsilon_t(z)$. Eq. (23) also indicates again that the important informational division is between aggregate shifts, $\beta m_t + v_t$, and relative shifts, $\varepsilon_t(z)$. In a more general model it would also become relevant to separate the βm_t part of the aggregate shifts from the v_t part – or, put another way, to separate the monetary shift, m_t, from the real shift, $v_t + \varepsilon_t(z)$. For example, this other type of informational division would arise if u_t were no longer generated by a random walk. Appendix 1 deals with this case and clarifies some aspects of the two types of information divisions: aggregate versus relative and monetary versus real.

The proposed criterion for monetary policy is to minimize the expected squared gap between $y_t(z)$ and $y_t^*(z)$, which is denoted by Ω. Substituting for $\theta_1 + \theta_2$ from eq. (11) and using eq. (23), the result is

$$
\begin{aligned}
\Omega &\equiv \mathrm{E}[y_t(z) - y_t^*(z)]^2 | I_t(z) \\
&= \frac{H^2\sigma_A^2\sigma_\varepsilon^2}{(\alpha\beta)^2(\sigma_A^2 + \sigma_\varepsilon^2)} \, .
\end{aligned}
\quad (24)
$$

This expression for the variance of output about its full information position will be used in the subsequent discussion of monetary policy.

3.2. The optimal money variance

Before introducing the possibility of monetary policy through feedback control on observed values of prices, outputs, etc., I consider here the role played by pure variance of money – that is, by σ_m^2. First, it is clear from eq. (23) that, if all the coefficients including $\theta_1 + \theta_2$ were fixed, then an increase in σ_m^2 would lead to an increased variance of $y_t(z)$ about $y_t^*(z)$. Accordingly, in the

Sargent and Wallace model, where all coefficients are fixed, it is trivial that $\sigma_m^2 = 0$ would be optimal (and, hence, they do not discuss this issue). On the other hand, in my model an increase in σ_m^2 has effects that operate through the θ-coefficients. Specifically, the coefficient on the aggregate disturbance term in eq. (23) is

$$1 - \theta_1 - \theta_2 = \frac{\sigma_\varepsilon^2}{\beta^2 \sigma_m^2 + \sigma_v^2 + \sigma_{\varepsilon_i}^2},$$

and this coefficient declines with σ_m^2. As σ_m^2 increases, individuals attribute a larger fraction of observed price movements to aggregate shocks and are, therefore, fooled less – in terms of the departure of $y_t(z)$ from $y_t^*(z)$ – for a given value of the aggregate shock, $\beta m_t + v_t$. In fact, as $\sigma_m^2 \to \infty$, the contribution of the aggregate disturbance term in eq. (23) to the output variance Ω, as calculated in eq. (24), approaches zero.[25] However, the contribution to Ω of the relative disturbance term in eq. (23), $(\theta_1 + \theta_2)\varepsilon_t(z)$, is an increasing function of σ_m^2, so that the overall effect on Ω depends on two offsetting forces.

The nature of the net effect is apparent from eq. (24). The form of this expression implies that Ω is an increasing function of both σ_A^2 (which equals $\beta^2 \sigma_m^2 + \sigma_v^2$) and σ_ε^2. Hence, it is true in this model that the variance of output about its full information position is minimized by setting $\sigma_m^2 = 0$.[26] The reason for this result is that the policy criterion dictates getting output as close as possible to its full information position. An increase in any of the underlying variances, σ_m^2, σ_v^2, or σ_ε^2, clouds the picture, in the sense of making current price information a less accurate signal for market participants, and therefore makes it more difficult for individuals to get output close to full information output. To the extent that the variance of money, σ_m^2, can be controlled,[27] the smallest possible value would be optimal.[28]

The conclusion that $\sigma_m^2 = 0$ is optimal is basically in the spirit of the constant growth rate rule that has been advocated particularly by Friedman (for example, in Friedman, (1960, chapter 4)), and earlier by Simons (1948, pp. 181–3).

[25]Because $(1 - \theta_1 - \theta_2)^2$ approaches zero faster than σ_m^2 approaches infinity.

[26]In an earlier version of this paper I obtained the result that $\sigma_m^2 = 0$ would minimize Ω only under some configurations of the underlying parameters, and that $\sigma_m^2 = \infty$ was optimal in some other cases. Those conclusions depended on a misspecification in which EP_t, rather than EP_{t+1}, entered into the supply and demand functions. Another way to end up with $\sigma_m^2 = \infty$ as an answer is to change the objective function to the minimization of the variance of 'aggregate' output y_t about $Ey_t|I_{t-1}$ (essentially the Sargent and Wallace criterion), where the aggregation eliminates the $\varepsilon_t(z)$ terms from the output expression of eq. (15). This objective would definitely call for $\sigma_m^2 = \infty$ if aggregate real shifts were absent; that is, if $u_t^d \equiv u_t^s \equiv 0$. In the case where aggregate real shifts are present, the criterion would typically lead to a positive, but finite, value for σ_m^2.

[27]If there are significant money-control-type costs associated with reducing σ_m^2, then these costs would have to be weighed against the benefits from a lower variance. This sort of trade-off would lead to the choice of a positive value for σ_m^2.

[28]This result remains valid when the u_t process is no longer a random walk. See appendix 1.

The present result indicates that monetary policy is best when it is most predictable. In particular, an increase in money variance is nonneutral and leads to an increased variance of output about its full information position because money variance clouds the real picture and reduces the value of observed prices as allocative signals.

It is also useful to note here that the predictability of future prices is maximized by setting $\sigma_m^2 = 0$. That is, the variance V of $P_{t+1}(z')$ about $EP_{t+1}|I_t(z)$, which is indicated in eq. (20), is an increasing function of σ_A^2 (and, hence, of σ_m^2) as long as $\alpha > \beta$ holds. Therefore, the introduction of a price variance criterion into the objective function would not alter the above result.

3.3. Monetary policy as feedback control

I now consider the implications of complicating the money supply rule from the simple form of eq. (4) to include feedback effects from observed economic variables. This extension would allow the monetary authority to perform the countercyclical function of increasing money more rapidly when output is relatively low or prices are relatively high, and expanding money less rapidly in the reverse situations. The implications of this sort of monetary behavior depend crucially on the information set that is available to the monetary authority. There are two cases that have sharply divergent implications. In the first case, the monetary authority does not have more information than any of the market participants. Formally, the authority's current information set is I_{t-1}, which includes all relevant information with a one-period lag, but does not include an observation on P_t.[29] In this situation monetary policy can react (say, countercyclically) only to economic variables that have already been perceived by market participants. In the second case, the monetary authority has superior information about (some) current economic variables. In an extreme case the authority's information set would be I_t, which includes an observation on P_t. In this case the authority's feedback rule for ΔM_t can include some economic variables, such as aggregate values of current prices and outputs, which are not yet fully perceived by market participants. Not surprisingly, it turns out that countercyclical policy can be more potent under the second case than under the first (and, further, that policy may have zero potency under the first case). Finally, I assume in both cases that the market participants and the monetary authority have the same information about the form of the monetary rule. That is, the form of the rule is, itself, assumed to be a part of the information set I_{t-1} (and, hence, of $I_t(z)$). I consider in a later section some implications of differential information about the form of the monetary rule.

[29]In this situation the monetary authority actually has less information than any of the market participants since each individual has a current price observation, $P_t(z)$, in his information set, $I_t(z)$.

3.3.1. The monetary authority lacks superior information about the economy. I consider first the situation where the monetary authority's information set is I_{t-1}. The feedback control problem can be illustrated in this case by prescribing a monetary rule of the form,

$$\Delta M_t = m_t - \gamma v_{t-1},\tag{25}$$

where, as before, $m_t \sim N(0, \sigma_m^2)$. Since v_{t-1} is last period's real shift to aggregate excess demand, the rule described by eq. (25) amounts to a countercyclical reaction to (one determinant of) last period's absolute price level if $\gamma > 0$. The form of the rule could be complicated to include a separate reaction to last period's 'aggregate' output or money stock, which would amount to introducing m_{t-1} and separate terms for v_{t-1}^d and v_{t-1}^s into eq. (25). The rule could also be extended to incorporate observations from period $t-2$ or earlier periods. However, these complications to the form of eq. (25) turn out to yield no additional insights, as should become clear from the subsequent discussion.[30]

When money is generated by the rule in eq. (25), the model can be solved out for prices and outputs using the same type of procedure as in section 2.2.[31] Since the formal procedure involves no important new elements, I will confine attention here to a presentation and discussion of the results. The solutions for $P_t(z)$, $EP_{t+1}|I_t(z)$, and $E\Delta M_{t+1}|I_t(z)$ turn out to be

$$P_t(z) = M_{t-1} + [\theta_1 + \theta_2 + (\beta/\alpha)(1 - \theta_1 - \theta_2) - \gamma\beta\theta_2]$$
$$\times [m_t + (1/\beta)(v_t + \varepsilon_t(z))] + (1/\beta)u_{t-1} - \gamma v_{t-1},$$

$$EP_{t+1}|I_t(z) = M_{t-1} + (\theta_1 + \theta_2 - \gamma\beta\theta_2)[m_t + (1/\beta)(v_t + \varepsilon_t(z))]$$
$$+ (1/\beta)u_{t-1} - \gamma v_{t-1},$$

$$E\Delta M_{t+1}|I_t(z) = -\gamma\beta\theta_2[m_t + (1/\beta)(v_t + \varepsilon_t(z))].$$

In contrast to the earlier case in which there were no feedbacks to money (eqs. (4), (10), and (13), and $E\Delta M_{t+1}|I_t(z) = 0$), the new elements concern the γ-terms. These terms are of two types: those pertaining to v_{t-1} and those associated with v_t. First, v_{t-1} is contained in the information set, $I_t(z)$. Hence, the negative effect of v_{t-1} on M_t, as implied by eq. (25) if $\gamma > 0$, is fully perceived. As is generally the case for the perceived part of M_t, $P_t(z)$ moves in proportion to money – that is, the $-\gamma v_{t-1}$ term appears in the $P_t(z)$ expression. Since eq. (25) implies that the effect of v_{t-1} on M_t would also carry over to

---

[30]I have not discussed the possibility of monetary reaction to the array of $\varepsilon_{t-1}(z)$. Since the monetary authority is assumed to possess only the aggregate instrument, ΔM_t, one would not expect the pattern of relative excess demands to be an important input into policy decisions. In any event introducing the array of $\varepsilon_{t-1}(z)$ into eq. (25) would not change the basic results.
[31]The form of the $P_t(z)$ solution in eq. (6) would now include the additional term, $\Pi_6 v_{t-1}$.

M_{t+1}, it follows that $EP_{t+1}|I_t(z)$ also moves in accordance with $-\gamma v_{t-1}$. Therefore, the negative reaction of ΔM_t to v_{t-1} does not produce any gaps either between $P_t(z)$ and $EP_{t+1}|I_t(z)$ or between $M_t + E\Delta M_{t+1}|I_t(z)$ and $EP_{t+1}|I_t(z)$.

A second type of effect arises because the current excess demand shift, v_t, will have an effect next period on ΔM_{t+1}. Since v_t is not contained in $I_t(z)$, market participants form an estimate of the feedback effect on next period's money based on the expectation $\gamma Ev_t|I_t(z) = \gamma \beta \theta_2[m_t + (1/\beta)(v_t + \varepsilon_t(z))]$. This term appears in the above expressions for $E\Delta M_{t+1}|I_t(z)$, $EP_{t+1}|I_t(z)$, and $P_t(z)$. Again, the response of ΔM_{t+1} to v_t does not produce any gaps either between $P_t(z)$ and $EP_{t+1}|I_t(z)$[32] or between $M_t + E\Delta M_{t+1}|I_t(z)$ and $EP_{t+1}|I_t(z)$.

The two feedback channels alter neither $P_t(z)$ relative to EP_{t+1} nor the wealth term, $M_t + E\Delta M_{t+1} - EP_{t+1}$. It follows that there will be no effect on commodity supply and demand, as given in eqs. (1) and (2), and therefore no effect on output, $y_t(z)$. Because the market participants know the form of the money rule, and take this behavior into account in forming expectations of future prices and monetary growth rates, the feedback from v_{t-1} to M_t has no effect on the entire distribution of output.[33] The level of output continues to be determined by eq. (15). It follows trivially that the choice of the feedback parameter, γ, is irrelevant to the determination of the variance of output about its full information position, as determined in eq. (24).[34]

3.3.2. The monetary authority possesses superior information about the economy.

The conclusions on the output effect of feedback control are radically different when the monetary authority has superior information that can be included in the money rule. The situation can be illustrated in the case where the authority has the information set I_t, which includes an observation of v_t.[35] In this case a

---

[32]Note that the supply and demand functions in eqs. (1) and (2) depend only on the expected real value of next period's money, $M_t + E\Delta M_{t+1} - EP_{t+1}$, which accords with the role of money as a store of value in this model. The current real money stock in market z, $M_t - P_t(z)$, might also enter these functions if the model incorporated the role of money as a mechanism for economizing on transaction costs (or if current real balances were simply included as a direct argument of individual utility functions). In that case $P_t(z)$ would not respond as much as $EP_{t+1}|I_t(z)$ to the expected movement in ΔM_{t+1}. The implied gap between $P_t(z)$ and EP_{t+1} would then lead to effects on output, though the effects on actual and full information output would coincide. This sort of effect is analogous to the effect of systematic money growth on actual and full information output, as discussed in appendix 3.

[33]This type of result was first presented by Sargent and Wallace (1975, section 4). Their assumptions about the monetary authority's information set are analogous to those that I make in this section.

[34]Generally, there will be a nonzero effect of changes in γ on the predictability of future prices. The main effect is the following. When γ is high, the effect of v_{t+1} on P_{t+1} is attenuated because of the offsetting feedback effect on ΔM_{t+2}. Hence (at least if γ is not too large) P_{t+1} can be made more predictable, based on $I_t(z)$, by setting a positive value of γ.

[35]I do not consider here the possibility of superior information about the configuration of the ε_t's. Since the policymaker is assumed to possess only the aggregate instrument, ΔM_t, this sort of information would, in any case, be of only second-order use. Further, it seems much less plausible that the policymaker would actually have superior information about the relative shifts.

possible form of the monetary rule is

$$\Delta M_t = m_t - \delta v_t. \tag{26}$$

Again, $\delta > 0$ describes a countercyclical monetary policy, but this time the response of ΔM_t is to v_t, which is not a part of the individual information sets, $I_t(z)$. Again, the solution for prices and outputs can be derived from a procedure of the type discussed in section 2.2. The price results are now[36]

$$P_t(z) = M_{t-1} + [\theta_1 + \theta_2 + (\beta/\alpha)(1 - \theta_1 - \theta_2)]$$
$$\times \{m_t + (1/\beta)[(1 - \beta\delta)v_t + \varepsilon_t(z)]\} + (1/\beta)u_{t-1}, \tag{27}$$

$$EP_{t+1}|I_t(z) = M_{t-1} + (\theta_1 + \theta_2)\{m_t + (1/\beta)[(1 - \beta\delta)v_t + \varepsilon_t(z)]\}$$
$$+ (1/\beta)u_{t-1}.$$

The feedback from v_t to ΔM_t implies that $\beta m_t + (1 - \beta\delta)v_t$ is now the aggregate excess demand shift that affects $P_t(z)$ and $EP_{t+1}|I_t(z)$. Therefore, the variance of aggregate demand is now

$$\sigma_A^2 = \beta^2\sigma_m^2 + (1 - \beta\delta)^2\sigma_v^2.$$

It is apparent that raising the feedback parameter, δ, will reduce σ_A^2 as long as $\delta < 1/\beta$ applies. Further, setting $\delta = 1/\beta$ would minimize σ_A^2 for a given value of σ_m^2. (The combination of $\delta = 1/\beta$ and $\sigma_m^2 = 0$ would yield $\sigma_A^2 = 0$.)

The formula for Ω, the variance of output about its full information position,[37] is still that given in eq. (24), and the formula for V, the variance of the absolute future price level, is still that given in eq. (20). In particular, reductions in σ_A^2 unambiguously reduce Ω, and such reductions also unambiguously reduce V if $\alpha > \beta$ applies. It is then clear that $\delta = 1/\beta$ (along with $\sigma_m^2 = 0$) yields the optimal money rule of the form of eq. (26). This parameter choice implies that the aggregate excess demand shift is $m_t + (1 - \beta\delta)v_t \equiv 0$. That is, there would be sufficient feedback from v_t to ΔM_t so that the direct effect of v_t on excess demand would be fully offset by an inverse movement of ΔM_t.[38]

Although the above form of stabilization policy seems obvious under the

---

[36]Given eq. (26), it follows that $E\Delta M_{t+1}|I_t(z) = 0$.

[37]The formula for $y_t(z)$ from eq. (15) is modified only in the coefficients of v_t^d and v_t^s. The new terms are

$$(1/\alpha)\{\alpha_s - (H/\beta)[(1 - \beta\delta)(\theta_1 + \theta_2) + \beta\delta]\}v_t^d,$$
$$(1/\alpha)\{\alpha_d + (H/\beta)[(1 - \beta\delta)(\theta_1 + \theta_2) + \beta\delta]\}v_t^s.$$

The formula for $y_t(z) - y_t^*(z)$ in eq. (23) is modified only by replacing v_t with $(1 - \beta\delta)v_t$. However, the $\theta_1 + \theta_2$ coefficient that appears in this expression now involves $(1 - \beta\delta)^2\sigma_v^2$, rather than σ_v^2 (see eq. (11)).

[38]This result can be generalized to a case where the policymaker has only partial information about current variables. As long as the monetary authority possesses some information that is not possessed by all market participants, there would be some potential role for countercyclical adjustments in money.

assumed superiority in the monetary authority's information set, the way that it works is somewhat subtle. In particular, the stabilization policy does not operate to eliminate any output effects of shifts in v_t^d or v_t^s, but, rather, it works by removing discrepancies between the movements of actual and full information output. Assume, for example, that there is no monetary feedback ($\delta = 0$), and that v_t^d is positive while v_t^s is zero. According to eq. (27), this unanticipated aggregate demand shift would affect prices in all markets equiproportionately – that is, there would be a shift in the absolute price level, but no shift in relative prices. However, participants in market z would not be able fully to distinguish this shift from a relative price change, and, therefore, the movement in output would depart from the movement in full information output. In the case where $H > 0$, eq. (23) indicates that actual output would increase too much in this situation. Suppose, now, that a stabilization policy is adopted that implies a negative response of ΔM_t to v_t so that the net disturbance, $(1 - \beta\delta)v_t$, is maintained at zero. Eq. (27) indicates that neither relative nor absolute prices would then be affected by the positive value of v_t^d. In that case there is no possibility of a confusion between absolute and relative shifts, and the movement in v_t^d cannot lead to a departure of actual from full information output. Further, as is clear from eq. (22), the movement in ΔM_t itself does not affect the response of full information output. Therefore, in this example, both actual and full information output would increase with the positive value of v_t^d in accordance with the coefficient shown in eq. (22).

Since the stabilization policy works by preventing a confusion between absolute and relative price changes, it is also clear that an alternative to the active stabilization policy would be the provision of the information about current economic variables. If the monetary authority actually had more rapid observations of v_t, they could convey this information to the public. This information would then augment the information set, $I_t(z)$, that is used to form expectations about P_{t+1}. Once v_t is observable, it is clear that shifts in v_t can no longer lead to confusions between relative and absolute price changes. Hence, as in the case of the countercyclical monetary policy described above, movements in v_t would not produce discrepancies between actual and full information output. In other words, when the monetary authority has superior information about the economy, the provision of the information to the public is an alternative to an active stabilization policy. An argument for the superiority of stabilization policy would have to be based on the costs of transmitting and using the relevant information.[39] In particular, it could be argued that the

---

[39]The active stabilization policy and the information-provision policy do have different implications for the predictability of future prices. The information-provision policy ($\delta = 0$) in eq. (26), but with v_t contained in $I_t(z)$, would involve a higher variance of future prices. Essentially, the movements in v_t and the associated movements in P_t would be perceived currently, but these movements would still not be predictable at date $t-1$. On the other hand, the stabilization policy described above completely eliminates fluctuations in P_t associated with movements in v_t, and therefore makes P_t more predictable at date $t-1$.

existence of an active stabilization policy motivates individuals to reduce expenditures that are aimed at augmenting their information sets. If there are
economies-of-scale in information production, there could be a net social gain
along these lines.[40]

3.3.3. The monetary authority has superior information about the monetary rule.

Taylor (1975) has stressed the idea that individuals would not have perfect
information about the form of the monetary rule. In this situation it is plausible
that the monetary authority would have better information than the general
public about its own future actions. In fact, this situation seems most plausible
when the policymaker lacks a consistent objective function, such as the minimization of the variance of output about its full information position.[41] In any
case, if the monetary authority has better information about its monetary rule,
there is the possibility of controlling money so as to systematically fool the
public. Taylor has pointed out that this sort of deception can be carried out
during 'transition' periods during which individuals are modifying their beliefs
(along Bayesian adaptation lines) about the form of policy.[42] In Taylor's model
there is also an optimal, nonzero amount of this deception. His model appears
to support this type of action because the policymaker's objective function
does not reflect individual preferences.[43] In my model, there appears to be no
basis for policy deception as long as the policymaker's objective is based on
minimizing the gap between actual and full information output.[44]

A simple form of policy deception arises when individuals believe that $\Delta M_t = m_t$, where $m_t \sim N(0, \sigma_m^2)$, but where the monetary authority knows (determines)
that m_t is generated by a distribution other than $N(0, \sigma_m^2)$. Consider, for example,
the case where m_t can be set by the monetary authority at any desired level,
while, in the 'short run', holding fixed people's belief that m_t has zero mean and
variance σ_m^2.[45] In this case it is clear that the choice of m_t has a systematic

---

[40]Of course, once this sort of information externality is introduced, it is also natural to
consider the negative externalities associated with governmental incentive and control.

[41]An unpredictable objective function would be one possible rationale for the existence of
m_t, the stochastic part of money.

[42]Sargent and Wallace (1974, p. 16) argue that there is no way for the monetary authority
to systematically fool the public, even in the short run.

[43]His objective function gives positive credit to reducing unemployment throughout the
relevant range. The analogy to my model would be to credit expansions of output even when it
was already above its full information position.

[44]The normative case for policy deception could be based on external effects, such as income
taxation, unemployment compensation, etc., that are not incorporated into my model. This
idea is discussed by Phelps (1972) and also by Hall (1973), who argues: '. . . the benefits of
inflation derive from the use of expansionary policy to trick economic agents into behaving
in socially preferable ways even though their behavior is not in their own interest . . .'. Prescott
(1975) downplays the importance of external effects in this context. In any case the possible
external effects seem to have more pertinence for long-term allocative policies, such as the
design of tax and welfare system, than for countercyclical monetary policy.

[45]The monetary authority might, instead, be reacting to v_{t-1} by a feedback rule of the
form of eq. (25), but individuals currently believe that $\gamma = 0$.

effect on current output, as determined in eq. (15). However, it is also clear from eq. (23) that the expected squared gap between actual and full information output would be minimized by choosing $m_t = 0$.[46] Given the objective of minimizing gaps between actual and full information output, it is not surprising that optimal behavior rules out policy deception. In this sort of framework the best monetary policy is always the policy that is most predictable.[47] The obvious policy implication is for the monetary authority to make known in advance its intentions about money growth,[48] which is again the basic philosophy behind the constant growth rate rule.

4. Conclusions

I will conclude by highlighting some of the main results that deal with the effects of money variance and with the role of monetary policy. An increased variance of money makes it more difficult for individuals to react appropriately to the real shifts in the economy. There are two important types of responses to an increased money variance. First, since individuals react by attributing a larger fraction of observed price movements to monetary causes, there is a smaller effect of a given size monetary disturbance on output – that is, the magnitude of the Phillips curve slope is smaller. Second, the associated compounding of individual information problems leads both to a higher variance of output about its full (current) information position and to a reduced predictability of future prices. It also leads to an increase in the variance of relative prices across markets.

From the standpoint of monetary policy, it is clear that pure variance of money is harmful, essentially because it clouds the real picture for individuals. The analysis of monetary policy as feedback control is more complicated since the results hinge on the relative information positions of the monetary authority and the public. When the authority lacks superior information, the feedback to money must be based on economic variables that have already been perceived by the public. In this circumstance the choice of feedback control parameters has no implications for the entire distribution of output. On the other hand, if the monetary authority has superior information about the economy –

---

[46]If the monetary authority sets $m_t = 0$ continually, this action would also lead people to believe (along Bayesian lines) that $\sigma_m^2 = 0$. I have not dealt explicitly with the effects of fooling people about the value of σ_m^2. Presumably, the variance of actual about full information output is minimized when perceptions about σ_m^2 are correct.

[47]There is a sense in which this conclusion is violated for the case where the monetary authority has superior information about the economy. In particular, the feedback rule from v_t to ΔM_t described by eq. (26) would be ineffective if people fully perceived the countercyclical money response, $-\delta v_t$, while still remaining in the dark about v_t. On the other hand, it is desirable even in this case for people to know the form of the monetary rule.

[48]More specifically, the Federal Reserve should publicize, as rapidly as possible, the proceedings of its Open Market Committee.

which, for some reason, it does not provide to the public directly – then the appropriate feedback response to the extra information can move output closer to its full information position.

Basically, the conclusions for monetary policy are in accord with the philosophy behind Friedman's proposal for a constant growth rate rule. It is only to the extent that the monetary authority has superior economic information (as well as the appropriate objectives), and to the extent that providing information to the public is costly, that there is a call for departures from the constant growth rate rule. Further, if the attempt to use countercyclical policy to exploit the superior information results in a higher variance of money, σ_m^2, there would be a tradeoff between the beneficial effects from the countercyclical elements (the negative correlation between v_t and ΔM_t) and the adverse effects from pure monetary variance.[49]

It may be useful to discuss the role of feedback control of money in the case of a concrete example.[50] The United States economy in 1974 was affected by two important real shocks: the oil cartel and the shortfall of agricultural harvests. Although my model has been constructed to deal with a closed economy, it seems that either of these shocks can be represented by a downward movement in aggregate real supply, v_t^s, and a lesser downward movement in aggregate real demand, v_t^d. (I am abstracting here from effects on relative supply and demand, which would be quantitatively important for these shocks, but which would not affect the essential parts of my story.) It follows that output (in a 'typical' market which experiences zero relative shifts) would fall while prices would rise. What is the role for monetary policy in this situation? The present analysis suggests that there is a substantive role only to the extent that the monetary authority has better information than the public about the disturbances, or, possibly, about their implications for the economy. Perhaps the most obvious observation about the oil and agricultural shocks is the extent to which they are perceived. Hence, the approach in this paper argues that there is no role for monetary policy in offsetting these real shifts.[51,52] Adverse shifts like the oil and agricultural crises will reduce output and cause painful relative adjustments no matter what the reaction of the monetary authority. Added monetary noise would only complicate and lengthen the process of adjustment.

[49]This type of tradeoff is discussed in Friedman (1953).

[50]Gordon (1975) discusses the same example. Perhaps not surprisingly, he reaches very different conclusions.

[51]Further, to the extent that there is any role it would be a contraction of ΔM_t in response to the positive value of $v_t \equiv v_t^d - v_t^s$.

[52]The present analysis implies that having the monetary authority announce that there had been an oil or agricultural crisis (or, perhaps, telling people that these crises meant lower output and higher prices) would be equivalent to the appropriate active response of money. In this case it seems that both the announcement and the active policy would have negligible effects. In fact, the announcement would be somewhat preferable since it would not involve the danger of introducing added variance into the money supply.

Appendix 1: Results when u_t is a first-order Markov Process

I consider here the case where the real excess demand shift, u_t, is generated by a first-order Markov Process,

$$u_t = \lambda u_{t-1} + v_t,$$

where

$$0 \leq \lambda \leq 1.$$

Under this specification the magnitude of λ determines the extent to which the current shift, v_t, persists in its effect on u_{t+1}, and, hence, on P_{t+1}. The case treated in the main text corresponds to $\lambda = 1$ – that is, to the situation where v_t affects u_{t+1} on a one-to-one basis.

The solution for prices and outputs can be derived in accordance with the general procedure developed in section 2.2 of the text. Since no new elements are involved, I will simply indicate the results. It is convenient to define the parameter,

$$\hat{\lambda} = \frac{\lambda}{\lambda + (\alpha/\beta)(1-\lambda)}.$$

If $\alpha > \beta$ then the $\hat{\lambda}$ parameter satisfies the conditions $0 \leq \hat{\lambda} \leq \lambda \leq 1$, $\hat{\lambda} \to 0$ as $\lambda \to 0$, and $\hat{\lambda} \to 1$ as $\lambda \to 1$. Recalling that $H \equiv \alpha_s \beta_d - \alpha_d \beta_s$, the results for prices and outputs are now

$$P_t(z) = M_{t-1} + [\theta_1 + \hat{\lambda}\theta_2 + (\beta/\alpha)(1 - \theta_1 - \hat{\lambda}\theta_2)]$$
$$\times [m_t + (1/\beta)(v_t + \varepsilon_t(z))] + (\hat{\lambda}/\beta)u_{t-1},$$

$$EP_{t+1}|I_t(z) = M_{t-1} + (\theta_1 + \hat{\lambda}\theta_2)[m_t + (1/\beta)(v_t + \varepsilon_t(z))]$$
$$+ (\lambda\hat{\lambda}/\beta)u_{t-1},$$

$$y_t(z) = (H/\alpha)(1 - \theta_1 - \hat{\lambda}\theta_2)m_t + (1/\alpha)[\alpha_s - (H/\beta)(\theta_1 + \hat{\lambda}\theta_2)]$$
$$\times [v_t^d + \varepsilon_t^d(z)] + (1/\alpha)[\alpha_d + (H/\beta)(\theta_1 + \hat{\lambda}\theta_2)][v_t^s + \varepsilon_t^s(z)]$$
$$+ \lambda\left[\frac{\alpha_s(1-\lambda) + \beta_s\lambda}{\alpha(1-\lambda) + \beta\lambda}\right]u_{t-1}^d + \lambda\left[\frac{\alpha_d(1-\lambda) + \beta_d\lambda}{\alpha(1-\lambda) + \beta\lambda}\right]u_{t-1}^s,$$

$$y_t^*(z) = (1/\alpha)[\alpha_s - (H/\beta)\hat{\lambda}]v_t^d + (1/\alpha)[\alpha_d + (H/\beta)\hat{\lambda}]v_t^s + (\alpha_s/\alpha)\varepsilon_t^d(z)$$
$$+ (\alpha_d/\alpha)\varepsilon_t^s(z) + \lambda\left[\frac{\alpha_s(1-\lambda) + \beta_s\lambda}{\alpha(1-\lambda) + \beta\lambda}\right]u_{t-1}^d$$
$$+ \lambda\left[\frac{\alpha_d(1-\lambda) + \beta_d\lambda}{\alpha(1-\lambda) + \beta\lambda}\right]u_{t-1}^s,$$

$$y_t(z) - y_t^*(z) = (H/\alpha\beta)[\beta m_t + \hat{\lambda}v_t - (\theta_1 + \hat{\lambda}\theta_2)(\beta m_t + v_t + \varepsilon_t(z))],$$

$$\Omega \equiv E[y_t(z) - y_t^*(z)]^2 | I_t(z)$$

$$= \frac{H^2}{(\alpha\beta)^2(\sigma_A^2 + \sigma_\varepsilon^2)} \left[(1 - \hat{\lambda})^2 \beta^2 \sigma_m^2 \sigma_v^2 + \beta^2 \sigma_m^2 \sigma_\varepsilon^2 + (\hat{\lambda})^2 \sigma_v^2 \sigma_\varepsilon^2 \right],$$

where $\sigma_A^2 \equiv \beta^2\sigma_m^2 + \sigma_v^2$ in the last expression. The original results in section 2.2 of the text correspond, in each case, to $\lambda = \hat{\lambda} = 1$.

The principal new results from allowing $\hat{\lambda} \neq 1$ are brought out in the above expression for Ω. When $\hat{\lambda} = 1$, the aggregate real shift, v_t, is permanent, in the sense of affecting u_{t+1} on a one-to-one basis. More importantly, the monetary variable, M_t, and the aggregate real shift, u_t, are in this case generated by processes of the same form – that is, by random walks. In this situation the current disturbance associated with money, βm_t, and the current movement in the aggregate real disturbance, v_t, have identical implications for the future price level, P_{t+1}. Therefore, when $\hat{\lambda} = 1$, it is unnecessary for individuals who are interested in forecasting P_{t+1} to separate out the βm_t part of the current excess demand shift from the v_t part. The only concern is with separating the total aggregate shift, $\beta m_t + v_t$, from the relative shift, $\varepsilon_t(z)$ (since $\varepsilon_t(z)$ is purely transitory and has no impact on P_{t+1}). In the Ω-expression, $\hat{\lambda} = 1$ implies that the $\sigma_m^2\sigma_v^2$ interaction term vanishes, and the remaining terms can be combined into an interaction term between σ_ε^2 and $\beta^2\sigma_m^2 + \sigma_v^2 \equiv \sigma_A^2$ (as in eq. (24)). In this case the problem of separating permanent from transitory shifts in order to forecast P_{t+1} amounts to separating aggregate from relative shifts.

The other polar case is $\hat{\lambda} = 0$, which corresponds to the v_t shifts being purely transitory. In that case v_t and $\varepsilon_t(z)$ are generated by processes of the same form and the $\sigma_v^2\sigma_\varepsilon^2$ interaction term vanishes from the Ω-expression. The remaining terms can then be combined into an interaction term involving $\beta^2\sigma_m^2$ and $\sigma_v^2 + \sigma_\varepsilon^2$. That is, the separation between permanent and transitory reduces in this case to a separation between monetary and real.

In the general case where $\hat{\lambda}$ is in the interval between zero and one, all three interaction terms appear in the Ω-expression. Individuals would then be concerned with the full separation of the current excess demand shift, $\beta m_t + v_t + \varepsilon_t(z)$, into its three components. The separation between permanent and transitory would entail two types of divisions of current excess demand shifts: aggregate versus relative and monetary versus real.

From the standpoint of monetary policy, the important aspect of the extended model is that Ω is still a strictly increasing function of σ_m^2. (This property can be verified from straightforward differentiation of the Ω-expression.) Hence, the compounding of the information problem to include a separation of monetary versus real along with a separation of aggregate versus relative does not alter the conclusion that monetary noise makes the information problem more difficult.

Finally, it can be noted that the extension of the model to a first-order Markov process for u_t has been carried out within the framework where the monetary disturbance, m_t, and the relative shift, $\varepsilon_t(z)$, are purely white noise processes. It would be possible to introduce some serial dependence into these processes. However, it is already apparent from the above discussion of the u_t process that the crucial consideration is the relation between the processes that generate M_t, u_t and $\varepsilon_t(z)$. When these three processes assume different forms there will be an information problem associated with dividing currently observed excess demand shifts into its three components. The above case, in which the u_t-process is first-order Markov (with $\hat{\lambda} \neq 0$ or 1) and m_t and $\varepsilon_t(z)$ are white noise, is one way in which the processes for M_t, u_t, and $\varepsilon_t(z)$ can take on different forms. Further alteration of the m_t or $\varepsilon_t(z)$ processes would not seem to change the basic picture, at least in terms of the implications for money variance, σ_m^2.

Appendix 2: Systematic growth in money and output

This section extends the analysis of the text in two respects. First, the systematic growth rate of money, g in eq. (4), is allowed to be nonzero. Second, the growth rate of k_t, the systematic part of excess demand which is defined as $-\beta\rho$ in eq. (5), is allowed to be nonzero. It is clear that the introduction of these systematic growth elements (which are included in the information set, $I_t(z)$) would not affect the gap between actual and full information output. Therefore, the present discussion is limited to the effects of systematic growth on $P_t(z)$, $EP_{t+1}|I_t(z)$, and $y_t(z)$. The analysis here returns to the case where u_t is generated by a random walk ($\hat{\lambda} = 1$, in the terminology of appendix 1).

Formally, the extended model can be solved by the method of section 2.2 of the text if the solution form for $P_t(z)$ in eq. (6) is extended to include a time trend and a constant term – that is, $\Pi_6 t + \Pi_7$. Additional complications to the systematic parts of M_t and k_t – for example, to allow nonconstant growth rates – would be reflected as additional terms in the solution form for $P_t(z)$. Given the extended form of the solution, the procedure for solving the model is the same as that employed in section 2.2.

The solution for $P_t(z)$ coincides with eq. (10) except for the inclusion of systematic effects associated with g and ρ. The extended result is

$$P_t(z) = M_{t-1} + g + [\theta_1 + \theta_2 + (\beta/\alpha)(1 - \theta_1 - \theta_2)][m_t + (1/\beta)(v_t + \varepsilon_t(z))]$$
$$+ (1/\beta)u_{t-1} - \rho t + (\alpha/\beta)(g - \rho) + \rho.$$

Since $M_{t-1} + g$ is now the fully perceived part of M_t, this term has a one-to-one effect on $P_t(z)$. The $-\rho t$ term indicates that the systematic growth of k_t at rate $-\beta\rho$ would generate a systematic growth in the price level at rate $-\rho$ if M were constant. With M growing steadily at rate g, the net systematic

c

growth rate of the price level is $g-\rho$. This systematic rate of inflation appears additionally in the term $(\alpha/\beta)(g-\rho)$ as a positive effect on $P_t(z)$ for a given value of the nominal money stock. Equivalently, systematic inflation reduces the (expected) holding of real balances. I will discuss below the meaning of the final term, $+\rho$, in the $P_t(z)$ expression.

The expected price level for next period is now

$$EP_{t+1}|I_t(z) = M_{t-1}+2g+(\theta_1+\theta_2)[m_t+(1/\beta)(v_t+\varepsilon_t(z))]$$

$$+(1/\beta)u_{t-1}-\rho(t+1)+(\alpha/\beta)(g-\rho)+\rho.$$

In particular, the gap between $P_t(z)$ and $EP_{t+1}|I_t(z)$ now includes the term $-(g-\rho)$, which is the negative of the systematic rate of inflation. In this model, where commodity supply and demand depend on $P_t(z)-EP_{t+1}|I_t(z)$, it is this effect of systematic growth that leads to influences on output.

The solution for output is determined by substituting the price results into the commodity supply or demand function, as given in eqs. (1) and (2). The result for $y_t(z)$ coincides with eq. (15) except for the new systematic effects,

$$y_t(z) = (\beta_s/\beta)k_t^d+(\beta_d/\beta)k_t^s-(H/\beta)(g-\rho)+\ldots,$$

where the terms that appear in eq. (15) have been omitted. In determining output it is necessary to specify separately the systematic demand and supply, k_t^d and k_t^s, as well as the excess demand, k_t. I assume that individuals plan the systematic growth rate of real balances (real wealth) to equal the systematic growth rate of output. From the above expressions for $P_t(z)$ and $EP_{t+1}|I_t(z)$, it is clear that the systematic growth rate of real balances is ρ. From the $y_t(z)$ expression it is clear that the systematic growth rate of output depends on the systematic growth rates of k_t^d and k_t^s. The condition that the systematic growth of real balances coincides with the systematic growth of output therefore implies a condition on the time paths of k_t^d and k_t^s. Using also the condition that $k_t = -\beta\rho t$, and setting $k_0^d = k_0^s = 0$ for convenience, it can be determined that

$$k_t^d = \rho(1-\beta_s)t,$$

$$k_t^s = \rho(1+\beta_d)t.$$

Substitution into the above expression for $y_t(z)$ yields

$$y_t(z) = \rho t-(H/\beta)(g-\rho)+\ldots.$$

That is, the systematic growth rate of output is, indeed, equal to ρ.

The other property of the output expression is that an increase in the systematic inflation rate, $g - \rho$, reduces output (both actual and full information) if $H > 0$. The mechanism is as follows. An increase in $g - \rho$ implies a lower real rate of return on money, which is the only store of value in the model. Accordingly, there is a substitution effect that reduces current labor supply and raises current consumption demand.[53] This shift raises output when $H > 0$. Of course, this sort of effect is operative here because money serves as the only store of value. Further, the present analysis does not deal with any benefits of holding money that are associated with transaction costs. For these reasons, it seems that the present model is probably more useful for an analysis of unperceived monetary change than for an analysis of systematic inflation.

Finally, I can now comment on the presence of the $+\rho$ terms in the above price expressions. In eqs. (1) and (2), excess commodity demand depends on expected next period's real balances, $M_t + E\Delta M_{t+1}|I_t(z) - EP_{t+1}|I_t(z)$. This formulation is reasonable as long as desired real balances are constant. More generally, it is a gap between expected and desired real balances that would produce an effect on excess commodity demand. It is now apparent that (desired) real balances grow at rate ρ in this model. If the effects of real balances on excess commodity demand are adjusted to take account of this systematic growth in desired real balances, the $+\rho$ terms would no longer appear in the above price expressions. The expression for $y_t(z)$ would be unaffected by this adjustment. Of course, no adjustment at all is required for the case in the text where $\rho = 0$ was assumed.

[53] In a life-cycle model these effects would also alter the distribution of wealth by age. I have not dealt with this type of distribution effect.

References

Barro, R.J., 1972, A theory of monopolistic price adjustment, Review of Economic Studies, January, 17–26.

Barro, R.J. and H.I. Grossman, 1975, Money, employment, and inflation (Cambridge University Press, Cambridge).

Cairnes, J.E., 1873, The course of depreciation, in: Essays in political economy (Kelley, London).

Friedman, M., 1953, The effects of a full-employment policy on economic stability: A formal analysis, in: Essays in positive economics (University of Chicago Press, Chicago).

Friedman, M., 1960, A program for monetary stability (Fordham, New York).

Friedman, M., 1968, The role of monetary policy, American Economic Review, March, 1–17.

Gordon, R.J., 1975, Alternative responses of policy to external supply shocks, Brookings Papers on Economic Activity, no. 1.

Graham, F.D., 1930, Exchange, prices and production in hyper-inflation: Germany, 1920–23 (Princeton University Press, Princeton).

Hall, R.E., 1975, The Phillips curve and macroeconomic policy, in: K. Brunner and A. Meltzer, eds., The Phillips curve and labor markets (North-Holland, Amsterdam).

Lucas, R., 1972, Expectations and the neutrality of money, Journal of Economic Theory, April, 103–24.

Lucas, R., 1973, Some international evidence on output–inflation tradeoffs, American Economic Review, June, 326–34.

Lucas, R., 1975, An equilibrium model of the business cycle, Journal of Political Economy, December, 1113–44.

Lucas, R. and L. Rapping, 1969, Real wages, employment, and inflation, Journal of Political Economy, September/October, 721–54.

Mills, F.C., 1927, The behavior of prices (N.B.E.R., New York).

Mortensen, D.T., 1975, Job matching under imperfect information, in: O. Ashenfelter, ed., Evaluating the labor market effects of social programs, forthcoming.

Phelps, E.S., 1972, Inflation policy and unemployment theory (Norton, New York).

Prescott, E.C., 1975, Efficiency of the natural rate, Journal of Political Economy, December.

Sargent, T. and N. Wallace, 1974, Rational expectations and the theory of economic policy, presented at the Seminar on Rational Expectations at the Federal Reserve Bank of Minneapolis, October.

Sargent, T. and N. Wallace, 1975, 'Rational' expectations, the optimal monetary instrument, and the optimal money supply rule, Journal of Political Economy, April, 241–54.

Simons, H., 1948, Economic policy for a free society (University of Chicago Press, Chicago).

Taylor, J., 1975, Monetary policy during a transition to rational expectations, Journal of Political Economy, October, 1009–22.

Vining, D., 1974, The relationship between relative and general prices, unpublished.

A Capital Market in an Equilibrium Business Cycle Model*

This paper extends previous equilibrium *business cycle* models of Lucas (1973, 1975) and Barro (1976) by incorporating an economy-wide capital market. One aspect of this extension is that the relative price that appears in the supply and demand functions in local commodity markets becomes an anticipated real rate of return on earning assets, rather than a ratio of actual to expected prices. The analysis brings in as a central feature a portfolio balance schedule in the form of an aggregate money demand function. The distinction between the nominal and real rates of return is an important element in the model.

From the standpoint of expectation formation, the key aspect of the extended model is that observation of the economy-wide nominal rate of return conveys current global information to individuals. In this respect the present analysis is distinguished from Lucas's (1975) model, which considered only local (internal) finance. However, my analysis does not deal with the dynamics of capital accumulation, as considered by Lucas, and does not incorporate any other elements, such as inventory holdings, multiperiod lags in the acquisition of information, or the adjustment costs for changing employment that were treated by Sargent (1977), that could produce persisting effects of monetary and other disturbances.

In order to retain the real effects of monetary surprises in the model, it is necessary that the observation of the current nominal rate of return, together with an observation of a current local commodity price, not convey full information about contemporaneous disturbances. Limitation of current information is achieved in the present framework by introducing a contemporaneously unobserved disturbance to the aggregate money demand function, along with an aggregate money supply

*This research was supported by the National Science Foundation. I have benefited from comments by Moses Abramowitz, Bob Hall, Zvi Hercowitz, Robert King, and Leo Leiderman.

Reprinted from *Econometrica*, 48, September 1980, 1393–1417, by permission of The Econometric Society, Evanston, Illinois.

shock and an array of disturbances to local excess commodity demands. Aggregate shocks to the commodity market (to the extent that they were not directly and immediately observable) could serve a similar purpose.

With respect to the effect of money supply shocks on output, the model yields results that are similar to those generated in earlier models. Notably, incomplete current information about the nature of underlying economic disturbances can produce a positive relation between money shocks and the level of output. Furthermore, the coefficient that connects money disturbances to output responses tends to be inversely related to the variance of the money shocks.

A new result concerns the behavior of the anticipated real rate of return on earning assets. Because this variable is the pertinent relative price for commodity supply and demand decisions, it turns out to be unambiguous that positive money surprises raise the anticipated real rate of return. In fact, this response provides the essential channel in this equilibrium model by which a money shock can raise the supply of commodities and thereby increase output. However, it is possible through a sort of *liquidity* effect that positive money surprises can depress the economy-wide nominal interest rate. Given the increase in the real interest rate, this liquidity effect must involve a decrease in the anticipated rate of inflation. The downward movement of the nominal interest rate is less likely to obtain if money shocks exhibit positive serial correlation because the perceived part of money movements would then have a direct positive impact on anticipated inflation.

Since the relative price variable in the commodity supply and demand functions is a real rate of return on earning assets, rather than a ratio of actual to expected prices, there is a less clear connection than in previous models between money shocks and the current price level. Although the typical pattern would still be a positive, but less than one-to-one, short-run response of prices to money shocks, it is now possible that the required positive movement of the anticipated real rate of return would reflect an increase in the nominal interest rate rather than (or as a partial substitute for) a rise in the ratio of current to expected future prices. Abstracting from effects of serial correlation in the money supply process, the model suggests that a strong positive response of the current price level to money shocks would be associated with a strong negative response of the nominal interest rate and vice versa.

The first section sets up the model and presents the basic equilibrium conditions. The analysis proceeds, as in Barro (1976), by postulating "plausible" forms for the supply and demand functions, rather than by presenting and solving an explicit underlying maximization problem. There is, however, an extended discussion of the specification of the relative price and wealth variables in the commodity supply and demand functions. The second section solves the model under conditions of full current information. Although these results involve an independence of the "real" variables from monetary disturbances (including the shock to the aggregate money demand function), they provide a useful frame of reference for the subsequent analysis. The third section solves the model under a specification of incomplete current information, where individuals are limited in their current knowledge of the economy to observations of the economy-wide nominal interest rate and a single local commodity price. A central aspect of the solution involves inferences from the observed current nominal interest rate and local price level to the expected value of the contemporaneously unobserved money shock. The final part of this section provides some interpretations of the principal analytical results.

Setup of the Model

In the current period each individual transacts in two markets: a local commodity market indexed by z, and an economy-wide capital or loanable-funds market that deals in homogeneous, riskless, one-period loans. The number of commodity markets and the number of individuals are assumed constant, so that separate notation is not used below to distinguish aggregate from per capita quantities. The logarithm of the current price on the local commodity market is designated by $P_t(z)$ and the nominal, one-period rate of return on the capital market is denoted by R_t. Aside from holding capital market claims, individuals can hold fiat money, which is a liability of the "government." Changes in the aggregate quantity of money occur through positive or negative transfers from the government to individuals. The size of the transfer varies randomly across individuals and is independent of an individual's own holdings of cash. The analysis does not deal with any deadweight losses associated with governmental transfer–tax programs. The logarithm of the aggregate nominal quantity of money, denoted by M_t, is determined from

$$M_t \equiv M_{t-1} + \mu + m_t, \tag{1}$$

where μ is the constant long-run growth rate of money and m_t indicates the extent to which the current money growth rate departs from μ. I assume that m_t is generated in accordance with the first-order stochastic process,

$$m_t = \rho m_{t-1} + n_t, \tag{2}$$

where $\rho \gtreqless 0$, $|\rho| < 1$, and n_t, the current innovation to money growth, is normally, independently distributed with zero mean and variance σ_n^2. In parts of the subsequent analysis the values of M_t and m_t are currently unobservable, but the lagged values, M_{t-1} and m_{t-1}, are assumed throughout to be contained in current individual information sets.

Each individual's portfolio allocation problem can be viewed as involving a tradeoff between the rate-of-return differential for holding capital market claims rather than money, R_t, and the marginal transactions benefits from holding cash.[1] Overall portfolio balance entails equality between the total amount of cash outstanding and the aggregate demand for money, which I assume can be described in the

---

[1]If these net benefits are always positive then portfolio balance would require R_t to be positive. The form of the money demand function, equation (3) below, does not exhibit this property, although a modification along these lines would not seem to have important implications for the main analysis.

semi-log form,

$$M_t = M_t^d = P_t - \gamma R_t + \delta y_t + \phi_t, \tag{3}$$

where the constant, which would include the fixed number of individuals, has been normalized to zero. In equation (3), M_t is again in logarithmic terms, P_t is the (unweighted) average across markets of the local (log of) commodity prices, $\gamma > 0$ measures the interest rate sensitivity of real money demand, y_t is the (unweighted) average across markets of the local (log of) commodity outputs, and $\delta > 0$ is the elasticity of "per capita" real balances demanded with respect to "per capita output." The shock to aggregate money demand, ϕ_t, is assumed to be independently, normally distributed with zero mean and variance σ_ϕ^2. The realized value of ϕ_t is currently unobservable in some of the subsequent analysis.

The postulated commodity supply and demand functions for market z involve the specification of a relative price term and a wealth variable.

Specification of the Relative Price Variable

The relative price term compares current sale (purchase) opportunities in market z with those anticipated for next period in a randomly selected market. For example, a sale this period is evaluated at the (log of) current price $P_t(z)$ plus the nominal rate of return from date t to $t+1$, R_t, to obtain a comparison with the expected (log of) price next period, $E_z P_{t+1}$. (The subscript z indicates that the expectation of P_{t+1} is conditioned on information available currently in market z.) The relative price term is then $r_t(z) \equiv P_t(z) - E_z P_{t+1} + R_t$—that is, the anticipated one-period real rate of return from the perspective of market z. It is this expression that would be considered in contemplating a shift of labor services, commodity purchases, and so on, from date t to date $t+1$, assuming that any funds (plus or minus) held over time earn nominal interest at rate R_t. By comparison, the earlier analysis in Lucas (1973) and Barro (1976) amounts to treating $R_t = 0$, which is appropriate in a model where the only store of value is money that bears a zero nominal rate of return. The logarithm of local commodity supply, $y_t^s(z)$, is assumed to be positively related to $r_t(z)$, while the log of local demand, $y_t^d(z)$, is negatively related. The impact on demand amounts to the usual positive substitution effect on saving of the anticipated real rate of return. The nature of the income effect associated with a change in $r_t(z)$ is discussed in the section below that deals with the specification of a wealth variable.

In the present model it turns out that expected future values of r are constant—essentially, departures of $r(z)$ from the "normal" real rate of return represent a temporary situation that cannot be predicted to arise in one direction or the other for future periods. Therefore, it is only the current value of the perceived real rate of return that will appear in the commodity demand and supply functions.

The present treatment of the anticipated real rate of return, $r_t(z)$, considers only the supply and demand effects associated with the conditional first moment of P_{t+1}. Generally, higher moments of the conditional distribution of the future price level would also be relevant. For example, suppose that the pertinent relative price variable for determining commodity demand and supply were $E_z[\hat{P}_t(z) e^{R_t}/$

$\hat{P}_{t+1}(z')$], where a caret denotes the level of a variable rather than its logarithm, and z' specifies the randomly selected market visited next period. Assuming $\hat{P}_{t+1}(z')$ to be log-normally distributed, the log of this expected relative price variable is given by[2]

$$P_t(z) + R_t - E_z P_{t+1} + \tfrac{1}{2}\sigma^2,$$

where P_{t+1} is the average across the markets of $P_{t+1}(z')$ and σ^2 is the conditional variance of $P_{t+1}(z')$. This expression differs from the $r_t(z)$ variable specified above by the inclusion of the variance term, $\tfrac{1}{2}\sigma^2$. As long as σ^2 is constant, the use of this expression rather than $r_t(z)$ would modify the subsequent analysis only by adding effects of once-and-for-all shifts in σ^2 on the mean (natural) values of output and the real rate of return. It would also be necessary to relate σ^2 to the underlying parameters of the model, including the variances of the exogenous disturbance terms. Additional variance effects on the supply and demand functions would, of course, arise in a serious analysis of individual choice under uncertainty.

Specification of the Money-Wealth Variable

Since the model does not encompass changes in physical or human capital, the specified wealth variable considers only movements in the money stock.[3] The net money–wealth variable that is pertinent to commodity demand and supply involves four elements: current money stocks, expected future monetary transfers from the government, current money demand, and expected future money demand.

Let $\hat{M}_t(z)$ denote the quantity of nominal money held at the start of the period (before any market trading occurs, but after the transfers from the government) by the aggregate of individuals located currently in market z. Individuals anticipate for future periods an infusion of cash that will accrue as transfer payments from the government. The size of the transfer varies randomly across individuals—in particular, the amount is independent of individual money holdings or of current or future market location. The expected individual nominal transfer for period $t + i$ is therefore equal, aside from a constant of proportionality, to the expected change in total money outstanding for the period, $E_z(\hat{M}_{t+i} - \hat{M}_{t+i-1})$, where $i \geqslant 1$.

Denote the sequence of anticipated future one-period nominal interest rates as $R_{t+1}, R_{t+2}, \ldots$. I treat these future yields as though they were known with certainty, although this assumption is not crucial for the results obtained later.[4] The discount factor applicable to date $t + i$ is then given by

$$\nu_i = \frac{1}{(1 + R_t)(1 + R_{t+1})\cdots(1 + R_{t+i-1})}.$$

[2]See Aitchison and Brown (1969, p. 8).
[3]A change in $r_t(z)$ would generally have an income effect. See the following discussion.
[4]The important condition is $\nu_i = (1+R_{t+i})\nu_{i+1}$, where ν_i is the discount factor for date $t + i$, as defined later.

The nominal present value of current money holdings plus expected future transfers is equal to

$$\hat{M}_t(z) + \sum_{i=1}^{\infty} v_i E_z(\hat{M}_{t+i} - \hat{M}_{t+i-1}),$$

where constants of proportionality have been omitted.

Commodity demand and supply will be influenced by this wealth variable net of the expected portion of wealth *expended* on current and future demands for cash. This net expression would appear in an intertemporal budget equation that involved also the present value of nominal commodity sales and purchases, with the v_i, as defined above, used as discount factors. If the nominal demand for money in period $t+i$ by individuals who are located *at date t* in market z is $\widehat{M}_{t+i}^d(z)$, then the nominal interest earnings in period $t+i+1$ for these individuals are reduced by $R_{t+i}\widehat{M}_{t+i}^d(z)$ relative to a situation where zero cash is held. The expected nominal present value of these interest payments foregone is given by

$$\frac{R_t \hat{M}_t^d(z)}{(1 + R_t)} + \sum_{i=1}^{\infty} v_{i+1} R_{t+i} E_z \hat{M}_{t+i}^d(z).$$

Therefore, the net monetary wealth variable for current participants of market z can be written as

$$\hat{M}_t(z) + \sum_{i=1}^{\infty} v_i E_z(\hat{M}_{t+i} - \hat{M}_{t+i-1}) - \frac{R_t \hat{M}_t^d(z)}{(1 + R_t)} - \sum_{i=1}^{\infty} v_{i+1} R_{t+i} E_z \hat{M}_{t+i}^d(z).$$

Using the condition, $v_i = (1 + R_{t+i})v_{i+1}$, the second term can be modified to yield the equivalent net wealth expression,

$$\hat{M}_t(z) - \frac{1}{(1 + R_t)} E_z \hat{M}_t + \sum_{i=1}^{\infty} v_{i+1} R_{t+i} E_z \hat{M}_{t+i} - \frac{R_t \hat{M}_t^d(z)}{(1 + R_t)}$$
$$- \sum_{i=1}^{\infty} v_{i+1} R_{t+i} E_z \hat{M}_{t+i}^d(z).$$

Suppose now that individuals are identical in the sense that their expected nominal demands for cash in period $t + i$, $E_z \hat{M}_{t+i}^d(z)$, where $i \geqslant 1$, is equal, aside from a constant of proportionality, to the expected total nominal demand for the period, $E_z \hat{M}_{t+i}^d$. The two summations terms above can then be written as

$$\sum_{i=1}^{\infty} v_{i+1} R_{t+i} E_z(\hat{M}_{t+i} - \hat{M}_{t+i}^d),$$

which equals zero since individuals appropriately anticipate portfolio balance to obtain in every (future) period. The simplified net wealth expression can then be written in two equivalent forms:

$$[\hat{M}_t(z) - E_z \hat{M}_t] - \frac{R_t}{(1 + R_t)}[\hat{M}_t^d(z) - E_z \hat{M}_t] = \frac{1}{(1 + R_t)}(\hat{M}_t - E_z \hat{M}_t)$$
$$+ \frac{1}{(1 + R_t)}[\hat{M}_t(z) - \hat{M}_t] + \frac{R_t}{(1 + R_t)}[\hat{M}_t(z) - \hat{M}_t^d(z)]. \qquad (4)$$

116

The first form of the net wealth expression in equation (4) indicates that a net monetary wealth effect arises in market z only when the money held in this market at the start of the period, $\hat{M}_t(z)$, or the local demand for money, $\overparen{M_t^d}(z)$, differs from the perceived value of the aggregate money stock, $E_z\hat{M}_t$. Equal movements in $\hat{M}_t(z)$, $\overparen{M_t^d}(z)$, and $E_z\hat{M}_t$ yield no net effect because the interest foregone associated with current and expected future money demand exactly offsets the present value of current cash plus expected future transfers. For a given value of $E_z\hat{M}_t$, the net wealth position is raised by an increase in $\hat{M}_t(z)$ and lowered by an increase in $\overparen{M_t^d}(z)$ (because of the interest foregone, $R_t\overline{M_t^d}(z)$, on this period's relatively high cash holdings).

The second form of the net wealth expression in equation (4) is convenient because it separates out the last two terms, which add to zero in summations across the markets. The middle term depends on $\hat{M}_t(z) - \hat{M}_t$, which expresses the relative cash position of participants of market z at the start of the period.[5] Since this term adds to zero in summations across the markets, it may represent a shift to relative commodity demand and supply, but it would not (in a linear model) represent an aggregate shift. Since relative commodity demand and supply disturbances to market z are included separately below, it is satisfactory to omit further consideration of this term in the construction of the money–wealth variable.

The last part of the net wealth expression in equation (4) depends on $\hat{M}_t(z) - \hat{M}_t^d(z)$.[6] Since $\hat{M}_t(z)$ represents cash held at the start of the period by participants of market z, portfolio balance does not require this term to equal zero. That is, market z could turn out to be a net importer or exporter of cash during period t. However, overall portfolio balance for the current period does require this term to add to zero (in equilibrium) in summations across the markets. As in the case above, this term can be viewed as a component of the relative commodity demand and supply terms that are introduced separately. Therefore, this term may also be neglected in the construction of the money–wealth variable.

The key element in the money–wealth variable is the first term on the right side of equation (4), which involves the expression, $(\hat{M}_t - E_z\hat{M}_t)$. Note that, since $E_z\hat{M}_t \neq \hat{M}_t$ in each market or on average over z, this term can represent an aggregate net wealth effect that does not vanish in summations across the markets.

Commodity demand and supply will depend on the "real value" of the term, $(\hat{M}_t - E_z\hat{M}_t)/(1+R_t)$. If the real value were defined as the ratio of this nominal magnitude to the current local price level $\hat{P}_t(z)$, then a change in $r_t(z)$ would—with this *real wealth* concept held fixed—involve an important income effect. Since the real rate of return expected at date t for date $t+1$ onward turns out to be constant in the present model, the natural definition of real wealth is in terms of date $t+1$ commodity values. With this wealth concept held fixed, a change in $r_t(z)$ has an

---

[5]This term corresponds to Lucas's (1972) mechanism for generating relative disturbances across markets.

[6]This term is analogous to Mishan's (1958) "cash balance effect [that] comes into operation when the cash available to the community for transactions purposes . . . diverges from the amount of cash that the community desires to hold for this purpose [p. 107]." This concept appears also in Archibald and Lipsey (1958).

income effect that involves only the one-period opportunity for a high (or low) anticipated real rate of return. Since this income effect can reasonably be neglected in a context where decisions are based on *permanent income* over a long horizon, it is then satisfactory to assume that the substitution effects of $r_t(z)$, as discussed earlier, are, in fact, the dominant responses to a change in the current anticipated real rate of return. The expected real value for date $t+1$ of the money–wealth variable, abstracting from the two terms on the right side of equation (4) that cancel in summations across the markets, is

$$\frac{1}{(1 + R_t)} (\hat{M}_t - E_z \hat{M}_t) \cdot (1 + R_t) E_z(1/\hat{P}_{t+1}) = (\hat{M}_t - E_z \hat{M}_t) E_z(1/\hat{P}_{t+1}). \quad (5)$$

In order to remain within the setting of a linear model, it is necessary to make some approximations to the form of the money–wealth variable. Basically, these approximations amount to neglecting some effects of higher moments of the distribution of money growth—that is, errors that are of the same order of magnitude as those committed earlier when the future price variance was neglected as a component of $r_t(z)$. From equation (1), assuming $|\mu| \ll 1$, it is assumed that

$$\hat{M}_t \approx \hat{M}_{t-1}(1+\mu)(1+m_t),$$

where m_t is the nonsystematic part of the money growth rate. With $\hat{M}_{t-1}$ observable at date t, $E_z \hat{M}_t$ is similarly approximated by $\hat{M}_{t-1}(1+\mu)(1+E_z m_t)$, which neglects an effect of a term that depends on the conditional variance of m_t. The money–wealth variable can then be approximated by

$$(m_t - E_z m_t)\hat{M}_{t-1}(1+\mu)E_z(1/\hat{P}_{t+1}). \quad (6)$$

The principal implication of this analysis is that the net money–wealth variable in expression (6) depends on discrepancies between actual and currently perceived money growth, $m_t - E_z m_t$. The net money–wealth variable equals zero when $m_t = E_z m_t$, independently of the anticipated rate of growth of money or prices. It should be noted from the forms of expressions (4) and (5) that this general type of result does not hinge on the approximations made earlier. Furthermore, this conclusion does not depend on the form of the money demand function—which did not enter the analysis—or on the specification of individual information sets, other than their inclusion of the last period's money stock.

Two aspects of the derivation of the net money–wealth variable in the form of equation (6) should be stressed. First, the analysis involves the capitalization of transfers and interest foregone over an infinite horizon. In this context it is not surprising that an increase in current real balances that is accompanied by an equal, permanent increase in the demand for real balances would not generate a net wealth effect that would influence commodity demand and supply.[7]

---

[7]In this respect the analysis parallels the infinite horizon, optimizing model of Sidrauski (1967). The superneutrality of money in his model—that is, the independence of the steady-state real interest rate and

Finally, the major limitation of the present analysis is its failure to incorporate the real role of money as an economizer of transaction costs, and so on—that is, to bring in the real factors that underlie the demand for money. Although these considerations would not seem to invalidate the specification of the net wealth term in expression (6), some other effects might be missed. For example, an increase in the average inflation rate that reduces the average holdings of real cash and correspondingly raises average transaction costs incurred could also influence the work-leisure decision, the demands for productive factors, and so forth. These effects would depend on cross substitutions between the demand and supply of commodities and the demand for money. Sidrauski's (1967) deterministic model, in which real balances provide utility, labor supply is exogenous, and utility is additive over time with a constant utility rate of discount, is an example of a setting where these effects do not arise in the steady state.

Specification of Commodity Supply and Demand Functions

Formally, the local commodity supply and demand functions are written as the semi-log expressions,

$$y_t^s(z) = k^s(z) + \alpha_s r_t(z) - \beta_s(m_t - E_z m_t) + \epsilon_t^s(z), \tag{7}$$

$$y_t^d(z) = k^d(z) - \alpha_d r_t(z) + \beta_d(m_t - E_z m_t) + \epsilon_t^d(z), \tag{8}$$

where y denotes the log of the quantity of commodities (and services), the k terms—assumed to be invariant over time—represent any systematic supply and demand forces that are not captured by the other terms, $r_t(z) \equiv P_t(z) - E_z P_{t+1} + R_t$ is the relative price term discussed earlier, $(\alpha_s, \alpha_d) \geq 0$ are relative price elasticities, $(\beta_s, \beta_d) \geq 0$ are wealth elasticities, and the $\epsilon_t(z)$'s represent local shocks to commodity supply and demand. The realized values of these shocks are not currently observable in some of the subsequent analysis. Aggregate real shocks could be added to equations (7) and (8), as in Barro (1976, pp. 4,5), without altering the nature of the main analysis. The present model does not deal with capital accumula-

---

capital–labor ratio from the growth rate of money—depends on this infinite horizon setup. For additional discussion see Barro and Fischer (1976, Section 3). In a finite horizon setting the liquidation value of terminal real balances would produce a positive net wealth effect when actual and desired real cash rose by the same amounts. The issue is analogous to the question of whether interest-bearing government bonds constitute net wealth. The finiteness of life can generate a net wealth effect for shifts between public debt and taxes because the tax liabilities on future generations are not fully counted. Similarly, a net wealth effect from the level of real money balances would result if the interest foregone associated with the demand for money (net of government transfers) by future generations were not considered. As in the interest-bearing public debt case discussed in Barro (1974), the presence of operative intergenerational transfers can make finite-lived individuals act as though they were infinitely lived with respect to calculations of effective wealth. With a tie to subsequent generations and the knowledge that descendants will also have a demand for money (as well as a claim to future government transfers), an increase in actual and permanently desired real cash balances would not exert a direct wealth effect on commodity demand and supply. In this sense the derivation of the net money–wealth term in the form of equation (6) can apply even when the finiteness of life is brought into the model.

tion, inventory changes, population growth, technological change, and so on, which could be described by exogenous or endogenous movements over time in the k terms of equations (7) and (8). Note that the α_d term in equation (8) corresponds to the usual inverse effect on commodity demand (investment and/or consumption) of the anticipated real rate of return. The α_s term in equation (8) corresponds to the type of relative price effect on supply (of labor services, etc.) that was stressed in Lucas and Rapping (1969). As seems appropriate, this relative price is measured by an anticipated real rate of return—that is, in a manner that is symmetric to the specification of commodity demand.[8]

In order to preserve the linearity of the model (so as to be able to calculate expectations), I have entered the money–wealth variable from expression (6) as a linear term in $(m_t - E_z m_t)$. Essentially, the dependence of the β coefficients attached to this variable in equations (7) and (8) on the level of normal real balances has been lost in this restricted specification. The β_d term in equation (8) expresses the usual positive wealth effect on demand. The β_s term in equation (7) can be viewed as a negative wealth effect on the supply of services—that is, a positive wealth effect on leisure. The general analysis would not be altered—although some ambiguities would be resolved—if the wealth effect on the supply side were omitted.

It is convenient to use the definitions,

$$\alpha \equiv \alpha_s + \alpha_d,$$

$$\beta \equiv \beta_s + \beta_d,$$

$$k = k(z) \equiv k^d(z) - k^s(z),[9]$$

$$\epsilon_t(z) \equiv \epsilon_t^d(z) - \epsilon_t^s(z),$$

where $\epsilon_t(z)$ is assumed to be normally, independently distributed with zero mean and variance σ_ϵ^2. The values of the $\epsilon_t(z)$'s are assumed to net to zero in summations across the markets.[10]

Market-Clearing Conditions

The local commodity price, $\hat{P}_t(z)$—or, equivalently, the anticipated real rate of return from the perspective of market z, $r_t(z)$—must be such as to satisfy the local

[8]Sargent (1973, p. 434) and Sargent and Wallace (1975, pp. 242-243) specify a model in which commodity demand depends on the anticipated real rate of return, but where commodity supply depends on the ratio of the current price to the price that was anticipated for today as of last period.

[9]The equality $k = k(z)$ for all z follows from an arbitrage condition (in the absence of mobility costs over one period of time) that requires all markets to look equally desirable, ex ante, from the standpoint of suppliers and demanders.

[10]This netting to zero is essentially a matter of defining a relative disturbance to local commodity markets. Aggregate real commodity shocks could be considered separately in equations (7) and (8). Serial independence of the $\epsilon(z)$'s can be viewed as a consequence of the arbitrage condition described in note 9.

market-clearing condition, $y_t^s(z) = y_t^d(z)$. This equilibrium condition follows from the constraint that commodities not travel from one local market to another during the current period. However, the existence of a global capital market means that a particular market z can assume a net export (import) position in cash that corresponds to the opposite net position in interest-bearing assets. If relative shocks to money supply and demand in market z are neglected (or viewed as part of the $\epsilon(z)$ terms, as in the present analysis), the net cash and interest-bearing asset positions of market z will depend, from equation (3), on the relative values of local commodity price and output, which will turn out to depend on the realized values of the local commodity market shocks, $\epsilon_t^d(z)$ and $\epsilon_t^s(z)$.

Using equations (7) and (8), the local commodity market-clearing condition requires

$$r_t(z) = (1/\alpha)[k + \beta(m_t - E_z m_t) + \epsilon_t(z)], \tag{9}$$

which implies the expression for local (log of) output,

$$y_t(z) = (\alpha_s/\alpha)[k^d(z) + \epsilon_t^d(z)] + (\alpha_d/\alpha)[k^s(z) + \epsilon_t^s(z)]$$
$$+ [(\alpha_s\beta_d - \alpha_d\beta_s)/\alpha](m_t - E_z m_t). \tag{10}$$

It follows that economy-wide average values, for which the $\epsilon_t(z)$ terms vanish, are given by

$$r_t = (1/\alpha)[k + \beta(m_t - \overline{E_z m_t})], \tag{11}$$

and

$$y_t = (\alpha_s/\alpha)k^d + (\alpha_d/\alpha)k^s + [(\alpha_s\beta_d - \alpha_d\beta_s)/\alpha](m_t - \overline{E_z m_t}), \tag{12}$$

where $\overline{E_z m_t}$ is the economy-wide average value of $E_z m_t$. It is convenient to define

$$y^* \equiv (\alpha_s/\alpha)k^d + (\alpha_d/\alpha)k^s,$$

which is the level of y_t that corresponds to $m_t = \overline{E_z m_t}$ in equation (12).

It is useful to note that equations (9)–(12) have been derived without regard to the form of the demand function for money, the form of the process for m_t, or any specification of current information sets other than their inclusion of M_{t-1}. Equations (9)–(12) are not final solutions for anticipated real rates of return and outputs because they contain the endogenous expectation, $E_z m_t$. However, several results are already apparent:

1. $r_t(z)$ and $y_t(z)$ will depend only on *real* factors—that is, the k and ϵ terms in the present setup—unless money growth differs from its perceived value, $m_t \neq E_z m_t$.[11] Of course, this property depends on the form of the net money–wealth term, as given in expression (6).

[11]An interaction between monetary *neutrality* results for output and interest rates has been stressed by Sargent (1973, pp. 442–444).

2. The anticipated real rate of return is positively related to unperceived money shocks. Typical Keynesian analysis under fixed wages and/or prices argues that (unperceived?) monetary expansion has a depressing, *liquidity* effect on the (nominal and real) rate of return,[12] which leads to an expansion of aggregate demand. Since this scenario leaves unexplained the motivation for increased supply, it is necessary to view output determination in this context as involving an initial excess supply–quantity rationing situation in which production and sales and/or employment are willingly raised without additional price incentives in response to increases in aggregate demand. In the present equilibrium context the initial monetary expansion produces an excess demand for commodities that must be closed by an increase in the anticipated real rate of return.

3. Output can be positively related to unperceived monetary expansion. Demand is directly stimulated (in accordance with the coefficient β_d) by the monetary movement, and supply is raised (in accordance with the coefficient α_s) by the increase in the anticipated real rate of return. However, because of the offsetting wealth and relative price effects, as represented by the coefficients β_s and α_d, the sign of the output response is generally ambiguous. The net effect depends on the same combination of elasticities, $\alpha_s \beta_d - \alpha_d \beta_s$, that appeared in my earlier model that omitted a capital market (1976, p. 11). If the dominant influences are the wealth effect on demand (β_d) and the relative price effect on supply (α_s)—in particular, if the wealth effect on supply β_s is minor—then unperceived monetary expansion will have a positive output effect.

The full solution of the model involves also the determination of R_t and $P_t(z)$. Defining the combination of supply and demand parameters,

$$H \equiv \alpha_s \beta_d - \alpha_d \beta_s,$$

the nominal rate of return can be written from equation (3), with y_t substituted from equation (12) and M_t from equation (1), as

$$R_t = -(1/\gamma)\{M_{t-1}+\mu + m_t - P_t - \phi_t - \delta[y^*+(H/\alpha)(m_t - \overline{E_z m_t})]\}, \quad (13)$$

where y^* is defined after equation (12). The solution for $P_t(z)$ can be written by using the condition $P_t(z) \equiv r_t(z) + E_z P_{t+1} - R_t$, where $r_t(z)$ is determined from equation (9) and R_t from equation (13), as

$$P_t(z) = \frac{k}{\alpha} + \frac{\beta}{\alpha}(m_t - E_z m_t) + \frac{1}{\alpha}\epsilon_t(z) + E_z P_{t+1} \quad (14)$$

$$+ \frac{1}{\gamma}\left\{M_{t-1} + \mu + m_t - P_t - \phi_t - \delta\left[y^* + \frac{H}{\alpha}(m_t - \overline{E_z m_t})\right]\right\}.$$

Note that $E_z P_{t+1}$ and $E_z m_t$ are expectational variables contained on the right side of equation (14).

---

[12]The downward effect of money on the rate of return in this type of model follows unambiguously only if a direct wealth effect of money on consumer demand is omitted.

The solution of the model hinges on the structure of current local information. I assume throughout that information on all lagged variables, including M_{t-1} and m_{t-1}, is available during period t. I work out first the case of full current information—which includes direct observations or sufficient indirect information to infer the values of the three current shocks, m_t, ϕ_t and $\epsilon_t(z)$—and second the case where current information is limited to that contained in the observation of the economy-wide nominal interest rate R_t and a single local commodity price $P_t(z)$.[13] The background of the full current information case is useful in discerning the monetary effects on output, the anticipated real rate of return, and so on, that emerge under conditions of incomplete current information.

Solution of the Model under Full Current Information

Since $E_z m_t = m_t$ obtains under complete current information, the solutions for $r_t(z)$ and $y_t(z)$ follow immediately from equations (9) and (10). Using asterisks to denote the full current information case, the results are

$$r_t^*(z) = (1/\alpha)[k + \epsilon_t(z)],$$

$$y_t^*(z) = (\alpha_s/\alpha)[k^d(z) + \epsilon_t^d(z)] + (\alpha_d/\alpha)[k^s(z) + \epsilon_t^s(z)]. \qquad (15)$$

Therefore, in terms of economy-wide average values, the results are

$$r_t^* = k/\alpha,$$

$$y_t^* = (\alpha_s/\alpha)k^d + (\alpha_d/\alpha)k^s \equiv y^*. \qquad (16)$$

Given the availability of full current information, the average across markets of the anticipated real rate of return corresponds to its *natural* value, k/α, and is independent of the quantity of money, M_t, the current money shock, m_t (or n_t), the aggregate money demand shock, ϕ_t, or the long-run money growth rate, μ. The absence of anticipated inflation-type effects on real rates of return and output depends on the form of the net money–wealth term in expression (6). The average anticipated real rate of return would be affected positively by any aggregate real disturbances that affected excess commodity demand. The local anticipated real rate of return, $r_t(z)$, is positively related to the local excess commodity demand shock, $\epsilon_t(z)$.

As with the anticipated real rate of return, the level of output under conditions of full current information is independent of M_t, m_t, ϕ_t, or μ.[14] The (geometric)

---

[13]It is assumed throughout that the observation of one's own transfer from the government conveys negligible additional information over the observations of R_t and $P_t(z)$. Similarly, the analysis neglects the information provided by observations of one's own money demand shift.

[14]The locally anticipated real rate of return and level of output also respond in the same manner to permanent demand or supply forces, $k^d(z)$ and $k^s(z)$, as to temporary stimuli, $\epsilon_t^d(z)$ and $\epsilon_t^s(z)$. The

average of outputs across the markets is fixed at its *natural* value, $y^* \equiv (\alpha_s/\alpha)k^d + (\alpha_d/\alpha)k^s$.

As a prelude to the incomplete current information case, it is useful to apply a solution procedure for $P_t(z)$ and R_t under full current information that is more formal than would be necessary for this case alone. The method is the one of undetermined coefficients that has been applied before in models that omitted a global capital market in Lucas (1973, 1975) and Barro (1976). Specifically, given the form of the price solution in equation (14)—which involves the expectations, $E_z P_{t+1}$ and $E_z m_t$—and given that m_t is generated from the first-order process that is shown in equation (2), it is apparent for the full current information case that the present "state of the economy" for a local commodity market would be fully described by a specification of values for the variables, $[M_{t-1}, m_t, \phi_t, \epsilon_t(z)]$. I limit attention in the present analysis to solutions that are determined as a stationary function of this state vector—that is, nonstationary price solutions are not considered.

In the present linear model, the local price solution will end up as a linear function of the state variables—that is,

$$P_t(z) = \pi_0 + \pi_1 M_{t-1} + \pi_2 m_t + \pi_3 \phi_t + \pi_4 \epsilon_t(z), \tag{17}$$

where the π's are a set of yet-to-be-determined coefficients. The (geometric) average price across the markets is determined by averaging the $\epsilon_t(z)$'s to zero in equation (17) to be

$$P_t = \pi_0 + \pi_1 M_{t-1} + \pi_2 m_t + \pi_3 \phi_t. \tag{18}$$

The expected price for next period in a randomly selected market is given by taking expectations of an updated form of equation (18) to be

$$E_z P_{t+1} = \pi_0 + \pi_1(M_{t-1} + \mu + E_z m_t) + \rho \pi_2 E_z m_t, \tag{19}$$

where equations (1) and (2) and the conditions, $E_z \phi_{t+1} = E_z \epsilon_{t+1}(z) = 0$, have been used. Under full current information, $E_z m_t = m_t$ can be substituted in equation (19).

The forms for $P_t(z)$, P_t, and $E_z P_{t+1}$ (and the condition $E_z m_t = m_t$) can be substituted into the price level relation that is shown in equation (14). The five π coefficients are then determined by requiring this price condition to hold identically

---

distinction between permanent and temporary shock effects that arose in my earlier model (1976, Appendix 1) does not appear here because of the adjustment of the nominal interest rate (to the value of k in equation (23) below). The permanent–temporary distinction would reemerge if the commodity excess demand response to (perceived) *permanent* movements in $r_t(z)$ were differentiated from the response to *temporary* (perceived) changes. It would be anticipated that excess commodity demand would be substantially more responsive—because of the larger set of intertemporal substitution possibilities—to movements in $r_t(z)$ that were viewed as transitory opportunities for above or below normal real rates of return.

in $[M_{t-1}, m_t, \phi_t, \epsilon_t(z)]$. The solution from this straightforward exercise turns out to be

$$\pi_0^* = \gamma k/\alpha - \delta y^* + \mu(1 + \gamma),$$

$$\pi_1^* = 1,$$

$$\pi_2^* = 1 + \gamma\rho/(1 + \gamma - \gamma\rho),$$

$$\pi_3^* = -1/(1 + \gamma),$$

$$\pi_4^* = 1/\alpha.$$

The implied price level solutions are then

$$P_t^*(z) = \frac{\gamma k}{\alpha} - \delta y^* + \mu\gamma + (M_{t-1} + \mu + m_t) + m_t \left(\frac{\gamma\rho}{1 + \gamma - \gamma\rho} \right)$$
$$- \frac{\phi_t}{1 + \gamma} + \frac{\epsilon_t(z)}{\alpha}, \tag{20}$$

and

$$(E_z P_{t+1})^* = \frac{\gamma k}{\alpha} - \delta y^* + \mu\gamma + (M_{t-1} + \mu + m_t) + \mu$$
$$+ \rho m_t \left(\frac{1 + \gamma}{1 + \gamma - \gamma\rho} \right), \tag{21}$$

where $(M_{t-1} + \mu + m_t) = M_t$ from equation (1) could be substituted in the preceding expressions. Note that, via inverse effects on money demand, there is a negative effect on the price level of normal output y^* and a positive effect of the long-run money growth rate μ. As would be expected, the level of the nominal money stock has a one-to-one, positive price level effect.

The anticipated rate of inflation from the perspective of market z is given by

$$(E_z P_{t+1})^* - P_t^*(z) = \mu + \frac{\rho m_t}{(1 + \gamma - \gamma\rho)} + \frac{\phi_t}{1 + \gamma} - \frac{\epsilon_t(z)}{\alpha}. \tag{22}$$

The average across markets of the expected rate of inflation is influenced positively by the long-run money growth rate μ, by the short-run part of anticipated money growth as represented here by ρm_t, and by the (temporary) aggregate money demand shift, ϕ_t.

Finally, the nominal rate of return, which corresponds to the sum of the average anticipated real rate r_t^* from equation (16) and the average across markets of the anticipated inflation rates shown in equation (22), is equal to

$$R_t^* = \frac{k}{\alpha} + \mu + \frac{\rho m_t}{(1 + \gamma - \gamma\rho)} + \frac{\phi_t}{1 + \gamma}. \tag{23}$$

The nominal interest rate is independent of the level of the money stock, but varies one to one with the long-run money growth rate μ. The excess of current money expansion over μ, m_t, has a temporary positive effect on anticipated inflation if

$\rho > 0$, which implies a positive effect of m_t on R_t^*. The effect of monetary disturbances on the nominal rate of return becomes substantially more complicated and interesting under conditions of incomplete current information, as discussed in the next section.

Solution of the Model under Incomplete Current Information

The full current information setup is now replaced by a specification in which current information for a participant of market z is limited to that contained in the observations of the local commodity price, $P_t(z)$, and the global nominal interest rate, R_t. Because this analysis becomes algebraically very complicated, I have simplified the model by eliminating serial correlation in the money growth process—that is, by assuming $\rho = 0$ in equation (2). In this restricted specification m_t is independently, normally distributed with zero mean and variance σ_m^2. This simplification of the model is probably not serious because the main effect of allowing $\rho \neq 0$ seems to be the corresponding influence of the perceived part of m_t on the anticipated inflation rate and the nominal rate of return, as shown in equations (22) and (23). These effects of serial correlation in money growth did not have any impact on the anticipated real rates of return or levels of output, as given in equation (15), because these variables depend, as shown in equations (9) and (10), only on the unperceived part of money growth, $m_t - E_z m_t$.

The basic equilibrium conditions that are expressed in terms of $r_t(z)$, $y_t(z)$, R_t, and $P_t(z)$ in equations (9), (10), (13), and (14) continue to apply. The forms of the solutions for $P_t(z)$, P_t, and $E_z P_{t+1}$ that are shown in equations (17)–(19) also remain valid.[15] The key difference in the incomplete information setup is that the $E_z m_t$ terms that appear in equations (14) and (19) cannot simply be replaced by m_t.

In the present context $E_z m_t$ is conditioned on the observations of $P_t(z)$ and R_t (and M_{t-1}). It is apparent from equation (17) that the current information contained in the observation of $P_t(z)$ amounts to knowledge of a certain linear combination of the three current shocks—$\pi_2 m_t + \pi_3 \phi_t + \pi_4 \epsilon_t(z)$. Equation (13), which reflects averaging out of market-specific effects, indicates that the observation of R_t conveys information about a particular linear combination of the two aggregate disturbances, which can be denoted as $c_2 m_t + c_3 \phi_t$, where the c's are yet-to-be-determined coefficients. If the model had contained only a single aggregate shock (or no market-specific shock)—for example, if $\sigma_\phi^2 = 0$ had been assumed[16]—then the observations

---

[15]The term $\pi_5 m_{t-1}$ would have to be added to equations (17) and (18) if $\rho \neq 0$ were permitted. The term $\rho \pi_5 E_z m_t$ would then appear in equation (19).

[16]However, the equilibrium solution can break down in the present model when $\sigma_\phi^2 = 0$. The problem is that the observed nominal interest rate cannot impart information about the underlying money shock when the interest rate is invariant with money—as one would expect when $\sigma_\phi^2 = 0$. The introduction of a nonzero value for ρ would eliminate this problem. A more general discussion of this type of equilibrium problem is contained in King (1978).

II THE EQUILIBRIUM APPROACH TO BUSINESS CYCLES

of $P_t(z)$ and R_t would amount to full current information. In other words, the setup with one type of relative disturbance and two types of aggregate disturbances is the simplest stochastic structure within the present general framework that would reveal the consequences of incomplete current information. It would, of course, be possible to introduce additional shocks—for example, aggregate real disturbances to the commodity market can readily be incorporated.

Under the assumption of normally distributed shocks, the conditional expectation of m_t will turn out, as discussed in the Appendix, to be a linear combination of the two pieces of current information—that is,

$$E_z m_t = b_1[\pi_2 m_t + \pi_3 \phi_t + \pi_4 \epsilon_t(z)] + b_2(c_2 m_t + c_3 \phi_t). \tag{24}$$

The formulae for the b_1 and b_2 coefficients are derived in the Appendix.

The average value $\overline{E_z m_t}$, which appears in equations (13) and (14), can be calculated by subtracting $b_1 \pi_4 \epsilon_t(z)$ from the $E_z m_t$ expression that is shown in equation (24). Note that it is now not possible to determine the anticipated real rate of return and the level of output before obtaining the solutions for $P_t(z)$ and R_t. Because $r_t(z)$ and $y_t(z)$ depend on $E_z m_t$, which depends in turn on the realized values of $P_t(z)$ and R_t, it is now necessary to start with the full solution of the model.

The two c coefficients, which express the dependence of R_t on m_t and ϕ_t, can be readily related to the π coefficients by using the expression for R_t that is given in equation (13). Substituting on the right side for P_t from equation (18) and for $\overline{E_z m_t}$ from the use of equation (24), and writing $R_t = \cdots + c_2 m_t + c_3 \phi_t$ (where the dots denote dependence on M_{t-1} and a constant, which are not of interest here) leads to the conditions,

$$c_2(1 + b_2 \delta H/\gamma\alpha) = -(1/\gamma)[1 - \delta H/\alpha - \pi_2(1 - b_1 \delta H/\alpha)],$$

$$c_3(1 + b_2 \delta H/\gamma\alpha) = (1/\gamma)[1 + \pi_3(1 - b_1 \delta H/\alpha)],$$

where it may be recalled that $H \equiv \alpha_s \beta_d - \alpha_d \beta_s$.

The solution for the π coefficients now involves the use of the price level condition from equation (14). The procedure is first to substitute for $P_t(z)$ from equation (17), $E_z m_t$ from equation (24), $E_z P_{t+1}$ from equation (19), and P_t from equation (18), using the preceding two conditions to substitute out for the c_2 and c_3 coefficients in the expression for $E_z m_t$. The five π coefficients are then determined, as in the full current information case, by requiring the resulting equation to hold identically in $[M_{t-1}, m_t, \phi_t, \epsilon_t(z)]$. Not surprisingly, the constant, π_0, and the M_{t-1} coefficient, π_1, correspond to the full current information values. However, the other three coefficients generally differ from those associated with full current information. After a large amount of algebra, the solution for these coefficients turns out to be

$$\pi_2 = \frac{(1 - b_2)(\alpha - \beta - \delta H) + \beta(1 + \gamma)}{(b_1 - b_2)(\alpha - \beta - \delta H) + [\alpha(1 - b_1) + b_1\beta](1 + \gamma)},$$

$$\pi_3 = -\frac{(1-b_2)\alpha + b_2\beta}{(b_1 - b_2)(\alpha - \beta - \delta H) + [\alpha(1-b_1) + b_1\beta](1+\gamma)}, \quad (25)$$

$$\pi_4 = \frac{1}{\alpha(1-b_1) + b_1\beta}.$$

Defining the denominator of the π_2 and π_3 expressions as

$$A \equiv (b_1 - b_2)(\alpha - \beta - \delta H) + [\alpha(1-b_1) + b_1\beta](1+\gamma)$$

and neglecting the constant and M_{t-1} parts of the answer (which correspond to those from the full current information case), the price level solutions are given from equations (17) and (19) by

$$P_t(z) = \cdots + (1/A)[(1-b_2)(\alpha - \beta - \delta H) + \beta(1+\gamma)]m_t$$
$$- (1/A)[(1-b_2)\alpha + b_2\beta]\phi_t + \epsilon_t(z)/[\alpha(1-b_1) + b_1\beta], \quad (26)$$

and

$$E_z P_{t+1} = \cdots + (1/A)[(b_1 - b_2)(\alpha - \beta - \delta H) + b_1\beta(1+\gamma)]m_t$$
$$- (\alpha/A)(b_1 - b_2)\phi_t + b_1\epsilon_t(z)/[\alpha(1-b_1) + b_1\beta]. \quad (27)$$

These results imply the anticipated inflation rate from the perspective of market z,

$$E_z P_{t+1} - P_t(z) = \cdots - (1/A)(1-b_1)(\alpha + \beta\gamma - \delta H)m_t + (1/A)[\alpha(1-b_1) + b_2\beta]\phi_t$$
$$- (1-b_1)\epsilon_t(z)/[\alpha(1-b_1) + b_1\beta]. \quad (28)$$

The solution for the nominal rate of return, which is found by means of the preceding conditions for the c coefficients, is

$$R_t = \cdots - (1/A)(1-b_1)(\alpha - \beta - \delta H)m_t + (1/A)[\alpha(1-b_1) + b_1\beta]\phi_t. \quad (29)$$

The locally anticipated real rate of return is determined from the use of equations (9) and (24) to be

$$r_t(z) = r_t^*(z) + (1/A)(1-b_1)\beta(1+\gamma)m_t + (1/A)(b_1 - b_2)\beta\phi_t$$
$$- (\beta/\alpha)b_1\epsilon_t(z)/[\alpha(1-b_1) + b_1\beta], \quad (30)$$

where $r_t^*(z)$ is the full current information solution (which includes a dependence on $\epsilon_t(z)$) that is shown in equation (15). Finally, the result for local output is

$$y_t(z) = y_t^*(z) + (\alpha_s\beta_d - \alpha_d\beta_s)\{(1/A)(1-b_1)(1+\gamma)m_t + (1/A)(b_1 - b_2)\phi_t$$
$$- (b_1/\alpha)\epsilon_t(z)/[\alpha(1-b_1) + b_1\beta]\}, \quad (31)$$

where $y_t^*(z)$ is the full current information solution (which includes a dependence on $\epsilon_t^d(z)$ and $\epsilon_t^s(z)$), as shown in equation (15).

The above solutions involve the b_1 and b_2 coefficients. The analysis in the Appendix relates these coefficients to the underlying parameters of the model, including the variances, σ_m^2, σ_ϕ^2, and σ_ϵ^2. The Appendix calculations do raise the possibility of multiple solutions for b_1 and b_2, although a unique solution is guaranteed for a plausible range of parameter values. Since I do not presently understand the economics of the multiple solution case, I have limited attention in the text to situations where (b_1, b_2) are uniquely determined. For present purposes, the most important properties of the solutions for b_1 and b_2—in the case of a unique solution—are, assuming that σ_m^2, σ_ϕ^2, and σ_ϵ^2 are all nonzero,

$$0 < b_1 < 1,$$

$$-\infty < b_2 < 1 \qquad \text{if } (\alpha - \beta - \delta H) > 0,$$

$$b_1 > b_2 \qquad \text{if and only if } (\alpha - \beta - \delta H) > 0.$$

The analysis implies also that the A parameter, as defined before equation (26), is unambiguously positive.

I focus the analysis on the case where $H \equiv \alpha_s \beta_d - \alpha_d \beta_s > 0$ and $\alpha - \beta - \delta H \equiv \alpha - \beta - \delta(\alpha_s \beta_d - \alpha_d \beta_s) > 0$. If the income elasticity of money demand, δ, were equal to unity and if α_d and β_s were negligible, this last condition would, assuming $\beta < 1$, require $\alpha > \beta/(1-\beta)$. Larger values of $\alpha_d \beta_s$ imply a less stringent condition—for example, $\alpha > \beta$ would be required when $\alpha_d \beta_s = \alpha_s \beta_d$. In general the assumed inequality requires a high relative price elasticity of excess commodity demand, α, in comparison to the wealth elasticity, β.

Effects of Money Shocks

Consider now the effects of a money shock, m_t. The central conclusion, which was suggested much earlier from the form of equation (9), is that the anticipated real rate of return, $r_t(z)$, rises with m_t, as shown in equation (30). (Note that $1 - b_1 > 0$ and $A > 0$ apply.) Unanticipated monetary expansion causes excess commodity demand, which requires an increase in the anticipated real rate of return in order to restore market clearing. These movements imply a positive response of output to m_t (assuming that $\alpha_s \beta_d - \alpha_d \beta_s > 0$), as shown in equation (31). However, as $\sigma_m^2 \to \infty$, the results from the Appendix imply that $b_1 \to 1$ (all price movements are viewed in this situation as reflecting monetary stimuli on a one-to-one basis), while A remains finite, so that the coefficients on m_t in the $r_t(z)$ and $y_t(z)$ expressions approach zero.[17] When monetary disturbances become the primary source of price fluctuations, the confusion between monetary and other disturbances vanishes, which implies a disappearance of the *real* effects of m_t (on $r_t(z)$ and $y_t(z)$). This phenomenon is an example of Lucas's (1973) effect of monetary variance on the slope of the "Phillips curve."

[17]I have as yet been unable to ascertain whether the relation between σ_m^2 and these coefficients is monotonic.

A basic implication of the model is that the responses of $P_t(z)$, $E_z P_{t+1}$, and R_t to m_t must be consistent with the positive response of $r_t(z) \equiv P_t(z) - E_z P_{t+1} + R_t$. However, the response of the three individual components of the anticipated real rate of return turns out to be sensitive to changes in the specification of the model. In the present setup, assuming $\alpha > \beta + \delta H$, it follows from equation (26) (using the definition of A and the condition $b_2 < 1$) that $P_t(z)$ responds positively and less than one to one with m_t. It also follows from equation (27) (recalling that $b_1 > b_2$) that $E_z P_{t+1}$ responds positively and less than one to one with m_t. Furthermore, the response of $E_z P_{t+1}$ is smaller than that of P_t, so that the anticipated inflation rate, as shown in equation (28), declines with m_t. Finally, equation (29) indicates a negative response of the nominal interest rate to m_t. This behavior corresponds to the usual *liquidity* effect of monetary expansion—with the quantity of money rising more than prices in the *short run*, as implied by equation (26), aggregate portfolio balance requires a decline in R_t (assuming, as guaranteed by the condition $\alpha > \beta + \delta H$, that the rise in y_t does not, by itself, raise money demand sufficiently to balance the increase in supply). Note that the downward response of R_t to m_t is consistent with the upward movement of $r_t(z)$. The intervening variable between the nominal and anticipated real interest rates, which is the expected rate of inflation, moves downward sufficiently—that is, $P_t(z)$ rises sufficiently relative to $E_z P_{t+1}$—to allow R_t and $r_t(z)$ to respond in opposite directions to monetary disturbances. The *short-run flexibility* of the anticipated inflation rate is obviously a crucial element in this analysis. If inflationary expectations responded only sluggishly to current disturbances, it would not be possible for the nominal interest rate to move substantially in the short run in a direction opposite to that of the anticipated real rate of return.

The pattern of response to monetary shocks may be altered if the relative price sensitivity of excess demand, α, is sufficiently weak so that $\alpha < \beta + \delta H$ applies. Equation (29) indicates that R_t would now be positively related to m_t—because the response of money demand from the output channel is stronger than before. The response of $P_t(z)$ to m_t becomes of ambiguous sign and would be negative if $\alpha - \beta - \delta H$ were negative and of sufficient magnitude. However, the response of $E_z P_{t+1}$ to m_t that is shown in equation (27) is still positive (as can be seen by substituting for $b_1 - b_2$ from the formula given in the Appendix), so that the anticipated inflation rate now rises with m_t. A conclusion here is that a weak contemporaneous response of prices to money shocks is possible if it is accompanied by a positive relation between money shocks and the nominal rate of return. The positive response of the anticipated real rate of return now involves an increase in the nominal interest rate that exceeds the rise in the anticipated inflation rate. In the previous (perhaps more likely) case, the rise in $r_t(z)$ involved a decline in the anticipated inflation rate that dominated over a decline in the nominal rate of return.

Another consideration that would affect the relation of money shocks to prices and the nominal interest rate involves serial correlation in the money growth process. This possibility was considered in the initial analysis in the form, $m_t = \rho m_{t-1} + n_t$, but was dropped subsequently on computational grounds. This extension

130

would not seem substantially to alter the determination of $r_t(z)$ and $y_t(z)$, which depend from equations (9) and (10) only on the unperceived parts of monetary expansion. However, anticipated future growth rates of money would involve the term, $\rho E_z m_t = \rho(\rho m_{t-1} + E_z n_t)$. For the case where $\rho > 0$, the current monetary innovation n_t would raise $E_z n_t$ and thereby raise the short-term anticipated money growth rate. This expectation would produce an increase in the short-term anticipated inflation rate and *thereby* raise the nominal interest rate. (A positive effect on price levels would also arise here because of the inverse dependence of money demand on R_t.) The negative *liquidity* effect of monetary expansion on R_t that is shown in equation (29) (when $\alpha > \beta + \delta H$ applies) would therefore be offset by this direct money growth anticipation effect.

Because of the various possibilities for the effects of monetary surprises on price levels and the nominal interest rate, it seems that the most interesting conclusion from the present analysis is that the average anticipated real rate of return, $r_t \equiv P_t - E_z P_{t+1} + R_t$, would rise with m_t. This result is of special interest because it distinguishes qualitatively an implication of the *equilibrium business cycle* approach from the hypothesis of an inverse effect of m_t on r_t that would arise under usual Keynesian analysis.

It is worth emphasizing that the model's results discussed above apply to the anticipated real rate of return—which is the variable that affects commodity supply and demand—and not directly to the realized value of this return. In fact, under the present partial information setup that involves the setting of an economy-wide nominal interest rate, it turns out that the anticipated and realized real rates of return respond in opposite directions to money shocks. Aside from effects that involve the dependence of P_{t+1} on realized values of date $t+1$ disturbances, the economy-wide average anticipated real rate of return differs from the average realized return because of a difference between the economy-wide average value of $E_z P_{t+1}$ and the value of this expectation that would have been formed under full date t information. The latter expectation, labeled EP_{t+1}, follows immediately from updated forms of equations (26) and (20) as $EP_{t+1} = \cdots + m_t$—that is, under full current information, the effect on EP_{t+1} of m_t is one to one (assuming $\rho = 0$) and the effect of ϕ_t is nil. The economy-wide average realized real rate of return depends on the realized values of date $t+1$ disturbances and on the expression, $R_t - (EP_{t+1} - P_t)$. The last term is determined, using the preceding expression for EP_{t+1} and the formulae for $P_t(z)$ and R_t from equations (26) and (29), as

$$R_t - (EP_{t+1} - P_t) = \cdots - (1/A)(1-b_1)(\alpha-\beta)(1+\gamma)m_t$$
$$- (1/A)(b_1 - b_2)(\alpha-\beta)\phi_t. \qquad (32)$$

In contrast with the anticipated real rates of return, as shown in equation (30), the average realized rate moves inversely to m_t.

It seems clear that this result could not obtain if the capital market specified a real interest rate rather than a nominal rate. In the context of an economy-wide real interest rate, the movements in anticipated and realized real rates of return would be coincident and would involve a positive response to money shocks. The *indexation* of nominal returns on financial assets to the average realized value of inflation would therefore alter the model's conclusions concerning the behavior of realized real rates of return.[18]

Effects of Money Demand Shocks

Consider now the impact of an aggregate money demand shock, ϕ_t. The model yields the surprising conclusion that this disturbance has a positive effect on output. However, it should be stressed that the present analysis does not admit the possibility of negative correlation between the money demand shock and a disturbance to aggregate excess commodity demand (which was not included in the model). The existence of this sort of correlation would likely reverse the association between money demand shocks and output movements.

It is clear from equations (9) and (10) that the effect of ϕ_t on $r_t(z)$ and $y_t(z)$ would operate in the present framework solely through an effect on $E_z m_t$. An increase in ϕ_t implies, as would be expected, a decrease in $P_t(z)$ from equation (26) (assuming $\alpha > \beta + \delta H$ so that $b_2 < 1$) and an increase in R_t from equation (29). The former effect leads, in accordance with the coefficient b_1, to a decrease in $E_z m_t$. The latter effect involves, through the coefficient b_2, an ambiguous effect on $E_z m_t$. However, if the latter effect is positive, it must, assuming $\alpha > \beta + \delta H$, be of smaller magnitude than the former effect. Therefore, $E_z m_t$ declines with ϕ_t, which implies—for a given value of m_t—that $r_t(z)$ and $y_t(z)$ would increase. Although a money demand shock is contractionary in the sense of reducing price levels, it is expansionary in terms of leading, via an increase in $(m_t - E_z m_t)$ and a corresponding increase in anticipated real rates of return, to an increase in outputs. It is worth noting that the present example is one in which an output expansion is accompanied by a decline in current prices relative to expected future prices. The result in equation (32) indicates that the effect on realized real rates of return is again opposite to that on anticipated returns.

Effects of Relative Shocks

Finally, a relative excess demand shock $\epsilon_t(z)$ raises $P_t(z)$ (and does not affect R_t) and thereby implies an increase in $E_z m_t$. Consequently, $r_t(z)$ and $y_t(z)$ are determined below their full current information values, as shown in equations (30) and (31). The output solution in equation (31) implies that, in comparison with the full current information case (and assuming $\alpha > \beta + \delta H$ and $\alpha_s \beta_d - \alpha_d \beta_s > 0$), the incomplete current information solution involves *excessive* response to the global

---

[18]The simultaneous presence of economy-wide nominal and real interest rates would imply a qualitative shift in the information structure of the model. The two pieces of current global information implied by this setup would seem to constitute full current information in the present model that includes only two types of aggregate shocks. A satisfactory analysis of this model would seem to require the introduction of additional disturbance terms.

disturbances, m_t and ϕ_t, and *insufficient* response to the local disturbances, $\epsilon_t(z)$. Similar behavior emerged in the model without a global capital market that was constructed in my earlier paper (Barro, 1976, p. 17), although the aggregate money demand–portfolio shock, ϕ_t, did not enter into that analysis.

Concluding Remarks

This theoretical study has focused on the anticipated real rate of return on earning assets as the relative price variable that links monetary shocks to output responses. A monetary disturbance that creates excess demand for commodities raises this anticipated return and thereby eliminates the excess demand. If this relative price variable does have a key role in the transmission of monetary effects, it is likely that the same variable would be important for analyzing the output effects of other variables, such as government purchases of goods and services (see Hall, 1978, and Evans, 1978, in this context). For example, the rate of return mechanism might explain the tendency of total output to rise strongly during wartime. A possible analysis would involve the following elements: (a) Aggregate demand rises initially because the government spending is, first, not a close substitute for private consumption or investment, and second, is not perceived as permanent. These two considerations imply a small initial offsetting decrease in private commodity demand. (b) The consequent increase in the anticipated real rate of return would reduce private demand and also stimulate an increase in the overall supply of goods and services. A strong response on the supply side might account for the observed responsiveness of total output to wartime spending.

There are numerous related issues that could be pursued theoretically—notably, a mechanism for explaining the persisting output effects of monetary and other disturbances could be added to the model. However, I suspect that empirical research would potentially constitute the most fruitful complement to the present theoretical analysis. Key empirical questions are whether monetary disturbances exert the hypothesized positive contemporaneous effect on the anticipated real rate of return and whether the response of this relative price variable can be documented as a central channel for the transmission of real effects of monetary disturbances. The treatment of expectations will be a crucial part of this empirical analysis.

Appendix: Derivation of the Conditional Expectation of Money Growth

The conditional expectation, $E_z m_t$, is expressed in equation (24) in terms of the two pieces of current information and the two coefficients, b_1 and b_2. The b_1 coefficient multiplies the current information implicit in the observation of $P_t(z)$, $\pi_2 m_t + \pi_3 \phi_t + \pi_4 \epsilon_t(z)$, while the b_2 coefficient applies to the current information contained in the observation of R_t, $c_2 m_t + c_3 \phi_t$. The three π coefficients are shown in equation (25), while the two c-coefficients are those attached to m_t and ϕ_t in the formula for R_t in equation (29).

Since the three current disturbances, m_t, ϕ_t, and $\epsilon_t(z)$, are independently, normally distributed with zero mean and known variances, the determination of the b_1 and b_2 coefficients emerges from a straightforward, but tedious, calculation of a conditional expectation. A formula for the present multivariate normal case appears in Graybill (1961, p. 63). An intuitive feel for this formula can be obtained by viewing b_1 and b_2 as least-squares estimates—using the known population variances and covariances—that would emerge from a regression of m_t on the two variables, $\pi_2 m_t + \pi_3 \phi_t + \pi_4 \epsilon_t(z)$ and $c_2 m_t + c_3 \phi_t$. The results can be written from the usual least-squares regression formulae as

$$b_1 = -(c_3/\Delta)(c_2\pi_3 - c_3\pi_2)\sigma_m^2\sigma_\phi^2,$$

$$b_2 = (1/\Delta)[\pi_3(c_2\pi_3 - c_3\pi_2)\sigma_m^2\sigma_\phi^2 + (\pi_4)^2 c_2\sigma_m^2\sigma_\epsilon^2],$$

where the determinant Δ is given by

$$\Delta = (c_2\pi_3 - c_3\pi_2)^2\sigma_m^2\sigma_\phi^2 + (c_2\pi_4)^2\sigma_m^2\sigma_\epsilon^2 + (c_3\pi_4)^2\sigma_\phi^2\sigma_\epsilon^2.$$

After substitution for the π and c coefficients and a substantial amount of manipulation, the two b coefficients can be expressed as

$$b_1 = \frac{\alpha\beta\sigma_m^2\sigma_\phi^2}{\alpha\beta\sigma_m^2\sigma_\phi^2 + \left[\dfrac{(1 - b_1)(\alpha - \beta - \delta H)}{\alpha(1 - b_1) + b_1\beta}\right]^2\sigma_m^2\sigma_\epsilon^2 + \sigma_\phi^2\sigma_\epsilon^2}, \tag{A1}$$

$$b_2 = \frac{\alpha\beta\sigma_m^2\sigma_\phi^2 - \dfrac{(1 - b_1)(\alpha - \beta - \delta H)}{[\alpha(1 - b_1) + b_1\beta]^2}\left\{(1 + \gamma)[\alpha(1 - b_1) + b_1\beta] + b_1(\alpha - \beta - \delta H)\right\}\sigma_m^2\sigma_\epsilon^2}{\alpha\beta\sigma_m^2\sigma_\phi^2 - b_1(1 - b_1)\left[\dfrac{\alpha - \beta - \delta H}{\alpha(1 - b_1) + b_1\beta}\right]^2\sigma_m^2\sigma_\epsilon^2 + \sigma_\phi^2\sigma_\epsilon^2}. \tag{A2}$$

Unfortunately, the solutions for b_1 and b_2 cannot be written as closed-form expressions.

The solution in equation (A1) can be expressed as a cubic in the coefficient b_1. It is possible to obtain necessary and sufficient conditions in terms of the parameters (σ_m^2, σ_ϕ^2, σ_ϵ^2, α, β, δH) for the existence of a single real root. The general conditions are very complicated, but a sufficient condition for one real root turns out to be

$$(\beta^2\sigma_\phi^2)/\sigma_\epsilon^2 > (8/27)[(\alpha - \beta - \delta H)/\alpha]^2. \tag{A3}$$

Therefore, if σ_ϕ^2 is not too small relative to σ_ϵ^2 and/or if $|\alpha - \beta - \delta H|$ is small, a single real root is guaranteed. However, there seems to be a range of parameter values that yield three real roots for b_1.

The solution in equation (A2) relates b_2 one to one to the value of b_1. Therefore, a unique solution for b_1 implies a unique solution for b_2 and vice versa.

There seems to be a range of parameter values that yield three separate real solutions for (b_1, b_2). I do not presently see the economic meaning of these multiple equilibria. For some discussion of this type of problem, see King (1978). For present purposes I carry out the rest of the analysis under the assumption that the parameter values are such as to imply a single real solution for (b_1, b_2).

It is convenient to have an expression for the difference between b_1 and b_2, which can be written as

$$(b_1 - b_2) = \frac{(1 - b_1)(1 + \gamma)(\alpha - \beta - \delta H)\sigma_m^2 \sigma_\epsilon^2}{[\alpha(1 - b_1) + b_1\beta]\left\{\alpha\beta\sigma_m^2\sigma_\phi^2 - b_1(1 - b_1)\left[\dfrac{\alpha - \beta - \delta H}{[\alpha(1 - b_1) + b_1\beta]}\right]^2 \sigma_m^2\sigma_\epsilon^2 + \sigma_\phi^2\sigma_\epsilon^2\right\}} \cdot \text{(A4)}$$

The subsequent discussion assumes that the parameters $(\sigma_m^2, \sigma_\phi^2, \sigma_\epsilon^2, \alpha, \beta)$ are all positive. The condition $0 < b_1 < 1$ then follows from inspection of equation (A1).

The condition $b_2 < 1$ if $\alpha - \beta - \delta H > 0$ is implied by equation (A2). The result follows if the denominator on the right side of the equation can be shown to be positive because the second term of the numerator (which is negative if $\alpha - \beta - \delta H > 0$) can, since $0 < b_1 < 1$, be readily shown to be of larger magnitude than the middle term of the denominator. The denominator is positive for some values of $(\sigma_m^2, \sigma_\phi^2, \sigma_\epsilon^2)$—for example, as $\sigma_m^2 \to 0$ and $b_1 \to 0$, the denominator would become positive since $\sigma_\phi^2\sigma_\epsilon^2 \neq 0$. Further, the denominator cannot pass through zero because this expression equalling zero can be shown to be inconsistent with the expression for b_1 that is given in equation (A1). With b_2 a continuous function of the σ^2's (in the case of unique solutions for b_1 and b_2), it follows that the denominator must be positive throughout.

The condition $b_1 > b_2$ if and only if $\alpha - \beta - \delta H > 0$ follows from equation (A4), because $0 < b_1 < 1$ and the expression in large brackets in the denominator of the right side of the equation is positive from the argument in the preceding paragraph. It also follows from the form of the expression for $(b_1 - b_2)$ in equation (A4) that the A parameter, as defined above equation (26) in the text, is unambiguously positive.

The following limiting conditions for the b coefficients are implied by equations (A1) and (A2):

$$\sigma_m^2 \to 0 \quad \Rightarrow (b_1, b_2) \to 0,$$

$$\sigma_m^2 \to \infty \quad \Rightarrow (b_1, b_2) \to 1,$$

$$\sigma_\phi^2 \to 0 \quad \Rightarrow b_1 \to 0, \qquad b_2 \to -\infty \cdot \text{sign}(\alpha - \beta - \delta H),$$

$$\sigma_\phi^2 \to \infty \quad \Rightarrow (b_1, b_2) \to \frac{\alpha\beta\sigma_m^2}{\alpha\beta\sigma_m^2 + \sigma_\epsilon^2} \, \epsilon \, [0,1],$$

$$\sigma_\epsilon^2 \to 0 \quad \Rightarrow (b_1, b_2) \to 1,$$

$$\sigma_\epsilon^2 \to \infty \quad \Rightarrow b_1 \to 0, \qquad b_2 \to -\frac{(\alpha - \beta - \delta H)(1 + \gamma)\sigma_m^2}{\alpha\sigma_\phi^2} =$$

$$-(+) \cdot \text{sign}(\alpha - \beta - \delta H).$$

References

Aitchison, J., and J. A. C. Brown, *The Lognormal Distribution,* Cambridge, University Press, 1969.

Archibald, G. C., and R. G. Lipsey, "Monetary and Value Theory: A Critique of Lange and Patinkin," *Review of Economic Studies,* 26, October 1958, 1–22.

Barro, R. J., "Are Government Bonds Net Wealth?" *Journal of Political Economy,* 82, November–December 1974, 1095–1117.

Barro, R. J., "Rational Expectations and the Role of Monetary Policy," *Journal of Monetary Economics,* 2, January 1976, 1–32.

Barro, R. J., and S. Fischer, "Recent Developments in Monetary Theory," *Journal of Monetary Economics,* 2, April 1976, 133–167.

Evans, P., "The Timing and Duration of Fiscal Policy in a Neoclassical Model," unpublished, Stanford University, 1978.

Graybill, F. A., *An Introduction to Linear Statistical Models,* vol. 1, New York, McGraw-Hill, 1961.

Hall, R. E., "Intertemporal Substitution and Aggregate Fluctuations," unpublished, 1978.

King, R., "Asset Markets and the Neutrality of Money," unpublished, University of Rochester, 1978.

Lucas, R. E., "Expectations and the Neutrality of Money," *Journal of Economic Theory,* 4, April 1972, 103–124.

Lucas, R. E., "Some International Evidence on Output-Inflation Tradeoffs," *American Economic Review,* 63, June 1973, 326–334.

Lucas, R. E., "An Equilibrium Model of the Business Cycle," *Journal of Political Economy,* 83, December 1975, 1113–1144.

Lucas, R. E., and L. Rapping, "Real Wages, Employment and Inflation," *Journal of Political Economy,* 77, September–October 1969, 721–754.

Mishan, E. J., "A Fallacy in the Interpretation of the Cash Balance Effect," *Economica,* 25, May 1958, 106–118.

Sargent, T. J., "Rational Expectations, the Real Rate of Interest, and the Natural Rate of Unemployment," *Brookings Papers on Economic Activity,* 2, 1973, 429–472.

Sargent, T. J., "The Persistence of Aggregate Employment and the Neutrality of Money," unpublished, 1977.

Sargent, T. J., and N. Wallace, "Rational Expectations, the Optimal Monetary Instrument, and the Optimal Money Supply Rule," *Journal of Political Economy,* 83, April 1975, 241–254.

Sidrauski, M., "Rational Choice and Patterns of Growth in a Monetary Economy," *American Economic Review,* proceedings, 57, May 1967, 534–544.

5

Unanticipated Money Growth and Economic Activity in the United States*

The hypothesis that forms the basis of this empirical study is that only the unanticipated components of movements in money affect real economic variables like the unemployment rate or the level of output. This hypothesis is explicit in *rational expectation* monetary models, such as those of Lucas (1972, 1973), Sargent and Wallace (1975), and Barro (1976). However, the proposition that only the unanticipated part of money movements has real effects is clearly more general than the specific setting of these models.

In order to implement and test the hypothesis empirically, it is necessary to quantify the notions of anticipated and unanticipated money movements. Accordingly, the first part of the analysis specifies a simple model of the money growth process. The variables that turn out empirically to have a systematic effect on U.S. money growth, using annual observations from 1941 to 1978, are a measure of federal government expenditures relative to "normal," a lagged unemployment rate, and two lagged values of money growth. Anticipated money growth is then viewed as the prediction that could have been obtained by exploiting the systematic relation between money growth and this set of independent variables.

The measure of unanticipated money growth—actual growth less the anticipated portion—that is obtained in the first section is used in the second section as an explanatory variable for the unemployment rate and real GNP, which are the real economic variables that are focused on in the present study. Over the 1946–1978

*This chapter updates results reported in my previously published works: "Unanticipated Money Growth and Unemployment in the United States," *American Economic Review*, March 1977; "Unanticipated Money, Output, and the Price Level in the United States," *Journal of Political Economy*, August 1978; "Unanticipated Money Growth and Unemployment in the United States: Reply," *American Economic Review*, December 1979; and "Unanticipated Money and Economic Activity," Part I, in S. Fischer, ed., *Rational Expectations and Economic Policy*, 1980. This research was supported by the National Science Foundation.

period, the contemporaneous and one annual lag value of the constructed measure of unanticipated money growth turn out to have effects that are significantly negative on the unemployment rate and positive on output. Furthermore, the hypothesis that only the unanticipated part of money expansion influences these real variables receives support from some empirical tests.

The third section extends the framework to a consideration of the price level and hence to the rate of inflation. The nature of the monetary influence on the price level is more complicated than that for output or the unemployment rate, because both anticipated and unanticipated movements in money must be taken into account. In fact, a key hypothesis to be tested is that anticipated movements in the money stock (with expected rate of inflation-type effects held fixed) would be reflected in one-to-one, contemporaneous movements of the price level. Although the estimated monetary effects on the price level accord in important respects with the theoretical propositions, there are also some substantial empirical puzzles. The unexplained results include an estimated response of the price level to monetary shocks that is elongated substantially relative to the response of output, and some cross-equation coefficient discrepancies between the money growth and price level equations.

Analysis of Money Growth

Setup of the Equation

The money growth equation applies to annual observations for the 1941–1978 period. The dependent variable is the logarithmic first difference of the annual average of the M1 concept of the money stock.[1] Independent variables are those described in Barro (1977, pp. 101–104); which include a measure of real federal expenditures relative to normal, the lagged unemployment rate, and two lagged values of money growth.

The federal spending variable is intended to capture an aspect of the revenue motive for money creation. If inflationary finance is less subject to adjustment costs than are other forms of taxation, the money growth rate would be especially sensitive to short-run changes in real federal spending.[2] On the other hand, permanent expansions of spending may be met principally by conventional taxation; empirically, the effect on money growth of current real federal spending is insignificant once the influences of real spending relative to normal has been held fixed.

The federal spending variable is defined as

$$FEDV \equiv \log(FED) - [\log(FED)]^*,$$

where FED is real federal expenditure (nominal spending divided by the GNP

---

[1]Earlier investigations in Barro (1975) indicated far less explanatory power for the unemployment rate or output from the M2 or high-powered money definitions of the money stock.

[2]This effect is at least diminished by the possibility of issuing interest-bearing debt. See Barro (1979a).

deflator) and [log(FED)]* is an exponentially declining distributed lag of log(FED), using an adaptation coefficient of $\beta = .2$ per year (see note 7 on the choice of β).[3] Values of $FEDV$ corresponding to this value of β are tabulated from 1941 to 1978 in Table 3. It would be preferable to base the $FEDV$ variable on a dynamic model in which the actual time series process for federal expenditure was utilized to generate predictions of future values of spending. Some progress along these lines is reported in another paper, Barro (1979c).

The money growth rate equation includes also a measure of lagged unemployment. A positive response of money growth to this variable could reflect at least two elements. First, there would be the conventional countercyclical policy response to the level of economic activity. (However, the subsequent analysis raises questions concerning the efficacy of this type of policy.) Second, a decline in real income lowers holdings of real balances, which would reduce the amount of government revenue from high-powered money issue for a given value of the money growth rate. An offsetting expansion of money growth is likely to result.

Finally, the money growth equation includes as *explanatory* variables two lagged values of money growth. These lagged dependent variables would pick up any elements of serial dependence or lagged adjustment that have not been captured by the other independent variables.[4]

The form of the systematic part of the money growth rate equation is

$$DM_t = \alpha_0 + \alpha_1 DM_{t-1} + \alpha_2 DM_{t-2} + \alpha_3 FEDV_t + \alpha_4 \log[U/(1-U)]_{t-1}, \quad (1)$$

where M_t is an annual average of the M1 definition of the money stock,[5] $DM_t \equiv \log(M_t/M_{t-1})$, $FEDV_t \equiv \log(FED_t) - [\log(FED)]_t^*$, as defined above and in the notes to Table 3, and U is the annual average unemployment rate in the total labor force, which includes military personnel. The form in which the unemployment rate enters corresponds to the specification of the unemployment rate equation as set out below. Over the sample, where U is much less than 1, the α_4 coefficient relates proportional changes in the unemployment rate approximately to percentage point changes of the money growth rate.

The estimation of equation (1) weighs the World War II observations less heavily

[3]As defined, the $FEDV$ variable is not normalized to make its long-run average value equal zero. Secular growth of the public sector implies that the typical measured value of $FEDV$ is positive. It turns out that constant growth of real expenditures at rate g would generate a $FEDV$ value of $g(1-\beta)/\beta$, which equals $4g$ at $\beta = .2$. An adjustment of the $FEDV$ variable for this effect would alter only the constant term in the money growth rate equation. From 1949 to 1978, the average annual growth rate g is .047, so that the corresponding *long-run average* value of $FEDV$ is .19. However, real growth of the public sector at almost 5% per year would not be permanently sustainable.

[4]Values of the federal government deficit relative to GNP are insignificant in a money growth equation when the $FEDV$ variable is also included. Lagged values of inflation rates or interest rates were also unimportant. However, lagged change-in-interest-rate variables do have some explanatory value for money growth (in a negative direction!), which would be worth further examination.

[5]The data before 1947 from Friedman and Schwartz (1970, Table 2) have been adjusted upward by about 1½% to take account of a later revision in the money stock concept. This refinement affects the money growth rate only for 1947. See the notes to Table 2.

than the postwar values. This differential weighting is appropriate because of the larger error variance that apparently prevailed before 1946.[6] The observations on each variable (including the constant) from 1941 to 1945 are multiplied by .36; a value that was determined jointly with the estimation of the coefficients in equation (1) from a maximum likelihood criterion. Each observation from 1946 to 1978 receives a unit weight in the estimation.

Separately Estimated Money Growth Rate Equation

Using the weighting scheme described above and employing annual observations from 1941 to 1978, the least-squares estimates of the money growth rate equation are, with standard errors in parentheses,

$$DM_t = \underset{(.023)}{.097} + \underset{(.14)}{.48DM_{t-1}} + \underset{(.12)}{.17DM_{t-2}} + \underset{(.015)}{.071FEDV_t} + \underset{(.008)}{.031 \cdot \log[U/(1 - U)]_{t-1}},$$

$$\hat{\sigma} = .014, D - W = 1.9, \tag{2}$$

where $\hat{\sigma}$ is the standard error of estimate that is applicable to the error term for the post–World War II period. Residual serial correlation is not a problem for the estimated equation, as measured either by the Durbin–Watson statistic of 1.9 or by more appropriate direct estimation of an autoregressive process for the error term.

Consider first the coefficient on the federal expenditure variable $FEDV$.[7] The estimated value of .071 implies that a 10% increase in federal expenditure—holding fixed the normal value of expenditure and lagged values of money growth—would raise DM_t by about 7/10 of a percentage point per year. Historically, the extreme values of the $FEDV$ variable have occurred during and immediately following wars. For example, the 1943 value of $FEDV = 1.37$ implies (with lagged values of DM held fixed, so that .071 is the applicable *short-run* coefficient) that DM_t would be 8.4 percentage points per year higher than if $FEDV$ had taken on its average value (note 3). On the other hand, the 1947 value of $FEDV = -.34$ implies that DM_t would be 3.8 percentage points per year below that corresponding to the average value of $FEDV$.

Consider next the coefficient on the lagged unemployment rate variable. The estimated value of .031 implies that a 10% increase in U—that is, an increase by roughly one-half percentage point starting from $U = .05$—would imply a reaction

---

[6]Examination of residuals from equations that are extended to the pre-1941 period suggests that the shift in error variance pertains to a change to a more predictable year-to-year monetary process in the "Full Employment Act" period following World War II, rather than to an effect of the war, per se. Detailed analysis of this change would require a satisfactory specification of the money growth equation for the interwar period, which has not yet been accomplished.

[7]Based only on the fit of the money growth equation, the maximum likelihood estimate of the adaptation coefficient β is close to .20, with an asymptotic 95% confidence interval of (.10, .50). Since the results for the unemployment rate, output, and the price level were not sensitive to variations in β over an interval from .15 to .40, I have limited the reported results to the case where $\beta = .20$.

of next year's money growth rate by about 3/10 of a percentage point per year. In other words each one percentage point change in the unemployment rate feeds back on next year's money growth rate by the amount of roughly 6/10 of a percentage point per year.

Finally, the regression results indicate positive persistence effects with an estimated coefficient for DM_{t-1} of .48 and DM_{t-2} of .17. The remaining analysis is not altered appreciably if the marginally significant DM_{t-2} variable is deleted from the equation. However, the estimated coefficient of this variable does differ significantly from zero in some of the jointly estimated systems of equations that are discussed in the following.

A notable aspect of the estimated equation is that it implies a normal, or long-run average, value for the money growth rate. For given values of the constant term and the federal expenditure and unemployment rate variables, the equation specifies the mean value of DM; both in a short-run context conditional on realizations for DM_{t-1} and DM_{t-2}, and also in a long-run unconditional sense. For example, if the unemployment rate is 4.6%, the average estimated *natural rate* during the 1960s as discussed later, and if the *FEDV* variable takes on its "average" value of .19 (note 3), the implied long-run mean value of DM is 4.7% per year. For a natural unemployment rate of 6.3%, which turns out to be the estimate for 1978, the corresponding long-run mean value for DM is 7.7% per year.[8]

Prior Predictions of Money Growth Rates

For the present analysis, the purpose of fitting a money growth rate equation is to obtain a division of total monetary change into anticipated and unanticipated components. There is a basic problem to consider in using an estimated equation to specify the concept of anticipated money growth. Consider the formulation of this anticipation for date t, $\widehat{DM}_t$. This anticipation could be based on information that was available up to date $t-1$, and might include also partial information applicable to date t. However, $\widehat{DM}_t$ should not be based on any information that becomes available only after date t. For example, if the estimated values from the DM regression for the 1941–1978 period were used to obtain $\widehat{DM}$ for 1950, then information subsequent to 1950 would be used to "predict" that year's money growth rate. Specifically, later observations on $(DM, FEDV, U)$ would be used to estimate the coefficients of the DM relation, and these coefficients would then be applied to the 1950 values of the independent variables to obtain $\widehat{DM}$ for 1950. However, it should be noted that the manner in which later observations affect earlier values of $\widehat{DM}$ is solely through pinning down the estimates of the coefficients in the DM equation. If individuals have information about the money growth structure beyond that conveyed in prior observations—for example, from the experiences of other countries or on theoretical grounds—then the use of the overall sample period, 1941–1978, may be reasonable even for the earlier dates.

[8]At the 1979 value of $FEDV = .13$, the long-run mean value of DM would be only 6.0% per year.

A procedure that avoids the use of later observations to generate earlier predictions involves obtaining $\widehat{DM}_t$ from a regression in which the coefficients are estimated from data only up to date $t-1$. In this approach there would be as many DM equations, each incorporating data up to $t-1$, as there were predicted values $\widehat{DM}_t$. In this context it would also be natural to consider the possibility of time-varying coefficients, which would entail weighting the observations so that more recent information was counted more heavily in forming predictions.[9]

In an earlier study (Barro, 1975), I constructed money growth rate predictions that were based solely on prior observations. Since it turned out that the implications for the analysis of unemployment, output, and the price level were minor, I have not included this discussion. For the present analysis I use the estimated values of DM from the overall sample 1941 to 1978 to form a time series of anticipated money growth, $\widehat{DM}$. Unanticipated money growth is then given by $DMR \equiv DM - \widehat{DM}$.[10]

Analysis of the Unemployment Rate and Output

Setup of the Analysis

The effects of monetary expansion on the unemployment rate and output are measured by the impact of current and lagged values of unanticipated money growth, $DMR \equiv DM - \widehat{DM}$. The number of lags to introduce was not established from a priori reasoning, although the models of Lucas (1975) and others discussed in my survey paper (this volume, paper no. 2) provide a general theoretical rationale for persisting real effects of monetary surprises. Empirically, it turns out that the current and one annual lag value of DMR have significant effects on the unemployment rate and output.[11]

In addition to monetary influences, the unemployment rate and output equations include the contemporaneous value of real federal purchases. Lagged values of this variable turned out to be unimportant. A change of concept either to total government purchases or to defense purchases has a minor effect on the results. A detailed theoretical and empirical analysis of the role of government purchases is contained in Barro (1979c).[12] The output equation includes also a time trend, which is intended to capture the secular movement of "normal" output.

[9]Heavier weighting of recent observations can be rationalized along the lines of the adaptive regression model, as discussed in Cooley and Prescott (1973). A similar procedure that uses the Kalman filter is discussed in Germany and Srivistava (1979).

[10]Note that $\widehat{DM}_t$ is calculated from the contemporaneous value of $FEDV$, rather than from a lagged value. The rationale is that the principal movements in $FEDV$, which are dominated by changes in wartime activity, would be perceived sufficiently rapidly to influence $\widehat{DM}$ without a lag. For example, in 1946 the value of $\widehat{DM}$ is much lower than in 1945 because of the contemporaneous downward movement in $FEDV$.

[11]In earlier analyses that used as an explanatory variable a measure of military personnel (see note 12), a second annual lag of the monetary shock was also significant.

[12]The federal purchases variable replaces a related measure of military personnel that was used earlier (Barro, 1977, pp. 106–107). The role of the military variable in unemployment rate equations that were

The forms of the unemployment rate and output equations are[13]

$$\log[U/(1-U)]_t = a_0 + a_1 DMR_t + a_2 DMR_{t-1} + a_3(G/Y)_t + \epsilon_t^U, \qquad (3)$$

$$\log(Y_t) = b_0 + b_1 DMR_t + b_2 DMR_{t-1} + b_3 \cdot \log(G_t) + b_4 \cdot t + \epsilon_t^Y. \qquad (4)$$

The new variables included in equations (3) and (4) are G, federal purchases in 1972 dollars; Y, GNP in 1972 dollars; t, time trend; ϵ_t, stochastic error terms with the usual desirable properties including serial independence. I consider below some effects of allowing for first-order autoregressive processes for the error terms. The possible endogeneity with respect to ϵ_t^U of the Y variable, which appears through the G/Y variable in equation (3), could cause some estimation problems. However, the estimates were altered negligibly when the variable $(G/\hat{Y})_t$ was used as an instrument for $(G/Y)_t$, where $\hat{Y}_t$ is an estimated value of Y_t based on equation (4). I report only the results with $(G/Y)_t$ included directly in the form of equation (3).

Estimated Equations Based on Separate Estimates of
Unanticipated Money Growth

I consider first estimation of unemployment rate and output equations for which the *DMR* values are the residuals from the separately estimated money growth rate equation (2). This procedure seemed attractive initially because it permitted a separation between estimates of the monetary process and the use of these estimates to explain other variables. This two-stage procedure yields consistent estimates, but there is an efficiency loss from preventing the coefficient estimates in equation (2) from weighing the effects on the fit of the other equations through the calculation of the *DMR* series. An efficient technique entails joint, maximum likelihood estimation of equations (1), (3), and (4), taking account of the cross-equation restrictions implied by the definition $DMR_t \equiv DM_t - \widehat{DM}_t$, where $\widehat{DM}_t$ is an estimated value from equation (1). Further discussion of this issue appears in Leiderman (1980), and more general cross-equation estimation issues are considered in Hansen and Sargent (1979a,b). Jointly estimated systems and related tests of cross-equation coefficient restrictions appear later in this section.

With residuals from equation (2) used to measure the *DMR* variable, the esti-

---

stratified by sex and age and the results in output and price level equations were difficult to reconcile with my original interpretation of this variable (Barro, 1978, pp. 553, 555, 566–567). I have also excluded a minimum wage rate variable (Barro, 1977, p. 107), because its effect is now insignificant in unemployment rate equations (with the military variable excluded or, in any case, for samples starting in 1949 rather than 1946). This variable is also insignificant in output equations. I have been unable to isolate real effects of terms-of-trade or unemployment insurance variables.

[13] The logistic form for equation (3) confines the unemployment rate to the interval $(0,1)$; in particular, the marginal effect of the *DMR* variable on U approaches zero as $U \to 0$ or $U \to 1$. For the sample period, $\log(U)$ provides a satisfactory approximation to the dependent variable. It appears that the very low unemployment rates during World War II would be better explained if the lower asymptote for U were set at a positive value in the neighborhood of .005 rather than at 0; that is, if the dependent variable took the form, $\log[(U - .005)/(1 - U)]$. See the discussion later in this chapter.

mated unemployment rate equation for annual observations from 1946–1978 is, with standard errors in parentheses,

$$\log[U/(1 - U)]_t = -2.41 - 4.9DMR_t - 11.3DMR_{t-1} - 5.3(G/Y)_t,$$
$$(.13) \quad (2.4) \quad\quad (2.4) \quad\quad (1.1)$$

$$R^2 = .65, \quad \hat{\sigma} = .18, \quad D - W = 1.4. \tag{5}$$

There is some question whether the specified equation accords with the immediate post–World War II experience; in particular, the actual values of the unemployment rates for 1947–1948 of .038 and .037 are well below the corresponding estimates of .054 and .055, respectively. In any event the fit and residual serial correlation properties of the equation are improved substantially if the sample begins in 1949 rather than 1946.[14] Over the 1949–1978 period the estimated equation is

$$\log[U/(1 - U)]_t = -2.25 - 5.8DMR_t - 10.8DMR_{t-1} - 6.4(G/Y)_t,$$
$$(.11) \quad (2.0) \quad\quad (2.0) \quad\quad (0.9)$$

$$R^2 = .78, \quad \hat{\sigma} = .14, \quad D - W = 1.7. \tag{6}$$

For the case of real GNP, the estimated equation for annual observations from 1946–1978 is

$$\log(Y_t) = 2.92 + 1.00DMR_t + 1.09DMR_{t-1} + .070 \cdot \log(G_t) + .0330 \cdot t,$$
$$(.04) \quad (.23) \quad\quad (.23) \quad\quad (.013) \quad\quad (.0004)$$

$$R^2 = .998, \quad \hat{\sigma} = .017, \quad D - W = 1.5. \tag{7}$$

No important changes occur in the estimated output equation if the immediate post–World War II observations are deleted.

Equations (5)–(7) exhibit a moderate amount of positive serial correlation in the residuals. However, the estimated coefficients and standard errors are altered only in minor ways if explicit estimation of a first-order autoregressive error process is included. For the unemployment rate equation over a 1947–1978 sample, the estimated autoregressive error coefficient is $\hat{\rho} = .33$, s.e. $= .19$, with the other estimates differing negligibly from those shown in equation (5). Similarly, for the output equation over 1947–1978, the estimate is $\hat{\rho} = .27$, s.e. $= .19$, with little changes in the other estimates from those shown in equation (7). Lagged dependent variables also do not play a major role if added to the equations. The estimated

[14]This discrepancy did not appear in my original estimates (Barro, 1977, p. 108) because of the inclusion of the military personnel and minimum wage rate variables (see note 12). The apparently warranted modification to the money stock data before 1947 (note 5) also worsens the fit for 1947–1948.

coefficient for $\log(U/1 - U)_{t-1}$, when added to equation (5), is .19, s.e. $= .11$, and in equation (6) is .14, s.e. $= .12$. For equation (7), the estimated coefficient of the added variable $\log(Y_{t-1})$ is .10, s.e. $= .07$. Finally, a check for robustness in the output equation was carried out by reestimating in first-difference form. The results for the 1947–1978 sample are

$$D\log(Y_t) = \begin{array}{cccc} .033 & + \ 0.84D(DMR_t) & + \ 0.90D(DMR_{t-1}) & + \ .059D\log(G_t), \\ (.004) & (.23) & (.23) & (.024) \end{array}$$

$$R^2 = .53, \quad \hat{\sigma} = .020, \quad D - W = 2.5, \tag{8}$$

where D is the first difference operator. Note that the estimated constant corresponds now to the estimated time trend in equation (7). A comparison with equation (7) indicates that the estimated coefficients are robust to first differencing. This type of comparison has been suggested as a test of specification by Plosser and Schwert (1978).

Equations (5)–(7) indicate significant expansionary effects of the current and 1-year lagged monetary shocks.[15] Additional lagged terms, considered out as far as 7 years, were individually and jointly insignificant in the unemployment rate and output equations. For the unemployment rate equation, there is a triangular lag pattern with a peak effect after 1 year. If the DMR_{t-2} value is added to the form of equation (5) for the 1946–1978 sample, the estimated coefficient is -2.7, s.e. $= 2.0$. Similar results apply for the 1949–1978 period. For the output equation there appears to be a shorter average lag response to a monetary stimulus, with roughly equal coefficients applying to the contemporaneous and 1-year lagged shocks. In this case the estimated coefficient on the DMR_{t-2} variable in the form of equation (7) turns out to be .10, s.e. $= .19$.

The triangular pattern of response to monetary shocks is defined better in results obtained from quarterly data, as reported in Barro and Rush (1980, Table 1). The principal monetary effects on output and the unemployment rate emerge in that study with a lag between 1 and 6 quarters. However, these results are characterized by substantial serial correlation in the residuals. The quarterly estimates also require further examination for the effects of seasonality.

Returning to the results from annual data, the real federal purchases variables are also significantly expansionary in equations (5)–(7). More detailed aspects of these

---

[15]The estimated coefficient of DMR_t would be biased—probably toward zero—if there were contemporaneous positive feedback from U to DM_t. The response of money growth to lagged unemployment was already taken into account in forming the anticipated money growth rate $\widehat{DM}_t$. The variable DMR_t could be omitted from the estimated equation and treated as part of the error term (as in Leiderman, 1980, p. 74), in which case the other coefficient estimates are altered negligibly from those shown in equations (5)–(7). The simultaneity problem implied by within-period policy feedback is likely to be less serious with quarterly data, which are utilized in Barro and Rush (1980, Part II).

estimated equations will be discussed after the implementation of a number of statistical tests.

Results with Total Money Growth Rates

Unemployment rate and output regressions have also been run based on total money growth rates DM, rather than on the unanticipated part of growth DMR. For an unemployment rate regression over the 1946–1978 sample that includes a contemporaneous and one lagged value of DM, the estimated monetary coefficients are individually and jointly insignificantly different from zero. The fit improves somewhat as more lagged values are included; the estimated equation that includes the contemporaneous and four annual lagged values of DM is, for the 1946–1978 sample,

$$\log[U/(1 - U)]_t = -1.78 - 2.6DM_t - 3.9DM_{t-1} + 2.0DM_{t-2} + 2.5DM_{t-3}$$
$$\quad\quad (.27)\quad (2.6)\quad\quad (2.8)\quad\quad\quad (2.5)\quad\quad\quad (1.8)$$

$$- 4.1DM_{t-4} - 8.5(G/Y)_t ,$$
$$\quad (1.5)\quad\quad\quad (1.8)$$

$$R^2 = .52, \quad \hat{\sigma} = .22, \quad D - W = 1.6. \tag{9}$$

The F value for the joint hypothesis that all five DM coefficients are zero is $F^5_{26} = 2.6$, which just equals the 5% critical value. The fit of the unemployment rate equation with four lagged values of DM is poorer than that obtained in equation (5) with one lagged value of the DMR variable. It is also useful to note that the estimated coefficients on the DM_{t-2} and DM_{t-3} variables are positive; that is, in the contractionary direction.

For output regressions, the principal explanatory power from the DM variables is provided by the contemporaneous effect. The estimated equation that includes four lagged values of DM is

$$\log(Y_t) = 3.02 + 0.88DM_t + 0.34DM_{t-1} - 0.18DM_{t-2} - 0.18DM_{t-3}$$
$$\quad\quad (.14)\quad\quad (.26)\quad\quad\quad (.37)\quad\quad\quad (.24)\quad\quad\quad (.18)$$

$$+ 0.13DM_{t-4} + .074 \cdot \log(G_t) + .0316 \cdot t,$$
$$\quad (.20)\quad\quad\quad (.035)\quad\quad\quad\quad\quad (.0006)$$

$$R^2 = .997, \quad \hat{\sigma} = .020, \quad D - W = 1.1. \tag{10}$$

In this case the F value for joint significance of the five DM coefficients is $F^5_{25} = 5.5$, which exceeds the 5% critical value of 2.5. The fit is poorer than that obtained with one lag of the DMR variable in equation (7). Again, the point estimates of coefficients on the DM_{t-2} and DM_{t-3} variables indicate a contractionary effect.

Tests That Only Unanticipated Components of Money Growth
Affect the Unemployment Rate and Output

A key hypothesis of this study is that only the unanticipated part of money growth influences real variables like the unemployment rate and output. One way to test this proposition is to run regressions that include simultaneously sets of DMR and DM variables and then examine whether the deletion of the DM variables, which amounts to a set of linear restrictions on the coefficients, produces a significant worsening of the fit. For the unemployment rate equation over the 1946–1978 sample, with a contemporaneous and one annual lag of the DMR and DM variables considered, the resulting test statistic is $F^2_{27} = 3.7$, 5% critical value $= 3.4$. When four lagged values of each monetary variable are included, the result is $F^5_{21} = 3.0$, 5% critical value $= 2.7$. The F values are reduced greatly—to .6 and .3, respectively—if the sample is limited to the 1949–1978 period. For the output equation over the 1946–1978 sample, the corresponding test statistic with one lag of each monetary variable is $F^2_{26} = .7$, 5% critical value $= 3.4$. The result with four lags of each variable is $F^5_{20} = .3$, 5% critical value $= 2.7$. Despite the cases of marginal rejection at the 5% level for the unemployment rate equation over the 1946–1978 sample, the overall outcome supports the hypothesis that actual money growth is unimportant for the determination of the real variables, given the values of the monetary shocks DMR. It should also be noted that the equivalent test statistics would apply for the hypothesis that anticipated money growth $\widehat{DM}$ is irrelevant for the unemployment rate and output, given the values of the DMR variables.

In order to assess the power of the preceding tests it is useful to consider the reverse hypothesis associated with deleting the DMR variables while retaining the DM values. For the unemployment rate equation over the 1946–1978 sample, the resulting test statistic with one lag of the monetary variables is $F^2_{27} = 16.9$, 5% critical value $= 3.4$. The outcome with four lags of each variable is $F^5_{21} = 8.0$, 5% critical value $= 2.7$. For the 1949–1978 sample, the corresponding statistics are $F^2_{24} = 12.6$ and $F^5_{18} = 4.3$, respectively. For the output equation over the 1946–1978 sample, the statistics associated with deletion of the set of DMR values are, with one lag of each monetary variable, $F^2_{26} = 7.0$, 5% critical value $= 3.4$; and with four lags of each, $F^5_{20} = 2.0$, 5% critical value $= 2.7$. Overall, the reverse hypothesis of irrelevance for the DMR variables can be rejected at the 5% level except for the case of output with four lags of each monetary variable included. Accordingly, there is an indication that the findings on the unimportance of the DM variables do not arise because the sets of DM and DMR variables are closely correlated.

A point to stress about the preceding statistical tests is that they can be carried out only because predictors of DM_t other than its own history have been included in the money growth rate equation. For example, suppose that $\widehat{DM}_t$ were generated solely as a function of DM_{t-1}; say, $\widehat{DM}_t = \alpha_0 + \alpha_1 DM_{t-1}$. In this circumstance a regression of the unemployment rate or output on a series of DMR values, where $DMR \equiv DM - \widehat{DM}$, could not fit better than a regression on a series of DM values that included one additional lag term. If no truncation were imposed ex ante on the number of lag values to admit, the *DMR* and *DM* forms would be observationally equivalent, which implies that testing of *natural rate hypotheses* could not proceed. In the cases discussed earlier, the superior fits of the *DMR* form of the unemployment rate and output equations reflect the impact of the additional variables— namely, the federal expenditure and lagged unemployment measures—that were included in the money growth equation but were excluded ex ante from entering directly into the unemployment rate or output expressions, as shown in equations (3) and (4). A general discussion of the identifying role of these types of exclusion restrictions appear in the fifth section of paper no. 2 in this volume; related material on the testing of natural rate hypotheses appears in Sargent (1976a, 1976b).

Further perspective on the distinction between actual and unanticipated money specifications can be obtained by substituting into the estimated unemployment rate and output relations from equations (5)–(7), using the condition $DMR_t \equiv DM - \widehat{DM}_t$, where $\widehat{DM}_t$ is calculated from the estimated money growth rate relation in equation (2). The resulting *reduced form* expresses the unemployment rate or output as a function of $(DM_t, \ldots, DM_{t-3})$; $(FEDV_t, FEDV_{t-1})$; (U_{t-1}, U_{t-2}); and $(G/Y)_t$ (with log (G_t) replacing $(G/Y)_t$ and a time trend added for the case of output). Specifically, the coefficients that derive from this substitution are listed as constrained values in Table 1. It is also possible to estimate the reduced forms in a direct, unconstrained fashion; a procedure that yields the estimated coefficients and standard errors that are listed as unconstrained values in Table 1.

The *DMR* forms impose a set of restrictions on the manner in which the reduced form independent variables influence the unemployment rate and output. Specifically, the use of equations (3) and (4) with *DMR* values derived from the separately estimated equation (2) amounts to reducing the number of free coefficients from 10 in the unconstrained reduced form (11 for output) to 4 in the *DMR* form (5 for output). If the unanticipated money specification in equations (3) and (4) is appropriate, these six coefficient restrictions should not significantly worsen the fit of an unemployment rate or output equation; heuristically, the constrained coefficients shown in Table 1 should not differ "excessively" from the unconstrained values (taking account of standard errors). An overall hypothesis test can be constructed from the usual comparison of restricted and unrestricted sums of squared residuals. The outcome of this test for the unemployment rate equation over the 1946–1978 sample is $F_{23}^6 = 3.0$, 5% critical value $= 2.5$; and over the 1949–1978 sample, $F_{20}^6 = .5$, 5% critical value $= 2.6$. The result for the output equation over the 1946–1978 sample is $F_{22}^6 = .4$, 5% critical value $= 2.6$. Therefore, the null hypothesis associated with the unanticipated money form is accepted for output and for the 1949–1978 unemployment rate sample, but just rejected at the 5% level for the unemployment rate over the 1946–1978 period. The results correspond to those of the earlier comparison tests for the *DMR* and *DM* forms; namely, overall support for the null hypothesis implied by the unanticipated money form, but some indication of difficulty with the immediate post–World War II observations for the unemployment rate.

Table 1
Constrained and Freely Estimated Coefficients of Reduced Forms

(1)	Unemployment rate 1946–1978		Unemployment rate 1949–1978		Output 1946–1978	
	(2) Constrained	(3) Unconstrained	(4) Constrained	(5) Unconstrained	(6) Constrained	(7) Unconstrained
Constant	−.36	−.50 (.39)	−.65	−.50 (.41)	2.72	2.69 (.16)
DM_t	−4.9	−6.8 (2.2)	−5.8	−6.0 (2.5)	1.00	1.09 (.26)
DM_{t-1}	−9.0	−7.6 (2.6)	−8.0	−7.5 (2.9)	.61	.52 (.31)
DM_{t-2}	6.2	3.5 (1.9)	6.1	4.2 (2.9)	−.69	−.46 (.25)
DM_{t-3}	1.9	2.5 (1.5)	1.8	4.0 (2.6)	−.18	−.19 (.18)
$FEDV_t$	.35	.96 (.50)	.41	.58 (.98)	−.071	−.118 (.087)
$FEDV_{t-1}$	.81	1.24 (.29)	.77	.96 (.53)	−.078	−.074 (.037)
$\log[U/(1-U)]_{t-1}$	.15	.32 (.18)	.18	.31 (.23)	−.031	−.033 (.023)
$\log[U/(1-U)]_{t-2}$	.35	.21 (.16)	.33	.31 (.22)	−.034	−.018 (.020)
$(G/Y)_t$	−5.3	−7.6 (1.9)	−6.4	−5.4 (3.6)	—	—
$\log(G_t)$	—	—	—	—	.070	.100 (.041)
t	—	—	—	—	.0330	.0324 (.0009)

Notes: Constrained coefficients in columns 2, 4, and 6 follow from combination of the estimated coefficients shown in equations 5, 6, and 7, respectively, with the estimated coefficients from the money growth rate equation (2). The calculations use the definition $DMR = DM - \widehat{DM}$. Unconstrained coefficient values in columns 3, 5, and 7 are derived directly from least-squares estimates using the variables indicated in column 1 as regressors. The dependent variable for columns 3 and 5 is $\log[U/(1-U)]$, while that for column 7 is $\log(Y)$. See the text and Tables 2 and 3 for definitions of variables.

The listing of the reduced form coefficients in Table 1 illustrates the points about observational equivalence that were mentioned earlier. Namely, the DMR form of the unemployment rate and output equations are equivalent to forms that contains DM values (in this case up to DM_{t-3}), along with the $FEDV$ and lagged U variables (up to $FEDV_{t-1}$ and U_{t-2}, respectively) that were included in the DM relation. The exclusion of the $FEDV$ and lagged U variables from the form of the unemployment rate and output relations, equations (3) and (4), constitutes a set of identifying restrictions that permits an observational separation between the DMR and DM forms of the equations. The above tests of the distinction between these two forms then amount to tests of the joint hypothesis that (a) $\widehat{DM}$ is generated in accordance with equation (2); (b) monetary movements influence the unemployment rate and output only in the form $DMR \equiv DM - \widehat{DM}$; and ($c$) the $FEDV$ and lagged U variables that appear in equation (2) do not enter directly in equations (3) and (4). Of course, the acceptance of the joint null hypothesis provides some support for each element of the hypothesis; namely, for (a) and (b), which were the main objects of interest.

It would be possible to interpret the estimated reduced forms for the unemployment rate and output in Table 1 as indicating the influence of actual money growth DM, along with direct influences of the $FEDV$, lagged U, and G variables, with the coefficients of the DM, $FEDV$, and lagged U variables satisfying the restrictions implied by the DMR form out of pure coincidence. However, this interpretation leaves some results that require additional explanation; in particular, the contractionary effects of the $FEDV$ variables and of some of the lagged money growth rate variables in the reduced form. These findings are readily explained by a model that involves expansionary effects of monetary shocks.

Jointly Estimated Equations and Tests

The statistical tests based on Table 1 involve a problem that derives from the two-stage estimation procedure. The constrained values shown in the table apply only if the coefficient estimates of the money growth rate equation (2) are regarded as known constants, rather than as values that are subject to estimation error. In particular, the two-stage procedure allows insufficient scope for the constrained estimates to fit the unemployment rate, output and money growth rate equations in a joint sense.

An efficient procedure involves joint estimation of the money growth, unemployment rate, and output equations. Specifically, write the money growth equations as $DM_t = F(X_t) + DMR_t$, where X_t is a set of predictors for monetary movements; in the present case $F(X_t) = \alpha_0 + \alpha_1 DM_{t-1} + \alpha_2 DM_{t-2} + \alpha_3 FEDV_t + \alpha_4 \cdot \log[U/(1-U)]_{t-1}$. The condition, $DMR_t \equiv DM_t - F(X_t)$, with a corresponding substitution for DMR_{t-1}, can then be applied to the unemployment rate and output equations. The system can be estimated in an unrestricted manner by allowing separate coefficients on the variables; $DM_{t-1}, DM_{t-2}, \ldots$, which are contained in $F(X_t)$, and so on, in each of the equations. The underlying unanticipated money growth hypothesis—which amounts to a set of nonlinear coefficient restrictions across the equations—is that $F(X_t)$ in the unemployment rate and output equations corresponds to the coefficients in the money growth rate equation. A likelihood ratio test can be carried out to check whether the imposition of these restrictions on the joint estimation produces a statistically significant deterioration of the fit, in which case the underlying hypothesis would be rejected.

The joint estimates for the money growth, unemployment rate, and output equations, which are subject to the restrictions implied by the unanticipated money growth hypothesis and which comprise the same sample periods and weighting scheme for the DM equation that are shown above in equations (2), (5), and (7), are[16]

$$
\begin{aligned}
DM_t = \ & .099 \ + \ .24DM_{t-1} \ + \ .27DM_{t-2} \ + \ .113\text{FEDV}_t \\
& (.015) \quad (.08) \qquad\quad (.07) \qquad\quad (.010)
\end{aligned}
$$

$$
\begin{aligned}
& + \ .032 \ \cdot \ \log[U/(1 \ - \ U)]_{t-1} , \\
& \ \ (.005)
\end{aligned}
$$

$$
\hat{\sigma} = .015, \quad D - W = 1.5, \tag{11}
$$

$$
\begin{aligned}
\log[U/(1 \ - \ U)]_t = \ & -2.19 \ - \ 6.1DMR_t \ - \ 10.9DMR_{t-1} \ - \ 7.2(G/Y)_t , \\
& \ \ (.13) \quad (1.7) \qquad\quad (1.8) \qquad\qquad (1.1)
\end{aligned}
$$

$$
\hat{\sigma} = .12, \quad D - W = 1.8, \tag{12}
$$

$$
\begin{aligned}
\log(Y_t) = \ & 2.80 \ + \ 1.09DMR_t \ + \ 0.74DMR_{t-1} \ + \ .105 \quad \log(G_t) \\
& (.03) \quad (.18) \qquad\qquad (.20) \qquad\quad (.013)
\end{aligned}
$$

$$
\begin{aligned}
& + \ .0327 \ \cdot \ t, \\
& \ \ (.0004)
\end{aligned}
$$

$$
\hat{\sigma} = .014, \quad D - W = 1.6. \tag{13}
$$

The results for the same specification except for a change in the unemployment rate sample to 1949–1978 are

$$
\begin{aligned}
DM_t = \ & .098 \ + \ .41DM_{t-1} \ + \ .18DM_{t-2} \ + \ .081\text{FEDV}_t \\
& (.015) \quad (.09) \qquad\quad (.07) \qquad\quad (.009)
\end{aligned}
$$

$$
\begin{aligned}
& + \ .031 \ \cdot \ \log[U/(1 \ - \ U)]_{t-1} , \\
& \ \ (.005)
\end{aligned}
$$

$$
\hat{\sigma} = .013, \quad D - W = 1.8, \tag{14}
$$

[16]The estimation, carried out with the TSP regression package, includes contemporaneous covariances for the error terms across the equations. However, the covariance of the money growth error term with that in the other equations is zero by construction. There is a minor problem in that the presently used computer program allows for different numbers of observations across equations only by introducing some extra observations (for the U and Y equations) that are then set to zero on both sides of the equations. This procedure inflates the apparent degrees of freedom and thereby leads to an underestimate of standard errors of coefficient estimates and disturbances.

$$\log[U/(1 - U)]_t = -2.20 - 6.0DMR_t - 10.6DMR_{t-1} - 6.9(G/Y)_t ,$$
$$(.12) \quad (1.6) \quad \quad (1.7) \quad \quad (1.6)$$

$$\hat{\sigma} = .12, \quad D - W = 1.7, \tag{15}$$

$$\log(Y_t) = 2.88 + 1.01DMR_t + .99DMR_{t-1} + .081 \cdot \log(G_t)$$
$$(.03) \quad (.19) \quad \quad (.22) \quad \quad (.014)$$
$$+ .0329 \cdot t,$$
$$(.0004)$$

$$\hat{\sigma} = .014, \quad D - W = 1.6. \tag{16}$$

Note that the coefficient standard errors shown in parentheses and the $\hat{\sigma}$ values are asymptotic estimates, which are not adjusted for degrees of freedom, and are therefore not comparable directly to those shown in earlier equations.

As would be expected in the present case, the shift to joint estimation implies some improvements in the fit of the unemployment rate and output equations and worsening in the fit of the money growth rate equations. The principal changes in estimated coefficients and standard errors apply to the money growth equations. For equation (14), which corresponds to the 1949–1978 unemployment rate sample, the main changes are the reduction in standard errors for the estimated coefficients of the FEDV and lagged U variables. These reduced standard errors reflect the important role of these variables for the calculation of the DMR series and thereby for the estimation of the other two equations, which is now taken into account in the calculation of coefficient standard errors for the money growth equation. In equation (11), which is associated with the inclusion of the 1946–1948 values for the unemployment rate, the shifts in estimated coefficients for the DM_{t-1} and $FEDV_t$ variables are substantial. These changes reflect the attempt to change parts of the DMR series in order to reduce the large unemployment rate residuals for 1947–1948.

The three equations have been fitted also with the relaxation of the cross-equation restrictions implied by the unanticipated money growth hypothesis. A comparison of the unrestricted and constrained results leads to the calculation of a value for $-2 \cdot \log$(likelihood ratio) for a test of the cross-equation restrictions. This statistic is distributed asymptotically as a χ^2 variable with 12 df. For the case corresponding to equations (11)–(13), where observations from 1946–1948 of the unemployment rate are included, the value of the test statistic turns out to be 34.4, as compared to a 5% critical value of 21.0 and a 1% value of 26.2. (The use of the higher critical value may be reasonable because of the lack of adjustment for degrees of freedom in this asymptotic test.) In the situation corresponding to equations (14)–(16), where the unemployment rate sample is limited to 1949–1978, the test statistic is 18.0, with the same critical values applying. The cross-equation restrictions implied by the unanticipated money form are accepted at the 5 (or 1) % level if the 1946–1948 observations on the unemployment rate are excluded and rejected in the reverse case. Accordingly, the outcome of this joint test parallels the results of tests from the two-stage estimation procedure, which were discussed earlier.

The joint estimation technique becomes important when a large number of candidate variables is considered for the money growth rate equation. For example, the introduction of numerous irrelevant variables into this equation would produce important errors-in-variables problems for a DMR series that was constructed with a finite data sample from a separately estimated money growth rate equation. The estimates of the DMR coefficients in unemployment rate and output equations would then tend to be biased substantially toward zero. Joint estimation of the money growth rate equation with the other equations avoids much of this problem. An example of this phenomenon appears in my discussion (Barro, 1979b) of the comment by Small (1979). Of course, the joint estimation procedure does not eliminate sensitivity of the estimates and tests to specification errors in the money growth rate equation, such as omission of important money growth predictors. In this respect see Germany and Srivastava (1979) and McCallum (1979).

Properties of the Estimated Unemployment Rate and
Output Equations

I will discuss now some detailed properties of the jointly estimated equations (14)–(16), which are based on the 1949–1978 sample for the unemployment rate. The coefficient estimate of -11 on the DMR_{t-1} variable in equation (15) implies that a 1 percentage point money shock would reduce next year's unemployment rate by 11%; that is, by about ½ percentage point at an initial unemployment rate of 5%. The estimated contemporaneous effect is smaller, corresponding to a reduction in the unemployment rate by about 3/10 of a percentage point. Equation (16) indicates that a 1 percentage point money shock would raise this year's and next year's levels of output by about 1% each. Aside from a slightly longer lag in the response of the unemployment rate, the results exhibit an Okun's Law type relation in which money-induced increases in output and reductions in percentage points of the unemployment rate are associated on about a 2½-to-1 basis.

It should be stressed that the lag patterns for money growth that are described in equations (15) and (16) refer to unanticipated rather than actual monetary movements. The implied pattern in terms of actual money growth—given the form of the estimated money growth rate equation—is approximated by the array of constrained coefficients that are shown in columns 4 and 6 of Table 1. Because of the positive effects of the DM_{t-1} and DM_{t-2} variables on the current value of anticipated money growth, the lag pattern for the unemployment rate or output in terms of DM values differs markedly from that in terms of the DMR variables. Two important differences are, first, the *mean* lag effect from DM to the real variables is shorter than that associated with the DMR values; and second, contractionary monetary effects can appear in the DM form even when the DMR coefficients are restricted to be expansionary.

The estimated federal purchases' coefficient of -6.9 in equation (15) implies that a 10% increase in these purchases would reduce the unemployment rate by about 4/10 of a percentage point. This computation assumes that the initial unemployment rate is .05 and that the G/Y variable initially takes on its mean value for the 1946–1978 sample, which was .10. Correspondingly, equation (16) implies that a 10% increase in real federal purchases would raise real GNP by about 8/10 of a percent. The coefficient estimate .081 on the $\log(G_t)$ variable in equation (16) implies, at a value $G/Y = .10$, that each unit increase in G raises output by about .8 units. Further discussion of these effects is contained in Barro (1979c).

Given the estimated relation from equation (15), it is possible to calculate values of the unemployment rate associated with $DMR = 0$ for all t; that is, with fully anticipated current and past monetary growth. I will refer to these unemployment rates as natural values, denoted by UNAT.[17] In the present setup the natural unemployment rate depends only on the values of the federal purchases ratio, G/Y, and the constant term. Values of UNAT derived from equation (15) and the values of G/Y shown in Table 3 are indicated in Table 2. Tables 2 and 3 contain also actual and estimated values and residuals of money growth rates from equation (14), of the unemployment rate based on equation (15),[18] and of output growth based on equation (16). The basic patterns since World War II for money growth, the unemployment rate, and output are as follows.

With the reduction of military spending after World War II, the estimated natural unemployment rate rose[19] to about 4½% in 1946 and from 5½ to 6% for 1947–1950. The natural rate falls as low as 3% during the Korean War, remains in the range between 4.1 and 5.0% from 1955 to 1969, and rises after the Vietnamese War to a value of 6.3% in 1978.

The end of World War II involved a large cutback in money growth from annual rates above 15% through 1945 to 6.8% in 1946, 3.6% in 1947, and .4% in 1948. However, the estimated money growth rate equation implies that this cutback was anticipated because of the sharp decline in federal expenditure. In fact, the estimated values, $\widehat{DM} = 5.5\%$ for 1946 and 2.8% for 1947, imply that these years were ones of unanticipated monetary expansion. Correspondingly, the estimated values for the unemployment rate (extrapolated from the 1949–1978 sample) are somewhat below the estimated natural values for 1946–1948. However, the actual values of the unemployment rate for 1947–1948 are unaccountably low, which is surprising in that the same discrepancy does not arise for output growth rates in Table 3.

The monetary contraction for 1948–1949 accounts for the excess of estimated

---

[17]Because of nonlinearities, these values differ from expected unemployment rates derived from equation (15) with an additive, constant variance error term. The gap between the expected unemployment rate and the natural rate, as defined, increases with the variance of the error term and with the variance of the DMR variable.

[18]No adjustment was made for nonlinearities in calculating these values from a transformation of the dependent variable, $\log[U/(1-U)]$.

[19]The functional form appears to underestimate the natural unemployment rate during the extreme conditions of World War II (see note 13).

Table 2
Values of Money Growth and Unemployment Rates

(1) Date	(2) DM	(3) $\widehat{DM}$	(4) DMR	(5) U	(6) $\hat{U}$	(7) $U\text{-}\hat{U}$	(8) UNAT
1941	.160	.179	−.019	.064	—	—	.038
2	.179	.216	−.037	.035	(.017)	(.018)	.011
3	.265	.207	.058	.017	(.005)	(.011)	.005
4	.162	.206	−.044	.012	(.003)	(.009)	.004
1945	.150	.139	.011	.019	(.009)	(.010)	.006
6	.068	.055	.013	.042	(.037)	(.005)	.045
7	.034	.028	.006	.038	(.051)	(−.013)	.061
8	.004	.008	−.003	.037	(.055)	(−.018)	.057
9	−.010	.003	−.013	.058	.058	.000	.053
1950	.026	.006	.020	.051	.058	−.007	.057
1	.044	.032	.012	.032	.030	.002	.040
2	.049	.039	.010	.029	.026	.003	.031
3	.024	.041	−.017	.028	.030	−.002	.030
4	.015	.019	−.003	.053	.044	.009	.036
1955	.031	.027	.004	.042	.043	−.001	.042
6	.012	.024	−.012	.040	.044	−.004	.043
7	.005	.020	−.015	.041	.052	−.011	.042
8	.012	.018	−.006	.065	.049	.016	.041
9	.037	.033	.004	.053	.045	.008	.044
1960	−.001	.035	−.036	.053	.053	.000	.045
1	.021	.028	−.007	.065	.065	.000	.044
2	.022	.038	−.017	.053	.051	.002	.043
3	.029	.034	−.005	.055	.055	.000	.045
4	.039	.037	.002	.050	.049	.001	.047
1965	.042	.039	.003	.044	.048	−.004	.050
6	.044	.043	.001	.036	.046	−.010	.048
7	.039	.041	−.003	.037	.045	−.008	.045
8	.068	.040	.027	.034	.040	−.006	.045
9	.061	.044	.017	.034	.033	.001	.048
1970	.038	.045	−.007	.048	.045	.003	.051
1	.065	.045	.020	.057	.052	.005	.055
2	.068	.059	.009	.054	.044	.010	.057
3	.072	.062	.010	.047	.052	−.005	.060
4	.053	.059	−.006	.054	.056	−.002	.060
1975	.042	.059	−.018	.083	.070	.013	.060
6	.050	.061	−.012	.075	.078	−.003	.061
7	.069	.060	.009	.069	.066	.003	.062
8	.079	.065	.014	.059	.054	.005	.063
				Predicted Values			
(Data through 1978)							
1979	—	.068	—	—	.056	—	.063
1980	—	.064	—	—	.063	—	
1981	—	.064	—	—	—	—	
1982	—	.064	—	—	—	—	
1983	—	.063	—	—	↓	—	↓
. . .	—	. . .	—	—		—	
∞	—	.063	—	—	.063	—	.063

(continued)

Table 2 *(Continued)*

(1) Date	(2) DM	(3) $\widehat{DM}$	(4) DMR	(5) U	(6) $\hat{U}$	(7) $U\text{-}\hat{U}$	(8) UNAT
(Data through 1979)							
1979	.076[a]	.067	.009	.057	.053	.004	.064
1980	—	.062	—	—	.059	—	
1981	—	.059	—	—	.064	—	
1982	—	.060	—	—	—	—	
1983	—	.060	—	—	↓	—	↓
. . .	—	. . .	—	—		—	
∞	—	.060	—	—	.064	—	.064

Notes: $DM_t = \log(M_t/M_{t-1})$, where M is an annual average of the M1 definition of the money stock from the *Federal Reserve Bulletin,* incorporating revisions of data through November 1979. Data before 1947 are from Friedman and Schwartz (1970, Table 2). (See note 5.) $\widehat{DM}$ is the estimated value from equation (14). $DMR \equiv DM - \widehat{DM}$.

U is the unemployment rate in the total labor force, which includes military personnel. Data appear, for example, in the *Economic Report of the President,* various issues. $\hat{U}$ is the estimated value based on equation (15) (see note 18). UNAT is derived from equation (15) with all DMR values set equal to zero.

Predicted values for the unemployment rate are based on equation (15), using the 1978 value of G/Y for the first set and the 1979 value for the second set. Future values of the DMR variable are set to zero. The second set of predictions uses the value $DMR = .009$ for 1979.

Predicted values for the money growth rate are based on equation (14), using the 1978 value for the $FEDV$ variable in the first set and the 1979 value in the second set. The lagged unemployment rate is set equal to its predicted value in these calculations.

[a] Based on the M1-B definition of the money stock, which includes NOW accounts, etc. Data are from Federal Reserve releases of February 1980. Values of DM before 1979 would not be affected appreciably by this change of definition.

unemployment rates above the natural values for 1949–1950. The Korean War years of 1951–1953 involve a combination of the sharp rise in federal purchases with unanticipated monetary expansion for 1950–1952 (above the amount associated normally with the federal spending increase) to yield unemployment rate estimates in the vicinity of 3% for 1951–1953. Negative values of the DMR variable for 1953–1954 account for part of the rise in the unemployment rate estimate for 1954. Small values of the DMR variables for 1954–1955 are associated with estimated unemployment rates that are close to the natural values for 1955–1956.

Monetary contraction for 1956–1958 implies an increase in estimated unemployment rates for 1957–1958, but the timing does not accord with the strong peak in the unemployment rate for 1958. A similar discrepancy appears in the estimated output equation. The equations are back on track in 1960.

An especially interesting monetary episode is the absolute contraction of money that occurred during 1960. This behavior represented the first absolute decline in money since 1949, but more significantly, the estimate for anticipated money growth for 1960 is 3.5% per year, as contrasted with .3% for 1949. Therefore, the unanticipated monetary contraction for 1960 was -3.6%; the largest absolute value of the DMR variable for the post–World War II period. This monetary contraction accounts for the sharp rise in the estimated unemployment rate for 1961 to 6.5%,

Table 3

Values of Output Growth, Inflation, and Other Variables

(1) Date	(2) DY	(3) $\widehat{DY}$	(4) DY-$\widehat{DY}$	(5) DP	(6) $\widehat{DP}$	(7) DP-$\widehat{DP}$	(8) FEDV	(9) G/Y	(10) R
1941	.143						.803	.148	.0277
2	.136	(.048)	(.089)	.100	(.077)	(.023)	1.356	.333	.0283
3	.148	(.058)	(.090)	.045	(.242)	(−.197)	1.369	.448	.0273
4	.073	(−.056)	(.129)	.019	(.329)	(−.310)	1.161	.437	.0272
1945	−.014	(−.153)	(.139)	.024	(.452)	(−.428)	.812	.416	.0262
6	−.157	−.161	.003	.144	(.368)	(−.224)	−.131	.122	.0253
7	−.020	−.014	−.005	.124	(.209)	(−.084)	−.338	.077	.0261
8	.041	.035	.006	.066	.075	−.009	−.196	.087	.0282
9	.006	.019	−.013	−.009	.013	−.022	−.016	.100	.0266
1950	.084	.066	.017	.019	.016	.003	−.033	.088	.0262
1	.078	.084	−.007	.067	.054	.013	.199	.141	.0286
2	.037	.052	−.014	.012	.013	−.001	.307	.179	.0296
3	.038	.024	.014	.015	.023	−.008	.303	.184	.0320
4	−.013	−.009	−.004	.013	.009	.004	.151	.155	.0290
1955	.065	.051	.014	.022	.030	−.009	.090	.133	.0306
6	.021	.010	.011	.031	.033	−.003	.089	.128	.0336
7	.018	.006	.012	.033	.035	−.002	.123	.132	.0389
8	−.002	.030	−.032	.017	.012	.004	.167	.137	.0379
9	.058	.083	−.025	.021	.040	−.019	.139	.127	.0438
1960	.023	.026	−.003	.018	.007	.010	.116	.123	.0441
1	.025	.030	−.005	.009	.020	−.011	.157	.127	.0435
2	.056	.063	−.007	.019	.034	−.016	.179	.129	.0433
3	.039	.041	−.003	.014	.026	−.012	.157	.123	.0426
4	.051	.053	−.002	.015	.016	−.001	.143	.115	.0440
1965	.057	.042	.015	.022	.006	.016	.136	.109	.0449
6	.058	.026	.032	.033	.023	.010	.207	.115	.0513
7	.027	.005	.022	.028	.031	−.003	.244	.124	.0551
8	.043	.039	.004	.045	.069	−.025	.243	.122	.0618
9	.025	.044	−.018	.048	.072	−.023	.190	.113	.0703
1970	−.003	.009	−.012	.053	.075	−.022	.174	.103	.0804
1	.030	.044	−.014	.049	.037	.012	.164	.094	.0739
2	.056	.061	−.005	.041	.034	.006	.189	.087	.0721
3	.053	.024	.029	.056	.056	.000	.170	.078	.0744
4	−.014	−.012	−.002	.092	.105	−.013	.160	.079	.0857
1975	−.013	.008	−.021	.092	.092	.000	.195	.080	.0883
6	.057	.048	.009	.050	.055	−.005	.143	.076	.0843
7	.052	.055	−.003	.058	.061	−.003	.148	.075	.0802
8	.043	.059	−.016	.070	.076	−.006	.140	.070	.0873
				Predicted Values					
Data through 1978									
1979	—	.042	—	—	.045	—	(.140)	(.070)	(.0916)
1980	—	.022	—	—	.036	—			
1981	—	.036	—	—	.054	—			
1982	—	↓	—	—	.060	—	↓	↓	↓
1983	—		—	—	.056	—			
. . .	—		—	—	. . .	—			
∞	—	.036	—	—	.049	—			

(continued)

157

Table 3 (*Continued*)

(1) Date	(2) DY	(3) $\widehat{DY}$	(4) $DY\text{-}\widehat{DY}$	(5) DP	(6) $\widehat{DP}$	(7) $DP\text{-}\widehat{DP}$	(8) $FEDV$	(9) G/Y	(10) R
Data through 1979									
1979	.022	.049	−.027	.085	.068	.017	.127	.069	.0963
1980	—	.022	—	—	.179	—			(.127)
1	—	.027	—	—	.058	—			(.129)
2	—	.036	—	—	.061	—			
3	—	↓	—	—	.060	—	↓	↓	↓
. . .	—	. . .	—	—	. . .	—			
∞	—	.036	—	—	.046	—			

Notes: Y is real GNP, P is the GNP deflator, and G is real federal purchases (all 1972 base). Data are from recent issues of the *U.S. Survey of Current Business* and from *The National Income and Product Accounts of the United States, 1929–1974*.

$DY_t \equiv \log(Y_t/Y_{t-1})$. $\widehat{DY}_t \equiv \widehat{\log(Y_t)} - \log(Y_{t-1})$, where $\widehat{\log(Y_t)}$ is the estimated value from equation (16).

$DP_t \equiv \log(P_t/P_{t-1})$. $\widehat{DP}_t \equiv \widehat{\log(P_t)} - \log(P_{t-1})$, where $\widehat{\log(P_t)}$ is the estimated value from equation (21).

$FEDV_t \equiv \log(FED_t) - [\log(FED)]_t^*$, where FED is nominal federal expenditure divided by the GNP deflator. Nominal federal spending is obtained from the sources indicated above. $[\log(FED)]_t^* \equiv 0.2 \cdot \log(FED_t) + 0.8[\log(FED)]_{t-1}^*$.

R is the annual average Aaa corporate bond rate, as given in the *Federal Reserve Bulletin*, various issues.

Predicted values for output growth and inflation are based on equations (16) and (21), respectively. The predictions assume growth in G from the 1978 value (1979 value for the second set) at a rate of .036 per year. The first set of predictions uses values of $DMR = 0$ for 1979 onward and sets R equal to its end-of-1978 value. The second set assumes $DMR = .009$ for 1979, sets the 1979 value and the January–February 1980 values for R equal to their actual values, and sets later values of R equal to the March 7, 1980, value.

which corresponds to the actual value and is about 2 percentage points above the estimated natural rate for that year. Similar behavior appears in the estimated output equation.

Negative values for the *DMR* variable for 1961–1963 account for the 1 percentage point gap between the estimated unemployment rate and the natural value that persists through 1963. Values of the *DMR* variable from 1963–1967 are small in magnitude (although quarterly observations would show much less appearance of monetary stability), which implies estimated unemployment rates that are close to the natural values for 1964–1967. The unemployment rate and output equations underestimate somewhat the boom for 1965–1967.

The sharp monetary expansion for 1968–1969 implies lower estimated unemployment rates for those years, which conform to the actual values. From 1969–1978 the reduction in the federal purchases ratio leads to a gradual rise in the estimated natural unemployment rate from 4.8% in 1969 to 6.3% in 1978. Accordingly, the monetary expansion for 1971–1973 is estimated to be consistent with unemployment rates in the vicinity of 5%, which is about 1 percentage point below the estimated natural rate for 1973.

Monetary contraction relative to anticipations for 1974–1976 implies an increase in the estimated unemployment rate to 7.0% for 1975 and 7.8% for 1976. The estimated timing does not accord with observations of the unemployment rate and output growth, which place the trough of the recession in 1975. The unemployment rate residual of .013 for 1975 is actually smaller than the 1958 value of .016, although the nonmonetary nature of part of the more recent 1975 recession has received more frequent (recent) attention. The estimated values of the unemployment rate and output for 1976 are close to the actual values. Finally, the monetary expansion for 1977–1978 brings the estimated unemployment rate for 1978 almost 1 percentage point below the natural value (and ½ point below the actual value.)

Tables 2 and 3 contain predictions for money growth, the unemployment rate, and output growth for 1979 and later years. The first set of predictions incorporates data through 1978, while the second set provides estimates for the unemployment rate and output growth that are conditioned on observed monetary behavior through the end of 1979. Predictions listed here for money growth from 1980 onward are conditioned on observed monetary, unemployment rate, and federal spending data through 1979. Based on observations through 1979, the estimated money growth rate for 1979 was 6.7% per year, with a small decrease thereafter to a long-run value of 6.0% per year. The actual value of money growth for 1979, based on the new M1-B concept that includes NOW accounts and other checkable, interest-bearing deposits, is 7.6%, which implies a *DMR* value of .009. Since the corresponding growth rate of the old M1 concept of money for 1979 was only 5.0% (which would imply a *DMR* value of −.017), the shift in money stock concept has a substantial effect on predictions. However, the estimates prior to 1979 would not be materially altered by this definitional change.

Using observations through 1978, the predicted unemployment rates are 5.6% for 1979—compared to an actual value of 5.7%—and 6.3%, the estimated natural rate, for 1980 onward. Correspondingly, the predicted values for output growth are 4.2% for 1979—compared to an actual value of 2.2%—2.2% for 1980, and 3.6% per year for 1981 onward.

With data for 1979 incorporated, including the value $DMR = .009$, the "predicted" unemployment rates become 5.3% for 1979 (which is below the actual value of 5.7%), 5.9% for 1980, and 6.4% for 1981 onward. The corresponding predictions for output growth become 4.9% for 1979 (compared to the actual value of 2.2%), 2.2% for 1980, 2.7% for 1981, and 3.6% for 1982 onward. Accordingly, the predictions based on 1979 data and the new M1-B concept of money do not indicate a recession for 1980–1981. [These predictions were not conditioned on the monetary contraction that occurred during 1980.]

Price Level Estimates

Setup of the Price Equation

In order to derive the form of a price equation, I begin with an expression for the demand for money,

$$\log(M_t) - \log(P_t) = c_0 + c_1 \cdot \log(X_t) - c_2 R_t + c_3 t + \epsilon_t^m, \qquad (17)$$

where M is the nominal money stock, P is the price level (GNP deflator), X is a measure of real expenditure pertinent to money demand, R is a nominal interest rate (measured emprically by the Aaa corporate bond rate; see later), t is a time trend, and ϵ_t^m is a random term that is not necessarily independent of the stochastic term, ϵ_t^Y, in the output equation (4). The coefficients satisfy the conditions $c_1 > 0$, $c_2 > 0$, $c_3 \gtreqless 0$, with the last coefficient reflecting any trend elements in money demand associated with the development of financial institutions, and so on. The formulation in equation (17) neglects any lags in the adjustment of money demand to changes in X, R, or other variables.

The real expenditure determinant of money demand, X, is assumed to be linearly related to real GNP for a given value of real federal purchases of goods and services, G. For a given value of total GNP, an increase in G reduces the volume of expenditure pertinent to money demand (especially since federal government holdings of money are excluded from the money stock definition), so that X is related inversely to G. I use the specification,

$$X = \lambda(Y - \gamma G), \tag{18}$$

where $\lambda > 0$ and $0 \leq \gamma \leq 1$. The exclusion of state and local purchases from the G variable amounts to treating state and local governments as comparable to the private sector in terms of money demand behavior. (Empirically, for the period considered, it is not possible to distinguish the definition of G exclusive of state and local purchases from that inclusive of these purchases.) The present formulation neglects also any effect of government transfer activities on money demand. (Empirically, the inclusion of federal or total government transfers in the G variable does not have a significant effect on the results.)

Using equations (17) and (18) and the approximation $\log(Y - \gamma G) \approx \log(Y) - \gamma G/Y$, which is satisfactory over the sample period since $\gamma G/Y \ll 1$ applies, leads to the price level equation,

$$\log(P_t) = \text{constant} + \log(M_t) - c_1\log(Y_t) + c_1\gamma(G/Y)_t + c_2R_t - c_3t - \epsilon_t^m.$$

Substituting for $\log(Y_t)$ from equation (4) then applies

$$\log(P_t) = \text{constant} + \log(M_t) - c_1(b_1DMR_t + b_2DMR_{t-1}) - c_1b_3\log(G_t)$$
$$+ c_1\gamma(G/Y)_t + c_2R_t - (c_1b_4 + c_3)t - (\epsilon_t^m + c_1\epsilon_t^Y). \tag{19}$$

The empirical work approximates equation (19) by combining the two G variables in a form involving $\log(G_t)$. The sign of this variable is generally ambiguous, since it depends on a comparison of the b_3 and γ parameters.

Abstracting for the moment from endogeneity of the interest rate, equation (19) implies the following hypotheses concerning monetary effects on the price level:

1. Given current and lagged DMR values and the nominal interest rate R_t, which would reflect anticipated inflation rates, there is a one-to-one effect of $\log(M_t)$ on $\log(P_t)$. Fully perceived movements in the money stock—which correspond to

changes in M_t while holding fixed current and lagged DMR values (weighted in accordance with their effects on current output)—have equiproportionate, contemporaneous effects on the price level.

2. Current and lagged values of the DMR variable have negative effects on the price level, for given values of M_t, R_t, and so on. The pattern of lagged DMR effects corresponds, with the opposite sign, to the pattern in the output equation. If real money demand is unit elastic in real expenditure ($c_1 = 1$), then the DMR pattern in the price level equation corresponds in magnitude and shape to the pattern in the output equation.[20] More generally, the DMR patterns would correspond in shape but not necessarily in magnitude.

3. Given M_t and the DMR values (and R_t, etc.), lagged values of the money stock—M_{t-1}, M_{t-2}, ... —or, equivalently, current and lagged values of actual money growth—DM_t, DM_{t-1}, ... —are irrelevant for the determination of the price level.

4. In the present formulation, changes in expected inflation rates that correspond to changes in expected growth rates of money or other variables are reflected in the nominal interest rate R_t. I have not yet successfully explored the relation between *exogenous* monetary movements and R_t. However, an increase in R_t, for given values of the DMR variables, and so on, has a positive effect on P_t.

Estimated Price Equation

One problem with estimation of equation (19) is the likely endogeneity of R_t; that is, the probable correlation between R_t and the error term of equation (19). (It can be noted that this estimation problem is equivalent to the familiar one of estimating the coefficient of a nominal interest rate as one of the right-hand variables in a money demand function.) Since I have not yet developed an analysis that relates the interest rate to exogenous variables such as money shocks, expected growth rates of money, and other factors, I have carried out estimation of the price equation with a lagged interest rate variable, R_{t-1}, used as an instrument for R_t.[21] The use of R_{t-1} as an instrument would eliminate correlation between the interest rate variable and the error term of equation (19)—thereby leading to consistent estimation at the expense of some lost efficiency—if the error term were itself serially uncorrelated. The estimation of the price equation might be improved by the development of a successful empirical model of interest rate determination. However, the main shortcoming of the present procedure may not be with estimation of the coefficients in equation (19), but rather with the lack of a full reduced-form description of the influence of money, and so on, on the price level. The channels of monetary effects on prices that involve variations in the nominal interest rate are not

---

[20]Equivalently, nominal income would in this case be invariant with the DMR variables for given values of M_t and R_t.

[21]An OLS regression of R_t on R_{t-1} alone from 1948 to 1978 yields

$$R_t = \underset{(.002)}{.002} + \underset{(.04)}{1.01 R_{t-1}}, \qquad R^2 = .96, \ D - W = 1.7, \ \hat{\sigma} = .004.$$

observed when the interest rate variable is held fixed separately, as in the present analysis.

From some preliminary work, it became clear that the immediate post–World War II observations on the price level were heavily influenced by a residual effect of the extensive wartime controls (see the following for a formal analysis of this period). Accordingly, I concentrate the empirical analysis on price equations that are estimated over the 1948–1978 period. It also turned out that additional lagged values of the DMR variable were significant when added to equation (19), so the reported results include the values $DMR_t, \ldots, DMR_{t-5}$.

The estimates of equation (19) for the 1948–1978 period are

$$
\begin{aligned}
\log(P_t) = {} & -4.30 + 1.01 \cdot \log(M_t) - .68DMR_t - 1.69DMR_{t-1} \\
& (.27) (.05) (.20) (.27) \\[4pt]
& - 1.87DMR_{t-2} - 1.42DMR_{t-3} - .65DMR_{t-4} - .32DMR_{t-5} \\
& (.31) \phantom{DMR_{t-2} -1.}(.25) \phantom{DMR_{t-3} -.}(.19) \phantom{DMR_{t-4} -.}(.16) \\[4pt]
& - .0165 \cdot t + .079 \cdot \log(G_t) \\
& (.0029) (.021) \\[4pt]
& + 5.0 \cdot R_t, \qquad \hat{\sigma} = .0136, \ DW = 1.6, \\
& (1.4)
\end{aligned}
\tag{20}
$$

where P is the GNP deflator (1972 base), R is the Aaa corporate bond rate,[22] and R_{t-1} has been used as an instrument for R_t in the estimation. Ordinary least-squares estimates are similar except for a substantial reduction in the estimated coefficient of R_t.[23]

The estimated coefficient of the $\log(M_t)$ variable in equation (20), 1.01, s.e. = .05, conforms with the null hypothesis of a unit coefficient. With lagged values of the money stock excluded (tests of this proposition are carried out below), the hypothesis of a unit coefficient on $\log(M_t)$ can be viewed as a test for the absence of money illusion. In this sense this hypothesis may be regarded as being on a different level—less specific to the expectational theory under test but essential for confidence in the other results—from the other propositions to be considered. If the coefficient of the $\log(M_t)$ variable is constrained to equal unity—which amounts to using the log of real balances as a dependent variable—the estimated price equation becomes

---

[22] Short-term interest rates—including 3-month Treasury Bill rates, the commercial paper rate, and the rate on savings and loan shares—were insignificant when added to the price equation.

[23] The OLS estimates are

$$
\begin{aligned}
\log(P_t) = {} & -4.52 + .96 \cdot \log(M_t) - .68DMR_t - 1.23DMR_{t-1} - 1.35DMR_{t-2} \\
& (.30) (.14) (.20) (.33) \phantom{DMR_{t-1} -1.}(.37) \\[4pt]
& - 1.04DMR_{t-3} - .55DMR_{t-4} - .22DMR_{t-5} - .0102 \cdot t + .052 \cdot \log(G_t) \\
& (.32) \phantom{DMR_{t-3} -.}(.29) \phantom{DMR_{t-4} -.}(.21) \phantom{DMR_{t-5} -.}(.0051) (.019) \\[4pt]
& + 2.7 \cdot R_t, \qquad \hat{\sigma} = .122, \ DW = 1.4. \\
& (.8)
\end{aligned}
$$

$$\log(P_t) = -4.28 + \log(M_t) - .68DMR_t - 1.70DMR_{t-1} - 1.88DMR_{t-2}$$
$$(.18)(.20)(.26)(.29)$$

$$-\ 1.42DMR_{t-3} - .64DMR_{t-4} - .32DMR_{t-5} - .0164 \cdot t$$
$$(.25)(.18)(.16)(.0029)$$

$$+\ .079 \cdot \log(G_t) + 5.0 \cdot R_t, \quad \hat{\sigma} = .0134,\ DW = 1.6.\ (21)$$
$$(.020)(1.2)$$

Not surprisingly, considering the closeness to unity of the estimated $\log(M_t)$ coefficient in equation (20), these estimates are similar to those obtained without the coefficient constraint. Again, the OLS estimates differ mainly in the estimated coefficient of R_t.[24]

The estimated coefficients and standard errors for the price equation are robust to estimation of a first-order autoregressive error process (under OLS estimation, since the instrument R_{t-1} is inappropriate in this case). The estimated autoregressive coefficient for the error term over the 1949–1978 sample is .40, s.e. $= .28$, in the form of equation (20); and .23, s.e. $= .24$, in the form of equation (21). The estimates are also similar if equations (20) and (21) are reestimated by OLS in first-difference form.[25] Finally, the inclusion of lagged dependent variables also

[24]The OLS estimates are

$$\log(P_t) = -4.59 + \log(M_t) - .69DMR_t - 1.29DMR_{t-1} - 1.43DMR_{t-2} - 1.10DMR_{t-3}$$
$$(.11)(.19)(.22)(.23)(.20)$$

$$-\ .61DMR_{t-4} - .25DMR_{t-5} - .0114 \cdot t + .055 \cdot \log(G_t) + 2.8 \cdot R_t,$$
$$(.17)(.14)(.0016)(.014)(.7)$$

$$\hat{\sigma} = .0118,\ DW = 1.5.$$

[25]When the coefficient of $\log(M_t)$ is unconstrained, the OLS estimate in first-difference form for the 1949–1978 sample are

$$D[\log(P_t)] = -.0066 + .91DM_t - .75D(DMR_t) - 1.26D(DMR_{t-1}) - 1.36D(DMR_{t-2})$$
$$(.0060)(.14)(.21)(.29)(.31)$$

$$-\ 1.03D(DMR_{t-3}) - .58D(DMR_{t-4}) - .22D(DMR_{t-5}) + .044D[\log(G_t)]$$
$$(.28)(.23)(.14)(.024)$$

$$+\ 2.6DR_t, \quad \hat{\sigma} = .0138,\ DW = 2.2,$$
$$(.8)$$

where D is the first-difference operator. With the coefficient of $\log(M_t)$ constrained to equal unity, the results are

$$D[\log(P_t)] = -.0099 + DM_t - .81D(DMR_t) - 1.33D(DMR_{t-1}) - 1.40D(DMR_{t-2})$$
$$(.0031)(.19)(.27)(.29)$$

$$-\ 1.05D(DMR_{t-3}) - .59D(DMR_{t-4}) - .23D(DMR_{t-5}) + .046D[\log(G_t)]$$
$$(.27)(.23)(.14)(.023)$$

$$+\ 2.5DR_t, \quad \hat{\sigma} = .0136,\ DW = 2.2.$$
$$(.8)$$

These results are close to OLS estimates in level form, as shown above in notes 23 and 24.

does not have a major impact on the estimates. The estimated coefficient of $\log(P_{t-1})$ in the form of equation (20)—under OLS for the 1948–1978 sample—is .29, s.e. = .16; whereas that for the lagged dependent variable, $\log(P/M)_{t-1}$, in equation (21) is .30, s.e. = .14.

All six of the estimated *DMR* coefficients in equation (21) are negative—that is, conforming in sign to the underlying theory—and all are individually significantly different from zero. The precision with which the lagged response of the price level to unanticipated money growth is estimated and the smooth triangular shape of the lag pattern are striking features of the results. On the other hand, the estimated lagged response of the price level to monetary shocks is elongated substantially relative to that for the unemployment rate and output, as shown in equations (5) and (7). Notably, the estimated coefficients on the *DMR* variables are significantly negative in the price equation up to a lag of 4–5 years, while the principal unemployment rate and output stimuli are completed after a 1-year lag. Put another way, an unanticipated increase (though not an anticipated rise) in the money stock is estimated to take over 5 years to filter through to an equiproportional move in the price level. The net impact of a money shock on the price level would actually be negative over part of the distributed lag response period.

The appearance of differing lag response patterns across the output and price level equations can be confirmed by formal statistical tests, which are carried out in Barro (1978, pp. 567–571). That paper (pp. 568–571) attempts also to account for this discrepancy by introducing a form of lagged adjustment into the money demand function. However, this line of argument does not convincingly explain the magnitude of the differences between the lag patterns. It is worth noting that the type of sluggish price adjustment that appears in equation (21) also cannot readily be explained by models of the "disequilibrium" (Barro and Grossman, 1976, Chapter 2) or contracting variety (e.g., Taylor, 1980). These theories seem to account only for a pattern of price stickiness that corresponds to the patterns of output and unemployment rate stickiness.

Although the above problem raises questions about the specification of the price equation, it seems useful to consider the outcome of some additional tests. As in the case of output and unemployment rate equations, it is possible to compare the performance of the set of *DMR* variables in equations (20) and (21) with that of a set of *DM* values. A joint test from the perspective of equation (20) that the coefficient of $\log(M_t)$ is unity and that the set of variables $(DM_t, \ldots, DM_{t-5})$ is irrelevant—which corresponds to the proposition that fully anticipated monetary change has an immediate, equiproportional effect on the price level—yields the statistic $F_{14}^7 = 4.9$, which exceeds the 5% critical value of 2.8. The reverse test associated with deletion of the *DMR* variables produces the statistic $F_{14}^7 = 17.7$. Accordingly, these results again indicate a preference for the *DMR* form of the equation, but the failure to accept the null hypothesis on the irrelevance of the *DM* variables suggests some type of misspecification. A similar conclusion emerges from cross-equation tests of coefficient restrictions that are calculated from joint estimates of money growth and price level equations. In the form where the coefficient of $\log(M_t)$ is maintained to be unity, a test of the coefficient restrictions implied by the *DMR* form of the price equation yields the test statistic [for $-2 \cdot$ log (likelihood ratio)] of 49.8, which exceeds the 1% χ^2 value with 14 d.f. of 29.1. Although there are insufficient observations to rely heavily on this asymptotic test, the outcome does accord with the other pieces of negative evidence on the specification of the price equation.

Considering these results, I will discuss only briefly the other estimated coefficients in the price equations. The coefficient on log(G_t), which was ambiguous in sign on theoretical grounds, is estimated in equation (21) to be positive. This result is dominated by the sharply upward movement in G for the Korean War; in particular, the coefficient estimate of .079 implies that the increase in G from 1950 to 1951 raised the price level for 1951 by 4.3%, which helps to explain the rise by 7.3% in the actual price level. The estimated negative time trend coefficient of -1.6% per year from equation (21) suggests that the output trend of 3.3% per year from equation (7) was offset by a negative trend in money demand of about -1.7% per year, assuming a unit real expenditure elasticity of real money demand. Finally, the estimated R_t coefficient of 5.0 in equation (21) corresponds to an elasticity of money demand with respect to the long-term interest rate of $-.26$ at the sample mean value of R over the 1948–1978 sample (which was .052) and an elasticity of $-.44$ at the 1978 value of R (.087). The interest rate variable is important in *accounting* for some of the strong price increases since the late 1960s. The movement of R from .045 in 1965 to .087 in 1978 contributes 1.6 percentage points per year to the average inflation rate over that period. The strong interplay between velocity shifts and changes in the price level implies that variations in R will be associated—although not necessarily in a causal sense—with magnified short-run fluctuations in the price level. Notably, a change by 1 percentage point in the annual average long-term interest rate would correspond to a movement by 5 percentage points in the annual average price level. Although a complete analysis would require a study of interest rate determination in the context of changes in anticipated inflation rates, the present results suggest that unpredictability of changes in long-term interest rates would be associated with magnified unpredictability of inflation rates.

I have considered the stability of the price equations over different sample periods. The World War II controls seem to have exerted an important downward effect on prive level observations from 1943 to 1947. The hypothesis can be decisively rejected that the 1947 and/or 1946 observations can be included with the 1948–1978 values in the forms of equations (20) or (21). Extrapolation of the price level estimates from equation (21) indicates that the reported price levels are below the estimated values by 8.1% in 1947, 22% in 1946, 42% in 1945, 31% in 1944, and 19% in 1943. Interestingly, the equation fits satisfactorily for 1942, where the actual price exceeds the extrapolated estimate by 2.6%. If the price discrepancies associated with World War II are regarded primarily as measurement errors, the reported price increase by 14.5% from 1945 to 1946 would be converted to an estimated decrease by 6.0%; the reported increase by 12.4% from 1946 to 1947 to an estimated decrease by 1.5%; and the reported increase by 6.6% from 1947 to 1948 to an estimated decrease by 1.0%. On the other hand, the reported average annual wartime inflation rate of 2.9% from 1942 to 1945 would be converted to an estimated average rate of 18.0%. In other words, the estimated values show the typical pattern of sharp price increase during wartime followed by some declines in the postwar period.

There is no indication of downward effects on the price level from the two post-World War II general price control programs, which were the Korean War controls for 1951-1952 and the more recent experiment from August 1971 through roughly 1973. Extrapolated residuals from a relation of the form of equation (21) that was estimated over the sample (1948-1950, 1953-1970, 1974-1978) are typically positive for the price control years: +3.7% for 1951, +1.8% for 1952, +1.9% for 1971, +0.5% for 1972, and −1.0% for 1973. Although the results could be influenced by endogeneity of the control programs or by effects of controls on explanatory variables like the interest rate, it is difficult to see how the post-1948 experience can be used to argue that controls significantly depress the price level,[26] even if one abstracts from the distinction between the reported and actual price levels during a controlled period. See Barro (1978, pp. 572-573) for some further discussion.

It is worth examining whether the estimated price equations show signs of the post-1974 breakdown in the money demand function that was noted by Enzler, Johnson, and Paulus (1976) and Goldfeld (1976), but disputed by Hamburger (1977). A test of the null hypothesis that the 1974-1978 observations can be grouped with the 1948-1973 values yields the statistics $F_{15}^5 = .6$, 5% critical value $= 2.9$, in the form of equation (20); and $F_{16}^5 = .7$, 5% critical value $= 2.8$, for the form of equation (21) where the restriction is maintained that the $\log(M_t)$ coefficient equals one. Therefore, these results support the hypothesis of unchanged structure before and after 1974.

Table 3 contains actual values of inflation rates (for the GNP deflator) and estimated values, which are calculated as differences between the estimated log of the price level from equation (21) and lagged values of the log of the actual price level. Except for the questionable value for 1948, as discussed above, and the sharp price increase for 1951, there is little inflation to explain until the late 1960s. The estimated equation *accounts* for the higher recent values of inflation from the stepup in monetary growth rates and from the increase in nominal interest rates, as mentioned earlier. The reduced growth rate of federal purchases since the late 1970s is a negative contributor to the recent estimated price level movements.

Inflation rate estimates, based on monetary observations through 1979 and interest rate data through March 7, 1980, are 6.8% for 1979 (compared to an actual value of 8.5%) and 17.9% for 1980. The predicted inflation rates exhibit a typically declining pattern thereafter, with a 1981 value of only 5.8% and a long-run value of 4.6% per year. Note that the inflation rate predictions of 4.5% for 1979 and 3.6%

---

[26]This conclusion seems to agree with that reached by Feige and Pearce (1976, p. 295) and to conflict with results obtained by Gordon (1975, p. 640). However, it is difficult to make a satisfactory comparison with Gordon's results, because his measurement of the price level by the private deflator exclusive of food and energy components involves a mixing up of absolute and relative price movements.

for 1980, which were based on data through 1978, are raised dramatically to 6.8% and 17.9%, respectively, by the inclusion of recent data. The sharp rise in interest rates—including the increase by more than 3 percentage points in the Aaa corporate bond rate from the average for 1979 to the value for March 7, 1980—is the main element in this change.

The long-run estimate for a monetary growth rate of 6.0% per year is not consistent with sustained annual inflation rates in the vicinity of 10%, although this behavior can be "explained" in the short-run via the increases in velocity that are produced by "exogenous" rises in interest rates. In fact, current long-term interest rates in excess of 10% are probably best regarded as a prediction of a shift in the monetary process away from the one that I have estimated from data through 1978 and toward a new structure that involves a higher mean rate of expansion. Subsequent observations will indicate whether a reformulation of the monetary process is required; the alternative seems to be that current nominal interest rates contain excessive predictions of long-term inflation.

Concluding Observations

The present empirical results from annual, post–World War II data indicate strong expansionary effects of current and lagged monetary shocks on the unemployment rate and output. Subject to some identification problems for testing natural rate hypotheses, as discussed earlier, the statistical tests indicate that the unemployment rate and output respond to the surprise parts of money movements rather than to systematic monetary policy. The details of monetary effects on business fluctuations emerge more clearly from the quarterly U.S. data that are examined in Barro and Rush (1980, Part II), but additional work is needed in that context to account for residual serial correlation and to deal with problems of seasonality.

The results reveal substantial contemporaneous expansionary effects of federal purchases. Further analysis of these effects, which focuses on the theoretical and empirical distinction between temporary and permanent government purchases, is contained in Barro (1979c).

The estimated price level equations are consistent with some of the underlying natural rate hypotheses, but they also reveal some serious specification problems. The most notable puzzle involves the substantial elongation in the lagged response of prices to money shocks, as compared with the behavior of output and the unemployment rate.

The present results do not reveal the channels of effect by which movements in money or government purchases are communicated to variations in the unemployment rate and output. Theoretical analyses, as in Lucas (1972, 1973, 1975) and Barro (1976, 1980), stress the role of intertemporal substitution variables like prices relative to expected future prices and anticipated real rates of return on earning assets. Improvement of the price equation is an important element for a study of these types of relative price variables. The analysis will also have to encompass the determination of nominal interest rates, which appear through their influence on velocity as *explanatory* variables in the price equations. Nominal interest rates enter also into anticipated real rate-of-return calculations.

The methods for analyzing post–World War II behavior in the present study would be usefully applied to long-period time series data for the United States. The possibility of isolating different monetary regimes, such as the one prevailing during the gold standard period prior to World War I and the one associated with the volatile monetary behavior of the interwar years, improves the chances for testing natural rate hypotheses and thereby making reliable inferences for policy. Cross-crountry evidence, as utilized by Lucas (1973), would be useful for similar reasons.

References

Barro, R. J., "Unanticipated Money Growth and Unemployment in the United States," working paper, University of Rochester, July 1975.

Barro, R. J., "Rational Expectations and the Role of Monetary Policy," *Journal of Monetary Economics,* 2, January 1976, 1–32.

Barro, R. J., "Unanticipated Money Growth and Unemployment in the United States," *American Economic Review,* 67, March 1977, 101–115.

Barro, R. J., "Unanticipated Money, Output, and the Price Level in the United States," *Journal of Political Economy,* 86, August 1978, 549–580.

Barro, R. J., "On the Determination of the Public Debt," *Journal of Political Economy,* 87, October 1979a, 940–971.

Barro, R. J., "Unanticipated Money Growth and Unemployment in the United States: Reply," *American Economic Review,* 69, December 1979b, 1004–1009.

Barro, R. J., "Output Effects of Government Purchases," unpublished, University of Rochester, December 1979c.

Barro, R. J., "A Capital Market in an Equilibrium Business Cycle Model," *Econometrica,* 48, 1980.

Barro, R. J., and H. I. Grossman, *Money, Employment, and Inflation,* Cambridge, Cambridge University Press, 1976.

Barro, R. J., and M. Rush, "Unanticipated Money and Economic Activity," in S. Fischer, ed., *Rational Expectations and Economic Policy,* Chicago, University of Chicago Press for the National Bureau of Economic Research, 1980.

Cooley, T. F., and E. C. Prescott, "Varying Parameter Regression: A Theory and Some Applications," *Annals of Economics and Social Measurement,* 2, 1973, 463–474.

Enzler, J., L. Johnson, and J. Paulus, "Some Problems of Money Demand," *Brookings Papers on Economic Activity,* 1, 1976, 261–280.

Feige, E. L., and D. K. Pearce, "Inflation and Incomes Policy: An Application of Time Series Models," *Journal of Monetary Economics,* supplement, 1976, 273–302.

Friedman, M., and A. J. Schwartz, *Monetary Statistics of the United States,* New York, Columbia University Press, 1970.

Germany, J. D., and S. Srivastava, "Empirical Estimates of Unanticipated Policy: Issues in Stability and Identification," unpublished, M.I.T., June 1979.

Goldfeld, S. M., "The Case of the Missing Money," *Brookings Papers on Economic Activity,* 3, 1976, 683–730.

Gordon, R. J., "The Impact of Aggregate Demand on Prices," *Brookings Papers on Economic Activity,* 3, 1975, 613–670.

Hamburger, M. J., "Behavior of the Money Stock: Is there a Puzzle," *Journal of Monetary Economics,* 3, July, 1977, 266–288.

Hansen, L. P., and T. J. Sargent, "Formulating and Estimating Dynamic Linear Rational Expectations Models," unpublished, Federal Reserve Bank of Minneapolis, March 1979a.

Hansen, L. P., and T. J. Sargent, "Linear Rational Expectations Models for Dynamically Interrelated Variables," unpublished, Federal Reserve Bank of Minneapolis, July, 1979b.

Leiderman, L., "Macroeconometric Testing of the Rational Expectations and Structural Neutrality Hypotheses for the United States," *Journal of Monetary Economics,* 6, January 1980, 69-82.

Lucas, R. E., "Expectations and the Neutrality of Money," *Journal of Economic Theory,* 4, April 1972, 103-124.

Lucas, R. E., "Some International Evidence on Output-Inflation Tradeoffs," *American Economic Review,* 63, June 1973, 326-334.

Lucas, R. E., "An Equilibrium Model of the Business Cycle," *Journal of Political Economy,* 83, December 1975, 1113-1144.

McCallum, B. T., "The Current State of the Policy-Ineffectiveness Debate," *American Economic Review,* proceedings, 69, May 1979, 240-245.

Plosser, C. I., and G. W. Schwert, "Money, Income and Sunspots: Measuring Economic Relationships and the Effects of Differencing," *Journal of Monetary Economics,* 4, November 1978, 637-660.

Sargent, T. J., *Testing for Neutrality and Rationality,* Federal Reserve Bank of Minneapolis, June 1976a.

Sargent, T. J., "The Observational Equivalence of Natural and Unnatural Rate Theories of Macroeconomics," *Journal of Political Economy,* 84, June 1976b, 631-640.

Sargent, T. J., and N. Wallace, "Rational Expectations, the Optimal Monetary Instrument, and the Optimal Money Supply Rule," *Journal of Political Economy,* 83, April 1975, 214-254.

Small, D. H., "Unanticipated Money Growth and Unemployment in the United States: Comment," *American Economic Review,* 69, December 1979, 996-1003.

Taylor, J. B., "Aggregate Dynamics and Staggered Contracts," *Journal of Political Economy,* 88, February 1980, 1-23.

ALTERNATIVE APPROACHES TO MACROECONOMICS

This section discusses *Keynesian-style* macroeconomics. The first two papers (nos. 6,7) are the basis for the non-market-clearing analysis that Herschel Grossman and I have addressed in our book, *Money, Employment, and Inflation*. I have been asked frequently about the relation of this work to my subsequent research on *equilibrium-style* macroanalysis. Putting aside frivolous remarks concerning schizophrenia and the desirability of maintaining a diversified portfolio of views, I have managed to construct something of an explanation. Before the late 1960s and early 1970s, the Keynesian model was the only serious theory of business fluctuations. Accordingly, it was a major concern to resolve some internal inconsistencies in this standard framework, which involved such issues as the nature of the labor market analysis, the role of effective demand, the meaning of quantity variables as arguments in the consumption and other functions, the significance of Walras' Law in a setting where all markets could apparently be in simultaneous excess supply, the asymmetric treatment of commodity supply and demand, and so on. In the narrow sense of clarifying some of these matters, I think that Grossman's and my analysis, in conjunction with the earlier work of Patinkin and Clower, has been basically successful.

It was apparent throughout that crucial elements of our and others' analysis relied on unexplained failures of wages and prices to adjust instantaneously to clear markets. Although the importance of this assumption was clear, it seemed a reasonable modeling strategy to develop implications of the non-market-clearing model without at each stage questioning this key building block. At the time we thought also that the slow adjustment of wages and prices might eventually receive an independent explanation that was consistent with individual rationality. (An approach that assumes direct costs of price adjustment is carried out in paper no. 8. The shortcoming of this type of model is that these direct costs of adjustment are unlikely to be of sufficient quantitative importance to play a major role in business cycles.)

171

Somewhat later I appreciated that imperfect flexibility of wages and prices was only a proxy in Keynesian models for a more general type of malfunctioning of the private sector with respect to the execution of mutually advantageous production and exchange. This point is clear in long-term contracting analyses (discussed in paper no. 9), which can account for some wage-price rigidites at the same time that they make *full employment* consistent with these rigidities. The crucial missing link in Keynesian models concerns the nature of the private sector inefficiencies that allow government intervention via the usual macropolicy instruments to improve economic outcomes. Elements of imperfect information, mobility costs, and the like—which have been stressed as influences on business fluctuations in the equilibrium-type models—tend to inhibit government actions as much as they do those of the private sector.

A General Disequilibrium Model of Income and Employment

WITH HERSCHEL I. GROSSMAN

As is now well understood, the key to the Keynesian theory of income determination is the assumption that the vector of prices, wages, and interest rates does not move instantaneously from one full employment equilibrium position to another. By implication, Keynesian economics rejects the market equilibrium framework for analyzing the determination of quantities bought, sold, and produced. This framework is associated with Walras and Marshall, both of whom proceeded as if all markets were continuously cleared. Walras rationalized this procedure by incorporating recontracting arrangements, while Marshall did so by regarding price adjustments to be an instantaneous response to momentary discrepancies between quantities supplied and demanded.

By rejecting these rationalizations, Keynesian theory proposes as a general case a system of markets which are not always cleared. Keynes was, tacitly at least, concerned with the general theoretical problem of the intermarket relationships in such a system. The failure of a market to clear implies that, for at least some individuals, actual quantities transacted diverge from the quantities which they supply or demand. Thus, the natural focus of Keynesian analysis is on the implications for behavior in one market of the existence of such a divergence in another

* Assistant professor and associate professor of economics, respectively, Brown University. National Science Foundation Grants GS-2419 and GS-3246 supported this research.

market. Indeed, some recent writers, such as Robert Clower and Axel Leijonhufvud, have argued very convincingly that this focus is the crucial distinguishing feature of Keynesian economics.

Unfortunately, the evolution of conventional post-Keynesian macroeconomics failed to interpret the Keynesian system in this light.[1] Instead, conventional analysis has chronically attempted to coax Keynesian results out of a framework of general market equilibrium. The result has been to leave conventional macroeconomics with an embarrassingly weak choice-theoretic basis, and to associate with it important implications which are difficult to reconcile with observed phenomena.

A classic example of such a difficulty concerns the relationship between the level of employment and the real wage rate. In the conventional analysis, the demand for labor is inversely and uniquely related to the level of real wages. This assumption accords with Keynes; who, in this respect, had adhered to received pre-Keynesian doctrine.[2] Given this assump-

[1] See Leijonhufvud.

[2] Keynes wrote:
... with a given organization, equipment and technique, real wages and the volume of output (and hence of employment) are uniquely correlated, so that, in general, an increase in employment can only occur to the accompaniment of a decline in the rate of real wages. Thus, I am not disputing this vital fact which the classical economists have (rightly) asserted. ... The real wage earned by a unit of labor has a unique inverse correlation with the volume of employment. [1936, p. 17]

173

Reprinted from *American Economic Review*, 61(1), March 1971, 82–93, by permission of American Economic Association, Nashville, Tennessee, and the authors.

tion, cyclical variations in the quantity of labor demanded and the amount of employment must imply countercyclical variation in real wage rates. As is well known, however, such a pattern of real wages has not been observed.[3]

A few authors have pointed out the inappropriateness of attempts to force Keynesian analysis into a market equilibrium framework. Contributions by Don Patinkin (1956) and Clower, in particular, represent important attempts to reconstruct macroeconomic theory within an explicitly disequilibrium context.

In the unfortunately neglected chapter 13 of *Money, Interest, and Prices*, Patinkin analyzed involuntary unemployment in a context of explicit market disequilibrium; and he showed that the misleading implications of the conventional analysis regarding the real wage are a direct consequence of its general equilibrium character.[4] Patinkin presented a theory in which involuntary unemployment of labor can arise as a consequence of disequilibrium, in particular, excess supply in the market for current output. In this theory, the inability of firms to sell the quantity of output given by their supply schedule causes them to demand a smaller quantity of labor than that given by their conventional (or notional) demand schedule. The immediate significance of this theory is that it is able to generate unemployment without placing any restrictions on the level

or movement of the real wage.[5] Unemployment of labor requires only that the vector of prices and wages implies a deficiency of demand for current output. As Patinkin suggests, this interpretation of the proximate cause of unemployment is more Keynesian than Keynes' own discussion.

The essence of Patinkin's theory is causality running from the level of excess supply in the market for current output to the state of excess supply in the market for labor. Patinkin thereby explains the proximate cause of cyclical unemployment, but his analysis involves only partial, rather than general, disequilibrium. At the least, a general disequilibrium model would, in addition, incorporate the possibility of a reverse influence of the level of excess supply in the labor market upon the state of excess supply in the market for current output.

Clower's important paper develops a theory emphasizing this causal relationship. He presents a derivation of the Keynesian consumption function in which he interprets the relationship between consumption and income as a manifestation of disequilibrium in the labor market. This approach to explaining household behavior is obviously similar to Patinkin's analysis of the firm. The only significant difference is that Clower's households have a choice between consuming and saving, so that his problem is explicitly choice theoretic. However, if Patinkin's approach were generalized to a multi-input production function, the resulting analysis would be formally analogous to Clower's.

The analysis in this paper builds on the

---

[3] The evidence has been recently reviewed by Edwin Kuh, esp. pp. 246–48; and Ronald Bodkin. Keynes (1939) recognized this discrepancy, and offered a rather contrived explanation for it in terms of monopoly and procyclical variation in demand elasticities. More recently, Kuh attempted to explain this discrepancy in terms of a fixed proportions production function in the short run.

[4] Chapter 13 also appears, apparently unchanged, in the second edition of *Money, Interest, and Prices* (1965). Patinkin had first presented some of the essentials of this analysis i̓ ᵃn earlier article (1949). A similar formulation appeaɪ ˙n Edgar Edwards.

[5] Patinkin's theory does not involve any restrictions either upon the substitutability among factors of production or upon demand elasticities. (See fn. 3.) Of course, this theory does not deny that an excessive level of real wages can be an independent cause of unemployment. But, a clear analytical distinction is made between unemployment due to this cause, and unemployment which occurs even when the level of real wages is not excessive.

foundations laid down by the Patinkin and Clower analyses of a depressed economy. Our purpose is to develop a generalized analysis of both booms and depressions as disequilibrium phenomena.[6] Section I sketches the analytical framework employed. Section II reviews and generalizes Patinkin's analysis of the labor market and involuntary unemployment. Section III develops a distinction, implied by Patinkin's analysis, between two concepts of unemployment; one associated with excess supply in the labor market and the other associated with equilibrium in the labor market but with disequilibrium elsewhere in the system. Section IV reviews Clower's analysis and shows how it is formally analogous to Patinkin's. Section V joins the Patinkin and Clower analyses into a model of an economy experiencing deficient aggregate demand. Section VI formulates an analogous model of an economy experiencing excessive aggregate demand. Finally, Section VII summarizes the main results.

I. Analytical Framework

The following discussion utilizes a simple aggregative framework which involves three economic goods—labor services, consumable commodities. and fiat money—and two forms of economic decision making unit—firms and households. Labor services are the only variable input into the production process. Other inputs have a fixed quantity, no alternative use, and zero user cost. Consumable commodities are the only form of current output; there is no investment.[7] Money is the only store of

[6] The analysis by Robert Solow and Joseph Stiglitz, although they emphasize different questions, is somewhat similar to the present approach. However, their analytical format does differ from ours in at least three substantial respects: First, they do not discuss the choice-theoretic basis for the theory. Second, the equilibrium price level is indeterminate in their model. Third, by introducing restrictions on the rate of change of employment, they complicate matters and obscure what would seem to be essential in the intermarket effects of disequilibrium.

[7] It should be clear that the incorporation of investment and a market for securities would alter none of the conclusions advanced in this paper.

value, and it also serves as a medium of exchange and unit of account. The nominal quantity of money is exogenous and constant.

Firms demand labor and supply commodities. They attempt to maximize profits. Households supply labor and demand commodities and money balances. They also receive the profits of the firms according to a predetermined distribution pattern. Households attempt to maximize utility. Each firm and household is an atomistic competitor in the markets for both commodities and labor.

Following Patinkin (1956, 1965), each of the flow variables in the model—commodities, labor services, and the increment to money balances—is for simplicity expressed as the quantity which accrues over a finite unit of time, say a week, so that each assumes the dimensions of a stock. The model thus includes the following variables:

y = quantity of commodities
x = quantity of labor services
m = increment to real money balances (in commodity units)
π = quantity of real profits (in commodity units)
M = initial stock of nominal money balances
P = money price of commodities
w = real wage rate (in commodity units)

Throughout the following discussion, the method of analysis is to take a particular vector of the price level and real wage rate as given, and to work out the levels of income and employment implied by that vector. This procedure represents a non-Marshallian, or Keynesian, extreme, and following John Hicks may be denoted as the "fix-price method." The analysis does, of course, have implications for the appropriate specification of the forces making for changes in prices and wages. This paper does not explicitly investigate these implications, although we do consider a parenthetical example concerning the model's implications for the cyclical behavior of real wages.[8]

II. Patinkin's Analysis of the Labor Market

Consider the behavior of the representative firm under the provisional assumption that it regards profit maximization as being constrained only by the production function. In particular, the firm perceives that it can purchase all the labor which it demands and sell all the output which it supplies at the existing levels of w and P. Thus, profits are given by

$$\pi = y^S - wx^D,$$

where the superscripts indicate supply and demand quantities. Assuming the production function to be

$$y = F(x),$$

with positive and diminishing marginal product, profit maximization implies

$$x^D = x^D(w),$$

such that $\partial F/\partial x = w$, and

$$y^S = F(x^D)$$

Patinkin (1956, 1965) contrasts the above to a situation in which commodities are in excess supply. Voluntary exchange implies that actual total sales will equal the total quantity demanded. The representative firm will not be able to sell its notional supply y^S.[9] Let y represent its actual demand-determined sales, where $y < y^S$.[10] Then, the profit maximization

problem becomes simply to select the minimum quantity of labor necessary to produce output quantity y.[11] In other words, the firm maximizes

$$\pi = y - wx^{D'},$$

subject to $y = F(x)$. The variable $x^{D'}$ may be denoted as the effective demand for labor. Profit maximization now implies

$$(1) \qquad x^{D'} = F^{-1}(y) \quad \text{for } \frac{dF}{dx} \geq w$$

The constraint of $y < y^S$ implies $x^{D'} < x^D$, with $x^{D'}$ approaching x^D as y approaches y^S.[12]

___
this apportionment within a framework of voluntary exchange.

The inability of a firm to sell its desired output at the going price violates an assumption of the perfectly competitive model. Kenneth Arrow has stressed this inconsistency of perfect competition with disequilibrium. Essentially, he argues that economic units which act as perfect competitors in equilibrium must (at least in certain respects) perform as monopolists in disequilibrium. In this paper we focus on the reaction of economic units to given (equilibrium or disequilibrium) price levels. If, in addition, one wished to analyze explicitly the dynamics of price adjustment, it would be necessary to discard the perfectly competitive paradigm of the producer as a price taker. (In this regard, see Barro 1970, 1971.)

[11] This analysis abstracts from inventory accumulation or decumulation. For simplicity, we assume throughout that output always adjusts instantaneously to equal the smaller of supply and demand. Permitting inventory accumulation would not affect the essentials of the analysis, although it would introduce a complication analogous to the inclusion of an additional input. In general, we might obtain $dy/dt = k[\min (y^D, y^S) - y]$, where $k = k(w, y) > 0$. A similar gradual adjustment process for employment might also be possible, as in Solow and Stiglitz.

[12] The choice-theoretic nature of the problem becomes much more interesting when there is more than one form of input. Assume profits to be given by $\pi = y - w_1 x_1^{D'} - w_2 x_2^{D'}$, where the production function is $y = F(x_1, x_2)$, which has the usual convexity properties. Profit maximization now implies

$$(1.1) \qquad x_1^{D'} = x_1^{D'}\left(\frac{w_1}{w_2}, y\right)$$

$$(1.2) \qquad x_2^{D'} = x_2^{D'}\left(\frac{w_1}{w_2}, y\right)$$

such that at output y, $(\partial F/\partial X_1)/(\partial F/\partial X_2) = (w_1/w_2)$. In reducing output y^S to y, the firm must now make a decision regarding optimal input combinations. However, as y approaches y^S, $x_1^{D'}$ and $x_2^{D'}$ approach x_1^D and x_2^D.

___
[8] Grossman develops a more general model of multimarket disequilibrium based on Clower's choice-theoretic paradigm, and focuses in detail on the implications of this model for the disequilibrium behavior of prices and interest.

[9] We assume here that the firm would actually like to sell y^S. Such behavior may not always be optimal. For example, Section VI discusses a situation of excess demand for labor in which the firm's effective supply $y^{S'}$ is less than y^S. However, we assume for simplicity that excess demand for labor never coexists with excess supply of commodities and vice versa. Grossman presents a more general treatment of multi-market disequilibria which allows for the coexistence of excess supply in one market and excess demand in another, as well as excess supply or demand in both.

[10] In principle, y need not be less than y^S for every firm. The apportionment of the actual sales among the firms depends upon established queuing or rationing procedures. Grossman presents an explicit analysis of

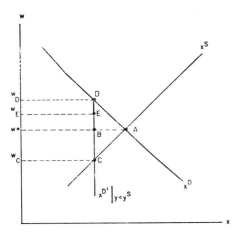

FIGURE 1. THE LABOR MARKET WITH EXCESS SUPPLY
OF COMMODITIES

The essential implication of equation (1) is that the effective demand for labor can vary even with the real wage fixed. Given voluntary exchange, employment cannot exceed the effective demand for labor. The quantity of employment thus is not uniquely associated with the real wage.

III. The Concept of Unemployment

Figure 1 depicts the preceding analysis of the labor market. The notional demand schedule for labor x^D is downward sloping. If $y = y^S$, the effective demand for labor $x^{D'}$ coincides with the notional demand. If $y < y^S$, the effective demand is independent of the real wage and less than the notional demand. The (notional) supply schedule for labor x^S, which will be derived below, is shown as upward sloping.

Figure 1 suggests a distinction between two concepts of unemployment—involuntary unemployment associated with excess (effective) labor supply, and voluntary unemployment associated with equilibrium in the labor market, but with disequilibrium elsewhere in the system. Suppose that initially the commodity market is in equilibrium, so that $y = y^S$ and $x^{D'} = x^D$, and that initially the real wage is w^*. Thus, the labor market is in equilib-

rium at point A, which may be denoted as full employment general equilibrium. Now suppose, say because the price level P is too high, that commodity demand is lower so that $y < y^S$ and $x^{D'} < x^D$. At the real wage w^*, excess supply of labor will amount to quantity AB. Failure of the price level to adjust to clear the commodity market leads to excess supply in the labor market. This excess supply represents what we usually refer to as involuntary unemployment. It is also what the Bureau of Labor Statistics ideally intends to represent by its statistical measure of unemployment—those seeking but not obtaining work at the going real wage. Involuntary unemployment clearly does not require a rise in the real wage above the level consistent with full employment equilibrium.

Now suppose that the real wage were to decline to w_C, so that the supply and effective demand for labor are equilibrated at point C. At point C, involuntary unemployment has vanished, but clearly this situation is not optimal. The reduced real wage has induced AB man-hours of labor to leave the labor force. Employment remains AB man-hours below the level associated with general equilibrium. Involuntary, i.e., excess supply, unemployment has been replaced by voluntary unemployment.[13]

The conclusion is that too high a real wage was not the cause of the lower employment, and a reduction in the real wage

[13] In terms of the *BLS* unemployment statistic, it is not clear that "zero" unemployment would be measured at w_C. If the higher wage, w^*, were (at least for a time) viewed as "normal," a considerable proportion of job seekers at wage w_C would be those willing to work at w^*, but not at w_C. These people are in the labor market seeking information on possible employment opportunities at (or above) w^*, and would not actually be willing to work at the going wage (see Armen Alchian). To the extent that the *BLS* measure includes this type of frustrated job seeker, the index will be a better measure of the gap between actual and general equilibrium employment BA, while simultaneously being a poorer index of those seeking but not obtaining employment at the going wage w_C.

is only a superficial cure. The real cause of the problem was the fall in commodity demand, and only a reflation of commodity demand can restore employment to the proper level.

The above analysis suggests the following cyclical patterns of real wages and employment: A decline in commodity demand and output produces a decline in employment with a corresponding excess supply of labor (point B). To the extent that real wages decline in response to this excess supply, a fall in real wages toward w_C will accompany (follow upon) the decline in employment. If, at point C or at some intermediate point between B and C, some action is taken to restore effective commodity demand, excess demand for labor (or, at least reduced excess supply) will result. In that case, a rising real wage may accompany the recovery of output and employment. Thus, disequilibrium analysis of the labor market suggests that real wages may move procyclically. This result differs from the conventional view that employment and real wages must be inversely related.

The present model can also be used to analyze involuntary unemployment which results from an excessive real wage. Clearly, if the real wage were above w^*, no stimulation of commodity demand could bring about full employment equilibrium, unless the real wage were reduced. This classical type of involuntary unemployment should be clearly distinguished from the type of unemployment discussed above, which arises, with the real wage at or below w^*, from a deficiency of demand for commodities.

IV. Clower's Analysis of the Consumption Function

In order to close the model, we must also analyze household behavior. Consider the behavior of the representative household under the provisional assumption that it regards utility maximization as being sub-

ject only to the budget constraint. In particular, the household perceives that it can sell all the labor which it supplies and purchase all the commodities which it demands at the existing levels of w and P. Assume the utility function to be

$$U = U\left(x^S, y^D, \frac{M}{P} + m^D\right),$$

with the partial derivatives $U_1 < 0$, $U_2 > 0$ and $U_3 > 0$. The budget constraint is

$$\pi + wx^S = y^D + m^D$$

x^S, y^D, and m^D may be denoted as the notional supply of labor, the notional demand for commodities, and the notional demand for additional money balances. Utility maximization in general will imply that x^S, y^D, and m^D are each functions of w, M/P, and π. For simplicity, we shall assume that x^S depends only on the real wage. The important point is that the notional demand functions for commodities and additional money balances do not have the forms of the usual consumption and saving functions with income as an argument, because the household simultaneously chooses the quantity of labor to sell.

Clower contrasts the above notional process to a situation in which labor services are in excess supply. Given voluntary exchange, actual total employment in this situation equals the total quantity demanded. Thus, the representative household is unable to sell its notional labor supply x^S and obtain its implied notional labor income wx^S.[14] Labor income is no longer a choice variable which is maximized out, but is instead exogenously given. We may assume that the representative household is able to obtain the quantity of employment x, where $x < x^S$

[14] We assume that the household would actually like to sell x^S. As indicated in fn. 9, we assume for simplicity that excess demand for commodities never coexists with excess supply of labor.

so that its total income is $wx+\pi$. In this case, the utility maximization problem amounts to the optimal disposition of this income.

In other words, the household maximizes

$$U\left(x, y^{D'}, \frac{M}{P} + m^{D'}\right)$$

subject to $\pi+wx=y^{D'}+m^{D'}$. The variables $y^{D'}$ and $m^{D'}$ may be denoted as the effective demands for commodities and additional money balances. Utility maximization now implies

$$(2) \qquad y^{D'} = y^{D'}\left(\pi + wx, \frac{M}{P}\right),$$

and

$$(3) \qquad m^{D'} = m^{D'}\left(\pi + wx, \frac{M}{P}\right)$$

Note that, in aggregate, $\pi+wx=y=F(x)$. Thus, since all income accrues to the households, consumption and saving demand depend ultimately only on the level of employment and real money balances and not on the real wage rate. The constraint $x<x^S$ would generally imply $y^{D'}<y^D$ and $m^{D'}<m^D$, but as x approaches x^S, $y^{D'}$ and $m^{D'}$ approach y^D and m^D.[15]

The important property of equations (2) and (3) is that they do have the form of the usual Keynesian consumption and saving functions. Labor income enters the consumption and saving functions as it represents the constraint upon the demand for current output imposed by the excess supply of labor.

[15] To the extent that long-run employment (income) exceeds current employment (income), a household may be more willing to maintain a higher demand for commodities at the expense of money balances. In this case effective commodity demand would remain closer to notional demand, and the "income multiplier" (as depicted later in Figure 4) would be smaller. In general, the size of the effect of quantity constraints on effective demands will depend on whether the constraint is viewed as "permanent" or "transitory."

The formal analogy between the Clower and Patinkin models should be apparent from the derivations of equations (2), (3) and equation (1), or more particularly equations (1.1) and (1.2) in footnote 12. Patinkin's model involves profit maximization subject to an output constraint, whereas Clower's model involves utility maximization subject to an employment constraint.

V. General Disequilibrium Involving Excess Supply

In Patinkin's analysis, the effective demand for labor was derived for a given level of demand for current output. To close this model, the demand for current output must be explained. In Clower's analysis, the effective demand for current output was derived for a given level of demand for labor. To close this model, the demand for labor must be explained. Thus, the Patinkin and Clower analyses are essential complements. When appropriately joined, they form a complete picture of the determination of output and employment in a depressed economy.

Figure 2 depicts Clower's analysis of the commodity market. The notional supply schedule for commodities is a downward sloping function of the real wage. The two notional demand schedules are upward sloping functions, reflecting the effect of substitutability between consumption and leisure as well as a positive income effect. As the real wage rate rises, leisure becomes relatively more expensive, and households tend to work and consume more. The schedule corresponding to the general equilibrium price level P^* passes through the point A. At point A, which corresponds to point A in Figure 1, P^* and w^* are consistent with simultaneous notional equilibrium in both the labor and commodity markets. The other notional commodity demand schedule in Figure 2 corresponds to the higher price level P_1. Because of the real balance effect, this

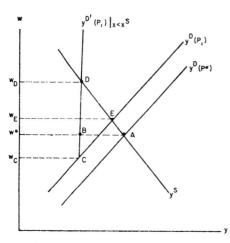

FIGURE 2. THE COMMODITY MARKET WITH
EXCESS SUPPLY OF LABOR

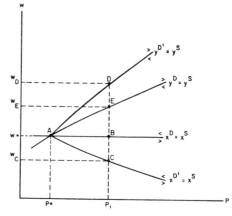

FIGURE 3. INTERACTION OF EXCESS
SUPPLY IN BOTH MARKETS

curve lies to the left of the curve associated with P^*.[16] If $x = x^s$, the effective demand for commodities coincides with the notional demand. If $x < x^s$, the effective demand is independent of the real wage, as noted above, and is less than the notional demand. The effective demand schedule shown in Figure 2 corresponds to the higher price level P_1. Points B, C, D, and E also correspond to the same points in Figure 1. This correspondence can be seen most clearly by explicitly depicting the interaction between the two markets, as is done in Figures 3 and 4.

Figure 3 illustrates the relationship between the existence of excess supply in one market and the other. In Figure 3, the points A, B, C, D, and E coincide with the same points in Figures 1 and 2. The four loci separate the regions of inequality between the indicated supply and demand

concepts. The locus $x^D = x^S$ is horizontal because, by assumption, both x^D and x^S depend only on the real wage. The locus $y^D = y^S$ is upward sloping because as shown in Figure 2, y^S is a decreasing function of the real wage, whereas y^D is an increasing function of the real wage (substitution and income effect) and a decreasing function of the price level (real balance effect). These loci intersect at point A, which depicts full employment general equilibrium. Points B, C, D, and E are all associated with a price level P_1, which is higher than the equilibrium price level P^*.[17] Point B, for example, would be consistent with notional equilibrium in the labor market, but implies excess supply in the commodity market. The essential point of Patinkin's analysis is that the effective demand for labor is smaller than the notional demand when commodities are in excess supply. Thus, the locus $x^{D'} = x^S$ exists to the right of point A and lies everywhere below the locus $x^D = x^S$. The existence of excess supply in the commodity market enlarges the region of excess supply in the labor market. Similarly, according to Clower's

---

[16] As the model is constructed, only y^D and m^D of the five notional schedules; x^D, x^S, y^D, y^S, and m^D depend on the price level independently of the real wage. In a more general model, real balances would affect x^D, x^S, and y^S, and the price level would affect these schedules also. By ignoring this possibility, the exposition is simplified without losing any of the essence of the analysis. Of course, if none of the five schedules were influenced by the price level, prices would not be determined within the model.

[17] We could, of course, just as well think of these points as being associated with a nominal money supply which is too small.

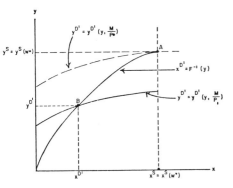

FIGURE 4. OUTPUT AND EMPLOYMENT WITH EXCESS
SUPPLY IN BOTH MARKETS

analysis, the effective demand for commodities is less than the notional demand when labor is in excess supply. Thus, the locus $y^{D'}=y^S$ exists to the right of point A and lies everywhere above the locus $y^D=y^S$. The existence of excess supply in the labor market also enlarges the region of excess supply in the commodity market.

Figure 4 illustrates the determination of the actual quantities of current output and employment when there is excess supply in both markets. In particular, Figure 4 has been drawn under the assumption that the existing wage-price vector is (w^*, P_1), that is that the economy is at point B of Figures 1, 2, and 3. Given voluntary exchange, x and y are determined by $x=\min[x^{D'}, x^S]$ and $y=\min[y^{D'}, y^S]$. The solid locus $x^{D'}=F^{-1}(y)$ describes firm behavior for values of y less than y^S. The solid locus $y^{D'}=y^{D'}(y, M/P_1)$ describes household behavior for values of x less than x^S. The intersection of these two loci determines the values of x and y corresponding to point B. Point A, full employment equilibrium, is at the intersection of y^S and x^S. Since at point B the real wage is consistent with full employment equilibrium, a movement from B to A involves on net only a fall in the price level from P_1 to P^*. In Figure 4, this fall in P is represented by an upward shift in $y^{D'}$ to the dashed locus $y^{D'}(y, M/P^*)$, which intersects $x^{D'}$ at

point A. The income multiplier in this case is given by the ratio of the difference between y^S and $y^{D'}(B)$ to the vertical distance between the two curves $y^{D'}(P^*)$ and $y^{D'}(P_1)$. Figure 4 is simply the Keynesian cross diagram with employment replacing income on the horizontal axis.

VI. General Disequilibrium Involving Excess Demand

The preceding discussion has concentrated on the case of excess supply in the markets for both commodities and labor. However, analogous considerations clearly apply to the boom situation of excess demand for both commodities and labor.

First, consider the behavior of the representative firm when there is excess demand for labor. The representative firm will be be able to obtain the quantity of labor x, where $x<x^D$. The firm then must maximize

$$\pi = y^{S'} - wx$$

subject to $y=F(x)$. The variable $y^{S'}$ may be denoted as the effective supply of commodities. The problem is simply to produce as much output as possible with the available labor. The solution is

(4) $y^{S'} = F(x)$ for $\dfrac{dF}{dx} \geq w$

Figure 5 depicts the commodity market in this situation, and is analogous to Figure 2. The price level P_2 is assumed to be below P^*.

Next, consider the behavior of the representative household when there is excess demand for commodities. The representative household will be able to obtain the quantity of commodities y, where $y<y^D$. The household then has to choose between either saving, i.e., accumulating as money balances the income which it cannot spend on consumption, or substituting leisure for the unobtainable commodities by supplying less labor, or some combination of the

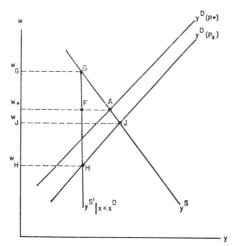

FIGURE 5. THE COMMODITY MARKET WITH
EXCESS DEMAND FOR LABOR

two. Formally, the household's problem is to maximize

$$U\left(x^{S\prime}, y, \frac{M}{P} + m^{D\prime}\right)$$

subject to $\pi + wx^{S\prime} = y + m^{D\prime}$

The variable $x^{S\prime}$ may be denoted as the effective supply of labor. Utility maximization now implies

(5) $x^{S\prime} = x^{S\prime}\left(w, \frac{M}{P}, \pi, y\right),$

and

(6) $m^{D\prime} = m^{D\prime}\left(w, \frac{M}{P}, \pi, y\right)$

This theory stresses the fact that a household may react to frustrated commodity demand in two ways. First, the household may save the income which cannot be spent on consumption (in this model, solely by augmenting money balances). This option corresponds to the classical concept of forced saving, or, more precisely, what D. H. Robertson defined as "automatic lacking." Second, the household may increase leisure by reducing its supply of labor. The second option prob-

ably becomes more important when excess commodity demand is chronic, as in wartime or during other periods of rationing and price controls.[18] However, given that consumption, saving, and leisure in aggregate are substitutes, in general some combination of the two options will always be optimal. Excess demand will generally result in some fall in output.

Classical analysis, in which labor supply is solely a function of the real wage, assumes that households channel all frustrated commodity demand into forced saving. The possibility of reduced labor supply is ignored. However, the inclusion of this option is especially interesting, since it has the apparently paradoxical implication that excess commodity demand can result in decreased employment and output.

Figure 6, which is analogous to Figure 1, depicts the labor market in this situation. Two important observations should be stressed. First, too low a real wage, that is a real wage below the level consistent with general equilibrium, is not a necessary condition for excess demand for labor, even though the notional demand and supply for labor are both assumed to depend only upon the real wage. This observation is obviously the converse of the earlier observation that the effective demand for labor is not uniquely associated with the real wage. If commodities are in excess demand so that, given voluntary exchange, $y < y^D$, which in turn implies $x^{S\prime} < x^S$, at real wage w^* excess demand for labor will amount to quantity AF.

Second, with commodities in excess demand, the quantity of employment will generally be below the full employment level. The explanation of this apparent

[18] For example, R. Vicker, a recent visitor to the Soviet Union, reports the effects of suppressed inflation upon output: "Goods produced for sale in state retail outlets are snapped up more and more quickly, and the remaining excess of income over things to spend it on dilutes the incentive of Soviet workers."

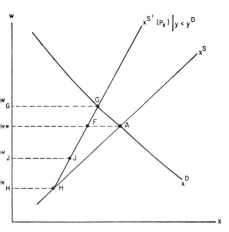

FIGURE 6. THE LABOR MARKET WITH EXCESS
DEMAND FOR COMMODITIES

paradox, as indicated above, is twofold: 1) the quantity of employment can be no greater than the quantity supplied; and 2) when their consumption plans are frustrated households will generally substitute leisure and thus supply less labor at any given real wage. Notice that even if the real wage should rise sufficiently, i.e., to w_G, to eliminate the excess demand for labor, the level of employment would still be below that obtaining at general equilibrium.

Finally, Figures 7 and 8, which are analogous to Figures 3 and 4, depict the interaction between the two markets with excess demand in both. Points A, F, G, H, and J in Figure 7 coincide with the same points in Figures 5 and 6. Figure 8 is drawn under the assumption that the existing wage-price vector is (w^*, P_2), that is, that the economy is at point F. The details of the construction of these diagrams are left as an exercise for the reader.

VII. Summary

This paper describes the application of a general disequilibrium approach to familiar problems of macro-analysis. Some familiar results, such as the notion that insufficient commodity demand produces unemployment, are arrived at in a much more satisfactory manner than is possible under more conventional analysis. In addition, the specific inclusion of disequilibrium elements leads to some nonfamiliar results.

The impact of excess supply of commodities on labor demand removes the one-to-one classical relationship between real wage and employment. In a general disequilibrium situation, unemployment can coexist with "non-excessive" real wages, and a procyclical pattern of real wages is consistent with the theoretical model.

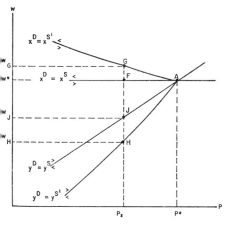

FIGURE 7. INTERACTION OF EXCESS DE-
MAND IN BOTH MARKETS

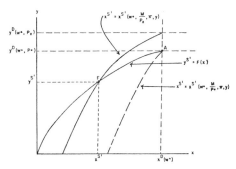

FIGURE 8. OUTPUT AND EMPLOYMENT WITH EXCESS
DEMAND IN BOTH MARKETS

The disequilibrium analysis of the commodity market is formally parallel to the analysis of the labor market. The Keynesian consumption function emerges as a manifestation of the impact of excess labor supply on commodity demand. In this respect conventional macro-analysis is seen to be asymmetric. On the one hand, the disequilibrium impact of excess labor supply is implicitly recognized by entering income as a separate argument in the consumption function. However, on the other hand, the impact of excess commodity supply is neglected by adhering to the classical labor demand function which involves only the real wage. Because of this peculiar asymmetry, previous analyses of unemployment have had to rely on such contrived devices as a countercyclical pattern of real wages or fixed proportion production functions.

The framework for analyzing the excess supply, depression case is directly applicable to an analysis of sustained excess demand. The classical concept of forced saving is one aspect of the impact of excess commodity demand on household decision making. The forced saving solution is, however, incomplete, since labor supply would also react inversely to a prolonged frustration of commodity demand. To the extent that labor supply declines in response to excess commodity demand, increases in commodity demand lead to reduced employment, rather than to increased (forced) saving.

REFERENCES

A. A. Alchian, "Information Costs, Pricing, and Resource Unemployment," *Western Econ. J.*, June 1969, 7, 109–28.

K. J. Arrow, "Toward a Theory of Price Adjustment," in M. Abramowitz, ed., *The Allocation of Economic Resources*, Stanford 1959.

R. J. Barro, "A Theory of Monopolistic Price Adjustment," read at Econometric Society Meetings, Detroit, Dec. 1970.

———, "A Theory of Optimal Adjustment," forthcoming 1971.

R. G. Bodkin, "Real Wages and Cyclical Variations in Employment," *Can. J. Econ.*, Aug. 1969, 2, 353–74.

R. Clower, "The Keynesian Counter-Revolution: A Theoretical Appraisal," in F. H. Hahn and F. P. R. Brechling, eds., *The Theory of Interest Rates*, London 1965.

E. O. Edwards, "Classical and Keynesian Employment Theories: A Reconciliation," *Quart. J. Econ.*, Aug. 1959, 73, 407–28.

H. I. Grossman, "Money, Interest, and Prices in Market Disequilibrium," *J. Polit. Econ.*, forthcoming 1971.

J. Hicks, *Capital and Growth*, New York, 1965.

J. M. Keynes, *The General Theory of Employment, Interest, and Money*, New York 1936.

———, "Relative Movements of Real Wages and Output," *Econ. J.*, Mar. 1939, 49, 34–51.

E. Kuh, "Unemployment, Production Functions, and Effective Demand," *J. Polit. Econ.*, June 1966, 74, 238–49.

A. Leijonhufvud, *On Keynesian Economics and the Economics of Keynes*, New York 1968.

D. Patinkin, "Involuntary Unemployment and the Keynesian Supply Function," *Econ. J.*, Sept. 1949, 59, 360–83.

———, *Money, Interest, and Prices*, 1956: 2d ed. New York 1965.

D. H. Robertson, *Banking Policy and the Price Level*, London 1926.

R. M. Solow and J. E. Stiglitz, "Output, Employment, and Wages in the Short Run," *Quart. J. Econ.*, Nov. 1968, 82, 537–60.

R. Vicker, "USSR: Rising Income, Black Markets," *The Wall Street Journal*, Apr. 21, 1970.

7

Suppressed Inflation and the Supply Multiplier[1,2]

WITH HERSCHEL I. GROSSMAN

Suppressed inflation describes a situation in which, at existing wages and prices, the aggregate demands for current output and labour services exceed the corresponding aggregate supplies. Suppressed inflation is the opposite of suppressed deflation, in which aggregate supplies of output and labour exceed aggregate demands. Both suppressed inflation and suppressed deflation involve non-wage and non-price rationing. In suppressed inflation, purchases of goods and labour services are rationed. In suppressed deflation, sales are rationed.

Suppressed inflation and suppressed deflation both result from the inability of wages and prices to adjust instantaneously, in response to shifts in aggregate demand or supply, to satisfy the conditions for general market clearing. This inability can result either from effective legal constraints—that is, the imposition of price and wage ceilings or floors—or from natural frictions in the workings of the market mechanism.[3] However, whatever the cause of wage and price stickiness, the resulting failure of markets to clear has profound consequences for the determination of output and employment.

In the case of suppressed deflation, standard macro-economic analysis has long recognized these consequences. In contrast, suppressed inflation, although empirically not a rare phenomenon, has been the subject of little systematic theoretical analysis. In addition, the standard macro-economic paradigm fails even to recognize the analogy between suppressed inflation and suppressed deflation.

A central aspect of the received theory of suppressed deflation is the demand multiplier. This theoretical construct was first discovered by Kahn [7] and expanded by Keynes [8] and quickly became part of conventional wisdom. Assume, starting from a position of general market clearing and full employment, an autonomous reduction in aggregate demand for current output.[4] Maintaining full employment would require a fall in the price level and nominal wage rate, but prices and wages are sticky. The initial effect of the reduced demand will be the emergence of excess supply in the output market. This excess supply induces the representative firm to reduce output to what it can sell, which is less than what it desires to sell at current wages and prices, and to reduce its effective

[1] *First version received August 1972; final version received February 1973 (Eds.).*
[2] The National Science Foundation has supported this research.
[3] A variety of rationalizations may be offered for such frictions. However, such analysis is beyond the scope of the present paper. See [4] for a general discussion of market-clearing frictions. Barro [1] develops a micro-economic model which rationalizes market-clearing frictions.
[4] This paragraph summarizes the analysis which is worked out in [2] and [3, Ch. II].

185

Reprinted from *The Review of Economic Studies*, 41, January 1974, 87–104, by permission of *The Review of Economic Studies*, and the authors.

demand for labour services accordingly.[1] This action by firms creates excess supply in the labour market, which restricts the representative household's employment and income below what the household desires at current wages and prices and forces it to reduce its effective consumption and savings demand accordingly. This response by households will further restrict the sales of the firms, who in turn will further reduce employment, and so on. Output and employment will converge to levels determined by the interaction of the marginal productivity of labour and the marginal propensities to consume and to save. The total change in output will equal the product of the initial autonomous reduction in aggregate demand and the demand multiplier. The demand multiplier of suppressed deflation equals the inverse of the marginal propensity to save.

The main point of the present paper is that the existence of suppressed inflation has consequences which are completely analogous to the recognized consequences of suppressed deflation,[2] which have just been described. Suppressed inflation constrains the behaviour of firms and households in the same manner as does suppressed deflation. On the one hand, excess demand for labour services means that the representative firm is unable to purchase the quantity of labour services which it notionally demands and that it must reduce its effective supply of output accordingly. On the other hand, excess demand for current output means that the representative household is unable to purchase the quantity of consumables which it notionally demands. It will typically respond by both increasing its effective savings demand and decreasing its effective labour supply accordingly. Employment cannot exceed the quantity of labour services supplied, and the level of employment constrains the level of output according to the production function. Hence, to the extent that households reduce their effective labour supply, employment and output must also decline. Thus, excess demand for current output will generally cause employment and output to be below their general-market-clearing levels. Although many descriptive accounts of actual suppressed inflations mention this phenomenon,[3] the existing literature seems to contain no systematic theoretical or empirical analyses of it. Moreover, the analogy between the analyses of suppressed inflation and deflation means that in suppressed inflation, as in suppressed deflation, the convergence of employment and output involves a multiplier process.

The discussion which follows considers in detail the two essential aspects of an analysis of suppressed inflation. Specifically, it develops an intertemporal analysis of the household utility maximization problem in the context of suppressed inflation. Then, it develops the concept of the supply multiplier which determines the levels of output and employment in a suppressed inflation. Section I sketches the analytical framework employed. Section II deals with the behaviour of firms. Sections III and IV analyse the behaviour of households in contexts of general market clearing and suppressed inflation. Section V explains the supply multiplier. Finally, Section VI considers some possible extensions of the analysis of household behaviour under suppressed inflation.

---

[1] In another version of this story, prices fall sufficiently to clear the output market, and the reduction in the demand for labour services results from the consequent rise in real wage rates—see [8]. This version, which implies countercyclical variation in real wage rates, does not alter the rest of the multiplier story.

[2] We first noted this analogy in [2]. However, that paper dealt only implicitly with the essential intertemporal nature of the household utility maximization problem and it did not develop the concept of the supply multiplier.

[3] Cf., for example, the following quotations:

Excess demand for commodities (which leads to difficulties for the workers in spending their money incomes in some reasonable way) makes workers inclined not to work so much. This situation has become well known in most countries since the Second World War.—Hansen [5, p. 188].

After the collapse of Germany in 1945 . . . most people had no inducement to earn more money than was required to buy the rations at prices which were, on the whole, still fixed at the pre-war level. It was profitable for a man to be absent one or two days a week from his job if he could use the time to cultivate his own garden, to forage on the countryside for food, or to operate in the black market.—Lutz [9, p. 122].

Goods produced for sale in state retail outlets are snapped up more and more quickly, and the remaining excess of income over things to spend it on dilutes the incentive of Soviet workers.—Vicker [11].

I. ANALYTICAL FRAMEWORK

Consider a simple aggregative framework which involves three economic goods—labour services, consumable commodities, and fiat money—and two forms of economic decision-making unit—firms and households.[1] Labour services are the only variable input into the production process. Other inputs have a fixed quantity, no alternative use, and zero user cost. Consumable commodities are the only form of current output; there are no investment goods and the consumables are not storable. Money is the only store of value, and it also serves as a medium of exchange and unit of account. Transactions involving money are costless, and receipts and disbursements of money are perfectly synchronized. The nominal stock of money is exogenous and constant.

Firms demand labour and supply commodities. They attempt to maximize profits. Households may be either working or retired. Working households supply labour and demand consumables and money balances. Retired households demand consumables and money balances. Households also receive the profits of the firms according to a predetermined pattern. Households attempt to maximize utility. Each firm and each household is both a wage and price taker.[2]

The analytical framework thus includes the following variables:

l = flow of labour services, measured in man-hours per year,

c = flow of consumables, measured in physical units per year,

π = flow of profits, measured in units of consumables per year,

M = nominal stock of money balances, measured in dollars,

m = flow of nominal money balances, measured in dollars per year, where $m = dM/dt$,

P = the price of consumables, which is the number of dollars per unit of consumables, and

W = the nominal wage rate, which is the number of dollars per man-hour of labour services.

The real wage rate, which is the number of units of consumables per man-hour of labour services, is given by the ratio W/P. The superscripts s and d denote the quantity supplied or demanded, respectively, of the attached variable. Variables written without a superscript denote the actual flow exchanged or the actual stock held.

An asterisk denotes the prices and quantities which correspond to general market clearing—that is, to the equation of demand and supply in both the labour and commodity markets. Hence, $(W/P)^*$ and P^* are the general-market-clearing values of the real wage rate and the price level, and l^* and c^* are the general-market-clearing values of employment and output.[3]

As in the conventional demand-multiplier analysis, the procedure in the following discussion is to take a particular vector of the price level and real wage rate as given, and to work out the levels of employment and output implied by that vector. In particular, the discussion focuses on a combination of that real wage rate which would be consistent

[1] The analysis of the behaviour of firms, working households, and retired households considers the " representative " unit; that is, a unit whose behaviour, except for its atomistic scale, is identical to the behaviour of the aggregate of such units. The representative unit is essentially an average unit. Consequently, we are able to move freely between the individual and the aggregate, and we use the same notation to represent both. Note, however, that in employing the concept of the representative unit we abstract from distributional effects. Therefore, the validity of the analysis depends either on the smallness of changes in distribution, or on the negligible impact on variables of interest of those variations in distribution which do occur. In addition, for simplicity, the analytical framework does not include capital goods, earning assets, or a government sector. See [3] for extensions along these lines. Such extensions do not affect the main points of the present analysis. See also Section VI below.

[2] This assumption implies that a third party is setting wages and prices, which accords readily with a situation of wage and price ceilings. Alternatively, if either firms or households themselves are responsible for setting wages and prices, the model of firm or household behaviour must be specified somewhat differently, but the general conclusions reached below would still obtain. Cf. [4].

[3] To economize on space, this paper does not analyse the determination of general-market-clearing quantities. Cf. [3, Ch. I].

with general market clearing—$(W/P)^*$—and a price level which is lower than that which would be consistent with general market clearing—$P<P^*$. In other words, our interest is in a situation in which the price level and nominal wage rate are too low—that is, in which an inflation of the price level and nominal wage rate is being suppressed—but in which " relative prices ", represented in this framework by the real wage rate, are at the " correct " level.

II. THE BEHAVIOUR OF FIRMS

The conventional neoclassical theory of the competitive firm implicitly assumes a general-market-clearing situation. In this theory, the representative firm regards profit maximization as being constrained only by the production function. In particular, the representative firm perceives that it can purchase all the labour which it demands and sell all the output which it supplies at the existing levels of W and P. Thus, profits are given by

$$\pi = c^s - \frac{W}{P} l^d.$$

Assume the production function to exhibit a positive and diminishing marginal product, that is

$$c = c(l), \text{ with } \frac{\partial c}{\partial l} > 0 \text{ and } \frac{\partial^2 c}{\partial l^2} < 0.$$

Profit maximization involves choosing l^d and c^s to equate the marginal product of labour to the real wage rate.[1] The implied labour demand and consumables supply functions are [2]

$$l^d = l^d \left(\underset{(-)}{\frac{W}{P}} \right) \qquad \qquad ...(1)$$

and

$$c^s = c^s \left(\underset{(-)}{\frac{W}{P}} \right) \equiv c \left[l^d \left(\frac{W}{P} \right) \right], \qquad ...(2)$$

such that $\partial c/\partial l = W/P$. Denote l^d as the notional demand for labour and c^s as the notional supply of consumables.

This neoclassical analysis does not apply to a situation of suppressed inflation. Although firms are not constrained by excess demand for consumables, they are constrained by excess demand for labour services. Under suppressed inflation, voluntary exchange implies that actual employment will equal the total quantity supplied. The representative firm will not be able to obtain its notional demand l^d. In the neoclassical analysis, purchases of labour services were a choice variable. In contrast, under suppressed inflation the representative firm acts as a quantity taker with respect to employment, in addition to acting as a wage and price taker. Let l represent its actual supply-determined purchases of labour services, where $l<l^d$.[3] Profit maximization now implies producing as much output as possible with the available labour. Denote this maximum quantity as the effective supply of consumables, and represent it by $c^{s'}$. Formally, the representative

---

[1] Assuming neither output nor input to be storable, and abstracting from adjustment costs, profit maximization is not an intertemporal problem.

[2] The sign in parentheses below an argument of a function indicates the sign of the derivative, partial or total as the case may be, of the dependent variable with respect to that argument.

[3] As with prices and wages in a general-equilibrium model, the determination of the actual value of l involves the market interaction of firm and household behaviour. Section V below analyses this interaction. However, as with wages and prices in the conventional competitive model, the atomistic firm ignores its own contribution to the market process which determines l.

firm's problem is to choose $c^{s'}$ so as to maximize $\pi = c^{s'} - (W/P)l$, subject to the production function. The solution is to select [1]

$$c^{s'} = c^{s'}(l) \equiv c(l) \text{ for } l < l^d\left(\frac{W}{P}\right). \qquad ...(3)$$

The constraint of $l < l^d$ implies $c^{s'} < c^s$, with $c^{s'}$ approaching c^s as l approaches l^d. The constraint on employment forces the representative firm to operate in a region where $\partial c/\partial l$ exceeds W/P.

In the conventional neoclassical analysis, the notional supply of consumables was a function of the real wage rate, as in equation (2), but was not a function of employment. Employment was maximized out as a separate choice variable. In contrast, in equation (3), the effective supply of consumables is a function of the given level of employment. The level of labour supply here imposes employment as a constraint upon the effective supply of consumables. Equation (3) implies that the effective supply of consumables can vary even with the real wage rate fixed. Changes in the level of the constraint l determine effective consumables supply independently of changes in W/P, as long as $l < l^d(W/P)$.

III. THE BEHAVIOUR OF HOUSEHOLDS UNDER GENERAL MARKET CLEARING

The conventional neoclassical theory of household behaviour also implicitly assumes a general-market-clearing situation. In this theory, the representative household perceives that it can sell all the labour which it supplies and can purchase all the consumables which it demands at the existing levels of W and P. If utility at time t depends directly upon the level of consumption at time t and inversely upon the intensity of work at time t, the momentary utility function may be specified as

$$u(t) = u\underset{(+)\quad(-)}{\left[c^d(t), \ l^s(t)\right]}.$$

We should be careful to note that " consumption ", c, refers here to consumables purchased for money in the market place and that " work ", l, refers to employment for money wages obtained in the market place. By definition, all time not spent " working " in the market is spent at " leisure ". This analysis does not distinguish between various possible leisure time activities, such as rest and home production.

The theory assumes that the representative household attempts to maximize total utility over its planning horizon, N,[2]

$$U = \int_0^N u(t)dt.$$

[1] This analysis generalizes readily to the multi-input case. In this case, if purchases of all inputs are constrained, we may interpret l as a vector of input quantities. However, if purchases of some inputs are unconstrained, the choice problem is slightly more complex. Consider the two-input case, in which purchases of the first input are constrained at level $l_1 < l_1^d$. The firm's problem is to choose $c^{s'}$ and $l^{d'}$ so as to maximize

$$\pi = c^{s'} - (W_1/P)l_1 - (W_2/P)l_2^{d'},$$

subject to the production constraint

$$c^{s'} = c(l_1, l_2^{d'}).$$

The solution is to select

$$c^{s'} = \underset{(-)\quad(+)}{c^{s'}(W_2/P, l_1)},$$

and

$$l_2^{d'} = \underset{(-)\quad(?)}{l_2^{d'}(W_2/P, l_1)},$$

such that $\dfrac{\partial c}{\partial l_2^{d'}}(l_1, l_2^{d'}) = W_2/P$. The effect of l_1 upon $l_2^{d'}$ depends upon the sign of $\partial^2 c/\partial l_1 \partial l_2^{d'}$.

[2] The total utility expression can be generalized to include a discount factor for the instantaneous utility flow $u(t)$. In addition, intertemporal dependence among utility flows at different points of time can be introduced. These complications would not affect the general forms of the resulting supply and demand functions and are not treated explicitly here.

The planning horizon consists of N' working years and $N-N'$ retirement years. We treat N' and N as exogenously determined parameters. For households which are currently retired, $N' = 0$.

Holdings of money balances provide a medium which ties together the time paths of c^d and l^s. By appropriate management of its money balance over time, money being the only store of value in this model, the household can select from among a wide range of lifetime consumption and employment patterns. Assuming P to be constant, the household's income consists of its wage income plus its profit income. Saving, which is the rate of change of real money holdings, is the difference between real income and consumption. Thus, during working years, saving demand conforms to

$$\frac{1}{P}\left(\frac{dM}{dt}\right)^d \equiv \frac{m^d}{P} = \frac{W}{P}\,l^s + \pi - c^d. \qquad \qquad ...(4)$$

By determining its consumption and employment, the household simultaneously determines the rate of change of its real money balance. Only two of these three decisions are independent. Equation (4) applies also to retired households, but with l^s set at zero. With P constant over time, planned real asset holdings at any point of time, $M(t)/P$, can be calculated by adding to initial real asset holdings, $M(0)/P$, the integral of m^d/P from time 0 to time t.

Since no utility accrues from consumption beyond the planning horizon, the households optimal life plan entails the exhaustion of asset holdings at date N. Assuming that the household takes W, P and π to be exogenous and constant over time, its planned time path of consumption and work will satisfy

$$\frac{M(N)}{P} = \frac{M(0)}{P} + N\pi + \frac{W}{P}\int_0^{N'} l^s(t)dt - \int_0^N c^d(t)dt = 0. \qquad ...(5)$$

This condition says that total consumption until its planning horizon must equal the sum of total real wages earned until retirement plus total profits received until its planning horizon plus its present holding of real money balances. The latter two items would delimit lifetime consumption if no work were performed and they represent a basic constraint upon household behaviour. Refer to this constraint as non-wage wealth, and denote its value by Ω, where

$$\Omega \equiv \frac{M(0)}{P} + N\pi.$$

Again, equation (5) also applies to retired households, but with wage earnings set at zero.

The optimal time pattern of consumption and employment depends upon the specification of the momentary utility function, upon the additive nature of lifetime utility, upon the lengths of the working and planning horizons, N' and N, upon the relative price of leisure and consumption during working years, which is the real wage rate W/P, and upon Ω. In particular, given the values of N' and N, the maximization of U, subject to the asset exhaustion condition of equation (5), requires, for working households, the following time pattern for l^s and c^d:[1] The level of l^s is constant from now, date 0, until retirement, date N'. The level of c^d is constant from date 0 until date N' and is also constant, but possibly at a different level, from date N' until the planning horizon, date N. If consumption and employment were independent influences upon utility, before- and after-retirement levels of consumption would be the same—that is c^d would be constant from date 0 until date N.[2] Given the saving specification of equation (4), these time paths for

---

[1] The appendix presents an explicit derivation of these results. The maximization of U is also subject to the inequality constraints $[c^d(t), l^s(t), M(t)] \geqq 0$. We assume these constraints to be ineffective, except for $M(N) = 0$, and we therefore deal only with interior solutions for c^d and l^s, subject to equation (5).

[2] The existence of earning assets would alter these conclusions by tilting the life plane toward more work and less consumption in early years. Cf. [3, Ch. III]. However, the inclusion of earning assets would not alter the major conclusions reached in this paper.

l^s and c^d also imply a constant value for m^d/P until retirement and a constant negative value for m^d/P after retirement.[1] In particular, the maximization calculus implies that the current levels of c^d, l^s, and m^d/P for the representative working household are determined by functions of the following form:

$$c^d = c^d(\Omega, W/P), \qquad \qquad \qquad \text{...(6)}$$
$$\quad \;\; {\scriptstyle(+)\;\;(+)}$$

$$l^s = l^s(\Omega, W/P), \qquad \qquad \qquad \text{...(7)}$$
$$\quad \;\; {\scriptstyle(-)\;\;(?)}$$

$$\frac{m^d}{P} = \frac{m^d}{P}(\Omega, W/P, \pi). \qquad \qquad \text{...(8)}$$
$$\qquad \quad {\scriptstyle(-)\;\;(+)\;\;(+)}$$

Assuming that consumables and leisure are both normal goods, the signs of these partial derivatives are all unambiguous, except for the effect of W/P upon l^s. This sign depends on the relative magnitudes of the substitution and income effects. Denote c^d as the notional demand for consumables, l^s as the notional supply of labour services, and m^d/P as the notional saving demand.

Retired households differ from working households in that, for retired households, l^s is zero and no possibility exists for substitution between consumption and leisure. Consequently, the real wage rate has no effect upon the optimal behaviour of retired households. However, the direction of the effect of Ω and π on c^d and m^d/P for retired households is the same as that for working households. Thus, the aggregate notional demand and supply functions, which combine the behaviour of working and retired households, have the same form as the functions given in equations (6)-(8), where Ω and π are now interpreted as aggregate quantities.[2] Aggregate Ω has the same definition as individual Ω, but with $M(0)/P$ and π representing aggregates and N representing the average number of years until the planning horizon for all households.

IV. THE BEHAVIOUR OF HOUSEHOLDS UNDER SUPPRESSED INFLATION

The neoclassical analysis of the preceding section again does not apply to a situation of suppressed inflation. Although households are not constrained by excess demand in the labour market, they are constrained by excess demand for consumables. Actual consumption cannot exceed the total quantity of consumables supplied. Consequently, under suppressed inflation the representative household will not be able to purchase the quantity c^d. In the neoclassical analysis, consumption was a choice variable. In contrast, under suppressed inflation the representative household acts as a quantity taker with respect to consumption, in addition to acting as a wage and price taker. Let c represent its actual supply-determined purchases of consumables, where $c < c^d$.[3] Given this constraint, the representative working household must choose some combination of two options: it can continue to accept employment equal to its notional supply l^s, thereby maintaining its notional income, and then save, i.e. accumulate as money balances, the portion of this

---

[1] Whether m^d/P is positive or negative during working years depends upon the value of $M(0)/P$.

[2] This formulation abstracts from the effects of the distribution of wealth both among working and retired households and between these two groups. In fact, such effects may be important. For example, working and retired households should have predictably different reactions to changes in non-wage wealth. In particular, *ceteris paribus*, an increase in the share of a given aggregate Ω owned by retired households would have the following effects. Working households would decrease their notional consumption demand and increase their notional labour supply and saving. However, retired households would increase their notional consumption demand and decrease their saving, and because of their shorter planning horizons, their changes in consumption and saving would tend to outweigh those of the working households. Consequently, on balance c^d and l^s would tend to rise, and m^d/P would tend to fall.

[3] As with l, the determination of the actual value of c also involves the market interaction of firm and household behaviour. However, as with the atomistic firm, the atomistic household also ignores its own contribution to the market process.

income which it would like to consume currently but cannot. Alternatively, it can accept less employment, substituting leisure for the current consumption which it cannot obtain.

Utility maximization remains an intertemporal problem. The choice of optimal time paths, including the current values, for effective labour supply and effective savings demand depends not only upon the current consumption constraint which the representative working household directly perceives, but also upon the expected future time path of this constraint up to date N. These expectations could take many forms, and Section VI below considers some general possibilities. However, the main analysis assumes the following simple specification: the representative household expects to be effectively constrained to the current level of consumption, c, for a period of $\hat{N}$ years, where $\hat{N} < N$, and expects to be unconstrained for the remaining $(\hat{N} - N)$ years. The length of the constraint period, $\hat{N}$, is treated as exogenous.

This specification has two important properties: first, the anticipated future shortfall of consumption below demand is larger the larger the present shortfall. Second, the representative household does not anticipate the shortages to persist indefinitely—that is, the household expects to be unconstrained at some time in the future. In addition, we assume for most of our analysis that, for the representative working household, $\hat{N} < N'$— that is, the period of anticipated effective constraint ends before retirement.

Given the above specification, the representative working household's formal problem is to maximize

$$U = \int_0^{\hat{N}} u[c, l^{s'}(t)]dt + \int_{\hat{N}}^{N'} u[c^{d'}(t), l^{s'}(t)]dt + \int_{N'}^{N} u[c^{d'}(t), 0]dt,$$

subject to given and constant values of W, P, π, and c, to given values of $\hat{N}$, N, and N', and to initial real asset holdings, $M(0)/P$.[1] Denote $l^{s'}$, $c^{d'}$, and $m^{d'}/P$ as effective supplies and demands. In contrast to the notional supplies and demands, the effective supplies and demands are chosen subject to the perceived constraint on purchases of consumables. The working household's life plan now involves three subperiods: the initial period from time 0 to time $\hat{N}$, during which consumption is determined exogenously at the effective constraint level and during which labour supply and saving demand are the only choice variables; a second period from time $\hat{N}$ to time N', during which consumption demand, labour supply, and saving demand are all choice variables; and the retirement period from time N' to time N, during which consumption demand and saving demand are choice variables and labour supply is set at zero.

The relationship between savings demand, labour supply, and consumption for the three subperiods has the following form:

$$\frac{m^{d'}}{P} = \begin{cases} \dfrac{W}{P} l^{s'} + \pi - c, & \text{for } t = 0, \ldots, \hat{N}, \\[2mm] \dfrac{W}{P} l^{s'} + \pi - c^{d'}, & \text{for } t = \hat{N}, \ldots, N', \\[2mm] \pi - c^{d'}, & \text{for } t = N', \ldots, N. \end{cases} \qquad \ldots(9)$$

---

[1] The actual value of π depends upon the actual values of c and l, which depend in turn upon the market interaction of firm and household behaviour. Again, the atomistic household ignores its own contribution to the market process. However, is it consistent for the household to take W, P, and π to be constant over time? Because the current shortages reflect suppressed inflation, the expectation that the shortages will end at date $\hat{N}$, may imply an expectation of higher values of W and P after date $\hat{N}$. Such an expectation would influence current household behaviour. However, if the current excess demand reflects a temporary disruption of supply factors, resulting from, for example, war or famine, the ending of shortages need not imply higher wages and prices. Similarly, the expectation that shortages will end at date $\hat{N}$, may or may not be consistent with the expected constancy of π. More generally, should household expectations be constrained to be consistent in the above sense? The evaluation of the consistency of expectations requires a valid model of the economic system, something which the representative household does not possess.

Optimal behaviour again entails the exhaustion of asset holdings at date N. Therefore, the choice of $l^{s'}(t)$ and $c^{d'}(t)$ will satisfy

$$\frac{M(N)}{P} = \frac{M(0)}{P} + N\pi - \hat{N}c + \frac{W}{P}\int_0^{N'} l^{s'}(t)dt - \int_{\hat{N}}^{N} c^{d'}(t)dt$$

$$\equiv \Omega - \hat{N}c + \frac{W}{P}\int_0^{N'} l^{s'}(t)dt - \int_{\hat{N}}^{N} c^{d'}(t)dt = 0. \qquad \ldots(10)$$

The maximization of U now yields optimal time paths for $l^{s'}$ until retirement and for $c^{d'}$ during the unconstrained years.[1] The solution is somewhat more complicated than that for the general-market-clearing case. The effective labour supply, $l^{s'}$, is constant from time 0 to time $\hat{N}$, and also constant, but possibly at a different level, from time $\hat{N}$ to time N'. The effective consumption demand, $c^{d'}$, is constant from time $\hat{N}$ to time N', and also constant, but possibly at a different level, from time N' to time N. However, if leisure and consumption are independent influences on utility, $l^{s'}$ will be constant over the entire working period, and $c^{d'}$ will be constant over the entire unconstrained period after date $\hat{N}$. In this case the asset-exhaustion condition of equation (10) simplifies to

$$\Omega - \hat{N}c + N'\frac{W}{P}l^{s'} - (N - \hat{N})c^{d'} = 0. \qquad \ldots(10.1)$$

Since c is below c^d during the constraint period, $l^{s'}$ will be below the notional supply, l^s, and $c^{d'}$ after date $\hat{N}$ will exceed notional demand, c^d. These results reflect the substitution of both increased leisure during working years and increased consumption during the unconstrained years for the desired but unobtainable consumption during the constrained years. Given the saving specification of equation (9), these planned time paths for $l^{s'}$ and $c^{d'}$ also imply a constant value for $m^{d'}/P$ from date 0 to date $\hat{N}$, a smaller constant value from date $\hat{N}$ to date N', and a constant negative value after retirement. Since saving is undertaken during working years solely to provide for consumption after retirement, and since, given $\hat{N} < N'$, $(N - N')c^{d'}$ exceeds $(N - N')c^d$, $m^{d'}/P$ from date 0 to date $\hat{N}$ must exceed m^d/P.[2] In particular, the maximization calculus implies that the current levels of $l^{s'}$ and $m^{d'}/P$ for the representative working household are determined by functions of the following form:

$$l^{s'} = l^{s'}(\underset{(-)}{\Omega - \hat{N}c}, \underset{(?)}{W/P}, \underset{(-)}{\hat{N}}) \qquad \ldots(11)$$

and

$$\frac{m^{d'}}{P} = \frac{m^{d'}}{P}(\underset{(-)}{\Omega - \hat{N}c}, \underset{(+)}{W/P}, \underset{(-)}{\hat{N}}, \underset{(+)}{\pi - c}). \qquad \ldots(12)$$

The signs of these partial derivatives are all unambiguous, except for the effect of W/P upon $l^{s'}$.[3]

In equations (7) and (8) the notional supply of labour and demand for savings were

---

[1] The maximization is now subject to the values of W/P, Ω, N', N, $\hat{N}$, c, and condition (10). The appendix again presents an explicit derivation of the results.

[2] Whether $m^{d'}/P$ is positive or negative during the working years again depends upon the value of $M(0)/P$. The excess of current $m^{d'}/P$ over m^d/P reflects the excess of $c^{d'}$ over c^d during the retirement years, which have been assumed to be unconstrained. However, if the anticipated consumption constraint extended into the retirement years, i.e., $\hat{N} > N'$, the relationship between current values of $m^{d'}/P$ and m^d/P would be ambiguous. Moreover, if $\hat{N} = N$—so that there were no possibility of substituting increased consumption during unconstrained retirement years for the frustrated demand during constrained years —current $m^{d'}/P$ would be less than m^d/P.

[3] Since substitution between consumption and leisure is now limited to increasing $c^{d'}$ during the unconstrained years at the expense of leisure during working years, the substitution effect of W/P on $l^{s'}$ is weaker than the corresponding effect on l^s. Hence, it is more likely that the income effect will dominate, in which case W/P would have a negative effect on labour supply.

not functions of the level of consumption. Consumption was maximized out as a separate choice variable. In contrast, in equations (11) and (12), the effective supply of labour and demand for savings are functions of the given level of consumption. The level of supply of consumables here imposes consumption as a constraint upon the effective supply of labour and demand for savings. In the $l^{s'}$ and $m^{d'}/P$ functions, the obtainable total of consumption during the constrained years, given by $\hat{N}c$, enters as an exogenous charge against non-wage wealth, Ω. Changes in $\Omega - \hat{N}c$ now have an effect which is analogous to the effect that changes in Ω had in the l^s and m^d/P functions. In the $m^{d'}/P$ function, current consumption, c, enters again as a charge against current non-wage income π. Changes in $\pi - c$ now have an effect which is analogous to the effect that changes in π had in the m^d/P function.

Equations (11) and (12) contain $\hat{N}$ as a separate argument. With Ω and c (but not $\Omega - \hat{N}c$) fixed, an increase in $\hat{N}$ reduces both the period of unconstrained consumption and the amount of net non-wage resources, $\Omega - \hat{N}c$. The first effect would tend to raise $c^{d'}$ during the remaining unconstrained years and lower $l^{s'}$ during the working years. The second effect has opposite implications. However, the net effect is unambiguous. An increase in $\hat{N}$ implies more years of consumption at level c and less years at level $c^{d'}$. Since $c^{d'} > c$, more resources are available for spending either on $c^{d'}$ over the reduced number of unconstrained years or on leisure during the working years. Hence, the full effect would be a rise in $c^{d'}$ and a fall in $l^{s'}$. Since current $l^{s'}$ falls, current $m^{d'}/P$ must also fall when $\hat{N}$ rises. In general, the larger is $\hat{N}$, the more the representative household reacts to a given value of c by reducing labour supply and the less by increasing saving— that is, the greater the difference between l^s and $l^{s'}$ and the smaller the difference between $m^{d'}/P$ and m^d/P.

With regard to the value of $\hat{N}$, two extreme cases are worth noting. First, the representative working household may regard the current constraint on consumption as purely transitory—that is, $\hat{N} = 0$. In this case the constraint has a negligible effect on the household's life plan, and the household will not significantly reduce labour supply— that is, $l^{s'} = l^s$. The household will increase $m^{d'}/P$ over m^d/P by about as much as the shortfall of c below c^d. Second, the representative working household may regard the constraint on consumption as permanent—that is, $\hat{N} = N$, which involves a relaxation of our earlier assumption that $\hat{N} < N'$. In this case, because the household thinks that consumption will also be constrained below the notional level during retirement years, it will reduce current saving below the notional level—that is, $m^{d'}/P < m^d/P$. The household will reduce its effective labour supply so that its labour income falls by even more than the current shortfall of c below c^d.[1]

These extreme possibilities notwithstanding, the representative working household typically responds to a constraint upon current consumption by exercising two options— an increase in current saving to pay for an increase in planned consumption during unconstrained retirement years and a decrease in current labour supply. The induced increase in saving corresponds to the classical concept of forced saving, or, more precisely, to what Robertson [10] defined as " automatic lacking ". Classical analysis, in which labour supply is principally determined by the real wage rate, implicitly assumed that households channel all frustrated consumption demand into forced saving, and did not consider the alternative possibility of an increase in leisure. According to the above analysis, this classical result would apply only when the excess demand for consumables was regarded as a purely transitory phenomenon. Alternatively, if the representative working household anticipated a permanent supply-imposed constraint upon consumption, it would increase leisure so much as to reduce labour income by more than the current shortfall of consumption

---

[1] In this case, the household works only the minimum amount to pay for the available consumption. It sets $l^{s'}$ so that $N'(W/P)l^{s'} = Nc - \Omega$. The elasticity of $l^{s'}$ with respect to W/P would be minus unity. Because substitution possibilities do not exist, the income effect of a change in W/P must dominate. Moreover, W/P would have no effect on $m^{d'}/P$.

below notional demand, so that current saving would actually fall. In this case an excess demand for consumables would lead to less saving rather than more.

Most realistic situations would presumably fall somewhere between these two extremes. In general, the longer the anticipated duration of the shortfall of consumption below notional demand, the greater will be the reduction in effective labour supply below the notional level and the lower will be the rate of saving. However, from a qualitative standpoint, we should stress that there will be some reduction in labour supply so long as the representative working household regards a supply-imposed constraint on consumption as anything more than a transitory phenomenon. The likelihood of some reduction in labour supply is especially interesting, since, as the next section stresses, it has the apparently paradoxical implication that excess demand for consumables can result in decreased employment and output.

With regard to households who are currently retired, because they do not have the option of reducing labour supply, the full impact of a constraint on consumption would be on saving. Their effective saving demand would be

$$\frac{m^{d'}}{P} = \pi - c > \frac{m^d}{P} = \pi - c^d.$$

However, the direction of effect of $\pi - c$ upon $m^{d'}/P$ for retired households is the same as for working households. Therefore, the aggregate effective labour supply and savings demand functions, which combine the behaviour of working and retired households, have the same form as the functions given in equations (11) and (12), where Ω, π, and c are now interpreted as aggregate quantities.

V. THE DETERMINATION OF OUTPUT AND EMPLOYMENT UNDER SUPPRESSED INFLATION

The preceding analyses of firm and household behaviour may be combined to provide, for a given wage-price vector, a complete picture of the determination of output and employment under general excess-demand conditions. When a particular market is experiencing excess demand, voluntary exchange implies that the actual level of transactions will be supply determined. According to the analyses of the preceding two sections, when either the consumables market or the labour market is experiencing excess demand, an effective supply, given by either equation (3) or (11), prevails in the other market. Consequently, when both markets are experiencing excess demand, output and employment are determined by the effective supplies of consumables and labour services—that is,[1,2]

$$c = c^{s'}(l) < c^d(\Omega, W/P) \qquad \qquad ...(13)$$
$$\scriptstyle (+) \qquad (+) \ (+)$$

[1] It is not necessary to deal explicitly with the effective demand for money, $m^{d'}/P$. Combining the representative household's current budget equation, $(W/P)l^{s'} + \pi = c + m^{d'}/P$, and the representative firm's profit equation, $\pi = c^{s'} - (W/P)l$, yields an economy-wide budget equation which is analogous to Walras' Law, $(W/P)(l - l^{s'}) + (c - c^{s'}) + m^{d'}/P = 0$. Hence, $m^{d'}/P = 0$ holds automatically from this budget equation when conditions (13) and (14) are satisfied. If a nonzero flow supply of money balances, m^s/P, had been introduced—corresponding, for example, to a transfer payment from government—this condition would generalize to $m^{d'}/P = m^s/P$.

[2] Conditions (13) and (14) specify the effective supply in each market to be less than the notional demand. The present discussion is not concerned with specifying the precise amount of effective excess demand in the two markets. However, it is worth noting that the actual demands may differ from the notional demands in this context. First, households may attempt, despite the constraint on current consumption, to substitute increased current consumption for future consumption which they do not expect to obtain. Second, if buyers think that actual purchases are directly related to demands expressed, they may express demands in excess of their desired purchases. Cf. Hansen [5]. Third, if there are costs associated with the expression of offers to purchase, the representative household or firm may not bother to make offers which are not expected to be successful. This last effect would tend to reduce actual below notional demand and would tend to offset the first two effects.

and

$$l = l^{s'}(\Omega - \hat{N}c, \; W/P, \; \hat{N}) < l^{d}(W/P). \qquad \ldots(14)$$
$$\underset{(-)}{} \quad \underset{(?)}{} \; \underset{(-)}{} \quad \underset{(-)}{}$$

In order for conditions (13) and (14) to be relevant, the existing wage-price vector must be such that excess demand exists in both the consumables and the labour market. The present analysis considers the combination $(W/P)^*$—the general-market-clearing real wage rate—and P_1—a price level which is below the general-market-clearing price level P^*.[1]

When W and P are such that excess demand exists in both markets, conditions (13) and (14) determine the levels of output and employment. Condition (13) relates c to l. With c so determined, given the exogenous variables—M, $\hat{N}$, N', N, P, and W—$l^{s'}$ depends only upon l. Therefore, given condition (13), condition (14) determines l. In effect, the level of l determines an amount of consumption, $c^s(l)$, and an amount of profit income, $c^s(l) - lW/P$, which together determine the amount of non-wage wealth net of consumption during constrained years, $\Omega - \hat{N}c$. Given $\hat{N}$ and W/P, $\Omega - \hat{N}c$ determines $l^{s'}$. According to equation (14), the level of l must be such that the level of $l^{s'}$ so determined is equal to l itself.

The implications for output and employment of the real wage-price vector $[(W/P)^*, P_1]$ may perhaps be seen most clearly by considering the following thought experiment. Suppose that initially the real wage-price vector was $[(W/P)^*, P^*]$, consistent with general market clearing. Now suppose that M is increased, which has the effect of raising the general-market-clearing price level and nominal wage rate equiproportionally. With the actual price level and nominal wage rate fixed, the situation would now be described by the real wage-price vector $[(W/P)^*, P_1]$, where P_1 is below the new general-market-clearing price level.[2]

The initial effect of such a disturbance would be an increase in the notional demand for consumables, given by equation (7), and a decrease in the notional supply of labour services, given by equation (8). The disturbance thus creates excess demand in both markets. As an immediate consequence, the representative working household perceives a supply-imposed constraint upon its consumption, which causes it to reduce its effective supply of labour services below its notional supply. At the same time, the representative firm perceives a supply-imposed constraint upon its employment, which both reduces its profits and causes it to reduce its effective supply of consumables below its notional supply. However, these initial effects are just the beginning of the story. The induced reduction in effective labour supply implies a further constraint upon employment, which causes a further reduction in profits and effective supply of consumables. At the same time, the induced reduction in effective consumables supply implies a further constraint upon consumption, which induces a further reduction in effective labour supply; while the induced reduction in profits implies a reduction in non-wage wealth, which creates a partially offsetting stimulus to effective labour supply. This entire process cumulates until the actual levels of output and employment settle well below their general-market-clearing levels.

The preceding paragraph describes a multiplier process, by which an initial decline in employment, brought about either by a decline in the notional labour supply function and/or by a decline in the effective labour supply below the notional level, causes a decline

---

[1] See [3, Ch. II] for a general specification of those wage-price vectors which lead to excess demand in both markets.

[2] A more general dynamic analysis would deal with the simultaneous adjustment of both quantities and prices. The analysis and discussion in the text concentrates on the determination of equilibrium quantities for given prices. This analysis is empirically useful to the extent that quantity adjustment is rapid relative to price adjustment. This condition obviously applies to situations of wage and price controls, but may also provide a good approximation to the implications of natural frictions in the working of the market mechanism.

in output which leads to further declines in employment, and so on.[1]   An appropriate name for this phenomenon would seem to be the " supply multiplier ".   Notice that the supply multiplier is completely analogous to the conventional demand multiplier, discussed in the introduction to the present paper, by which an initial decrease in demand for current output brings about a decrease in employment and income which leads to further decreases in demand for output, and so on.   The essential difference between the two multipliers concerns their respective frames of reference.   The conventional demand multiplier is applicable to a situation of general excess supply, in which output and employment are constrained by demand.   The supply multiplier refers to a situation of general excess demand, in which output and employment are constrained by supply.

The actual convergence of employment and output in the thought experiment described above will be determined by the interaction between the household's marginal propensity to work given a change in consumables available for purchase and the marginal productivity of labour.   The outcome of this cumulative process can be determined analytically from equations (13) and (14).   Differentiation of equation (14), holding W/P and $\hat{N}$ fixed, yields the following relationship between exogenous changes in M/P and the level of employment:

$$dl = \frac{1}{1 - \dfrac{\partial l^{s'}}{\partial l}} \frac{\partial l^{s'}}{\partial(\Omega - \hat{N}c)} d\left(\frac{M}{P}\right), \qquad \ldots(15)$$

where

$$\frac{\partial l^{s'}}{\partial l} = \left[-\hat{N}\frac{W}{P} + (N - \hat{N})\frac{\partial \pi}{\partial l} \right] \frac{\partial l^{s'}}{\partial(\Omega - \hat{N}c)}^2. \qquad \ldots(16)$$

Once the effect of an exogenous disturbance on the level of employment is known, the effect on the level of output is apparent from equation (13)—in particular,

$$dc = \frac{\partial c^{s'}}{\partial l} dl.$$

According to equation (15), in a situation of suppressed inflation, the ultimate negative effect upon employment of an increase in M/P results from two components.   First, the increase in M/P implies an increase in $\Omega - \hat{N}c$ which directly induces a decline in effective labour supply and employment.   This effect is given by the term, $[\partial l^{s'}/\partial(\Omega - \hat{N}c)]d(M/P)$, in equation (15).   Second, this decrease in employment means less output and hence less consumption, a constraint which induces further decreases in effective labour supply and employment.   However, the reduction in employment also means less profit, which boosts effective labour supply and thereby offsets the effect of less consumption.   The net effect here depends upon the term $1/(1 - \partial l^{s'}/\partial l)$, which magnifies the direct effect of the disturbance in equation (15).   This term is the supply multiplier, and it is completely analogous to the

---

[1] The following simple dynamic model captures the spirit of this verbal sketch.   Suppose that the effective labour supply and employment of any particular individual during the current period depends upon the values of Ω and c which he perceived during the preceding period—that is,

$$l_t = l_t^{s'} = l^{s'}(\Omega_{t-1} - \hat{N}c_{t-1}, W/P, \hat{N}).$$

Aggregation of this discrete-time decision-making framework over all individuals yields as a continuous approximation

$$dl/dt = l^{s'}(\Omega - \hat{N}c, W/P, \hat{N}) - l.$$

Given that output is not storable, c conforms to the contemporaneous relationship

$$c = c^{s'}(l).$$

This model is stable and converges to the solution determined by equations (13) and (14), if $\partial l^{s'}/\partial l$, as specified in equation (16), is less than unity.   Storability of output makes the stability analysis slightly more complex.
[2] The term in the brackets represents $\partial(\Omega - \hat{N}c)/\partial l$.   The form in which we have expressed this term follows immediately by using the definition of profit, $\pi \equiv c - (W/P)l$, to eliminate c in the expression $\Omega - \hat{N}c \equiv M/P + (N - \hat{N})\pi - \hat{N}lW/P$.

demand multiplier, which equals the reciprocal of one minus the propensity to consume. However, in the excess demand case which we are now considering, it is the marginal propensity to work, $\partial l^{s'}/\partial l$, rather than the marginal propensity to consume, which enters into the determination of employment and output.

As is the case with the demand multiplier, one would expect the supply multiplier to be finite but greater than unity. These bounds require that $\partial l^{s'}/\partial l$, as given by equation (16), be less than unity but greater than zero. The condition for a finite multiplier, $\partial l^{s'}/\partial l < 1$, is unambiguously satisfied. From equation (16), we see that this condition requires

$$\frac{1}{\partial l^{s'}/\partial(\Omega-\hat{N}c)} < -\hat{N}\frac{W}{P}+(N-\hat{N})\frac{d\pi}{dl}. \qquad ...(16.1)$$

The simplified asset-exhaustion condition of equation (10.1) implies

$$\frac{\partial l^{s'}}{\partial(\Omega-\hat{N}c)} = -\frac{1}{N'(W/P)}+\frac{N-\hat{N}}{N'(W/P)}\frac{\partial c^{d'}}{\partial(\Omega-\hat{N}c)} > -\frac{1}{N'(W/P)},$$

which implies

$$\frac{1}{\partial l^{s'}/\partial(\Omega-\hat{N}c)} < -N'\frac{W}{P} < -\hat{N}\frac{W}{P},$$

since $\hat{N} < N'$. Finally, the condition $\partial c/\partial l \geqq W/P$ implies

$$\frac{\partial\pi}{\partial l} = \frac{\partial c}{\partial l}-\frac{W}{P} \geqq 0,$$

so that condition (16.1) must be satisfied.[1]

In contrast, the condition for a supply multiplier greater than unity, $\partial l^{s'}/\partial l > 0$, is *not* unambiguously satisfied. From equation (16), we see that this condition requires

$$-\hat{N}\frac{W}{P}+(N-\hat{N})\frac{\partial\pi}{\partial l} < 0. \qquad ...(16.2)$$

In the neighbourhood of general market clearing, where $\partial\pi/\partial l = \partial c/\partial l - W/P \approx 0$, condition (16.2) is satisfied. However, as l falls below l^*, $\partial c/\partial l$ and $\partial\pi/\partial l$ become larger, and eventually condition (16.2) would be violated. When the gap between l^* and l is sufficiently large, the supply multiplier becomes a dampener. This result reflects the offsetting effects which enter into the supply multiplier. A decline in l implies both a reduction in c which depresses $l^{s'}$ and a reduction in π which raises $l^{s'}$. At a sufficiently low level of employment, the second effect dominates.[2]

Two important implications of the above analysis should be stressed. First, although the firms' notional demand for labour depends only on the real wage rate, the real wage rate which is consistent with general market clearing may also be associated with a positive amount of excess demand for labour. Thus, "too low" a level of the real wage rate is not a necessary condition for the existence of excess demand for labour. This observation

[1] If $\hat{N} > N'$, condition (16.1) may not be satisfied. In fact, $\hat{N} = N$ would imply

$$\frac{\partial l^{s'}}{\partial l} = \frac{N}{N'} > 1.$$

In other words, if households believed that the current constraint on consumption would be permanent, the supply multiplier would be implosive. A non-implosive multiplier requires either that the anticipated constraint be limited in duration, as we have been assuming, or that the anticipated future level of the constraint change by less than one-for-one in response to changes in the current constraint. See the discussion in Section VI below.
[2] It is interesting to note that a parallel result does not arise in the general excess supply (demand multiplier) case. In that situation a fall in c produces a fall in π which reinforces the effect of a fall in l as a depressing influence on consumption demand. Consequently, the demand multiplier is unambiguously greater than unity.

parallels the observation that excess supply of labour does not require a real wage rate above the level associated with general market clearing. Excess demand arises in the current case solely because the price level and nominal wage rate are " too low "—that is, because P and W are equiproportionately below P^* and W^*.

The second important implication is that too low a price and nominal wage level and the consequent excess demand for consumables and labour services causes employment and output to be below general-market-clearing levels. This result obtained because households react both to their increased real money balances and to the frustration of their consumption plans by reducing their effective supply of labour services. Given voluntary exchange, employment cannot exceed the quantity supplied, and by the production function, the level of output is constrained by the level of employment.

In standard macro-economic analysis, excessive price and nominal wage levels lead to deficient demand for consumables which depresses output and employment below the full employment level. Here, we see that deficient price and nominal wage levels lead to excessive demand for consumables and also lead to depressed levels of output and employment. Thus, we must not conclude that, because deficient demand for consumables and labour services is bad, excessive demand must be good. The fact is that any chronic failure of markets to clear will lead to a shortfall of output and employment. Both output and employment are maximized at the general-market-clearing wage-price vector.[1]

VI. EXTENSIONS OF THE ANALYSIS OF HOUSEHOLD BEHAVIOUR

This section discusses briefly some directions for extending the simplified model of household behaviour, subject to excess demand for consumables, which was constructed in Section IV.[2] In that model the representative household expected the current constraint on consumption to persist from time 0 to time $\hat{N}$, but expected to be unconstrained after time $\hat{N}$. Two types of objections to this framework arise immediately. First, the anticipated constraint level, c, is based solely on current experience, and the expected duration of the constraint, $\hat{N}$, is totally exogenous. Second, during the constrained period, the household is assumed to be able to purchase consumables up to quantity c merely by paying the going price, P, but is is assumed to be unable to purchase any amount of consumables above c at any price. Consider these objections in turn.

In a more general framework the expected constraint on consumption at various times in the future would depend on the experience of past, as well as present, consumption constraints, and on the supposed implications of special circumstances, such as war or famine, for future constraints. For the determination of the effect of current suppressed inflation upon current employment and output, the important consideration would be the relationship between the current consumption constraint and the expected future time path of consumption constraints. In particular, the weaker the relationship between the current constraint level and the " average " constraint level which is anticipated for the future, the smaller would be the short-run supply multiplier. Moreover, because past, as well as present, constraints would influence expectations, this extended framework would also involve an important dynamic element. The more persistent the shortfall of consumption below notional demand, the larger would be the average expected future consumption shortfall. In effect, the long-run supply multiplier would be larger than the short-run supply multiplier. This conclusion is analogous to the observation that the

---

[1] For a diagrammatic representation of analysis leading to these results, see [2] and [3, Ch. II].
[2] We do not discuss here extensions of the model which involve the introduction of additional types of goods or economic units. For example, the model could be enlarged to include private investment, earning assets, and government behaviour. One interesting aspect of this type of extension is that the total shortfall of output below commodity demand would now have to be divided among various types of demands—in particular, some frustration of private investment demand and of government consumption and investment demand would generally appear along with the frustration of private consumption demand. However, the main conclusions from the present analysis would seem to hold even in this type of extended framework.

long-run demand multiplier will exceed the short-run multiplier when consumption demand depends on " permanent " income, rather than simply on current income.

Another interesting and analytically more challenging extension would involve relaxing the assumption that the consumption constraint is absolute. In a framework of legally enforced rationing and price control, this rigid assumption could be relaxed by introducing " black markets ". These extra-legal markets would present the household with the opportunity of purchasing an unconstrained quantity, but at a higher price, which would include the implicit costs of engaging in illegal activities. More generally, each household could recognize that the level of its individual constraint depends, in part, on the extent of its own activity in search, exhortation, bribery, etc. The amount available for purchase by each household would become an increasing function of the price which the household is willing to pay where this price includes the value of time devoted to search activity. The macro-economic implications of such a formulation are an interesting subject for further analysis.

APPENDIX

The working household's choice of $c^d(t)$ and $l^s(t)$ in Section III involves the following maximization problem:

$$\text{Maximize } U = \int_0^{N'} u[c^d(t), l^s(t)]dt + \int_{N'}^{N} u[c^d(t), 0]dt,$$

subject to the inequality conditions $c^d(t), l^s(t), M(t) \geq 0$, to the initial value of real assets, $M(0)/P$, to given constant values of P, W, π, N' and N, and to the saving condition,

$$\frac{1}{P}\left(\frac{dM}{dt}\right)^d = \begin{cases} \dfrac{W}{P}\, l^s + \pi - c^d & \text{for } t = 0, ..., N', \\ \pi - c^d & \text{for } t = N', ..., N. \end{cases}$$

The solution entails the exhaustion of assets at date N,

$$\frac{M(N)}{P} = \frac{M(0)}{P} + N\pi + \frac{W}{P}\int_0^{N'} l^s(t)dt - \int_0^{N} c^d(t)dt = 0.$$

The interior solution for $c^d(t)$ and $l^s(t)$ satisfies the following marginal conditions:

$$\frac{\partial u}{\partial c^d(t)} = \lambda \text{ for all } t = 0, ..., N$$

and

$$\frac{\partial u}{\partial l^s(t)} = -\lambda\frac{W}{P} \text{ for all } t = 0, ..., N',$$

where λ is a constant which is determined to satisfy the asset-exhaustion condition. These marginal conditions imply

$$c^d(t) = c^d(0) \quad \text{for all} \quad t = 0, ..., N',$$

$$c^d(t) = c^d(N) \quad \text{for all} \quad t = N', ..., N,$$

$$l^s(t) = l^s(0) \quad \text{for all} \quad t = 0, ..., N'.$$

Further, if consumption and work are independent influences on utility—that is, if

$$\partial^2 u/\partial c\partial l = 0$$

—then $c^d(0) = c^d(N)$. In this case the asset-exhaustion condition simplifies to

$$\frac{M(N)}{P} = \frac{M(0)}{P} + N\pi + N'\frac{W}{P}l^s - Nc^d = 0.$$

The working household's choice of $c^{d'}(t)$ and $l^{s'}(t)$ in Section IV involves the following maximization problem:

$$\text{Maximize } U = \int_0^{\hat{N}} u[c, \, l^{s'}(t)]dt + \int_{\hat{N}}^{N'} u[c^{d'}(t), \, l^{s'}(t)]dt + \int_{N'}^{N} u[c^{d'}(t), \, 0]dt,$$

subject to the inequality conditions $c^{d'}(t)$, $l^{s'}(t)$, $M(t) \geqq 0$, to the initial value of real assets, $M(0)/P$, to given constant values of c, $\hat{N}$, W, P, π, N' and N, and to the saving condition,

$$\frac{1}{P}\left(\frac{dM}{dt}\right)^{d'} = \begin{cases} \dfrac{W}{P}l^{s'} + \pi - c & \text{for } t = 0, \, ..., \, \hat{N}, \\[2mm] \dfrac{W}{P}l^{s'} + \pi - c^{d'} & \text{for } t = \hat{N}, \, ..., \, N', \\[2mm] \pi - c^{d'} & \text{for } t = N', \, ..., \, N. \end{cases}$$

The solution again entails the exhaustion of assets at date N,

$$\frac{M(N)}{P} = \frac{M(0)}{P} + N\pi - \hat{N}c + \frac{W}{P}\int_0^{N'} l^{s'}(t)dt - \int_{\hat{N}}^{N} c^{d'}(t)dt = 0.$$

The interior solution for $c^{d'}$ and $l^{s'}$ satisfies the following marginal conditions:

$$\frac{\partial u}{\partial c^{d'}(t)} = \lambda \qquad \text{for all } t = \hat{N}, \, ..., \, N,$$

and

$$\frac{\partial u}{\partial l^{s'}(t)} = -\lambda \frac{W}{P} \quad \text{for all } t = 0, \, ..., \, N',$$

where λ is again a constant which is determined from the asset-exhaustion condition. These marginal conditions imply

$$c^{d'}(t) = c^{d'}(\hat{N}) \quad \text{for all } t = \hat{N}, \, ..., \, N',$$

$$c^{d'}(t) = c^{d'}(N) \quad \text{for all } t = N', \, ..., \, N,$$

$$l^{s'}(t) = l^{s'}(0) \quad \text{for all } t = 0, \, ..., \, \hat{N},$$

$$l^{s'}(t) = l^{s'}(N') \quad \text{for all } t = \hat{N}, \, ..., \, N'.$$

Concerning $l^{s'}(0)$, the form of the function, for fixed values of N' and N, is

$$l^{s'} = l^{s'}(\Omega - \hat{N}c, \, W/P, \, \hat{N}, \, c).$$

The presence of c in the function reflects the ambiguous effect of the level of consumption on the marginal disutility of work. If this effect is assumed to be nil—that is, if

$$\partial^2 u/\partial c \partial l = 0$$

—then c could not appear as a separate argument, as in equation (11). This assumption also implies that $c^{d'}(\hat{N}) = c^{d'}(N)$ and that $l^{s'}(0) = l^{s'}(N')$.

For a discussion of the nature and form of these types of intertemporal maximization problems, see, for example, [6, Ch. 14].

REFERENCES

[1] Barro, R. J. " A Theory of Monopolistic Price Adjustment ", *Review of Economic Studies*, **39** (January 1972), 17-26.

[2] Barro, R. J. and Grossman, H. I. " A General Disequilibrium Model of Income and Employment ", *American Economic Review*, **61** (March 1971), 82-93.

[3] Barro, R. J. and Grossman, H. I. " Money, Employment, and Inflation " (un-published manuscript, 1973).

[4] Grossman, H. I. " Aggregate Demand and Employment ", read at Western Economic Association meetings (August 1972).

[5] Hansen, B. *A Study in the Theory of Inflation* (New York, 1951).

[6] Intriligator, M. D. *Mathematical Optimization and Economic Theory* (Englewood Cliffs, 1971).

[7] Kahn, R. F. " The Relation of Home Investment to Unemployment ", *Economic Journal*, **41** (June 1931), 173-198.

[8] Keynes, J. M. *The General Theory of Employment, Interest, and Money* (New York, 1936).

[9] Lutz, F. A. " The German Currency Reform and the Revival of the German Economy ", *Economica*, **16** (May 1949), 122-142.

[10] Robertson, D. H. *Banking Policy and the Price Level* (London, 1926).

[11] Vicker, R. " USSR: Rising Income, Black Markets ", *The Wall Street Journal* (April 21, 1970).

A Theory of Monopolistic Price Adjustment [1,2]

The theory of price adjustment has been dominated by the idea that prices rise in the presence of excess demand and fall in the presence of excess supply. In the simplest version of this law of supply and demand, the rate of price change is directly proportional to the amount of excess demand:

$$\frac{1}{P}\frac{dP}{dt} = k(Q^d - Q^s) \qquad \qquad ...(1)$$

where, k is a positive constant. Such devices as an auctioneer and recontracting have been introduced to rationalize this type of price-change mechanism. However, the distinctive feature of this type of model is that variations in price are generated by the workings of the " market " and are, therefore, separate from the actions of individual market participants. Further, while demand and supply functions may be formulated in accordance with maximizing principles, the mechanics of price change is essentially *ad hoc*, and seemingly reflects no one's maximizing behaviour.[3]

In general, optimal price adjustment depends on certain " institutional " characteristics under which trading occurs; for example, the form of competition, the presence or absence of trading devices such as an auctioneer, and the determination of which market participants call out prices in the absence of a specific marketeer. While it would be an interesting study to relate these market features to the underlying characteristics of goods and traders, the present analysis abstracts from this type of question. The analysis focuses on a market with one (monopolistic) seller and many (perfectly-competitive) buyers. The seller is taken as the unambiguous price-setter, while the buyers are regarded as unambiguous price-takers. Within this framework, the response of prices to " disequilibrium " emerges as the pattern which maximizes the monopolist's conception of profit. In one sense this restriction to monopoly is a limitation, since perfect competition and oligopoly should also be considered. On the other hand, as Arrow [2] has pointed out, the existence of disequilibrium (excess demand or supply) is inconsistent with certain assumptions of the perfectly competitive model. In particular, the firm's assumption that it is confronted with a perfectly elastic demand curve must be discarded in disequilibrium if the firm is ever to change price. In this sense the response of prices to disequilibrium is essentially a monopolistic phenomenon even if the individual units perform as perfect competitors in equilibrium. Therefore, it

[1] *First version received August 1970; final version received June 1971 (Eds.).*
[2] Earlier versions of this paper were presented at the Workshop on Lags in Economic Behaviour at the University of Chicago, July, 1970; and at the Econometric Society Meetings, Detroit, December 1970. I am grateful for helpful comments from Marc Nerlove and for research support from National Science Foundation grant GS-3246.

[3] This gap in standard analysis has been pointed out by Arrow [2, p. 43]; " [Equation (1) is] the well-known ' Law of Supply and Demand.' . . . The Law of Supply and Demand may be a useful basis for interpreting some empirical phenomena . . . however, the Law is not on the same logical level as the hypotheses underlying [demand and supply functions]. It is not explained whose decision it is to change prices in accordance with [equation (1)]."

Similarly, Koopmans [6, p. 179] argues: " If . . . the net rate of increase in price is assumed to be proportional to the excess of demand over supply, whose behaviour is thereby expressed? And how is that behaviour motivated? "

203

Reprinted from *The Review of Economic Studies*, 39, January 1972, 17–26, by permission of *The Review of Economic Studies*.

seems clear that a theory of monopolistic price adjustment is a prerequisite to a general theory of price adjustment.

While the principal motivation for this paper is a consideration of optimal price adjustment, the formal analysis applies to a larger class of optimal adjustment problems. The basic methodological approach may be outlined as follows. Abstracting from adjustment costs, the optimal value (target) of some control variable X depends on some variable(s) y: $X^d = X^d(y)$. If the actual value of X differs from X^d, an out-of-equilibrium cost (per period) results equal to: $Z(X^d - X)$. In the price adjustment case, Z indicates the cost of maintaining price so that marginal revenue departs from marginal cost. For the simple model considered in Section I, the following important properties are satisfied: (1) Z has a unique minimum point at $X^d = X$, and (2) Z is symmetric in $(X^d - X)$ and increases monotonically with $| X^d - X |$.

In addition to the out-of-equilibrium cost, there is some cost associated with adjustments of X (price). In this paper attention is limited to lump-sum adjustment costs. That is, some cost is incurred each time an adjustment of price is made, but the cost is independent of the amount or direction of adjustment.

Given the nature of the out-of-equilibrium and adjustment costs, optimal adjustment of X depends on the anticipated future behaviour of the target, X^d. In this paper target movements are produced by shifts in demand, which are in turn generated by a symmetric, stochastic process. In other words the decision-maker regards X^d as, at least in part, a temporary target, but he has no information on the direction of future change. Given the adjustment cost specification, optimal adjustment behaviour takes a discrete form—either make a discrete adjustment of X (so as to equate X to X^d in the model being considered), or make no adjustment. However, in a certain expected sense, optimal price adjustment may be approximated in the form of equation (1). In this form the model determines the (optimal) adjustment coefficient, k, as a function of underlying parameters.

I. STATIC OPTIMIZATION MODEL

A monopolistic firm produces a homogenous output flow Y. The cost of producing Y is solely a function of current output:

$$\text{COST} = C(Y) \qquad (C'(Y)>0) \qquad \qquad ...(2)$$

The possibility of storing up finished product as an inventory is omitted.[1]

The firm is aware of a downward-sloping demand curve for its product:

$$Y^d = Q(P)+u \qquad (Q'(P)<0) \qquad \qquad ...(3)$$

where, P is unit price and u is an additive term. The variable u is later treated as a stochastic element which encompasses all price-independent (nonsystematic) variations in demand.

The firm maximizes profit, subject to its demand constraint[2]:

Maximize: $\qquad\qquad\qquad \pi = PY - C(Y) \qquad\qquad\qquad\qquad ...(4)$

Subject to: $\qquad\qquad\qquad Y = Y^d = Q(P)+u \qquad\qquad\qquad ...(5)$

The first-order condition for a maximum is the equation of marginal revenue to marginal cost:

$$P + \frac{Q(P)+u}{Q'(P)} = C'(Y) \qquad\qquad\qquad ...(6)$$

---

[1] The firm's product may be viewed as a service which is immediately " perishable ". The simultaneous consideration of optimal inventory policy with optimal price-change policy appears to be a difficult problem.

[2] Since $\pi = PY - C(Y)$, the optimum P for a given value of Y is the highest price which is consistent with $Y \le Y^d = Q(P)+u$. Since $Q'(P)<0$, this price is the one that just equates Y to Y^d. Therefore, $Y = Y^d$ may be treated as an equality constraint in deriving interior maximization conditions.

Equation (6), together with equation (5), determines optimal values of P and Y.[1]

Returning to the demand curve of equation (3), it is of interest to examine the impact of changes in u (nonsystematic variations in demand) on profit. Differentiating π with respect to u, and using equations (5) and (6):

$$\frac{d\pi}{du} = P - C'(Y)$$

If u is varied from an initial value, u_0, to a final value, u_1, the corresponding change in profit is:

$$\Delta\pi_{(u_0, u_1)} = \int_{u_0}^{u_1} \left(\frac{d\pi}{du}\right) du = \int_{u_0}^{u_1} [P - C'(Y)] du$$

where P and Y are constrained to satisfy equations (5) and (6) along the integration path. The evaluation of the above integral depends on knowledge of the functions, $Q(P)$ and $C(Y)$. Since a general treatment is impossible, explicit functional representations of $Q(P)$ and $C(Y)$ have been used. If $Q(P)$ is a linear function in P, and $C(Y)$ is a quadratic in Y (or, more generally, if $Q(P)$ and $C(Y)$ can be satisfactorily approximated by linear and quadratic functions, respectively, for the relevant range of values), the solution is straight-forward. Using:

$$Q(P) = \alpha - \beta P \qquad (\alpha, \beta > 0)$$
$$C(Y) = a + bY + cY^2 \quad (a, b > 0) \qquad \text{...(7)}$$

and setting $u_0 = 0$ and $u_1 = u$, for convenience, the solution is[2]:

$$\Delta\pi_{(0, u)} = \frac{(\alpha - b\beta)}{2\beta(1 + c\beta)} u + \frac{1}{4\beta(1 + c\beta)} u^2 \qquad \text{...(8)}$$

The change of profit in equation (8) corresponds to a continuous adjustment of price (and output) to variations in u. In order to derive the cost of being out of equilibrium, it is necessary to compare the above change in profit to that which would occur if the firm did not adjust price as u varied. Assume that price is fixed at a level which equates marginal revenue to marginal cost for $u = 0$. This " constrained " price, $\hat{P}$, is determined from:

$$\hat{P} + \frac{Q(\hat{P})}{Q'(\hat{P})} = C'(Y) \Big|_{Y = Q(\hat{P})} \qquad \text{...(9)}$$

Given the price $\hat{P}$, the firm selects a value of current output, $\hat{Y}$, to maximize profit[3]:

Maximize: $\qquad \hat{\pi} = \hat{P}\hat{Y} - C(\hat{Y})$

Subject to: $\qquad \hat{Y} \leq Y^d = Q(\hat{P}) + u.$

Temporarily ignoring the demand constraint, the condition for optimal output (that is, maximum output supply) is:

$$\hat{P} = C'(Y) \big|_{Y = \hat{Y}_{max}} \qquad \text{...(10)}$$

When the price level is fixed (at $\hat{P}$), the monopolistic firm is willing to expand output until

---

[1] The second-order condition for a maximum is:
$$Q'(P)[2 - C''(Y)Q'(P)] + Q''(P)[P - C'(Y)] < 0.$$
The attainment of an interior maximum is also subject to the condition that maximum profit be positive.
[2] The second-order maximum condition is satisfied if $c\beta > -1$. The condition that profit be positive is:
$$\pi = \frac{(\alpha - b\beta + u)^2}{4\beta(1 + c\beta)} - a > 0.$$
[3] No distinction is made between " short " and " long " run costs in the function, $C(Y)$, and future levels of demand are assumed to be independent of the firm's current output decision.

price and marginal cost are equated.[1] The maximal output ($\hat{Y}_{max}$ in equation (10)) necessarily exceeds the demand at $u = 0$, since the determination of $\hat{P}$ involved the equation of
marginal revenue to marginal cost at $u = 0$, and price exceeds marginal revenue ($Q'(P)<0$).
Therefore, with a fixed price level, the firm responds to increases in u by meeting the extra
demand until marginal cost is raised sufficiently to equal price (such a point will exist only
if $C''(Y)>0$ over a sufficient range). Beyond this point (for as long as price remains fixed),
a portion of demand goes unsatisfied.

There also exists a minimum value of u, u_{min}, such that $\hat{\pi}$ is negative for $u \leqq u_{min}$.
In this simple model, production is cut off entirely when u falls below u_{min}.

If u can be guaranteed to lie within the range, $u_{min} \leqq u \leqq u_{max}$, the demand condition
may be treated as an equality constraint (see footnote 1, p. 23). In this case $\hat{Y} = Y^d$,
together with equation (9), determines the price and output ($\hat{P}$ and $\hat{Y}$) of a " fixed-price
monopolist ".

Writing $\hat{\pi} = \hat{P} \hat{Y} - C(\hat{Y})$ and using $\dfrac{d\hat{P}}{du} = 0$, the change in profit with respect to changes

in u (for $u_{min} \leqq u \leqq u_{max}$) is:

$$\frac{d\hat{\pi}}{du} = \hat{P} - C'(Y)\big|_{Y = \hat{Y}}.$$

The total change in profit induced by a change in u from u_0 to u_1 is:

$$\Delta\hat{\pi}_{(u_0, u_1)} = \int_{u_0}^{u_1} [\hat{P} - C'(Y)\big|_{Y = \hat{Y}}]du$$

$$= \hat{P}(u_1 - u_0) - C(Y)\big|_{Y = Q(\hat{P})+u_1} + C(Y)\big|_{Y = Q(\hat{P})+u_0}.$$

Using the forms of $Q(P)$ and $C(Y)$ in equation (7) and substituting $u_0 = 0$, $u_1 = u$, the
solution is:

$$\Delta\hat{\pi}_{(0, u)} = \frac{(\alpha - b\beta)}{2\beta(1 + c\beta)} u - cu^2. \qquad \qquad ...(11)$$

Equation (11) gives the change in profit when price is maintained at the value corresponding to $u = 0$, while equation (8) indicates the profit change when price is continuously
adjusted in an " optimal " manner. The " gain " from price adjustment is given by the
difference between these two expressions:

$$\Delta\pi_{(0, u)} - \Delta\hat{\pi}_{(0, u)} = \frac{(1 + 2c\beta)^2}{4\beta(1 + c\beta)} u^2 = \theta u^2 \qquad \qquad ...(12)$$

$$\left(\theta = \frac{(1 + 2c\beta)^2}{4\beta(1 + c\beta)} > 0 \text{ if } c\beta > -1, \text{ the second-order condition}; \ u_{min} \leqq u \leqq u_{max}\right)$$

Equation (12) indicates the profit foregone (cost of being out of equilibrium) from not
adjusting price while demand has varied by an amount u. The cost is seen to depend on
the square of the " neglected " demand variation (u^2). The symmetry of this cost should
be emphasized. Because the cost of neglecting variations in demand depends only on the
magnitude of the variation, and not on the direction, the final price-change mechanism
turns out to be symmetric.

For a given amount of disequilibrium (u), the out-of-equilibrium cost decreases with
the price sensitivity of demand, β, and (if the second-order condition, $c\beta > -1$, is satisfied)
increases with the slope of the marginal cost curve ($C''(Y) = 2c$).

---

[1] In terms of output determination, the monopolist acts like a perfect competitor in " disequilibrium "
(while P is fixed) since the connection between output and price is temporarily " neglected ". This conclusion
may be contrasted with that of Arrow [2], who observes that perfect competitors must, with respect to price
decisions, act like monopolists in disequilibrium.

II. OPTIMIZATION SUBJECT TO STOCHASTIC DEMAND

If price (and output) could be adjusted instantaneously at zero cost, and no delays in perception were involved, it would be unnecessary ever to forego the profit indicated in equation (12). As u (demand) varied, optimal policy would involve the necessary variation in price in order to continuously maintain marginal revenue = marginal cost. However, if some cost is attached to making changes in price, this cost should be weighed against the cost of being out of equilibrium. The precise form of optimal policy depends on the nature of the adjustment costs, as well as on the (expected) future behaviour of u (assuming that the other functions and parameters are fixed).

Shifts in price involve direct administrative costs to the producer (seller) and they also impose information costs on customers. Each time price is adjusted it is necessary for buyers to learn the new price. This type of information and related search cost has been discussed by Alchian [1]. In terms of the model of Section I, information costs would be transmitted indirectly to the producer by shifts in the demand curve. In particular, a firm with a more variable price history is likely to experience a lower demand (smaller α in equation (7)) for any current price level. Therefore, any decision to change price should consider the impact of this change on the firm's price " reliability " and, hence, on the level of its demand curve.

The administrative costs associated with price changes are straightforward, and can reasonably be described as a lump-sum amount, independent of the size or direction of adjustment. For the purposes of the current analysis, it is assumed that the total cost imputed to each price adjustment may be represented in this simple form; that is, a lump-sum (dollar) amount, γ. This form of adjustment cost leads to an optimal control problem which can be solved analytically. However, since information costs are likely to be more important empirically than administrative costs, it would be useful to extend the analysis to include adjustment costs which operate indirectly through effects on the demand curve.

Variations in output are assumed to incur zero adjustment costs. The inclusion of output adjustment costs would require a consideration of inventories and an explicit treatment of factor adjustment costs. These considerations go beyond the scope of the present paper.

The additive demand component, u, of Section I is treated as an observable random variable which is generated by a symmetric random walk. The walk is regarded as having zero origin, unit step size,[1] and a constant time interval between steps equal to τ. Two important properties of this stochastic process are absence of trend and serial independence.

In determining its price-adjustment behaviour, the firm is assumed to adopt a policy of " (S, s) " form.[2] In accordance with this type of policy, the firm selects ceiling and floor values for demand (h_c and $-h_f$) at which price adjustments occur. For example, if u attains the ceiling, the firm effectively revises its view of the demand function by adding the amount h_c. Assuming that the process originated at $u = 0$, the new " effective " demand function after a ceiling hit would be:

$$Y_1^d = Y_0^d + h_c = \alpha_0 - \beta_0 P + h_c. \qquad \ldots(13)$$

Subject to this revised view of the demand curve, the firm determines a new (higher) price level (so as to equate marginal revenue to marginal cost) and maintains this price until a new ceiling or floor hit occurs. For the linear demand function of equation (7), the

---

[1] As long as the steps are of equal size, a unit step size may be chosen by taking the appropriate normalization for output units. One problem with the random walk process is its nonstationarity. Modification of the process to achieve stationarity would be useful, but it is not immediately clear how to proceed without introducing other undesirable properties into the model.

[2] Scarf [9] presents an optimality proof for the (S, s) policy form in a similar context. However, his model constrains the stochastic movement to be in a single direction. Eppen and Fama [4] provide numerical proofs for (S, s)-type optimality in two-sided stochastic models which are analogous to the one used in this paper.

addition of h_c to Y_0^d in equation (13) can be viewed as a shift in the constant term:

$$\alpha_1 = \alpha_0 + h_c.$$

Since the out-of-equilibrium cost (equation (12)) is independent of α (and, since γ is independent of α), the trade-off between adjustment and out-of-equilibrium costs is not affected by this "revision" of the demand curve. Accordingly, the stochastic process may be treated as though it were repetitive, with u returning to the origin each time an adjustment in price (that is, α) occurs. It also follows that once optimal ceiling and floor values have been found, these values remain optimal after future price adjustments have occurred.

Letting m denote the number of price adjustments which occur over some time interval T, the total expected cost per unit of time may be written as (using equation (12)):

$$E\left[\frac{\text{Cost}}{\text{Time}}\right] = \gamma \cdot E(m/T) + E(\Delta\pi - \Delta\hat{\pi}) = \gamma \cdot E(m/T) + \theta \cdot E(u^2). \qquad ...(14)$$

The firm is assumed to select ceiling and floor values (h_c and $-h_f$) so as to minimize this expected cost per time.[1] Since the out-of-equilibrium cost is symmetric in u, the optimal solution is symmetric: $h_c = h_f = h$. Given this symmetry, the essential problem is to relate the expectations which appear in equation (14) to the choice of h. The solution utilizes previous work of Feller [5] and Miller and Orr [7].

For a symmetric random walk with return point at zero and absorbing barriers at $\pm h$, the expected duration (expected amount of time between barrier contacts) is[2]:

$$D = h^2\tau$$

where, τ is the amount of time per step. The expected number of barrier contacts (price adjustments) per unit of time approaches $1/D$ as the planning horizon becomes large [7, p. 421]:

$$E(m/T) \approx 1/D = \frac{1}{h^2\tau}.$$

The variance of the Bernoulli process involved in the symmetric random walk may be derived as: $\sigma_t^2 = t/\tau$, where t denotes the total elapsed time since the start (from the origin) at time zero.[3] The "daily" variance is:

$$\sigma^2 = \sigma_t^2(t = 1) = \frac{1}{\tau}.$$

The parameter σ^2 may be viewed as a measure of variability of demand. The expected adjustment cost per unit of time may then be written as:

$$\gamma \cdot E(m/T) \approx \gamma\sigma^2/h^2. \qquad ...(15)$$

Note that a higher h reduces the expected adjustment cost per time.

The expected out-of-equilibrium cost is given from equation (14) as: $\theta \cdot E(u^2)$. $E(u^2)$ may be calculated by deriving the density function of u. The difference equation and boundary conditions which determine $f(u)$ are (using steady-state occupancy probabilities):

$$f(u) = \tfrac{1}{2}[f(u+1) + f(u-1)] \quad (-h+1 \leq u \leq h-1; \; u \neq 0)$$
$$f(h) = f(-h) = 0$$
$$f(0) = \tfrac{1}{2}[f(1) + f(-1) + f(h-1) + f(-h+1)]$$
$$\sum_{u=-h}^{h} f(u) = 1.$$

---

[1] The firm is assumed to be risk-neutral, hence, only the expected value of cost per time is considered. If information costs (on customers) of price adjustments were included, the different attitudes toward risk of firms and customers would become important.

[2] This result follows with some modifications from Feller [5, p. 349].

[3] This "unconstrained" variance is derived independently of the barrier positions, and does not correspond to $E(u^2)$, which is derived below.

The difference equation can be solved to yield the density function:

$$f(u) = \begin{cases} \dfrac{1}{h}\left(1-\dfrac{u}{h}\right) & (0 \leq u \leq h) \\[2ex] \dfrac{1}{h}\left(1+\dfrac{u}{h}\right) & (-h \leq u \leq 0) \end{cases} \quad \text{...(16)}$$

Using equation (16) and $h \geq 1$, $E(u^2)$ is eventually determined as:

$$E(u^2) \approx h^2/6.$$

Therefore, the expected out-of-equilibrium cost is:

$$\theta \cdot E(u^2) \approx \frac{\theta h^2}{6}. \quad \text{...(17)}$$

Note that a higher h increases the expected out-of-equilibrium cost.

Using equations (15) and (17), total expected cost per time may be expressed as a function of h:

$$E\left[\frac{\text{Cost}}{\text{Time}}\right] \approx \frac{\gamma\sigma^2}{h^2} + \frac{\theta h^2}{6}. \quad \text{...(18)}$$

The value of h^2 that minimizes this expected cost per time is[1]:

$$(\hat{h})^2 = \sigma \cdot \sqrt{\frac{6\gamma}{\theta}} \quad \left(\theta = \frac{(1+2c\beta)^2}{4\beta(1+c\beta)}\right). \quad \text{...(19)}$$

If a firm selects its critical ceiling and floor values for demand according to equation (19), the reaction to changes in u (variations in demand) depends on the position of u relative to $\pm\hat{h}$. If an increase in u produces a contact with the upper barrier, the firm will react with a discrete upward shift in price. If u decreases sufficiently to reach $-\hat{h}$, an equal size fall in price will occur. For intermediate variations in u which do not involve barrier contacts, no price change will occur.

Although an individual firm's optimal price-adjustment behaviour is fundamentally of this discrete decision type, some further insights can be gained by considering expected price-change behaviour. Starting from (observed) disequilibrium u, consider the expected price change which occurs over the interval up to (and including) the first adjustment of price.

The probability of the random walk terminating at $+\hat{h}$ (therefore, resulting in an increase in the firm's price), given that the walk originated at u, is [5, p. 345]:

$$\Pr(+\hat{h}) = \tfrac{1}{2}\left(1 + \frac{u}{\hat{h}}\right).$$

The corresponding probability of terminating at $-\hat{h}$ (reducing price) is:

$$\Pr(-\hat{h}) = \tfrac{1}{2}\left(1 - \frac{u}{\hat{h}}\right).$$

For the simple demand and cost curves that have been employed in this analysis (equation (7)), the corresponding discrete price changes are: $\pm\dfrac{\hat{h}}{2\beta}\left(\dfrac{1+2c\beta}{1+c\beta}\right)$. Therefore, the net

---

[1] The condition of Section I which guarantees that a fixed-price monopolist meets demand completely, $u_{min} \leq u \leq u_{max}$, translates into: $-u_{min} \geq \hat{h} \leq u_{max}$, with $\hat{h}$ determined from equation (19). If the parameter values are such that this last inequality is satisfied, the monopolist will, in fact, always meet demand.

expected price change at the first adjustment time (starting from u) is:

$$E(\Delta P) = \frac{\hat{h}}{2\beta}\left(\frac{1+2c\beta}{1+c\beta}\right)[\text{Pr}\,(+\hat{h})-\text{Pr}\,(-\hat{h})]$$

$$= \frac{1}{2\beta}\left(\frac{1+2c\beta}{1+c\beta}\right)u. \qquad\qquad\qquad ...(20)$$

The expected duration of the walk which originates at u (average time to first price adjustment) is [5, p. 349]:

$$D_u = \frac{\hat{h}^2-u^2}{\sigma^2}.$$

Therefore, the expected price change per time up to (and including) the first price adjustment may be approximated by[1]:

$$\left(\frac{\overline{\Delta P}}{\Delta T}\right) \approx \frac{E(\Delta P)}{D_u} = \frac{\sigma^2}{2\beta}\left(\frac{1+2c\beta}{1+c\beta}\right)\frac{u}{\hat{h}^2-u^2}.$$

If the initial disequilibrium is small relative to that value which would cause a shift in price: $|u| \le \hat{h}$, one may approximate:

$$\left(\frac{\overline{\Delta P}}{\Delta T}\right) \approx \frac{\sigma^2}{2\beta}\left(\frac{1+2c\beta}{1+c\beta}\right)\frac{u}{\hat{h}^2} \quad (|u| \le \hat{h}). \qquad ...(21)$$

Viewing " output supply " as the output corresponding to $u = 0$, u may be replaced by current excess demand: $u = Y^d - Y^s$. Substituting for $\hat{h}^2$ from equation (19) and dividing both sides of equation (21) by P, one obtains[2]:

$$\frac{1}{P}\left(\frac{\overline{\Delta P}}{\Delta T}\right) \approx k(Y^d - Y^s)$$

$$k = \frac{\sigma(1+2c\beta)^2}{4P\sqrt{6\gamma}[\beta(1+c\beta)]^{\frac{3}{2}}}. \qquad\qquad ...(22)$$

In the above expression σ^2 is the " daily " variance of u (demand), γ is the lump-sum price-adjustment cost, β is the (constant) price sensitivity of demand, and c measures the (constant) slope of the marginal cost function ($C''(Y) = 2c$).

The expected price change behaviour described in equation (22) has the form of the conventional law of supply and demand given in equation (1). However, it should be stressed that equation (22) involves an averaging (over time) of discrete behaviour, so that optimal price adjustment (at least at the individual firm level) cannot be accurately described by a differential equation. An important feature of equation (22) is its symmetry. This result derives from symmetry in the out-of-equilibrium and adjustment costs, and from the symmetry of the stochastic demand process.

---

[1] In order to calculate $\left(\frac{\overline{\Delta P}}{\Delta T}\right)$ exactly, it would be necessary to sum over an explicit expression for the density of first absorption time. Unfortunately, this calculation does not appear feasible. Therefore, a ratio of expectations has been taken as an approximation to the expectation of the ratio.

[2] The presence of P in the expression for k in equation (22) may be interpreted by expressing the nominal price-adjustment cost as: $\gamma = \gamma^*\bar{P}$, the demand sensitivity as: $\beta = \beta^*/\bar{P}$, and the cost coefficient as: $c = c^*\bar{P}$, where $\bar{P}$ is the " overall " price level. In terms of starred variables, the adjustment coefficient is:

$$k = \frac{\sigma(1+2c^*\beta^*)^2}{4\left(\frac{P}{\bar{P}}\right)\sqrt{6\gamma^*}[\beta^*(1+c^*\beta^*)]^{3/2}}.$$

Therefore, the relative price, $P/\bar{P}$, influences k, but proportional shifts in P and $\bar{P}$ (with β^*, c^*, γ^* fixed) leave k unchanged.

The coefficient of proportionality (k) between average price change per time and excess demand is explicitly related to the parameters of the model.

1. The coefficient is positively related to the variance of demand, σ^2. This result emerges as the outcome of two offsetting forces. First, a larger demand variance implies an increased frequency of price adjustment for a given ceiling value, $\hat{h}$ (equation (15)). Second, this effect is partially offset by the positive relation between $\hat{h}$ and σ^2 (equation (19)). The net effect is a positive relation between k and σ^2.

2. The coefficient is inversely related to the lump-sum cost of price adjustment, γ.

3. The coefficient is inversely related to the price-sensitivity of demand, β. A larger demand sensitivity reduces the out-of-equilibrium cost (equation (12)), and it also decreases the size of the price adjustment which is necessary to re-attain " equilibrium ". Both of these effects tend to lower the responsiveness of price to excess demand.

4. The coefficient is positively related to c (given the second-order condition, $c\beta > -1$) which measures the slope of the marginal cost curve $(C''(Y) = 2c)$. This result reflects the increase in out-of-equilibrium cost (equation (12)) which accompanies a rise in $C''(Y)$. Since this cost is raised, the firm is motivated to raise price more frequently (by reducing $\hat{h}$) and k is increased.

III. EXTENSIONS OF THE MODEL

1. An important extension of the model is the inclusion of anticipated trends in underlying variables (such as, overall price level, costs, systematic demand shifts) which lead to an expected trend in a firm's target price level. This modification would alter the form of the average price change relation in equation (22) to include the anticipated trend of the target price along with a measure of current excess demand.

2. In the model used in this paper, adjustment costs were assumed to be solely lump-sum and symmetric. This set-up appears reasonable if one considers purely administrative costs of price change, but information costs (which are actually transmitted to the firm indirectly via shifts in the demand curve) may be more appropriately modelled by also including costs which depend on the amount or the speed of adjustment. In the optimal investment literature initiated by Eisner and Strotz [3; see, in particular, p. 69], speed-dependent adjustment costs (for example, costs which vary with the square of the amount of adjustment) were emphasized as the essential rationale for partial adjustment behaviour. However, the incorporation of speed-dependent (say, quadratic) adjustment costs into the current model does not alter the one-shot (bang-bang) adjustment behaviour which emerged in Section II. The inclusion of costs which vary with the amount and/or speed of adjustment (with symmetry retained) implies that discrete adjustment from the barriers, $\pm h$, should be made to non-zero return points, $\pm R$, respectively; that is, the common return point at zero disappears, but the basic form of adjustment is the same, as long as no indivisibilities or " large " jumpiness in the stochastic process are introduced. A more complicated adjustment cost function which does lead to partial (discrete) adjustment is the following: lump-sum, decision-type costs are incurred at the initiation of adjustment, but these costs do not recur as long as adjustment in successive periods is merely a continuation of the original decision. Subsequent adjustment periods are characterized by another type of lump-sum cost and also by speed-dependent adjustment costs. Under the above specification, adjustment will again not occur until the stochastic variable (u) reaches a critical barrier $(\pm h)$. At this point, adjustment will be initiated, but the return point $(\pm R)$ will not be attained in a single step. Rather, a finite number of periods will be used to move from $\pm h$ to $\pm R$, thus implying a form of partial adjustment. While this extended model does lead to partial adjustment, the idea of a non-recurring decision cost may be more applicable to optimal investment behaviour[1] than to optimal pricing policy. In any case

[1] Asymmetry in the adjustment costs may also be appropriate in models of optimal capital accumulation.

one-shot adjustment does not appear unreasonable for optimal price policy, though it does appear unreasonable for optimal capital stock accumulation. It would, therefore, be of considerable interest to apply a modified version of the model to the problem of optimal capital accumulation.

3. Since the current price adjustment model is limited to the framework of monopoly, it would be useful to generalize to a framework of oligopoly. This extension requires a mechanism for allocating demand among different firms, and it also requires a specification of firm interaction. Some developments along this line are contained in the papers in Phelps [8], though these papers omit lump-sum adjustment costs, and therefore, do not deal with discrete adjustment behaviour.

In an oligopoly model it would be interesting to consider some measures of overall price change by averaging over individual firm behaviour. It seems likely that individual adjustment will still be of the one-shot variety, but average response may be describable as a smooth function. In other words the conventional law of supply and demand (equation (1)) may well be satisfactory as an approximation in the aggregate, although it misses the discrete response at the individual unit level.

4. Finally, the model could be usefully extended to include wage (factor-cost) adjustment and to include optimal inventory holding along with optimal pricing policy.

REFERENCES

[1] Alchian, A. A. " Information Costs, Pricing and Resource Unemployment ", *Western Economic Journal* (1969), **7**, 109-128.

[2] Arrow, K. J. " Toward a Theory of Price Adjustment ", in M. Abramowitz, ed., *The Allocation of Economic Resources* (Stanford, Stanford University Press, 1959).

[3] Eisner, R. and Strotz, R. " Determinants of Business Investment ", in: Commission on Money and Credit, *Impacts of Monetary Policy* (Englewood Cliffs, New Jersey, 1963).

[4] Eppen, G. and Fama, E. " Solutions for Cash Balance and Simple Dynamic Portfolio Problems ", *Journal of Business* (1968), **41**, 94-112.

[5] Feller, W. *An Introduction to Probability Theory and its Applications*, Vol. I, 3rd ed. (New York, John Wiley and Sons, 1968).

[6] Koopmans, T. C. *Three Essays on the State of Economic Science* (New York, McGraw-Hill, 1957).

[7] Miller, M. H. and Orr, D. " A Model of the Demand for Money by Firms ", *Quarterly Journal of Economics* (1966), **80**, 413-435.

[8] Phelps, E. S., *et al.* *Microeconomic Foundations of Employment and Inflation Theory* (New York, 1970).

[9] Scarf, H. " The Optimality of (S, s) Policies in the Dynamic Inventory Problem ", in K. J. Arrow, S. Karlin and P. Suppes, eds., *Mathematical Methods in the Social Sciences*, 1959 (Stanford, Stanford University Press, 1960).

Long-Term Contracting, Sticky Prices, and Monetary Policy *

1. Introduction

A key element in Keynesian-type analyses of economic fluctuations is the assumption of stickiness in the adjustment of some prices to excess demands. In particular, when wages and prices are maintained for substantial periods at non-market clearing values, it becomes interesting to examine the implications of sustained excess demand or supply in the labor and commodity markets. The application of non-price rationing rules to determine quantities of employment and output, the implications of these rules for quantity constraints perceived by individual market participants, and the spillover effects of these constraints from one market to another then become central ingredients of Keynesian multiplier analysis.[1] Although this approach has some attractive features for explaining the cyclical behavior of employment and output, there is a weak theoretical link in the nonexplanation for the failure of wages and prices to move rapidly to clear markets without the application of nonprice rationing rules.

Some recent developments in labor market contracting theory [Baily (1974), Azariadis (1975), Gordon (1974)] have rationalized a sluggish response of wages to changing economic conditions. Workers and firms are viewed as engaging in long-term (explicit or implicit) contracts that specify in advance the (possibly state-dependent) wage rates that workers will receive over the life of the contract. The motivation for long-term contracts in these models derives from an insurance element. Because the owners of the firms are assumed to be less risk averse (possibly due to self-selection) or to have better access to capital markets, it becomes mutually advantageous to enter into a long-term arrangement in which the firms assume at least the main portion of the under-

*This research was supported by the U.S. Department of Labor (ASPER). I am grateful for helpful comments from Costas Azariadis, Jo Anna Gray, Herschel Grossman and Zvi Hercowitz.
[1] A full discussion of this topic is contained in Barro and Grossman (1976, ch. 2).

213

Reprinted from *Journal of Monetary Economics*, 3, July 1977, 305–316, by permission of North-Holland Publishing Company, Amsterdam.

lying risk by guaranteeing the workers a fixed (state-invariant) wage rate.[2,3] Hence, the long-term contracting approach seems to firm up a weak link in Keynesian analysis by providing a theoretical rationale for the slow adjustment of wages and prices.

The long-term contracting approach has, in fact, been used by Gray (1976) and Fischer (1977a, b) to rationalize wage stickiness in a macro model. The presence of sticky wages in their models implies that monetary disturbances can affect employment and output, even when the disturbances are recognized, contemporaneously, as monetary in nature. A related conclusion is that feed-back rules for monetary policy can be an effective stabilization device. The crux of the argument in the present paper is that the Gray and Fischer models produce this conclusion because the contracting approach is applied only to one aspect of the labor market – wage determination – and not to the other aspect – employment determination. When optimal contractual arrangements are specified for determining employment, the output and employment effects of currently perceived monetary disturbances disappear. In other words, the link between contracting theory and sticky prices does not produce a reconciliation between the standard Keynesian model and rational behavior.

2. The Gray–Fischer analysis

I will outline here the type of model used by Gray (1976) and Fischer (1977a, b).[4] The framework is closer in details to Gray's, but the essential aspects accord also with Fischer's model.

Assume a log-linear production function for output, y, in terms of labor

---

[2]In the absence of 'transaction costs' that involve contract enforcement, the insurance element actually argues for a constant income, rather than a constant wage. This conclusion follows from the analysis of Shavell (1976). See also Grossman (1975). However, the distinction between sticky wages and sticky labor incomes is not an important consideration for the main analysis in this paper.

[3]Alternatively, (explicit or implicit) long-term contracts with a prior specification of payment schedules could be rationalized by assuming that the work arrangement required at least one of the parties to acquire a substantial amount of specific human capital. In this case job turnover would entail 'mobility costs.' Prior specification of payments – to the extent that they could be enforced by legal means or by 'reputation' – would be a mechanism for preventing ex post 'monopoly exploitation' of the specific capital. The specific human capital idea was developed by Becker (1962). The same basic idea appears under the heading, 'idiosyncratic exchange,' in Williamson, Wachter and Harris (1975). The importance of mobility costs in long-term labor arrangements is stressed in Baily (1977).

[4]A similar analysis is carried out by Phelps and Taylor (1977), but without relating price rigidities to long-term contracting. They observe (p. 4), ' . . . we surmise (but do not model) that there are costs or losses incurred by too-frequent or too-precipitate revisions of price lists and wage scales.' An explicit price adjustment model of this type is developed in Barro (1972). However, the drawback of this type of model is that it relies on direct 'price adjustment costs,' which do not seem to be quantitatively important. The attractive feature of the contracting approach is its potential for a quantitative reconciliation between sticky prices and rational behavior.

input, l,

$$\log (y) = A + \alpha \log (l) + u, \tag{1}$$

where $0 < \alpha < 1$ and u is a stochastic term, generated by a white-noise process with variance σ_u^2, that represents an aggregate real shock to productivity. The implied demand for labor function, corresponding to an equation of the marginal product of labor to the real wage, w/P, is

$$\log (l^d) = B - \frac{1}{1-\alpha} \log (w/P) + \frac{1}{1-\alpha} u, \tag{2}$$

where $B \equiv (1/1-\alpha)[A + \log (\alpha)]$. The supply of labor function is, normalizing the constant to zero,

$$\log (l^s) = \beta \log (w/P), \tag{3}$$

where $\beta \geqq 0$ is assumed. Following the earlier models for convenience, I do not introduce any stochastic elements into the labor supply function.

The demand for real money balances, M/P, is unit elastic with respect to real income, y,[5] and depends also on a stochastic shift term, v_1 – that is,

$$\log (M) - \log (P) = C + \log (y) + v_1.$$

The log of the money stock differs from its expected value, $\overline{\log M}$, by a stochastic term, v_2,

$$\log (M) = \overline{\log M} + v_2.$$

Defining $v \equiv v_2 - v_1$ (which represents the sum of unanticipated movements in the log of the money stock and in the log of velocity), the price level is determined from

$$\log (P) = -C + \overline{\log M} - \log (y) + v, \tag{4}$$

where v is assumed to be generated by a white noise process with variance σ_v^2.

In the case of a nonindexed fixed nominal wage contract, the nominal wage is set (over the life of the contract) before the realization of the stochastic terms, u and v. One possible setting of w would be at the value that corresponds to an equality of l^d and l^s when the stochastic terms take on their expected values ($u = v = 0$). Although optimal (and competitive) fixed-wage contracts would

---

[5]The analysis could be modified without substantial changes to allow a non-unit income elasticity and also to introduce an interest rate variable. See Fischer (1977b, appendix).

not generally specify this value of w (as implied, for example, by the analysis of Azariadis (1975, section V)), it is convenient and harmless to carry out the main exposition by assuming that the wage is set in this manner. Normalizing by setting $A = -\log(\alpha)$, so that $B = 0$, then implies that $\log(w) = 0$. If C is also set to equal $\overline{\log M} - A$, then the values associated with $u = v = 0$ are $\log(P) = \log(l) = 0$ and $\log(y) = -\log(\alpha)$.

Since the realizations of u and v will generally be nonzero, there will be a discrepancy, ex post, between l^d and l^s. The completion of the model requires a rule for determining l (and, hence, y from eq. (1)) in this circumstance. The specification of quantity determination rules is, of course, as much a part of the long-term contractual arrangement as is the agreement about wage schedules. Gray and Fischer deal with contracts in which employment is always determined along the l^d curve, as given in eq. (2). Although I argue below that the form of the employment rule is the key to their results, it can be noted here that two alternative rules: $l = l^s$ and $l = \text{Min}(l^d, l^s)$ (the 'short-end' rule) would not change the basic picture. For the $l = l^d$ rule, the values of w/P, l, and y can be determined as functions of the disturbances, u and v, by solving through eqs. (1), (2) and (4). The results for the normalized system are

$$\log(w/P) = u - (1-\alpha)v,$$
$$\log(l) = v, \tag{5}$$
$$\log(y) = -\log(\alpha) + \alpha v + u.$$

It is useful to note also the values of the real wage and employment that correspond to an equality between l^d and l^s for nonzero values of u and v. These market-clearing values of w/P and l, marked by an asterisk, can be determined from eqs. (2) and (3) to be

$$\log(w/P)^* = \frac{u}{1+\beta(1+\alpha)},$$
$$\log(l)^* = \beta u / [1 + \beta(1-\alpha)]. \tag{6}$$

Consider, first, the effect of a nominal disturbance, v, as depicted in fig. 1. A positive value of v raises the price level, which reduces the real wage since the nominal wage is fixed. Employment expands correspondingly along the l^d curve (though the associated rise in output implies a fall in the price level from eq. (4), which partly offsets the initial decline in the real wage). A negative value of v has an analogous depressing effect on employment. Hence, the model implies that unanticipated, but currently perceived, money shocks influence the levels of employment and output. (Note that monetary shocks have no effect

ɔn the market-clearing values, $(w/P)^*$ and l^*, as shown in eq. (6).) In Fischer's
(1977a) model with two-period contracts, this nonzero output effect of currently
perceived money shocks permits an activist role for monetary policy. The
monetary authority can act after it obtains information about next period's
values of u and the exogenous part of v, while some of the market participants
are constrained for another period to the contracted value of w.

The case of a real shock to productivity is depicted in fig. 2. A positive value
of u expands output for a given value of employment in accordance with eq. (1).

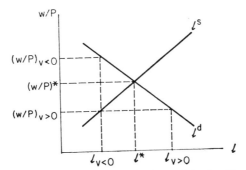

Fig. 1. Monetary shocks with fixed w and the $l = l^d$ rule.

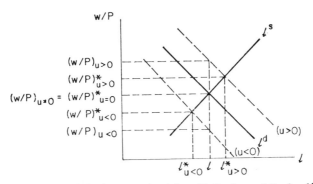

Fig. 2. Aggregate real shocks to productivity with fixed w and the $l = l^d$ rule.

There are two offsetting effects on employment itself. First, since the marginal
product of labor rises with u for a given value of l, there is a tendency for l^d
to rise, as indicated in eq. (2). Second, the direct effect of u on y implies a fall
in the price level from eq. (4), which leads to an increase in w/P and a fall in l^d.
In the present model, where real money demand is unit elastic with respect to y,
the movements in the marginal product of labor and in w/P are equal, so that
the net effect on employment is nil. Although this property is special to the

present model, it can be retained for expository convenience without affecting the main conclusions. Fig. 2 indicates that the same value of l arises for positive and negative values of u. On the other hand, the market-clearing value of employment, l^*, moves positively with u, corresponding to a movement of $(w/P)^*$ that is smaller in magnitude than the movement in w/P (associated with a fixed value of w).

The principal conclusion is that both types of shocks lead to a departure of employment, l, from the market-clearing value, l^*. The nominal shock, v, shifts l while l^* remains fixed. The real shock, u, shifts l^* while l remains fixed (or, more generally, does not shift by the same amount as l^*).

Given the $l = l^d$ rule, the source of the gaps between l and l^* is, of course, the prior contractual specification of the nominal wage, w. Gray and Fischer therefore consider the impact on employment determination of introducing some contractual flexibility into the nominal wage through an indexing rule. Gray uses the rule

$$\log (w) = \gamma \log (P), \tag{7}$$

where $0 \leqq \gamma \leqq 1$ (recall that the system has been normalized so that $\log (w) = \log (P) = 0$ applies when $u = v = 0$). For monetary shocks it is clear from fig. 1 that $l = l^*$, which is associated here with a constant value of w/P, would be maintained through full indexing where $\gamma = 1$. For aggregate real shocks to productivity as described in fig. 2, the maintenance of $l = l^*$ requires partial indexing – that is, a value of γ in the interval between 0 and 1. If the form of indexing is limited to that expressed in eq. (7), where the adjustment of w does not take account of the values of y or M, then there is no value of γ that maintains $l = l^*$ for all values of (u, v). However, Gray derives an optimal degree of indexing (dependent on σ_u^2 and σ_v^2), which is the value of γ that minimizes the expected squared gap between l and l^*.

3. The employment rule

The above type of model generates a dependence of employment on monetary shocks even when individuals have no problem currently in labeling the shocks as monetary. This result enables Fischer (1977a) to construct a money supply rule that has systematic (and possibly desirable) effects on the economy's time path of employment. As a related point the models imply that indexation of the nominal wage to the price level would alter the economy's response to monetary disturbances (of both the exogenous and policy variety). In this section I examine the sensitivity of these conclusions to the form of the rule for determining employment in 'non-market clearing' situations.

Return to the case of nonindexed contracts with fixed wages, and consider the effects of monetary shocks, as shown in fig. 1. Positive values of v lead to low values of w/P and high values of l, with the reverse applying for negative values of v. Put another way, positive money shocks imply that the marginal product of labor, as calculated from the l^d curve, is below the marginal value of time, as calculated from the l^s curve – and the reverse for negative money shocks.[6] Whenever there is a departure of the marginal product of labor from the marginal value of time there is, ex post, an unexploited opportunity for mutual gains from trade. Namely, any movement of l toward l^* (accompanied by appropriate side payments) would make both firms and workers better off. The puzzle, then, is why the parties would agree, ex ante, to a form of contract that imposes these sorts of ex post dead-weight losses.

Consider the situation from the ex ante position where the contract is set up between a firm and a worker before the value of the monetary shock, v, is realized. The two parties to the contract know that the v-shock will sometimes be positive and sometimes negative. If they agree on a fixed value of w and use an employment rule of the type proposed by Gray and Fischer,[7] they will be adopting a contract that imposes dead-weight losses for both positive and negative monetary disturbances. In the absence of any 'transaction costs' that would, for example, inhibit the possible contractual arrangements for making side payments between firms and workers, it is apparent that the employment rule would be selected in order to maximize the total pie possessed by the two parties. This total is maximized by specifying an employment rule that equates the marginal product of labor to the marginal value of time – that is, $l = l^*$ – in all circumstances.[8] In the case where there are only monetary disturbances, the employment rule is simple – namely, choose l to equal the constant value of l^* that is shown in fig. 1. Hence, in the case where w is fixed ex ante, monetary shocks would generate movements in w/P but no movements in l. In this situation the value of l is set at the intersection of the l^d and l^s curves, rather than being read off either curve at the prevailing value of w/P.

The situation is basically similar for the case of real shocks, although l^* is no longer constant. The optimal contingent contract would relate each value of u to a value of employment that corresponds to the equation of l^d to l^s. Employment would therefore be determined where the marginal product of labor is equated to the marginal value of time, though not necessarily to w/P itself.

Given this form of employment rule, which maximizes the total pie available to firms and workers, one can then consider optimal (and competitive) payment arrangements that would determine the split of the pie. For example, it may be

---

[6]In using a fixed l^s curve here and below I am neglecting the possible effects of (one-period) changes in income distribution on the marginal value of time. Note also that the marginal value of time would include unemployment compensation benefits. However, I am abstracting from any lump-sum costs or benefits associated with the work/no-work decision.

[7]The alternative rules, $l = l^s$ or $l = \text{Min } (l^d, l^s)$, entail the same sort of problems.

[8]This rule seems to be consistent with the more general criteria for employment determination that are set up by Azariadis (1975, parts IV and V) and Baily (1977, parts 3 and 4).

optimal for firms to perform the insurance function of guaranteeing to the workers, ex ante, a fixed (nominal or real) wage or income.[9] In this case long-term contracting may account for 'rigid' wages,[10] and may also explain the apparent nonwage rationing of jobs. For example, in the case of a contract that specifies a fixed nominal wage, a negative money shock would increase w/P above $(w/P)^*$ in fig. 1. The value of l^s associated with the 'prevailing' real wage would then exceed the amount of employment, l^*, which is determined at the intersection of the l^d and l^s curves. The gap between $l^s(w/P)$ and l^* appears to reflect non-wage rationing behavior. In fact, the situation is Pareto optimal because employment is determined where the marginal product of labor is equated to the marginal value of time. The 'excessive' real wage reflects a stochastic outcome whose possibility was fully considered in specifying the initial terms of the contract. Although this particular realization for w/P has implications for ex post income distribution in the current period, it has no implications for the determination of employment.

An important aspect of the rule that determines employment at the (possibly shifting) intersection of the l^d and l^s curves is that it implies a divorce of employment determination from perceived monetary disturbances. Hence, even with long-term contracts that specify fixed nominal wage rates, there would be no effects (from this channel) of money on employment, and, correspondingly, no stabilizing role for feedback monetary rules.

On the other hand, the opportunity to contract for a finite interval may have effects on natural rates of employment and output. For example, the workers' ability to utilize this type of insurance arrangement could produce a one-time shift in the l^s function by altering calculations on the marginal value of time. In the case of specific capital accumulation, as discussed in fn. 3 above, the opportunity to engage in long-term contracts would have efficiency aspects that could also influence the average level of employment. Further, since the slopes of the l^s and l^d schedules may be affected by the existence of long-term contracts, there could be some implications for the functional dependence of l^* on the real shock, u – or, in an extended model, on the portion of monetary shocks that were misperceived as real shocks. However, effects of this sort do not imply any policy role for feedback monetary rules.

With respect to indexing, it is apparent that nominal wage adjustment of the

[9]In the case of a contract that stipulates a fixed labor income, it is apparent that the rule which determines employment along the l^d (or l^s) curve would not be feasible. Ex post, the marginal cost of employment to the firm would be nil (as would the marginal gain to the worker). Accordingly, with a fixed income contract, a different type of employment rule must be specified – for example, a rule that l be determined at the intersection of the l^d and l^s curves, as proposed above.

[10]The approach may also account for the celebrated failure of real wages to move counter-cyclically, as pointed out by Gordon (1974, p. 456). A countercyclical movement of w/P in the face of aggregate demand shifts (for example, shifts in v) would be predicted from a model that determined l along the l^d curve.

form suggested in eq. (7) would not alter the conclusion that employment is determined at the l^* position. Any real effects of indexing would have to involve the implications of the opportunity to contract on an indexed basis for the underlying labor supply and demand curves, and, hence, for the determination of l^*.[11] The direct cyclical interplay between nominal disturbances and indexing that occurs in the Gray and Fischer models is entirely a consequence of the arbitrary rule for setting employment.

4. Incomplete information

In order to avoid the above conclusions on monetary policy, it is necessary to introduce some type of 'transaction cost' to prevent contracts from determining employment in the previously described manner that would otherwise be optimal. Of course, it should be noted that any costs of this sort will make contracting, per se, less desirable, and would therefore tend to move the economy toward spot market arrangements. In order to retain long-term contracting as a significant element in the analysis of monetary policy, it is necessary to concoct transaction costs that deter the proposed employment rule without deterring long-term contracting entirely. I discuss in this section some implications of incomplete information.

None of the preceding analysis assumed any ignorance of individuals about the current values of the monetary and real shocks. One obvious possibility is that market participants have incomplete current information about these disturbances. The partial information setup would beome more interesting in an expanded framework that included relative (industry or firm-specific) real shocks, in addition to the aggregate real shock (u). In this expanded context participants of localized markets might have current information sets that excluded observations on such global variables as the current absolute price level, money stock, and output. Notably, individuals might become uncertain about the real wages that they would be able to receive or pay either outside of their local environments or in future periods. The information problem that emanates from a confusion between relative (real) disturbances and monetary disturbances is the basis for a Phillips curve-type relationship in the extensive literature that includes Friedman (1968), Phelps (1970), and Lucas (1972, 1973). In these models the confusion between relative and absolute price changes implies shifts in the labor supply and demand functions, which lead to changes in employment associated with changes in the point of intersection between the l^d and l^s curves (l^*). However, these effects arise even in the absence of long-term contracts. The present issue concerns the additional implications of incomplete information that are associated with long-term contracting. For

---

[11]In this respect see Azariadis (1976).

this purpose I will abstract from any shifts in the l^d and l^s curves that might be produced by information confusion.

The operation of the employment rule, $l = l^*$, requires the contracting parties to have knowledge of the real shift, u, where I will limit attention here to the case of real shocks that are purely aggregate in nature (and, therefore, affect the absolute price level, as described above). If the value of u is perceived by the firms, who are directly affected by this 'productivity' shift, they may have a moral hazard-type incentive to misrepresent this value to the workers under fixed nominal wage contracts that contain the $l = l^*$ rule. For example, if there is a positive money shock, $v > 0$, firms would be willing to expand employment to the level, $l^d(w/P)$, which exceeds l^*. In this circumstance firms would be motivated to overstate their perception of the real shock, u, so as to substantiate a claim that l^* had increased. The incentive of workers would clearly be the opposite. In the case of a negative money shock, the roles would be reversed, with firms tending to understate the value of u and vice versa for workers.[12] In any event incomplete current information by one or both parties about the value of the real shock would prevent the exact achievement of the $l = l^*$ position. In comparison with spot market arrangements, long-term contracting does seem to involve a diminution of the signalling power of prices, in the sense of a decline in their ability to guide the economy toward the $l = l^*$ position.[13]

An important question is the implication of this result for the conclusions of the Gray–Fischer analysis. It remains true that monetary shocks do not affect the target employment position, l^*. Hence, even with incomplete current information, optimal contracts would contain the provision that employment be independent of the perceived part of money shocks. In his model with two-period contracts, Fischer (1977a) constructs a rule for setting the money supply that is contingent on outcomes during the previous period. Since the implied money movements in each period are, by assumption, fully perceived in that period, it follows that employment, determined in accordance with optimal contract provisions, would be independent of the form of the money supply rule. In other words, the Sargent–Wallace (1975) conclusion on the inefficacy of systematic feedback rules for monetary policy remains intact in a long-term contracting world with incomplete current information if the contracts contain the optimal provisions for employment determination.

If the labor contracts are indexed, then w will be adjusted in accordance with, say, the level of the observed (possibly lagged) absolute price level. However, the indexing rule does not exploit any information that the market participants

---

[12]These incentives to misrepresent the state of the world would not arise under the $l = l^d$ or $l = l^s$ rules. However, under the $l = l^*$ rule, the motivation of firms to misrepresent the value of l^* would be limited to the value of $l^d(w/P)$, while that for the workers would be limited to the value of $l^s(w/P)$.

[13]Although spot markets retain the information problem of distinguishing temporary price shifts from permanent ones and relative shifts from aggregate ones.

could not already have used to ascertain the position of l^*.[14] To the extent that the observed value of the absolute price level conveys information about l^*, this information would already have been incorporated into the determination of employment. The fact of indexing seems to have no additional implications for the setting of l.

5. Some conclusions

I observed at the outset that wage/price stickiness appeared to be a key under-pinning of Keynesian analysis. The puzzle then is why long-term contracting theory can (perhaps) account for wage/price stickiness without, at the same time, supporting Keynesian conclusions on monetary policy and in other areas. The explanation is that wage/price stickiness is not, per se, fundamental to Keynesian models. Rather, the crucial element – and the aspect that accurately marks this approach as 'non-market clearing' analysis – is the nonexecution of some *perceived* mutually advantageous trades[15] (where trades may include side payments). In the context of voluntary exchange on spot markets, it would not generally be possible to exhaust all perceived mutually advantageous trades unless all prices were 'flexible'. However, long-term contracts permit a separa-tion between mutually advantageous exchange and short-run price flexibility – it becomes possible to retain the former while abandoning the latter.

In order to support Keynesian results it is necessary to demonstrate a link between the potential for long-term contracts and the propensity of the private economy to experience cyclical phases of more or less missed (perceived) opportunities for mutually advantageous trade. It seems that any decrease in the cost of contracting would actually move the economy toward a position where, on average, a larger fraction of mutually desirable exhanges were accomplished. Even with transaction costs – say, for setting up contractual contingencies and for dealing with moral hazard-type problems – it would seem that an economy with some long-term contracting potential would come closer to carrying out its perceived opportunities for mutually advantageous trade than would an economy that was limited to spot arrangements. In this sense the potential for long-term contracting weakens the theoretical case for Keynesian analysis rather than supporting it.

[14]Some additional aspects of the noninformation role of indexing are discussed in Barro (1976).
[15]This view suggests a distinction between Keynesian analysis and the 'equilibrium' approach to business cycle theory that is exemplified by the work of Lucas, Sargent and Wallace et al. The former ('non-market clearing') model focuses on fluctuations in the quantity of perceived mutually advantageous trades that are not executed, while the latter ('market clearing' model) concentrates on fluctuations in the size of the gap between perceived and actual mutually advantageous trades as influenced by imperfect information, stochastic shocks, etc. It is clear from this distinction that first, the two approaches are not logically mutually exclusive, and second, they are distinguished on more than semantic grounds.

A specific conclusion from the present analysis is that long-term contracting does not account for a connection between perceived money movements and departures of employment from the (perceived) mutually advantageous position at $l = l^*$. Accordingly, the theoretical link between long-term contracting and activist rules for monetary policy has yet to be made. My own view is that contracting theory has more pertinence for natural rates of employment and output than for the business cycle. In fact, the principal contribution of the contracting approach to short-run macro-analysis may turn out to be its implication that some frequently discussed aspects of labor markets are a facade with respect to employment fluctuations. In this category one can list sticky wages, layoffs versus quits, and the failure of real wages to move countercyclically.

References

Azariadis, C., 1975, Implicit contracts and underemployment equilibria, Journal of Political Economy 83, December, 1183–1202.

Azariadis, C., 1976, Escalator clauses and the allocation of cyclical risks, unpublished.

Baily, M.N., 1974, Wages and employment under uncertain demand, Review of Economic Studies 41, January, 37–50.

Baily, M.N., 1977, On the theory of layoffs and unemployment, Econometrica.

Barro, R.J., 1972, A theory of monopolistic price adjustment, Review of Economic Studies 39, January, 17–26.

Barro, R.J., 1976, Indexation in a rational expectations model, Journal of Economic Theory 13, October, 229–244.

Barro, R.J. and H.I. Grossman, 1976, Money, employment, and inflation (Cambridge University Press, Cambridge).

Becker, G.S., 1962, Investment in human capital: A theoretical analysis, Journal of Political Economy, Supplement, 70, October, 9–44.

Fischer, S., 1977a, Long-term contracts, rational expectations and the optimal money supply rule, Journal of Political Economy, 85, February, 191–205.

Fischer, S., 1977b, Wage-indexation and macro-economic stability, Journal of Monetary Economics, supplement, January, 107–147.

Friedman, M., 1968, The role of monetary policy, American Economic Review 58, March, 1–17.

Gordon, D., 1974, A neo-classical theory of Keynesian unemployment, Economic Inquiry 12, December, 431–459.

Gray, J.A., 1976, Wage indexation: A macroeconomic approach, Journal of Monetary Economics 2, April.

Grossman, H.I., 1975, The nature of optimal labor contracts: Towards a theory of wage and employment adjustment, unpublished.

Lucas, R.E., 1972, Expectations and the neutrality of money, Journal of Economic Theory 4, April, 103–124.

Lucas, R.E., 1973, Some international evidence on output–inflation tradeoffs, American Economic Review 63, June, 326–334.

Phelps, E.S., 1970, The new microeconomics in employment and inflation theory, in: Phelps, ed., Microeconomic foundations of employment and inflation theory (Norton, New York).

Phelps, E.S. and J.B. Taylor, 1977, Stabilizing power of monetary policy under rational price expectations, Journal of Political Economy 85, February 7, 163–190.

Sargent, T.J. and N. Wallace, 1973, Rational expectations, the optimal monetary instrument, and the optimal money supply rule, Journal of Political Economy 83, April, 241–254.

Shavell, S., 1976, Sharing risks of deferred payments, Journal of Political Economy 84, February, 161–168.

Williamson, O., M. Wachter and J. Harris, 1975, Understanding the employment relation: The analysis of idiosyncratic exchange, Bell Journal of Economics, spring, 250–278.

IV

PUBLIC DEBT

This section considers the macroeconomic effects of public debt issue and carries out some positive theoretical and empirical analysis of the government's deficit decision. "Are Government Bonds Net Wealth?" (paper no. 11) discusses what I have since discovered is the Ricardian Equivalence Theorem on public debt. Within the context of an overlapping-generations model where individuals are finitely lived, the presence of operative intergenerational transfers is shown to eliminate the apparent net wealth effect of shifts between taxes and government deficits. Under these circumstances, a substitution of public debt issue for current taxation or a shift in the scale of an unfunded social security program would produce only offsetting changes in private intergenerational transfers and would therefore leave unchanged the values of interest rates, output, the price level, and so on. The final sections consider extensions that include inheritance taxes, imperfect private capital markets, and a preliminary discussion of uncertainty about future tax liabilities.

One shortcoming of the Ricardian view is that it leaves as indeterminate the government's choice between current taxation and deficit finance. The next paper (no. 12) modifies the framework to allow the excess burden produced by taxation to depend on the timing of tax rates, for a given present value of net government revenues. The model deals explicitly with direct *collection costs* for taxes (except in note 7), but the argument can be extended to encompass the indirect economic distortions that are usually stressed in public finance theory. If there is no special relationship between supply and demand elasticities of taxed commodities—for example, of labor services—and variables like the contemporaneous values of government spending or the real wage rate, then the minimization of overall excess burden entails a uniform time pattern of tax rates. The optimal pattern of deficits is then the one that smooths (expected) tax rates over time. The paper draws implications of this basic proposition for the reaction of public debt issue to temporarily large government expenditures as in wartime, to the business cycle, and to anticipated inflation. The empirical analysis demonstrates that quantitative counterparts of these three variables can account for the bulk of variations in the U.S. funded public debt since at least the 1920s.

The first paper in this section (no. 10) contains an expository treatment of the Ricardian Equivalence Theorem. There is a discussion of the various caveats: finite lives, imperfect private capital markets, uncertainty about future tax liabilities, misperception about taxes and deficits, the interplay between public finance decisions and the volume of government expenditures, and the relation of the timing of taxes to excess burden costs. The question of the perceived net wealth effect of public debt issue, which is the focus of the Ricardian Theorem, is related to concepts of public debt burden, crowding-out effects, and fiscal policy. The first part of the chapter contains some descriptive statistics on the long-term behavior of the funded public debt in the United States and the United Kingdom.

10

Public Debt and Taxes

The national debt, representing the accumulation of past choices to borrow rather than levy taxes, is frequently thought to constitute a burden on future generations. This burden is sometimes viewed as operating through direct income transfers from younger to older generations, and is sometimes described through the crowding-out of private capital formation. Alternatively, it has been argued that (domestically held) government bonds represent internally canceling debts and credits, and are therefore of negligible economic significance.

The first section of this chapter provides a brief examination of the historical development of national debt in the United States and the United Kingdom. In both cases, the principal increases in the ratio of debt to income are associated with wars and major economic contractions. The normal peacetime pattern, which applies also to the post–World War II period, is a declining debt–income ratio. The current ratios in both countries are not high by historical standards.

The next section discusses the effect of shifts between taxes and debt issue on perceived private wealth. The analysis centers around the so-called Ricardian theorem, that substitution of debt for taxes would not alter perceived private wealth. The sensitivity of this proposition is examined in relation to the finiteness of life, the imperfection of private capital markets, uncertainty about future tax liabilities, and some other factors. Finiteness of life would not be important if the typical individual were connected to future generations by private intergenerational transfers, either from parents to children (during life or at death) or from children to parents. The imperfection of capital markets is significant only if the government has some technical advantages over the private sector in the execution of loans—which is more likely to be important in underdeveloped countries than in developed countries

Reprinted from Michael J. Boskin, ed., *Federal Tax Reform* (1978). Reprinted with permission from the Institute for Contemporary Studies © 1978 by the Institute for Contemporary Studies, San Francisco, California.

such as the United States. Uncertainty about future tax liabilities has an ambiguous effect, but, overall, the Ricardian theorem stands up theoretically as a plausible first-order proposition.

The final section relates the wealth effect of debt issue to the central economic questions, which include the burden of the debt on future generations, the crowding-out of private investment, and fiscal policy. The analysis demonstrates that the validity of the Ricardian theorem rules out a public debt burden or a crowding-out effect on private investment. The theorem also ensures that fiscal policy, in the sense of tax changes accompanied by compensating adjustments of the government deficit, is impotent as a device for stabilizing the economy.

Some Data on Public Debt

Table 1 provides an overview of the behavior of the national debt in the United States since 1860. The first column shows the par value of nominal, interest-bearing federal debt net of holdings by U.S. government agencies and trust funds and the Federal Reserve. This concept of national debt is limited to the funded portion that corresponds to interest-bearing government bonds. As discussed by Feldstein (1974), the debt definition can be widened substantially to include the anticipated expenditures payable under social security and other governmental transfer programs. However, the present chapter limits consideration to the narrow national debt concept. The second column expresses the quantity of debt in real terms after division by a general price index (the GNP deflator), and the third column indicates the ratio of nominal debt to nominal gross national product. The quantity of public debt outstanding in 1860 amounted to only 1% of GNP.[1] During the Civil War, extensive deficit finance increased the debt–GNP ratio to about 25% in 1865. The long, essentially peacetime period that followed showed a steady decline of the national debt to about 2% of GNP in 1916. The figure rose sharply during World War I to a peak value of just under 30% of GNP, and then fell during the postwar period to about 14% in 1929. The large federal deficits and the decline in nominal income during the Great Depression increased the ratio to more than 40% in 1940. The ratio then increased sharply to just over 100% because of the vast debt issues of World War II. As in the peacetime periods following the Civil War and World War I, the debt–GNP ratio since World War II has steadily declined. However, because of the chronic inflation associated with the "new monetary standard,"[2] the debt figures expressed as dollars do not show the steady decline that characterized the earlier postwar periods. In 1974 the ratio fell below 20%, but increased to 24% in

---

[1] An interesting note about the pre-1860 period is the experience in 1835 when the national debt was entirely paid off and the government sought desperately for outlets for its surplus. Apparently this problem was solved by the motivation for deficit finance during the sharp economic contraction that began in 1837. For a discussion of this episode, see Dewey (1931, p. 221).

[2] See Klein (1975, pp. 461–484) on the significance for long-run price level behavior of the shift from the gold standard to a paper money regime.

Table 1

Values of Government Debt and Expenditures in the United States for Selected Years

Year	Federal government				State and local government			
	(1) B_f	(2) B_f/P	(3) B_f/Py	(4) G_f/Py	(5) B_{sl}	(6) B_{sl}/P	(7) B_{sl}/Py	(8) G_{sl}/Py
1860	.06	.4	.01[a]	.01[a]				
1865	2.22	8.7	.24[a]	.10[a]				
1867	2.24	8.8	.23[a]	.04[a]				
1880	1.71	9.1	.13	.02				
1902	.93	5.6	.041	.02	2.1	12.7	.09	.05
1916	.91	3.8	.018	.02	4.5	19.0	.09	.06[b]
1918	20.5	59.9	.26	.23	5.1	14.9	.06	
1922	21.6	67.1	.29	.04	7.9	24.5	.11	.08
1929	14.9	45.3	.14	.03	13.6	41.3	.13	.07
1940	41.5	142.6	.42	.10	16.4	56.4	.16	.08
1945	228.2	600.5	1.07	.40	13.4	35.3	.06	.04
1948	193.6	364.6	.75	.13	17.0	32.0	.07	.06
1956	198.1	314.9	.47	.17	44.5	70.7	.11	.08
1964	218.1	300.0	.34	.19	90.4	124.3	.14	.09
1974	269.9	231.9	.19	.21	211.2	181.4	.15	.11
1976	408.5	305.3	.24	.23	236.3	176.6	.14	.11

Source: Barro 1978a.

[a] Based on a trend value of real GNP.

[b] Value is for 1913.

Key: B_f is nominal, par value, interest-bearing federal debt in billions of dollars, net of holdings by federal agencies and trust funds and the Federal Reserve. Values since 1916 are at the end of the calendar year; earlier values are at midyear.

P is the GNP deflator (1972 = 1.0). y is real GNP (1972 dollars).

G_f is total nominal federal expenditure.

B_{sl} is the end-of-year value in billions of dollars of net nominal state and local government debt.

G_{sl} is total nominal state and local government expenditure less transfers from the federal government to the state and local sector.

1976 and 1977 as a consequence of the strong economic contraction. These figures show that the current debt–GNP ratio is not high by historical standards, and is well below the values that prevailed during the 1950s.

Over the past 50 years, federal spending has increased dramatically as a percentage of GNP, rising from 3% in 1929 to 23% in 1976 (see Table 1, column 4). Since World War II, this increased federal spending has been accompanied by a steady decline in the debt–GNP ratio.

State and local government debt and spending are shown in columns 5 through 7. Here, the debt–GNP ratio (column 7) has increased from 1902 (9%) to 1940 (16%), except during World War I, when the rise in nominal GNP reduced the ratio. After a sharp decline during World War II, the ratio of state and local government debt to GNP rose gradually to its pre–World War II level, which was attained by the mid-1960s. The ratio has remained steady at that value to the present.

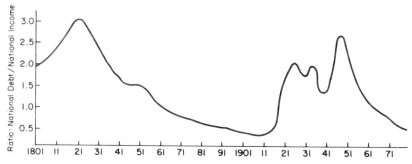

Figure 10.1. *Behavior of the British national debt* [from Benjamin and Kochin (1978)].

It is interesting to compare the U.S. experience with that of Great Britain. Figure 1, which is taken from on-going research by Benjamin and Kochin (1978), plots the ratio of British national debt to national income since 1801. As with the U.S. experience, there is a strong positive effect of major wars on the debt–income ratio. The extensive deficit finance of the Napoleonic Wars produced a debt–income ratio of almost 3.0 in 1821—a value almost three times the peak ratio reached in the United States in 1945. The British experience shows a long period of declining debt–income ratios from 1821 until the start of World War I. A strong increase in the ratio during the war was extended to the depressed economic period of the 1920s and early 1930s. A further sharp expansion of national debt occurred during World War II, although the peak debt–income ratio remained somewhat below that attained in 1821. Finally, as with the U.S. experience, the British debt/income ratio has steadily declined since World War II. Again, the current ratio of public debt to national income is not high by historical standards.

Economic Effects of the Debt-Tax Choice

What difference does it make for the economy if the national government finances its expenditures by debt rather than by taxation? The argument that there is no first-order difference, which dates back to Ricardo (1951, Vol. 1, pp. 244–248, Vol. 4, pp. 184–189), begins by observing that public debt issue implies a stream of future interest payments and possible repayments of principal. These future payments must be financed either by future taxes (including future money creation, which is a form of taxation that works through its effect on the price level) or by additional deficits, which would further increase future interest and principal payments. The option of financing interest payments solely through new debt issue raises the possibility that taxes could be escaped through perpetual deficit finance. But this possibility depends on a chain-letter mechanism in which individuals would be willing to hold ever-expanding amounts of public debt without regard to the government's limited capacity to raise revenue for debt repayment.[3] Generally, it

---

[3]In the case where the interest rate, net of expected inflation, on the public debt exceeds the long-run real growth rate of the economy (which turns out to be a necessary condition for the efficient operation of

seems safe to ignore this "free lunch" possibility, and to assume that debt issue implies a corresponding increase in the total of taxes that must be collected. As a simplification, I also assume that the future interest payments implied by current debt issue are exactly matched in magnitude and timing by additions to future taxes. This case, in which future interest payments are not financed by additional debt issue and in which future taxes are not high enough to retire outstanding debt, turns out to be adequate for examining the major economic effects of the debt–tax choice.

Suppose that an additional $1 million of current government expenditure is financed either by current taxes or debt. In the former case, individuals experience an additional one-time tax liability of $1 million. In the latter case, assuming the interest rate on government bonds to be 5% per year, government interest payments and, by assumption, tax collections are raised "forever" by $50,000 per year. (It is assumed that there are no direct administrative costs associated with public debt issue, and also that, aside from the difference in timing, the incidence of the $50,000 annual tax is identical to that of the lump-sum $1 million collection. Otherwise, an additional pure income redistribution effect would be added to the analysis.) Basically, the representative taxpayer would view the choice between debt issue and taxation as equivalent to the choice between a share of the $1 million current tax and a like share of the $50,000 annual tax in perpetuity. The two options would be viewed as equivalent—producing what economists call the Ricardian equivalence theorem on the public debt (see Ricardo 1951)[4]—under the following conditions: (a) there is no possibility of escaping part of the perpetual tax liability, either by dying (which introduces an effect of finite lives) or by leaving the jurisdiction of the government; (b) everyone can borrow and lend funds at the same interest rate as the government; (c) there is no certainty about future tax shares, which might be induced by uncertainty about individual income or other characteristics that determine tax shares; (d) the future tax liabilities implied by public debt are accurately perceived; (e) the volume of government expenditures is independent of the method of finance; and (f) no other channels exist for effects of the choice of finance method on the prices, rates of return, and so on, faced by individuals.

Considering the length of this list, it is obvious that not all of these conditions could be exactly satisfied. In evaluating these factors it is therefore useful to distinguish between first- and second-order effects and to weigh the likely balance of forces. I discuss, first, the various issues from the viewpoint of the effect of debt issue on how individuals evaluate their personal wealth—and second, the connec-

---

the private sector), perpetual deficit finance would require a continually rising ratio of public debt to national income. For a discussion of this and related matters, see Barro (1976, pp. 343–349). The chainletter aspect of perpetual deficit finance has been referred to as a Ponzi scheme by Miller and Upton (1974, p. 181) in honor of the "Boston 'money-manager' of the 1920s, who paid people 50% interest on funds deposited with him. He did so by using the proceeds of new deposits to pay off old depositors. While it worked, it was a good deal. Those who got in (and out) early made money, but the bubble eventually burst, and thse who still had deposits with Ponzi lost everything."

[4] A discussion of the Ricardian theorem is contained in Buchanan (1958, pp. 43–46, 114–122). See also de Marco (1936, 377–98) and Bailey (1971, 156–158).

tion of these wealth perceptions to the burden of the public debt argument, to crowding-out of private investments, and to fiscal policy.

Finite Lives and Related Matters

Suppose that interest payments and associated tax liabilities extend beyond the expected lifetime of the representative current taxpayer (as is clearly the case when the debt principal is "never" paid off). In this situation, an individual who is unconcerned with the welfare of his descendants, and who can borrow and lend at the same interest rate as the government, would be better off with a share of the $50,000 annual liability than with the like share of the single payment of $1 million. Consider an individual who expects to live 20 years, and who meets the one-time tax cost of his share of $1 million by reducing his interest-bearing assets by a like amount. Since these assets have a 5% yield, by assumption, annual income is reduced by the share of $50,000—the same annual cost that arises under the debt-finance option and which could have been met from the interest on the same assets, which could then have been maintained intact. Although the two finance options balance in this respect, there is a difference in the taxpayer's estate after 20 years. Under the tax option, the estate is reduced by the share of $1 million. Under the debt option, with no further tax payments required after 20 years (i.e., after death), this reduction does not apply. Anticipating this outcome, a taxpayer wishing to leave a zero (or fixed-size) estate, would therefore increase his lifetime expenditure under the debt option (financed by consuming the capital that would otherwise remain in the estate).[5] Thus, finite lives imply that the representative current taxpayer would perceive himself wealthier under debt issue than under taxation.

The choice of taxation versus debt produces a wealth effect associated with finite lives, because some of the future tax liabilities needed to pay future interest are shifted to members of later generations. If the added liabilities on descendants were fully counted in wealth calculations by current taxpayers, then the present distinction between the debt and tax options would disappear. Essentially, public debt issue enables members of current generations to die in a state of insolvency by leaving a debt for their descendants. Current taxpayers are "wealthier" if they view the implied governmental shifting of income across generations as desirable. In fact, most individuals already have private opportunities for shifting income across generations that they have chosen not to exercise. Parents make voluntary contributions to children in the form of educational investments, other expenses in the home, and bequests. Children—especially before the expansion of social security—provide support for aged parents. To the extent that private, voluntary, intergenerational transfers of this sort are operative—and casual observation suggests that such transfers, in the appropriate, broadly defined, sense, are pervasive—the shift from tax to

[5]The same conclusion applies if the taxpayer borrows to finance his share of the $1 million tax cost, assuming that such loans at 5% interest must be secured by life insurance.

debt finance (or, analogously, the introduction of a pay-as-you-go social security scheme) would not present the representative individual with a new opportunity for extracting funds from members of other generations. Rather, the private response to debt issue or to more social security would be to shift private, voluntary transfers by an amount sufficient to restore the balance of income across generations that was previously deemed optimal. In this case, a shift from tax to debt finance would not affect the perceived wealth of a finite-lived taxpayer.[6]

A taxpayer can also escape some part of the future taxes associated with debt by leaving the jurisdiction of the government. Presumably, this option is more pertinent for state and local governments than for the national government, and is generally more important where out-migration costs are low. However, the incentive for individuals to leave an area with a large accumulated debt would arise only where the quantity of government-owned real capital was not sufficient to generate income offsetting the debt-finance costs. At a local level, therefore, debt issue will tend to be associated more with large capital projects than with financing of current expenditures. One further consideration involves the capitalization of taxes—especially property taxes—into property values. To the extent that a higher flow of anticipated future taxes is already reflected in reduced property values (and, correspondingly, in a reduced annual cost of housing, etc.), individuals would not be motivated to move out of the jurisdiction with these higher future taxes.

Imperfect Private Capital Markets

The argument that debt and tax finance are equivalent depends also on the correspondence between private and governmental interest rates. Suppose, instead, that some individuals have poor collateral on private loan markets, and therefore face borrowing rates that are much higher than the government's rate, still assumed to be 5%. The high private borrowing rates would reflect both risk of default and administrative costs associated with the operation of loan markets. Suppose that the government reduces current taxes by $1,000 on an individual (Person A) with a high or infinite borrowing rate, and substitutes the issue of a $1000 bond, which would be held by a different individual or firm (Person B), who regards 5% per year from the government as a satisfactory rate of return. I assume that the $50 per year flow of taxes to finance the interest payments on the bond are levied on Person A, so that no direct redistribution of income results. The net outcome of this debt-creation

---

[6] A rigorous treatment of this private offset effect is contained in Barro (1974, pp. 1095–1117). A complication to the analysis arises when some taxpayers have more or less than the average number of descendants. For example, individuals without children may have no ties to future generations and are therefore made better off by debt issue, although such individuals must be matched by other persons with an above-average number of children who are likely to be made worse off by debt issue. A second-order wealth effect from debt issue would arise if these individual effects do not cancel out through aggregation. Another second-order effect is the stimulus of debt issue toward reduced family size, which would be motivated by the corresponding reduction in family liability for the stream of future taxes.

process is that Person A borrows $1000 at a 5% interest rate from Person B. With his high private borrowing rate, Person A is likely to be better off, because he may be willing to pay much more than 5% annual interest (even for a loan on which default is "impossible") in order to shift expenditures from the future to the present. Person B is satisfied, because the 5% yield is guaranteed by the government, although he would not accept such a return on a direct loan to Person A. Apparently, the shift to debt finance would therefore raise the average perceived wealth of current taxpayers.

The government's debt issue functions as a successful intermediation in the credit market, because it avoids the high transaction costs of private loan market operations that are implicit in the initially high borrowing rate of Person A. There is a hidden assumption that the government is more efficient than the private market in carrying out credit market operations. The omitted costs are those entailed by the collection of the flow of future taxes (rather than the single current tax) from Person A. If this individual is a poor credit risk who requires large "supervision" costs on the private market, he is likely, despite the government's coercive taxing powers, to be a similar risk on public loans. The argument that debt issue raises perceived wealth because of imperfect private capital markets assumes that the government is more efficient, at the margin, than the private market in carrying out the loan process.[7]

A related argument is that the superior marketability (which economists call liquidity) of public debt securities allows the government to sell its bonds at lower interest rates than those applicable to private obligations. This point seems to apply with most force to "high-powered" money—which consists, in the United States, of currency and reserves of commercial banks that are members of the Federal Reserve system—where the government has some clear monopoly power. In the United States, this monopoly position does not seem to extend significantly to interest-bearing debt, since the private market seems able to generate, at similar underlying administrative costs, close substitutes for both short- and long-term government securities. Therefore, from the liquidity standpoint, it seems unlikely that shifts between taxes and interest-bearing debt would, at the margin, significantly alter perceived private sector wealth in a developed country such as the United States.

Uncertainty about Future Taxes

It is often argued that, since the future individual tax liabilities implicit in public debt issue are unpredictable, they would be heavily discounted in calculations of wealth positions.[8] In fact, risk-averse individuals would tend to give higher, rather

---

[7]Private bail bondsmen are perhaps a response to a differential collection efficiency that favors the private sector. Casual observation of the federal government's student loan program suggests that relative government efficiency in the credit markets is actually an amusing idea.

[8]See, for example, Bailey (1971, pp. 157–158); Buchanan and Wagner (1977, pp. 17, 101, 130). The contrary view is taken in Buchanan (1967, pp. 258–260), and in Barro (1974, pp. 1113–1115).

than lower, weight to a given anticipated amount of future taxes when the uncertainty attached to these liabilities increases.[9] On this count, the substitution of debt issue for current taxation will tend to diminish perceived wealth.

Offsetting this conclusion, some future tax liabilities reflect movements in uncertain future individual incomes, rather than changes in other individual characteristics affecting tax liability, shifts in tax procedures, and so on. A positive association between individual taxes and incomes would buffer changes in individual disposable incomes, and would therefore offset the other effects of uncertainty in wealth calculations. The overall effect of uncertainty on the perceived wealth effect of debt issue is generally ambiguous.

Misperception of Future Taxes

It is also sometimes argued that the future taxes implicit in the public debt are largely ignored because of complexity in estimating them (Feldstein, 1976, p. 335; Buchanan and Wagner, 1977, p. 130). This problem, however, seems similar in its effects to uncertainty about future tax procedures as discussed earlier, which tend to magnify, rather than diminish, the average effective weight assigned to future taxes. In any event, it is unclear why misperceptions or "irrationality" would call particularly for underestimation of future taxes. At this level of analysis, one could just as well argue that government deficits, which are well publicized, make people nervous and induce them to feel poorer.

A more plausible argument is that unusual movements (either up or down) in the public debt—that is, government deficits not arising from the usual pattern associated with the business cycle, government expenditure changes, etc.—would be temporarily misperceived.[10] However, in a preliminary investigation (Barro, 1978c), I have been unable to isolate important effects of unusual (or usual) public debt movements on economic activity.

The Volume of Government Expenditure

The preceding analysis has treated the amount and composition of government spending as fixed, while considering some consequences of different methods of finance. Therefore, it has been possible to abstract the analysis from evaluations of government expenditure programs. It has, however, sometimes been argued that the existence of the debt-finance option effectively "cheapens" government expenditure, because deficits are politically more popular than taxes.[11] This argument is

[9]I am assuming that private insurance markets and other institutions are not sufficient to provide full diversification of relative tax risks.

[10]The adjustment of the measured government surplus to obtain a "full employment surplus" that takes account of the automatic stabilizer role of the tax system seems to be consistent with this viewpoint. The full employment surplus is discussed in Council of Economic Advisers (1962, pp. 78–81).

[11]Buchanan and Wagner (1977) present this hypothesis as the major theme of their book. They attempt to explain much of the rise in the U.S. federal spending/GNP ratio since World War II as a

equivalent to the proposition that a shift, at the margin, from taxes to debt would substantially raise perceived private sector wealth, since a move toward deficit finance would only be politically popular in this circumstance. Therefore, the same theoretical objections may be raised against it.

Public Debt and the Timing of Taxation

The set of arguments that includes finite lives, imperfect private capital markets, uncertainty about future taxes, and misperceptions of tax liabilities does not make an impressive a priori case for public debt issue to alter perceived private wealth in one direction or the other. In a country like the United States, in which the government's technical advantages at the margin in the loan process, or in creating liquidity are likely to be minimal, it is reasonable to conclude that substitution of debt issue for taxes will have a wealth effect of second-order magnitude (and of indeterminate direction).

One difficulty with this sort of negative conclusion is that it does not provide a basis for a positive theory of public debt issue. I have attempted to construct such a theory in another paper (Barro, 1978c) by focusing on the role of public debt issue as a mechanism for smoothing the time path of tax collection. Suppose that taxes entail collection costs or impose distortions on the private economy, and that these costs increase with the fraction of current national income that the government collects in taxes. Although public debt issue does not permit permanent escape from taxation, it does allow rearrangement of the timing of collections. With "collection costs" as an increasing function of the ratio of taxes to national income, the optimal method of public finance turns out to involve a pattern of debt issue that rules out any predictable changes in this ratio. This behavior raises a given total of tax revenues in a manner that minimizes the expected overall costs of collection.

Among the empirically important implications of this model, deficits would be used to finance temporary government expenditures, especially the large outlays during wartime, and debt issue would be large during recessions and small or negative during booms. During wartime, debt will avoid large temporary movements in the tax–income ratio; during recessions it will preserve stability of the tax–income ratio over the business cycle in the face of little cyclical fluctuation in government spending. Another result is that the debt–income ratio will tend to decline rather than remain constant during peacetime periods, to average out, ex ante, the large positive effects on debt issue of wars and severe contractions; and nominal debt will grow, other things equal, one to one with the anticipated rate of

---

response to a structural change to a "Keynesian debt policy" that made deficits politically more popular than before. However, this hypothesis seems to conflict with the observation that the federal debt/GNP ratio (Table 1) has actually fallen in the post–World War II period in a manner similar to that after World War I and the Civil War. Detailed empirical analysis of annual public debt movements that I have carried out, as discussed below, indicates that the economic structure that determines the amount of deficit finance has been reasonably stable since at least the 1920s.

growth of nominal national income. The last effect is especially important during the inflation of the last decade in the U.S., when much of the federal deficit for these years (although only about 30% of the total for 1975–1976) is associated merely with maintaining the anticipated real value of the outstanding interest-bearing public debt. Finally, the model also implies that certain variables—in particular, the size of the accumulated past debt and the level of government expenditure—would not be important determinants of current debt issue.

My empirical analysis suggests that the principal movements in publicly held, interest-bearing federal debt in the United States since World War I can be explained by three variables: (a) the movement in federal expenditures relative to "normal"—which captures, in particular, the strong response of debt issue to temporary wartime spending; (b) the movement in real GNP relative to trend, which captures the countercyclical response of debt issue; and (c) a one-to-one effect of the anticipated inflation rate on the growth rate of nominal debt. The effects of these three variables on debt issue appear to be reasonably stable over the post–World War I period. For example, the sharp expansion of federal debt for 1975–1976 emerges as a response of somewhat more than the usual size to the sharp contraction of output and to the high value of the anticipated rate of inflation. The overall extent of countercyclical debt movement is, actually, stronger than that called for by the model. However, results for the 1920s and 1930s appear similar in this respect to those for the post–World War II period. The evidence does indicate that the size of the outstanding debt (relative to GNP) and the level of government expenditure (as a fraction of GNP) are irrelevant to current debt issue. Overall, the analysis supports the theory of public debt that neglects direct wealth effects and focuses on the tax-smoothing role of deficits.

The Burden of the Public Debt

The sense in which the domestically owned national debt constitutes a burden on future generations has occupied substantial attention of economists.[12] This topic is intertwined with the wealth effect of debt issue, as can be illustrated for the case of finite-lived taxpayers that was discussed earlier. Suppose that the representative current taxpayer is unconcerned with his descendants and, therefore, experiences an increase in wealth when taxes are replaced by debt. As Buchanan (1958) has argued, the burden on future generations is direct and involves, in particular, the liability for taxes that greets members of future generations as they are born. This first-order argument for debt burden is independent of complications that involve the crowding-out of private investment, the direct role of government expenditure programs, the observation that the resources utilized by government for current expenditures must come out of current output, and so on. The debt burden on future generations is analogous to the one that might arise under a pay-as-you-go social

---

[12]See, for example, the papers in Ferguson (1964), and the review by Tobin (1965, pp. 679–682).

security scheme involving no government purchases of goods and services. Currently old individuals receiving retirement payments would benefit initially at the expense of the currently young taxpayers. These currently young individuals would be able to recoup a portion of their losses, because members of later generations will be born with the liability to pay taxes to finance social security benefits to retirees. Overall, there will be a transfer of wealth from younger generations (including the currently unborn) to older generations.

While this kind of analysis captures the essence of the public debt-burden argument, it is incomplete because it does not discuss the restoration of economic equilibrium after the initial boost to wealth perceptions. Basically, the rise in perceived wealth will increase consumer demand and, therefore, any increase in saving—which increases the supply of private loanable funds—must fall short of the rise in the government's demand for borrowings. The resulting excess of demand over supply will increase interest rates to restore equilibrium in the loanable funds market. The depressing effect of this higher required rate of return on private investment constitutes a crowding-out of public borrowing. Franco Modigliani (1961, pp. 730–755) has labeled the associated long-run decline in the economy's capital–labor ratio as the burden of the public debt on future generations (in the sense that each generation, in aggregate, bequeathes a smaller capital stock to its descendants). Although a capital stock reduction would be predicted under the above assumption about wealth perceptions, this effect is not the essence of the debt-burden argument, which has been captured above by the direct intergenerational income transfers that are implied by debt issue or social security.

The arguments for debt burden and for crowding-out of private investment hinge on the assumption that debt issue raises perceived wealth. Neither a burden on future generations nor crowding-out would occur in the case discussed earlier, where the public intergenerational transfers implied by debt issue or social security are fully offset by compensating adjustments in voluntary private transfers. For example, there may be no net change in income distribution across generations if parents react to debt issue by increasing transfers to their children, or if children react by reducing transfers to their aged parents. With the corresponding absence of a shift in perceived wealth, consumer demand would not be stimulated by the movement from taxes to debt issue. It follows that the supply of private loanable funds would rise one to one with the cut in current taxes (increase in current disposable income), so that the extra governmental demand for funds implied by its debt issue would be fully absorbed by the private sector without an increase in the rate of return. Under these circumstances—when public debt issue leaves unchanged the value of perceived wealth—the crowding-out of private investment would not arise.

Imperfect Private Capital Markets

Imperfect private capital markets (or the superior liquidity characteristics of government debt), which may be especially important for underdeveloped countries, also imply that public debt issue may raise perceived wealth. However, the analysis of debt burden and crowding-out for this case is quite different from that described earlier. Substitution of debt for taxation can work, in part, as an effective governmental intermediation in credit markets. By cutting current taxes, the government can place some funds in the hands of individuals with high (or infinite) borrowing rates who have correspondingly high opportunity rates of return for investment or consumption purposes. These individuals would respond to the tax cut by raising their demands for commodities and—as they exhaust the opportunities with the highest imputed rates of return—by correspondingly reducing the interest they would be willing to pay on borrowed funds. On the other hand—neglecting the government's collection costs for future taxes—individuals or firms with interest rates equal to the government's rate would be initially unaffected by the tax cut. Because of the net increase in private commodity demand, it again follows that the government's increased demand for loanable funds would exceed the increase in private supply. With debt issue, therefore, the interest rate on risk- and transaction cost-free loans will again rise. However, as shown above, the imputed rate of return for the individuals with high borrowing rates must fall. Therefore, the government's credit market intermediation implied by its debt issue leads to a convergence of rates of return across the economy. The net effect on investment versus consumption is ambiguous, but the diversion of funds from low opportunity rates of return to high rates is clear. In this event, if the government actually has a technical advantage in capital market operations, the perceived wealth increase associated with debt issue is neither an illusion nor an expropriation of future generations, but is rather a movement toward a more efficient allocation of resources. Although it is appropriate in this case to view debt issue as raising perceived private wealth, it would be inappropriate to speak of a public debt burden or of a crowding-out of private investment.

Fiscal Policy

The perceived wealth effect of public debt issue (produced in this case by a finite life effect, by imperfect private capital markets, or by other reasons for heavy discounting of future tax liabilities) is also a necessary condition for the efficacy of fiscal policy—that is, for the use of government deficits (surpluses) to stimulate (deflate) the economy.[13] Substitution of debt issue for taxation is assumed to raise perceived wealth, and thereby to increase aggregate demand. But if debt issue does not increase perceived wealth, the possibility of this sort of fiscal policy disappears. Therefore, the argument against a significant wealth effect of public debt issue is also an argument against the efficacy of fiscal policy.[14]

[13]I am abstracting here from the impact of changes in the level of government expenditures. That analysis would involve as a central element the economic function of these expenditures, as discussed in Bailey (1971, Chapter 9).
[14]It should not be inferred that a positive wealth effect of debt issue is sufficient to build a normative case for fiscal activism. Other considerations involve the adjustment of prices and rates of return, the timing of government policy, and the role of private expectations about government policy formation.

The weight of empirical evidence on the connection between public debt (or, analogously, the expected benefits less taxes implied by social security) and aggregate consumer demand suggests a minor impact of uncertain direction.[15] However, the evidence is surely not unanimous, and many estimation problems exist with this type of empirical analysis. Despite these results, which raise doubts about the possibility of important fiscal policy effects, some large econometric models nevertheless imply that "expansionary" fiscal policy would have a substantial positive impact on economic activity. These models essentially constrain a shift from taxes to debt to have a positive effect on consumer demand—usually by writing consumption as a positive function of current disposable income, without attempting to hold constant the value of anticipated future taxes.[16] This restricted specification unreasonably requires the response of consumer demand to a tax cut to be the same as that induced by a rise in real national income, independently of whether the tax cut is associated either with a deficit that would raise future taxes, or with a decline in the anticipated long-run government expenditures. Some analyses of income determination that do not impose these sorts of restrictions do not seem to show significant fiscal policy effects.[17]

It is thus fair to say that neither economic theories nor empirical analyses provide convincing evidence for the effectiveness of fiscal policy. The area of fiscal policy exhibits a wide gap between, on the one hand, the weight of theory and evidence, and, on the other hand, the general opinion of professional economists and policymakers.

References

Andersen, L. C., and J. L. Jordon, "Monetary and Fiscal Actions: A Test of Their Relative Importance in Economic Stabilization," Federal Reserve Bank of St. Louis, *Review*, November 1968.

Bailey, M. J., *National Income and the Price Level*, 2nd ed., New York, McGraw-Hill, 1971.

Barro, Robert J., "Are Government Bonds Net Wealth?" *Journal of Political Economy*, 82, November–December 1974, 1095–1117.

Barro, R. J., "Reply to Feldstein and Buchanan," *Journal of Political Economy*, 84, April 1976, 343–349.

Barro, R. J., "Unanticipated Money Growth and Unemployment in the United States," *American Economic Review*, 67, March 1977, 101–115.

Barro, R. J., "Comment from an Unreconstructed Ricardian," *Journal of Monetary Economics*, August 1978a, 569–581.

[15]The empirical literature includes Kochin (1974, pp. 385–394); Tanner (1970, pp. 473–485); David and Scadding (1974, pp. 225–249); Kormendi (1978); Feldstein (1974, pp. 905–926; 1977); Barro (1978b); Barro and MacDonald (1977); and Darby (1978).

[16]For example, in the Federal Reserve—MIT—Penn model, the key explanatory variable for consumption corresponds approximately to current personal disposable income (Modigliani 1971, p. 14). A similar current personal disposable income variable is used in the Brookings model, as reported in Suits and Sparks (1965, Chapter 7).

[17]The "St. Louis model" reduced-form equations, which use high-employment government expenditures rather than a deficit variable as a fiscal measure, are reported in Andersen and Jordon (1968, pp. 11–24). An updated view of this model is contained in Carlson (1978, pp. 13–19). Some reduced-form effects on unemployment and output of debt issue and of the "unanticipated" part of this issue are reported in Barro (1977, p. 114; 1978c, Section III).

Barro, R. J., *The Impact of Social Security on Private Savings—Evidence from the U.S. Time Series,* Washington, D.C., American Enterprise Institute, 1978b.

Barro, R. J., "On the Determination of the Public Debt," working paper, University of Rochester, March 1978c.

Barro, R. J., and G. MacDonald, "Social Security and Consumer Spending in an International Cross Section," working paper, University of Rochester, 1977.

Benjamin, D. K., and L. A. Kochin, "The British National Debt," working paper, University of Washington, 1978.

Buchanan, J. M., *Public Principles of Public Debt,* Homewood, Ill., Irwin, 1958.

Buchanan, J. M., *Public Finance in Democratic Process,* Chapel Hill, N.C., University of North Carolina Press, 1967.

Buchanan, J. M., and R. E. Wagner, *Democracy in Deficit,* New York, Academic Press, 1977.

Carlson, K. M., "Does the St. Louis Equation Now Believe in Fiscal Policy?" Federal Reserve Bank of St. Louis, *Review,* February 1978, 13–19.

Council of Economic Advisers, *Economic Report of the President,* Washington, D.C., Government Printing Office, 1962.

Darby, Michael R., "The Effects of Social Security on Income and the Capital Stock," working paper 95, UCLA, March 1978.

David, P. A., and J. Scadding, "Private Savings: Ultrarationality, Aggregation, and 'Dennison's Law,'" *Journal of Political Economy,* 82, March/April 1974, 225–249.

de Marco, A. de Viti, *First Principles of Public Finance,* Trans. E. Marget, London, Jonathan Cape, 1936.

Dewey, D. R., *Financial History of the United States,* 11th ed., New York, Longmans Green, 1931.

Feldstein, M., "Social Security, Induced Retirement, and Aggregate Capital Accumulation," *Journal of Political Economy,* 82, September–October 1974, 905–926.

Feldstein, M., "Perceived Wealth in Bonds and Social Security: A Comment," *Journal of Political Economy,* 84, April 1976, 331–336.

Feldstein, M., "Social Security and Private Savings: International Evidence in an Extended Life Cycle Model," in the *Economics of Public Services,* ed. M. S. Feldstein and R. Inman, London, Macmillan, 1977.

Ferguson, J. M., *Public Debt and Future Generations,* Chapel Hill, N.C., University of North Carolina Press, 1964.

Klein, B., "Our New Monetary Standard: The Measurement and Effects of Price Uncertainty: 1800–1973," *Economic Inquiry,* 13, December 1975, 461–484.

Kochin, Levis, "Are Future Taxes Anticipated by Consumers" *Journal of Money, Credit and Banking,* 6, August 1974, 385–394.

Kormendi, R. C., "Are Government Bonds Net Wealth? An Empirical Investigation," working paper, University of Chicago, Graduate School of Business, February 1978.

Miller, M., and C. Upton, *Macroeconomics: A Neoclassical Introduction,* Homewood, Ill., Irwin, 1974.

Modigliani, F., "Long-run Implications of Alternative Fiscal Policies and the Burden of the National Debt," *Economic Journal,* 71, December 1961, 730–755.

Modigliani, F., "Monetary Policy and Consumption: Linkages via Interest Rates and Wealth Effects in the FMP Model," in *Consumer Spending and Monetary Policy: The Linkages,* Conference Series No. 5, Boston: Federal Reserve Bank of Boston, June 1971.

Ricardo, D., *The Works and Correspondence of David Ricardo,* ed. P. Sraffa, Cambridge, Cambridge University Press, 1951.

Suits, D. B., and G. R. Sparks, "Consumption Regressions with Quarterly Data," in *The Brookings Quarterly Econometric Model of the U.S.,* ed. J. S. Duesenberry et al., Chicago, Rand McNally, 1965.

Tanner, J. E., "Empirical Evidence on the Short-Run Real Balance Effect in Canada," *Journal of Money, Credit and Banking,* 2, November 1970, 473–485.

Tobin, J., "The Burden of the Public Debt," *Journal of Finance,* 20, December 1965, 679–682.

11

Are Government Bonds Net Wealth?

The assumption that government bonds are perceived as net wealth by
the private sector is crucial in demonstrating real effects of shifts in the
stock of public debt. In particular, the standard effects of "expansionary"
fiscal policy on aggregate demand hinge on this assumption. Government
bonds will be perceived as net wealth only if their value exceeds the capitalized value of the implied stream of future tax liabilities. This paper
considers the effects on bond values and tax capitalization of finite
lives, imperfect private capital markets, a government monopoly in the
production of bond "liquidity services," and uncertainty about future
tax obligations. It is shown within the context of an overlapping-
generations model that finite lives will not be relevant to the capitalization of future tax liabilities so long as current generations are
connected to future generations by a chain of operative intergenerational
transfers (either in the direction from old to young or in the direction
from young to old). Applications of this result to social security and
to other types of imposed intergenerational transfer schemes are also
noted. In the presence of imperfect private capital markets, government
debt issue will increase net wealth if the government is more efficient,
at the margin, than the private market in carrying out the loan process.
Similarly, if the government has monopoly power in the production
of bond "liquidity services," then public debt issue will raise net wealth.
Finally, the existence of uncertainty with respect to individual future
tax liabilities implies that public debt issue may increase the overall
risk contained in household balance sheets and thereby effectively reduce household wealth.

The assumption that government bonds are perceived as net wealth by
the private sector plays an important role in theoretical analyses of
monetary and fiscal effects. This assumption appears, explicitly or implicitly, in demonstrating real effects of a shift in the stock of public debt

I have benefited from comments on earlier drafts by Gary Becker, Benjamin Eden,
Milton Friedman, Merton Miller, José Scheinkman, Jeremy Siegel, and Charles Upton.
The National Science Foundation has supported this research.
[*Journal of Political Economy*, 1974, vol. 82, no. 6]

1095

243

(see, e.g., Modigliani 1961, sec. IV; Mundell 1971; and Tobin 1971, chap. 5), and in establishing nonneutrality of changes in the stock of money (Metzler 1951, sec. VI). More generally, the assumption that government debt issue leads, at least in part, to an increase in the typical household's conception of its net wealth is crucial for demonstrating a positive effect on aggregate demand of "expansionary" fiscal policy, which is defined here as a substitution of debt for tax finance for a given level of government expenditure (see, e.g., Patinkin 1965, sec. XII.4; and Blinder and Solow 1973, pp. 324–25). The basic type of argument in a full-employment model is, following Modigliani (1961), that an increase in government debt implies an increase in perceived household wealth; hence, an increase in desired consumption (a component of aggregate demand) relative to saving; hence, an increase in interest rates; and, finally, a decline in the fraction of output which goes to capital accumulation. However, this line of reasoning hinges on the assumption that the increase in government debt leads to an increase in perceived household wealth. In a non-full employment context it remains true that the effect of public debt issue on aggregate demand (and, hence, on output and employment) hinges on the assumed increase in perceived household wealth.

It has been recognized for some time that the future taxes needed to finance government interest payments would imply an offset to the direct positive wealth effect. For example, in a paper originally published in 1952, Tobin (1971, p. 91) notes: "How is it possible that society merely by the device of incurring a debt to itself can deceive itself into believing that it is wealthier? Do not the additional taxes which are necessary to carry the interest charges reduce the value of other components of private wealth?" Bailey (1962, pp. 75–77) has gone somewhat further by arguing: "It is possible that households regard deficit financing as equivalent to taxation. The issue of a bond by the government to finance expenditures involves a liability for future interest payments and possible ultimate repayment of principal, and thus implies future taxes that would not be necessary if the expenditures were financed by current taxation. . . . If future tax liabilities implicit in deficit financing are accurately foreseen, the level at which total tax receipts are set is immaterial; the behavior of the community will be exactly the same as if the budget were continuously balanced."

There seem to be two major lines of argument that have been offered to defend the position that the offset of the future tax liabilities will be only partial.[1] One type of argument, based on finite lives, supposes that

---

[1] Of course, most analyses of government debt effects do not offer a specific defense for this position. For example, Blinder and Solow (1973, p. 325, n. 8) say: "This [analysis] includes government bonds as a net asset to the public. We are well aware of, but not persuaded by, the arguments which hold that such bonds are not seen as net worth by individuals because of the implied future tax liability."

the relevant horizon for the future taxes (which might correspond to the remaining average lifetimes of the current taxpayers) will be shorter than that for the interest payments. [2] Accordingly, a stream of equal values for interest payments and taxes will have a net positive present value. This argument has been used explicitly by Thompson (1967, p. 1200). The second type of argument, usually based on imperfect private capital markets, supposes that the relevant discount rate for tax liabilities will be higher than that for the interest payments. Hence, even with an infinite horizon for tax liabilities, a stream of equal values for interest payments and taxes will have a net positive present value. This argument has been used by Mundell (1971). [3]

The first part of this paper deals with the effect of government bond issue on the calculus of individual wealth in an overlapping-generations economy with physical capital where individuals have finite lives. No elements of "capital market imperfections" are introduced into this model. The key result here is that, so long as there is an operative intergenerational transfer (in the sense of an interior solution for the amount of bequest or gift across generations), there will be no net-wealth effect and, hence, no effect on aggregate demand or on interest rates of a marginal change in government debt. This result does not hinge on current generations' weighing the consumption or utility of future generations in any sense on an equal basis with own consumption, nor does it depend on current generations' placing any direct weight at all on the consumption or utility of any future generation other than the immediate descendant. Current generations act effectively as though they were infinite-lived when they are connected to future generations by a chain of operative inter-generational transfers.

The analysis then shows that social security payments are analogous to changes in government debt. Marginal changes in this type (or other types) of imposed intergenerational transfers have no real effects when current and future generations are already connected by a chain of operative discretionary transfers. The effects of inheritance taxes and of "transaction costs" for government bond issue and tax collections are also considered. It is shown that inheritance taxes do not affect the basic results, but that the presence of government transaction costs implies that the net-wealth effect of government bonds would actually be negative.

The second part of the paper deals with the existence of imperfect private capital markets. It is shown that, to the extent that public debt

---

[2] This type of argument applies to head taxes or to taxes based on wage income, but not to taxes which are based on the value of nonhuman assets. This distinction has been made by Mundell (1971, pp. 9, 10).

[3] A different line of argument that leads to a similar conclusion is that the government acts like a monopolist in the provision of the liquidity services yielded by its liabilities. I discuss this argument in part III, below.

issue entails a loan from low-discount-rate to high-discount-rate individuals, a positive net-wealth effect results if the government is more efficient than the private market in carrying out this sort of loan. If the government is more efficient only over a certain range, and if the public choice process determines the amount of government debt issue in accord with efficiency criteria, it is again true at the margin that the net-wealth effect of government bond issue is nil.

The third part of the paper discusses government debt as a bearer of nonpecuniary "liquidity services." It is shown that if the government acts like a competitive producer of these services, as would be dictated by a public choice process which reflects efficiency criteria, then the net-wealth effect of government bond issue would be zero on this count. More generally, the net-wealth effect would be positive if the government acts like a monopolist and would be negative if the government is an overproducer of liquidity services.

The last part of the paper deals with the risk characteristics of government debt and of the tax liabilities associated with the interest payments on this debt. It is argued that if relative tax liabilities are known, a change in government debt will not alter the overall risk contained in household balance sheets. When relative tax liabilities are uncertain, the effect of government debt issue on the overall risk may be positive or negative, depending on the nature of the tax system and on the transaction costs associated with private insurance arrangements.

I. The Effect of Finite Lives—a Model with Overlapping Generations

A. Setup of the Model

I use here a version of the Samuelson (1958)-Diamond (1965) overlapping-generations model with physical capital. Each individual lives two periods, which will be distinguished by the superscripts y (young) and o (old). Generations are numbered consecutively beginning with the generation which is currently old (subscript 1); followed by its descendant, which is currently young (subscript 2); followed by its descendant; and so on. I assume here that there are the same number of people, N, in each generation, and that all individuals are identical in terms of tastes and productivity. I also abstract from any technological change over time. The members of each generation work (a fixed amount of time set equal to one unit) only while young and receive an amount of wage income w. Expectations on w for future periods (i.e., for future generations) are assumed to be static at the current value. Asset holdings (A) take the form of equity capital (K). Subsequently, government bonds are introduced as an additional form in which assets can be held. The rate of return on assets is denoted by r and is assumed to be paid out once per period. Expectations on r for future periods are assumed to be static at the current value. A member of the ith generation holds the amount of assets A_i^y while young and the amount A_i^o while old. The asset holding while old constitutes the provision of a bequest, which is assumed to go to the immediate descendant, a member of generation $i + 1$. Since the focus of the analysis concerns shifts in tax liabilities and government debt for a given level of government expenditure, it is assumed for convenience that the government neither demands commodities nor provides public services. In this section, it is also assumed that the amounts of government debt and taxes are zero. Using the letter c to denote consumption, and assuming that consumption and receipt of interest income both occur at the start of the period, the budget equation for a member of generation 1, who is currently old, is

$$A_1^y + A_0^o = c_1^o + (1 - r)A_1^o. \tag{1}$$

The total resources available are the assets held while young, A_1^y, plus the bequest from the previous generation, A_0^o. The total expenditure is consumption while old, c_1^o, plus the bequest provision, A_1^o, which goes to a member of generation 2, less interest earnings at rate r on this asset holding.

The budget equation for members of generation 2 (and, more generally, for members of any generation $i \geq 2$) is, assuming that wage payments occur at the start of the young period,

$$w = c_2^y + (1 - r)A_2^y, \tag{2}$$

and, for the old period,

$$A_2^y + A_1^o = c_2^o + (1 - r)A_2^o. \tag{3}$$

A portion of the lifetime resources of a member of generation i goes to a bequest provision, A_i^o, which I assume is motivated by a concern for a member of generation $i + 1$. This concern could be modeled by introducing either the (anticipated) consumption levels or attainable utility of a member of generation $i + 1$ into the utility function for a member of the ith generation. For the purpose of the present analysis, the crucial condition is that this utility depend on the endowment of a member of generation $i + 1$ rather than, per se, on the gross bequest, A_i^o. (The distinction between the gross bequest and the net bequest, which determines the endowment of $i + 1$, will be discussed below.) So long as a member of generation i can transfer resources to a member of generation $i + 1$ only through the transfer of unrestricted purchasing power (which rules out the "merit good" case discussed in n. 8 below), the two types of models of interdependent preferences—concern with consumption levels and concern with attainable utility—will be equivalent in the sense of indirectly implying a concern for the endowment of a member of generation $i + 1$.

For present purposes, it is convenient to assume that the utility of a member of generation i depends solely on own two-period consumption, c_i^y and c_i^o, and on the attainable utility of his immediate descendant, U_{i+1}^*. The asterisk denotes the maximum value of utility, conditional on given values of endowment and prices. Hence, the utility function for a member of the ith generation has the form,[4]

$$U_i = U_i(c_i^y, c_i^o, U_{i+1}^*). \tag{4}$$

Subsequently, I consider the implications of entering the attainable utility of a member of the previous generation, U_{i-1}^*, as an additional argument of the U_i function.

Each member of generation 1 determines his allocation of resources to maximize U_1, subject to equations (1)–(4) and to the inequality conditions, $(c_i^y, c_i^o, A_i^o) \geq 0$ for all i. The key restriction here is that the bequest to the member of the next generation cannot be negative.[5] The choice of bequest, subject to this restriction, takes into account the effect of A_1^o on generation 2's resources, the impact of U_2^* on U_1, and the chain dependence of U_2 on U_3^*, of U_3 on U_4^*, etc. The solution to this problem will take the general form

$$c_1^o = c_1^o(A_1^y + A_0^o, w, r),$$

$$A_1^o = \frac{1}{1 - r}(A_1^y + A_0^o - c_1^o) = A_1^o(A_1^y + A_0^o, w, r). \tag{5}$$

Similarly, for members of generation 2 (and, more generally, for members of any generation $i \geq 2$), the solution would take the form,

$$c_2^y = c_2^y(A_1^o, w, r),$$

$$A_2^y = \frac{1}{1 - r}(w - c_2^y) = A_2^y(A_1^o, w, r),$$

$$c_2^o = c_2^o(A_2^y + A_1^o, w, r), \tag{6}$$

$$A_2^o = \frac{1}{1 - r}(A_2^y + A_1^o - c_2^o) = A_2^o(A_2^y + A_1^o, w, r).$$

---

[4] A member of generation i is assumed to be concerned with own consumption and with the attainable indifference surface of his descendant. Further, it is supposed that a member of generation i can attach a metric to generation $i + 1$'s indifference surface which makes it comparable to c_i^y and c_i^c in terms of generating U_i in the form of eq. (4). The nature of this sort of utility function is discussed in the general context of inter-dependent preferences in Becker (1974, sec. 3.A).

[5] I have not imposed the condition, $A_i^y \geq 0$, so that young individuals are allowed to issue interest-bearing debt on themselves. If issued, these debts are assumed to be perfect substitutes for equity capital. These debts correspond to the consumption loans which have been discussed by Samuelson (1958).

The model can be closed, as in Diamond (1965, pp. 1130–35), by specifying a constant-returns-to-scale production function that depends on the amounts of capital and labor input, and by equating the marginal products of capital and labor to r and w, respectively. The value of r for the current period would then be determined in order to equate the supply of assets to the demand—that is,

$$K(r, w) = A_1^o + A_2^y, \tag{7}$$

where $K(r, w)$ is such as to equate the marginal product of capital to r. The current demand for assets, $A_1^o + A_2^y$, depends, from equations (5) and (6), on r, w, and the previous period's value of K, which is equal to $A_1^y + A_0^o$. Since the number of people in each generation is assumed to equal a fixed number N, it is not necessary to enter this number explicitly into the aggregate asset demand in equation (7). Similarly, N is omitted from the aggregate formulations below. Since N is constant and technical change is not considered, the current and previous periods' values of K would be equal in a steady state.

With the marginal product of labor equated to w and with constant returns to scale, output is given by

$$. \quad y = rK + w. \tag{8}$$

Equations (2), (3), (7), and (8) imply a commodity market clearing condition,

$$c_1^o + c_2^y + \Delta K = y, \tag{9}$$

where ΔK denotes the change in capital stock from the previous to the current period. The value of ΔK would be zero in a steady state, but the present analysis is not restricted to steady-state situations.

B. Government Debt

Suppose now that the government issues an amount of debt, B, which can be thought of as taking the form of one-period, real-valued bonds. These bonds pay the specified amount of real interest, rB, in the current period and the specified real principal, B, in the next period.[6] It is supposed that asset holders regard equity and government bonds as perfect substitutes. It can be assumed, for simplicity, that the government bond issue takes the form of a helicopter drop to currently old (generation 1) households. Equivalently, it could be assumed that the bonds were sold on a competitive capital market, with the proceeds from this sale used to effect a lump-sum transfer payment to generation 1 households.

---

[6] The amount of bond issue would be limited by the government's collateral, in the sense of its taxing capacity to finance the interest and principal payments (see n. 12 below).

Allowing some portion of the proceeds to go to generation 2 households would not alter any of the basic conclusions.

The future interest payments on the government debt must be financed in some manner. Further, the principal may eventually be paid off— that is, the government may not reissue the bonds when they come due in the next period. I assume, provisionally, that the current period's interest payments are financed by a lump-sum tax levy on generation 2 households (while young), and that the principal is paid off at the beginning of the next period by an additional lump-sum tax levy on generation 2 households (while old). In this setup there is no direct effect of the government debt issue and its financing on generation 3 and later generations. I examine, subsequently, the implications of imposing some part of the taxes on generations of the more distant future.

The generation 1 budget constraint is now

$$A_1^y + A_0^o + B = c_1^o + (1 - r)A_1^o, \tag{10}$$

where B represents the lump-sum transfer payment, which is assumed to occur at the beginning of the period. For generation 2, the current budget constraint is now

$$w = c_2^y + (1 - r)A_2^y + rB, \tag{11}$$

where rB represents the tax levy for the government interest payments. The next period's budget constraint for generation 2 is now

$$A_2^y + A_1^o = c_2^o + (1 - r)A_2^o + B,$$

where B represents the tax levy for repayment of principal. The two constraints on generation 2 can be combined into a single two-period budget equation,

$$w + (1 - r)A_1^o - B = c_2^y + (1 - r)c_2^o + (1 - r)^2 A_2^o. \tag{12}$$

The form of equation (12) implies that the utility attainable by a member of generation 2 can be written in the indirect form,

$$U_2^* = f_2^*[(1 - r)A_1^o - B, w, r], \tag{13}$$

that is, the "net bequest," $(1 - r)A_1^o - B$, determines the "endowment" for members of generation 2.

From equation (10), it is also clear that c_1^o varies inversely with $(1 - r)A_1^o - B$ for a given value of $A_1^y + A_0^o$. Hence, given the predetermined value of c_1^y, and using equations (4), (10), and (13), U_1 can be written in the form,

$$U_1 = U_1(c_1^y, c_1^o, U_2^*) = f_1[(1 - r)A_1^o - B; c_1^y, A_1^y + A_0^o, w, r].$$

For given values of c_1^y, $A_1^y + A_0^o$, w, and r, the choice problem for members of generation 1 amounts to the optimal selection of the net bequest,

250

$(1 - r)A_1^o - B$, subject to the constraint that the gross bequest, A_1^o, be nonnegative. In particular, if the solution to this problem is associated with a value of A_1^o in the interior—that is, if the constraint, $A_1^o \geq 0$, is not binding—any marginal change in B would be met solely by a change in A_1^o that maintains the value of the net bequest, $(1 - r)A_1^o - B$. This response in A_1^o will keep unchanged the values of c_1^o, c_2^y, c_2^o, and A_2^o. Hence, the utility levels attained by members of generations 1, 2, etc., will be unaffected by the shift in B.

In terms of the effect on r, the current asset market clearing condition of equation (7) would now be modified to

$$K(r, w) + B = A_1^o + A_2^y. \tag{14}$$

The increase in B implies a one-to-one increase in the asset supply on the left-hand side of equation (14). However, A_1^o rises by $1/(1 - r)$ times the change in B in order to maintain the size of the net bequest, $(1 - r)A_1^o - B$. Further, with c_2^y fixed, the increase in rB (taxes) in equation (11) implies that A_2^y falls by $r/(1 - r)$ times the change in B. On net, total asset demand on the right-hand side of equation (14) rises one-to-one with B, so that no change in r is required to clear the asset market. Equivalently, the commodity market clearing condition, as expressed in equation (9), continues to hold at the initial value of r because the bond issue has no impact on aggregate demand.

Essentially, a positive value of B, financed by a tax levy on the next generation, enables a member of the old generation to "go out" insolvent by leaving a debt for his descendant. However, if, prior to the government bond issue, a member of the old generation had already selected a positive bequest, it is clear that this individual already had the option of shifting resources from his descendant to himself, but he had determined that such shifting, at the margin, was nonoptimal. Since the change in B does not alter the relevant opportunity set in this sense, it follows that—through the appropriate adjustment of the bequest—the values of current and future consumption and attained utility will be unaffected. On the other hand, if a member of generation 1 were initially at a corner where $A_1^o = 0$—in particular, if $A_1^o < 0$ would have been chosen had it been permissible—then an increase in B creates a relevant new opportunity. In this situation a generation 1 household would react by increasing c_1^o along with B, as long as the corner solution for A_1^o still applied. The upward shift in B would then correspond to an excess of earning-asset supply over demand (even after taking account of a shift in A_2^y), which would tend to raise the value of r. This increase in r would induce a drop in capital formation, which constitutes the real effect of government debt issue which has been described by Modigliani (1961). However, the main point is that the existence of this government debt effect hinges on a non-operative bequest motive—that is, on households being at the corner where the amount of bequest is zero.[7]

It should be stressed that the crucial consideration for the above result is an operative intergenerational transfer, rather than an operative bequest motive per se. For example, the transfer could take the form of parental expenditure on children's education, etc., during the overlapping tenure of parent and child.[8] Further, the transfer could be occurring in the direction opposite to that specified above. In particular, U_1^* could be entered as an argument of the U_2 function, and the possibility of gifts from the young to the old generation could be introduced. In that case the same conclusions on the effect of a change in the government debt would be reached if a "gift motive" were operative.[9] The mechanism through which changes in B were offset would then be an alteration in the amount of gifts from young to old, rather than an alteration of the amount of bequests from old to young.

The results will now be extended to a situation where the taxes which finance the government debt affect some generations which are not currently alive. The extension will be made explicitly only to generation 3, since the extension to generations further advanced in the future is straightforward.

Suppose now that the current period's interest payments are financed by a lump-sum tax levy on (young) generation 2, the next period's interest payments (on the reissued bonds) are financed by a lump-sum tax levy on (young) generation 3, and the principal is paid off by a lump-sum tax levy on (old) generation 3.[10] The generalization of the earlier results to this situation can be demonstrated by working backward from generation 3. By analogy to equation (13), the attainable utility of generation 3 can

---

[7] When households are not identical, the aggregate effect of government debt issue will depend on the fraction of households at a corner. As long as some households are in this situation, a shift in B will have some upward effect on r in this model. However, this effect would be "small" if the fraction of households at a corner were small. The role of a bequest motive in eliminating the perceived net-wealth effect of government debt has also been discussed by Miller and Upton (1974, pp. 176–79).

[8] The previous results on the effect of B might not hold if parents were concerned with specific consumption components of their children ("merit goods"), rather than with their children's attainable utility. Formally, U_i in eq. (4) could depend on (components of) c_{i+1}^y or c_{i+1}^o, rather than on U_{i+1}^*. If generation i can tie its aid to generation $i + 1$ to a specific type of expenditure (as could be the case for education), the previous results would not hold if this tied aid were an effective constraint—in the sense of forcing the next generation to "purchase" more of the item than it otherwise would—and if the parents were not making any other transfers which were equivalent to the transfer of general purchasing power. Becker (1974, sec. 3.C) presents a detailed discussion of the merit goods case in an analogous context.

[9] A model which allows for a reciprocal dependence between U_i and U_{i+1} is formally similar to the model discussed by Becker (1974, sec. 3.A) in the context of transfer payments among members of a family.

[10] I do not deal here with the possibility of net government debt issue during the old-age tenure of generation 2. No new considerations would arise here (see however, n. 12 below).

be written in the indirect form,

$$U_3^* = f_3^*[(1 - r)A_2^o - B, w, r],$$

where $(1 - r)A_2^o - B$ now determines the endowment for members of generation 3. Since generation 2 no longer pays off the government debt principal, its budget equation is modified from the form of equation (12) to

$$w + (1 - r)A_1^o - B = c_2^y + (1 - r)c_2^o + (1 - r)[(1 - r)A_2^o - B].$$

For given values of w, r, and the net bequest from generation 1, $(1 - r)A_1^o - B$, generation 2 would select an optimal value of the net bequest to generation 3, $(1 - r)A_2^o - B$. This net bequest would be invariant with B as long as the solution for A_2^o were interior. Assuming that this solution is interior, the attainable utility of generation 2 can be written in the indirect form,

$$U_2^* = f_2^*[(1 - r)A_1^o - B, w, r],$$

which coincides in form with equation (13). The situation has therefore been reduced to the previous case in which marginal changes in B led solely to changes in A_1^o which kept $(1 - r)A_1^o - B$ constant without affecting any values of consumption or attained utility.

The three-generation results generalize to the case in which taxes are levied on m generations, with the mth generation paying off the principal. By starting with generation m and progressing backward, it can be shown for all $2 \leq i \leq m - 1$ that, if A_i^o is interior, U_i^* can be written in an indirect form as a function of $(1 - r)A_{i-1}^o - B$. As long as all inheritance choices are interior[11] (as anticipated by current generations), shifts in B imply fully compensating shifts in bequests, so as to leave unchanged all values of consumption and attained utility.[12]

[11] Intuitively, if this condition is violated for some generations, the impact of these violations on current behavior should be less important the further in the future the violating generations. I make no claim to having proved this conjecture.

[12] This line of proof does not apply as $m \to \infty$. The main issue seems to be whether the assumption that the principal is eventually paid off is crucial. If the amount of outstanding government debt were constant, the impact of the principal on current decisions would become negligible for large m as long as $r > 0$. However, a difficulty arises here when B is allowed to grow over time. Suppose that the growth of B were limited to the growth of the government's collateral in the sense of its taxing capacity, which depends in turn on the growth of real income. Suppose that the growth rate of real income is equal to n, which can be viewed as the combined effects of population growth and technical progress, which are now allowed to be positive. In that case the present value of the principal would have to become negligible as $m \to \infty$ if $n < r$. The situation in which $n > r$ applies is inefficient in that it is associated with a capital stock in excess of the golden rule level (see, e.g., Diamond 1965, p. 1129). It is possible in Diamond's model (p. 1135) that the competitive equilibrium can be in this inefficient region. However, this situation is not possible in growth models where individuals are infinite lived and utility is discounted (see, e.g., Koopmans 1965). As long as intergenerational transfers are operative, the overlapping-generations model would seem to be equivalent to the infinite-life model in this respect— that is, the possibility of inefficiency in Diamond's model seems to hinge on finite lives with inoperative intergenerational transfers. Hence, when these transfers are operative, $n < r$ would be guaranteed, and the possibility of perpetual government finance by new debt issue could then be ruled out.

The results in this section have demonstrated that changes in government debt would not induce any alteration in consumption plans even in a model where (1) the present generations have finite lives, (2) the present generations may, in some sense, give lesser weight to the consumption or utility of future generations than they give to own consumption, and (3) the present generation may give no direct weight at all to the consumption or utility of generations beyond their immediate descendants (who are also finite-lived).

A sufficient condition for changes in government debt to have no impact on consumption plans and, hence, no effect on aggregate demand and interest rates is that the solution for the current generations' inheritances be interior, and that the solutions for future generations' inheritances (as perceived by current generations) also be interior. More generally, the result will hold as long as current generations are connected to all future generations by a chain of operative intergenerational transfers, either in the direction from old to young or in the direction from young to old.

The derivation of conditions under which the solution for intergenerational transfer would be interior appears to be a difficult problem and would seem to require some specialization of the form of the utility functions in order to make any headway. However, it seems clear that bequests are more likely to be positive the smaller the growth rate of w (assuming that w is now viewed as variable across generations), the higher the interest rate, the higher the relative weight of U_{i+1}^* in the U_i function, and the larger the value of B.[13] The reverse conditions favor a gift from young to old.[14]

C. Social Security Payments and Other Imposed Intergenerational Transfers

The above results on government debt also apply to social security payments.[15] Suppose that a scheme is instituted which immediately begins payments to the current old generation (generation 1) of amount S, financed by a lump-sum tax levy of amount S on the current young

---

[13] In a more general context B should be viewed as outstanding public debt less the value of physical capital held by the government.

[14] There is an alternative argument, which Gary Becker refers to as the "enforcement theory of giving," which suggests that bequest motives would typically be operative. Suppose that, instead of receiving utility from the perceived utility of his child, a parent is concerned with own consumption and with the amount of attention, etc., shown by his child during their overlapping tenure. Suppose, further, that the child has some information on the size of his parents' estate and that—acting as a good optimal controller— he regulates the amount of attention as a function of the estate size. In this situation the estate would surely be positive if parents place a high value on getting at least a small amount of attention, and if the child provides no attention when the estate is zero. However, although a positive estate could be guaranteed in this fashion, it seems that the previous conclusions about the marginal effect of B on consumption plans would not hold in this model. The nature of the interactions between parents and children would have to be analyzed more fully for this case.

[15] The view of social security as analogous to government debt has also been taken by Miller and Upton (1974, pp. 182–84).

generation (generation 2). Generation 2 expects to receive a transfer of amount S while old, financed by a lump-sum tax levy on (young) generation 3, etc. It is assumed here that an individual's payment received while old is independent of his own contribution to the scheme while young, and that neither the old receipt nor the young payment depends on the amount of work, income, etc. Assuming interior bequests (which would be guaranteed by a sufficiently high value of S), a change in S would induce the current old generation (generation 1) to maintain its choice of c_1^o and, correspondingly, to raise A_1^o by $1/(1 - r)$ times the change in S. This increased inheritance would just offset the increased tax liability imposed on (young) generation 2. With its consumption unchanged, generation 2 would use its own higher social security receipt to raise its bequest to generation 3, A_2^o, by $1/(1 - r)$ times the change in S. As in the case of changes in government debt, if the solutions for bequest are interior, the impact of a marginal change in S would be solely on the size of bequests and not at all on the pattern of consumption.[16] The same results would follow in the case of operative intergenerational transfers from young to old, with a marginal increase in S implying a corresponding reduction in the size of gifts from young to old.

The results for social security payments would apply also to other programs which amount to imposed intergenerational transfer schemes. In particular, public support of education involves a forced transfer of resources from old to young. In the main, this sort of imposed transfer would be offset by adjustments in the opposite direction of discretionary transfers.[17]

D. Inheritance Taxes

Suppose now that inheritances (or gifts) are taxed at a proportionate rate τ. In particular, the bequest from a member of generation i, A_i^o, yields a

[16] As in the case of government debt issue, the formal proof depends on the assumption that the scheme is eventually liquidated (see n. 12 above). The consumption patterns would also not be affected by a social security scheme that involved the accumulation of a government "trust fund." Assuming that the fund were held in the form of earning assets, an increase in the fund would be equivalent to a negative government debt issue. Real effects of a social security system would arise if the payments were contingent on the work behavior of the old generation. In that case there would be allocative effects produced by the disincentive to work in later years.

[17] On a theoretical level, government education programs will involve real effects to the extent that (1) there is an efficiency difference between public and private production of education, (2) public expenditure on education is pressed sufficiently far so that a reduction of discretionary transfers cannot occur on a one-for-one basis, and (3) there are distributional effects involving relative educational expenditures and tax liabilities across families. As an empirical matter, Peltzman (1973) has shown that public subsidies for higher education are offset to an extent of about 75 percent by reductions in private expenditures for higher education. However, Peltzman's 75 percent figure does not coincide with the desired estimate of the effect on discretionary transfers, since other components of discretionary transfers may also be affected and (on the other side) since not all private expenditures for education constitute intergenerational transfers.

net receipt to his descendant, a member of generation $i + 1$, of size $(1 - \tau)A_i^o$. Of course, the tax receipts must also go somewhere. Suppose that these receipts are transferred to members of generation $i + 1$ (while old) in accordance with a rule that is independent of the size of each individual's inheritance.

Since an individual's contribution to general tax revenue will typically be valued by him at less than an equal amount of own income, it is clear that an increase in τ will tend to lower the amount of intergenerational transfers. In particular, the higher the value of τ, the less likely that a bequest or gift motive will be operative. Suppose, however, that the value of τ is sufficiently low that all intergenerational transfers are operative, even if at reduced levels. In this case the previous results on the effect of a change in government debt remain valid.

Consider the situation in which the principal on the government debt is paid off by generation 2. Equation (10) continues to apply in the presence of inheritance taxes, but equation (12) must be modified to

$$w + (1 - r)(1 - \tau)A_1^o + (1 - r)\tau\overline{A_1^o} - B$$
$$= c_2^y + (1 - r)c_2^o + (1 - r)^2 A_2^o,$$

where $\tau\overline{A_1^o}$ represents the transfer to a member of (old) generation 2 corresponding to his share of the receipts from the total taxes paid on the average generation 1 bequest, $\overline{A_1^o}$. In deciding on a plan for consumption and intergenerational transfers, an individual is assumed to treat $\tau\overline{A_1^o}$ as exogenous. Consider the conjecture that, when B rises, each member of generation 1 continues to respond by maintaining the value of c_1^o and, hence, by maintaining the value of the net pretax bequest, $(1 - r)A_1^o - B$. This response requires an increase in A_1^o by $1/(1 - r)$ times the increase in B. Each individual's net posttax bequest would fall in this case, but this fall would be offset, at least on average, by an increase in the transfers to generation 2 which are financed from the inheritance tax receipts, $\tau\overline{A_1^o}$. In this circumstance, the individual values of c_2^y, c_2^o, and A_2^o—and, hence, the attained value of U_2—would remain fixed. Hence, by maintaining the net pretax bequest, each member of generation 1 achieves the same combination of c_1^o and U_2^* as before the shift in B. On the other hand, if an individual member of generation 1 decided to increase his net pretax bequest, while all other members held their net pretax bequests fixed, it would turn out for this individual that U_2^* would increase, while c_1^o would decrease. The terms on which an individual can exchange c_1^o for U_2^* depend on τ and r, and these terms have not been altered by the change in B. Further, when the transfer to generation 2 of size $\tau\overline{A_1^o}$ is included, there is also no change in an individual's overall wealth position. Therefore, the pattern which maintains the net pretax bequest—and thereby involves no shift in c_1^o or U_2^*—must be the optimal pattern for an individual. It follows that constancy of the net pretax bequest for all members of generation 1 is the equilibrium solution.[18] In this case, a marginal shift in B again has no effect on consumption patterns.

The basic conclusion here is that the existence of taxes on intergenerational transfers makes less likely an interior solution for these transfers, but if these transfers are operative, even if at reduced levels, the marginal effect of B on consumption plans—and, hence, on r—remains nil.

E. Bond Issue and Tax-Collection Costs

Suppose now that the issue of government debt and the collection of taxes to finance this debt involve transaction costs. In particular, in the case where the principal is paid off by generation 2, suppose that a net issue of B to generation 1 is now associated with a tax levy of $(1 + \gamma)rB$ on (young) generation 2 and a levy of $(1 + \gamma)B$ on (old) generation 2. That is, γ amounts to a proportional transaction cost associated with government debt issue and tax collection.[19] For simplicity, suppose now that the inheritance tax rate is zero. Equation (10) again remains valid, but equation (12) is now modified to

$$w + (1 - r)A_1^o - (1 + \gamma)B = c_2^y + (1 - r)c_2^o + (1 - r)^2 A_2^o. \qquad (15)$$

Consider, again, the conjecture that, when B rises, c_1^o and, hence, $(1 - r)A_1^o - B$ remain fixed. From equation (15), $\gamma > 0$ implies a negative-wealth effect on generation 2, so that U_2^* would fall. Since this effect would be anticipated by generation 1, it can be supposed in the normal case that A_1^o would actually rise by somewhat more than $1/(1 - r)$ times B, so that c_1^o would fall. In general, $\gamma > 0$ implies that an increase in B amounts to an overall negative-wealth effect, which would

---

[18] The equilibrium satisfies two properties: (1) each individual chooses his bequest optimally, subject to a given choice of bequests by all other individuals; and (2) all individuals choose the same value for their bequests. It can also be shown that the solution that maintains the net pretax bequest for all individuals is the unique equilibrium. Finally, it can be noted that the solution involves the assumption that each individual perceives the shift in the transfer term, $\tau \overline{A}_1^o$, associated with the average response of bequests to the change in B. Alternatively, if individuals treated $\tau \overline{A}_1^o$ as fixed, they would view an increase in B as, effectively, a negative change in wealth. The typical response would be a reduction in c_1^o, which would be associated with an increase in A_1^o by more than $1/(1 - r)$ times the change in B. In the aggregate, there would be an increase in desired saving, $A_2^o + A_1^y$, which would lead to a reduction in r and to an increase in capital formation. In particular, if the shift in transfers associated with inheritance tax revenues, $\tau \overline{A}_1^o$, is not perceived, the effects would be opposite to the standard case in which perceived net wealth rises with B.

[19] If the initial debt issue is associated with a decrease in other taxes, rather than an increase in transfers, there could be an offsetting reduction in transaction costs. The parameter γ, which is assumed to be positive, must be interpreted in this net sense.

typically involve reductions in both c_1^o and U_2^*. This effect can be seen by combining equations (10) and (15) into the single two-generation budget equation,

$$A_1^y + A_0^o - \gamma B + w = c_1^o + c_2^y + (1 - r)c_2^o + (1 - r)^2 A_2^o. \quad (16)$$

The decline in total resources on the left-hand side of equation (16) produced by an increase in B would typically be reflected in declines in all terms on the right-hand side—c_1^o, c_2^y, c_2^o, and A_2^o.

In this circumstance the effect on r of a shift in B would be unclear. The commodity market clearing condition of equation (9) would now be modified to include the resources devoted to bond and tax transactions. The revised market clearing condition would be

$$c_1^o + c_2^y + \Delta K + \gamma r B = y.$$

The effect of B on current r will depend on whether, for a given value of r, the sum, $c_1^o + c_2^y$, falls by more or less than the increase in $\gamma r B$. This relationship seems to be ambiguous.[20]

II. Imperfect Capital Markets

This part of the paper analyzes the implications of divergences among individual discount rates. This source of a net-wealth effect for government bonds has been stressed by Mundell (1971), who argues that, because of high discount rates for some individuals, the taxes which finance the government debt will not be fully capitalized—hence, an issue of government bonds will involve a net-wealth effect. To analyze this effect, it is necessary to construct a somewhat different model. Suppose that there are now two types of individuals—those who have a low discount rate, r_l, and those who have a high discount rate, r_h. It can be supposed that the high-discount-rate individuals have relatively "bad collateral," so that loans to these individuals involve high transaction costs, which are reflected in high (net-of-default-risk) borrowing rates.[21] In particular, suppose that the two discount rates are related according to

$$r_h = (1 + \lambda)r_l,$$

where $\lambda > 0$ represents the proportional transaction costs involved in the loan process.[22] I suppose in this part of the paper that both types of

[20] From eq. (16), the negative wealth effect is γB, which is the present value of the flow, $\gamma r B$. The sum, $c_1^o + c_2^y$, will fall by as much as $\gamma r B$ if the total "propensity to consume" associated with the negative "income" flow, $\gamma r B$, is equal to one.

[21] In this respect see Barro (1974).

[22] I am assuming that the r_h individuals are actually borrowing, so that r_h represents both their borrowing rate and their marginal discount rate. Alternatively, r_h could be viewed as a marginal discount rate which could be somewhere between the borrowing and lending rates, as in Hirshleifer (1958).

individuals are infinite-lived, since the effect of finite lives has already been examined above.

It is convenient to suppose that government debt now takes the form of a perpetuity that carries a real interest payment of i per year. Suppose that the government issues an additional bond of this type. This bond would be purchased by a low-discount-rate individual and would be evaluated as $B = i/r_l$.[23] Suppose then that the government uses the lump-sum proceeds from this sale, B, to effect a lump-sum transfer (or lump-sum tax reduction) to individuals, and suppose that a fraction α of this transfer goes to r_l discount rate individuals and a fraction $(1 - \alpha)$ to r_h discount rate individuals. Finally, the taxes for financing the government interest payments are $(1 + \gamma)i$, where γ represents, as in section IE, the proportional transaction costs associated with government bond sale and tax collection. Suppose that these taxes are distributed across discount rates in the same manner as the lump-sum proceeds[24]—that is, a fraction α to r_l individuals and a fraction $(1 - \alpha)$ to r_h individuals.

Consider, in turn, the wealth effects for the r_l and r_h groups. The bond sale itself involves no wealth effect for the r_l group. The lump-sum transfer to r_l individuals is $\alpha B = \alpha i/r_l$, while the present value of the r_l share of tax liabilities, discounted at rate r_l, is $(1 + \gamma)\alpha i/r_l$. Clearly, if $\gamma > 0$, the net-wealth effect for r_l individuals is negative, as it was in the case discussed in section IE, where all discount rates were equal.

For the r_h group, the lump-sum proceeds are $(1 - \alpha)B = (1 - \alpha)i/r_l$, while the present value of the tax liability, discounted at rate r_h, is $(1 + \gamma)(1 - \alpha)i/r_h$. Using $r_h = (1 + \lambda)r_l$, the net-wealth effect here can be expressed as

$$\frac{(1 - \alpha)i}{r_l}\left(1 - \frac{1 + \gamma}{1 + \lambda}\right) = \frac{(1 - \alpha)i}{r_l(1 + \lambda)}(\lambda - \gamma),$$

which is positive if $\lambda > \gamma$. That is, the net-wealth effect for the r_h group is positive if γ, which measures the government transaction costs for bond issue and tax collection, is smaller than λ, which measures the private transaction costs implicit in the existing pattern of (net-of-default-risk) discount rates. To the extent, $1 - \alpha$, that the transfer payment and tax liability involve the r_h group, the government bond issue amounts to effecting a loan from the low-discount-rate to the high-discount-rate individuals. On the other hand, this sort of transfer could already have

---

[23] This analysis abstracts from any "liquidity yield" of bonds (see part III, below).

[24] If the fractions for transfer and tax liability vary, then the wealth effects on the two discount-rate groups are likely to be in opposite directions. The net effect on current consumption demand would depend, in part, on relative propensities to consume, which are not obvious. In any event, this case would amount to the effect of income distribution on consumption demand, rather than the effect of government bond issue per se on net wealth and consumption demand.

been accomplished privately, except that the transaction costs, as measured by λ, made this transfer marginally unprofitable. Hence, the government-induced transfer implied by its bond issue can raise net wealth only if the government is more efficient than the private capital market in carrying out this sort of lending and borrowing operation.

Some additional observations can be made concerning this result. First, if the government is really more efficient than the private market in the lending process (presumably because the benefits of economies of scale [in information?] and the ability to coerce outweigh the problems of government incentive and control), it may be able to exploit this efficiency better by a direct-loan program, rather than by the sort of bond issue described above. In my simple model, a fraction α of transfers and tax liabilities involved the r_l group, and this process entailed a dead-weight loss to the extent that $\gamma > 0$. A program which limited the loan recipients to high-discount-rate individuals would be more efficient in this respect. However, the information requirements for this sort of program may be much greater than those for a program which does not attempt to discriminate—in the transfer and tax liability aspects—among discount rates. The crucial point which can make the bond issue work as a loan program is that the purchasers of the bonds automatically discriminate among themselves as to their discount rates.

Second, the government may be more efficient than the private market only over a certain range of B. In particular, there may be a sufficiently large value of B such that, at the margin, the net-wealth effect of government debt is zero. If the public choice process leads to this value of B (as it should on efficiency grounds), then, at the margin, the net-wealth effect of government bonds would be zero, despite the continued existence of "imperfect private capital markets."[25]

III. A Government Monopoly in Liquidity Services

Suppose now that government debt provides a form of "liquidity service" to the holder, in addition to the direct interest payments. Suppose that, at the margin, these services are valued at the amount L per bond per year. Hence, in the context where all individuals have the same discount rate, r, an additional perpetual government bond would be evaluated as

$$B = (i + L)/r.$$

The taxes for financing the government debt can be thought of as the interest costs, i, plus any costs involved with the process of creating

---

[25] Of course, government debt issue would be "productive" in a total sense even in the case where the marginal net wealth effect was nil. However, it is this marginal effect which enters into analyses of (marginal) fiscal and monetary policies.

liquidity services (which could involve the γ-type costs discussed above). Suppose that c denotes the marginal costs per bond per year associated with the production of liquidity services. Hence, at the margin, the wealth effect of a change in government debt will be

$$\frac{1}{r}(i + L) - \frac{1}{r}(i + c) = \frac{1}{r}(L - c).$$

If the public choice process is such as to motivate the government to act like a competitive producer of liquidity services (as it should on efficiency grounds), then $L = c$ and the marginal-wealth effect of government debt would be nil. On the other hand, if the government operates monopolistically, so that $L > c$, then the marginal-wealth effect of government debt would be positive.[26] However, it is also possible that the government overextends its production of liquidity services, so that $L < c$ and the marginal-wealth effect of government debt would be negative. This last case corresponds implicitly to the one discussed above in section IE, where $L = 0$ and $c > 0$ were assumed.

Of course, liquidity services can also be provided by private producers. If the types of services rendered by private and public debt instruments are close substitutes, and if the private market is competitive, then governmental monopoly power can arise here only to the extent that, at the margin, the government is more efficient than the private market as a producer of liquidity services. Even if the government is a more efficient producer over a certain range, a sufficient expansion of government "output" would eliminate this efficiency differential at the margin if the production of liquidity services is, at least eventually, subject to increasing marginal costs. As in the case of an imperfect private capital market, as discussed above, the net-wealth effect of government debt depends on the relative efficiency at the margin of government versus private production.

IV. Risk and Asset Substitutability

The previous sections have dealt with the net-wealth effect of government debt. I have not discussed explicitly in these sections the risk characteristics of government bonds, tax liabilities, and the other types of available assets and liabilities. Tobin (1971, p. 2) has argued: "The calculus of total wealth is less important than the change in the composition of private balance sheets that the government engineers by borrowing from the public—forcing on taxpayers a long-term debt of some uncertainty while providing bond-holders highly liquid and safe assets. Since no one else

---

[26] Of course, this observation would also apply to government money, which yields a zero rate of explicit interest. The usual real balance effect for outside money assumes that the marginal cost to the government of maintaining real balances is zero, and that the government acts like a monopolist in determining its supply of real balances.

can perform the same intermediation, the government's debt issues probably do, within limits, augment private wealth. Another way to make the point is to observe that future tax liabilities are likely to be capitalized at a higher discount rate than claims against the government." I have already considered, above, arguments for effectively discounting tax liabilities at a higher rate because of finite lives, imperfect private capital markets, and a government monopoly in the production of liquidity services, and these arguments need not be repeated here. In this part of the paper, I will consider briefly some implications of the risk characteristics of government bonds and of the future tax liabilities associated with the finance of these bonds.

Suppose, first, that there were no uncertainty about the relative burden of the (lump-sum) tax liabilities that finance the government debt. In this situation the uncertainty in an individual's real tax burden associated with government interest payments would reflect solely the variability over time in the real-interest payments themselves. In terms of present values, the variability in the tax liabilities would reflect the variability in prices and interest rates—that is, the same factors which lead to variability in real bond values. In particular, holdings of government debt—amounting to a claim to a certain fraction of total government interest payments—would be the perfect hedge against variations in tax liabilities.[27] In this context a simultaneous increase in government interest payments (i.e., government bonds) and in the tax liabilities for financing these payments would not involve any net shift in the risk composition of private balance sheets.[28]

Suppose now that the tax liabilities are subject to an additional variability concerning the relative burden across individuals. Suppose, first, that the variation in relative taxes is purely random, in the sense of being unrelated to variations in relative income, etc. In that case, it is clear that an individual's tax liability associated with government interest payments would be subject to a source of variability above that of the total interest payments. In particular, the fractional holdings of government bonds which corresponds to the expected fraction of tax liabilities would no longer provide a perfect hedge against variations in the tax liabilities. Of course, it would be possible for individuals to utilize private insurance markets to reduce the risks associated with variations in relative tax liability. However, to the extent that insurance arrangements entail transaction costs, the risk associated with relative liability would not generally be fully eliminated. In this case an increase in government bonds would produce a net increase in the risk contained in household balance

---

[27] I am ignoring here effects which relate to the maturity structure of the government debt. In order to provide a perfect hedge, an individual's holding of debt by maturity would have to correspond to the overall maturity distribution.

[28] There could be an effect on individuals who do not hold any government bonds (or assets subject to similar risks).

sheets—that is, there would be a decline in effective household wealth. The typical household reaction would be twofold: first, an increase in desired total saving, and, second, a shift in portfolio composition away from more risky assets, such as equity capital, and toward less risky assets. The impact on the equity rate of return, and, hence, on capital formation would depend on which of these two responses was the dominant force.

The above discussion would be altered to the extent that variations in tax liability reflect variations in income. In this context the variation in relative tax liabilities can serve to reduce the net variability in disposable income—that is, the income tax works, in part, like a public program of income insurance. If the income-offsetting feature of taxes were the dominant element in relative tax variability, then a shift in government bonds could lead to a reduction in the overall risk contained in household balance sheets. In that case the effects on desired total saving and on portfolio composition would be opposite to those described above. However, it should also be noted that the public program of income insurance which is implied by an income tax system will also involve transaction costs. There are costs associated with administration and with individual reporting effort, as well as "moral hazard" costs associated with incentives for earning income. A full analysis of the wealth effect of government bonds under different tax systems would have to involve a comparison of these types of public transaction costs against the transaction costs associated with the pooling of income risks under private insurance arrangements.

One final observation can be made here. The argument in the early literature for a net-wealth effect of government bonds—for example, that given by Modigliani (1961)—involved a neglect of the tax liabilities associated with the financing of the debt. Similarly, Tobin's argument for effects based on the risk composition of household balance sheets seems to neglect the tax liabilities as an element of these balance sheets. It seems clear that, either in the sense of effects on perceived total wealth, or in the sense of the risk composition of household portfolios, the impact of changes in government debt cannot be satisfactorily analyzed without an explicit treatment of the associated tax liabilities. Once the variability in relative tax liability is considered, there seem to be no clear results concerning the effect of government debt issue on the overall risk contained in household balance sheets. The net effect hinges on the extent to which variations in relative tax liability reflect variations in relative income, and on the transaction costs for public programs of income insurance relative to those of private programs.

V. Summary and Conclusions

This paper has focused on the question of whether an increase in government debt constitutes an increase in perceived household wealth. The effect of finite lives was examined within the context of an overlapping-generations model of the economy. It was shown that households would act as though they were infinitely lived, and, hence, that there would be no marginal net-wealth effect of government bonds, so long as there existed an operative chain of intergenerational transfers which connected current to future generations. Net-wealth effects associated with imperfect private capital markets and with a government monopoly in the production of liquidity services were shown to depend on the assumption that the government was more efficient, at the margin, than the private market either in the loan process or in the production of liquidity services. Further, the introduction of government transaction costs for bond issue and tax collection implied that the net-wealth effect of government bonds could be negative. Finally, a consideration of the risk characteristics of government debt and of the tax liabilities associated with the financing of this debt suggested that an increase in government bonds could raise the overall risk contained in household balance sheets. However, this effect depends on the nature of the tax system and on the transaction costs associated with private insurance arrangements.

The basic conclusion is that there is no persuasive theoretical case for treating government debt, at the margin, as a net component of perceived household wealth. The argument for a negative wealth effect seems, a priori, to be as convincing as the argument for a positive effect. Hence, the common assertion (as in Patinkin 1965, chap. 12, p. 289) that the marginal net-wealth effect of government bonds is somewhere between zero and one and is most likely to lie at some positive intermediate value has no a priori foundation. If, in fact, the marginal net-wealth effect were negligible, the implications for monetary and fiscal analysis would be far-reaching. In particular, in the case where the marginal net-wealth effect of government bonds is close to zero, (1) the Metzler-type argument for nonneutrality of changes in the stock of outside money would not be valid, (2) a change in the stock of government debt would have no effect on capital formation, and, more generally, (3) fiscal effects involving changes in the relative amounts of tax and debt finance for a given amount of public expenditure would have no effect on aggregate demand, interest rates, and capital formation.[29]

References

Bailey, M. J. *National Income and the Price Level.* New York: McGraw-Hill, 1962.
Barro, R. J. "The Loan Market, Collateral, and Rates of Interest." Center for Math. Studies in Bus. and Econ., Univ. Chicago, Report 7401, January 1974.

[29] The usual fiscal analysis involves a shift in the flow of government debt rather than a one-time shift in the stock. The zero net-wealth effect applies also to the flow case if individuals perceive the implications of the current flow for the future time path of the stock of government debt.

Becker, G. S. "A Theory of Social Interactions." *J.P.E.* 82, no. 6 (November/December 1974): 1063–93.

Blinder, A. S., and Solow, R. M. "Does Fiscal Policy Matter?" *J. Public Econ.* 2 (November 1973): 319–37.

Diamond, P. A. "National Debt in a Neoclassical Growth Model." *A.E.R.* 60 (December 1965): 1126–50.

Hirshleifer, J. "On the Theory of Optimal Investment Decisions." *J.P.E.* 66, no. 4 (August 1958): 329–52.

Koopmans, T. C. "On the Concept of Optimal Economic Growth." In *The Econometric Approach to Development Planning.* Amsterdam: North-Holland, 1965.

Metzler, L. "Wealth, Saving, and the Rate of Interest." *J.P.E.* 59, no. 2 (April 1951): 93–116.

Miller, M. H., and Upton, C. W. *Macroeconomics: A Neoclassical Introduction.* Homewood, Ill.: Irwin, 1974.

Modigliani, F. "Long-Run Implications of Alternative Fiscal Policies and the Burden of the National Debt." *Econ. J.* 71 (December 1961): 730–55.

Mundell, R. "Money, Debt, and the Rate of Interest." In *Monetary Theory,* edited by R. Mundell. Pacific Palisades, Calif.: Goodyear, 1971.

Patinkin, D. *Money, Interest, and Prices.* 2d ed. New York: Harper & Row, 1965.

Peltzman, S. "The Effect of Public Subsidies-in-Kind on Private Expenditures: The Case of Higher Education." *J.P.E.* 81, no. 1 (January/February 1973): 1–27.

Samuelson, P. A. "An Exact Consumption-Loan Model of Interest with or without the Social Contrivance of Money." *J.P.E.* 66, no. 6 (December 1958): 467–82.

Thompson, E. A. "Debt Instruments in Macroeconomic and Capital Theory." *A.E.R.* 67 (December 1967): 1196–1210.

Tobin, J. *Essays in Economics.* Vol. 1. *Macroeconomics.* Amsterdam: North-Holland, 1971.

12

On the Determination of the Public Debt

A public debt theory is constructed in which the Ricardian invariance theorem is valid as a first-order proposition but where the dependence of excess burden on the timing of taxation implies an optimal time path of debt issue. A central proposition is that deficits are varied in order to maintain expected constancy in tax rates. This behavior implies a positive effect on debt issue of temporary increases in government spending (as in wartime), a countercyclical response of debt to temporary income movements, and a one-to-one effect of expected inflation on nominal debt growth. Debt issue would be invariant with the outstanding debt-income ratio and, except for a minor effect, with the level of government spending. Hypotheses are tested on U.S. data since World War I. Results are basically in accord with the theory. It also turns out that a small set of explanatory variables can account for the principal movements in interest-bearing federal debt since the 1920s.

In a previous paper (Barro 1974) I discussed the "Ricardian" equivalence theorem on public debt[1]—that is, the proposition that shifts between debt and tax finance for a given amount of public expenditure would have no first-order effect on the real interest rate, volume of private investment, etc. This theorem surely remains controversial, although it seems to be evolving into a respectable viewpoint. In any event, proponents of the Ricardian view that the choice between debt

This research is being supported by the National Science Foundation. I have benefited from comments by Paul Evans, Milton Friedman, Bob Hall, Elhanan Helpman, Michael Parkin, John Shoven, David Starrett, George Stigler, and C. C. von Weizsäcker.

[1] I am grateful to Buchanan (1976) for pointing out that I was discussing this topic. The Ricardian equivalence proposition is presented in Ricardo (1951a, 1951b) and discussed in Buchanan (1958, chaps. 4 and 8). See O'Driscoll (1977) for an amusing discussion of whether Ricardo actually held to the Ricardian view.

[Journal of Political Economy, 1979, vol. 87, no. 5, pt. 1]
© 1979 by The University of Chicago. 0022-3808/79/8751-0003$02.56

and taxes does not matter are left with an embarrassing absence of a theory of public debt creation.[2] This paper develops a simple theory of "optimal" public finance that identifies some factors that would influence the choice between taxes and debt issue. The model accepts the Ricardian invariance theorem as a valid first-order proposition but introduces some second-order considerations involving the "excess burden" of taxation to obtain a determinate (optimal) amount of debt creation. It should be stressed that some typical features of public debt analysis, such as shifting of the tax burden to future generations, crowding out of private investment, etc., are excluded by the assumption that the Ricardian proposition is valid on the first order. Hence, the analysis concentrates on less familiar issues that would be dominated by the usual first-order effects—if these effects were, in fact, pertinent to the choice between debt and taxes.

The theoretical model is used to formulate several testable propositions concerning the determination of public debt issue. Principal hypotheses involve the positive effect on debt issue of temporary increases in government spending (especially important during war and postwar periods), the negative effect of temporary increases in income—that is, a countercyclical response of debt issue, and a one-to-one effect of the expected inflation rate on the growth rate of nominal debt. The theory also implies that the growth rate of debt would be independent of the debt-income ratio and would be affected at most in a minor way by the level of government expenditure.

The hypotheses are tested using the time-series data on public debt issue in the United States since World War I. The results are basically in accord with the underlying theory. In particular, the relation between debt issue and a small set of explanatory variables seems to be reasonably stable since World War I. However, the magnitude of countercyclical debt response is significantly larger than that implied by the theory. Although this phenomenon does not seem to be of recent origin, it does suggest that some additional element—such as governmental attempts at stabilization policy—would be needed to account for this behavior.

A Model of Public Debt Issue

The model applies to a large national government that has jurisdiction over a population of exogenous size. The analysis therefore neglects any effects of public debt policy on migration, which would be an important consideration for a local government. The govern-

---

[2] However, opponents of the Ricardian view seem also to lack an interesting positive theory of the public debt.

ment is assumed to finance its expenditures through two methods: current taxation and public debt issue. I do not deal here with currency issue, although for some purposes this type of finance could be included as one form of current taxation. The composition of taxes, by type or degree of graduation, is taken as given. The volume of real government expenditure, aside from interest payments on the public debt, during period t is denoted by G_t and is assumed to be exogenous. Hence, the present analysis does not deal with the determination of the size of the public sector. Future values of G and of other exogenous variables are treated as though known with certainty. Real tax revenue obtained by the government in each period is designated by τ_t, and aggregate real income (treated as exogenous) by Y_t. The real stock of public debt outstanding at the end of period t is denoted by b_t, where this debt can be assumed at this stage to take the form of one-period, single-coupon bonds that are issued at par. I assume initially that the price level, P, is (and is expected to be) constant over time, and the real (=nominal) rate of return on public and private debts, r, is also a constant.[3] The government's budget equation in each period is

$$G_t + rb_{t-1} = \tau_t + (b_t - b_{t-1}),\qquad(1)$$

where interest payments during period t are assumed to apply to the stock of debt outstanding at the beginning of the period.

The government's budget equation at each date t, together with an additional condition that rules out perpetual debt finance, implies the overall budget constraint,

$$\sum_1^\infty [G_t/(1 + r)^t] + b_0 = \sum_1^\infty [\tau_t/(1 + r)^t].\qquad(2)$$

This condition—which equates the present value of government expenditure (aside from interest payments) plus initial debt to the present value of taxes—follows from equation (1) as long as b is constrained to grow asymptotically at a rate below r.[4]

---

[3] Implicit in this condition is the assumption that the required real rate of return on public debt, relative to that on private debt, is invariant with the quantity of government debt outstanding. If the quantity of public debt approaches the government's collateral—in the sense of the present value of its future taxing capacity—then the risk of the government's default would have to be taken into account (see Barro 1976b, p. 343). Alternatively, if government debt were perceived as net wealth by the private sector, then the quantity of debt could influence real rates of return in the economy (see, e.g., Barro 1974, p. 1096).

[4] In the efficient case where r exceeds the growth rate of real income, this condition requires a bound on the asymptotic debt-income ratio (see Barro 1976b, pp. 343–45). Presumably, this ratio cannot, in fact, exceed the finite value implied by the government's collateral (n. 3 above).

The sum of the present value of government expenditures and the initial debt level, which appears on the left side of equation (2) and is exogenously given, determines the present value of government tax receipts. However, the fixity of this last present value leaves open the determination of the time pattern of taxes. It is assumed that taxation involves not only a one-to-one transfer of purchasing power from individuals to the government but also some collection costs and/or indirect misallocation costs that are imposed on the private economy. That is, the "production" of government revenue involves the using up of some resources in the sense of costs that are often referred to as "deadweight losses" or "excess burdens." For a given present value of net tax revenues (as fixed by the present value of expenditures and the initial debt level), the present value of these extra costs would generally depend on the distribution of taxes by type and timing. The present analysis, which focuses on the timing of taxes, abstracts from the determination of tax composition at a point in time. Essentially, the analysis of timing is conditional on the selection of an "optimal" tax composition that underlies the "production function" relation between net tax receipts and "excess burden" that is specified below.

For the case of direct collection costs for administration, enforcement, and so on, let Z_t represent the real cost incurred and Y_t the real national income in period t.[5] I assume that Z_t depends positively, with a positive second derivative, on the total net tax take for the period τ_t and negatively on the pool of contemporaneously taxable resources Y_t, but not on the values of taxes or incomes in other periods. Further, I neglect any special relation of collection costs to the contemporaneous government spending level G_t.[6] Finally, I assume the homogeneity condition that a doubling of net tax collections τ_t and potential tax pool Y_t doubles the collection cost Z_t. Therefore, the collection cost for period t can be written as

$$Z_t = F(\tau_t, Y_t) = \tau_t f(\tau_t/Y_t), \tag{3}$$

where $f' > 0$, and the function f is assumed to be invariant over time. The present value of collection costs is then given by

$$Z = \sum_{t=1}^{\infty} \tau_t f(\tau_t/Y_t)/(1 + r)^t. \tag{4}$$

---

[5] I have not included the collection costs as components of government spending in eq. (1), although the analysis could be altered in that manner without affecting any substantive results. Independence of national income levels from the choice of the time path of taxes is assumed to hold as a first-order approximation—essentially, the deadweight losses from taxation are assumed to constitute only a small fraction of GNP.

[6] Such an effect might arise if, e.g., the influence of war on "patriotism" lowers the administrative costs of raising taxes during wartime.

At the present time (date 1) the government is confronted by an exogenous series of planned expenditures, $G_1, G_2, \ldots$, which it must finance at each date; by a series of (anticipated) real income values, Y_1, $Y_2, \ldots$; the interest rate r; and an initial stock of debt, b_0. The overall budget condition in equation (2) fixes the present value of net tax collections. Given this present value, the government's objective is taken to be the minimization of the present value of the resources consumed by the process of revenue generation, Z, as shown in equation (4). This general form of the objective is similar to ones set up by Prescott (1977) and Barro (1976a).

The assumed objective of the government—that it pursues a cost-minimization policy involving the economization of revenue-raising costs—can be reconciled with various models of public sector behavior. For example, the setup seems consistent with a public-interest theory of government, with a model of self-interested politicians who are subject to "effective" electoral control, and with a model of a political dictator who maximizes own utility. The objective would not seem to apply if the institutional structure were such that "political income" was directly related to the amount of deadweight loss generated by the government.

The government's optimization problem amounts to choosing τ_1, τ_2, $\ldots$, to minimize the present value of revenue-raising costs, subject to the form of the cost function in equation (4) and the overall budget constraint in equation (2). The resulting first-order conditions, which can be obtained in the usual manner, require the marginal collection cost for raising taxes—$\partial Z_t / \partial \tau_t$—to be the same in all periods (without regard to the value of r, because tax revenue and the associated collection cost arise at the same point in time). With the homogeneous specification of costs in equation (4), these conditions require the tax rate, τ / Y, to be equal in all periods. The (planned) constancy of this ratio is the key to the subsequent analysis.[7] Given that the tax-income

[7] The choice of taxes over time can also be considered in terms of an objective that encompasses distortion costs on the private economy. I have considered only a simple model in which the representative individual receives utility from leisure and a single consumption good in each period, where any satisfaction provided by government services in various periods is separable from the utility provided by consumption and leisure, where interest income is untaxed, and where the present values of all producer prices are constant. This constancy would obtain if production were subject to constant returns to scale (which means that the model does not deal with capital accumulation in a serious way) and if the interest rate were fixed. One justification for the latter would be a small-country setting in which the domestic interest rate was tied to the exogenous return available internationally. The optimal taxation literature, as in Sandmo (1974) and Sadka (1977), can then be applied to determine the time pattern of consumption and leisure taxes that maximizes the utility of the representative individual, given the present value of tax collections. E.g., for the case where leisure in each period is untaxed, uniform consumption taxation over time emerges if the compensated elasticity of consumer demand in period i with respect to the present-value wage for any

ratio is constant, the level of taxes in each period is determined from the given values of $(Y_1, \ldots)$, $(G_1, \ldots)$, r, and b_0 in order to conform with the overall budget condition set out in equation (2). These values for taxes imply values for the government deficit in each period, $b_t - b_{t-1}$, in accordance with equation (1). The properties of the solution are illustrated below for particular specifications of the time paths of Y and G.

Constant Income and Government Expenditure

If Y is constant over time, the constancy of τ/Y implies constancy of τ. If G is also constant, the level of τ is determined immediately from equation (2), which specializes here to $G/r + b_0 = \tau/r$, so that $\tau = G + rb_0$. It follows from equation (1) that the government's budget is always in balance—that is, $b_t = b_{t-1} = b_0$ for all t. A notable aspect of this solution is that the initial debt is not amortized. The steady-state value of public debt is determined entirely by its initial value rather than as a function of G, Y, r, or the form of the collection cost function, f, in equation (3). A related implication is that the government deficit, $b_t - b_{t-1}$, is determined (to equal zero) independently of the values of b_0, G, Y, r, or the form of the f-function. This type of result continues to apply when complications are introduced into the specified time paths of G and Y.

Constant Rate of Growth of Income and Government Expenditure

Suppose now that aggregate real income grows at the constant rate ρ, so that $Y_t = Y_0(1 + \rho)^t$. In order for the present value of future income to be finite (i.e., to be in the efficient case referred to in n. 4 above), it must be that $r > \rho$. Government expenditure is assumed to grow at rate γ, so that $G_t = G_0(1 + \gamma)^t$. In order for $G/Y < 1$ to hold at all times, it must be that $\gamma \leqslant \rho < r$.[8] Clearly, $\rho = \gamma$ is the only specification within

---

period j is independent of the index i. (The results from Sandmo [p. 705, eq. 22] and Sadka [p. 389, eq. 8] can be extended to obtain this conclusion.) Essentially, this condition rules out any special relationship of complementarity or substitutability between leisure at date j and consumption at various dates—which would be violated if, e.g., contemporaneous leisure were a strong complement for consumption. Sandmo's analysis [p. 705, eq. 24] implies that the desired condition obtains if the utility function is weakly separable between work and consumption and homogeneous in consumption goods (so that the income elasticities for consumption at various dates are equal). More generally, it seems that approximate constancy of optimal tax rates would hold if leisure at one date were a close substitute for leisure at other dates and if consumption at one date were a close substitute for consumption at other dates. See Kydland and Prescott (1978, p. 18) on this point.

[8] However, it is clear empirically that $\gamma > \rho$ can prevail for long periods. E.g., for the United States from 1890 to 1976 the average growth rate of real GNP was 3.1 percent per year, while that of real federal expenditure was 5.8 percent per year.

the constant growth rate setup that allows for a positive, finite steady-state value of G/Y. However, examination of results for cases where $\rho \neq \gamma$ is permitted provides qualitative insights into more complicated situations where differences between ρ and γ prevail over finite intervals.

Since the tax-income ratio is still constant in the optimal solution it follows that taxes grow at the same rate as income—that is, $\tau_t = \tau_0(1 + \rho)^t$. Using the budget condition of equation (2) leads eventually to the result, $\tau_0 = [(r - \rho)/(1 + \rho)][G_0(1 + \gamma)/(r - \gamma) + b_0]$, which can be used to determine the value of taxes at any date. Using $\tau_1 = \tau_0(1 + \rho)$, $G_1 = G_0(1 + \gamma)$, and the government budget condition in equation (1) implies that the deficit in the current period is

$$b_1 - b_0 = \rho b_0 + [(\rho - \gamma)/(r - \gamma)]G_1. \qquad (5)$$

For the case where income and government expenditure grow at a common rate, $\rho = \gamma$, the conclusion from this extension is that (real) government debt also grows at this rate—$(b_1 - b_0)/b_0 = \rho$—rather than remaining constant over time. It is now the ratio of debt to income, b/Y, that remains fixed at its initial value, b_0/Y_0. The model therefore retains the property that the debt-income ratio is not determined within the model (by the values of G/Y, r, ρ, or the form of the f-function) but is rather fixed at its historically given "initial" value.

For $\rho \neq \gamma$ an additional effect is that the current deficit rises with ρ and falls with γ (for a given value of current government spending, G_1). When ρ exceeds γ, future values of G/Y will be lower than the current value. Consequently, the financing of expenditure becomes easier over time—in the sense of a diminished relative collection cost—so that the deferral of taxation is warranted. This deferral of taxation corresponds to current deficit finance, as reflected in the higher value of $b_1 - b_0$.[9]

Transitory Income and Government Expenditure

An empirically important extension to the model concerns temporary departures of government spending or aggregate income from "normal" values. This analysis applies especially to the role of wartime expenditures and depressions—both viewed as transitory phenomena—in the government debt creation process.

---

[9] In terms of the growth rate of b, the division of eq. (5) by b_0 indicates that the extra term is $[(\rho - \gamma)/(r - \gamma)](G_1/b_0)$. If $\rho > \gamma$, b grows faster than G over time, and the ratio G_t/b_{t-1} approaches zero. Hence, the asymptotic growth rate of b would still be ρ (and the asymptotic value of G/Y would be zero). Of course, if $\rho < \gamma$, G/Y would approach infinity, which would be a meaningless result. The main interest in the $(\rho - \gamma)$ term in eq. (5) would arise in situations where $\rho \neq \gamma$ applies over some finite period, but not in the steady state. The result for this more complicated situation would correspond qualitatively to that indicated in eq. (5).

Suppose that current government expenditure departs by a fraction ϵ from its trend value—that is, $G_1 = (1 + \epsilon)G_0(1 + \rho)$, and that the current value of income differs from its trend value by the fraction u—that is, $Y_1 = (1 + u)Y_0(1 + \rho)$, where G_0 and Y_0 are assumed (defined) to be along the respective trend lines. For convenience, I deal here with a case where the trend growth rates of G and Y are equal, since the main effect of unequal growth rates is brought out in equation (5). The expected departure of G from trend is assumed to persist (by the fraction ϵ) for k periods, while the departure of Y from trend is assumed to persist (by the fraction u) for n periods.[10] This specification could be generalized in obvious ways—for example, by altering the assumption that the anticipated fractional departures of G and Y away from trend, ϵ and u, were precisely constant over k and n periods, respectively. However, the present setup brings out two significant elements: first, the role of the magnitude of the departure of current G and Y from trend and, second, the impact of the perceived duration of departures from trend.

Optimal public finance still requires a constant (planned) ratio of taxes to income at all points in time. Accordingly, from date $n + 1$ onward, planned taxes still grow along with income at rate ρ. However, because of the transitory ($+$ or $-$) income over the first n periods, the taxes over this interval depart from trend by the factor, $1 + u$. Using these facts and the budget condition of equation (2)—which now includes the transitory government spending over the first k periods—it is possible to determine taxes at all points in time. The solution can be written in the form

$$\tau_t = [1/(1 + u)]\tau_1(1 + \rho)^{t-1} \text{ for } t = n + 1, n + 2, \ldots,$$

$$\tau_t = \tau_1(1 + \rho)^{t-1} \qquad \text{for } t = 1, \ldots, n, \tag{6}$$

$$\tau_1 = \frac{(1 + u)}{(1 + u) - u[(1 + \rho)/(1 + r)]^n}\Big(G_0(1 + \rho) + (r - \rho)b_0$$
$$+ \epsilon G_0(1 + \rho)\{1 - [(1 + \rho)/(1 + r)]^k\}\Big).$$

The above expression for τ_1, derived from the government's budget constraint in equation (2), can be interpreted as follows. The term in the right-hand parentheses measures the "permanent" level of required finance—the trend value of expenditures, $G_0(1 + \rho)$, plus the interest on the initial debt less the part that is financed by issue of debt along with the trend growth of income, $(r - \rho)b_0$, plus the effect of transitory expenditures. This last item is the amount of current transitory expenditure, $\epsilon G_0(1 + \rho)$, multiplied by a factor that accounts for duration. As $k \to 0$ (see n. 10 above) this factor approaches zero—that

---

[10] Although k and n must formally be integers within the present discrete framework, these restrictions are of no importance in interpreting the results.

is, purely transitory current government expenditure has no effect on current taxation. As $k \to \infty$ the factor approaches unity (assuming $r < \rho$)—signifying that the "transitory" component of government spending amounts in this case to permanent expenditure. Generally, the higher the expected duration of a given amount of current transitory government spending, the larger the amount of current taxation.

The other term on the right side of equation (6) accounts for transitory income. If the duration, n, of the departure of current income from trend were close to zero, then τ_1 would be a multiple, $1 + u$, of the permanent level of finance (in order to equate the current tax-income ratio to the future ratio). As n increases, the length of the period for which taxes will depart from trend by the factor $(1 + u)$ rises, which (if u is positive) diminishes the required amount of current taxation. As $n \to \infty$, the multiplication of trend income by $(1 + u)$ becomes permanent, so that the first term on the right side of equation (6) approaches unity (assuming $r > \rho$). In this situation taxes correspond to the permanent level of finance at all times rather than being multiplied by $(1 + u)$ over an interval of finite length n. Generally, current taxes are an increasing function of the amount of current transitory income, as measured by $(1 + u)$, and a decreasing function of the anticipated duration, n, of this transitory income.

With current taxes determined from equation (6), the current government deficit follows from the budget condition in equation (1) as $b_1 - b_0 = G_1 + rb_0 - \tau_1 \simeq [(1 + \rho)/(1 + r)]^k[\epsilon G_0(1 + \rho)] - [(1 + \rho)/(1 + r)]^n[G_0(1 + \rho) + rb_0]u + \rho b_0$, where the approximation involves neglecting the term, $u[(1 + \rho)/(1 + r)]^n$, relative to 1. Letting $\bar{G}_1 = G_0(1 + \rho)$ be the trend value of current government spending and $\bar{Y}_1 = Y_0(1 + \rho)$ be the trend value of current income, the solution can be rewritten from the definitions of ϵ and u as $b_1 - b_0 \simeq [(1 + \rho)/(1 + r)]^k(G_1 - \bar{G}_1) - [(1 + \rho)/(1 + r)]^n(\bar{G}_1 + rb_0)[(Y_1 - \bar{Y}_1)/\bar{Y}_1] + \rho b_0$, or, in growth rate terms,

$$(b_1 - b_0)/b_0 \simeq [(1 + \rho)/(1 + r)]^k(G_1 - \bar{G}_1)/b_0$$
$$- [(1 + \rho)/(1 + r)]^n[(\bar{G}_1 + rb_0)/b_0][(Y_1 - \bar{Y}_1)/\bar{Y}_1] + \rho. \quad (7)$$

The growth rate of debt in equation (7) departs from the trend income growth rate, ρ, in accordance with the value of two variables. The first variable is the departure of current government spending from normal, $G_1 - \bar{G}_1$, relative to the initial debt level. The coefficient of this variable, $[(1 + \rho)/(1 + r)]^k$, would be unity if the "extra" expenditure were entirely transitory ($k = 0$), less than unity (since $r > \rho$) if the duration were finite, and would approach zero as k approaches infinity (in which case the gap between G_1 and $\bar{G}_1$ would not actually represent a departure of spending from normal). The second variable is the proportional deviation of income from normal, $(Y_1 - \bar{Y}_1)/\bar{Y}_1$, multiplied by the normal level of government expenditure (including interest payments on the initial debt) relative to the initial debt. The coefficient of this variable, $[(1 + \rho)/(1 + r)]^n$, would be unity if departures of income from normal (booms and recessions) were entirely transitory $(n = 0)$, less than unity if this duration were finite, and would approach zero as n approaches infinity. If k and n are viewed as constants—that is, if systematic effects on perceived duration of transitory government expenditure or transitory income cannot be isolated—then the principal hypotheses derivable from equation (7) are that the $(G_1 - \bar{G}_1)$ variable has a coefficient that is positive but less than one, while the $(Y_1 - \bar{Y}_1)/\bar{Y}_1$ variable has a coefficient that is negative but less than one in magnitude. If the durations are themselves on the order of 2–5 years (corresponding roughly to the periods of business cycles and wars) and if the excess of r over ρ is in a range of 1–2 percent per year, then the magnitude of both coefficients is close to one. For example, if $r = 5$ percent per year (recall that r is a real rate of return) and $\rho = 3.5$ percent per year, then a horizon (k or n) of 2 years implies a coefficient magnitude of 0.97, while a horizon of 5 years implies a coefficient magnitude of 0.93.[11]

The response of the deficit to the income term in equation (7) corresponds partly to the "automatic stabilizer" property of a tax system by which revenues rise and the deficit falls with income for a given set of tax laws.[12] These income-induced changes in tax revenues (and also in some components of federal expenditure) are, in principle, filtered out in the construction of a "full-employment surplus" (see U.S. Council of Economic Advisers [1962, pp. 78–81] for a discussion of this concept). However, the present analysis would also incorporate changes in the tax "structure"—which would usually be labeled as "discretionary" fiscal changes—that are a response to income fluctuations. Further, the present model rationalizes a system of tax laws that allows for an automatic procyclical pattern of revenues as a convenient mechanism for stabilizing the tax-income ratio. This

---

[11] The model can also be used to analyze the effect of anticipated future blips in government expenditure or income. Current taxes and, hence, the current deficit would be affected here only to the extent that these anticipated future departures from normal have a substantial duration. The effects can be illustrated by the $(\rho - \gamma)$ term in eq. (5) from the model in which the trend growth rates of Y (ρ) and G (γ) were unequal. The anticipation of higher future values of income relative to government spending when $\rho > \gamma$ implies less incentive for current taxation. Therefore, the current deficit increases with $\rho - \gamma$. Similarly, the expectation that future government expenditures—say, for social security benefits—will increase relative to income should stimulate current taxation and, hence, move the government budget toward surplus.

[12] Any automatic response of government expenditure to income would be held constant by the $G - \bar{G}$ term in eq. (7).

rationale derives here from efficiency in revenue generation and not from stabilization policy considerations.[13]

The result in equation (7) implies that the debt-income ratio would be expected to remain constant on average but would rise in periods of abnormally high government spending or abnormally low aggregate income. However, as was also true in the simpler model above, the analysis does not determine a target or steady-state debt-income ratio. The ratio at any time reflects only the accumulation of realized values of government expenditure relative to normal and income relative to normal, which would have zero mean, ex ante, but do not have to add to zero, ex post. There is no force that causes the ratio of debt to income to approach some target value, which would itself depend on underlying parameters of the model.

In a more general model there may be a wide range within which the debt-income ratio can vary essentially freely in accordance with the shocks shown in equation (7), but there may be some eventual limits that come into play. A limit on the high side would arise when the debt-income ratio rises sufficiently to affect the probability of the government's default (n. 3 above). On the low side, public and private debts may become less perfect substitutes in terms of liquidity characteristics, etc., as the quantity of government bonds diminishes. The implied net worth aspect of public debt—corresponding to some monopoly power for the government in the sale of bonds—would then prescribe a target lower bound for the debt-income ratio. However, a zero value for B does not constitute a necessary lower bound, even if the B concept is limited to financial net worth (thereby not considering the value of governmentally owned real capital). There is nothing in the present analysis that rules out the possibility of the government's becoming a net creditor to the private sector. The last time this possibility arose for the federal government in the United States was in 1835 when the national debt was entirely paid off and the government sought desperately (!) for outlets for its surplus (Dewey 1931, p. 221). Apparently, the sharp contraction of 1837 solved this problem.

Changes in Prices

This section extends the model to allow for changes in the price level. Such changes enter the analysis because the government debt, which still takes the form of a one-period bond, is assumed to pay interest and principal in fixed nominal terms. Governmental finance through

[13] McCallum and Whitaker (in press) argue for automatic stabilizers as a device for stabilizing the economy in an environment where information on aggregate variables becomes available only with a lag.

currency issue is not considered here, and any price changes that occur are treated as exogenous with respect to the division of governmental finance between debt and taxes.[14] I first consider unanticipated price changes and then deal with anticipated inflation.

A one-time unexpected change in the price level can be modeled by allowing the current price level, P_1, to differ from P_0. Expectations of future price levels are assumed at this point to be static at P_1—that is, $P_t = P_1$ for all $t = 1, 2, \ldots$. Letting B_t denote the stock of nominal debt outstanding at the end of period t, the government's budget constraint from equation (1) is now modified to

$$G_t + r(B_{t-1}/P_t) = \tau_t + (B_t - B_{t-1})/P_t, \qquad (1')$$

where G and τ are still in real terms, r is still assumed to be constant, and $P_t = P_1 \neq P_0$ for all $t = 1, \ldots$. The entire analysis from before carries through in this case with the interpretation of the "real initial debt," b_0, as B_0/P_1. Accordingly, in equation (7), the dependent variable is now the growth rate of nominal debt, $(B_1 - B_0)/B_0$. On the right-hand side the first variable becomes $P_1(G_1 - \bar{G}_1)/B_0$, while the second now involves the term, $(P_1\bar{G}_1 + rB_0)/B_0$. As the arbitrary length of the "period" becomes small, the difference in dating of the variables in these two expressions becomes unimportant. The principal result here is that one-time changes in the price level (or the current actual inflation rate in a continuous time setup) do not affect the change (growth rate) of the nominal debt. This conclusion should be somewhat surprising, since one-time changes in the price level do alter the ratio of (real) debt to (real) income. If the model determined a steady-state value of the debt-income ratio, a shift in the actual ratio would have temporary effects on the government deficit. These effects do not arise here because the model does not, in fact, determine this sort of steady-state ratio.

To model anticipated inflation, suppose now that prices are expected to change at the constant rate π—that is, $P_t = P_0(1 + \pi)^t$. The nominal interest rate is given by $R \equiv r + \pi$. Although it is not crucial for present purposes, I assume that the real rate of interest, r, is invariant with inflation.[15] The previous analysis of the choice of taxes over time goes through completely in terms of real variables— *including* r. The only amendment to the previous analysis is that the

---

[14] As with the invariance of the rate of return, this assumption would be valid as a first-order proposition if government bonds were not perceived as net wealth by the private sector.

[15] Some theoretical—basically indeterminate—analysis of this issue is surveyed in Barro and Fischer (1976, sec. 3). If interest payments are subject to tax at rate θ, then the after-tax real rate of return is $\hat{r} = R(1 - \theta) - \pi$. Independence of $\hat{r}$ from π requires $R = (\hat{r} + \pi)/(1 - \theta)$, so that R would have to move more than one to one with π in this circumstance.

government budget constraint in equation (1') must be modified to reflect the distinction between the nominal and real interest rate—that is, the new specification is

$$G_t + R(B_{t-1}/P_t) = \tau_t + (B_t - B_{t-1})/P_t, \qquad (1'')$$

where $R \equiv r + \pi$. With taxes already set at the value determined in the preceding analysis (where $\pi = 0$), it follows that the "extra part" of current interest payments, $\pi(B_{t-1}/P_t)$, is financed entirely by extra issue of nominal debt. Equivalently, the growth rate of nominal debt, $(B_t - B_{t-1})/B_{t-1}$, is raised by the amount π—an amount that is just sufficient to offset the expected effect of price changes on the real value of the outstanding stock of debt. Therefore, the incorporation of the anticipated inflation effect into equation (7) yields the revised expression for the growth rate of nominal debt,

$$
\begin{aligned}
(B_1 - B_0)/B_0 = {} & [(1 + \rho)/(1 + r)]^k P_1 (G_1 - \bar{G}_1)/B_0 \\
& - [(1 + \rho)/(1 + r)]^n [(P_1 \bar{G}_1 + r B_0)/B_0][(Y_1 - \bar{Y}_1)/\bar{Y}_1] + \rho + \pi.
\end{aligned}
\qquad (8)
$$

Accordingly, the nominal government debt grows, ceteris paribus, at the trend growth rate of nominal income, $\rho + \pi$. Note especially that it is the expected inflation rate, π, and not the actual rate that influences the growth rate of nominal debt. The effects of the transitory government expenditure and income variables in equation (8) are the same as those discussed above.

Changes in the Rate of Return—Market versus Par Value of Government Debt

Abstracting for convenience from price-level changes, suppose now that the current rate of return on the one-period government debt, r, differs from that applicable in the previous period, r_0. It is assumed that anticipated rates of return for future periods are still equal to the current rate, r. In the case of the one-period debt that is being considered, the government's budget condition of equation (1) is now modified to

$$G_1 + r_0 b_0 = \tau_1 + (b_1 - b_0),$$
$$G_t + r b_{t-1} = \tau_t + (b_t - b_{t-1}), \quad t = 2, \dots, \qquad (1''')$$

where the b's refer throughout to the real par (initial) value of debt. These conditions can be shown to imply that the overall budget constraint is altered from the form of equation (3) to

$$\sum_1^\infty [G_t/(1 + r)^t] + b_0(1 + r_0)/(1 + r) = \sum_1^\infty [\tau_t/(1 + r)^t]. \qquad (3')$$

The budget constraint now involves the market value of the initial debt, $b_0^* = b_0(1 + r_0)/(1 + r)$, which is expressed as a present value at date 0 by means of the date 1 discount rate. Equation (3′) can be used to solve out for taxation over time, taking into account the constancy of the tax-income ratio in the optimal solution. The result is that the previous analysis goes through if all debt variables instead of being measured at par value are measured in terms of market value. Each market value is expressed as a present value at the corresponding date by means of the date 1 discount rate, r. (Note that the market value of debt at date 1, b_1^*, is equal to b_1 for the case of one-period debt.) It is important to stress that the modified "deficit" variable that emerges from these calculations, $b_1^* - b_0^*$, is not the change in the market value of debt as it would customarily be measured, but rather the difference in market value with the current discount rate, r, used in the calculations for *both* date 1 and date 0.

For the case of one-period, single-coupon debt, the solution can readily be expressed in terms of par values. Ignoring the temporary government expenditure and income variables and for the case where the trend growth rates of G and Y are equal (and where $\pi = 0$), the result is

$$(b_1 - b_0)/b_0 = \rho - (r - r_0)\left(\frac{1 + \rho}{1 + r}\right). \tag{9}$$

When r exceeds r_0, the market value b_0^* is below the par value b_0. Therefore, the achievement of a given change in the market value of debt requires a smaller value of b_1. Hence, the growth rate of debt measured at par value is related inversely to the change in the rate of return, $r - r_0$. Although the analysis is complicated by the inclusion of the temporary spending and income variables, it seems that this effect of the interest-rate change is the main new implication for the case of one-period debt.

In the empirically relevant situation where government debt exists with different maturity dates and various coupons, the main part of the analysis continues to go through. In particular, equation (3′) still holds in terms of the market value of the initial debt b_0^*, again expressed as a present value at date 0 by means of the date 1 discount rate, r. However, the formula for b_0^* is substantially more complicated than that shown in equation (3′). It remains true that all previous results on debt issue apply with the debt variables measured in market-value terms—expressed as present values at the corresponding date with r used as the discount rate. The difficulty arises in relating the market-value results, which involve complicated formulae for determining bond values, to the readily accessible figures on debt at par value. For the case of perpetual coupon bonds, where $b_0^* =$

$(r_0/r)b_0$, $b_1^* = b_1 - b_0 + (r_0/r)b_0$, with r_0 now interpreted as the average coupon rate on initially outstanding debt, the result in terms of par values is $(b_1 - b_0)/b_0 = \rho\,(r_0/r)$. The conclusion is again that an increase in r above r_0 reduces the growth rate of debt when expressed in terms of par values. However, the effect now depends on a positive value of ρ, since the amount of debt (at par or market value) would remain constant if $\rho = 0$.[16] Further, the relevant comparison is now between r and an average of rates applying to the outstanding debt, and the ratio, r_0/r, appears instead of the difference, $r - r_0$.

It seems that in the general case r would have to be compared with a complicated "average" value of past interest rates that took account of both quantities and maturities of the existing stock of debt. An additional complication arises in using par value figures when some portion of the debt is not issued at par. In any case the basic result from this section is that an increase in r above the average of preceding rates would reduce the growth rate of debt when measured in terms of par values.

Empirical Analysis

An interesting way to test the theory would be to examine directly the hypothesis that the planned tax-income ratio was constant. Since changes in this ratio should then reflect only new information about the time path of government expenditures, etc., the theory has the implication that changes in tax rates should be unpredictable from knowledge of any lagged variables, including prior changes in rates. An approach for testing this type of hypothesis was developed for analogous propositions about consumption in Hall (1978). The approach has obvious analogues to tests of efficient-markets hypotheses. I plan to explore this research avenue at a later time, but the present empirical investigation is limited to hypotheses and tests that directly concern public debt movements.

Setup of the Analysis

The form of the systematic part of the empirical equation to be applied to annual observations is derived from equation (8) as

$$\log (B_t/B_{t-1}) = \alpha_0 + \alpha_1\pi_t + \alpha_2[P_t(G_t - \bar{G}_t)/\bar{B}_t]$$
$$- \alpha_3[\log (Y_t/\bar{Y}_t)(P_t\bar{G}_t + r\bar{B}_t)/\bar{B}_t], \quad (10)$$

---

[16] Some effects would arise from the temporary government spending and income variables even when $\rho = 0$.

where B_t is the stock of nominal debt at the end of calendar year t, $\bar{B}_t$ is the average amount of debt outstanding during year t, π_t is the average anticipated rate of inflation during year t, P_t is the average price level for year t, G_t is real federal government expenditure (aside from interest payments) during year t, Y_t is aggregate real income (GNP) for year t, and $\bar{Y}_t$ is the level of normal income during year t. From the perspective of equation (8), the assumption that the α-coefficients in equation (10) are constant amounts to neglecting variations in the growth rate ρ, real interest rate r, and the durations of temporary government expenditure and income (k and n). The theory has the following implications for the coefficients. (1) α_0: This coefficient would equal the growth rate, ρ, if real income and government expenditure grow at the same rate. However, if government expenditures are expected to grow faster than income for some period, there would be a downward effect on the constant as indicated in a general way from the $(\rho - \gamma)$ term in equation (5).[17] (2) α_1: This coefficient should equal unity—the anticipated rate of inflation has a one-to-one effect on the growth rate of nominal debt. (3) α_2: This coefficient corresponds to $[(1 + \rho)/(1 + r)]^k$ in equation (8), which is below but close to unity. An interval of something like (0.8, 1.0) would appear to be a reasonable implication of the theory. (4) α_3: This coefficient corresponds to $[(1 + \rho)/(1 + r)]^n$ in equation (8), which is also below but close to unity. Again, an interval of something like (0.8, 1.0) appears reasonable.

The model implies also that certain variables would be irrelevant for the growth rate of public debt. In particular, the level of the outstanding stock of debt—relative, say, to the trend value of income—is excluded from equation (8). This proposition is tested by adding the variable, $B_{t-1}/(P_{t-1}\bar{Y}_{t-1})$—the previous year's ratio of real debt to normal real income—to the estimating equation. The theory also stresses the role of temporary government expenditure rather than the level of spending. (See, however, n. 17 above for a possible effect of the level.) Hence, the effect of a variable like $P_t\bar{G}_t/\bar{B}_t$—normal government spending relative to the stock of debt—is worth examining.

Measures of Variables

The present analysis considers evidence on the determination of public debt in the United States since 1917. I hope to extend the investigation to earlier dates but have encountered some data prob-

[17] An additional variable, $P_t\bar{G}_t/\bar{B}_t$, could be added to eq. (10) to pick up this effect. However, this variable is not significant in any of the empirical analysis (see below).

lems. One minor difficulty is that the available public debt data before 1916 refer to fiscal years, whereas the rest of the analysis is on a calendar-year basis. A more serious problem arises in the measurement of anticipated inflation (see below), which causes difficulties even for the post-1916 period.

The quantity of nominal debt, B, is measured as the outstanding stock of interest-bearing federal debt at par value in the hands of the "public" at the end of each calendar year.[18] In particular, the figures net out holdings of debt by the Federal Reserve, Social Security Administration, etc. I have not carried out the computations that would be required to adjust the par value measures for changes in rates of return, as discussed above. (Note that a market-value series, even if it were available, would not be the appropriate construct for present purposes.) The earlier analysis suggests that a change-in-interest-rate variable should then be added to equation (10). However, a proper measure of this variable would entail the construction of an appropriate average coupon rate on outstanding debt. Since this variable has not yet been constructed, I have limited consideration to the variable, $RG_t - RG_{t-1}$, where RG is an index of the interest rate on government bonds. Although there is a hint in the empirical results that this variable enters in the hypothesized manner, it turns out to be statistically insignificant and quantitatively unimportant. I am uncertain whether refinement of the measurement of this variable would materially affect the results.

The $\bar{B}_t$ variable, which scales the values of $G - \bar{G}$ and $\log (Y/\bar{Y})$ in equation (10), is measured as $\sqrt{B_t \cdot B_{t-1}}$. Since this construction introduces B_t into the right-hand side of equation (10), I have carried out the estimation using as instruments the values of the $G - \bar{G}$ and $\log (Y/\bar{Y})$ variables with B_{t-1} used instead of $\bar{B}_t$ as a scaling factor. It turns out that ordinary least-squares estimates differ negligibly from these instrumental estimates.

---

[18] See the notes to table 3 below for details on the public debt variable. The definition includes fully guaranteed securities that were issued by some New Deal agencies. These amounts are significant for 1934–44. Debt held by federal agencies and trust funds (but not by federally sponsored private corporations) and the Federal Reserve have been netted out. Non-interest-bearing components of government debt are excluded throughout. No adjustments have been made for government acquisitions of real capital or claims on the private sector or foreigners. Governmental "liability" for future social security benefits or other payments has not been included in the definition of public debt. It seems that expected future social security benefits and governmental acquisitions of capital, etc., would enter the present analysis as they affected the anticipated future value of federal expenditures or receipts. E.g., the anticipation of rapid growth in an expenditure component, such as social security benefits, would enter the analysis as indicated in n. 11 above. Expenditures on large capital projects, which are likely to represent a blip in spending, would tend to be mostly deficit financed.

For the 1948–76 period I have constructed an expected rate-of-inflation variable, π, based on the estimated equation for the GNP deflator in an earlier study of mine (1978). This variable, which refers to the expected rate of change of the GNP deflator over a 1-year horizon, is tabulated in table 1 and is discussed in detail in the notes to that table. I do not presently have an analysis of price determination before 1948 to use for the construction of the π-variable. (The World War II price controls cause difficulty for the years immediately prior to 1948.) For the 1948–76 period it turns out that a long-term interest-rate variable proxies satisfactorily for π. Specifically, the estimated after-tax nominal rate on corporate bonds, $R(1 - \theta)$, where θ is an estimate of the tax rate,[19] would measure the anticipated rate of inflation (up to a constant) over the average period of the bonds if the anticipated after-tax real rate of return were fixed.[20] This interest-rate variable is available also for the pre-1948 period, but the assumption of a constant anticipated real rate of return over the entire 1917–76 sample is doubtful. Specifically, the nominal yields (see table 1) relative to actual price changes during the interwar period are much higher than those since 1941. The likely anticipated deflation after World War I is, in particular, not captured by the interest-rate variable for 1919–21. I have presently used the $R(1 - \theta)$ variable for the 1922–76 sample but have included a dummy variable for the 1922–40 years to allow for a different (presumably higher) anticipated real rate of return over that period. I have not included the 1917–21 years in the main analysis, although extrapolations of the estimates to those years are examined. The present procedure for measuring π before 1948 is obviously not satisfactory, and I hope to construct a more appropriate variable, especially for the planned extension of the analysis to the pre–World War I period.[21]

I have based my measurement of normal real federal expenditure, $\bar{G}$, on the variable that worked satisfactorily in my previous studies of

[19] I have calculated this rate as the ratio of federal plus state and local personal income tax payments to personal income, although this measure may underestimate the average marginal rate for bondholders.

[20] Replacing $R(1 - \theta)$ by R produces a negligible change in the results. The government bond rate, RG, yields basically similar results. A short-term interest-rate variable—specifically, that on prime commercial paper—was insignificant when used instead of a long-term rate as a proxy for π in the government debt equation. A likely interpretation is that variations in anticipated real rates of return are important in the short-term rate.

[21] I have not attempted to calculate the π variable as a distributed lag of actual rates of price change. That type of relation would seem much different over a gold standard regime (1880–1914 and, to a lesser extent, 1919–33) as compared with a fiat money regime. The distributed lag of inflation approach fails especially in episodes like 1919–21, where experience appears to be dominated by a return to normal levels of prices rather than a continuation of past rates of price change.

TABLE 1

VALUES OF INDEPENDENT VARIABLES

	π	$R(1-\theta)$	log $(Y/\bar{Y})$	$P\bar{G}/\bar{B}$	$P(G-\bar{G})/\bar{B}$	$\dfrac{P\bar{G}\cdot\log\ (Y/\bar{Y})}{\bar{B}}$	$G/\bar{Y}$
1916	...	.045	−.051	...	...	...	.016
1917	...	.045	−.070	.75	1.908	−.052	.102
1918	...	.054	.021	.29	1.218	.006	.230
1919	...	.054	−.040	.21	.312	−.009	.142
1920	...	.060	−.110	.24	−.021	−.026	.053
1921	...	.059	−.226	.21	−.022	−.049	.052
1922	...	.050	−.104	.21	−.060	−.021	.039
1923	...	.051	−.015	.21	−.061	−.003	.037
1924	...	.050	−.042	.21	−.063	−.009	.034
1925	...	.048	.013	.22	−.059	.003	.034
1926	...	.047	.050	.22	−.062	.011	.033
1927	...	.045	.020	.23	−.059	.005	.032
1928	...	.045	.000	.25	−.053	.000	.033
1929	...	.047	.040	.25	−.084	.010	.026
1930	...	.045	−.084	.25	−.061	−.021	.028
1931	...	.045	−.189	.24	.034	−.045	.046
1932	...	.050	−.363	.20	−.013	−.073	.038
1933	...	.044	−.409	.18	.018	−.075	.048
1934	...	.040	−.359	.19	.081	−.070	.068
1935	...	.036	−.298	.18	.050	−.055	.067
1936	...	.032	−.196	.19	.086	−.037	.087
1937	...	.032	−.176	.20	.019	−.035	.068
1938	...	.031	−.243	.21	.037	−.050	.079
1939	...	.030	−.195	.21	.028	−.041	.081
1940	...	.028	−.148	.22	.032	−.032	.086
1941	...	.027	−.029	.24	.192	−.007	.159
1942	...	.027	.082	.26	.536	.021	.385
1943	...	.024	.206	.23	.503	.048	.549
1944	...	.024	.253	.23	.350	.057	.585
1945	...	.023	.214	.22	.179	.048	.493
1946	...	.023	.033	.23	−.070	.008	.175
1947	...	.023	−.022	.26	−.110	−.006	.125
1948	−.002	.026	−.017	.27	−.092	−.004	.133
1949	−.002	.025	−.046	.27	−.057	−.012	.153
1950	.002	.024	.002	.27	−.060	.001	.143
1951	.022	.026	.044	.30	−.007	.013	.187
1952	.027	.026	.046	.33	.029	.016	.215
1953	.038	.028	.049	.36	.029	.018	.221
1954	.019	.026	.001	.37	−.026	.000	.191
1955	.024	.027	.030	.38	−.048	.011	.176
1956	.015	.030	.016	.41	−.052	.007	.174
1957	.010	.035	−.002	.45	−.043	−.001	.180
1958	.010	.034	−.039	:47	−.026	−.018	.190
1959	.019	.039	−.016	.48	−.039	−.008	.184
1960	.020	.039	−.029	.50	−.051	−.014	.179
1961	.013	.039	−.039	.52	−.034	−.021	.187
1962	.022	.038	−.019	.54	−.024	−.010	.192
1963	.009	.038	−.015	.57	−.037	−.009	.189
1964	.014	.040	.001	.59	−.046	.000	.186
1965	.018	.040	.023	.62	−.053	.014	.184

95⁸

TABLE 1 *(Continued)*

| | | log | | | $P\bar{G}\cdot\log (Y/\bar{Y})$ | |
	π	$R(1-\theta)$	$(Y/\bar{Y})$	$P\bar{G}/\bar{B}$	$P(G-\bar{G})/\bar{B}$	$\bar{B}$	$G/\bar{Y}$
1966	.026	.046	.045	.68	−.011	.030	.199
1967	.030	.049	.036	.74	.015	.027	.213
1968	.029	.054	.044	.80	.015	.035	.217
1969	.035	.061	.034	.87	−.029	.030	.208
1970	.041	.070	−.005	.96	−.047	−.005	.207
1971	.050	.065	−.011	.99	−.058	−.011	.205
1972	.062	.063	.010	1.00	−.034	.010	.211
1973	.061	.065	.027	1.07	−.055	.029	.220
1974	.061	.075	−.025	1.21	−.078	−.030	.207
1975	.060	.078	−.079	1.20	−.032	−.095	.218
1976	.062	.074	−.055	1.08	−.044	−.059	.217

NOTE.—$\pi_t \equiv \log (P_{t+1}) - \log (P_t)$, where $\log (P_{t+1})$ and $\log (P_t)$ are predicted and estimated values, respectively, of the GNP deflator from the equation in Barro (1978, eq. 13). These calculations are based on lagged values of money growth and the unemployment rate and on contemporaneous values of the interest rate and federal spending. R from 1919 is Moody's Aaa index of corporate bond rates and for 1916–18 is the average of Durand's yield on 10- and 20-year bonds, adjusted by +.0048 to conform with the overlap for 1919–21 (U.S. Council of Economic Advisers 1977, p. 260; U.S. Bureau of the Census 1975, pp. 1003–4). θ is the ratio of federal plus state and local personal income tax payments to personal income (U.S. Council of Economic Advisers 1977, p. 210; U.S. Department of Commerce 1976, pp. 97, 108, 334, 340–41, July 1977, pp. 31, 32, and 1973, p. 188; U.S. Bureau of the Census 1975, p. 1107). Y is real GNP (1972 base) and P is the GNP deflator (1972=1.0) from U.S. Council of Economic Advisers (1977, pp. 188, 190); U.S. Department of Commerce (1976, pp. 324, 349). Figures before 1929 are based on data from ibid. 1973, series A1, p. 182 and series B61, p. 222. Log $(\bar{Y})$ is a trend value of real GNP, calculated as 1946–76: $2.985 + .0354 \cdot t$, 1915–45: $3.912 + .0250 \cdot t$, 1880–1914: $3.291 + .0359 \cdot t$, where t is time with 1858=1. G is nominal total federal expenditure divided by the GNP deflator. Expenditure data are from U.S. Council of Economic Advisers (1977, p. 270). Data before 1929 are from Firestone (1960, table A-3). $\bar{B}_t \equiv \sqrt{B_t \cdot B_{t-1}}$.

money growth (1977, 1978). This variable is a distributed lag of total real federal spending using an adaptation coefficient of 0.2 per year. The variable has been modified here to take account of the long-term growth rate of real federal spending, which is estimated as 5.6 percent per year—the average growth rate from 1860 to 1976. Presumably, this measurement could be improved by relating the concept of normal spending to the actual time-series behavior of the federal spending series. Another problem is that the variable includes government interest payments as a part of government expenditure. This inclusion would be unimportant for the calculation of $G - \bar{G}$ in equation (10) but would have some effect on the last term in the equation, which involves the expression, $P\bar{G} + r\bar{B}$. Essentially, it is only the real interest rate part of government interest payments that should be included as a part of real government expenditure (see above). The portion of interest payments, $\pi\bar{B}$, that reflects anticipated inflation corresponds also to finance by issue of nominal debt at rate π. These payments play no role in influencing taxes, etc., and should be excluded from the term in equation (10). Since I believe this consideration to be quantitatively unimportant in terms of the manner it enters into equation (10), I have not attempted to adjust government expenditure by eliminating a portion of interest payments.

The departure of income from normal, $\log (Y/\bar{Y})$, is calculated for the 1946–76 period from my previous (1978) analysis of output (real GNP). Log $(\bar{Y}_t)$ is calculated along the trend line, with a growth rate of 3.54 percent per year, that is implied by that analysis. I have also calculated a pure trend relation for real GNP over the 1880–1914 period, which reveals a strikingly similar growth rate of 3.59 percent per year. From 1915 to 1945 (for lack of a better procedure), I connected the fitted trend values for real GNP from 1914 and 1946 along a constant growth line, which implied an average growth rate of 2.50 percent per year.[22] The values of $\log (Y/\bar{Y})$ are indicated, along with the values of the $P\bar{G} \cdot \log (Y/\bar{Y})$ variable, in table 1.

Finally, the P variable is measured by the average value of the GNP deflator for the year.

Empirical Results

Table 2 describes the estimates of equation (10) for various sample periods. Although there is an indication that the error variance during World War II (1941–47 sample) exceeds that before 1941 (1922–40), which exceeds that of the recent period (1948–76), I have presently dealt only with unweighted regressions. The Durbin-Watson statistics suggest absence of serial correlation in the residuals. Further, if a lagged dependent variable, DB_{t-1}, is added to the equation its estimated coefficient differs insignificantly from zero over all sample periods.

Estimates are shown in table 2 with the coefficient of the expected inflation variable (π for 1948–76 or the $R[1 - \theta]$ variable for all sample periods) unrestricted and with this coefficient restricted to equal unity. The unrestricted estimates of this coefficient differ insignificantly from one at the 5 percent level in all cases. For example, for the 1948–76 period the estimated π-coefficient is 1.12, SE = 0.22; while that on $R(1 - \theta)$ is 1.32, SE = 0.25. A comparison of results based on the π and $R(1 - \theta)$ variables for this sample suggests that the interest-rate variable is a satisfactory proxy for anticipated inflation. However, as noted above, this outcome for the post-1948 period does not guarantee the appropriateness of the interest-rate variable for earlier years. For the 1922–76 sample the estimate of the $R(1 - \theta)$ coefficient is 1.44, SE = 0.28, while that for the 1922–40, 1948–76 sample is 1.31, SE = 0.27. Again, these estimates do not differ

---

[22] In other words, although the post–World War II growth rate of output coincides with that from 1880–1914, the position of real GNP implied by the 1880–1914 trend line has not been reattained after the Great Depression and World War II.

TABLE 2

ESTIMATED PUBLIC DEBT GROWTH-RATE EQUATIONS

(SEs in Parentheses)

Sample	Constant	Pre-1941 Dummy	π	$R(1-\theta)$	$P(G-\bar{G})$ $\bar{B}$	$P\bar{G}\cdot\log(Y/\bar{Y})$ $\bar{B}$	R^2	D-W	$\hat{\sigma}$	SSE
1948–76	.011(.010)	...	1.12(.22)	...	.61(.16)	−1.75(.17)	.87	1.8	.022	.0124
1948–76	.015(.007)	...	1.0	...	.62(.15)	−1.77(.16)	.87	1.7	.022	.0125
1948–76	−.011(.013)	...	...	1.32(.25)	.77(.15)	−1.69(.17)	.88	1.8	.022	.0117
1948–76	.003(.007)	...	...	1.0	.76(.15)	−1.77(.16)	.87	1.6	.022	.0125
1941–76	.002(.013)	...	...	1.26(.29)	1.02(.03)	−1.78(.19)	.97	2.1	.026	.0224
1941–76	.012(.004)	...	...	1.0	1.02(.03)	−1.84(.18)	.97	2.1	.026	.0230
1922–76	−.006(.012)	−.058(.009)	...	1.44(.28)	1.01(.03)	−1.62(.14)	.95	2.2	.028	.0389
1922–76	.012(.005)	−.059(.009)	...	1.0	.99(.03)	−1.67(.14)	.95	2.1	.028	.0407
1922–40, 1948–76	−.010(.012)	−.054(.008)	...	1.31(.27)	.78(.10)	−1.75(.14)	.89	2.0	.025	.0260
1922–40, 1948–76	.002(.006)	−.056(.008)	...	1.0	.74(.09)	−1.79(.14)	.89	1.9	.025	.0269
1922–40	−.070(.059)	...	...	1.32(1.56)	.71(.33)	−1.92(.46)	.90	2.2	.031	.0141
1922–40	−.059(.015)	...	...	1.0	.66(.20)	−1.97(.39)	.90	2.2	.030	.0142
1941–47	−.59(.72)	...	...	26(29)	.83(.25)	−0.40(2.00)	.98	3.0	.048	.0068
1941–47	.017(.027)	...	...	1.0	1.02(.10)	−1.91(.90)	.97	3.1	.048	.0092
1922–29	−.20(.42)	...	...	3.2(9.2)	−.01(1.70)	−0.83(2.04)	.22	3.1	.037	.0054
1922–29	−.109(.092)	...	...	1.0	−.15(1.45)	−1.18(1.27)	.19	3.1	.033	.0056
1930–40	−.077(.067)	...	...	1.3(2.1)	.70(.37)	−2.09(.82)	.79	1.8	.033	.0076
1930–40	−.069(.028)	...	...	1.0	.67(.25)	−2.17(.57)	.79	1.8	.031	.0077

NOTE.—The dependent variable for each regression is $DB_t \equiv \log(B_t) - \log(B_{t-1})$. Variables are tabulated and defined in table 1. Equations with 1.0 indicated in the π or $R(1-\theta)$ column have the value of this coefficient constrained to equal one. D-W is the Durbin-Watson statistic, $\hat{\sigma}$ is the standard error of estimate, SSE is the error sum of squares.

significantly from one at the 5 percent level. Since the theoretical value of unity is in accord with these results, and since an (appropriate) restriction of this coefficient would sharpen the remaining analysis, I focus the subsequent discussion on the restricted form of the government debt equation.

The 1922–76 and 1922–40, 1948–76 samples indicate a significantly negative coefficient for a pre-1941 dummy variable with a magnitude of 0.05–0.06 per year. From the perspective of the $R(1 - \theta)$ variable as an expected inflation-rate proxy, the interpretation would be that the average anticipated (after-tax) real rate of return before 1941 was higher by 0.05–0.06 per year than that after 1941. Clearly, the interpretation could also be that other factors reduced the average growth rate of nominal debt before 1941 by 0.05–0.06 per year (or by some part of that amount) below that of the post-1941 period. Without a direct measure of anticipated inflation it is not possible to compare the constant term before 1941 with that of the later years. However, this difficulty does not prevent a comparison of the other coefficients across the different samples.

With the inclusion of the pre-1941 dummy variable, the hypothesis of a stable set of coefficients across the various sample periods is accepted. That is, the empirical evidence is in accord with a single set of coefficients for the temporary government expenditure and income variables. The following F-tests (with 5 percent critical values shown in parentheses)[23] arise for tests of the common coefficient hypothesis for the indicated samples and for cases where the coefficient of the $R(1 - \theta)$ variable is restricted to equal unity. (The results are similar in cases where the $R(1 - \theta)$ coefficient is unrestricted.)

1941–47; 1948–76: $F_{30}^3 = 0.6$ (2.9),
1922–40; 1948–76: $F_{42}^2 = 0.0$ (3.2),
1922–40; 1941–47; 1948–76: $F_{46}^5 = 1.2$ (2.4),
1922–29; 1930–40: $F_{13}^3 = 0.3$ (3.4).

Hence, the results are consistent with the hypothesis that the response of government debt to temporary movements in government spending or in aggregate income has been stable since 1922. The results are also consistent with a single constant over the 1922–29 and 1930–40 subsamples and over the 1941–47 and 1948–76 subsamples.

For the case where the $R(1 - \theta)$ variable is employed with a coefficient restricted to unity and for the 1922–40, 1948–76 sample, the estimated coefficient of the temporary federal spending variable,

---

[23] Heteroscedasticity across the different subperiods would have some effect on these F-values.

$P(G - \bar{G})/\bar{B}$, is 0.78, SE = 0.10. Over the World War II sample, 1941–47, the estimated coefficient is 1.02, SE = 0.10, which dominates the overall sample (1922–76) estimate, 1.01, SE = 0.03. These estimates are in accord with the underlying hypothesis of a coefficient in an interval of roughly (0.8, 1.0). A lagged value of the $G - \bar{G}$ variable is insignificant when added to the debt equation.

It is worth noting from table 1 that the constructed $G - \bar{G}$ variable, which incorporates a trend growth rate of 5.6 percent per year, is negative except for wartime years (1917–19, 1941–45, 1952–53, 1967–68) and the period of rapid government expansion during the Great Depression (1931 and 1933–40). The temporary government spending variable can average to zero, ex ante, only if expenditure bulges associated with large wars are offset by a much larger number of years with small negative values. Hence, the typical peacetime value (1920–30 and 1946–76 except for 1952–53 and 1967–68 in the present sample) shows a negative value of the $G - \bar{G}$ variable, which produces a declining, rather than a constant, debt-income ratio as the normal peacetime pattern. In this respect the ratio of debt to normal income, as shown in table 3, declined from a peak value of 0.29 in 1919 to a trough of 0.15 in 1930 (before rising during the Depression), and declined from a peak value of 1.33 in 1945 to a trough of 0.19 in 1974 (before rising slightly to 0.23 in 1976). The basic pattern of peacetime decline in the debt-income ratio appears similar after the two world wars, although the starting ratio is much lower in 1919 than in 1945, and the period following World War I contains a much smaller number of non-Depression, peacetime years than that following World War II. The period following the Civil War seems to exhibit the same general pattern as that following the two world wars. The peak debt–nominal income ratio (based on June figures for the public debt) was about 0.25 in 1866 and declined from there over a long, almost entirely peacetime period to a trough of 0.02 in 1916. The $G - \bar{G}$ variable, as measured in the present analysis, would be negative throughout the 1866–1916 period except for a small positive value in 1892 and for the years of the Spanish-American War, 1898–99.

The estimated coefficient of the temporary income variable, log $(Y/\bar{Y}) \cdot P\bar{G}/\bar{B}$, over the 1922–76 sample is -1.67, SE = 0.14. (A lagged value of this variable is insignificant if added to the equation.) The estimated coefficient of the log $(Y/\bar{Y})$ variable significantly exceeds in magnitude the value, 1.0, that appears as the upper limit of the ex ante interval on this coefficient. Hence, there is an indication that the magnitude of typical countercyclical debt response has exceeded the amount that would be dictated purely from efficient public finance considerations. There is, however, no indication that this

TABLE 3

Actual and Estimated Values of Public Debt

	1922–76 Equation, $R(1-\theta)$ Coefficient = 1			1948–76 Equation, π-Coefficient = 1			
	DB (1)	$\hat{DB}$ (2)	DBR (3)	$\hat{DB}$ (4)	DBR (5)	B (6)	$B/(\bar{Y}\cdot P)$ (7)
1916	...	...	...	...	...	.91	.02
1917	2.040	(1.976)	(.065)	...	...	7.0	.11
1918	1.075	(1.203)	(−1.29)	...	...	20.5	.26
1919	.166	(.331)	(−.165)	...	...	24.2	.29
1920	−.038	(.036)	(−.074)	...	...	23.3	.24
1921	−.039	(.071)	(−.110)	...	...	22.4	.27
1922	−.036	−.020	−.017	...	...	21.6	.26
1923	−.038	−.051	.014	...	...	20.8	.24
1924	−.049	−.045	−.004	...	...	19.8	.23
1925	.000	−.062	.062	...	...	19.8	.22
1926	−.112	−.080	−.032	...	...	17.7	.19
1927	−.064	−.067	.003	...	...	16.6	.18
1928	−.049	−.054	.005	...	...	15.8	.16
1929	−.059	−.101	.042	...	...	14.9	.15
1930	−.007	−.027	.020	...	...	14.8	.15
1931	.084	.107	−.023	...	...	16.1	.18
1932	.123	.111	.012	...	...	18.2	.22
1933	.162	.142	.020	...	...	21.4	.26
1934	.167	.189	−.022	...	...	25.3	.27
1935	.177	.131	.046	...	...	30.2	.31
1936	.104	.132	−.028	...	...	33.5	.33
1937	.029	.062	−.033	...	...	34.5	.32
1938	.043	.105	−.062	...	...	36.0	.33
1939	.070	.079	−.009	...	...	38.6	.35
1940	.072	.066	.006	...	...	41.5	.36
1941	.245	.242	.003	...	...	53.0	.41
1942	.583	.536	.047	...	...	94.9	.65
1943	.407	.454	−.047	...	...	142.6	.91
1944	.301	.288	.012	...	...	192.6	1.18
1945	.170	.133	.036	...	...	228.2	1.33
1946	−.097	−.047	−.050	...	...	207.2	1.02
1947	−.030	−.064	.034	...	...	201.0	.84
1948	−.038	−.046	.008	−.037	−.001	193.6	.74
1949	.035	.001	.034	−.001	.035	200.4	.74
1950	−.014	−.024	.010	−.021	.007	197.6	.69
1951	−.018	.008	−.027	.009	−.027	194.0	.61
1952	.019	.041	−.022	.033	−.014	197.7	.60
1953	.019	.040	−.021	.040	−.021	201.5	.58
1954	.013	.012	.001	.017	−.004	204.1	.56
1955	.000	−.027	.026	−.011	.011	204.0	.53
1956	−.029	−.020	−.010	−.013	−.016	198.1	.48
1957	−.011	.006	−.017	.000	−.011	195.9	.44
1958	.033	.051	−.019	.041	−.009	202.4	.43
1959	.035	.025	.009	.024	.011	209.6	.42
1960	−.014	.025	−.039	.029	−.043	206.6	.40
1961	.022	.052	−.029	.044	−.021	211.3	.39
1962	.018	.044	−.026	.040	−.021	215.2	.37
1963	.006	.028	−.022	.016	−.011	216.4	.36
1964	.008	.006	.002	−.001	.008	218.1	.34

964

TABLE 3 (Continued)

	1922–76 Equation, $R(1-\theta)$ Coefficient=1			1948–76 Equation, π-Coefficient=1			
	DB (1)	$\widehat{DB}$ (2)	DBR (3)	$\widehat{DB}$ (4)	DBR (5)	B (6)	$B/(\bar{Y}\cdot P)$ (7)
1965	−.009	−.023	.014	−.025	.016	216.1	.32
1966	−.006	−.004	−.001	−.021	.015	214.9	.30
1967	.018	.031	−.013	.006	.012	218.9	.29
1968	.030	.023	.007	−.009	.039	225.6	.27
1969	−.025	−.005	−.020	−.021	−.004	220.0	.24
1970	.036	.044	−.008	.035	.001	228.0	.23
1971	.076	.038	.038	.048	.028	246.1	.23
1972	.057	.025	.032	.038	.019	260.5	.22
1973	−.003	−.027	.023	−.011	.007	259.6	.20
1974	.039	.060	−.021	.081	−.042	269.9	.19
1975	.255	.217	.038	.224	.032	348.4	.21
1976	.159	.141	.018	.154	.006	408.5	.23

Sources.—From 1916 to 1938, Board of Governors of the Federal Reserve System 1943, pp. 509–12 and issues of the *Federal Reserve Bulletin* (for holdings by the Federal Reserve). From 1939 to 1976, U.S. Council of Economic Advisers 1970, p. 255, 1976, p. 253, 1977, pp. 274–75: *Treasury Bulletin* (June 1977), p. 68; Board of Governors of the Federal Reserve System 1976, pp. 868, 869, 882. $B/(\bar{Y}\cdot P)$ is the ratio of B to the nominal value of trend GNP. See table 3 for the definitions of $\bar{Y}$ and P.

Note.—$DB_t \equiv \log (B_t) - \log (B_{t-1})$, $\widehat{DB}$ in col. 2 is the estimated value from the 1922–76 equation with the $R(1-\theta)$ coefficient constrained to equal one; in col. 4 it is the estimated value from the 1948–76 equation with the π-coefficient constrained to equal one. $DBR \equiv DB - \widehat{DB}$, B is the end-of-year value in billions of dollars of privately held interest-bearing public debt at nominal par value. The gross debt includes fully guaranteed securities issued by the Federal Home Mortgage Corporation, Home Owners Loan Corporation, Reconstruction Finance Corporation, Commodity Credit Corporation, U.S. Housing Authority, and Federal Housing Administration. The amounts of these issues are significant from 1934–44. Non-interest-bearing debt has been excluded. The figures are net of holdings by the Federal Reserve and government agencies and trust funds.

behavior is a recent phenomenon. In particular, the estimated coefficient of the temporary income variable over the 1922–40 sample is −1.97, SE = 0.39. Although the pre-Depression years, 1922–29, are a part of this sample, it is clear from the separate coefficient estimate and standard error for this period, −1.18, SE = 1.27, that only a moderate amount of information on this coefficient is provided by the addition of these data. A meaningful test for a shift in counter-cyclical debt response beginning with the New Deal would have to bring in earlier evidence from the Gold Standard period.[24] I plan to carry out this extension at a later time.

The estimated constant term for the 1922–76 sample (with the coefficient of the $R[1 - \theta]$ variable restricted to unity) is 0.012, SE = .005. (Since the dummy variable applies to the 1922–40 period, the

[24] One suggested explanation for the "excessive" countercyclical debt response is that it reflects the cross-sectional graduation of income tax rates, which might affect the time-series relation of taxes to income if there were substantial adjustment costs for changing tax laws over the business cycle. Under this interpretation, the countercyclical response would be weaker during the pre–World War I, non–income tax period.

constant for these years would be $0.012 - 0.059 = -0.047$.) Theoretically, with the value of $R(1 - \theta)$ rather than π held fixed, the constant should correspond to the difference between ρ, the growth rate of real GNP, and the anticipated after-tax real rate of return. Since the average growth rate of real GNP from 1922 to 1976 was 0.032 per year, the constant corresponds to an anticipated after-tax real rate of return for the post-1941 period of 0.020 per year.[25]

The Level of Debt

The theory predicts that the level of debt or the debt-income ratio would be irrelevant for current debt issue. I have tested this proposition by adding the variable, $B_{t-1}/(P_{t-1}\bar{Y}_{t-1})$, to the estimating equation. The estimated coefficient of this variable differs insignificantly from zero in all cases—for example, over the 1922–76 period with the coefficient of the $R(1 - \theta)$ variable restricted to unity, the estimated coefficient is -0.012, SE $= 0.018$. This result supports the surprising proposition of the theory that the debt-income ratio does not have a "target" value but rather moves "randomly" in accordance with the realizations for the federal expenditure and income shocks.

Level of Federal Spending

The theory stresses the role of temporary government expenditure, as opposed to the level of spending (see, however, n. 17 above). If the variable, $P_t\bar{G}_t/B_t$, is added to the debt equation, its estimated coefficient differs insignificantly from zero in all cases. For example, over the 1922–76 sample with the coefficient of the $R(1 - \theta)$ variable again restricted to one, the estimated coefficient is 0.022, SE $= 0.017$.

Change in Interest Rate

An increase in interest rates should reduce the growth rate of public debt when measured at par values (see above). For the case where the $R(1 - \theta)$ coefficient is constrained to one and for the 1922–76 sample, the estimated coefficient of the variable, $RG_t - RG_{t-1}$, is -0.7, SE $= 1.3$. A failure to isolate a significant effect of this variable may stem from improper measurement, since RG_{t-1} should be replaced by an

[25] However, over the 1948–76 period with the π variable held fixed, the estimated constant is 0.015, SE $= 0.007$, which is well below the growth rate of real GNP. A possible interpretation is that the anticipated real rate of return for the post-1941 period is actually close to zero, and that the constant is below the growth rate because of the expectation that government spending will rise faster than income over time (see above).

appropriately weighted average of past coupon rates. Therefore, the effect of this variable may be worth further examination.

The Experience of Debt Issue from 1917 to 1976

Table 3 contains values for the actual growth rate of nominal public debt, DB, since 1917. Estimated values and residuals from the 1922–76 equation (with the coefficient of the $R[1 - \theta]$ variable set to one and with the estimates extrapolated to 1917–21) and from the 1948–76 equation with the coefficient of the π-variable set to one are also indicated. Values of the independent variables used in the estimating equations are shown in table 1.

The extrapolation of the 1922–76 equation captures well the extraordinarily high growth rates of public debt (starting from a low base of less than \$1 billion of debt in 1916) during World War I, 1917–18. The equation substantially overestimates the growth rate of debt from 1919 to 1921. I suspect that this underestimation arises because a strong anticipated deflation after the war is not captured by the interest-rate variable. However, this conjecture cannot be tested without a direct measure of anticipated inflation.

The 1922–29 period exhibits negative values of DB, which are consistent with the negative values of $G - \bar{G}$ during this period and with the absence of any important economic contraction from 1923 to 1929. The strongly positive growth rates of debt from 1931 to 1940 reflect, first, the countercyclical response to the depression (with a peak effect from 1932 to 1934) and, second, the impact of a sharp increase in federal spending, especially from 1934 to 1936. The value of +0.08 for the $P(G - \bar{G})/B$ variable in 1934, as contrasted with −0.08 for 1929, implies, by itself, that the value of $\hat{DB}$ for 1934 exceeds that for 1929 by 0.26 per year. The even sharper rise in federal spending during World War II accounts for the vast increase in debt for 1941–45.

The first years of the post–World War II period, 1946–48, show negative growth rates of debt, which are associated with the sharp cutback in federal spending. This pattern is interrupted by the 1949 recession but is resumed in 1950. The expansion of federal spending associated with the Korean War, especially in 1952–53, is reflected in higher growth rates of debt. The 1954 "recession" is offset by a substantial drop in the federal spending variable to produce a moderate growth rate of debt for that year. Throughout the period from 1955 to 1965, the relatively slow growth in federal spending (relative to the average since 1860 of 5.6 percent per year) is a factor that lowers the growth of debt.

The boom in 1955 produces an estimated value $\hat{DB}$ of −0.027, although the actual value of zero is substantially higher. From 1956 to 1958 the values of DB are below the estimated values—in particular, the expansion of debt during the 1958 contraction is less vigorous than would have been expected. This pattern of weaker than expected debt expansion applies also to the 1960–63 period. This relationship is reversed for 1964–65—apparently reflecting the positive effect on debt issue of the celebrated 1964–65 tax cuts. However, the residual from the 1922–76 equation for 1964 is only 0.004. The 1965 residual, 0.014, shows a more substantial effect. An expansionary factor for 1967–68 is the rise in federal spending associated with the Vietnam War. An interesting note about the 1968 observation is that it shows a positive residual, which confirms the general belief that the "tax surcharge" for that year was quantitatively trivial. However, a negative residual does appear for 1969.

During the 1970s the federal spending variable is again a negative contributor to the growth of debt. However, the anticipated rate of inflation becomes a significant positive element during this period— π rises from 0.014 in 1964 to 0.030 in 1967 and from 0.029 in 1968 to 0.062 in 1972, remaining at about 6 percent per year through 1976; the interest-rate variable, $R(1 - \theta)$, rises steadily from 0.040 in 1964 to 0.070 in 1970, and then varies between 0.063 and 0.078 for the 1970–76 period. For the early 1970s the expected inflation factor is substantially offset only by the strong boom in 1973, which produces a single year of negative growth in the nominal debt. The recession that begins in 1974 returns the growth rate of debt to the positive range.

The vast debt explosion for 1975–76 has been widely noted. It is therefore of interest that the present analysis seems to account for this behavior reasonably well—the 1922–76 equation yields a value for $\hat{DB}$ of 0.22, as compared with an actual value of 0.26. For 1976 the $\hat{DB}$ value is 0.14, as compared with an actual value of 0.16. It is important to note that the federal spending variable is not an element in these high values of debt growth. The major contributor is the strong recession (output 8 percent below trend in 1975), which produces a value of the pertinent variable, $\log(Y/\bar{Y}) \cdot P\bar{G}/B$, for 1975 that is the highest magnitude, 0.095, of the entire 1922–76 sample! The effect of a given proportionate shortfall of income (in this case by 8 percent) on debt issue depends multiplicatively on the normal level of federal spending, because the product of $\log(Y/\bar{Y})$ and $\bar{G}$ indicates (if $G = \bar{G}$) the amount by which real taxes would be reduced if the tax-income ratio were to be kept constant. Because the value of $\bar{G}$ is much higher in 1975 than during the depth of the Great Depression in 1933 (where $\log[Y/\bar{Y}] = -0.40$), the smaller percentage output shortfall in 1975 is converted into a larger overall effect on debt issue. According to the 1922–76 equation, the temporary income variable for 1975 raises $\hat{DB}$ by 0.16 per year (relative to a situation in which log $[Y/\bar{Y}]$ = 0)—that is, it accounts for $47 billion out of the total debt increment during 1975 of $78 billion. The second positive element for 1975 is the high anticipated rate of inflation (π = 0.060), which affects the value of $\hat{DB}$ on a one-to-one basis and thereby accounts for $17 billion of debt issue (relative to a situation where π = 0).

For 1976 the reduced value of $\hat{DB}$ reflects principally the smaller magnitude of the temporary-income variable. The value of π (0.062) remains high for this year.

It may be of interest to carry out a formal test of the hypothesis that the apparent debt explosion for 1975–76 is consistent with earlier experience.[26] A test that the 1975–76 observations conform with those from 1922 to 1974 yields the statistic, F_{49}^2 = 1.9, 5 percent critical value = 3.2. Therefore, the hypothesis of an unchanged structure for 1975–76 is accepted by this test. An extrapolation of an equation that is estimated over the 1922–74 period yields values for 1975 of $\hat{DB}$ = 0.196, residual = 0.059; and for 1976 of $\hat{DB}$ = 0.127, residual = 0.032. Hence, the observed values of $\hat{DB}$ for 1975–76 are above the extrapolated estimates from the 1922–74 experience, but not significantly so.

Concluding Remarks

Natural extensions to the present analysis of public debt behavior have been noted in parts of the discussion above. Theoretical possibilities include the incorporation of currency issue, a rigorous application of optimal taxation theory to public debt determination (n. 7 above), and an explicit treatment of uncertainty about future government spending, national income, and so on. On an empirical level it would be useful to improve the measure of anticipated inflation to include a proper treatment of change-in-interest-rate effects, to test directly propositions concerning the unpredictability of federal tax rate changes, and to extend the analysis to earlier U.S. data. An investigation of the debt-creation process in the United Kingdom, which is currently being carried out by Benjamin and Kochin (1978), should provide interesting comparative evidence.

I have also begun a study that utilizes the present analysis to examine the effects of shifts between public debt and taxes on economic activity. This analysis stresses the distinction between customary debt movements—which may be measurable as the estimated value from a public debt equation—and the surprise part of these shifts. Theoreti-

---

[26] A difficulty with this test is that it is motivated entirely by the observation of a "high" realized value of DB. The statistical properties of the usual tests would therefore not hold.

cally, the latter parts would have a stronger impact on output—in fact, the former parts would be neutral in some models. However, my preliminary results have not isolated important output effects of either component of public debt movements. The public debt theory developed in the present paper suggests a possible difficulty in isolating the business-cycle effects of the temporary tax changes that are associated with the usual view of fiscal policy. If the theory has some empirical validity, so that the principal movements in federal tax rates have, in fact, represented permanent changes—in the sense that future changes in rates were unpredictable—then the historical data would not provide much evidence about the impact of temporary changes in federal taxes.

References

Barro, Robert J. "Are Government Bonds Net Wealth?" *J.P.E.* 82, no. 6 (November/December 1974): 1095–1117.
———. "Optimal Revenue Collection and the Money Growth Rate." Unpublished paper, Univ. Rochester, 1976. (*a*)
———. "Reply to Feldstein and Buchanan." *J.P.E.* 84, no. 2 (April 1976): 343–49. (*b*)
———. "Unanticipated Money Growth and Unemployment in the United States." *A.E.R.* 67 (March 1977): 101–15.
———. "Unanticipated Money, Output, and the Price Level in the United States." *J.P.E.* 86, no. 4 (August 1978): 549–80.
Barro, Robert J., and Fischer, Stanley. "Recent Developments in Monetary Theory." *J. Monetary Econ.* 2 (April 1976): 133–67.
Benjamin, Daniel K., and Kochin, Levis A. "The British National Debt." Unpublished paper, Univ. Washington, 1978.
Board of Governors of the Federal Reserve System. *Banking and Monetary Statistics.* Washington: Federal Reserve, 1943.
———. *Banking and Monetary Statistics, 1941–70.* Washington: Federal Reserve, 1976.
Buchanan, James M. *Public Principles of Public Debt.* Homewood, Ill.: Irwin, 1958.
———. "Barro on the Ricardian Equivalence Theorem." *J.P.E.* 84, no. 2 (April 1976): 337–42.
Dewey, D. R. *Financial History of the United States.* 11th ed. London: Longmans Green, 1931.
Federal Reserve Bulletin, various issues.
Firestone, John M. *Federal Receipts and Expenditures during Business Cycles.* Princeton, N.J.: Princeton Univ. Press, 1960.
Hall, Robert E. "Stochastic Implications of the Life Cycle–Permanent Income Hypothesis: Theory and Evidence." *J.P.E.* 86, no. 6 (December 1978): 971–87.
Kydland, Finn, and Prescott, Edward C. "On the Possibility and Desirability of Stabilization Policy." Paper presented at the N.B.E.R. Conference on Rational Expectations and Economic Policy, Bald Peak, N.H., October 1978.

McCallum, Bennett T., and Whitaker, J. K. "The Effectiveness of Fiscal Feedback Rules and Automatic Stabilizers under Rational Expectations." *J. Monetary Econ.*, in press.

O'Driscoll, Gerald P., Jr. "The Ricardian Nonequivalence Theorem." *J.P.E.* 85, no. 2 (February 1977): 207–10.

Prescott, Edward C. "Should Control Theory Be Used for Economic Stabilization?" In *Optimal Policies, Control Theory and Technology Exports*. Supplement to the *J. Monetary Econ.*, 1977.

Ricardo, David. "On the Principles of Political Economy and Taxation." In *The Works and Correspondence of David Ricardo*, edited by P. Sraffa. Vol. 1. Cambridge: Cambridge Univ. Press, 1951. (*a*)

———. "Funding System." In *The Works and Correspondence of David Ricardo*, edited by P. Sraffa. Vol. 4. Cambridge: Cambridge Univ. Press, 1951. (*b*)

Sadka, Efraim. "A Theorem on Uniform Taxation." *J. Public Econ.* 7 (June 1977): 387–91.

Sandmo, Agnar. "A Note on the Structure of Optimal Taxation." *A.E.R.* 64 (September 1974): 701–6.

Treasury Bulletin (June 1977).

U.S. Bureau of the Census. *Historical Statistics of the United States, Colonial Times to 1970.* Washington: Government Printing Office, 1975.

U.S. Council of Economic Advisers. *Economic Report of the President.* Washington: Government Printing Office, 1962, 1970, 1976, 1977.

U.S. Department of Commerce. *Long Term Economic Growth, 1860–1970.* Washington: Government Printing Office, 1973.

———. *The National Income and Product Accounts of the United States, 1929–74.* Washington: Government Printing Office, 1976.

———. *Survey of Current Business.* Washington: Government Printing Office, July 1977.

V
MONEY DEMAND AND RELATED TOPICS

The first two papers in this section involve the inventory approach to money demand. The first paper (no. 13), which derives from my Ph.D. thesis, analyzes the effect of anticipated inflation on the frequency of wage (and other) payments. In a simple framework that limits the use of interest-bearing assets as a store of working balances, there is a straightforward inverse link between these transaction frequencies and the quantity of average real-money balances held by employers and workers. The analysis also encompasses a negative response of the fraction of monetized transactions to increases in the expected inflation rate. A model of stochastically varying inflation rates with lumpy costs of altering transaction patterns is used to relate average real money holdings to a distributed lag of current and past inflation rates. In this formulation the *speed of adjustment* for reactions of real money demand to the current rate of inflation turns out to rise with the expected inflation rate. Empirical estimates of the model and hypothesis tests are carried out for four cases of post–World War I hyperinflation.

The next paper (no. 14, which is jointly written by Tony Santomero) uses the inventory approach to relate money demand to income, transaction costs, and the rate-of-return differential between earning assets and demand deposits. The principal empirical novelty is the derivation of a time series for the implicit interest rate on demand deposits, which was obtained for the 1950–1968 period by surveying banks on the manner in which they remitted service charges on some types of demand accounts in accordance with average levels of customer deposit balances. The empirical results on household money holdings indicate substantial explanatory power for this variable. The findings also support some hypotheses about coefficient magnitudes that were derived from the underlying inventory-type model of money demand.

The final paper (no. 15) deals with a very different topic. The theory of money supply and price level determination is developed under conditions of fixed values for the price of gold and the ratio of total money supply to the reserve gold stock. Comparative statics techniques are used to analyze the economic effects of gold discoveries, changes in real income, shifts in the ratio of money to the reserve gold stock, variations in the price of gold, and movements in velocity. Also considered are the effects of devaluation, increased international adoption of the gold standard, and the consequences of a variety of alternative commodity standards: bimetallism, symmetallism, and commodity-reserve currency. Partly, this theoretical analysis is of historical interest—useful for understanding the nature of money and inflation at earlier times, perhaps as recently as the period until the movement away from fixed exchange rates and the remnants of the gold standard in 1971. More importantly, the severity of recent inflationary problems in the United States and internationally suggests that implementation of some form of new monetary standard will become imperative. Commodity standards and constitutionally restricted fiat money arrangements seem to be the main candidates for this type of new regime. Accordingly, an understanding of the workings of the gold standard is important for the present-day choice of monetary institutions.

13

Inflation, the Payments Period, and the Demand for Money

Part I of this paper develops a model of economic response to inflation. Sections A, B, and C consider the maximizing behavior of employers and employees in the context of a steady rate of inflation. Since the rate of price change can be translated into an effective cost of holding money, a higher rate provides increased incentive for economizing on cash balances. Two methods of economizing are considered: first, (Sections A and B), reductions of the time interval between various types of payments (increases in "velocity") and, second (Section C), decreases in the fraction of "monetized" transactions.

With a given fraction of monetized transactions, the selection of the optimal length of time between (wage and other types of) payments involves a tradeoff of the inventory type. Given some fixed (real) cost of making payments, a higher rate of price change reduces the optimal-payment interval (increases velocity) and produces a corresponding reduction in average real money holdings.

The demand-for-money function which is implied by optimal-payments period selection approaches an inflation-rate elasticity of $-1/2$ as the rate of inflation becomes large (relative to real rates of return in the economy). However, this formulation assumes that the fraction of monetized transactions is unaffected by changes in the inflation rate. In fact, "money" may be viewed as a medium which provides certain transactions benefits (in terms of physical convenience, general acceptability, et cetera) in comparison with alternative media. At a higher rate of price change, the cost of retaining money as a payments medium is increased (relative to

The author is grateful for helpful comments from Zvi Griliches, Michael Connolly, Gary Becker, Milton Friedman, Herschel Grossman, and Marc Nerlove. This paper is a portion of the author's Ph.D. thesis at Harvard University.

301

that for stable-valued substitutes, such as payments in kind or foreign exchange). If this inflationary cost is weighed against money's transactions benefits, the fraction of expenditures for which it pays to retain money is inversely related to the rate of price change. The combination of this money-substitute effect with the previously described velocity mechanism produces an increasing (absolute) elasticity of money demand to the rate of inflation.

The analysis of Sections A, B, and C assumes a constant rate of price change. Section D extends the analysis to consider the optimal response to rates of inflation which vary over time. Basically, if no costs of adjustment or lags in perception are involved, the steady-state solution would be optimal at all times. Accordingly, if lags in perception are neglected, the optimal response to changing rates of inflation involves a weighing of adjustment costs (for example, costs of instituting changes in the payments period) against "out-of-equilibrium" costs (that is, costs of not adhering to the steady-state rules at all times). The model of Section D assumes that actual rates of price change are generated by a symmetric, stochastic process (a random walk), and that individuals adopt an adjustment policy of the (S, s) inventory form. According to this type of policy, variations in the inflation rate produce no response (in, say, the payments period or the fraction of monetized transactions) until some critical gap between actual and statically optimal levels appears. At this point some discrete adjustment of decision variables is performed in accordance with the optimal steady-state relationships. No subsequent adjustments occur until a new gap of the critical size appears.

The (S, s) response model is used to obtain an aggregate mechanism for generating "effective" rates of inflation (the rate which is relevant for key decision variables, and, therefore, for demand for money). The mechanism is similar in form to earlier models of the adaptive-expectations type (Cagan 1956), although the current model reflects solely an adjustment lag. A key implication of maximizing behavior is the dependence of the response coefficient on the (effective) rate of inflation itself.

The theory of Part I is applied in Part II to an empirical study of demand for money. The data derive from four cases of post–World War I hyperinflation (Austria, Germany, Hungary, and Poland), which were previously studied by Cagan (1956) and Allais (1966). Substantial space is devoted to constructing null hypotheses which embody the theoretical implications of Part I. Basically, these null hypotheses involve a priori conjectures on the coefficients of regression equations. The (nonlinear, iterative) empirical estimation and testing confirms the bulk of these conjectures, and, therefore, provides support for the underlying theory. Comments on the statistical results and avenues for future research are indicated at the end of the paper.

1. A Model of the Payments Period and the Demand for Money

A. The Basic Steady-State Model

The model is developed with reference to a business firm, which is subsequently viewed as an employer. Assume that prices in an economy are rising uniformly at a continuous rate, r_p, so that:

$$P(t) = P_0 e^{r_p t}, \qquad (1)$$

where, P_0 is the price level at time zero.

A firm (for example, a store) is receiving a continuously rising stream of money income given by:

$$Y(t) = Y_0 e^{r_p t}, \qquad (2)$$

where, Y_0 is the income level at time zero.

Money income is assumed to be rising at the same rate, r_p, as prices, so that real income is constant. The firm's alternative to retaining its income flow as cash (which is depreciating in value at the rate of inflation, r_p) is to hold some alternative stable-valued asset, such as physical commodities or foreign exchange (it is assumed for simplicity that real interest bearing assets are unavailable). However, there is some cost or bother associated with the conversion of cash into a stable-valued asset, so that transfers are not made continuously. That is, the firm accumulates money over a period and converts a lump amount to an alternative asset at some transfer date. The nature of the relevant transfer cost is complex, since it may involve personal bother or waste of time, wage payments to employees, actual brokerage charges for foreign exchange or other financial transactions, et cetera. In general the cost involves some elements which are related to the price level and others which are of an income-forgone nature.[1] However, when prices and income grow at the same rate, it is expected that the money value of the transfer cost also grows at this rate. Accordingly, if $a(t)$ represents the money cost of transfers at time t (regarded for simplicity as being independent of the amount transferred), we have:

$$a(t) = a_0 e^{r_p t}, \qquad (3)$$

where a_0 is the money cost at time zero.

The presence of interest and transfer-cost elements produces a tradeoff which amounts to an optimization problem for the firm. A general formulation of the problem is the following: Given that a transfer from cash to stable asset was made at some time t_0, choose the future transfer

---

[1] That is, a substantial element in transfer activity is the expenditure of a certain amount of time, so that transactions productivity may not grow, even if overall real per capita income is rising.

dates, t_1, t_2, ... so as to achieve an optimal tradeoff between the interest cost of holding cash and the transfer cost of making more frequent asset conversions.

Mathematically, the optimization is as follows: After the transfer at time t_0, consider the interval (t_0, t_1) where t_1 is the first optional transfer date. In a time differential, dt, the increment to money holding is given by $dM = Y dt = Y_0 e^{r_p t} dt$. Therefore, the addition to interest cost (in terms of "t_1-money") is given by:

$$dZ = dM[e^{r_p(t_1 - t)} - 1] = Y_0 e^{r_p t}[e^{r_p(t_1 - t)} - 1]dt.$$

The total interest cost (in "t_1-money") for the interval (t_0, t_1), is then:

$$Z(t_0, t_1) = Y_0 \int_{t_0}^{t_1} e^{r_p t}[e^{r_p(t_1 - t)} - 1]dt$$

$$= Y_0[e^{r_p t_1 (t_1 - t_0)} - \frac{1}{r_p}(e^{r_p t_1} - e^{r_p t_0})].$$

Since the employer's opportunity-cost rate is equal to r_p, this cost can be expressed as "time-zero money" by discounting by the factor, $e^{-r_p t_1}$. Denoting this discounted amount (to time zero) as Z^*, we have:

$$Z^*(t_0, t_1) = Y_0 \left\{ t_1 - t_0 - \frac{1}{r_p}[1 - e^{r_p(t_0 - t_1)}] \right\}. \tag{4}$$

Similarly, for any interval (t_k, t_{k+1}), the result is:

$$Z^*(t_k, t_{k+1}) = Y_0 \left\{ t_{k+1} - t_k - \frac{1}{r_p}[1 - e^{r_p(t_k - t_{k+1})}] \right\}. \tag{5}$$

The total interest cost up to the nth transfer date, t_n, is the sum of n terms of the form of equation (5), so that:

$$Z^*(t_0, t_n) = Y_0 \left\{ t_n - t_0 - \frac{1}{r_p}[n - e^{r_p(t_0 - t_1)} - \ldots - e^{r_p(t_{n-1} - t_n)}] \right\}. \tag{6}$$

The nominal amount of transfer cost for any interval, (t_k, t_{k+1}), is $a_0 e^{r_p t_{k+1}}$, so that the discounted cost is a_0. Therefore, the total discounted transfer cost for the interval, (t_0, t_n), is given by:

$$A^*(t_0, t_n) = a_0 n. \tag{7}$$

The total discounted cost, Z_T^*, for the interval (t_0, t_n), is given by the sum of equations (6) and (7):

$$Z_T^* = Y_0 \left\{ t_n - t_0 - \frac{1}{r_p}[n - e^{r_p(t_0 - t_1)} - \ldots - e^{r_p(t_{n-1} - t_n)}] \right\} + a_0 n. \tag{8}$$

The optimization problem can be formulated as follows. Given a time interval, $T = t_n - t_0$, with the constraint that the final transfer be made at time t_n, choose n and $t_1, t_2, \ldots, t_{n-1}$ so that Z_T^* is a minimum. A necessary condition for a minimum is $\partial Z_T^*/\partial t_k = 0$ for $k = 1, \ldots, n - 1$. Therefore, $Y_0(-e^{r_p t_{k-1}} e^{-r_p t_k} + e^{-r_p t_{k+1}} e^{r_p t_k}) = 0$. Rearranging terms, we have $e^{2 r_p t_k} = e^{r_p(t_{k-1} + t_{k+1})}$ Therefore:

$$t_k = \frac{1}{2}\left(t_{k-1} + t_{k+1}\right) \text{ for } k = 1, \ldots, n-1. \tag{9}$$

In other words, the optimal transfer points are evenly spaced when prices, income, and transfer costs grow at the same rate.[2]

The result in equation (9) implies that equation (8) can be simplified to:

$$Z_T^* = Y_0\left[T - \frac{n}{r_p}(1 - e^{-r_p T/n})\right] + a_0 n, \tag{10}$$

where use has been made of the conditions $(t_k - t_{k+1}) = -T/n$, and $(t_n - t_0) = T$. The minimization problem then reduces to choosing n, the number of transfers in time T, so that (10) is a minimum. Accordingly,[3]

$$\frac{\partial Z_T^*}{\partial n} = Y_0\left[\frac{n}{r_p}(e^{-r_p T/n})\frac{r_p T}{n^2} - \frac{1}{r_p}(1 - e^{-r_p T/n})\right] + a_0 = 0.$$

Therefore: $Y_0 e^{-r_p T/n}(1/r_p + T/n) - Y_0/r_p + a_0 = 0$. Expanding the exponential in a power series:

$$Y_0\left(\frac{1}{r_p} + \frac{T}{n}\right) \sum_{i=0}^{\infty}\left\{\left[(-1)^i\left(\frac{r_p T}{n}\right)^i\right]/i!\right\} - \frac{Y_0}{r_p} + a_0 = 0.$$

Simplifying, we eventually obtain:

$$\frac{a_0}{Y_0} = r_p(T/n)^2 \cdot \sum_{i=0}^{\infty}\left\{[(-1)^i]/[(i+2)i!]\left(r_p \frac{T}{n}\right)^i\right\}. \tag{11}$$

[2] If real income is not constant, a sufficient condition for equally spaced transfers is that money income and transfer cost grow at the same rate. (This result is valid even if some nonzero real rate of discount is appropriate. In this case the opportunity cost of holding money is $r = r^* + r_p$, where r^* is the real rate of discount and r_p is the rate of price change.) Stated somewhat differently, as long as transfer costs are completely of an income-forgone nature, the optimal transfer points are equally spaced.

[3] At first sight, the treatment of n (number of transfers in time T) as a continuous variable is suspect. However, the selection of n in this manner amounts to a choice of T/n (time between payments), which can properly be regarded as continuous. The optimization runs into some trouble if T is retained as a finite horizon (amounting to the constraint that an integral number of transfers must occur in a specified length of time, such as a week or a month), in which case the calculus solution must be regarded as an approximation. However, the nature of the objective function guarantees that the true optimum will be close, in the sense that an integer adjacent to the calculus result will be the optimal value. (That is, the second derivative of the cost expression in equation [10] is $(\partial^2 Z_T^*)/(\partial n^2) = Y_0 e^{-r_p T/n}(r_p/n)(T/n)^2$, which is positive when r_p is positive. Therefore, the objective function is "single troughed," and an integer adjacent to the calculus solution is the optimal value.)

If $r_p(T/n) \ll 1$, we may approximate $a_0/Y_0 \approx \frac{1}{2}r_p(T/n)^2$. Therefore:

$$\frac{T}{n} \approx \sqrt{(2a_0)/(r_p Y_0)}. \tag{12}$$

Corresponding to this solution, $r_p T/n = \sqrt{(2a_0 r_p)/Y_0}$, which will be much less than 1 for conceivable values of a_0, r_p, and Y_0, so that the exponential approximation is appropriate. The second-order condition is also satisfied, so that the solution of equation (12) corresponds to a minimum for Z_T^*.

Applying the exponential approximation, $e^{-r_p T/n} \approx 1 - r_p T/n + \frac{1}{2}$ $(r_p T/n)^2$, directly to equation (10), we obtain for later use an expression (dependent on T/n) for total (discounted) employer cost over time T:

$$Z \text{ employer} \approx \frac{1}{2}\frac{Y_0}{P_0} r_p(T/n)T + (a_0/P_0) \cdot n. \tag{13}$$

The first term in this expression amounts to the interest cost over time T on the employer's average money balance:

$$(M/P) \text{ employer} \approx \frac{1}{2}\frac{Y_0}{P_0}\frac{T}{n} = \frac{1}{2}\frac{Y}{P}\frac{T}{n}. \tag{14}$$

Therefore, the determination of T/n in equation (12) implies an employer average money demand in the form of equation (14). Since the solution for T/n in equation (12) is modified by a consideration of employee behavior, this implied demand-for-money function is not discussed at this point.

B. The Payments Period

Equation (12) indicates the optimal time spacing for conversions of employer cash holdings to alternative stable-valued assets, such as commodities and foreign exchange, on the assumption that these assets represent an ultimate destination for employer funds. In fact, a substantial fraction of employer income is destined for wage payments to employees (or other types of payments), so that the indirect route, cash to stable asset (to cash) to payments, may be nonoptimal. That is, if wage payments (or other payments) are regarded by the employer as fixed in *real* terms, the rendering of these payments is (from the employer standpoint) equivalent to the transfer of cash to a stable-valued asset. In other words, if $a(t)$ in equation (3) is reinterpreted as the cost of making wage payments, and if the rendering of these payments is substituted for the conversion of cash to a stable-valued asset, then the model will (with the qualifications noted below) describe the determination of the payments period during inflation.

From the employer standpoint, the interpretation of the time interval of equation (12) as a payments period assumes that the indirect route, cash to stable asset to payments, will not be used. Whether, in fact, an asset would be considered for this type of intermediate function depends on the cost of moving in and out of the asset, and the real rate of return that accrues on it. In particular, an asset will be used only if the transfer cost is small relative to the cost of making wage payments, and/or the real rate of return is substantial. One possible type of satisfactory asset is a stable-valued (or real interest bearing) deposit or short-term bill.

At least during extreme inflationary experiences, the available assets do not conform well to the conditions suggested above.[4] Rather, the available assets appear to serve two other types of functions. First, there are assets whose transactions-cost and return characteristics make them suitable as a long-term store of wealth, but not as a temporary abode for funds earmarked for payments over the relatively short term.[5] This class includes real investment opportunities, accumulation of types of physical commodities, and so forth.

The second category consists of assets which themselves acquire means-of-payments properties during extreme inflation. When a sufficiently high rate of inflation is attained, it becomes worthwhile to use certain substitute transactions media (such as foreign exchange, private tokens, and certain commodities) in order to avoid the costs associated with the use of the depreciating currency. However, while the existence of such money substitutes has a substantial impact on the demand for money, the effect does not operate via the intermediary mechanism described above. That is, as long as the usual money supply is retained for receipts and payments, these types of assets do not enter the analysis.[6] A discussion of these assets as substitute means of payments is contained in Section C below. For the remainder of this section, it is assumed that the usual money supply is retained for all transactions purposes, and that no satisfactory inter-mediate assets exist.[7]

A more serious qualification to the interpretation of equation (12) as a

---

[4] In a complete model, the types of available assets would themselves be endog-enous. However, the absence of "short-term," real interest bearing assets during extreme inflations seems to reflect the uncertainty of the inflationary course, rather than the intensity, per se. Since the introduction of uncertainty does not seem critical for the prime areas of interest of the steady-state model, it seems desirable to main-tain the assumption of certainty and to regard the types of available assets as exog-enous.

[5] It is assumed implicitly that the payments period will not exceed some relatively short time interval. This constraint derives from the employee behavior (discussed below), which serves to make an overly long period unprofitable to the employer.

[6] Essentially, if these assets could serve as a profitable intermediate asset, they could more profitably serve as a complete means-of-payments substitute.

[7] The impact of stable-valued, readily accessible intermediate assets is discussed below in n. 17.

payments period involves the behavior of employees. The original presentation of the model (with the substitution of wage payments for transfers to stable-valued assets) tacitly assumes that employees are indifferent to the length of the payments period, and are concerned only with the (apparent) real wage rate. In fact, increases in the period impose certain costs on employees, which must be weighed in determining the optimal length of time between payments.[8]

The first type of employee cost derives from the delay in real payment implied by a lengthened payments period.[9] The second cost involves the relationship between the payments period and average employee money holdings.

The cost imputed to delayed real wage payment depends on the use of these payments. If delayed payment implies a reduction in employee savings, the (real) lending rate is relevant. If the delay results in increased borrowings, the (real) borrowing rate is appropriate. In many cases (particularly during extreme inflation, when financial markets are highly imperfect) neither borrowing nor lending is involved, and the impact is directly on postponed consumption.[10] That is, if (real) lending rates are low and (real) borrowing rates are high, an intermediate marginal impatience rate is most likely to apply. In any case, there exists some (real) rate r^* (not necessarily identical for all individuals)[11] at which payment delays are discounted.[12]

[8] See Friedman 1956, p. 13.

[9] It is assumed that wage payments are made subsequent to the rendering of services. This assumption is discussed below in n. 12.

[10] Behavior in markets where borrowing and lending rates differ is discussed in Hirshleifer 1958.

[11] The discount rate may not be independent of T/n (delays need not be discounted linearly), but this complication is neglected here.

[12] The question of advanced versus deferred wage payments (see n. 9) can be treated as follows. Let r_B denote the real employee borrowing rate (and also the rate at which employers are willing to lend to employees); r^* the marginal impatience rate of employees (which is assumed to equal the rate at which employees are willing to lend to employers—that is, lending to employers is viewed as a riskless investment by employees); and r_L the real rate of return (or riskless lending rate) on employer (and employee) wealth holdings, where $r_B \geq r^* \geq r_L$. It is assumed that the employer borrowing rate (and, therefore, also the employer marginal impatience rate) is approximately equal to r_L, so that r_L unambiguously represents the marginal rate of return on employer funds. Therefore, in this view the essential distinction between employees and employers is the relative position of borrowing rates.

Assume that the (real) amount X/P is paid from employers to employees at some nonzero payment interval. An advance of wages amounts to a loan (of the average quantity, $[1/2]/[X/P]$), from employers to employees while a deferral implies a loan in the opposite direction. An advance (employer to employee loan) is valued by employers at the rate $-r_B$, and by employees at the rate r^*. The net (nonpositive) rate of return associated with advance payment is therefore $-r_B + r^*$. Similarly, the rate of return on deferrals (employee to employer loans) is $-r^* + r_L$. Therefore, advances and deferrals both involve nonpositive rates of return in comparison with the zero rate of return attached to perfect synchronization of payments (abstracting from transactions costs). Given that payments are not to be perfectly synchronized

If the nominal wage rate is denoted by w, the amount of nominal wage payment (for a period, T/n) is given by $X = w(T/n)$.[13] Consider the interval between the payments points, t_0 and t_1. At t_1, employees receive a quantity of real wage payment, $X/P = w/P(T/n)$, in payment for services between t_0 and t_1. Assuming that employees conduct expenditures at a uniform rate and just exhaust a single wage payment over the time interval, T/n, the average deferred time between wage accruals and employee expenditure is T/n. The cost of this delay for a single payments period (ignoring compounding during the short interval, T/n)[14] is $r^*(X/P)T/n = r^*(w/P)(T/n)^2$. The cost for n periods (that is, for a time T) is therefore:

$$Z_{r*} = r^*(w/P)(T/n)T. \qquad (15)$$

The average employee real money balance (assuming the absence of intermediate assets) can be approximated by:

$$\overline{M/P} \approx \frac{1}{2}\frac{X}{P} = \frac{1}{2}\frac{w}{p}(T/n). \qquad (16)$$

The corresponding employee interest cost (that is, the inflationary loss on money holdings, neglecting compounding, over the time T) is given by:

$$Z_r \approx (\overline{M/P})\, r_p T = \frac{1}{2}\frac{w}{p}r_p\left(\frac{T}{n}\right)T. \qquad (17)$$

The total employee cost for time T (the sum of expressions [15] and [17]) is therefore:

$$Z\text{ employee} = \frac{1}{2}\frac{w}{P}\cdot\frac{T}{n}T(r_p + 2r^*). \qquad (18)$$

Expression (18), above, may overstate employee costs, since it excludes any deviation of expenditures from a uniform flow. In fact, as inflation intensifies, employees are (*ceteris paribus*) motivated to concentrate

---

(because of transactions costs), the optimal payments scheme is the one with the least negative rate of return. (As in the rest of the analysis, concern is only with obtaining a "Pareto-optimal type" solution, and is not with the division of costs and benefits between employers and employees. See n. 15 below.) *Therefore, deferred payment is preferred to advanced payment if and only if:* $(r^* - r_L) < (r_B - r^*)$. (It should be noted that, at least as long as r^* is independent of the length of delays, any intermediate payments solution corresponds to a weighted average of the two extreme rates of return, and is therefore inferior to one of the extreme solutions, unless these are themselves equivalent.) Since the model assumes that payments are deferred, the appropriate (real) discount rate for payments delays is $(r^* - r_L)$; $(r_L = 0$ has also been assumed). In general the discount rate can be written as: min $[(r_B - r^*);$ $(r^* - r_L)]$.

[13] It is assumed that employment—numbers of man-hours worked per week—does not change. In this case, T/n is an acceptable proxy for total man-hours worked.

[14] This and subsequent approximations which ignore compounding are formally equivalent to the infinite series approximation involved in the derivation of equation (12). The validity of the approximation depends throughout on $(r_p + r^*)(T/n) \ll 1$.

expenditures closer to payment times in order to reduce money holdings and incur smaller losses from inflation. However, a preliminary model of this behavior suggests that the general relationship between average money holdings and the rate of inflation is not materially altered by a consideration of this motive. This conclusion is further supported by the observation that, while employees desire to concentrate expenditures shortly *after* wage payments, employers have a symmetric desire to concentrate expenditures just *before* payments. The balancing of these forces could generate a "weekly seasonal" of rate of price change that would discourage the concentration of expenditures either just after or just before wage payments, and tend to restore the system to a uniform pattern of expenditure. In any case, the assumption of uniform patterns is retained in the body of this paper.

With the assumption of uniform expenditure streams, total real costs over time T (the sum of employer and employee costs) are given (from equations [13] and [18]) by:

$$Z_{\text{total}} \approx T\left\{\left[\frac{1}{2}\left(\frac{Y}{P} + \frac{w}{p}\right)r_p + \frac{w}{P}r^*\right]\frac{T}{n} + \frac{a}{p}\frac{n}{T}\right\}. \tag{19}$$

The optimal-payments period is that value of T/n which minimizes this total cost expression.[15] Accordingly, we have: $\partial Z/\partial(T/n) = T[\frac{1}{2}(Y/P + w/p)r_p + w/p\,r^* - (a/p)/(T/n)^2] = 0$. Therefore:

$$\frac{T}{n} = \sqrt{(a/P)\Big/\left[\frac{1}{2}\left(\frac{Y}{P} + \frac{w}{P}\right)r_p + \frac{w}{P}r^*\right]}. \tag{20}$$

If we assume $w/P \approx Y/P$,[16] we can write:[17]

$$\frac{T}{n} \approx \sqrt{(a/P)/[Y/P(r_p + r^*)]}. \tag{21}$$

The second-order minimum condition is satisfied for this solution.

[15] This cost minimization guarantees a Pareto-optimal situation with respect to employers and employees. For example, if employees were willing to pay some amount (in the form, say, of a reduced explicit wage) for a reduction in the payments period, and employers were willing to accept some lesser amount as compensation for this reduction, it is assumed that the reduction of the payments period takes place. The division of costs and benefits between employers and employees is not discussed explicitly—largely because it does not seem necessary for the desired results.

[16] In effect, Y corresponds to the total money flow into a business and w to the total money flow out of a business. (That is, w comprises rentals, payments to other businesses, net earnings, et cetera, as well as payments to labor—although the real discount rate, r^*, may depend on the particular form of payment.) Therefore, systematic deviations between Y/P and w/P can occur only through intermediate inflationary losses. This loss relates to the cost of inflation (equations [19] and [22]) and increases with $(r_p + r^*)^{1/2}$. However, as long as r_p is less than astronomical, this cost remains small relative to Y/P, so that the approximation $Y/P \approx w/p$ should be sustainable.

[17] The payments-period relationship, equation (21), can be readily extended to the case where satisfactory intermediate assets exist (see previous discussion). In one

TABLE 1

RELATIONSHIP BETWEEN PAYMENTS PERIOD
AND RATE OF INFLATION*

r_p (% per Month)	T/n (Months)
0	.5 (2 per month)
1	.35 (3 per month)
3	.25 (1 per week)
15	.125 (2 per week)
50	.07 (every 2 days)
200	.035 (daily)

* As implied by equation (21).

While it is possible to discuss only orders of magnitude, it is interesting
to explore the relationship between the payments period and the rate of
inflation implied by equation (21). For example, taking parameter values
of $Y = \$400$ per month, $a = \$1.00$ (only the ratio a/Y is of importance in
equation [21]), and $r^* = .01$ per month, the relationship as shown in
table 1 holds.

While the exact relationship depends on the arbitrary specification of
parameters, the overall magnitudes accord with observations from some
extreme inflationary experiences.[18] An interesting implication of the above

---

plausible situation, employers have available (at a transfer cost which, in the overall
cost calculation, is low enough to make the asset worthwhile) an alternative asset
with (riskless) real rate of return, r_L, and employees have available no satisfactory
alternative asset. In this case the real rate of return on employer money holdings is
changed from $-r_p$ to r_L, and the remainder of the model is unchanged. Therefore,
$(r_p + r^*)$ in equation (21) is replaced by $(r^* - \frac{1}{2}r_p - \frac{1}{2}r_L)$ to yield the new optimal
payments period. If employees have access to a similar satisfactory asset, $(r_p + r^*)$
in equation (21) is replaced by $(r^* - r_L)$. In this case, the determination of a finite
payments period requires the real discount rate of employees (r^*) to exceed the
underlying (riskless) real rate of return (r_L).

It should be noted that the decision to employ an alternative asset involves a
weighing of the rate of return against the cost of transactions relative to the volume
of transactions. Therefore, considering their larger scale of transactions, employers
are more likely than employees to find a particular asset (with given rate of return
and transactions-cost characteristics) satisfactory, so that the first case (with rate:
$r^* + \frac{1}{2}r_p - \frac{1}{2}r_L$) may be the most realistic—at least for developed countries like the
United States. For countries that are experiencing extreme inflations (such as those
studied in Part II of this paper) the complete exclusion of intermediate assets seems
most realistic, and equation (21) applies directly.

[18] For example, in 1923, the final year of the German hyperinflation, "it became
the custom to make an advance of wages on Tuesday the balance being paid on Friday.
Later, some firms used to pay wages three times a week, or even daily" (Bresciani-
Turroni 1937, p. 303). The range of ("effective") rates of inflation in this period was
20–300 percent per month (see table A2). Similarly, during the Austrian hyperinflation, "the salaries of the state officials, which used to be issued at the end of the
month, were paid to them during 1922 in instalments three times per month" (Walre
de Bordes 1924, p. 163). During 1922 the (effective) rate of inflation reached a peak
value of about 45 percent per month (see table A1).

relationship is the comparatively minor adjustment in the payments period necessitated by astronomical rates of inflation. Even at the extraordinary rate of 200 percent per month, payments are made only once per day. While this high frequency of payment involves additional bother (amounting to one-half of the inflationary cost of equation [22]), it cannot be viewed as an intolerable burden. Therefore, it is not surprising that (depending on the types of substitute payments media available) the benefits of money as a transactions medium could outweigh the inflationary cost, and induce persons to retain money at rates of inflation (as high, say as 100–200 percent per month) at which casual analysis might suggest a total flight from money.[19]

Substituting the result of equation (21) into equation (19), using $Y/P \approx w/P$, we obtain an expression for total (minimized) inflationary cost over time T:[20]

$$Z_{\text{total}} \approx 2T\sqrt{a/P(Y/P)(r_p + r^*)}. \tag{22}$$

C. The Demand for Money and Money Substitutes

Using the approximation for employer money balances in equation (14) and the analogous expression for employees in equation (16), aggregate real balances can be expressed as:

$$\overline{M/P} = \overline{M/P}_{\text{employers}} + \overline{M/P}_{\text{employees}}$$

$$\approx \frac{1}{2}\frac{Y}{P}\frac{T}{n} + \frac{1}{2}\frac{w}{P}\frac{T}{n}. \tag{23}$$

Taking $Y/P \approx w/P$ and substituting for T/n from equation (21), we obtain (omitting the bar over M/P):

$$M/P \approx \sqrt{\frac{(a/P)(Y/P)}{(r_p + r^*)}}. \tag{24}$$

If transfer costs (a/P) are totally of an income-forgone nature $(a/P \sim Y/P)$, then:

$$M/P \approx \frac{A\,Y/P}{\sqrt{r_p + r^*}}, \tag{25}$$

where $A = \sqrt{(a/P)/(Y/P)}$ is taken as a positive constant.

In the analysis of Sections A and B, money was retained as the sole payments medium. Within this framework, there emerged an inverse

---

[19] In this regard see Keynes 1924, pp. 48–50.
[20] The cost due to the inflation rate r_p requires a subtraction of the r^* portion from equation (22):

$$Z_{r_p} = 2T\sqrt{\frac{a}{P}\frac{Y}{P}}(\sqrt{r_p + r^*} - \sqrt{r^*}).$$

relation between real cash balances and the inflation rate (equations [24] and [25]). The mechanism by which cash holdings were reduced in response to a higher rate of inflation involved the reduction of the time period between transactions (that is, an increase in velocity). An additional mechanism by which cash holdings could be reduced involves the substitution of some alternative asset (foreign exchange, private tokens, payments in kind, and so on) as a transactions medium. By reducing the set of transactions to which money is applied, average cash holdings can be reduced, even if transaction periods (velocity) remain constant.

Letting $\Phi(r_p)$ denote the fraction of transactions (as a function of the inflation rate) which are conducted via some substitute medium, and assuming that the analysis of Sections A and B applies to the $100(1 - \Phi)$ percent of transactions for which money is retained, we have from equation (25):

$$M/P \approx \frac{[1 - \Phi(r_p)] \cdot A \, Y/P}{\sqrt{r_p + r^*}}. \qquad (26)$$

The elasticity of real cash balances with respect to the inflation rate is (from equation [26]):

$$\frac{\partial(M/P)}{\partial r_p} \cdot \frac{r_p}{M/P} = -\frac{1}{2}\left(\frac{r_p}{r_p + r^*}\right) - \frac{r_p \cdot \Phi'(r_p)}{1 - \Phi(r_p)}. \qquad (27)$$

Therefore, if the percentage of monetized transactions does not respond to $r_p[\Phi'(r_p) = 0, \Phi(r_p) < 1]$, the elasticity is given by the first term on the right-hand side of equation (27). In this form (with $r^* > 0$), the (absolute) elasticity rises from zero at $r_p = 0$ and asymptotically approaches $\frac{1}{2}$ as r_p becomes large relative to r^*. On the other hand, if the percentage of substitutes responds positively to the rate of inflation $[\Phi'(r_p) > 0]$, the right-hand term in equation (27) adds (possibly in an increasing fashion) to the (absolute) elasticity. Stated another way, if the percentage of money substitutes is constrained to be unresponsive to the inflation rate (and, therefore, if increases in velocity are the only method for reducing real money holdings),[21] there would exist a limiting elasticity of real cash balances to the inflation rate. When the possibility of varying the percentage of monetized transactions is recognized, there exists the potential for an indefinitely increasing elasticity.

Once the percentage of monetized transactions $(1 - \Phi)$ is regarded as a behaviorally determined magnitude, it is necessary to construct an explicit cost-benefit framework for determining the mode which payments take. If money is used for a volume of transactions corresponding to

---

[21] It should be recalled that variations in the shape of expenditure streams have been ruled out. However, this type of variation does not appear to be a potential source of an increasing inflation-rate elasticity.

Y/P, the inflationary cost per unit of time is (from equation [22], using $A = \sqrt{[a/P]/[Y/P]}$):

$$\frac{Z_{r_p}}{T} = 2A(Y/P)(\sqrt{r_p + r^*} - \sqrt{r^*}).\tag{28}$$

If a *stable-valued* asset is substituted as the transactions medium, the above cost could be avoided. Therefore, the decision to employ money or the substitute involves a comparison of the inflationary cost (equation [28]) with the benefits of money as a transactions medium (in terms of physical convenience, general acceptability, et cetera). The size of this benefit cannot be readily quantified, since it depends on the type of transaction and the individuals involved. For example, the benefit is likely to increase as one moves along the following list: (1) transactions within a family, (2) regular dealings with a local merchant, (3) dealings in new locations, (4) payments by mail, (5) dealings in securities markets. In any case, it seems feasible to group transactions into homogeneous classes, within which the benefit per amount of transaction is constant. That is, for the ith group of transactions, the benefit (per unit of time) of employing money is:

$$B_i = (\Psi/P)_i(1 - \Phi_i)(Y/P)_i,\tag{29}$$

where, $(1 - \Phi_i)$ is the fraction of the ith group's transactions which use money; and $(\Psi/P)_i$ is a constant for the ith group. The net benefit from employing money (over the stable-valued substitute) is (from equations [29] and [28]):

$$R_i = (1 - \Phi_i)(Y/P)_i[(\Psi/P)_i - 2A(\sqrt{r_p + r^*} - \sqrt{r^*})].\tag{30}$$

If the expression in brackets is positive, it will be advantageous to employ money for all transactions of the ith group ($\Phi_i = 0$), while if the bracket expression is negative, the ith group should abandon money entirely ($\Phi_i = 1$). Therefore, the criterion for employing *substitutes* for the entire volume of transactions corresponding to $(Y/P)_i$ is:

$$(\Psi/P)_i < 2A(\sqrt{r_p + r^*} - \sqrt{r^*}).\tag{31}$$

Given the group criterion of equation (31), and assuming that A, r_p, and r^* do not vary among different groups, the overall percentage of substitute transactions as a function of r_p is determined by the joint distribution of $(\Psi/P)_i$ and $(Y/P)_i$. In the absence of direct empirical evidence on this distribution, an aggregate relation for subsequent empirical analysis is derived from the following (semiheroic) assumptions: (1) $(\Psi/P)_i$ and $(Y/P)_i$ are independently distributed; (2) the distribution of $(\Psi/P)_i$ satisfies certain boundary conditions,[22] and can be adequately described by a (second-order) gamma distribution (Hogg and Craig 1965, pp. 91–93):

$$P_r[(\Psi/P)_i \leq x] = 1 - (1 + \lambda x)e^{-\lambda x} \quad (x \geq 0),$$
$$P_r[(\Psi/P)_i \leq x] = 0 \qquad\qquad\qquad (x < 0), \tag{32}$$

where, P_r may be interpreted as a cumulative probability. With the above assumptions, the overall percentage of substitute transactions is:

$$\Phi = P_r[(\Psi/P)_i \leq 2A(\sqrt{r_p + r^*} - \sqrt{r^*})]. \tag{33}$$

Letting $k = 2A\lambda$, we obtain from equation (32):[23]

$$\Phi = 1 - [1 + k(\sqrt{r_p + r^*} - \sqrt{r^*})]e^{-k(\sqrt{r_p + r^*} - \sqrt{r^*})} \quad (r_p \geq 0),$$
$$\Phi = 0 \qquad\qquad\qquad\qquad\qquad\qquad\qquad (r_p < 0). \tag{34}$$

Using equation (26) we obtain the demand-for-money function:

$$M/P = \frac{AY/P}{\sqrt{r_p + r^*}}[1 + k(\sqrt{r_p + r^*} - \sqrt{r^*})]e^{-k(\sqrt{r_p + r^*} - \sqrt{r^*})}, \quad (r_p \geq 0),$$
$$\tag{35}$$

$$M/P = \frac{AY/P}{\sqrt{r_p + r^*}} \qquad\qquad\qquad\qquad (-r^* < r_p < 0).^{24}$$

In equation (32), the "expected value" of $(\Psi/P)_i$ is $\overline{(\Psi/P)} = 2/\lambda$. Therefore, in equations (34) and (35), $k = 4A/\overline{(\Psi/P)}$ is a parameter which is inversely related to the average cost of employing money substitutes. The higher this average cost, the smaller the percentage of money substitutes (equation [34]), and the larger the demand for the conventional money supply (equation [35]) for a given value of r_p.[25]

The inflation-rate elasticity from equation [35] for large values of r_p is:

$$\frac{\partial(M/P)}{\partial r_p} \cdot \frac{r_p}{M/P} \approx -\frac{1}{2}\left(1 + \frac{k^2 r_p}{1 + k\sqrt{r_p}}\right) \quad (r_p \gg r^*). \tag{36}$$

---

[22] (1) $f(x) = 0$ for $x \leq 0$ (see n. 24), (2) $f(x)$ is skewed to the left for positive values of x, (3) $f(x)$ is approximately exponentially declining for large values of x. While the (second-order) gamma distribution is only one possible distribution that satisfies these properties, some others which might be considered (such as, log normal) have cumulative distributions which cannot be integrated in closed form.

[23] By adopting the boundary condition $\Phi(r_p = 0) = 0$, we ignore the possible use of money substitutes when $r_p < 0$. Actually, a positive rate of return on money holdings ($r_p < 0$) may be required in order to induce certain nonmonetary sectors of the economy (especially prevalent in underdeveloped countries) to employ the conventional money supply.

[24] The situation with $r_p \leq r^*$ is unstable because the real rate of return on money holdings ($-r_p$) exceeds the marginal impatience rate, r^*. The stability properties of the system will be discussed in a later paper.

[25] The percentage of money-substitute transactions, as a function of the rate of inflation, is illustrated in the table below. Parameter values of $k = 1.25$ (months $^{1/2}$) (the empirical estimate for Germany) and $r^* = .01$ per month have been used.

Therefore, the (absolute) elasticity increases with r_p beyond $\frac{1}{2}$, with the rate of increase depending on k. While the precise form of equation (36) hinges on the assumed distributions of $(\Psi/P)_i$ and $(Y/P)_i$, the general behavior depends only on an increasing tendency to adopt substitutes as r_p rises, and has already been described in equation (27).

In equation (35), which assumes that transactions costs, a/P, rise proportionately with Y/P, the elasticity of real cash balances with respect to real income is constant at $+1.0$. If transactions costs rise less than in proportion to Y/P, the elasticity is reduced and "economies-of-scale" in cash balances are realized. If transactions costs rise more than in proportion to Y/P, the elasticity exceeds $+1.0$ and money is a "luxury." [26]

D. The "Effective" Rate of Inflation

Equation (35) indicates the quantity of real money holdings, M/P, corresponding to a steady rate of inflation, r_p. If the inflation rate varies over time, equation (35) does not carry over directly, since the underlying optimization assumes that the single rate r_p persists forever (or, at least, that all economic actors behave as though they believe in a constant rate). If the rate of inflation is not constant, we can *define* an effective rate of inflation, π_t^e, as that "perpetual" rate which corresponds to the current (demand for) real balances in the form of equation (35). That is:

$$(M/P)_t^D \equiv \frac{A\,Y/P}{\sqrt{\pi_t^e + r^*}}\,[1 + k(\sqrt{\pi_t^e + r^*} - \sqrt{r^*})]\,e^{-k(\sqrt{\pi_t^e + r^*} - \sqrt{r^*})} \quad (\pi_t^e \geq 0),$$

$$(37)$$

$$(M/P)_t^D \equiv \frac{A\,Y/P}{\sqrt{\pi_t^e + r^*}} \qquad (-r^* < \pi_t^e < 0),$$

where, we maintain the assumption that Y/P and r^* are fixed.

r_p (% per month)	$\Phi(\%)$
0	0
1	0.2
3	0.8
15	5.5
50	18.0
200	49.2

Therefore, if the form of the distribution and the estimated k value are accepted, money substitutes become important only under the most extreme inflationary conditions.

[26] This result assumes that changes in Y/P do not, *ceteris paribus*, produce changes in the percentage of transactions which are monetized. One might argue that an increase in overall real income (development) is associated with shifts to types of

If π_t denotes the actual rate of inflation, $(1/P)(dP)/(dt)$, at time t, the steady-state model suggests the boundary condition: $\pi_t = r_p = $ constant, for $t = -\infty, +\infty \Rightarrow \pi_t^e = r_p$, where, π_t at future times may be interpreted here as a fully expected ($\pi_t = r_p$ with probability 1) rate of inflation.

In the general case we require behavioral assumptions that go beyond the steady-state model.

The statement that $(M/P)_t^D$ is related to π_t^e in the form of equation (37) amounts to the statement that π_t^e determines such fundamental decision variables as the payments period and the percentage of money substitutes in a manner which leads to the prescribed form for money demand. Accordingly, T/n (for those transactions which retain the conventional money supply) is given from equation (21) as:

$$(T/n)_t \equiv \sqrt{\frac{a/P}{Y/P(\pi_t^e + r^*)}}, \tag{38}$$

and the percentage of money substitutes by:[27]

$$\Phi_t \equiv 1 - [1 + k(\sqrt{\pi_t^e + r^*} - \sqrt{r^*})]e^{-k(\sqrt{\pi_t^e + r^*} - \sqrt{r^*})} \quad (\pi_t^e \geq 0),$$
$$\Phi_t \equiv 0 \quad\quad\quad\quad\quad\quad\quad\quad\quad\quad\quad\quad\quad\quad\quad\quad (\pi_t^e < 0). \tag{39}$$

Presumably, values of $(T/n)_t$ and Φ_t (with implied values of π_t^e) are chosen over time so as to minimize some conception of inflationary costs. In attempting to quantify these costs below, we neglect the influence of money substitutes (take $k \approx 0$) in order to keep the algebra manageable.[28]

Assume that the actual rate of price change, π_t, prevails over some time interval, T. The cost associated with maintaining an effective rate, π_t^e, over this interval is:

$$Z = T\left[\overline{(M/P)}(\pi_t + r^*) + \frac{n}{T} \cdot \frac{a}{P}\right] = T\left[\frac{Y}{P}\frac{T}{n}(\pi_t + r^*) + \frac{n}{T}\frac{a}{P}\right]. \tag{40}$$

---

transactions in which the benefits of money as a payments medium are high ($\overline{\Psi/P}$ increases as $\overline{Y/P}$ increases—though this is likely to contradict the previous simplifying assumption that $[\Psi/P]_i$ and $[Y/P]_i$ are independently distributed). In this case the income elasticity is raised, and money is more likely to emerge as a luxury.

[27] It is assumed that the same π_t^e value is appropriate for T/n, Φ, and any other decision variables that are relevant for $(M/P)^D$.

[28] Essentially, we concentrate on the payments period as a decision variable, and therefore restrict attention to individuals who retain the conventional money supply. As far as relative shifts in and out of substitutes (changes in Φ) differ from relative shifts in the payments period, some error will be introduced in the generation of π^e. The error is likely to be small for small values of Φ (see n. 24), and may become important as Φ becomes large. However, the direction of error is not immediately clear, and further analysis would be required to ascertain it.

Substituting for T/n from equation (38) (with $A = \sqrt{[a/P]/[Y/P]}$) we obtain after simplifying:

$$Z = \frac{T \cdot A Y/P}{\sqrt{\pi_t^e + r^*}} (\pi_t + r^* + \pi_t^e + r^*). \tag{41}$$

If π_t^e is set equal to the actual rate, π_t, the cost is (assuming $\pi_t + r^* > 0$):

$$\mathbf{Z} = 2T(A Y/P) \sqrt{\pi_t + r^*}. \tag{42}$$

Therefore, the cost of maintaining an effective rate different from the actual rate (over time T) is (after simplifying):

$$Z - \mathbf{Z} = \frac{T \cdot A Y/P}{\sqrt{\pi_t^e + r^*}} (\sqrt{\pi_t + r^*} - \sqrt{\pi_t^e + r^*})^2. \tag{43}$$

Clearly, the minimum cost, $Z - \mathbf{Z} = 0$, obtains at $\pi_t^e = \pi_t$.

Presumably, if π_t were perceived instantaneously, and π_t^e (that is, T/n and other implied decision variables) could be adjusted costlessly with a zero time lag, we would always have $\pi_t^e = \pi_t$. Assuming that the lag in perception of π_t can be neglected, the essential characteristic for the existence of $\pi_t^e \neq \pi_t$ is a nonzero cost associated with changes in π^e (that is, with changes in T/n, et cetera). Let α denote the real (fixed) cost attached to making changes in π^e (the cost is assumed to be invariant with the amount of the change). In general, if π^e is varied more frequently, the α cost rises, but the average cost of being out of equilibrium (setting $\sqrt{\pi^e + r^*} \neq \sqrt{\pi + r^*}$ is equation [43]) declines. The complete description of the tradeoff requires a specification of the mechanism by which π is generated.

The model adopted here involves the application of an (S,s) policy to a stochastic inventory model of the type utilized by Miller and Orr (1966) in a different context. Assume that at time zero an economic unit has just adjusted its effective rate to equal the current actual rate ($\pi_0^e = \pi_0$). Future actual rates are assumed to be observed as averages over discrete time periods: $\pi_\tau, \pi_{2\tau}, \ldots$, with a fixed observation interval, τ. The variable, $\sqrt{\pi_t + r^*}$, is assumed to follow a symmetric random walk with fixed step size ϵ, beginning at $\sqrt{\pi_0 + r^*}$ at time zero. That is, $\sqrt{\pi_\tau + r^*} = \sqrt{\pi_0 + r^*} + \epsilon$ with probability $\frac{1}{2}$, and $\sqrt{\pi_0 + r^*} - \epsilon$ with probability $\frac{1}{2}$; $\sqrt{\pi_{2\tau} + r^*} = \sqrt{\pi_\tau + r^*} \pm \epsilon$ with $\frac{1}{2}$ probability each, and so on. The economic unit selects ceiling and floor values of $\sqrt{\pi + r^*}$, $\sqrt{\pi_0 + r^*} + h_u$ and $\sqrt{\pi_0 + r^*} - h_L$, at which adjustments in π^e occur (that is, the unit sets $\sqrt{\pi^e + r^*} = \sqrt{\pi_0 + r^*} + h_u$ if the ceiling is reached, and $\sqrt{\pi^e + r^*} = \sqrt{\pi_0 + r^*} - h_L$ if the floor is reached).[29] Because the cost of being out of equilibrium is

---

[29] The realism of this process can be questioned on two (interrelated) levels: (1) Do individuals behave this way? (2) Does the actual course of rates of price change approximate a random walk? Since π_t is endogenous at the aggregate level, the second

symmetric about π_0, an optimal solution involves $h_u = h_L = h$.[30] The higher the selected value of h, the smaller the adjustment (α) cost, but the larger the average out-of-equilibrium cost. The tradeoff is formalized below.

Let $x = (\sqrt{\pi_t + r^*} - \sqrt{\pi_0^e + r^*})/\epsilon$ denote the random variable (with zero origin and unit step size) which is subject to the random walk. The density of x is determined by the difference equation:

$$f(x, t) = \frac{1}{2} f(x - 1, t - 1) + \frac{1}{2} f(x + 1, t - 1); x \neq 0; -\frac{h}{\epsilon} < x < \frac{h}{\epsilon}.$$

$$(44)$$

Confining attention to the steady-state distribution defined by:

$$f(x) = \frac{1}{2} f(x - 1) + \frac{1}{2} f(x + 1); x \neq 0; -\frac{h}{\epsilon} < x < \frac{h}{\epsilon}, \quad (45)$$

with boundary conditions:

$$f(h/\epsilon) = f(-h/\epsilon) = 0,$$

$$f(0) = \frac{1}{2}\left[f\left(\frac{h}{\epsilon} - 1\right) + f(-1)\right] + \frac{1}{2}\left[f\left(-\frac{h}{\epsilon} + 1\right) + f(+1)\right]. \quad (46)$$

$$\sum_{x = -h/\epsilon}^{h/\epsilon} f(x) = 1,$$

the equation can be solved in the form $f(x) = A_1 + B_1 x$ ($x \geq 0$), $f(x) = A_2 + B_2 x$ ($x \leq 0$).

---

question involves, in particular, the behavior of the rate of change of the money supply. Because the random-walk process is nonstationary, it is unlikely to provide a realistic long-run description of the rate of price change or of the rate of change of the money supply. Nevertheless, the process may provide a useful basis for short-run analysis of individual adjustment behavior. In any case the important assumptions seem to be: (1) a fixed perception interval, τ, (2) the symmetric nature of the walk, and (3) serial independence. The second assumption reflects a (long-run) neutral stance toward acceleration or deceleration of prices, and appears to be reasonable. The third assumption (which rules out extrapolations of the recent π_t trend) is more questionable. Serial dependence would affect the form, though not the general nature, of the results. The first assumption is critical for the model, and reflects a segment of behavior that has not been considered at all. Essentially, the random-walk process regards any observed value of π_t as the best estimate of future π values. Accordingly, no distinction is made between expected and actual rates of inflation, and the explanation for $\pi_t^e \neq \pi_t$ derives solely from costs of adjustment of π^e. As the perception interval (τ) tends to zero, the model implies that each instantaneous value of $(1/p)(dp)/(dt)$ is, by itself, the best estimate of future π_t's. Maintaining a finite value of τ substitutes an average value of $(1/p)(dp)/(dt)$ for an instantaneous value, but does not change the fundamental problem. A complete model would consider both expectational and adjustment factors in the formation of the effective rate (π^e), and would remove the ad hoc perception interval that was necessitated by the lack of an expectations mechanism.

[30] This is a slight approximation, based on the discussion in n. 34 below.

Using the four boundary conditions to evaluate the constants, the solution is:

$$f(x) = \frac{\epsilon}{h}\left(1 - \frac{\epsilon x}{h}\right) \quad (x \geq 0),$$

$$f(x) = \frac{\epsilon}{h}\left(1 + \frac{\epsilon x}{h}\right) \quad (x \leq 0). \tag{47}$$

In equation (43) the cost of being out of equilibrium depends on $(\epsilon x)^2 = (\sqrt{\pi_t + r^*} - \sqrt{\pi_0^e + r^*})^2$. Using the density function of equation (47), the average out-of-equilibrium cost (per unit of time) can be calculated as:[31]

$$\frac{E(Z - \mathbf{Z})}{T} = \frac{A\,Y/P}{\sqrt{\pi_0^e + r^*}} \cdot E(\epsilon x)^2 \approx \frac{A\,Y/P}{\sqrt{\pi_0^e + r^*}}\left(\frac{h^2}{6}\right), \tag{48}$$

where, E denotes an expected value. As suggested above, the (expected) out-of-equilibrium cost increases with h.

The second cost element (α cost) involves the expected number of π^e adjustments per unit of time. Feller has shown[32] that the expected duration (expected number of trials between hits at the ceiling or floor) for the random-walk process under consideration is:

$$D = h^2/\epsilon^2(\text{ expected number of trials}). \tag{49}$$

The above expression for D can be converted to time units by multiplying by τ (time per trial) to obtain:

$$D = \frac{h^2\tau}{\epsilon^2} \text{ (expected number of time units).} \tag{50}$$

---

[31]
$$E(x^2) = \frac{\epsilon}{h}\left[\sum_0^{h/\epsilon} x^2\left(1 - \frac{\epsilon x}{h}\right) + \sum_0^{-h/\epsilon} x^2\left(1 + \frac{\epsilon x}{h}\right)\right]$$

$$= \frac{2\epsilon}{h}\left[\sum_0^{h/\epsilon} x^2 - \frac{\epsilon}{h}\sum_0^{h/\epsilon} x^3\right]$$

$$= \frac{2\epsilon}{h}\left[\frac{h/\epsilon}{6}\left(\frac{2h}{\epsilon} + 1\right)\left(\frac{h}{\epsilon} + 1\right) - \frac{\epsilon}{h}\left(\frac{(h/\epsilon)^2(h/\epsilon + 1)^2}{4}\right)\right]$$

$$= (h/\epsilon + 1)\left[\frac{2h/\epsilon + 1}{3} - \frac{h/\epsilon + 1}{2}\right]$$

$$= \frac{(h/\epsilon)^2 - 1}{6} = \frac{1}{\epsilon^2}\left(\frac{h^2 - \epsilon^2}{6}\right)$$

$$\approx \frac{h^2}{6\epsilon^2} \text{ if } h/\epsilon \gg 1.$$

Therefore, $E(\epsilon x)^2 \approx h^2/6$.

[32] Feller 1968, p. 349. In Feller's model, the barriers are at 0 and a, with an intermediate starting point at z; while in our model, the barriers are at $\pm h$, with a starting point of 0. However, Feller's results are readily adaptable to our case.

The above expression measures the expected amount of time between contacts with the upper or lower barrier (that is, between adjustments of π^e). The expected number of contacts (adjustments) per unit of time can be approximated by $1/D$ (see Miller and Orr 1966, p. 421).

Letting m denote the number of contacts in time T, we have:

$$E(m/T) \approx 1/D = \frac{\epsilon^2}{h^2 \tau}. \tag{51}$$

As suggested above, the higher h, the lower the (expected) number of adjustments per time, and the lower the associated (expected) α cost.

The variance of the Bernoulli process involved in the symmetric random walk can be derived (as a function of time) as $\sigma_t^2 = (\epsilon^2/\tau) \cdot t$, where t denotes the total elapsed time since the start at time zero.[33] At $t = 1$ (month) the variance is:

$$\sigma^2 = \frac{\epsilon^2}{\tau} = \text{monthly variance of } \sqrt{\pi_t + r^*}. \tag{52}$$

Therefore, the expected adjustment cost per unit of time may be written (from equation [51]) as:

$$E(Z_\alpha) = \alpha \cdot E(m/T) = \alpha \cdot \frac{\sigma^2}{h^2}. \tag{53}$$

The total expected cost per unit of time (as a function of h) is (from equations [48] and [53]):[34]

$$E(\text{cost/time}) = \frac{E(Z - \mathbf{Z})}{T} + \alpha \cdot E(m/T)$$

$$= \frac{A Y/P}{6\sqrt{\pi_0^e + r^*}} \cdot h^2 + \alpha \cdot \frac{\sigma^2}{h^2}. \tag{54}$$

The value of h^2 that minimize this expected cost is given from $\partial(\text{Cost})/\partial h^2 = 0$ as:

$$\hat{h}^2 = \left(\frac{6\alpha}{A Y/P}\right)^{1/2} \sigma(\pi_0^e + r^*)^{1/4}. \tag{55}$$

On an individual level, π^e is shifted or kept constant according to whether a newly observed value of π_t is sufficient to reach a ceiling or floor (with the ceiling and floor positions determined from equation [55]). The

---

[33] See Miller and Orr, p. 419. This unconstrained variance is, of course, derived independently of the barrier positions at $\pm h$, and, therefore, does not correspond to $E(\epsilon x)^2$, which was calculated above.

[34] This analysis neglects the fact that subsequent starting points do not correspond to the initial point ($\sqrt{\pi_0^e + r^*}$). In fact, the starting points conform to a modified symmetric random walk with stochastic time interval and varying step size. Since the process is symmetric, neglecting it may be a satisfactory first approximation.

aggregate π^e behavior depends on the proportion of units that attain ceilings or floors in a particular time interval. An approximation to the aggregate response is described below.

Assume that a particular value of $\epsilon x = \sqrt{\pi_t + r^*} - \sqrt{\pi_0^e + r^*}$ prevails at some time. The likely conclusion of the random walk which originates at x (that is, the relative probabilities of hitting the ceiling or floor first) depends on the position of x relative to h and $-h$. It can be shown that (see Feller 1968, p. 345):

$$Pr(+h) = \frac{h + \epsilon x}{2h},$$

$$Pr(-h) = \frac{h - \epsilon x}{2h},$$

(56)

where $Pr(+h)$ is the probability of terminating at $+h$ when the process originates at x, and analogously for $Pr(-h)$.

The expected duration of the walk which originates at x is (Feller, p. 349):

$$D_x = \frac{(h - \epsilon x)(h + \epsilon x)}{\sigma^2}.$$

(57)

Therefore, the expected number of adjustments per time is:

$$E(m/T) \approx 1/D_x = \frac{\sigma^2}{(h - \epsilon x)(h + \epsilon x)}.$$

(58)

The expected number of ceiling hits per time can be approximated by:

$$E\left(\frac{m+}{T}\right) \approx Pr(+h) \cdot E(m/T) \approx \frac{\sigma^2}{2h(h - \epsilon x)}.$$

(59)

Similarly, the expected number of floor hits is:

$$E\left(\frac{m-}{T}\right) \approx Pr(-h) \cdot E(m/T) \approx \frac{\sigma^2}{2h(h + \epsilon x)}.$$

(60)

Each ceiling hit produces an increase in (an individual's) $\sqrt{\pi^e + r^*}$ by h, and each floor hit a reduction by h. The net (expected) change in $\sqrt{\pi^e + r^*}$ is given by:

$$\frac{d}{dt}\left(\sqrt{\pi^e + r^*}\right) \approx h \cdot \left[E\left(\frac{m+}{T}\right) - E\left(\frac{m-}{T}\right)\right]$$

(61)

$$= \frac{\sigma^2}{2}\left(\frac{1}{h - \epsilon x} - \frac{1}{h + \epsilon x}\right) = \frac{\sigma^2 \epsilon x}{h^2 - (\epsilon x)^2} \approx \frac{\sigma^2 \epsilon x}{h^2}$$

$$\text{(if } h \gg \epsilon x).[35]$$

[35] That is, the original (in effect, average aggregate) deviation, $\sqrt{\pi_t + r^*} - \sqrt{\pi_t^e + r^*}$, is assumed to be small relative to that deviation (h) which produces a shift in π.

Substituting $\epsilon x = (\sqrt{\pi_t + r^*} - \sqrt{\pi_0^e + r^*})$, and $h^2 = \hat{h}^2$ from equation (55):

$$\frac{d}{dt}\sqrt{\pi^e + r^*} \approx \left(\frac{A\,Y/P}{6\alpha}\right)^{1/2}\sigma(\pi_0^e + r^*)^{-1/4}(\sqrt{\pi_t + r^*} - \sqrt{\pi_0^e + r^*}).$$
(62)

Equation (62) describes the expected change over time in (an individual's) $\sqrt{\pi^e + r^*}$ as a function of the current gap $(\sqrt{\pi_t + r^*} - \sqrt{\pi_0^e + r^*})$. With the additional (difficult to evaluate) assumption that the average aggregate value of $\sqrt{\pi_t + r^*} - \sqrt{\pi_0^e + r^*}$ yields a satisfactory approximation to average behavior in the form of equation (62), the relationship can be used to explain the trend over time in the average aggregate value of π_t^e, which is assumed to be relevant for aggregate money demand in the form of equation (37).

The first term on the right side of equation (62), $[(A\,Y/P)/6\alpha]^{1/2}$, may perhaps be satisfactorily regarded as a constant. However, σ, the square root of the monthly variance of $\sqrt{\pi + r^*}$, generally depends on the intensity of inflation. Provisionally, this dependence is approximated in the following manner.

Let $\mu = (1/M)(dM/dt)$ denote the proportionate rate of change of the money stock. The corresponding amount of inflationary-financed (government) expenditure is: $G_M = \mu \cdot M/P$. Assuming $M/P \approx M/P^D$ and $\pi^e \approx \mu$, we have (from equation [37] with $k \approx 0$):

$$\frac{dG_M}{dt} = \frac{d}{dt}(\mu \cdot M/P) \approx \frac{M/P}{2}\left(1 + \frac{r^*}{\mu + r^*}\right)\frac{d\mu}{dt}.$$
(63)

Therefore:

$$\frac{d\mu}{dt} \approx \frac{2}{M/P}\left(1 - \frac{r^*}{\mu + 2r^*}\right)\frac{dG_M}{dt}.$$
(64)

If government expenditure is financed by a combination of money creation and tax revenues ($G = G_M + G_T$) we have:

$$\frac{dG}{dt} = \frac{dG_M}{dt} + \frac{dG_T}{dt}.$$
(65)

If the primary function of inflationary finance is to offset (unexpected?) variations in tax revenue (that is, $dG/dt \approx 0$), we have:

$$\frac{dG_M}{dt} \approx -\frac{dG_T}{dt}.$$
(66)

Letting θ denote the proportional rate of change of nominal tax revenues, we have:

$$\frac{dG_T}{dt} = G_T[\theta - \pi].$$
(67)

Therefore, the magnitude of fluctuation in tax revenues depends on the average magnitude of $|\theta - \pi|$. Provisionally, we assume that this average size is proportional to π^e. In this case:

$$\left|\frac{dG_T}{dt}\right| \approx g \cdot \pi^e \ (g = \text{constant}).\tag{68}$$

Therefore, from equations (66) and (64):

$$\left|\frac{d\mu}{dt}\right| \approx \frac{2g\pi^e}{M/P}\left(1 - \frac{r^*}{\mu + 2r^*}\right).\tag{69}$$

Using $\mu \approx \pi^e$, $M/P \approx M/P^D$, and substituting from equation (37):

$$\left|\frac{d}{dt}\sqrt{\mu + r^*}\right| \approx \frac{g}{A\,Y/P}\frac{\pi^e}{1 - \Phi}\left(1 - \frac{r^*}{\pi^e + 2r^*}\right),\tag{70}$$

where Φ is given by equation (39).

If $|d/(dt)\sqrt{\pi + r^*}|$ can be approximated by $|d/(dt)\sqrt{\mu + r^*}|$, and if σ (the monthly standard deviation of $\sqrt{\pi + r^*}$) is proportional to $|d/(dt) \times \sqrt{\pi + r^*}|$, we have (from equation [62]) a mechanism for generating effective rates of inflation:

$$\frac{d}{dt}\sqrt{\pi^e + r^*} \approx b \cdot \frac{\pi^e}{(\pi^e + r^*)^{1/4}}\left(\frac{1}{1 - \Phi}\right)\left(1 - \frac{r^*}{\pi^e + 2r^*}\right)$$
$$\times (\sqrt{\pi + r^*} - \sqrt{\pi^e + r^*}),\tag{71}$$

where $b = \text{constant} > 0$.

If $\pi^e \gg r^*$:

$$\frac{d}{dt}\sqrt{\pi^e} \approx b \cdot (\pi^e)^{3/4}\left(\frac{1}{1 - \Phi}\right)(\sqrt{\pi} - \sqrt{\pi^e}).\tag{72}$$

The mechanism in equations (71) and (72) may be compared with the original adaptive-expectations model (Cagan, p. 37): ﹣

$$\frac{d}{dt}(\pi^e) = \gamma(\pi - \pi^e), (\gamma > 0).\tag{73}$$

The new mechanism differs in two respects. First, as a reflection of the underlying inflationary costs, the mechanism (equations [71] and [72]) emerges in square root, rather than linear, form. Second, the coefficient of adjustment is not constant, but increases with the rate of inflation (with $(\pi^e)^{3/4}[1/(1 - \Phi)]$ in equation [72]). Cagan's empirical results suggested that a rising adjustment coefficient might be a more appropriate mechanism (Cagan, pp. 58–64). The current model provides a theoretically derived mechanism of this type, which is used for an empirical study in the second part of this paper.

II. Empirical Results on Demand for Money during Hyperinflations

The theoretical model of demand for money has been applied to data on four post–World War I hyperinflations (Austria, Germany, Hungary, Poland) previously studied by Cagan (1956)[36] and Allais (1966). The data for each case differ somewhat from that employed by Cagan, and are described briefly in the Appendix tables. The demand-for-money function is derived from the theoretical model (equations [37] and [39]):

$$\log (M/P^D)_t = \alpha_1 + \alpha_2 \cdot \log (\pi^e + r^*)_t + \log (1 - \Phi_t) + u_t, \quad (74)$$

where:

$$(1 - \Phi_t) = [1 + k(\sqrt{\pi^e + r^*} - \sqrt{r^*})_t]e^{-k(\sqrt{\pi^e + r^*} - \sqrt{r^*})t}, (\pi^e_t \geq 0); \quad (75)$$

$$(1 - \Phi_t) = 1, \qquad\qquad\qquad (- r^*_t < \pi^e_t < 0);$$

and u_t is thought of as an independently, normally distributed disturbance term. In the theoretical model, $\alpha_1 = \log (A Y/P)$ (though this coefficient is likely to be affected by aggregation) and $\alpha_2 = -0.5$. We have assumed, additionally, for the current empirical study that $Y/P \approx$ constant; $r^* \approx$ constant ≈ 0; $(M/P^D)_t \approx (M/P)_t$.

The accuracy of $Y/P \approx$ constant for the relatively short hyperinflationary experiences under consideration has been discussed in Cagan (pp. 97–114). The type of information that Cagan considers can be used to construct rough employment indices for the four cases. These indices are contained in the Appendix tables. Considering the coverage and accuracy of the basic data, the indices seem fairly reliable (as a general indicator) for Austria and Germany, less reliable for Poland, and mostly unreliable for Hungary. The overall indication is that variations in real income were small relative to changes in the inflation rate, so that taking $Y/P \approx$ constant may be satisfactory (though this conclusion is especially questionable for Hungary and uncertain for Poland). Because of the crude nature of the employment data, the addition of real income to the regression equations has not been attempted.

In general, the real rate of discount (r^*) should be somewhat above the (riskless) real rate of return in an economy. Average real rates of return during the hyperinflations were apparently small and possibly negative. Accordingly, we expect values of r^* near zero, and, in any case, negligible in comparison with the inflation-rate variable (π^e). Therefore, we have set $r^* = 0$ and have not attempted to estimate r^* from the data.

---

[36] Three cases from Cagan's original seven have been excluded: post–World War I Russia and World War II Greece and Hungary. The Russian case was excluded because the assumption of constant real income appeared unreasonable and adequate income data was unavailable. The money-supply data for Greece was unreliable (Cagan, p. 106), and the variation in real income during the war was apparently substantial (*International Labor Review*, December 1945, p. 650). The available data for Hungary covers too brief a period to provide a useful test of the model.

The possible error involved with taking $M/P^D = M/P$ is not explicitly considered in this paper.

The effective rate of inflation (π^e) in equations (74) and (75) is assumed to be generated by the mechanism of equation (72):

$$\frac{d}{dt}\sqrt{\pi^e} = b(\pi^e)^{3/4}\left(\frac{1}{1-\Phi}\right)(\sqrt{\pi} - \sqrt{\pi^e}), \qquad (76)$$

where, Φ is given in equation (75). Since the model is applied to discrete (monthly) data, a discrete approximation has been used:[37]

$$\sqrt{\pi_t^e} \approx \beta_t \cdot \sqrt{\bar{\pi}_t} + (1 - \beta_t)\sqrt{\pi_{t-1}^e},$$

$$\beta_t = 1 - e^{-b(\bar{\pi}_t^e)^{3/4}}\left(\frac{1}{1-\bar{\Phi}_t}\right), \qquad (77)$$

where, $\bar{\pi}_t$ is the average rate of price change over the interval $(t - 1, t)$, $\bar{\pi}_t^e = \frac{1}{2}(\pi_t^e + \pi_{t-1}^e)$, and $\bar{\Phi}_t = \Phi(\bar{\pi}_t^e)$.

The coefficients to be estimated for each case are α_1, α_2, k, and b. The method of estimation is a nonlinear iterative routine for minimizing the sum of squared residuals in each regression. This procedure corresponds to maximum likelihood estimation if the error disturbances (u_t) are independently and normally distributed.[38] Since the primary objective is to test the theory, we list the a priori conjectures on each coefficient:

1. $\alpha_1 = \log(AY/P)$: Without information on real income levels, this coefficient depends on arbitrary index levels, and cannot be tested.

2. $\alpha_2 = -0.5$: This point value is the strongest a priori information to be tested.

3. k: This parameter determines the percentage of money substitutes (Φ) as a function of π^e (equation [75]). The higher k, the larger the percentage of substitutes and the smaller the demand for money at a given value of π^e: $k = 4A/(\overline{\Psi/P}) = 4\sqrt{a/Y}/(\overline{\Psi/P})$ (see Section IC), where a/Y is the ratio of transactions cost to transactions volume and $\overline{\Psi/P}$ is the average cost of employing money substitutes (per amount of transaction). To obtain some notion of the order of magnitude of k, we assume (taking time units of months), $0.5/400 \le a/Y \le 2.0/400$, $.10 \le \overline{\Psi/P} \le .20$. Correspondingly, the limiting values of k are $0.7 \le k \le 2.8$ (months$^{1/2}$).

---

[37] Negative values of $\bar{\pi}_t$ were set equal to zero in order to obtain $\sqrt{\bar{\pi}_t}$ in equation (77). In fact, few negative values occurred so that no major adjustment was required. Nevertheless, the necessity for this adjustment reflects an incompleteness in the generation mechanism for π^e, which may stem from the lack of an expectations mechanism (see n. 29).

[38] See Cagan, pp. 93–94. One problem with the estimation is that P_t influences both sides of the equation. This problem is not serious when $\beta_t \ll 1$, but may become important for the most extreme observations. Unfortunately, obtaining a reduced form equation does not seem possible.

Obviously, this limit is both wide and arbitrary, but $k > 0$ is a fundamental implication of the theory: $k = 0$ (an infinite cost for money substitutes) corresponds to a constant inflation-rate elasticity, while $k > 0$ corresponds to an increasing (absolute) elasticity. The model is supported if $k = 0$ can be rejected in favor of $k > 0$.

The k parameter may also be viewed in terms of its variation among different cases. The theory suggests (for given values of a/Y) that k is larger the smaller the value of $\overline{\Psi}/P$. Therefore, higher k values correspond to situations where money substitutes are more readily available (that is, less costly). However, there is little a priori basis for determining relative $\overline{\Psi}/P$ values among the cases studied, so that equality among the k values forms the basic null hypothesis.

4. b: This coefficient determines the speed with which effective rates of inflation (π^e) respond to actual rates (π) (equation [77]). A priori, we expect $b > 0$ and approximately equal for each case: $b = 0$ implies that π^e does not respond at all to changes in π, therefore, $b = 0$ should be rejectable in favor of $b > 0$. Order-of-magnitude notions of b were not derived.

The a priori conjectures on the coefficients are tested by means of the likelihood ratio (λ). The asymptotic χ^2 distribution of $-2 \log_e \lambda$ is utilized to construct 95 percent confidence intervals for each coefficient.[39] These intervals can then be used to construct acceptance regions for two-sided (5 percent) tests of the a priori conjectures on each coefficient.[40] The tests were applied independently for each coefficient in order to obtain separate conclusions on each conjecture. While these tests depend on asymptotic distribution theory and are not actually independent, the greatest hedge on their validity seems to be the assumed serial independence of the errors.

The likelihood ratio was also used to test the joint null hypothesis, $\alpha_2 = -0.5$, for the four cases combined, and to test the null hypothesis of equality for α_2, k, and b coefficients among the different cases.

The basic empirical results are contained in table 2. This table contains point estimates and 95 percent confidence intervals for the coefficients of each regression, along with various measures of the fit. The overall estimates of α_2, k, and b are based on a combined regression for the four cases. For example, the overall estimate of α_2 ($-.515$) is that value which

---

[39] $-2 \log_e(\lambda) \sim \chi^2(\rho)$, where ρ is the number of restrictions contained in the null hypothesis (see Cagan, pp. 93–96). In the present case we have:

$$-2 \log_e \lambda = T[\log_e (SSE^*/\hat{SSE})] \sim \chi^2(\rho),$$

where $\hat{SSE}$ is the overall minimum error sum of squares, SSE^* is the minimum subject to ρ restrictions, and T is the number of observations.

[40] If the null hypothesis involves an interval rather than a point value, the (maximum) type one error probability corresponding to a 95 percent confidence interval is below .05.

TABLE 2

EMPIRICAL RESULTS

$$\text{Log } (M/P)_t = \hat{\alpha}_1 + \hat{\alpha}_2 \cdot \text{Log } (\pi_t^e) + \text{Log } (1 - \hat{\Phi}_t)$$

Country	Period	T	$\hat{\alpha}_1$	$\hat{\alpha}_2$	$\hat{k}$	$\hat{b}$	AAE	SEE	R^2	D.-W.
Austria	1/21–12/22	24	.82	−.545 (−.46, −.62)	1.45 (.68, 2.11)	0.70 (.61, .77)	.038	.048	.987	1.67
Germany	1/21–8/23	32	.50	−.516 (−.49, −.54)	1.25 (1.13, 1.35)	0.82 (.77, .87)	.042	.050	.996	1.14
Hungary	10/21–2/24	29	−.73	−.578 (−.43, −.69)	0.95 (0−, 2.45)	0.93 (.70, 1.19)	.092	.114	.935	0.48
Poland	1/22–1/24	25	.46	−.417 (−.34, −.51)	1.70 (1.30, 2.01)	0.85 (.74, .97)	.046	.056	.990	0.78
Overall	. . .	110	. . .	−0.515	1.27	0.805	. . .	. . .	. . .	. . .

NOTES.—All data are monthly. All logarithms are base e. T is the number of observations; AAE is the average absolute error (which, $\times 100$, corresponds to the approximate average percentage error, since natural logarithms were used); SEE (standard error of estimate) is the root-mean-square residual, which corresponds to the maximum likelihood estimate of the standard error of the disturbance term; R^2 is the coefficient of determination; D.-W. is the Durbin-Watson statistic. 95 percent confidence intervals are indicated in parentheses below each point estimate.

yields a minimum overall sum of (weighted)[41] squared residuals in the constrained regression where α_2 estimates are equal for each case. Accordingly, this regression involves the imposition of three independent restrictions on the fit. Overall estimates of k (1.27) and b (0.805) are obtained in a similar manner.

Evaluation of Empirical Results

1. Coefficient Estimates

α_2 *estimates.*—The a priori value of -0.5 is within the 95 percent confidence interval for each case. Therefore, the null hypothesis, $\alpha_2 = -0.5$, is accepted at the .05 level for each case. The strongest result is provided by the German case, for which the 95 percent confidence interval $(-.49, -.54)$ is especially narrow.

An overall test of equality among the four α_2 values involves the likelihood ratio with 3 df, based on the overall estimate of α_2 $(-.515)$.[42] The relevant statistic is $-2 \log_e \lambda = 5.42$, which is less than $\chi^2(3)_{.05} = 7.82$, so that the null hypothesis of equality among the α_2's is accepted at the .05 level.

The overall hypothesis, $\alpha_2 = -0.5$, can be tested by constraining $\alpha_2 = -0.5$ in each case. The resulting statistic is: $-2 \log_e \lambda = 7.40$, which is less than $\chi^2(4)_{.05} = 9.49$. Therefore, the overall null hypothesis $\alpha_2 = -0.5$, is accepted at the .05 level.

Because of the restrictive nature of the null hypothesis ($\alpha_2 = -0.5$, a point value) the empirical results for the α_2 coefficients provide strong support for the underlying theory.

k *estimates.*—The point estimates of k are, in each case, positive and within the a priori interval, $0.7 \le k \le 2.8$. Therefore, the null hypothesis that each k lies within this interval is accepted. The null hypothesis, $k = 0$, is rejected at the 5 percent level in favor of $k > 0$ for Austria,

---

[41] The weighting scheme follows from the usual treatment of heteroscedastic disturbances. Let $(\hat{SEE})_i = \sqrt{(\hat{SSE}/T)_i}$ denote the estimated standard error of the residuals from the unconstrained regression for the ith case. In performing an overall regression, the observations for the ith case are weighted by $1/SEE_i = \sqrt{T_i/\hat{SSE}_i}$. Therefore, we wish to minimize the overall weighted sum of squared residuals:

$$\sum_{i=1}^{4} T_i \frac{SSE_i^*}{\hat{SSE}_i},$$

where SSE_i^* is the (restricted) sum of squared residuals for the ith case in the overall regression, and the summation is over the (four) cases in the sample.

[42] Based on the weighting scheme of n. 41 above, and the likelihood-ratio distribution discussed in n. 39 above, we have:

$$\sum_{i=1}^{4} T_i \left\{ \log_e \left[\frac{\sum T_i (SSE_i^*/\hat{SSE}_i)}{\sum T_i} \right] \right\} \sim \chi^2(3).$$

Germany, and Poland, but must be accepted for Hungary. Therefore, three of the four cases considered substantiate an increasing inflation-rate elasticity, as was suggested by the money-substitute section of the theory.

The null hypothesis of equality among k values for the four cases corresponds to a statistic: $-2 \log_e \lambda = 5.19$, which is less than $\chi^2(3)_{.05} = 7.82$. Therefore, equality among the k's is accepted at the .05 level. The implication is that no significant divergence existed in the availability of money substitutes among the four cases considered.

b estimates.—The point estimates are positive in each case, and significantly greater than zero. The null hypothesis of equality among the four cases corresponds to a statistic: $-2 \log_e \lambda = 9.22$, which is greater than $\chi^2(3)_{.05} = 7.82$ (though less than $\chi^2(3)_{.02} = 9.84$). Therefore, equality among the b coefficients is rejected at the .05 level. Observation of the individual confidence intervals suggests that the chief "cause" of rejection is the low b estimate for Austria, relative to those for Germany and Poland. Since there are no obvious theoretical grounds for divergence among b values, this result may be symptomatic of some flaw in the mechanism by which π^e is generated.

2. The Overall Fit and Comparison with Cagan's Results

In general the regression fits for Austria, Germany, and Poland (in terms of standard error of estimate [SEE]) are "good," and apparently quite similar.[43] The average errors for Hungary appear to be significantly higher than those for the other three cases.

Some perspective on the fit may be gained by a comparison with Cagan's results. Table 3 contains regression results in the form of Cagan's model:[44]

$$\log (M/P)_t = \hat{\alpha}_3 + \hat{\alpha}_4 \hat{\pi}_t^e,$$
$$\hat{\pi}_t^e = \hat{\beta}\pi_t + (1 - \hat{\beta})\hat{\pi}_{t-1}^e. \tag{78}$$

In general, the average errors in Cagan's form are about twice as large as those in table 2, and the serial correlation of residuals is substantially more pronounced (see below).

3. Autocorrelation of Residuals

A major cause of concern in the empirical results (table 2) is the generally low Durbin-Watson statistic, which indicates positive serial correlation

---

[43] No statistical tests for equality among error variances have been attempted.

[44] Cagan's model has been refitted here because of minor differences in data and in periods of observation, and because the original study did not include some of the desired statistical measures.

TABLE 3

CAGAN MODEL

$$\log (M/P)_t = \hat{\alpha}_3 + \hat{\alpha}_4 \cdot \hat{\pi}_t^e$$
$$\hat{\pi}_t^e = \hat{\beta}\pi_t + (1 - \hat{\beta})\hat{\pi}_{t-1}^e$$

Country	$\hat{\alpha}_3$	$\hat{\alpha}_4$	$\hat{\beta}$	AAE	SEE	R^2	D-W.
Austria.	2.67	−4.09	.171	.069	.090	.955	.53
		(−3.6, −4.5)	(.15, .21)				
Germany	2.43	−3.79	.176	.108	.127	.976	.25
		(−3.3, −4.3)	(.14, .21)				
Hungary	1.40	−5.53	.139	.114	.142	.898	.31
		(−4.6, −6.9)	(.10, .20)				
Poland	1.64	−2.56	.291	.091	.109	.963	.32
		(−2.1, −3.3)	(.18, .43)				

NOTE.—See table 2. Sample periods the same.

of residuals for Hungary and Poland, and possible positive correlation for Germany. Only in the Austrian case can serial correlation be ruled out.[45]

In principle, serial correlation does not produce inconsistency in point estimates, although it does reduce efficiency. The impact on statistical tests is likely to be more serious since the underlying distribution theory requires serially independent errors. One approach to the problem involves the explicit specification of a residual process which exhibits serial correlation (for example, a first-order Markov process). However, since the presence of serial correlation is likely to be an indicator of some sort of misspecification, the best remedy is a fuller specification of the model. This attempt at fuller specification constitutes a useful area for future research. At this point it is clear that the statistical results for Austria and Germany are considerably more reliable than those for Hungary and Poland. Despite the problem of serial correlation, it seems clear that the empirical results provide considerable support for the theory developed in Part I.

III. Extensions of the Model

Future extensions of the model aimed particularly at removing residual serial correlation will involve: (a) inclusion of additional explanatory variables, such as real income and seasonal factors; (b) further investiga-

[45] While the Durbin-Watson test is not strictly applicable to this nonlinear model, it should provide a useful measure of autocorrelation. Assuming that the model comprises four independent variables (plus a constant term), the statistics for Hungary and Poland indicate positive serial correlation at the 1 percent level. The German statistic indicates positive correlation at the 5 percent level, but is inconclusive at 2.5 percent. The Austrian statistic is inconclusive at 5 percent, but the null hypothesis of serial independence is accepted at 2.5 percent (see Durbin and Watson 1951, pp. 173–75).

tion of the effective rate of inflation mechanism, possibly involving the introduction of an expectations mechanism; (c) reconsideration of the assumption of continuous equilibrium between actual and desired money balances.

The theoretical results will be extended to a consideration of inflationary finance and the welfare cost of inflation.

The model will be applied to an empirical study of the inflationary experiences in Latin America and in other countries.

Appendix

TABLE A1

AUSTRIA

End-of-Month	β_t	π_t	π_t^e	Log $(M/P)_t$ (Actual)	Log $(M/P)_t$ (Estimated)	Residual	Employment Index
1921:							
January . . .	.076	.060	.052	2.349	2.385	−.036	99.3
February . .	.072	.156	.058	2.314	2.325	−.011	99.5
March . . .	.083	.068	.058	2.314	2.317	−.003	99.7
April	.080	.045	.057	2.363	2.329	.034	99.8
May	.079	.006	.051	2.370	2.394	−.024	99.8
June	.076	.144	.057	2.317	2.335	−.019	99.8
July.	.077	−.108	.048	2.509	2.429	.080	99.7
August . . .	.078	.275	.059	2.313	2.308	.005	99.8
September . .	.089	.292	.073	2.212	2.186	.025	99.9
October . . .	.113	.496	.102	1.974	1.983	−.008	100.0
November . .	.144	.597	.148	1.678	1.747	−.069	100.0
December . .	.184	.375	.182	1.670	1.612	.059	99.6
1922:							
January . . .	.213	.357	.214	1.579	1.502	.077	98.7
February . .	.201	.142	.199	1.587	1.553	.034	98.2
March . . .	.194	.027	.153	1.716	1.726	−.009	98.3
April	.169	.154	.153	1.698	1.724	−.027	98.1
May	.187	.343	.183	1.493	1.608	−.115	98.5
June	.203	.297	.204	1.529	1.536	−.007	98.9
July.	.254	.654	.294	1.232	1.281	−.049	99.0
August . . .	.348	.852	.455	0.923	0.953	−0.29	99.0
September . .	.344	.108	.309	1.339	1.246	.093	98.7
October . . .	.260	.024	.204	1.580	1.534	.046	97.6
November . .	.184	−.047	.136	1.766	1.800	−.034	96.1
December . .	.142	−.036	.100	1.980	1.993	−.013	94.2

Notes to Appendix Data

Units for β_t, π_t, and π_t^e are per month. Employment indices are based on $100.0 = $ full employment in June 1920 (see the discussion for Austria below). 1. Austria: M is an end-of-month index of the note circulation of the Austrian Republic (Walre de Bordes 1924, pp. 48–50); P, from December 1920 is the end-of-month cost-of-living index (excluding housing) of the Osterreiche Volkswirt (Walre de Bordes, pp. 88, 89). From January 1919 to December 1920, an index of food prices for a working family has been used

TABLE A2

GERMANY

Midmonth	β_t	π_t	π_t^e	Log $(M/P)_t$ (Actual)	Log $(M/P)_t$ (Estimated)	Residual	Employment Index
1921:							
January . . .	.057	.018	.029	2.416	2.317	.099	95.8
February . .	.052	−.029	.026	2.435	2.374	.061	95.6
March . . .	.048	−.008	.023	2.452	2.426	.026	96.6
April	.046	−.010	.021	2.469	2.476	−.007	96.5
May	.043	−.006	.019	2.483	2.523	−.039	96.7
June	.042	.042	.020	2.465	2.502	−.037	97.4
July.	.044	.070	.022	2.425	2.463	−.038	97.9
August . . .	.047	.064	.023	2.385	2.428	−.043	98.3
September . .	.048	.032	.024	2.400	2.419	−.020	99.2
October . . .	.050	.091	.026	2.368	2.369	−.002	99.4
November . .	.055	.168	.030	2.272	2.282	−.010	99.2
December . .	.060	.085	.033	2.293	2.240	.053	99.1
1922:							
January . . .	.064	.056	.034	2.302	2.219	.083	97.4
February . .	.066	.190	.041	2.146	2.127	.018	98.0
March . . .	.074	.177	.048	2.038	2.043	−.005	99.7
April	.086	.174	.055	1.944	1.960	−.016	99.9
May	.093	.104	.059	1.903	1.923	−.019	100.1
June	.097	.086	.062	1.921	1.901	.020	100.3
July.	.107	.262	.076	1.774	1.780	−.006	100.3
August . . .	.132	.358	.102	1.584	1.619	−.035	100.3
September . .	.169	.544	.152	1.295	1.385	−.091	100.2
October . . .	.221	.509	.212	1.120	1.180	−.060	99.6
November . .	.297	.717	.331	0.833	0.895	−.062	99.1
December . .	.357	.442	.369	0.890	0.822	.068	98.3
1923:							
January . . .	.390	.479	.410	0.786	0.750	.037	96.9
February . .	.457	.915	.616	0.544	0.456	.089	95.9
March . . .	.433	.096	.335	0.908	0.887	.022	95.5
April	.288	.004	.186	1.216	1.263	−.047	94.2
May	.231	.259	.202	1.163	1.213	−.050	95.0
June	.288	.725	.319	0.876	0.920	−.044	97.1
July.	.463	1.304	.692	0.463	0.365	.098	97.9
August . . .	.900	2.931	2.638	−0.966	−0.920	−.045	95.0

(*Statistische Nachrichten*, 1923, p. 195). Employment is based on the number of unemployed (receiving relief) for each month (Walre de Bordes, p. 11), and on interpolated population data from the *UN Demographic Yearbook*. The index is calculated as follows: N (employment) $= L$ (labor force) $- \Omega$ (number unemployed) $\approx a \cdot POP$ (total population) $- b \cdot U$ (number of unemployed from data) $= a \cdot [POP - (b/a)U]$, where we set $a \equiv 1$. Using Ω/L at October 1921 (the minimum unemployment date) $\approx .005$, b/a is determined and the index is calculated for each month.

2. Germany: M is an index of total legal tender (Sonderhefte zur *Wirtschaft und Statistik*, 1925, pp. 45 ff.). Until December 1922 figures are interpolated to the middle of the month from end-of-month data. For 1923, figures are available directly at the middle of the month; P is an index of the cost of living, available as a monthly average from February, 1920 to March, 1923 (*Statistisches Jahrbuch für das Deutsche Reich*, 1924/25, international

TABLE A3

HUNGARY

End-of-Month	β_t	π_t	π_t^e	Log $(M/P)_t$ (Actual)	Log $(M/P)_t$ (Estimated)	Residual	Employment Index
1921:							
October . . .	.077	.077	.038	1.253	1.138	.115	(89.2)
November . .	.083	.214	.048	1.092	1.012	.080	(89.4)
December . .	.086	−.006	.040	1.116	1.119	−.003	(89.7)
1922:							
January . . .	.076	−.018	.034	1.154	1.213	−.059	(89.9)
February . .	.066	.053	.035	1.147	1.193	−.046	(90.1)
March . . .	.078	.152	.041	1.086	1.097	−.011	(90.3)
April	.082	.085	.044	1.045	1.055	−.010	(90.5)
May	.086	.023	.042	1.066	1.084	−.018	(90.7)
June	.087	.165	.050	0.957	0.987	−.030	(90.9)
July.	.106	.299	.066	0.790	0.816	−.025	(91.1)
August . . .	.125	.207	.079	0.770	0.705	.066	(91.4)
September . .	.138	.225	.095	0.787	0.595	.192	(91.6)
October . . .	.160	.213	.111	0.755	0.501	.254	(91.8)
November . .	.148	−.010	.080	0.793	0.697	.096	92.0
December . .	.129	.024	.071	0.821	0.769	.052	(93.0)
1923:							
January . . .	.128	.142	.079	0.650	0.707	−.058	(93.9)
February . .	.121	.091	.080	0.586	0.696	−.110	(94.8)
March . . .	.157	.457	.119	0.220	0.456	−.236	95.8
April	.183	.243	.139	0.181	0.362	−.181	95.5
May	.196	.118	.134	0.238	0.381	−.142	98.4
June	.214	.444	.186	0.070	0.178	−.108	(98.3)
July.	.294	.683	.299	−0.234	−0.133	−.101	98.1
August . . .	.362	.481	.360	−0.146	−0.258	.112	99.1
September . .	.350	.186	.293	0.061	−0.119	.180	98.2
October . . .	.299	.058	.204	0.238	0.118	.120	98.4
November . .	.238	.082	.170	0.295	0.234	.061	97.6
December . .	.224	.121	.158	0.261	0.279	−.018	97.7
1924:							
January . . .	.220	.173	.162	0.240	0.266	−.026	96.9
February . .	.241	.560	.236	−0.119	0.024	−.143	94.7

table 1). From April 1923 the index is available on a weekly basis (*Wirtschaft und Statistik*, January 1924, p. 12). From November 1915 to February 1920 use has been made of an index of the retail price of food (*International Labour Review*, September 1921, p. 301; October 1921, p. 84). The employment index is based on the percentage of unemployed trade union members (Bresciani-Turroni 1937, p. 449) and on interpolated population figures (*UN Demographic Yearbook*).

3. Hungary: *M* is an end-of-month index of total note circulation (Young 1925, p. 321; *Statistisches Jahrbuch für das Deutsche Reich*, 1926, international table 23); *P*, from July, 1921 to November, 1923, is an index of retail prices (Young 1925, p. 322), which apparently relates to the end of the month (*Annuaire Statistique Hongrois*, 1931, p. 126). From December 1923, *P* is an end-of-month index of the cost-of-living (*Statistisches Jahrbuch für das Deutsche Reich*, 1924/25, p. 86*). The indices were joined together by means of the overlap in November 1923. From January 1918 to July 1921 an index of the

TABLE A4

POLAND

Midmonth	β_t	π_t	π_t^e	Log $(M/P)_t$ (Actual)	Log $(M/P)_t$ (Estimated)	Residual	Employment Index
1922:							
January . . .	.116	0.003	.062	1.610	1.552	.058	89.3
February . .	.100	0.026	.058	1.621	1.586	.036	90.5
March . . .	.099	0.089	.060	1.560	1.563	−.004	92.8
April . . . .,	.107	0.115	.066	1.473	1.525	−.052	94.3
May	.112	0.088	.068	1.435	1.508	−.073	95.6
June	.114	0.069	.068	1.438	1.507	−.069	97.7
July.	.118	0.143	.075	1.394	1.456	−.062	98.6
August . . .	.130	0.142	.083	1.378	1.410	−.032	99.7
September . .	.139	0.173	.093	1.370	1.350	.020	100.0
October. . .	.152	0.177	.104	1.400	1.293	.107	100.6
November . .	.173	0.289	.130	1.293	1.179	.114	100.7
December . .	.204	0.303	.159	1.152	1.068	.084	100.0
1923:							
January . . .	.252	0.419	.213	0.892	0.901	−.009	99.8
February . .	.307	0.509	.290	0.605	0.712	−.107	98.5
March . . .	.346	0.311	.298	0.662	0.696	−.035	98.1
April . . .	.322	0.095	.220	0.910	0.882	.028	98.4
May	.270	0.125	.192	0.984	0.962	.022	99.7
June	.268	0.297	.218	0.904	0.888	.016	100.9
July.	.320	0.497	.295	0.662	0.702	−.040	101.7
August . . .	.396	0.503	.371	0.487	0.551	−.064	102.4
September . .	.428	0.385	.377	0.566	0.540	.026	102.9
October. . .	.608	1.229	.836	−0.037	−0.081	.044	102.8
November . .	.738	0.802	.811	−0.048	−0.054	.006	102.6
December . .	.764	0.983	.941	−0.168	−0.188	.020	102.4
1924:							
January . . .	.800	0.940	.940	−0.222	−0.188	−.034	100.5

price of food for a working family was used (*Annuaire Statistique Hongrois,* 1919–22, pp. 102, 193). The employment index is based on numbers of unemployed (*International Labour Review,* September 1925, pp. 347–48, and *Statistisches Jahrbuch für das Deutsche Reich,* 1926, international table 23), and on interpolated population figures (*UN Demographic Yearbook*). The unemployment percentage is assumed to be 6.5 percent in January 1924 (*International Labour Review,* September 1925, p. 349), and the index is calculated by the method described above for Austria. Values in parentheses have been obtained by interpolation.

4. Poland: *M* is an index of note circulation (Young 1925, p. 347). Figures have been interpolated to the middle of the month from end-of-month data; *P*, from November 1921 to October, 1923, is an index of the cost of living, apparently referring to the middle of the month (League of Nations, *Monthly Bulletin of Statistics,* 1920–21, vol. 2, no. 12, p. 18, and later issues). Published figures under this heading for months prior to November 1921 actually refer to wholesale prices. From November 1923 the data relates to the second half of the month, and has been interpolated to the middle of the month (*Monthly Bulletin,* 1923, vol. 4, no. 11, p. 3). Prior to November 1921, retail price indices are apparently unavailable, and an index of wholesale prices has been used (*International Labour Review,* October 1921, p. 77). The employment

index is based on numbers of unemployed (*Statistisches Jahrbuch für das Deutsche Reich*, 1924/25, international table 13), and on interpolated population figures (*UN Demographic Yearbook*). The percentage of unemployed on September 1923 is assumed to be 3 percent, and the index is calculated by the method described above for Austria.

References

Allais, M. "A Restatement of the Quantity Theory of Money." *A.E.R.* 56 (December 1966):1123–57.

Bresciani-Turroni, C. *The Economics of Inflation*. London: Allen & Unwin, 1937.

Cagan, P. "The Monetary Dynamics of Hyperinflation." In *Studies in the Quantity Theory of Money*, edited by M. Friedman. Chicago: Univ. Chicago Press, 1956.

Durbin, J., and G. S. Watson. "Testing for Serial Correlation in Least Squares Regression II." *Biometrica* 38 (June 1951):159–78.

Feller, W. *An Introduction to Probability Theory and its Applications*. Vol. 1, 3d ed. New York: Wiley, 1968.

Friedman, M. "The Quantity Theory of Money—a Restatement." In *Studies in the Quantity Theory of Money*, edited by M. Friedman. Chicago: Univ. Chicago Press, 1956.

Hirshleifer, J. "On the Theory of Optimal Investment Decisions." *J.P.E.* 66 (August 1958):329–52.

Hogg, R., and A. Craig. *Introduction to Mathematical Statistics*. 2d ed. New York: Macmillan, 1965.

Keynes, J. M. *A Tract on Monetary Reform*. London: Macmillan, 1924.

Miller, M. H., and D. Orr. "A Model of the Demand for Money by Firms." *Q.J.E.* 80 (August 1966):413–35.

Sonderhefte zur *Wirtschaft und Statistik*. "Zahlen zur Geldentwertung in Deutschland 1914 bis 1923." Berlin: Hobbung, 1925.

Statistisches Jahrbuch für das Deutsche Reich, 1924/25 and 1926. Berlin: Statistisches Reichsamt, 1925, 1926.

Walre de Bordes, J. van. *The Austrian Crown*. London: King, 1924.

Young, J. P. *European Currency and Finance*. Vol. 2. Washington: Government Printing Office, 1925.

Household Money Holdings and the Demand Deposit Rate*

WITH ANTHONY M. SANTOMERO

INTRODUCTION

A MAJOR CONCLUSION FROM RECENT empirical studies[1] is that demand for money is inversely related to the interest rate. Interest rate variables contained in previous studies range over a variety of financial assets and include both short- and long-term rates. In general, however, the opportunity cost of holding money is measured by the absolute rate of return on some alternative asset—that is, the (marginal) rate of return on money is implicitly taken to be zero.[2]

In fact, at least one component of (narrowly-defined) money, demand deposits, bears a form of interest which should be taken into account in determining the opportunity cost of holding money. We argue in Section I that the relevant return on demand deposits for the United States is the rate at which charges are remitted or services rendered in accordance with deposit balances. A private survey of commercial banks has enabled us to compile a time series measure of the demand deposit rate (r_D) for the post-World War II period. The results indicate that r_D has

*The authors are grateful to Herschel Grossman for a number of helpful suggestions, and appreciate the demand deposit rate information which was supplied by the respondents to the commercial bank survey. Useful comments were also provided by members of the Money and Banking Workshop at the University of Chicago and by members of the Brown University Monetary Economics Seminar. National Science Foundation Grant GS-3246 supported this research.

[1]For a summary of the recent literature, see Laidler [8], Ch. 8.
[2]Apparent exceptions to this approach are Lee [9], Feige [5], and Cagan [3]. These authors all use a measure of bank service charges as a measure of rate of return on demand accounts. However, as discussed below, the level of service charges is not an appropriate measure of marginal rate of return on demand deposits.

ROBERT J. BARRO *is associate professor of economics at Brown University and visiting associate professor of economics at the University of Chicago.* ANTHONY M. SANTOMERO *is assistant professor of economics at Bernard Baruch College, City University of New York.*

Reprinted from *Journal of Money, Credit, and Banking,* 4(2), May 1972, 397–413. Copyright © 1972 by the Ohio State University Press. Reprinted by permission of Ohio State University Press, Columbus, and the authors.

been significantly positive and has changed considerably from 1950 to 1968. This time series of r_D should be of interest independently of the other results which are discussed in this paper.

In order to design an appropriate test for the influence of the r_D variable on demand for money, we first construct an illustrative theoretical model of household transactions demand in Section II. Employing a division of holdings and expenditures into currency and demand deposit components, the model uses an inventory-optimization approach to explain the money-demand behavior of an individual household. The theory derives an explicit demand function for total money, and also explains the division of holdings between currency and demand deposits. The major qualitative conclusions from this model of transactions demand are: (1) demand for money is inversely related to the differential interest return between alternative "liquid" assets (e.g., savings deposits) and demand deposits; (2) demand for currency is insensitive to the interest rate on alternative liquid assets, but is inversely dependent on the demand deposit rate; and (3) the ratio of currency to total money holdings is independent of "income."

Section III presents an empirical test of the theory, emphasizing the impact of the demand deposit interest rate on money demand. The empirical findings confirm hypotheses which were suggested by the theory of Section II, and substantiate the importance of r_D as an explanatory factor in money demand.

I. THE RATE OF RETURN ON DEMAND DEPOSITS

In most studies of demand for money in the United States, the interest rate on demand deposits has not been included as an explanatory variable because the payment of explicit interest on demand accounts has been prohibited for some time. However, even a casual view of commercial banking suggests that the provision of services (or remission of charges) in accordance with deposit balances provides an effective means for paying demand deposit interest. Given this potential for "evading" the legal restriction, one would also expect that the effective demand deposit rate would not be constant over time, but would vary according to the overall pattern of market rates.

In some previous studies of the demand for money, where the theoretical importance of the demand deposit rate was recognized, r_D was incorrectly measured as the difference between explicit interest payments and average service charges. The general procedure follows that introduced by Cagan [3], who stated (p. 305):[3] "While all deposits once paid interest, the average return on demand deposits has been negative since 1934 because service charges have exceeded interest payments."

---

[3]Similarly, in Edgar Feige's analysis of liquid assets [5, p. 19], he says, "with respect to demand deposits. . . . The interest return is negative and is represented by total service charges divided by average demand deposit balances. . . ."

Finally, in Lee's study [9, p. 1169], he states, "The yield on traditionally defined money is derived as the weighted average of rates of return on demand deposits (the negative of service charges) and currency (zero)."

However, the relevant rate of return on demand deposits is that which applies to marginal holdings. In this context fixed monthly service charges or charges per check or per deposit are not relevant (although these types of charges would affect transactions costs, and may have some indirect impact on the proportion of total expenditures made by check, see Section II). Therefore, service charges should not be deducted from interest payments to measure r_D. Further, the appropriate measure of interest payments at a time when explicit interest is prohibited is not the explicit payment (zero); but the rate at which charges are remitted (or services rendered) as a function of deposit balances.

We have obtained an approximate measure of r_D for the United States from 1950 to 1968 by surveying major commercial banks on the rates at which they have remitted service charges as a function of demand deposit balances. The resulting time series is contained in Table 1. The data indicate that the effective rate on demand deposits has been significantly positive and has varied considerably over the last two decades in the United States.

Since the time series on r_D represents a new piece of data which should be of substantial interest for its own sake, we present some details of the methods used to construct the series. The top 100 commercial banks were asked to provide a time series on the rate at which they have remitted service charges as a function of average balances for various types of demand accounts. The rate information that was used refers to the remission rate on smaller size regular accounts (that is, commercial account rates were excluded, as far as possible, since a rate which is relevant for household decision-making is desired). Usable information was obtained from 23 banks, which represent 21 per cent of the total demand deposit holdings of commercial banks in 1967. The typical information received from a single bank indicated three or four instances since 1950 when changes in the remission rate occurred (for example, shifts from $0.10 per month per $100 of balances to $0.15 and $0.20, etc.). The volume and apparent accuracy of the information improves for the later years. Therefore, more confidence can be placed in the recent r_D figures. Variations in the rate appear to have become more frequent in recent years and a roughly constant differential has been maintained since 1960 between the rate paid at savings and loan associations, r_S, (see Table 1) and r_D, although a substantial advance has occurred in the level of both rates.[3.5]

The r_D rate indicated in Table 1 is an unweighted mean of those banks from which information was obtained. It is thought that this equal-weight procedure provides a better measure of the overall national rate for households than a scheme which weighted by the deposit volume of the banks in the sample. (A weighting by total deposit volume would give an undue weight to New York banks, where the

---

[3.5]In a very recent study, Klein [7] argues that, if restrictions on the payment of demand deposit interest are entirely ineffective, r_D would be proportional to the interest rate on bank investment assets. In this context r_D would be expected to maintain a roughly constant proportion to r_S rather than a constant differential. However, the constant of proportionality in Klein's model does vary with bank's reserve-deposit ratio. Direct costs of paying interest on demand accounts and changes in the competitiveness of the banking industry would also affect Klein's result.

TABLE 1

Data for Regression Equations*

	M	$\log\left(\dfrac{Y}{PN}\right)$	r_S	r_D	$r_S - r_D$
1950	53.0	5.022	.0252	.0143	.0109
1951	56.2	5.019	.0258	.0143	.0115
1952	58.1	5.031	.0269	.0143	.0126
1953	59.4	5.061	.0281	.0143	.0138
1954	60.5	5.062	.0287	.0150	.0137
1955	61.6	5.112	.0294	.0150	.0144
1956	62.4	5.120	.0303	.0150	.0153
1957	61.7	5.125	.0326	.0157	.0169
1958	62.1	5.116	.0338	.0157	.0181
1959	64.4	5.156	.0353	.0159	.0194
1960	63.5	5.168	.0386	.0172	.0214
1961	64.4	5.172	.0390	.0172	.0218
1962	66.0	5.205	.0408	.0172	.0236
1963	70.2	5.233	.0417	.0177	.0240
1964	75.8	5.274	.0418	.0180	.0238
1965	83.4	5.324	.0423	.0193	.0230
1966	87.0	5.364	.0445	.0212	.0233
1967	94.5	5.382	.0467	.0226	.0241
1968	102.2	5.422	.0467	.0242	.0225

*Data Sources for Tables 1 and 2:
M: Annual average of money holdings of households and nonprofit organizations (billions of dollars) from the Federal Reserve Flow-of-Funds Accounts. The numbers were obtained on request from the Division of Research and Statistics of the Board of Governors of the Federal Reserve. Figures from 1952 to 1968 are averages of quarterly data. Numbers for 1950 and 1951 and based on year-end values. Data for 1968 is preliminary.
Y: Personal consumption expenditure (billions of dollars) from *U.S. Survey of Current Business*, July, 1968, July, 1969, and summary issue: *The National Income and Product Accounts of the United States, 1929-1965.*
P: Implicit price deflator for personal consumption expenditure (1958 = 1.0); sources as above for Y.
N: Total resident population in units of 10^8 people. Sources as above for Y and *Statistical Abstract of the United States, 1969.*
r_S: Average annual dividend rate on shares of savings and loan associations. Data was obtained from the Office of Research and Home Finance of the Federal Home Loan Bank Board.
r_D: Imputed marginal (annual) rate of return on demand deposits at commercial banks.

(Source: Private survey)

preponderance of deposits is in business, rather than in personal, accounts). In any case the general character of the calculated r_D series is not sensitive to shifts in the weighting scheme.

The measurement of r_D involves a basic conceptual problem since not all types of demand accounts involve the remission of charges as a function of average balances. Further, simple remission of charges is not the only vehicle by which banks can effectively pay interest on deposit holdings. For example, banks often supply loans (on attractive terms and in guaranteed amounts) on the basis of deposit balances (compensating balances), and they provide other types of customer services in at least rough relation to deposit holdings. These methods of paying interest are, however, likely to be more important for firms than for households. By concentrating on the service charge remission rate on types of accounts for which this method of remission applies, we are able to obtain a quantitative time series measure of r_D. Implicitly, it is being assumed that (at least on average) the return on other types of household accounts, for which the method of paying interest may be more subtle, can be approximated by the measured r_D value. While this last point is surely disputable, the r_D figures in Table 1 are likely to provide a better measure of the rate of return on demand deposits than $r_D \approx 0$ or $r_D \approx$ constant. In any case, the empirical results of Section III suggest that using this r_D variable significantly improves the explanation of household money demand.

Finally, the time series measure of r_D would improve with increased coverage of banks, as well as with more detailed information from individual banks on the manner in which charges are remitted or services rendered in accordance with deposit balances. This type of information could be obtained in sufficient detail on a continuing basis only if some official body, such as the Federal Reserve or the FDIC, deemed it worthwhile, and required regular reporting of the necessary information. However, by collecting this data the Federal Reserve would be implicitly admitting that its legal restrictions did not rule out the payment of demand deposit interest. We believe that the empirical results using the r_D series in this paper demonstrate the importance of this variable, and make the gathering of data on the effective demand-deposit rate a worthwhile public project.

II. THEORETICAL MODEL OF HOUSEHOLD DEMAND FOR MONEY

The basic aim of this section is to develop a theory of demand for money which explicitly includes a rate of return on demand deposits. The model described below is limited to a consideration of household transactions demand subject to simple assumptions about receipt and expenditure patterns. Nevertheless, the results should be useful in indicating how r_D influences money demand and in suggesting empirical tests to be carried out in Section III.

The basic vehicle of analysis is a version of the inventory-type optimization model, which has been applied previously by Baumol [2] and Tobin [11].

It is assumed that an economic unit (a "household") receives a lump-sum income payment, X, at (fixed) payment interval, T.[4] The unit conducts expenditures at a uniform rate, $Y = X/T$, so as to exhaust one income payment just prior to the next receipt of funds. The total expenditure is divided between hX of currency (C) and $(1 - h)X$ of demand deposits (D), with h determined exogenously (see footnote 9). In addition to C and D, a third alternative for holding "working balances" is a "savings deposit" (S).[5] The three assets pay interest rates on *marginal* holdings of r_C, r_D and r_S, respectively, where $r_C < 0$ (indicating possible losses and storage

---

[4]The payments period is viewed as an exogenous variable in this model. An endogenous determination of the period is considered in Barro [1], Sections IA and IB.

[5]The term, working balances, has been employed by Tobin. "Savings deposits" is a proxy term for "liquid," interest-bearing assets that are included in the working balance.

costs), $r_D \geqslant 0$, and $r_S > r_D$. The interest rates and expenditure flows are assumed to be perfectly foreseen with no possibility of changes during the period.

The completion of the model requires a specification of the costs associated with transfers of funds among the three available assets, and some information about the form of the income receipt.

It is assumed that the major cost involved in movements between C and D or S is a "going-to-the-bank" cost, which, once paid, allows unlimited transfers in any direction. That is, the payment of some fixed cost, α, permits any allocation of funds among C, D and S. A transfer from D to C only (cashing a check) does not involve a bank trip, and is assumed to cost some fixed amount, β, where $\beta < \alpha$.

The form of the income receipt is assumed to be such that it "necessitates" a trip to the bank at the start of each period.[6] In this case the initial allocation of funds may be treated as an optional (that is, optimal) division among C, D, and S.

The objective of the economic unit is taken as the maximization of profit (interest earnings on average holdings of the three assets, less transactions costs incurred) over the interval T. Let n denote the number of bank trips (including the "required" initial trip) which occur over time T. An optimal solution involves equally-spaced trips, each of which concludes with a money balance: $M = C + D = X/n$.[7] The implied trip times are: $0, T/n, 2T/n, \ldots, (n-1)T/n$. Let m denote the number of check-cashings which occur during each sub-interval, T/n. An optimal solution involves equally-spaced check-cashings, each of which concludes with a currency total: $C = 1/(m+1)(hX/n)$.

Let Ω (working balances) denote the sum of the three assets $(S + D + C)$. From the above discussion (and the assumed uniformity of expenditure flows) average asset holdings as a function of n and m are:

$$\overline{\Omega} = \overline{S} + \overline{D} + \overline{C} = X/2$$

$$\overline{M} = \overline{D} + \overline{C} = \frac{1}{2}\left(\frac{X}{n}\right)$$

$$\overline{S} = \overline{\Omega} - \overline{M} = \frac{X}{2}\left(1 - \frac{1}{n}\right)$$

$$\overline{C} = \frac{1}{2(m+1)}\left(\frac{hX}{n}\right)$$

[6]If the unit concludes each period with zero working balances, an initial bank trip is required if the mode of income receipt is (1) currency, (2) direct accrual in S, or (3) payment by check. However, if the income receipt accrues directly in D, the unit may pay the check-cashing cost (β) to obtain some currency, and avoid the larger bank-trip cost (α) as long as no S is desired.

[7]The resulting quantity of money just suffices to meet expenditures over the interval, T/n, after which a new bank trip occurs. The optimality of equally-spaced trips is discussed in Tobin [11, p. 247], in a somewhat different context.

Discounting of returns is omitted in this model, since the payments period is assumed to be short, in the sense that

$$|r_S T|, |r_D T|, |r_C T| \ll 1.$$

$$\overline{D} = \overline{M} - \overline{C} = \frac{1}{2}\frac{X}{n}\left(1 - \frac{h}{m+1}\right). \tag{1}$$

Profit over time T, as a function of n and m, is given by:

$$\pi(n,m) = \overline{S} \cdot r_S T + \overline{D} \cdot r_D T + \overline{C} \cdot r_C T - n\alpha - nm\beta. \tag{2}$$

Substituting from equation (1) and simplifying:

$$\pi(n,m) = \frac{XT}{2}\left[r_S - \frac{1}{n}\left(r_S - r_D + \frac{h}{m+1}(r_D - r_C)\right)\right] - n\alpha - nm\beta. \tag{3}$$

The unit selects values of n and m (n^* and m^*) which maximize π. Assuming that n and m can be satisfactorily treated as continuous variables, and that an interior solution applies, the first-order maximization conditions can be expressed as (using $X = YT$):

$$n^* = T\sqrt{\frac{Y\left(r_S - r_D + \frac{h}{m^*+1}(r_D - r_C)\right)}{2(\alpha + m^*\beta)}},$$

$$(m^* + 1) = \frac{T}{n^*}\sqrt{\frac{hY(r_D - r_C)}{2\beta}}. \tag{4}$$

Simplifying, we eventually obtain:[8]

$$n^* = T\sqrt{\frac{Y(r_S - r_D)}{2(\alpha - \beta)}},$$

$$(m^* + 1) = \sqrt{\frac{h(\alpha - \beta)(r_D - r_C)}{\beta(r_S - r_D)}}. \tag{5}$$

[8]For continuous variates the interior solutions of equation (5) are subject to the inequality constraints: $n^* \geq 1$, $m^* \geq 0$. Subject to these inequalities, the solutions can be shown to yield a global profit maximum. The inequality conditions translate into the parametric inequalities:

$$T^2 Y(r_S - r_D) \geq 2(\alpha - \beta); \qquad h(\alpha - \beta)(r_D - r_C) \geq \beta(r_S - r_D).$$

The above inequalities are assumed to be satisfied (for "most" individuals) and attention is therefore restricted to interior solutions. It should be noted that the paradoxical behavior of n^* and m^* in equation (5) associated with the limiting cases: $\beta \longrightarrow \alpha$, $r_D \longrightarrow r_S$, $r_C \longrightarrow r_D$ is ruled out when the interior inequalities are satisfied. As $\beta \longrightarrow \alpha$, the second inequality is eventually violated, at which point m^* reaches and remains equal to zero (although equation (5) indicates an economically-meaningless, negative value for m^*). Qualitatively, if the check-cashing cost is not sufficiently below the going-to-the-bank cost, it does not pay to use the demand deposit as a temporary store of funds which are eventually spent in the form of currency.
Similarly, as $r_C \longrightarrow r_D$, the use of the demand deposit as a temporary store of currency-destined funds becomes less worthwhile, and m^* eventually reaches and remains equal to zero

Substituting the solutions of equation (5) into the relevant portions of equation (1), average holdings of currency and total money are:

$$\overline{C} = \sqrt{\frac{hY\beta}{2(r_D - r_C)}},$$

$$\overline{M} = \sqrt{\frac{Y(\alpha - \beta)}{2(r_S - r_D)}}. \tag{6}$$

The ratio of currency to money holdings is, therefore,

$$\overline{C}/\overline{M} = \sqrt{\frac{h\beta(r_S - r_D)}{(\alpha - \beta)(r_D - r_C)}}. \tag{7}$$

The major qualitative conclusions from equations (6) and (7) are:[9]

1. The demand for money is inversely related to an interest rate variable which measures the differential return between alternative liquid assets and demand deposits $(r_S - r_D)$.

(when the second inequality constraint becomes effective). Finally, as $r_D \longrightarrow r_S$, the use of the savings deposit becomes less worthwhile. Accordingly, n^* eventually attains the value 1, at which point the first inequality constraint becomes operative (although $n^* \longrightarrow 0$ as $r_D \longrightarrow r_S$ in equation (5)).

The solutions of equation (5) are additionally restricted to integral values (in the region: $n^* \geqslant 1$, $m^* \geqslant 0$). If one substitutes the integer optimum of m in the n^* solution of equation (4), the integer optimum, $\hat{n}$, is determined from:

$$\hat{n}(\hat{n} - 1) \leqslant n^* \leqslant \hat{n}(\hat{n} + 1); \qquad (\hat{n} \geqslant 1)$$

That is, $\hat{n}$ is adjacent to the continuous n^* value.

Similarly, if one substitutes the integer optimum of n in the m^* expression, one has:

$$\hat{m}(\hat{m} + 1) \leqslant m^* + 1 \leqslant (\hat{m} + 1)(\hat{m} + 2); \qquad (\hat{m} \geqslant 0)$$

Therefore, $\hat{m}$ is adjacent to m^*.

Since we are eventually interested in an aggregate money-demand function, one could proceed, in principle, by aggregating over individual, integer-constrained solutions. Unfortunately, since the integer optima cannot be expressed in a simple form, this direct aggregation is not feasible. Further, since the continuous solution appears to provide a reasonable approximation to the individual integral solutions (at least, when $n^* \geqslant 1$, $m^* \geqslant 0$ is satisfied), and since aggregation involves averaging over numerous discrete values (for various values of Y, T, α, β, r_S, r_D, r_C), it appears reasonable to proceed on the basis of the continuous solution.

[9]Substituting the optimal values of n and m from equation (5) into the profit expression of equation (3), one obtains:

$$\pi(n^*, m^*) = T\left[r_S\left(\frac{YT}{2}\right) - \sqrt{2Y}\left(\sqrt{(\alpha - \beta)(r_S - r_D)} + \sqrt{h\beta(r_D - r_C)}\right)\right].$$

Therefore, (maximized) profit is an inverse function of $\sqrt{h}$. If h could be reduced costlessly, the optimal value would be $h = 0$ (all expenditures by check). In fact, the process of reducing h involves an increase in check-use costs (positive costs include explicit bank charges and bother costs, while the receipt value of checks is a negative cost). The trade-off between this check-use cost and the above profit expression could be exploited to determine the optimal expenditure proportion, which would provide an endogenous determination of h. The authors hope to proceed further along this line of analysis at a later date.

2. Demand for currency is insensitive to the interest rate on alternative liquid assets (r_S), but is inversely related to the demand deposit rate.

3. While currency and total money holdings are both positively related to Y, the ratio of currency to money is independent of "income" (for a given expenditure proportion). The ratio is positively related to the interest rate variable: $(r_S - r_D)/(r_D - r_C)$. Essentially, since it is only the demand deposit component of money holdings which is sensitive to "the" interest rate $(r_S - r_D)$, an increase in this rate (with $(r_D - r_C)$ fixed) must raise the share of currency in total holdings.

Although the forms in equation (6) derive from a fairly simple underlying model, they are useful in formulating empirical tests. In particular, the expression for $\overline{M}$ indicates that $(r_S - r_D)$ is the relevant interest rate variable for household money demand, and the form also suggests hypotheses for interest rate and income elasticities of demand, as discussed in the next section.

III. EMPIRICAL STUDY OF HOUSEHOLD MONEY HOLDINGS

In order to carry out a full empirical test of the model developed in Section II, it is necessary to measure, in addition to r_D, the fraction of expenditures which are conducted via currency (h). Unfortunately, we have been unable to obtain a satisfactory measure of this variable for the United States. Because of this data limitation, the empirical analysis in this section is limited to a consideration of total (household) money holdings. Since the results in this area turn out to be satisfactory, it would be useful to obtain a measure of h in order to test additional aspects of the theory.

The Empirical Framework

From equation (6) we may write for the ith "household" at the tth time period:

$$M_{it}^D = \sqrt{\frac{(\alpha - \beta)_{it} Y_{it}}{2(r_S - r_D)_{it}}} \; (v_{it}), \tag{8}$$

where, M_{it}^D is the demand for nominal money balances by the ith household at time t, α is the going-to-the-bank cost, β is the check-cashing cost, Y is the flow (nominal) household expenditure, r_S is the interest rate on an alternative liquid asset, r_D is the (marginal) rate of return on demand deposits, and v_{it} is treated as a multiplicative stochastic disturbance term.

If the same interest rates apply for all households, equation (8) may be rewritten (in real terms) as:

$$\left(\frac{M}{P}\right)_{it}^D = \frac{1}{\sqrt{2(r_S - r_D)_t}} \sqrt{\left(\frac{\alpha - \beta}{P}\right)_{it} \left(\frac{Y}{P}\right)_{it}} \; (v_{it}).$$

If the distribution across households of transactions costs and expenditure flows has remained constant over time, money demand may be aggregated in a simple form to yield:

$$\left(\frac{M}{PN}\right)_t^D = \frac{1}{N_t}\sum_{i=1}^{N_t}\left(\frac{M}{P}\right)_{it}^D = (\text{constant})\cdot\frac{1}{\sqrt{2(r_S-r_D)}}\sqrt{\left(\frac{\alpha-\beta}{P}\right)_t\left(\frac{Y}{PN}\right)_t}\cdot v_t.$$

(9)

where, M^D is aggregate money demand, P is the price level (assumed to be the same for all households), N is the number of households, $(\alpha - \beta/P)$ is an average real transactions cost, Y is aggregate expenditure, v is an (in general fairly complicated) aggregate disturbance term, and (constant) depends on the form of the transactions-cost/expenditure distribution but does not vary over time if the distribution remains unchanged.

In the statistical analysis it is assumed that the number of households may be measured by (that is, retains a proportional relationship to) total population. In this case equation (9) describes the dependence of real per capita money demand on real per capita expenditure and other factors.

Taking logarithms of equation (9), we obtain:

$$\log\left(\frac{M}{PN}\right)_t^D = (\text{constant}) + \frac{1}{2}\cdot\log\left(\frac{\alpha-\beta}{P}\right)_t + \frac{1}{2}\cdot\log\left(\frac{Y}{PN}\right)_t$$

$$-\frac{1}{2}\cdot\log(r_S-r_D)_t + u_t$$

(10)

where, $u_t = \log(v_t)$ is assumed to be independently, normally distributed.[10]

The main difficulty with the use of equation (10) is that the real transactions-cost term, $(\alpha - \beta/P)_t$, is not observable. If real transfer costs were assumed to be constant over time, this variable could be combined into the constant term and the estimation could proceed. However, if one considers the nature of the costs involved, it is very unlikely that transactions costs would remain fixed while real per capita expenditure, and, more pertinently, real value of time, was rising. To a considerable extent, the cost involved in going to the bank or cashing a check involves the expenditure of a certain amount of time. As the value of time rises, this type of transactions cost would increase proportionately.

As far as the process of conducting transactions were subject to some real productivity advance, transfer costs would rise less than time valuation. For example, average transactions costs (time involved in transactions) would decrease with the following changes: (1) an increase in the number of bank branch offices, (2) the

---

[10]From the aggregation in equation (9), v_t depends on the number of household units (population); hence u_t is likely to be heteroscedastic. Considering the relatively small change in population over the sample period, it did not seem necessary to introduce this complication.

introduction of banking-by-mail, (3) an increase in the number of types of accounts available. If this type of technical advance occurs sufficiently rapidly, the effect of increased value of time would be offset and real transfer costs would remain unchanged (or possibly even be reduced).

In terms of estimation the form ultimately used does not explicitly include the transactions-cost term:

$$\log\left(\frac{M}{PN}\right)^D_t = \alpha_1 + \alpha_2 \cdot \log\left(\frac{Y}{PN}\right)_t + \alpha_3 \cdot \log\left(r_S - r_D\right)_t + u_t \qquad (11)$$

In order to obtain some a priori notion of the expenditure coefficient (α_2), it is necessary to have some idea of the implicit relationship between $(\alpha - \beta/P)_t$ and $(Y/PN)_t$ (assuming that transactions costs are independent of the interest rate variable). The total effect of $\log(Y/PN)$ on $\log(M/PN)$ includes the direct effect $(+\frac{1}{2})$, and also an indirect effect. This indirect effect involves the impact of $\log(\alpha - \beta/P)$ on $\log(M/PN)$ $(+\frac{1}{2})$ and the implicit relationship between $\log(\alpha - \beta/P)$ and $\log(Y/PN)$. That is:

$$\alpha_2 = \frac{1}{2} + \frac{1}{2} \cdot b\left(\frac{\alpha - \beta}{P}\right), \frac{Y}{P} \qquad (12)$$

where, b may be thought of as the regression coefficient of $\log(\alpha - \beta/P)$ on $\log(Y/P)$.

Since a theory of the relationship between transactions costs and per capita expenditure has not been developed, we resort to some empirical measurements. For the statistical study below, real per capita consumption expenditure is used as a measure of (Y/PN). Over the period 1950 to 1967 in the United States, the increase in average real wages (adjusted by the rise in the average percentage tax rate) was 1.34 times the increase in real per capita consumption.[11] Therefore, one can take as an approximation for the real value of time (v):

$$\log v_t \approx \text{constant} + 1.34 \cdot \log\left(\frac{Y}{PN}\right)_t$$

If no transactions productivity advance had occurred over the sample period, $(\alpha - \beta/P)_t$ would be proportional to v_t, and 1.34 would be a measure of b in equa-

---

[11]An index of real wage rates (average compensation per man-hour in the total private economy, from *Statistical Abstract of the United States*, 1969, deflated by the implicit price deflator for consumption expenditure) rose from 78.05 to 132.3 from 1950 to 1967. The fraction of personal tax and nontax payments in personal income rose from 0.09 to 0.13 over this period.

While the relative long-term trends in real wages and real per capita expenditure may indicate the general relation between real value of time and real per capita transactions, available wage indices are unlikely to provide a useful short-term measure of transactions costs. Therefore, the wage rate has not been included as a separate explanatory variable for regression analysis.

tion (12). In this case the measured income elasticity of money demand (α_2) would be about 1.2.

To the extent that productivity advance has occurred, the measured income elasticity is reduced. If the advance just offsets the increase in value of time, the elasticity is: $\alpha_2 = 0.5$. If the extent of productivity advance exceeded the increase in value of time (which, however, seems unlikely), α_2 would be below 0.5. Therefore it is difficult to place a firm lower bound on α_2.

In any case the major result is that a (measured) income elasticity of money demand in excess of 1 is not inconsistent with the theory. This result contradicts the conventional view that inventory models of money demand are necessarily associated with "economies-of-scale" in cash balances ($\alpha_2 < 1$). The key element which is typically neglected is transactions costs. As transaction volume increases, economies-of-scale are realized only to the extent that transactions costs rise less than transactions volume. Since transaction costs depend largely on value of time, and since value of time may increase even faster than transactions volume, diseconomies-of-scale (money being a "luxury") is quite compatible with the inventory approach.[12]

Since the theory of Section II is intended to apply to households, we have measured r_S in equation (11) by the average rate paid on deposits ("shares") at savings and loan associations.[13] This type of asset appears more relevant as a component of household working balances than some other possibilities; such as Treasury bills, commercial paper, long-term bonds, equities, etc. Time deposits at commercial banks (exclusive of commercial-type instruments, such as certificates-of-deposits)[14] and mutual savings deposits would also be important for households, and it might eventually be worth combining rate information on these assets with the savings association yields.

The final consideration for estimation of equation (11) is the empirical measurement of demand for money. We assume that actual (annual average) real balances of households are a satisfactory approximation to real demand over the sample period considered (1950 to 1968, United States). The empirical measure of M is taken from the household sector of the flow-of-funds accounts, since it is this portion of money holdings to which the theory applies.[15] The final form for estima-

---

[12]It is assumed throughout that the fraction of expenditures which are "monetized" remains fixed over time. This assumption would not be appropriate if "interest rates" became extreme (as occurs during hyperinflations), and it would also not be valid for a "developing" economy. (See Barro [1], Section IC.) The process of development is likely to be associated with an increasing transactions benefit of money, which would result in a higher percentage of monetized transactions over time. This effect would tend to raise the observed expenditure elasticity of money demand, and make it more likely that money would emerge as a "luxury."

[13]This choice is supported by empirical results obtained by Lee [9, p. 1175], who observes: "the demand for money is highly sensitive to changes in the yield on savings and loan shares, and savings and loan shares are the closest substitute for money."

[14]The time deposit rate may cause difficulty since this asset may be subject to the same type of implicit service returns as demand deposits. Therefore, measured time deposit rates may underestimate the true rate of return on this asset.

[15]There are well-known difficulties with flow-of-funds data, but it seems best to use an approximation to our desired measure (household money holdings) rather than use total money holdings. Hamburger [6] also made use of household flow-of-funds data in his empirical study.

tion is:

$$\log\left(\frac{M}{PN}\right)_t = \alpha_1 + \alpha_2 \cdot \log\left(\frac{Y}{PN}\right)_t + \alpha_3 \cdot \log\left(r_S - r_D\right)_t + u_t \tag{13}$$

where, the null hypotheses suggested by the theory are:[16]

$$\alpha_2 < 1.2,$$

$$\alpha_3 \approx -0.5.$$

Log $(M/PN)_t$ is taken as the dependent variable for a regression in the form of equation (13). The rationale for this specification is that nominal money balances, M_t, may be viewed as exogenous, while the price level, P_t, is determined endogenously to satisfy the stochastic relation of equation (16).[17] Put another way, the equation of money demand and supply is viewed as guaranteed by suitable variations in the price level. Particularly since we are using annual (rather than quarterly or monthly) data, we believe that this specification may be a reasonable approximation. However, it is certainly clear that many authors who have used log $(M/PN)_t$ (or log $(M/P)_t$) as a dependent variable in regression analysis would not accept this implication of their own specification.

Empirical Results

The data used to estimate equation (13) are annual observations for the United States from 1950 to 1968 of the variables indicated in Tables 1 and 2. The least-

[16]The constant interest rate elasticity of −0.5 depends, to some extent, on certain omissions in the theoretical model of Section II. Two general types of omissions are: (1) the assumption that an interior solution (equation (5)) applies for all units, which effectively removes the aggregation problem; and (2) the assumption that certain elements are either absent or exogenously determined. Santomero [10] has extended the model by incorporating commodity inventories as an additional household asset, and by including an endogenous payments period. At this point there are a number of data and estimation problems which prevent estimation of the extended model. However, by viewing household commodity holdings as an omitted relevant variable, and by making assumptions about sample correlations between some unobservable elements and the included regression variables, Santomero [10, pp. 114-22] calculates the impact on the expected regression coefficient, $E(\hat{\alpha}_3)$, of equation (13). Depending on assumptions about the unobserved elements, he estimates an interval for $E(\hat{\alpha}_3)$ of: [−0.5, −0.8]. Therefore, this interval, rather than the point value of −0.5, is the appropriate null hypothesis for the extended model which includes commodity inventories.

The endogeneity of the payments period also affects the interest rate elasticity, but estimates of this effect are confounded by aggregation problems. There is some indication that an explicit treatment of aggregation in which some fraction of units did not conform to an interior solution (equation (5) and footnote 8) would reduce the interest elasticity, that is, reduce $E(\hat{\alpha}_3)$ in equation (13). This effect would then offset the effect of commodity inventories on $E(\hat{\alpha}_3)$, but quantitative estimates of the net effect have not been obtained at this time.

[17]There is some problem with this specification since we are dealing only with household money holdings, and not with the total money supply or high-powered money. However, given that one is to apply a single-equation estimating technique (which appears worth doing, at least as a preliminary step, because of its simplicity), the choice of P_t as "the" endogenous variable appears most reasonable. In this case, $M_t, N_t, (Y/PN)_t$ and $(r_S - r_D)_t$ are taken as exogenous.

TABLE 2

Actual versus Estimated Values for Equation (14)

	$\text{Log}\left(\dfrac{M}{PN}\right)$ (Actual)	$\text{Log}\left(\dfrac{M}{PN}\right)$ (Estimated)	Residual
1950	3.740	3.761	−.021
1951	3.718	3.728	−.010
1952	3.714	3.691	.023
1953	3.708	3.673	.036
1954	3.699	3.678	.021
1955	3.695	3.703	−.008
1956	3.667	3.678	−.010
1957	3.608	3.628	−.020
1958	3.574	3.581	−.006
1959	3.580	3.585	−.004
1960	3.535	3.543	−.009
1961	3.522	3.537	−.014
1962	3.522	3.528	−.005
1963	3.556	3.548	.009
1964	3.608	3.595	.012
1965	3.678	3.667	.011
1966	3.685	3.701	−.015
1967	3.731	3.701	.030
1968	3.764	3.781	−.017

squares regression results (using natural logarithms and indicating standard errors in parentheses) are:

$$\log\left(\frac{M}{PN}\right)_t = \underset{(0.46)}{-3.96} + \underset{(.068)}{1.044}\ \log\left(\frac{Y}{PN}\right)_t \underset{(.031)}{-0.549}\ \log\,(r_S - r_D)_t\,.$$

$$S.E.E. = 0.019, DW = 1.46, R^2 = 0.95. \tag{14}$$

A tabulation of actual versus estimated values and residuals is contained in Table 2.

The most interesting result from the regression equation is the estimated interest rate coefficient, $\hat{\alpha}_3 = -0.549$. The t-statistic for the null value suggested by the transactions demand model, $\alpha_3 = -0.5$, is $t_{16} = 1.6$, so that the null hypothesis is accepted at the 5 percent, type-I error level. Since the estimated standard error (.031) is quite small, this result is of considerable interest. Although the inventory-theoretic model discussed in Section II is, at least superficially, founded on very simple assumptions (see footnote 16), its implications for interest rate elasticity of money demand are borne out by this empirical test.

The above result depends on the specification of the interest rate variable in equation (14) to measure the *differential* return between an alternative liquid asset (here, savings deposits) and demand deposits, rather than the absolute return. If r_S alone is used as the interest rate measure, the regression equation is:

$$\log (M/PN)_t = -8.89 + 1.715 \cdot \log \left(\frac{Y}{PN}\right)_t - 1.092 \cdot \log (r_S)_t .$$
$$\quad\quad\quad\quad\quad (.97) \quad (.136) \quad\quad\quad\quad (.082)$$

$$S.E.E. = .024, DW = 1.36, R^2 = 0.92 \tag{15}$$

While the fit of this regression is worse than that of equation (14), the most interesting aspect is the large change in coefficient estimates. In particular, the hypothesis, $\alpha_3 = -0.5$, would not be accepted if the absolute interest rate measure were used as in equation (15). Within the context of the theoretical model of Section II, the "poor" results from equation (15) may be interpreted as a consequence of omitting a relevent variable, r_D.

On the one hand, the result of equation (14) demonstrates a substantial interest-elasticity of money demand $(-\frac{1}{2})$. On the other hand, this interest elasticity is with respect to the interest rate differential, $r_S - r_D$, and not with respect to the level of interest rates. Empirically, the rate differential has remained approximately constant in the United States since 1960, despite a considerable advance in the level of rates (Table 1). Therefore, the interest sensitivity of money demand with respect to (the level of) interest rates may, in fact, be small, and it is this elasticity which is often of interest in macroeconomic models.

The estimated coefficient of real per capita consumption expenditure in equation (14) is: $\hat{\alpha}_2 = 1.044$, standard error $= .068$. The estimated coefficient and small standard error suggest that the expenditure elasticity of money demand is very close to one.[18] This result is consistent with the theory, but is not required by it, since the model only restricted: $\alpha_2 < 1.2$. From the earlier discussion, a unit expenditure elasticity, in an equation which omits the transactions cost term, corresponds to a direct proportionality between real transactions costs and real per capita expenditure (here, consumption expenditure).

The Durbin-Watson statistic of equation (14) $(DW = 1.46)$ suggests absence of serial correlation in the residuals.[19] The standard-error-of-estimate indicates an equation error of approximately 1.9 percent (since natural logarithms were used).

A Further Test of the Model

The form in which the interest rate variable appears in equation (14) (as log $[r_S - r_D]$) is based on the theoretical model of Section II. The validity of this specification may be checked by generalizing the interest rate variable to be: log

[18]This estimated income coefficient is in marked contrast to that obtained by Hamburger [6] in his study of post-World War II household money holdings. Using first differences on quarterly data from 1952–1960, he concluded (p. 616): "These equations fail to indicate any strong short-run relationship between income and money for the household sector." The main sources of difference between our results and his is our inclusion of r_D and our measurement of r_S by the savings and loan rate, rather than by the return on long-term corporate bonds or on equities.

[19]At the 2.5 percent level, the critical values for a one-sided test against positive autocorrelation are (with nineteen observations and two independent variables plus a constant term): $d_L = 0.96, d_u = 1.41$. See Durbin and Watson [4], p. 174.

$(r_S - kr_D)$, where k is some unknown constant, and testing $k = 1$. Since k enters in a nonlinear manner, one must appeal to asymptotic distribution theory in order to estimate k and test the hypothesis, $k = 1$. Under our normality assumption, maximum likelihood estimation still corresponds to choosing estimates of k and the other parameters so as to minimize the sum of squared residuals. Further, confidence intervals may be constructed and hypothesis tests carried out by appealing to the asymptotic properties of the likelihood ratio.[20] The results of a search procedure yield the point estimate and 95 percent confidence interval for k.[21]

$$\hat{k} = 0.82; \quad [0.42, 1.19]$$

Therefore, a test of $k = 1$ is accepted at the five percent error level. Accordingly, the use of the rate differential, log $(r_S - r_D)$, in equation (14) is borne out by this empirical test.

IV. SUMMARY OF MAJOR CONCLUSIONS

The major impetus for this paper was the belief that the inclusion of an explicit rate of return on demand deposits would contribute significantly to the explanation of demand for money in the United States.

Section I of this paper presented the results of a private survey in which commercial banks provided information on rates at which they have remitted service charges as a function of demand deposit balances. In a period where explicit interest payments are prohibited, it is this type of remission rate that measures the marginal rate of return on deposit holdings. The survey data indicated that the rate of return on demand deposits in post-World War II United States has been significantly positive and has changed substantially over a twenty-year period.

Section II developed a simple model of transactions demand for a household-type economic unit. The results suggested that the relevant opportunity cost rate for money holdings is the differential between the rate on an alternative liquid asset and the demand deposit rate $(r_S - r_D)$. The theory also provided empirically-testable hypotheses on interest rate and income elasticities of money demand.

Section III used the demand deposit rate data of Section I to carry out empirical estimation and testing of the model developed in Section II. The results support the theoretical model and particularly confirm the importance of the demand deposit rate as an influence on money demand.

---

[20] For a more detailed discussion, see, for example, Theil [12], Ch. 8.
[21] The full regression results corresponding to $\hat{k} = 0.82$ are:

$$\log\left(\frac{M}{PN}\right)_t = -4.93 + 1.172 \log\left(\frac{Y}{PN}\right)_t - 0.651 \cdot \log (r_S - 0.82 \cdot r_D)$$

$$SEE = .018, \quad DW = 1.52, \quad R^2 = 0.95.$$

LITERATURE CITED

1. Barro, R. J. "Inflation, the Payments Period and the Demand for Money," *Journal of Political Economy*, 78 (November/December, 1970), 1228–63.

2. Baumol, W. J. "The Transactions Demand for Cash—An Inventory Theoretic Approach," *Quarterly Journal of Economics*, 66 (November, 1952), 545–56.

3. Cagan, P. "The Demand for Currency Relative to the Total Money Supply," *Journal of Political Economy*, 66 (August, 1958), 303–328.

4. Durbin, J. and G. S. Watson. "Testing for Serial Correlation in Least Squares Regression II," *Biometrika*, 38 (June, 1951), 159–78.

5. Feige, E. L. *The Demand for Liquid Assets: A Temporal Cross-Section Analysis*. Englewood Cliffs, N.J.: Prentice-Hall, 1964.

6. Hamburger, M. J. "The Demand for Money by Households, Money Substitutes and Monetary Policy," *Journal of Political Economy*, 74 (December, 1966), 600–623.

7. Klein, B. "The Payment of Interest on Commercial Bank Deposits and the Price of Money: A Study of the Demand for Money." Ph.D. Dissertation, University of Chicago, 1970.

8. Laidler, D. *The Demand for Money: Theories and Evidence*. Scranton, Pa.: International, 1969.

9. Lee, T. H. "Alternative Interest Rates and the Demand for Money: The Empirical Evidence," *American Economic Review*, 57 (December, 1967), 1168–81.

10. Santomero, A. "Optimal Transactions Behavior and the Demand for Money." Ph.D. Dissertation, Brown University, 1971.

11. Tobin, J. "The Interest-Elasticity of Transactions Demand for Cash," *Review of Economics and Statistics*, 38 (August, 1956), 241–47.

12. Theil, H. *Principles of Econometrics*. New York: Wiley, 1971.

15

Money and the Price Level under the Gold Standard*

This paper deals with the determination of the price level under the gold standard and related commodity standards (bimetallism, symmetallism, commodity-reserve currency). Since the "central bank" supports the nominal price of a reserve commodity such as gold under these systems, the determination of the absolute price level amounts to the determination of the relative price of the reserve commodity. In this sense the absolute price level becomes a determinate quantity that is amenable to usual supply and demand analyses, as applied to such things as gold production and non-monetary uses of gold. Although changes in the ratio of "money" to its commodity backing or shifts in velocity can influence the price level, the system possesses an important nominal anchor in the fixed price of the reserve commodity.

By way of contrast the absolute price level is determinate under a fiat (government-issue) currency system only up to the determination of the quantity of the fiat currency. Analysis of the price level involves, as its major element, a theory of government behaviour with respect to the quantity of money. In particular, there is no obvious nominal anchor that prescribes some likely limits to changes in the absolute price level.

The above discussion suggests that an important aspect of the gold standard or similar standards in relation to a fiat system is the (partial) separation of price level determination from governmental policy. This separation can be only partial since, at the level of the choice of a monetary regime, it is clear that the determination of money and prices cannot be divorced from the political process. The possibility for alterations in the underlying regime is exhibited by the gradual erosion of the international gold standard since 1914, and especially since the 1930s. The present analysis does not deal with this sort of change in the underlying "monetary constitution" (see Buchanan, 1962), but is rather confined to the workings of the system under a fixed monetary structure.

I. THE GOLD STANDARD

(A) Determination of the Price Level and the Money Stock

The framework of analysis is a closed economy that can represent either a single country or the world economy under fixed exchange rates. The stock of money,

* This research is being supported by the National Science Foundation. I have benefited from comments by Russ Boyer, Stanley Engerman, Herschel Grossman, Peter Howitt, David Laidler, Don McCloskey, Mark Rush, Nasser Saidi, Larry Sjaastad, Alan Stockman and two referees.

[13]

355

Reprinted from *Economic Journal*, 89, March 1979, by permission of Cambridge University Press, New York, New York.

denoted by M and denominated in a nominal unit such as dollars, represents a liability of the central bank(s). It can be assumed that money takes the physical form of a paper claim, rather than directly embodying gold or some other physical commodity. However, the bank is assumed to stand ready to buy or sell any amount of gold offered or demanded in exchange for money at the fixed (dollar) price, P_g.[1] If G_m represents the stock of gold held by the bank, then the supply of money would equal $P_g G_m$ under a strict commodity standard where the paper claims represent literal warehouse certificates, and would exceed this amount under a partial commodity standard. I assume that the total money supply is

$$M^s = (1/\lambda) P_g G_m,\qquad(1)$$

where the parameter λ, which satisfies $0 \leqslant \lambda \leqslant 1$, measures the gold "backing" of the monetary issue.[2]

The demand for circulating medium, M^d, is assumed to depend on the "general price level of commodities", P, on real income, y,[3] and on the opportunity cost rate for holding money rather than alternative assets. In the present set-up I assume that the principal alternative store of value is a commodity stock (or capital with a fixed real rate of return), so that the opportunity cost rate for holding money is measured by the expected rate of inflation, $\pi \equiv E(\dot{P}/P)$,[4] where a dot denotes a time derivative. Formally, money demand is represented by

$$M^d = k(\underset{(-)}{\pi}) Py,\qquad(2)$$

where the minus sign denotes a negative derivative which signifies that expected inflation and desired money holding are inversely related. The indicated unit income elasticity of money demand is convenient but not essential for the main analysis. The k-function can be thought of as an expression for the reciprocal of velocity.

The equation of money supply and demand from equations (1) and (2) implies the price level condition,

$$P = \frac{P_g G_m}{\lambda k(\pi) y}.\qquad(3)$$

In the subsequent analysis a principal issue is the implication of fixity in P_g – as guaranteed under the gold standard – for the short- and long-run behaviour of the general price level, P. Since equation (3) holds at all times, variations of P around P_g reflect movements in the right-hand-side variables, as represented in the combination, $G_m/(\lambda ky)$. For most of the analysis the variables k, λ, and y are treated as exogenous, although subject to disturbances.

---

[1] This set-up for a convertible currency is the one described by Ricardo (1821), p. 241.

[2] If money is defined to include commercial bank deposits, then the ratio of deposits to currency would influence the value of λ under a fractional-reserve banking system. Alternatively, if M is defined as high-powered money, then shifts in the deposit–currency ratio would influence the demand for "money", as represented by the k-function below.

[3] Real income would include the value added in the gold industry net of depreciation on gold stocks. Similarly, P would include P_g with an appropriate weight.

[4] Substitution between money and gold holdings implies that $E(\dot{P}_g/P_g)$ would enter as an additional negative argument of the money demand function. Since P_g is assumed constant, the inclusion of this term would not alter the subsequent analysis.

For purposes of exposition I have also carried out the main analysis in a setting that omits sustained growth in output, y. However, I have indicated the necessary modifications to incorporate growth. At the present stage the focus is on endogenous movements of the monetary gold stock, G_m.

As stressed by Fisher (1922), pp. 99 ff.,[1] the two key determinants of the monetary gold stock in a dynamic context are gold production and the extent to which gold is held for non-monetary purposes. Let g represent the rate at which new gold is produced. I assume that the current production function for a representative member of the gold mining industry can be expressed by the (real) cost function, $c(g)$, which describes the cost in commodity units for producing gold at rate g. Production is assumed to involve positive and increasing marginal cost – that is, $c', c'' > 0$.[2] The nominal cost for producing gold at rate g is $Pc(g)$, while the nominal revenue is $P_g g$ (with a common price for gold in monetary and non-monetary uses). Revenue-maximising behaviour on the part of gold producers, each of whom regards P_g and P as exogenous, entails

$$c'(g) = P_g/P, \qquad (4)$$

which implies a supply function for new gold of the form,

$$g^s = g^s \underset{(-)}{(P/P_g)}. \qquad (5)$$

Let G_n denote the stock of gold that is held for non-monetary (industrial, ornamental, etc.) uses. Gold held for these purposes is assumed to depreciate in an economic sense at the constant rate δ. (Gold held by the central bank is assumed not to depreciate.) Since the main analysis abstracts from real income growth, δG_n will turn out to measure the flow demand for gold in a steady state. More generally, this flow demand would also include the growth in G_m and G_n that is associated with sustained growth in y.

Non-monetary uses of gold would be deterred by a higher current relative price, P_g/P, but would be encouraged by expectations of higher future values of P_g/P. With P_g constant, expected future values of P_g/P vary inversely with π. Accordingly, I assume that the "target" stock of privately held gold is determined by a function of the form

$$f \underset{(+)\ (-)}{(P/P_g, \pi)}\, y,$$

which assumes, for convenience, a unit income elasticity. The underlying assumption that P_g is fixed seems to rule out the principal rationale for "speculative" gold hoards, so that the f-function should be thought of as pertaining to "real" uses of gold (for industry, ornamentation, etc.), rather than to a portfolio demand, per se. In this context it also seems natural to rule out rapid

---

[1] See also Thornton (1802), p. 266, Mill (1848), ch. IX, Friedman (1951), pp. 207 ff., and Whitaker (1976), section I. Niehans (1977), in an interesting recent contribution, also discusses some of the topics that I consider in my analysis.

[2] The exhaustible-resource property of gold could be captured by entering the accumulated stock of previously mined gold as a positive argument in the cost function. When the possibility of new discoveries and technical changes in mining are admitted, it is not clear that exhaustibility is an important characteristic over a relevant horizon. In any case the pertinent issue for subsequent analysis is the rate of "technical advance" in gold production relative to that in other industries – see section B2.

(that is, discrete) shifts in the non-monetary gold stock. Accordingly, I specify the non-monetary demand for gold in the form of a flow function,

$$g_n^d = \alpha[f(P/P_g, \pi)\,y - G_n] + \delta f(P/P_g, \pi)\,y. \qquad (6)$$
$$\underset{(+)\ (-)}{} \qquad \underset{(+)\ (-)}{}$$

Equation (6) assumes a desired gradual adjustment of G_n toward its target position in accordance with the adjustment parameter, $\alpha > 0$. In addition, g_n^d incorporates the "normal" replacement flow, $\delta f(\ldots)\,y$, that would be required to maintain the target value of G_n.[1] Note that the form of equation (6) implies that G_n has a negative effect on g_n^d. The form also implies $g_n^d = \delta f(\ldots)\,y = \delta G_n$ when G_n is equal to its target value. The net change in G_n at any point in time is given by

$$\dot{G}_n = g_n^d - \delta G_n = (\alpha + \delta)[f(P/P_g, \pi)\,y - G_n]. \qquad (7)$$
$$\underset{(+)\ (-)}{}$$

Finally, with the monetary authority standing ready to buy or sell any amount of gold at price P_g, the change in the monetary gold stock is given by

$$\dot{G}_m = g^s - g_n^d = g^s(P/P_g) - \alpha[f(P/P_g, \pi)\,y - G_n] - \delta f(P/P_g, \pi)\,y. \qquad (8)$$
$$\underset{(-)}{} \qquad \underset{(+)\ (-)}{} \qquad \underset{(+)\ (-)}{}$$

Consider the situation where y, λ, P_g, and the forms of the k- and f-functions are fixed. The steady state of the system described by equations (3), (7) and (8) corresponds to

$$\dot{P} = \dot{G}_m = \dot{G}_n = 0.$$

It can also be supposed that π, the expected value of $\dot{P}/P$, is equal to the actual value, zero, in the steady state. In order to simplify the analysis I assume at the outset that π is fixed at zero even when P is changing over time.

The steady-state values of P, G_m, and G_n, which will be denoted by asterisks, can be determined from equations (3), (7) and (8). Equations (8) and (7), together with $\dot{G}_m = \dot{G}_n = 0$, imply

$$g^s(P^*/P_g) = \delta f(P^*/P_g, \pi^*)\,y. \qquad (9)$$
$$\underset{(-)}{} \qquad \underset{(+)\ (-)}{}$$

This condition (together with $\pi^* = 0$) determines the steady-state value, P^*/P_g – and, hence, P^* – from the equality between gold production and the replacement demand for non-monetary gold.[2] In a model where y was continually increasing, the steady-state flow demand for gold would have additional components that reflected the growing demand for gold stocks in monetary and non-monetary uses.

---

[1] The alternative specification that substitutes δG_n for $\delta f(\ldots)\,y$ in equation (6) would seem appropriate if adjustment costs applied to the net change in G_n, which equals $g_n^d - \delta G_n$, rather than to alterations in the gross flow, g_n^d. The alternative assumes that changes in the gross flow that are associated with changes in actual depreciation, δG_n, do not involve any adjustment costs. Hence, the alternative has the odd property that a rise in G_n, for a given value of $f(\ldots)$, could raise the value of g_n^d. Although my preference is for the form of equation (6), the substitution of the alternative form would affect only a minor part of the dynamic analysis. (The form of the $\dot{G}_m$ expression, below, would be altered.)

[2] If the stock of previously mined gold were entered as a negative argument of the supply function (see note 2, p. 15 above), then P would not be constant in a steady state. Because of the depreciation of non-monetary gold stocks, P would have to fall continually in a steady state in order to provide the replacement flow of gold.

Equation (7) implies in a steady state that

$$G_n^* = f(P^*/P_g, \pi^*)\, y, \qquad (10)$$
$$\underset{(+)}{}\quad\underset{(-)}{}$$

which determines the value of G_n^* once P^* is set from equation (9). Finally, the money-supply-equals-money-demand condition, equation (3), implies

$$G_m^* = \lambda k(\pi^*)\, y P^*/P_g, \qquad (11)$$

which determines the steady-state value G_m^* (and, therefore, the money stock $M^* = (1/\lambda)\, P_g G_m^*$), once P^* is determined.

Consider a situation in which the outstanding gold stocks, G_m and G_n, are currently fixed at levels that need not correspond to a steady state. Given the values of y, π, and P_g, the value of G_m determines the current value of P from equation (3). With y, π, etc., constant, the movements of G_n and G_m (and hence, of P) are determined from equations (7) and (8).

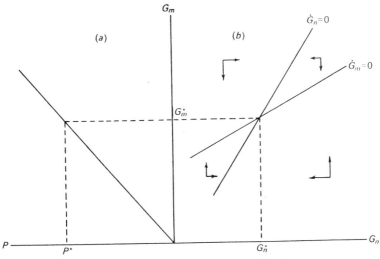

Fig. 1. Determination of price level and gold stocks.

Figs. 1 (a,b) depict the steady-state values, P^*, G_m^* and G_n^*, and also describe the dynamics of P, G_m and G_n. The line in Fig. 1 (a), based on equation (3), relates the value of P to the value of G_m. In Fig. 1 (b) the locus denoted by $\dot{G}_m = 0$ indicates combinations of G_n and G_m that yield $\dot{G}_m = 0$ in equation (8), taking into account the relation of P to G_m from equation (3). An increase in G_m raises P, which lowers g^s and raises g_n^d. Hence, $\dot{G}_m$ falls when G_m rises. Since an increase in G_n reduces g_n^d, which implies an increase in $\dot{G}_m$, the $\dot{G}_m = 0$ locus is positively sloped. Similarly, equation (7) implies that the $\dot{G}_n = 0$ locus is positively sloped. It can also be verified from equations (3), (7) and (8) that the $\dot{G}_n = 0$ locus has a steeper slope than the $\dot{G}_m = 0$ locus, so that the usual stability conditions are satisfied in this model (at least in the present case where π is fixed throughout at its steady-state value of zero). The slopes of the two loci and the stability conditions are derived in the appendix.

The following sections analyse the effects of various disturbances in the "short- and long-run". The focus is on the determination of P – notably, on the extent to which the gold standard insulates the price level from a variety of shocks.

(B) *Properties of the Model*

(1) *Technical Progress in Gold Production (Gold Discoveries)*

Consider a technical advance, discovery,[1] etc., that reduces the marginal cost of producing gold, $c'(g)$, for a given value of g. Since the supply function, g^s, shifts upward, equation (8) implies that $\dot{G}_m$ is higher for given values of P and G_n. Since there is no shift in the relationship between P and G_m from equation (3),[2] the Fig. 2(a) curve does not move, but the $\dot{G}_m = 0$ locus shifts upward in Fig. 2(b). (A higher value of G_m is now required, for a given value of G_n, to attain $\dot{G}_m = 0$.) The $\dot{G}_n = 0$ locus does not change, in accordance with equation (7).

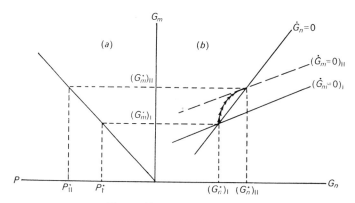

Fig. 2. Effect of gold discoveries.

Fig. 2(b) shows that G_m begins to rise in response to the disturbance. There is no immediate response in P or in $\dot{G}_n$. As G_m rises over time – as shown by the arrows in Fig. 2(b) – there is a corresponding increase in P, which leads to an increase in G_n and to a retardation in the growth of G_m. The new steady state is characterised by higher values of G_m^*, G_n^* and P^*, the increases in G_m^* and P^* being equiproportional. It also follows from equations (4), (5) and (9) that (for a given shift in marginal production cost, $c'(g)$) the proportional increase in P^* will be larger the larger the price elasticity of the supply function, g^s, and the smaller the magnitude of the price elasticity of the non-monetary gold demand function, f.

---

[1] This analysis abstracts from the possibly different intertemporal implications of changes in technique versus discoveries of new gold sources. (See notes 2, p. 15, and 2, p. 16, above.)

[2] Unless the contrary is noted, this and subsequent analyses neglect changes in y or π. Real income would change in the present case because of the technical advance in gold production. I have neglected this income effect because it is likely to be of second-order significance. See below for a discussion of expected inflation effects.

This analysis accords with Mill's[1] in predicting, first, a delayed and gradual rise of the price level in response to an increase in gold production, and, second, a coincident movement of P and G_m (and, hence, of M). However, these conclusions depend on the fixity of inflationary expectations, π, or on the constancy of velocity. If gold discoveries are perceived and if such discoveries are known to produce later increases in the price level, then π would increase at the time of the discovery. The induced fall in money demand, $k(\pi)$, implies, from equation (3), that P would rise for a given value of G_m.[2] (A full analysis of the impact of a shift in k is carried out in section 5, below.) In particular, there would be an initial jump in the price level before any movement occurred in G_m or the money stock. Hence, the workings of price expectations would eliminate part of the lagged response of P to gold discoveries and would produce a pattern where movements in P led movements in G_m and M.[3]

A natural assumption is that π corresponds to the time path of inflation that is generated by the model (rational expectations). However, I have not carried out this analysis within the present framework. One difficulty is that the various disturbances being considered here and below – to $c(g)$, y, λ, etc. – are presumably stochastic, which would have to be modelled explicitly in order to generate π in a rigorous manner. The information possessed by individuals about gold discoveries, etc., would also have to be specified. In any event the present mode of analysis may be adequate to ascertain the major types of responses to the indicated disturbances.

For evaluating the gold standard as a device for stabilising the general price level, the main implication of the present exercise is that volatility in conditions of gold production (associated with gold discoveries and changes in mining technique) would lead to volatility in the general price level.

Without working through the details it can be noted that shifts in nonmonetary gold demand – that is, movements in the f-function – have basically similar implications (although in the opposite direction) for the determination of the price level under the gold standard.[4]

(2) Changes in Real Income

Consider a one-time increase in real income, y, while holding fixed the technology of gold production. This example would reflect the secular pattern in the economy if gold mining were subject to less "technical advance" or to greater diseconomies-of-scale than the typical industry. The analysis deals initially with a one-time income change, although the effects of sustained income growth are also noted.

Equation (3) implies that P declines in inverse proportion to y for a given

---

[1] "Alterations…in the cost of production of the precious metals do not act upon the value of money except just in proportion as they increase or diminish its quantity…' (Mill, 1848, p. 29).

[2] There would also be a downward shift in the target stock of non-monetary gold, which would retard the acquisition of G_n.

[3] This behaviour also appears in the perfect-foresight model developed by Brock (1975).

[4] An upward shift in the f-function leads to decreases in P^* and G_m^* (which are in the same proportion), and to an increase in G_n^*. Again, if π is held fixed, the dynamic movement of P would lag behind the disturbance and would be coincident with the movement in G_m.

value of G_m (with π held fixed), so that the curve shown in Fig. 3 (a) shifts rightward. It follows from equation (7) that $\dot{G}_n$ increases for given values of G_m and G_n if and only if the magnitude of the price elasticity of the non-monetary gold target demand function, f, is less than one. Fig. 3 (b) depicts the case in which the elasticity equals one, so that there is no shift in the $\dot{G}_n = 0$ locus. In this situation equation (8) indicates that $\dot{G}_m$ rises for given values of G_m and G_n, because of the rise in g^s.

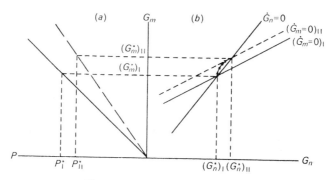

Fig. 3. Effect of increased real income.

Equation (9) implies that the increase in y leads, in the steady state, to a fall in P^*, as shown in Fig. 3 (a). The induced increase in g^s implies that G_m^*, which equals g^s/δ is a steady state, is increased. This property is exhibited in Fig. 3 (b). The net movement in G_m^*, as determined from equation (11), is generally ambiguous, although G_m^* must rise for the case depicted in Fig. 3.[1]

The most important response to a discrete rise in y is the immediate discrete fall in P. There is also, at least eventually, a period in which gold is accumulated in non-monetary form. The movement in G_m and the implied further movement in P are ambiguous. It is, however, unambiguous that the steady-state real stock of monetary gold – $P_g G_m^*/P^*$ – increases with y.

The basic conclusion is that output growth[2] – which dominates over "technical advances" in gold production – would imply secular decline in the price level. This result is often cited as a failing of the gold standard, although there would seem to be no objection to this sort of systematic – and hence, anticipated – deflation on business cycle grounds. The next sections consider the "remedies"

---

[1] Generally, G_m^* rises if and only if the sum of the absolute price elasticities of g^s and f exceeds one.

[2] If growth in output is sustained over time, a new element is that the corresponding steady decline in the price level would be anticipated in the steady state – that is, π^* would be negative. The forms of equations (6) and (7) would also have to be modified to incorporate the regular effect of changes in y and P on the flow demand for non-monetary gold. With growing real income and constant values for λ and k (and the assumed unit income elasticities for stock demands), it is possible to find a steady state in which the ratio of G_m to G_n remains constant only if the (steady-state value of the) price elasticity of the f-function is equal to minus one. In this case it can be shown that the steady-state inflation rate is $-\rho/(\eta_f + \eta_s) = -\rho/(1 + \eta_s)$, where $\rho = (1/y) \, dy/dt$, η_f is the magnitude of the price elasticity of the f-function, and η_s is the elasticity of g^s. Note that this inflation rate is invariant with shifts in the k- or f-functions or with changes in λ. See Mundell (1971), chs. 8 and 13, for some other aspects of the case of sustained output growth.

for secular deflation of paper gold creation and of changes in the nominal price of gold.

(3) "Paper Gold"

It is frequently argued that the deflationist tendency of the gold standard can be countered by supplementing the world's gold stock with some form of paper gold. For example, the plans suggested by Keynes (1943), Triffin (1960, part II), and Mundell (1971, pp. 135–6) can be viewed in this context. Recent forms of monetary supplement include international reserve holdings in the form of U.S. dollars and special drawing rights at the International Monetary Fund. In the present model the creation of paper gold can be modelled by a decrease in λ. Note that I retain the assumption that the central bank acts to maintain the (single) gold price, P_g.

Consider a one-time decrease in λ, which can be viewed as an increase in the money stock while holding fixed the initial amount of gold backing. Equation (3) indicates that P would rise for a given value of G_m, as represented by the leftward shift of the curve in Fig. 4 (a). It follows from equation (7) that $\dot{G}_n$ would rise for given values of G_m and G_n. Hence, the $\dot{G}_n = 0$ locus shifts rightward in Fig. 4 (b). Equation (8) implies that $\dot{G}_m$ would decline for given values of G_m and G_n, as indicated by the downward shift of the $\dot{G}_m = 0$ locus in Fig. 4 (b).

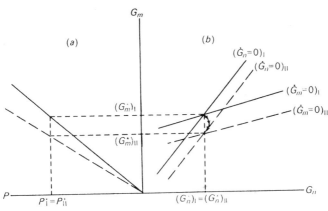

Fig. 4. Effect of increased paper gold or rise in velocity.

The exact position of the new steady state in Fig. 4 can be ascertained from equations (9)–(11). Equation (9) implies that P^* is invariant with λ. It follows from equation (10) that G_n^* is also unchanged. The downward movement in G_m^*, as shown in equation (11), is therefore proportional to the fall in λ, so that the steady-state money stock, $M^* = (1/\lambda)P_g G_m^*$, remains fixed.

Initially, with G_m (and π) held fixed, the effect of the increase in M is to increase P in proportion. This price change induces a rise over time in G_n and leads also to a drop in gold production. G_m falls over time on both counts, with P declining from its initially higher position in proportion to the decrease in G_m. Eventually, a point is reached where G_n is sufficiently high and P is sufficiently reduced so that G_n begins to fall. In the new steady state G_n and P have returned to their initial positions and the only net effect is the decline in G_m. Hence, the ultimate impact of increased paper money issue is to drive out part of the monetary gold stock without affecting the price level. In this sense – and as long as the value of P_g is actually maintained – paper gold does not counter the deflationary tendency of the gold standard. However, volatility of paper note issue (that is, of the ratio of money to its gold backing) would lead to short-run volatility of the general price level.[1]

It is worth noting that steady-state real balances, $M^*/P^* = P_g G_m^*/\lambda P^* = ky$, are invariant with λ, but the real value of the gold backing, $P_g G_m^*/P^*$, is positively related to λ.[2] Hence, the resource cost associated with the maintenance of the gold standard is, on this count, an increasing function of λ. Correspondingly, the monetary authority's steady-state "seigneurage" (in the sense of the *stock* of revenue from note issue)[3] can be written as $ky - P_g G_m^*/P^*$, which is negatively related to λ. However, the maximum (stock) amount of steady-state seigneurage – approached as $\lambda \to 0$ and $G_m^* \to 0$ – is M^*/P^*, which is fixed (for given values of y and π) at ky. In the steady state an excess of the lump-sum proceeds from note issue over ky is inconsistent with maintenance of the gold price, P_g. Attempts to secure additional revenue by issuing more paper currency would lead to more and more notes being presented to the central bank for conversion into gold at price P_g, which could lead to an increase in the gold price. (The next section deals with the effect of changes in P_g.) In this sense the paper gold route could eventually counter deflation by leading to the abandonment of the gold standard.[4] Mundell's (1971), pp. 133–5, discussion of the international economy during the decade after 1958 parallels this situation. The United States can be viewed as the world's central banker during this period.

The above analysis must be altered somewhat in the presence of sustained output growth. For present purposes the important consideration is that the steady-state flow demand for gold, which appears on the right side of equation (9), would include a term to account for the growth over time in G_m.[5] A decrease in λ would reduce the flow of gold for this purpose and would therefore tend

---

[1] Since P falls steadily after its initial discrete rise, π would tend to become negative. This decline in π would dampen the initial upward movement in P. More generally, the automatic response in π would seem to reduce the short-run price level variance associated with a given variance of λ.

[2] In this sense a partial commodity standard can "economise" on gold relative to a strict commodity standard. See Friedman (1951), pp. 215–6.

[3] In the model where y and P_g are constant, the flow of revenue from new note issue is zero in the steady state.

[4] Even before the standard was officially abandoned, paper gold issue could increase the price level by raising doubts about the maintenance of the price of gold. A rise in the expected future price of gold would reduce the demand for money and (depending on the reaction of π) also tend to raise the demand for non-monetary gold. The price level would rise with the decline in money demand, k, as shown in equation (3). Over time (with the actual value of P_g held fixed), there would be a tendency for G_n to rise and for G_m and M to decline (so that P would tend to return to its original value unless the actual value of P_g were altered).

[5] The term is $(\rho + \pi) \lambda k(\pi) P/P_g$, where ρ is the proportionate growth rate of y.

to raise P at any point in time. Although this channel implies that a lower value of λ would be associated with a higher level of the time path of P, there would still be no effect of λ on the steady-state inflation rate (see note 2, p. 20 above). Therefore it remains a valid conclusion that the (once-and-for-all)[1] choice of the proportional allocation of currency backing between gold and paper does not alter the connection between the gold standard and secular deflation. This connection seems inescapable with P_g held fixed if the gold-mining industry is perpetually less subject to "technical advance" than the rest of the economy.

(4) Changes in the Price of Gold

Consider a one-time increase in P_g in a non-growth context. It follows from equation (3) that, for given values of G_m, λ,[2] etc., P would increase equiproportionately. Further, equations (9)–(11) imply that this short-run solution, in which P/P_g, G_m and G_n are all unchanged, is also the new steady state.

For the case of sustained increases in P_g, the new element is that the associated increase in P would be anticipated, as reflected in a rise in π. This increase would reduce the real demand for money (k – see the analysis of this shift in the next section),[3] but would not alter the principal conclusion from above that the growth rate of P_g would be incorporated one-to-one in the steady-state growth rate of P. Notably, the growth rate of P_g could be engineered so as to offset the deflationary tendency of the gold standard.[4] Further (as suggested in the stable money proposal of Fisher, 1920, ch. IV), the value of P_g could be adjusted continuously so as to prevent even short-run fluctuations in P.

A difficulty with this "solution" is that it converts the problem of price level determination from an automatic mechanism under the gold standard (with P_g fixed) to a political choice of the time path of P_g. If this choice process is "reliable", then the gold standard could have been dispensed with all along and replaced by a paper standard (at the saving of the resource cost for maintaining monetary gold stocks). Under a paper standard it would "only" be necessary to ensure a "reasonable" growth rate of the quantity of fiat money.

(5) Shifts in Velocity

Consider a one-time decrease in real money demand, $k(\pi)$. In the context of a fractional-reserve banking system where M represents high-powered money, this shift could reflect an increase in the demand for deposits relative to currency.

---

[1] A steady decrease in λ would have a positive effect on the movement of P over time. However, this connection is subject to "diminishing returns". That is, as λ declines the flow demand for gold for monetary purposes becomes less important relative to the flow for non-monetary uses. If λ decreases at a constant rate, G_m/G_n would approach zero, and the steady-state value of π would still be the one given in note 2, p. 20 above.

[2] Fixity of λ implies that there is sufficient new currency issue to maintain the ratio of M to $P_g G_m$. If λ rises (which would occur, for example, if M were held fixed when P_g increased), the above analysis could be used to analyse the additional effects.

[3] Anticipated growth in P_g may also shift the demand for non-monetary gold – see note 4, p. 22 above.

[4] An exact offset would require setting $\dot{P}_g/P_g = \rho/(1 + \eta_s)$, where ρ is the growth rate of output and η_s is the price elasticity of g^s. See note 2, p. 20 above.

Equations (3), (7) and (8) indicate that this shock can be described exactly as in Fig. 4, which was constructed for the case of a decrease in λ. The immediate effects of the drop in money demand are a discrete increase in P, a tendency for G_m to fall over time, and a tendency for G_n to rise over time. As G_n rises and P falls along with G_m, the rising trend of G_n is diminished and eventually reversed. The new steady state involves a restoration of the initial values of P^* and G_n^*, with the only net effect being a decline in G_m^*. Real balances, $M/P^* = ky$, and the real value of monetary gold, $P_g G_m^*/P^*$, are both reduced in the new steady state. One implication of this exercise is that the endogenous movement of monetary gold stocks under the gold standard operates to buffer the price level against velocity shifts.[1]

As in the paper gold case, the analysis requires some modification in the presence of sustained output growth. A one-time reduction in k lowers the steady-state flow of gold that is required to maintain growth in G_m. On this count, the disturbance would produce an upward shift in the price level path. However, the steady-state inflation rate would be invariant with k (see note 2, p. 20 above).

(6) Some International Analysis

The model can be readily extended to a multiple country setting in which the gold standard prevails. Suppose that country i ($i = 1, ..., N$) is characterised by parameter values $P_{g_i}, \lambda_i, k_i, y_i$. The (fixed) exchange rate between country i and, say, country 1 is then P_{g_i}/P_{g_1}.[2] Arbitrage implies that the relative price of gold and (tradable) commodities would be the same in each country, so that P_i/P_{g_i} can be assumed to equal a common value, denoted by P/P_g. The equality between money demand and supply in each country at all points in time requires, from equations (1) and (2),

$$G_{m_i} = \lambda_i k_i y_i (P/P_g) \quad (i = 1, ..., N). \tag{12}$$

For a given current value of the world's monetary gold stock, G_m, equation (12) can be satisfied for all N countries by determining the allocation of G_m across countries[3] ($N-1$ independent conditions) and by determining the value of P/P_g – that is, by determining the "world price level". The latter condition can be seen by summing over equation (12) and rearranging terms to get

$$\frac{P}{P_g} = \frac{G_m}{\sum_i (\lambda_i k_i y_i)}. \tag{13}$$

In the long run P/P_g is determined by the equality between steady-state flow supply and demand for gold, as in equation (9). The world's monetary gold stock adjusts in the long run to satisfy equation (13) at this value of P/P_g.

---

[1] As in the case of a decrease in λ, a fall in π at the outset would improve this buffering action.

[2] Under a fixed exchange rate regime it is necessary for only one country to peg the price of gold directly.

[3] I am allowing instantaneous stock transfers of monetary gold (in exchange for commodities) across countries, although non-monetary gold still moves only in a smooth manner. The basic analysis would not seem to be altered if discrete shifts in G_{m_i} were ruled out (in which case equation (2) might be replaced by a flow demand for money function) or if discrete shifts in G_{n_i} were permitted.

Conditions for determining G_n in each country are analogous to those discussed in the one-country model.

In terms of volatility of general price levels, equation (13) indicates that the relevant influence is the variance of the world's "excess demand" for gold,

$$\left(\frac{1}{G_m}\right) \sum_i (\lambda_i k_i y_i).$$

Notably, if there is some independence across countries in movements of λ_i, k_i and y_i, then (because of a law-of-large-numbers effect) the variance of the general price level in each gold-standard country would tend to decline as the number of countries adhering to the standard increased.[1] In this sense the attractiveness of the set-up to a new country tends to rise with the number of countries that have already adopted the standard. However, it is possible that the inclusion into the gold-standard regime of a country with an especially volatile real demand, $\lambda_i k_i y_i$, would raise the variance of P/P_g. A mixing of countries with negative covariances of $\lambda_i k_i y_i$ would also tend to reduce the price level variance, although the empirical relevance of this point is not apparent.

I discuss below some examples of international disturbances that can be treated within the present framework.

(a) *Devaluation*. Consider a one-time devaluation in country j, which can be represented by an increase in P_{gj}. If λ_j remains fixed (implying that paper money in country j rises equiproportionately with the increased nominal value of that country's monetary gold holdings), then it is immediate from equations (12) and (13) that the only impact of the devaluation would be an equipro- portional increase in P_j. In particular, it follows from equation (13) and the fixity of P_{gi} for all the other countries that there is no spillover effect of the devaluation to prices abroad.

On the other hand, if λ_j is allowed to rise with the devaluation (which is, perhaps, the point of the devaluation), then it follows from equation (13) – for a given value of G_m – that P/P_g would decline. That is, P_i would fall in all countries $i \neq j$ that were maintaining the nominal price of gold (or were maintaining a fixed exchange rate with a country that was pegging the gold price). Further, P_j would rise less than equiproportionately with P_{gj} in the devaluing country.[2] The explanation of these effects, indicated in equation (12), is that the fraction of the world's monetary gold stock held in country j rises with the increase in λ_j.[3] The smaller remaining stock can satisfy the demand in other countries only with a decrease in P/P_g.

As in the one-country case analysed before, the long-run solution would also include the adjustment of G_m from gold production, etc. In the no-growth situation the steady-state effect of the devaluation on P/P_g would be nil,

---

[1] This analysis assumes that G_m is proportional to the number of countries on the gold standard. See below.

[2] This response is closer to equiproportional and the spillover effects to other countries are weaker the smaller the weight of country j in the world's overall demand for monetary gold – that is, the lower the value of $\lambda_j k_j y_j / \sum_i (\lambda_i k_i y_i)$.

[3] A "period" of balance-of-payments surpluses would be required for country j to obtain the additional gold.

although some long-run effect (to the level of the P/P_g path but not to the world inflation rate) would remain in a growth context.

(b) *Increased Adoption of the Gold Standard.* If an additional country, labelled $N+1$, adopts the gold standard, then

$$\sum_i (\lambda_i k_i y_i)$$

in equation (13) would rise with the inclusion of the term, $\lambda_{N+1} k_{N+1} y_{N+1}$. There would be a corresponding decline in P/P_g while G_m is held fixed.[1] Since $G_{m, N+1}$ will now be absorbed by country $N+1$ in accordance with equation (12), the remaining countries can be satisfied with the reduced amount of monetary gold only if P/P_g falls. As an example of this effect, the acquisition of large amounts of gold by the United States during the Resumption Period from 1875 to 1879 and somewhat thereafter (and, similarly, by Germany after 1871) should have exerted a depressing effect on prices in gold standard countries, such as England. Further, a country's (credible) announcement of a future plan to adopt the gold standard (as by the United States in 1875) would have an immediate downward effect on prices in gold standard countries – that is, even before the new country increased its gold holdings. The mechanism is a decline in the expected inflation rate, π, in the gold standard countries, which raises the demand for money (as well as the demand for non-monetary gold) and correspondingly lowers the price level.

The analysis can be extended in the usual way to consider the long-run effects when G_m is allowed to vary. In particular, for the no-growth case in which all countries are identical, the steady-state value of G_m would be proportional to the number of countries on the gold standard (see note 1, p. 25 above).

(c) *Multiple Commodity Standards.* It is, of course, possible for different groups of countries to adhere to different commodity standards – for example, there could be a gold standard group and a silver standard group (or a group of countries on a fiat standard, possibly tied together via fixed exchange rates). It should be noted that this multiple-standard set-up differs from bimetallism, which is discussed below. One observation on a multiple-standard world is that the exchange rate between, say, the gold and silver blocs would be determined by the relative price of gold and silver (which can be assumed to be the same within either bloc). Some empirical evidence that supports this proposition is presented in Sayers (1931) in a study of the Indian/English exchange rate during 1919–20, and in Fisher (1935), pp. 4–5 and chart 5, and Friedman and Schwartz (1963), pp. 361–2 and 489–90, in analyses of the Chinese exchange rate and price level from 1929 to 1935.

An interesting application of the analysis, which amounts to an extension of optimum currency area theory (Mundell, 1968, ch. 12), would be to a determination of the optimal groupings of countries and the optimal number of groups. (I am abstracting here from means-of-payments considerations involved with a particular country's use of a particular commodity for trans-

---

[1] I am assuming no change in world demand for non-monetary gold.

actions, and I am also not considering the transactions benefits derived from adherence to a fixed exchange rate regime.) From the perspective of price level variance it seems that (1) a country that has an especially low variance of demand – that is, of $\lambda_i k_i y_i$ – may find it advantageous to be isolated from the rest of the world; (2) with "free entry" to an existing commodity standard it seems infeasible to exclude from a group a "contaminating" country that has an especially high variance of demand; and (3) there could be incentive for an assortment among groups that exploits any negative covariances of demands. The empirical relevance of these propositions is not apparent.

II. OTHER COMMODITY STANDARDS

(A) Bimetallism

Two possible disadvantages of the gold standard (or an alternative single commodity standard, such as silver) are the short-run variability of prices in the face of volatile gold discoveries (and in the face of volatility in velocity and in the ratio of money to gold) and the tendency for secular deflation. Bimetallism has been advocated (Marshall, 1887, p. 204) as a mechanism for mitigating at least the short-run problem while remaining within the context of a commodity standard. I will first consider the usual form of bimetallism and then discuss Marshall's proposal for a "stable bimetallism", which is called symmetallism.

Returning to the context of a single closed economy, suppose now that gold and "silver" both serve as currency backing with

$$M^s = (1/\lambda) \quad (P_g G_m + P_s S_m), \tag{14}$$

where P_s is the nominal price of silver and S_m is the monetary silver stock. I assume that the circulating medium takes the form of paper notes, rather than gold or silver in a physical sense, so that there is no issue here concerning imperfect substitutability between gold and silver in monetary use. (See Chen, 1972, pp. 96 ff., on this point.) The form of bimetallism that I am presently considering involves (the attempt at) fixed nominal prices for both gold and silver within a single country – that is, P_g and P_s are both taken to be constant. Money demand still takes the form of equation (2), so that the price level is determined from

$$P = \frac{M}{k(\pi) y} = \frac{(P_g G_m + P_s S_m)}{\lambda k(\pi) y}. \tag{15}$$

The supply of new gold from the production side is again described by equation (5). A similar analysis of silver production leads to the supply function

$$s^s = s^s(P/P_s). \tag{16}$$
$$\quad\,\,(-)$$

I assume a flow demand function for silver in non-monetary use that parallels the gold specification in equation (6),[1]

$$s_n^d = \beta[h(P/P_s, \pi)y - S_n] + \epsilon h(P/P_s, \pi)y, \tag{17}$$
$$\quad\quad\,\,(+)\,\,(-) \quad\quad\quad\quad (+)\,\,(-)$$

---

[1] The price ratio, P_g/P_s, could be entered separately to account for substitutability between gold and silver in non-monetary use. This addition seems to be inconsequential.

where ϵ is the depreciation rate for the non-monetary silver stock, S_n. The movement of S_n over time is determined from

$$\dot{s}_n = (\beta + \epsilon) \, [h(P/P_s, \pi) \, y - S_n]. \qquad (18)$$

Finally, the change over time in S_m is

$$\dot{S}_m = s^s - s_n^d = s^s(P/P_s) - \beta[h(P/P_s, \pi) \, y - S_n] - \epsilon h(P/P_s, \pi) \, y. \qquad (19)$$

The basic difficulty with bimetallism, which has been discussed theoretically and in an historical perspective by Mill (1848), ch. x, Jevons (1884), ch. XIII, Laughlin (1896) and Fisher (1922), ch. VII, among others, can be seen by observing two of the conditions that ought to characterise a steady state. Consider the equalities between flow supplies and demands for gold and silver, respectively, when the non-monetary stock of each metal is at its target level. The steady-state condition for gold is, again,

$$g^s(P^*/P_g) = \delta f(P^*/P_g, \pi^*) \, y, \qquad (9)$$

while that for silver is

$$s^s(P^*/P_s) = \epsilon h(P^*/P_s, \pi^*) \, y. \qquad (20)$$

Ostensibly, equation (9) determines P^*/P_g, while equation (20) determines P^*/P_s. However, there is nothing to guarantee that the set values of P_g and P_s are consistent with both relative price conditions. The system has a steady state (with positive values of both G_m and S_m) that supports the set gold and silver prices only if the ratio, P_g/P_s, is consistent with the "natural" relative price that emerges from equations (9) and (20). Further, if P_g/P_s happens to be set appropriately, then the composition of the monetary backing in the steady state is indeterminate – that is, M^* is prescribed from equation (15), but the breakdown between G_m^* and S_m^* is not specified. To put the result differently, if P_g/P_s is originally "correct", any disturbance that would alter the values of P^*/P_g or P^*/P_s implied by equations (9) or (20) respectively (or any autonomous shift in the pegged ratio of P_g to P_s) would move the system toward a position where either G_m or S_m vanishes, so that the fixity of either P_g or P_s could not be maintained. For example, it can be verified that "technical advance" in silver production, as represented by an upward shift in the s^s function, would lead to the exhaustion of monetary gold stocks, G_m. The disturbance implies that the relative price, P_g/P_s, should rise. Under the form of bimetallism being considered, this relative price change can occur only by the exhaustion of G_m (as implied by Gresham's Law), after which P_g is free to rise. In this case equations (9) and (20) would determine the values of P_g^* and P^*, while equation (15) specifies the money stock (with the backing involving $G_m^* = 0$ and $S_m^* > 0$). Of course, this situation is precisely the silver standard (or, under an alternative shock, the gold standard) that has been analysed above.[1] An alternative out-

---

[1] Laughlin (1896), ch. III, discusses the effects of increased silver production up to 1820 in driving out monetary gold in the United States. He also discusses (ch. IV) the effects of a change in the pegged price ratio in 1834 (from 1:15 to 1:16 for gold versus silver) in tending to eliminate monetary silver, and (ch. V) the role of gold discoveries after 1850 in completing the elimination of silver money. According to Laughlin (p. 79), "...before 1834 the silver end was up. Now it was the gold end. How soon would it be the silver end again, if we adhered to such a system?"

come would be a compensating shift in the monetary authority's "pegged" price ratio, P_g/P_s. However, that alternative leaves unclear exactly what nominal price is held fixed under bimetallism.

(B) Symmetallism

Consider now Marshall's (1887, pp. 204–6; 1923, pp. 64 ff.) proposal for a "stable bimetallism", which is usually called symmetallism. Under this system the central bank does not attempt to stabilise the price of either gold or silver separately, but rather pegs the price of a reserve unit that corresponds to a specified combination of the two metals.[1] Define a reserve unit as γ_g (ounces) of gold and γ_s (ounces) of silver. If R represents the number of these units held as a currency reserve, then the monetary stocks of gold and silver are

$$G_m = \gamma_g R, \quad S_m = \gamma_s R. \tag{21}$$

If P_r denotes the price of a reserve unit, then the nominal value of the currency backing is

$$P_r R = P_g G_m + P_s S_m. \tag{22}$$

Equations (21) and (22) imply that the price of a reserve unit is

$$P_r = \gamma_g P_g + \gamma_s P_s,$$

that is, a combination of P_g and P_s, as set by the (fixed) weights, γ_g and γ_s.[2] Dividing through by P yields the more convenient condition,

$$P_r/P = \gamma_g P_g/P + \gamma_s P_s/P. \tag{23}$$

Under Symmetallism, the tie to the absolute price level is attained by pegging P_r. However, the problem of standard bimetallism is avoided since the fixity of P_r does not imply fixity of any relative price – notably, P/P_g and P/P_s are free to adjust to underlying shocks.

Equations (14)–(20), which were derived for bimetallism, continue to apply. Note that the money supply is now

$$M^s = (1/\lambda) P_r R = (1/\lambda) (P_g G_m + P_s S_m). \tag{24}$$

The money-supply-equals-money-demand condition, equation (15), determines the steady-state value of M and therefore the steady-state nominal value of reserve holdings, $P_r R^*$. Equation (21) then determines the composition of the monetary backing, given the weights, γ_g and γ_s. Equations (9) and (20) determine the steady-state values, P^*/P_g^* and P^*/P_s^*. Given these values, equation (23) and the fixed value of P_r determine the absolute price level, P^*.

The operation of the symmetallic system is analogous to that of the gold standard, except that steady-state price movements are now also induced by shifts in the flow excess supply of silver, and the dynamics of price movements are now also affected by the silver supply and demand elasticities. Essentially,

---

[1] An experimental coin made of "goloid" – a patented alloy of gold, silver and copper in which the ratio of silver to gold was 16 to 1 – was actually struck in 1878. A bill was proposed by Congressman Stephens (former Vice President of the Confederacy) to resolve the "silver question" by minting the goloid dollar. However, the measure did not get beyond the committee stage. One difficulty with the goloid coin is that it could not be distinguished from a silver coin in either colour or sonority. (See Judd, 1965, p. 177, and Hepburn, 1903, p. 299.)

[2] It is possible, but not necessary, to define the units so that P_r is a weighted average of P_g and P_s.

variability in P would now involve a weighting of the variability in P/P_s with that of P/P_g. If there is some independence in the shocks that produce changes in the silver relative price, P/P_s, from those that produce changes in P/P_g, and if P/P_s is not much more volatile than P/P_g, then there would be a law-of-average type gain – in terms of reduced variance of P – by moving from the gold standard to the bimetallic system. The choice of (relative) weights in the construction of the reserve unit could be determined from an (intertemporal) objective of minimising price level variance. The resulting weights would not necessarily bear a close relation to the relative weights of gold and silver (or other commodities that might have been chosen for the reserve unit) in national (world) product. For example, if P/P_g were more stable than P/P_s (which could arise from differences in fluctuations in the supply and demand functions and from differences in the elasticities of supply and demand), then gold would receive a higher weight than silver in the reserve unit even if gold's share of GNP were lower than silver's (which would reflect differences in the average levels of supply and demand for gold and silver).

(C) Commodity-Reserve Currency

The logic of symmetallism can be extended to include a variety of commodities in the reserve unit. This extended scheme, referred to as commodity-reserve currency, was proposed by Benjamin Graham (1937, 1944) and Frank Graham (1942), pp. 94–118, and was discussed in depth by Friedman (1951). (See also Luke, 1975, and Weber, 1976.) By analogy to the symmetallic case, the broadening of the currency base can produce further reductions in price level variance. Further, if the base includes products that resemble the overall commodity basket in terms of technical advance and scale characteristics, then the tendency toward secular deflation under the gold standard could be eliminated. At an ideal level it would be possible to achieve any desired degree of stability in a specified price index by designing the appropriate commodity-reserve bundle.

Friedman (1951) presents a quantitative criticism of commodity-reserve currency on the grounds that a feasible base would be very narrow and would therefore not guarantee more price stability than the gold standard. Friedman (pp. 223–9) eliminates a variety of commodities on the grounds of poor storage characteristics (oil, coal, manufactured products that are subject to obsolescence, perishable agricultural products) or on grounds of inelastic short-run supply conditions (storable agricultural products). In fact, these objections seem surmountable by substituting, say, a one-year future (or a future in the 11- to 12-month range to avoid infinite turnover frequency) for each physical commodity.[1] The use of futures not only eliminates significant storage costs, but

---

[1] Friedman (pp. 225–6) discusses some problems with the use of futures. Some of these problems relate to shifts of the reserve bundle between spot and future holdings of a particular commodity (along the lines suggested by B. Graham), which has arbitrary elements and can interfere with the relative price of future and spot commodities. However, this objection does not apply when a commodity *always* enters the reserve bundle in the form of a one-year future. Friedman also notes (p. 226) that "next year's wheat is not the same as this year's" – but a higher supply elasticity of next year's wheat suggests that this commodity may, in fact, be a more useful component of the commodity bundle than this year's wheat.

also removes the entire resource cost (except for transaction costs in futures markets) from this part of the currency base. The supply elasticity of, say, one-year-ahead wheat would also seem to be much higher than that of spot wheat. Further, if commodity-reserve currency were in operation, there would be an incentive for the creation of a much wider range of futures than currently exists (say, for standardised manufactured products like automobiles and other durables), which could then be used to augment the reserve base. It is, in fact, imaginable to have a commodity reserve that is based entirely on futures.[1]

Two remaining problems with the commodity-reserve proposal, also discussed by Friedman, are the difficulty in obtaining general acceptance and the possibility of political "tinkering" with the reserve base through changes in commodity weights. In these respects the gold standard is a superior system.

III. SOME CONCLUDING REMARKS

In relation to a fiat currency regime, the key element of a commodity standard is its potential for automaticity and consequent absence of political control over the quantity of money and the absolute price level. Essentially, the adoption of a commodity standard by any country would require a constitutional-type (political) decision that rules out the determination of the quantity of money over time through a series of political decisions. (See Buchanan, 1962.) It is not clear, *a priori*, that this sort of constitutional provision is more likely to obtain than, for example, a provision to expand the quantity of fiat money at a constant rate. In this context the choice among different monetary constitutions – such as the gold standard, a commodity-reserve standard, or a fiat standard with fixed rules for setting the quantity of money (possibly in relation to stabilising a specified price index) – may be less important than the decision to adopt *some* monetary constitution. On the other hand, the gold standard actually prevailed for a substantial period (even if from an "historical accident", rather than a constitutional choice process), whereas the world has yet to see a fiat currency system that has obvious "stability" properties.

University of Rochester   ROBERT J. BARRO

Date of receipt of final typescript: February 1978

REFERENCES

Brock, W. (1975). "A Simple Perfect Foresight Monetary Model." *Journal of Monetary Economics*, vol. 1 (April), pp. 133–50.
Buchanan, J. M. (1962). "Predictability: the Criterion of Monetary Constitutions." In *In Search of a Monetary Constitution* (ed. L. Yeager). Cambridge, Mass.: Harvard University Press.
Cagan, P. (1956). "The Monetary Dynamics of Hyperinflation." In *Studies in the Quantity Theory of Money* (ed. M. Friedman). University of Chicago Press.

[1] Friedman (pp. 225–6) objects that the use of futures "changes the fundamental character of the currency from a warehouse certificate to an evidence of debt". However, for commodity reserve purposes the relevant question concerns the quantitative variances (and covariances) in the relative prices, P/P_i, where P_i refers, say, to a one-year future in commodity i. This variance would be affected by, among other things, possible changes in the probability of fraud and inability to deliver on futures contracts. Qualitatively, it is not clear that these considerations differ from theft of commodity stocks, counterfeiting, changes in non-monetary demand for commodities, etc.

Chen, C. (1972). "Bimetallism: Theory and Controversy in Perspective." *History of Political Economy*, vol. 4 (Spring), pp. 89-112.

Fisher, I. (1920). *Stabilizing the Dollar*. New York: Macmillan.

—— (1922). *The Purchasing Power of Money*, 2nd ed. Reprinted by Augustus Kelley, New York, 1971.

—— (1935) "Are Booms and Depressions Transmitted Internationally through Monetary Standards?" *Bulletin of the International Statistical Institute*, vol. 28, pp. 1-29.

Friedman, M. (1951). "Commodity-Reserve Currency." *Journal of Political Economy*, vol. 59 (June), pp. 203-32. Reprinted in his *Essays in Positive Economics* (University of Chicago Press, 1953).

—— and Schwartz, A. J. (1963). *A Monetary History of the United States, 1867-1960*. Princeton University Press.

Goldman, S. M. (1972). "Hyperinflation and the Rate of Growth in the Money Supply." *Journal of Economic Theory*, vol. 5 (Oct.), pp. 250-7.

Graham, B. (1937). *Storage and Stability*. New York: McGraw-Hill.

—— (1944). *World Commodities and World Currency*. New York: McGraw-Hill.

Graham, F. D. (1942). *Social Goals and Economic Institutions*. Princeton: Princeton University Press.

Hepburn, A. B. (1903). *History of Coinage and Currency in the United States*. London: Macmillan.

Jevons, W. S. (1884). *Investigations in Currency and Finance*, reprinted by Augustus Kelley, New York, 1964.

Judd, J. H. (1965). *United States Pattern, Experimental and Trial Pieces*, 3rd ed. Racine, Wisc.: Whitman.

Keynes, J. M. *et al.* (1943). "Proposals by British Experts for an International Clearing Union" (April), reprinted in *Proceedings and Documents of the United Nations Monetary and Financial Conference*, vol. 2. Washington: U.S. Government Printing Office, 1948.

Laughlin, J. L. (1896). *History of Bimetallism in the United States*, 4th ed. New York: D. Appleton.

Luke, J. C. (1975). "Inflation-Free Pricing Rules for a Generalized Commodity-Reserve Currency." *Journal of Political Economy*, vol. 83 (August), pp. 779-90.

Marshall, A. (1887). "Remedies for Fluctuations of General Prices." Reprinted in *Memorials of Alfred Marshall* (ed. A. C. Pigou). London: Macmillan, 1925.

—— (1923). *Money, Credit and Commerce*. London: Macmillan.

Mill, J. S. (1848). *Principles of Political Economy*, vol. 2. Boston: Little, Brown.

Mundell, R. A. (1968). *International Economics*. New York: Macmillan.

—— (1971). *Monetary Theory*. Pacific Palisades: Goodyear.

Niehans, J. (1977). "Commodity Money." Unpublished (forthcoming as chapter 8 of book by Johns Hopkins University Press).

Ricardo, D. (1821). *The Principles of Political Economy and Taxation*, 3rd ed. Reprinted by J. M. Dent and Sons, London, 1911.

Sargent, T. J. and Wallace, N. (1973). "The Stability of Models of Money and Growth with Perfect Foresight." *Econometrica*, vol. 41 (Nov.), pp. 1043-8.

Sayers, R. S. (1931). "The Indian Exchange Problem 1919-20." *Economica*, vol. 11 (November), pp. 450-62.

Thornton, H. (1802). *An Enquiry into the Nature and Effects of the Paper Credit of Great Britain*. Reprinted by Allen and Unwin, London, 1937.

Triffin, R. (1960). *Gold and the Dollar Crisis*. New Haven: Yale University Press.

Weber, W. E. (1976). "Price Level Variability and Commodity Reserve Standards." Unpublished.

Whitaker, J. K. (1976). "An Essay on the Pure Theory of Commodity Money." Unpublished.

APPENDIX

The system that describes the motion of G_m and G_n can be written from equations (7) and (8) as

$$\dot{G}_m = g^s(P/P_g) - \alpha \underset{(+)}{[f(P/P_g)\,y - G_n]} - \delta \underset{(+)}{f(P/P_g)\,y}, \qquad (A\ 1)$$

with the $(-)$ under the first term,

$$\dot{G}_n = (\alpha + \delta) \underset{(+)}{[f(P/P_g)\,y - G_n]}. \qquad (A\ 2)$$

Equation (3) implies

$$\frac{P}{P_g} = \frac{G_m}{\lambda k y}, \qquad —$$

where λ, k, y, α and δ are all treated as constants for present purposes.

Defining $g^{s'} \equiv \partial g^s / \partial (P/P_g) < 0$ and $f' \equiv \partial f / \partial (P/P_g) > 0$ and taking partial derivatives of equations (A 1) and (A 2) yields

$$\frac{\partial \dot{G}_m}{\partial G_m} = -\frac{1}{\lambda k y} \left[(\alpha + \delta) y f' - g^{s'} \right] < 0,$$

$$\frac{\partial \dot{G}_m}{\partial G_n} = \alpha > 0,$$

$$\frac{\partial \dot{G}_n}{\partial G_m} = \frac{1}{(\lambda k y)} \left[(\alpha + \delta) y f' \right] > 0,$$

$$\frac{\partial \dot{G}_n}{\partial G_n} = -(\alpha + \delta) < 0.$$

The slope of the $\dot{G}_m$ locus in Fig. 1 is

$$-\left(\frac{\partial \dot{G}_m / \partial G_n}{\partial \dot{G}_m / \partial G_m} \right) = \frac{\alpha \lambda k y}{(\alpha + \delta) y f' - g^{s'}} > 0,$$

while that of the $\dot{G}_n$ locus is

$$-\frac{\partial \dot{G}_n / \partial G_n}{\partial \dot{G}_n / \partial G_m} = \frac{\lambda k}{f'} > 0.$$

Both slopes are positive since $f' > 0$ and $g^{s'} < 0$. It also follows that the $\dot{G}_n$ locus has a larger slope, as shown in Fig. 1.

The stability conditions are

$$\frac{\partial \dot{G}_m}{\partial G_m} + \frac{\partial \dot{G}_n}{\partial G_n} < 0$$

and

$$\left(\frac{\partial \dot{G}_m}{\partial G_m} \right) \left(\frac{\partial \dot{G}_n}{\partial G_n} \right) > \left(\frac{\partial \dot{G}_m}{\partial G_n} \right) \left(\frac{\partial \dot{G}_n}{\partial G_m} \right).$$

The first condition is satisfied immediately from above. The second condition corresponds to the proposition that the $\dot{G}_n$ locus is more steeply sloped than the $\dot{G}_m$ locus, which was also shown to hold above.

The stability conditions would also be satisfied if $\delta f(\ldots)$ in equation (6) were replaced by δG_n (note 1, p. 16 above), although the sign of $\partial \dot{G}_m / \partial G_n$ (and, hence, the inclination of the $\dot{G}_m$ locus) would then be indeterminate. A dependence of the expected inflation rate, π, on the time path of P or other variables leads to deeper stability questions of the sort discussed by Cagan (1956) and Goldman (1972) under adaptive expectations and by Sargent and Wallace (1973) in a deterministic, rational expectations setting.

REFERENCES FOR APPENDIX

Cagan, P. (1956). "The Monetary Dynamics of Hyperinflation" In *Studies in the Quantity Theory of Money* (ed. M. Friedman). University of Chicago Press.
Goldman, S. M. (1972). "Hyperinflation and the Rate of Growth in the Money Supply." *Journal of Economic Theory*, vol. 5 (Oct.), pp. 250-7.
Sargent, T. J. and Wallace, N. (1973). "The Stability of Models of Money and Growth with Perfect Foresight." *Econometrica*, 41 (Nov.), pp. 1043-8.

ECONOMIC THEORY, ECONOMETRICS, AND MATHEMATICAL ECONOMICS

Consulting Editor: Karl Shell

UNIVERSITY OF PENNSYLVANIA
PHILADELPHIA, PENNSYLVANIA

Edmund S. Phelps. **Studies in Macroeconomic Theory, Volume 1:** *Employment and Inflation.* **Volume 2:** *Redistribution and Growth.*

Marc Nerlove, David M. Grether, and José L. Carvalho. **Analysis of Economic Time Series:** *A Synthesis*

Thomas J. Sargent. **Macroeconomic Theory**

Jerry Green and José Alexander Scheinkman (Eds.). **General Equilibrium, Growth and Trade:** *Essays in Honor of Lionel McKenzie*

Michael J. Boskin (Ed.). **Economics and Human Welfare:** *Essays in Honor of Tibor Scitovsky*

Carlos Daganzo. **Multinomial Probit:** *The Theory and Its Application to Demand Forecasting*

L. R. Klein, M. Nerlove, and S. C. Tsiang (Eds.). **Quantitative Economics and Development:** *Essays in Memory of Ta-Chung Liu*

Giorgio P. Szegö. **Portfolio Theory:** *With Application to Bank Asset Management*

M June Flanders and Assaf Razin. **Development in an Inflationary World**

Thomas G. Cowing and Rodney E. Stevenson (Eds.). **Productivity Measurement in Regulated Industries**

Robert J. Barro (Ed.). **Money, Expectations, and Business Cycles:** *Essays in Macroeconomics*

In preparation

Giorgio Szegö (Ed.). **New Quantitative Techniques for Economic Analysis**